KF
4989
.M66x
2001
c.2

AF865072

The National Law of Treaty Implementation

In the government of this Commonwealth, the legislative department shall never exercise the executive and judicial powers, or either of them: The executive shall never exercise the legislative and judicial powers, or either of them: The judicial shall never exercise the legislative and executive powers, or either of them: to the end it may be a government of laws and not of men.

The Constitution of the Commonwealth of Massachusetts, "Part the First," art. XXX (1780), *reprinted in M. Connolly, The Constitution of the Commonwealth of Massachusetts* 3, 10 (1984).

The National Law of Treaty Implementation

John Norton Moore

Carolina Academic Press
Durham, North Carolina

Copyright © 2001
John Norton Moore
All Rights Reserved.

ISBN: 0-89089-647-X
LCCN: 2001087993

CAROLINA ACADEMIC PRESS
700 Kent Street
Durham, NC 27701
Telephone (919) 489-7486
Fax (919) 493-5668
www.cap-press.com

Printed in the United States of America

Preface

During the 1980's, a dispute arose over the correct legal meaning of the 1972 Anti-Ballistic Missile (ABM) Treaty between the United States and the then-Soviet Union. This Treaty, which had been a centerpiece of the SALT I negotiations under President Richard Nixon, was regarded by many as the centerpiece of strategic arms control. In this setting, President Reagan's proposal for a national missile defense, dubbed by its opponents as "star wars," gave rise to what quickly became a bitter legal dispute as to whether the Treaty prohibited development and testing of mobile ABM systems based on "other physical principles" (OPP) such as lasers or particle beams. It was eventually conceded on all sides that the Treaty prevented deployment of such mobile systems and it was broadly agreed that the Treaty permitted development and testing of fixed OPP based systems. The United States believed that the Treaty also broadly permitted research and, thus, within the United States, research was not part of the debate, although the U.S.S.R. continued to challenge this interpretation.

This debate, which became known as the "broad-narrow" debate about the meaning of the ABM Treaty, is still almost certainly *the* most complex and contentious legal debate in the history of United States foreign policy. At its height, both branches of Government, the Executive Branch and the Congress, were internally split about the correct meaning of the Treaty. Popularly, however, the debate became associated with the conflict between its principal antagonists, Senator Sam Nunn, the powerful Chairman of the Senate Armed Services Committee, for the "narrow" view restricting mobile OPP based systems, and Judge Abraham Sofaer, the Legal Adviser of the Department of State, for the "broad" view permitting development and testing of mobile OPP based systems. Both men produced massive studies in support of their positions.

In this context, I was requested by the Director of the Arms Control Agency to prepare for him a neutral analysis of the debate, summarizing the principal issues and positions and providing an analysis as to the more correct legal interpretation. Following assurances that I would have full access to all of the relevant records and negotiating history and that I would be completely independent in my review, I agreed to undertake the study. In doing so, however, I added the requirement that my work should also be completely *pro bono*, since any payment could be misconstrued in this contentious debate as payment for particular results. And I wrote into the contract that all of my notes, work materials of whatever kind, and, of course, the study itself must be permanently retained by the Government.

Approximately two years and nine months later, in September of 1989, I completed a multi-volume, 4000 page study of the issues. The study is, in most respects, highly classified and has never been released to the public. Although I have been authorized to talk about my conclusions, I have declined to do so until the study is declassified and released. Some years ago I requested declassification review of the study and was told that it had begun. To date, however, the contents of the study, as opposed to its existence, remain highly classified.

This monograph is the unclassified 607-page Volume IV of my study for the Director of the United States Arms Control Agency, an Agency now subsumed into the Department of State. The volume is entitled "The National Law of Treaty Implementation" and focuses on an issue in the debate which may well have the greatest significance for the future foreign relations law of the United States. That issue relates to a range of concerns about the standard for treaty interpretation under United States national law. During the debate, Senator Nunn and other proponents of the "narrow" interpretation argued that whatever the correct international legal interpretation of the Treaty, the President was bound to the interpretation of an Executive Branch witness and individual members of the Senate during the 1972 initial Senate advice and consent consideration of the Treaty. Although Senator Nunn believed the correct international legal interpretation to be the "narrow" interpretation, he offered this argument as an additional constitutional basis for his support for that position. Judge Sofaer, on the other hand, supported the traditional view that treaties have but one referent for interpretation, and that is the meaning agreed between the parties. Ultimately, the Senate became sufficiently attached to Senator Nunn's position, which I have termed the "dual" approach to treaty interpretation, that it developed and attached to subsequent treaty advice and consent resolutions its own view of the constitutional requirements for treaty interpretation. The first of these was adopted by the Senate on May 26, 1988, as a condition of Senate advice and consent to the INF Treaty and has become known as the "Biden Treaty Interpretation Condition". In turn this has generated a continuing constitutional debate about the treaty interpretation issues, as well as a less well recognized issue implicit in the debate, as to whether the Senate has any authority to attach "domestic conditions" to treaties at the time of advice and consent.

The correct constitutional answer to the "dual" versus "unitary" debate in treaty interpretation under the foreign relations law of the United States is of great importance for the Nation. Since this monograph addresses those issues, presenting the views of all sides in the debate more thoroughly than anything in print, I believed that it should be published and made generally available. This monograph presents the unedited version of Volume IV of the study for the Director of ACDA. It is, by its nature, a study that seeks to present both sides of the debate in full, as well as offer an outside appraisal for the Director. My own views about the issues, sharpened over the years since the study, are subsequently being published as *John Norton Moore, Treaty Interpretation, the Constitution and the Rule of Law,* forthcoming (Oceana Press, 2001).

The Annex to this monograph, *Summary Chart of Congressional Consideration of the "Broad-Narrow" Issue in Initial Consideration of the ABM Treaty*, is the original Annex D to the multi-volume study for the Director. It was reviewed for release by ACDA in December of 1992 and was released by the Director on December 7, 1992 in a letter to the author. This chart summarizes a detailed analysis of each separate consideration of the "broad-narrow" issue in the totality of initial Congressional consideration of the ABM Treaty. The lengthy analysis itself, part of the original study, remains classified. The chart, however, is useful in putting the underlying debate in a more specific context about full Congressional consideration of the ABM Treaty in 1972.

The "dual-unitary" debate about treaty interpretation is not the first constitutional debate about the treaty power in United States history. President George Washington's neutrality proclamation was the occasion of a lively debate between Hamilton and Madison as to the scope of the President's power. This debate, known as the Pacificus-Helvidius debate, is one of the classics in our constitutional history.[1] Subsequently, the 1950's witnessed the debate about the "Bricker Amendment" concerning the scope of the federal treaty power. More recently, the Vietnam War era produced debates about the modalities for entering into international agreements, whether treaties, international agreements pursuant to legislation, or Presidential agreements, and about the scope of authority to enter into "national commitments".[2] And the post-Vietnam 1970's produced a dramatic debate between the branches as to the President's authority to terminate treaties, following President Carter's normalization of relations with the People's Republic of China.[3] The "dual-unitary" debate about the proper mode of treaty interpretation under the Constitution is simply the latest in a long history of debates about the precise scope and operation of the treaty power. As such, of course, it builds upon the historical foundation of previous national treaty debates.

---

1 *See generally,* Alexander Hamilton, "First *Pacificus* Letter 29 June 1793," *reprinted in* 1 *W. Goldsmith, The Growth of Presidential Power* 398, 400-04 (1974); James Madison, "First *Helvidius* Letter August-September 1793," *reprinted in* 1 *W. Goldsmith, supra,* at 405, 407-10.

2 See generally, John Norton Moore, "Executive Agreements and Congressional Executive Relations," the Appendix to "Statement of John Norton Moore" (April 11, 1979), *in Treaty Termination Hearings Before the Senate Comm. On Foreign Relations, 96th Cong., 1st Sess. 400, 414 (1979).*

3 See generally "Statement of John Norton Moore for Treaty Termination Hearings," *supra* note 2, at 400.

The reader should also be aware that the post-Vietnam era produced a host of constitutional confrontations between the branches as to their respective authority in foreign affairs. Issues debated, in addition to various treaty issues, included a range of war power issues, information flow and executive privilege issues, and conduct and oversight of intelligence activities, among others. The Vietnam and immediate post-Vietnam eras saw increasing Congressional activism in response to what some believed was an "Imperial Presidency". More recently, there seems to be a move back to an historically more normal recognition of Executive Branch primacy in foreign affairs with parallel concerns expressed about an "Imperial Congress".

Hopefully, the materials in this monograph will assist in shedding light on the continuing debate between the branches in the conduct of foreign relations. At the least, it is hoped that they will aid in reducing the heat to light ratio of too much of this debate.

John Norton Moore
Charlottesville, Virginia
January 1, 2001

Acknowledgments

The views expressed in this monograph are solely those of the author and do not necessarily reflect the views of any agency or organization with which he is or has been affiliated, including the United States government, its Department of State, the United States Arms Control and Disarmament Agency (ACDA), the University of Virginia or the Center for National Security Law.

Thanks are due to Mrs. Christian Smith who provided editorial assistance in preparation of this volume in the original study prepared for the Director of ACDA. I would also like to thank Ms. Lauren Greenwood for flawlessly executing the Herculean task of translating an older version of WordPerfect into the finished manuscript.

Acknowledgments

Table of Contents

The National Law of Treaty Implementation

Legal Issues Under National Law Concerning Treaty Implementation and the Constitutional Structure for Separation of Powers in Foreign Policy

A. The Issues

In addition to its central focus on the appropriate interpretation of the ABM Treaty under international law, the "broad-narrow" debate has raised a series of legal issues concerning treaty implementation under national law. The thrust of this controversy has related to the relevance and weight to be accorded the record of Senate consideration of the ABM Treaty and the relative powers of the Senate, the Congress, and the President in implementation of treaties.[1] The immediate thrust

---

[1]*See generally* on this debate *Office of the Legal Adviser, U.S. Dep't of State, The ABM Treaty Studies: Part II: Ratification Process* (May 11, 1987) [hereinafter The ABM Treaty Studies, Part II]; Senator Sam Nunn, "Part One: The Senate Ratification Proceedings," in Senator Nunn's paper "Interpretation of the ABM Treaty" (May 19, 1987), in *The ABM Treaty and the Constitution: Joint Hearings Before the Senate Comms. on Foreign Relations and on the Judiciary*, 100th Cong., 1st Sess. 553, 560 (1987) [hereinafter *The ABM Treaty and the Constitution]*; Senator Ernest F. Hollings, "The ABM Treaty" (Statement of March 26, 1987); Assistant Attorney General Charles J. Cooper, "Memorandum to Abraham D. Sofaer, Legal Adviser, Department of State, Re: Relevance of Senate Ratification History to Treaty Interpretation" (U.S. Dep't of Justice, Office of Legal Counsel, April 9, 1987); *The ABM Treaty Interpretation Resolution: Report of the Senate Comm. on Foreign Relations Together with Additional Views, S. Rep. No.* 164, 100th Cong., 1st Sess. (Sept. 22, 1987) [hereinafter *The ABM Treaty Interpretation Resolution]; The INF Treaty: Report of the Senate Comm. on Foreign Relations, S. Exec Rep. No.* 15, 100th Cong., 2d Sess. (April 14, 1988) [hereinafter *The INF Treaty Report*]; Koplow, "Constitutional Bait and Switch: Executive Reinterpretation of Arms Control Treaties" (draft article of Nov. 1, 1988) [hereinafter Koplow Draft], forthcoming in 137 *U. Pennsylvania L. Rev.* (May 1989). Commentaries on the same theme to be published in this May issue of the *Pennsylvania University Law Review* include: Block, Casey & Rivkin, "The Senate's Pie-in-the-Sky Treaty Interpretation Power and the Quest for Legislative Supremacy"; Biden & Ritch, "The Treaty Power: Upholding a Constitutional Partnership"; Sofaer, "Treaty Interpretation: A Comment"; Trimble, "The Constitutional Common Law of Treaty Interpretation: A Reply to the Formalists"; Fisher, "Constitutional Participation in the Treaty Process" (developed from a speech, "Constitutional Underpinnings of the Treaty Powers," delivered at the Syracuse Conference on "Treaty Implementation and Interpretation Under the Constitution," March 10-11, 1989); Rostow, "The Reinterpretation Debate and Constitutional Law"; Nunn, "A Common-sense Definition of `Common Understanding.'" *Also see* Koh, Nowak, Rees & Sofaer, "The Treaty Power," in "Symposium: Foreign Affairs and the Constitution: The Roles of Congress, the President, and the Courts," 43 *U. Miami L. Rev.* 101 (Sept. 1988); Address

of this debate is whether the President remains free under national law to elect to act on the "broad" interpretation (at least absent a specific congressional ban as currently and in recent years has been attached on a yearly basis to Defense Authorization acts) or whether he may be bound to the "narrow" interpretation whatever the appropriate interpretation of the ABM Treaty under international law and regardless of any specific congressional ban. The debate, however, has proceeded more broadly with at least a bare majority of the Senate Foreign Relations Committee proposing in S. Res. 167[2] a method of treaty interpretation, at least under national law, that would require that "meaning is to be determined in light of what the Senate understands the treaty to mean when it gives its advice and consent" and "the Senate's understanding of a treaty cannot be informed by matters of which it is not aware." Moreover, Senators Byrd and Nunn have proposed a related "three principles"[3] of treaty interpretation; and, most recently, the Senate has attached a treaty interpretation condition to the resolution of ratification of the INF

---

by Abraham Sofaer, "Treaty Interpretation and Separation of Powers," to the American Law Institute, Chicago, Illinois (May 19, 1988). On March 10-11, 1989, a conference was held on "Treaty Implementation and Interpretation Under the Constitution," sponsored by the American Bar Association Standing Committee on Law and National Security and the Syracuse University College of Law, and it is expected that the proceedings will be published. *See*, and compare, particularly from this conference Fisher, "Constitutional Underpinnings of the Treaty Powers" [hereinafter Fisher, "Constitutional Underpinnings"], and Turner, "Constitutional Underpinnings of the Treaty Powers" [hereinafter Turner, "Constitutional Underpinnings"]. *Also see* a recent *Yale Law Journal* "Note," Lehmann, "Reinterpreting Advice and Consent: A Congressional Fast Track for Arms Control Treaties," 98 Yale L.J. 885 (March 1989).

[2]*See* "Text of S. Res. 167 (as reported)," in *The ABM Treaty Interpretation Resolution*, *supra* note 1, at 117-20. The key committee vote was 9-10, perfectly following party lines with all Democrats supporting S. Res. 167 and all Republicans supporting the alternative, *see The ABM Treaty Interpretation Resolution*, *supra* note 1, at 37.

S. Res. 167 has not become law but its theoretical underpinnings have led to the recent INF Treaty interpretation condition attached by the Senate to its advice and consent to the INF Treaty and discussed subsequently in this part.

[3]Letter from Senators Robert C. Byrd and Sam Nunn to Secretary of State George P. Shultz (Feb. 5, 1988).

Treaty.[4] To the extent that the approaches to treaty interpretation reflected in these related initiatives vary from the international standard as reflected in the Vienna Convention on the Law of Treaties, as they clearly seem to in a number of important respects;[5] it would require the United States to follow a dual mode of treaty interpretation, proceeding separately under both national and international law, which could require a result in individual cases at variance with well accepted principles of international law.

While these national law elements of the "broad-narrow" debate have tended to center on the relevance and weight of informal Senate ratification history to treaty interpretation (and particularly the legal effect of Executive branch statements made to the Senate during the advice and consent process), and the appropriate Senate, congressional, and presidential roles in treaty interpretation, full understanding of the debate and its implications both for the "broad-narrow" issue as well as future processes of treaty interpretation require focus on a range of individual but interrelated legal issues under national law, principally the national constitutional law of separation of powers in foreign policy concerning treaty implementation, and application of this law to the "broad-narrow" interpretation debate. Accordingly, this part of the overall study will be divided into four subsequent sections. These are: (B), which will focus on legal issues of separation of powers in foreign policy and the national law of treaty implementation; (C), which will provide an overview of the process of congressional consideration of the "broad-narrow" issue; (D), which will apply the law and the facts of treaty implementation to the "broad-narrow" dispute in parallel to all other parts of this study; and (E), which will provide a brief postscript on any constitutional issues posed by Senate Resolution 167, the "Byrd-Nunn three principles," and the INF Treaty interpretation condition. The heart of the legal discussion appears in section (B), immediately following this introduction to the issues. Section (B) will review the range of legal issues as follows:

1. An overview of the treaty power in the constitutional structure for separation of powers in foreign policy

---

[4]134 *Cong. Rec.* S6724 (daily ed. May 26, 1988) (Amendment No. 2305), 134 Cong. Rec. S6937 (daily ed. May 27, 1988) (Resolution of Ratification of the INF Treaty).

[5]This could include, *inter alia,* the relative legal effect to be given the negotiating record and record of ratification proceedings under national law.

a. General
b. The treaty power

2. Presidential authority to interpret treaties in the absence of congressional action

3. Relevance and weight of the record of Senate consideration of a treaty for interpretation of that treaty

   a. Threshold questions as to the goal of treaty interpretation under national law: the problem of unitary or dual standards for interpretation

   b. Questions of the relevance and weight to be accorded a range of elements in the process of Senate consideration: the problem of legislative (or treaty) history as an extrinsic aid to interpretation

   c. Questions of the level of generality in posing the issue of Senate purpose or intent: the problem of appropriate breadth of context and/or mistaken interpretation in Senate consideration for advice and consent

   d. A synthesis concerning relevance and weight of the record of Senate consideration

4. Issues of estoppel arising from the advice and consent process

5. The authority of a subsequent Senate or Congress to interpret a treaty consented to by a prior Senate

6. Presidential and congressional authority concerning suspension or termination of a treaty in whole or in part in response to prior breach of agreement

a. Presidential authority in the absence of congressional action

b. Congressional authority

7. Weight to be accorded Executive branch actions interpreting or implementing a treaty

8. Other potentially relevant national laws and a possible obligation of any administration to make known, at least to Congress, what it comes to believe may be a mistaken interpretation of an arms control agreement.

An outline of this section on the legal issues has been set out here to alert the reader that the legal issues are complex, and are not usefully subsumed under a single legal proposition. Indeed, they are broader than popularly assumed in much of the "broad-narrow" debate.

The reader should also be aware that while answers to some of these issues are clear, such as presidential authority to interpret treaties in the absence of congressional action, others, reflecting the underlying uncertainties of the constitutional scheme of separation of powers, are less clear or even unclear. These latter issues are likely to be the subject of competing constitutional theories, sometimes advanced in partisan debate as constitutionally self-evident, and may be expected to form the core of recurrent debates between Congress and the President concerning their appropriate roles in foreign policy. As Professor Louis Henkin reminds us in his seminal work on *Foreign Affairs and the Constitution*:

> The respective powers of President and Congress are established in the large, but the division I have described has not been accepted in all respects by all Presidents and all Congresses at all times, and in any event the generalizations leave ample areas of uncertainty. In principle, as in fact, recurrent competition for power has punctuated relations between President and Congress, throwing up the dominant, least-tractable constitutional issues of American foreign relations. That the Constitution is especially inarticulate in allocating foreign affairs powers; that a particular power can with equal logic and fair constitutional reading be claimed for the President or for Congress; that the powers of both President and

> Congress have been described in full, even extravagant adjectives ("vast," "plenary"); that instead of a "natural" separation of "executive" from "legislative" functions there has grown an irregular, uncertain division of each--all have served and nurtured political forces inviting to struggle. . . . Since, generally, these "boundary disputes" have not been resolved in court, they remain unresolved in principle and if the President has succeeded in winning most of them in fact, Congressional "irredentism" runs deep and erupts in almost every Congressional generation. Practice and sometimes even constitutional doctrine have been shaped by personal or partisan and other political relations between particular Presidents and particular Congresses (or Congressmen), sometimes too by particular issues: Lincoln and both Roosevelts effectively took power from fearful or friendly Congresses; the Vietnam war stirred Congressmen to reassert authority and confront the President.[6]

And as he points out in his "Introduction" to this book:

> Since the courts are not the principal arena the contests are fought within and between the political branches of government and are political rather than juridical. Since, usually, private interests are not directly at stake, the causes behind the issues tend to be "political" rather than economic or libertarian. Charges of Presidential usurpation, for a recurrent example, come principally from those who oppose the politics of his policies, as once from isolationist critics "on the right" of Franklin Roosevelt, more recently from anti-interventionist critics "on the left" of Lyndon Johnson or Richard Nixon; constitutional limitations on the Treaty Power are asserted by those who seek to preserve remnants of "States' rights" or to keep the United States free of naval foreign entanglements.[7]

---

[6] *L. Henkin, Foreign Affairs and the Constitution* 90 (1972).

[7] *Id.* at 6.

In a recent article, Professor Louis Henkin provides the following description of the recurrent tensions between the branches in the exercise of the treaty power:

CONSTITUTIONAL CONTROVERSIES ABOUT THE TREATY POWER

Constitutional controversies under the Treaty Power erupted early in our history, and during 200 years the infinite variety of international relations and of constitutional politics have continued to generate issues. Some of the controversies reflect differences as to the meaning or implications of the constitutional text; some reflect dissatisfaction with what the text has come to mean, or with how it has worked.

It is unnecessary to revisit the storms generated by the Jay Treaty of 1796, or even the Treaty of Versailles, now 70 years ago. We find uncertainties and controversies in our daily papers. In 1988, the Senate denied President Reagan's power to interpret the Anti-Ballistic Missile (ABM) Treaty other than as the Senate had interpreted it when the Senate consented to making that treaty. Later the Senate in effect declared its constitutional views on that issue as a condition of its consent to the Intermediate Nuclear Force (INF) Treaty. A few years ago the Senate challenged President Carter's authority to terminate the Defense Treaty with the Republic of China (Taiwan) without the consent of of [sic] Congress or at least of the Senate. Members of Congress went to court in an attempt to enjoin carrying out the Panama Canal Treaty, claiming that it was beyond the powers of the President and Senate under the Constitution.[6] [6. Edwards v. Carter, 580 F.2d 1055 (D.C. Cir. 1978), cert. denied, 436 U.S. 907 (1978); *see also infra* note 39.]

Other issues are older, but recur, and might yet trouble us again in the next century.[7] [7. One controversy, I hope, will not be resurrected: the campaign led by Senator Bricker to have the Constitution amended so as -- they thought -- to limit sharply the uses of the treaty power, and make it impossible for the United States to adhere to international human rights covenants.] Above all, repeatedly during 200 years, Senate and President have exchanged recriminations, the Senate accusing the President of frustrating the Senate's constitutional role, the President charging the Senate with abusing that role and embarrassing the United States in its relations with other countries. Again and again, during 200 years, Senators have challenged the President's authority to conclude international agreements as executive agreements without Senate consent.[8] [8. Senator Robert Dole went to court to try to prevent President Carter from returning the crown of St. Stephen to Hungary without a treaty approved by the Senate. See Dole v. Carter, 569 F.2d 1109 (10th Cir. 1977).] Every year during 200 years members of the House of Representatives have expressed resentment at their exclusion from treaty-making, and there have been innumerable proposals for amending the Constitution to undo that "error" of the Framers.

Despite the frequent uncertainties of the constitutional context of separation of powers in foreign policy, careful legal analysis as to the appropriate roles of Congress and the President is of fundamental importance for the preservation and effective growth of our constitutional system. The context suggests, however, that appropriate modesty in recognizing the real uncertainties of the legal map may be more frequently appropriate than charges that an opposing interpretation will precipitate a "constitutional crisis" or destroy the rule of law.

B. Separation of Powers in Foreign Policy and the National Law of Treaty Implementation

1. An overview of the treaty power in the constitutional structure for separation of powers in foreign policy

a. General

The doctrine of separation of powers is a major underpinning of the Constitution of the United States. The framers, familiar with the writings of John Locke and the Baron de Montesquieu, sought to create separate and distinct legislative, executive and judicial branches of government operating in a setting of checks and balances. This structure was motivated by the twin convictions that such separation of powers would work to preserve liberty and that it would promote efficiencies in carrying out the different forms of governmental power. In establishing a government of separate and distinct branches operating under checks and balances, the framers were concerned to avoid both a too dominant Executive, as in some periods of the history of the British Crown, and a too dominant legislature, as in their more recent experience with many state governments and under the Continental Congress and Articles of Confederation.[8]

Henkin, "Treaties in a Constitutional Democracy," 10 *Mich. J. Int'l L.* 406, 407-08 (Spring 1989).

[8]*See, e.g., A. Sofaer, War, Foreign Affairs, and Constitutional Power: The Origins* 6-25 (1976). Professor Harold J. Krent wrote recently in the Virginia Law Review:

> Although the Constitution places checks on all three branches, it circumscribes the legislature most rigidly. This result is not surprising because an overriding goal

---

of the framers in establishing a system of checks and balances was to limit the legislative power. Madison explained that "[i]n republican government, the legislative authority necessarily predominates" because the authority to set rules and policy makes the legislature the most powerful branch. Experience under the Articles of Confederation and various state constitutions had painfully proven that such power was subject to abuse; as Madison stated, "The legislative department is everywhere extending the sphere of its activity and drawing all power in its impetuous vortex." In particular, state legislators constructed a variety of inflationary schemes to aid debtors to the detriment of creditors both overseas and within the states. Such legislation not only led to a general decline in confidence (particularly among the moneyed classes), but also led indirectly to social unrest. Madison further stressed that in light of Congress's "constitutional powers being at once more extensive, and less susceptible of precise limits, it can, with the greater facility, mask, under complicated and indirect measures, the encroachments which it makes on the co-ordinate departments." Indeed, Madison noted that "the legislative department alone has access to the pockets of the people." Because of the inadequacy of circumscribing authority through a functionalist description of the powers to be exercised, the framers sought to restrain Congress through "internal" checks by circumscribing the ways it must act. Constructing safeguards internal to the legislature would check encroachment on the other branches and at the same time protect the public from arbitrary governance. In other words, as John Jay explained, "It surely does not follow that because they have given the power of making laws to the legislature, that therefore they should likewise give them power to do every other act of sovereignty by which the citizens are to be bound and affected."[41] [[41] The Federalist No. 64, supra note 21, at 394 (J. Jay). Although Jay was defending the Convention's choice not to give Congress the power to make treaties, his comments are illustrative of the general concern for limiting congressional power to legislation.]

The requirement of bicameralism constrains Congress's power by delimiting how it may act. The Federalist Papers explain that one "remedy . . . is to divide the legislature into different branches; and to render them, by different modes of election and different principles of action, as little connected with each other as the nature of their common functions and their common dependence on the society will admit." Legislative rule could result in the tyranny of the majority or in a legislature captured by faction. Requiring the concurrence of two distinct houses of Congress

> must be in all cases a salutary check on the government. It doubles the security to the people by requiring the concurrence of two distinct bodies in schemes of usurpation or perfidy . . . .

> . . . The necessity of a senate is not less indicated by the propensity of all single and numerous assemblies to yield to the impulse of sudden and violent passions, and to be seduced by factious leaders into intemperate and pernicious resolutions.

The requirement of bicameralism also preserves the separation of powers by limiting legislative authority vis-a-vis the other branches. Legislation potentially encroaching upon areas reserved to the other branches can only be passed if both houses concur. The judiciary and the executive, as well as the public, are therefore shielded to some extent from encroachments by factions.

Similarly, requiring presentment of legislation to the President plainly serves a critical separation of powers function. Hamilton feared that without a veto the legislature could gradually strip the executive of power, either "by successive resolutions" or "by a single vote." According to Hamilton, however, the veto

> not only serves as a shield to the executive, but it furnishes an additional security against the enaction of improper laws. It establishes a salutary check upon the legislative body, calculated to guard the community against the effects of faction, precipitancy, or of any impulse unfriendly to the public good, which may happen to influence a majority of that body.

The presentment requirement therefore ensures that the legislative branch will be accountable for its actions. By requiring the procedural step of presentment to the President, the framers circumscribed Congress's ability to pass laws that would encroach on the coordinate branches of government and harm the public at large.

. . . .

Although many participants in the Convention feared executive power, the primary architects of the Constitution were more suspicious of the legislative branch. For example, Madison stated that, in contrast to the nearly limitless power of the legislature, "the executive power being restrained within a narrower compass and being more simple in its nature . . . projects of usurpation . . . would immediately betray and defeat themselves." Montesquieu similarly had less fear of executive encroachments because "as the execution has its natural limits, it is useless to confine it; besides, the executive power is generally employed in momentary operations." As Justice Story later commented, Congress "must have a controlling influence over the executive power, since it holds at its own command all the resources, by which a chief magistrate could make himself formidable. . . . [I]t can unnerve the power of the sword by striking down the arm, which wields it."

The Constitution does not prescribe procedures comparable to the bicameralism and presentment requirements to constrain the executive. The framers rejected

Emphatically, separation of was not intended to be a one way street operating solely to limit executive power. It was at least equally fundamentally to serve as a check on legislative power. This fundamental underpinning of our constitutional system is reflected in the writings of theorists such as Locke and Montesquieu, framers such as James Madison, George Washington as the first American President, and repeated judicial statement, among other abundant sources. Thus Montesquieu wrote:

> In every government there are three sorts of power: the legislative; the executive in respect to things dependent on the law of nations; and the executive in regard to matters that depend on the civil law.
>
> . . . .
>
> The executive power, pursuant of what has been already said, ought to have a share in the legislature by the power of rejecting; otherwise it would soon be stripped of its prerogative. But should the legislative power usurp a share of the executive, the latter would be equally undone.[9]

James Madison wrote in *The Federalist* No. 49:

> The several departments being perfectly co-ordinate by the term of their common commission, neither of them, it is evident, can

---

> proposals to split the executive, and the President has never been required to present any planned action to Congress prior to execution.

Krent, "Separating the Strands in Separation of Powers Controversies," 74 *Va. L. Rev.* 1253, 1262-66 (1988) (footnotes omitted except note 41, included in brackets within text).

[9] 1 *Montesquieu, The Spirit of Laws* 151-52, 156-61 (T. Nugent trans., rev. ed. 1900). A recent article by Robert Wernick describes Montesquieu as "The Godfather of the American Constitution," and quotes Montesquieu's *The Spirit of Laws*: "`When the legislative and executive powers are united in the same person, or in the same body of magistrates, there can be no liberty.'" Wernick, "The Godfather of the American Constitution," 20 *Smithsonian* 183, 193 (Sept. 1989) (quoting Montesquieu, *The Spirit of Laws*, book 11, chapter 6).

> pretend to an exclusive or superior right of settling the boundaries between their respective powers.[10]

And Madison said during the debate over the establishment of the Department of Foreign Affairs on June 17, 1789:

> There is another maxim which ought to direct us in expounding the Constitution, and it is of great importance. It is laid down, in most of the Constitutions or bills of rights in the republics of America; it is to be found in the political writings of the most celebrated civilians, and is every where held as essential to the preservation of liberty, that the three great departments of government to be kept separate and distinct; and if in any case they are blended, it is in order to admit a partial qualification, in order more effectually to guard against an entire consolidation. I think, therefore, when we review the several parts of this Constitution, when it says that the Legislative powers shall be vested in a Congress of the United States, under certain exceptions, we must suppose they were intended to be kept separate in all cases in which they are not blended, and ought, consequently, to expound the Constitution so as to blend them as little as possible.[11]

President George Washington said in his Farewell Address, after months of annoyance over a constitutional debate with the House of Representatives which had requested and been refused the instructions and papers surrounding the negotiation of the Jay Treaty:

> It is important, likewise, that the habits of thinking in a free country should inspire caution in those intrusted with its administration to confine themselves within their respective constitutional spheres, avoiding in the exercise of the powers of one department to encroach upon another. The spirit of encroachment

---

[10]*The Federalist* No. 49, at 339 (J. Madison).

[11]James Madison, "Remarks During Debate on Establishing Department of Foreign Affairs," 1 *Annals of Cong.* 496-97 (1789).

> tends to consolidate the powers of all the departments in one, and thus to create, whatever the form of government, a real despotism.[12]

Similarly, the Supreme Court wrote in *Kendall v. United States* as early as 1838:

> The theory of the Constitution undoubtedly is that the great powers of the government are divided into separate departments: and so far as these powers are derived from the Constitution, the departments may be regarded as independent of each other. But beyond that, all are subject to regulations by law, touching the discharge of the duties required to be performed.
>
> The executive power is vested in a President, and as far as his powers are derived from the Constitution, he is beyond the reach of any other department, except in the mode prescribed by the constitution through the impeaching power.[13]

The important principle of separation of powers has not been simply a theoretical proposition in American constitutional law. In the case of *Myers v. United States,*[14] for example, the Supreme Court held that the requirement of Senate approval of executive officials was to be strictly construed and did not permit an act of Congress conditioning removal of such officials on Senate consent. Chief Justice Taft's Opinion of the Court in the *Myers* case emphasized the importance of a vital and living principle of separation of powers:

> [During Congressional debate, Representative James Madison said]: If there is a principle in our Constitution, indeed in any free Constitution, more sacred than another, it is that which separates the Legislative, Executive and Judicial powers. . . .

---

[12]1 *J. Richardson, Messages and Papers of the Presidents* 213 (Sept. 17, 1796). *See also* Younger, "Congressional Investigations and Executive Secrecy: A Study in the Separation of Powers," 20 U. of *Pittsburgh L. Rev.* 755, 756-58 (1959).

[13]Kendall v. United States, 37 U.S. (12 Pet.) 524, 610 (1838). *See also* Kilbourn v. Thompson, 103 U.S. 168, 190-91 (1881); Evans v. Gore, 253 U.S. 245, 247, 249 (1920); Myers v. United States, 272 U.S. 52, 116-18, 127-28, 151-52, 163-64 (1926).

[14]272 U.S. 52 (1926).

> Their union under the Confederation had not worked well, as the members of the Convention know. Montesquieu's view that the maintenance of independence as between the legislative, the executive and the judicial branches was security for the people had their full approval. . . . Accordingly, the Constitution was so framed as to vest in the Congress all legislative powers therein granted, to vest in the President the executive power, and to vest in one Supreme Court and such inferior courts as Congress might establish, the judicial power. From this division on principle, the reasonable construction of the Constitution must be that the branches should be kept separate in all cases in which they were not expressly blended, and the Constitution should be expounded to blend them no more than it affirmatively requires.[15]

Thus, the *Myers* case, with an explicit rooting in the constitutional principle of separation of powers, definitively established that the Constitution sets important limits on the exercise of congressional power which is, among other limits, also to be limited by the principle of separation of power.[16]

While the general principle of separation of powers is firmly established as constitutional doctrine, the precise parameters of congressional and presidential authority in foreign policy under that doctrine is clear on some issues and unclear

---

[15]*Id.* at 116-18.

[16]Specifically with respect to the treaty power, Story, in his *Commentaries on the Constitution of the United States*, writes:

> §1508. The power "to make treaties" is by the Constitution general . . . . But though the power is thus general and unrestricted, it is not to be so construed as to destroy the fundamental laws of the State. A power given by the Constitution cannot be construed to authorize a destruction of other powers given in the same instrument. It must be construed, therefore, in subordination to it; and cannot supersede or interfere with any other of its fundamental provisions. Each is equally obligatory, and of paramount authority within its scope; and no one embraces a right to annihilate any other.

2 *J. Story, Commentaries on the Constitution of the United States* 338-39 (5th ed. 1891) (footnote omitted).

on others. In the absence of Supreme Court consideration of most of these issues, partly as a result of the Court's policy of judicial restraint as embodied in the political question doctrine,[17] the constitutional parameters have pragmatically evolved from a combination of constitutional language concerning grants of specific foreign affairs powers, constitutional theories of the roles of Congress and the Presidency under the Constitution and the crucible of two hundred years of national practice.

In simplest outline, the Constitution provides in Article I, section 1, that "[a]ll legislative Powers herein granted shall be vested in a Congress of the United States, which shall consist of a Senate and House of Representatives." Pursuant to this grant Congress is given specific powers in Article 1, section 8, "[t]o regulate Commerce with foreign Nations," "[t]o define and punish Piracies and Felonies committed on the high Seas, and Offences against the Law of Nations; To declare War, grant Letters of Marque and Reprisal, and make Rules concerning Captures on Land and Water; To raise and support Armies," "[t]o provide and maintain a Navy; To make Rules for the Government and Regulation of the land and naval Forces; To provide for calling forth the Militia," and "[t]o provide for organizing, arming, and disciplining, the Militia." Congress was also given the general powers to tax and appropriate and "[t]o make all Laws which shall be necessary and proper for carrying into Execution the foregoing Powers, and all other Powers vested by this Constitution in the Government of the United States, or in any Department or Officer thereof." Article II, section 2, clause 2 also gives the Senate an advice and consent role with respect to treaties and the appointment of Ambassadors "and all other Officers of the United States."

Presidential powers in foreign policy are enumerated under Article II. The first sentence of Article II, section 1 provides, in terms contrastingly unqualified to the comparable grant of legislative authority to Congress in the first sentence of Article I, section 1, that "[t]he executive Power shall be vested in a President of the United States of America." Article II, section 2, clause 1 specifically says that in addition to this general grant of power "[t]he President shall be Commander in Chief of the Army and Navy of the United States," and Article II, section 2, clause 2 says:

---

[17]*See, e.g.*, Moore, "The Justiciability of Challenges to the Use of Military Forces Abroad" in *J.N. Moore, Law and the Indo-China War* 570 (1972) [hereinafter *J.N. Moore, Indo-China]*.

> He shall have Power, by and with the Advice and Consent of the Senate, to make Treaties, provided two thirds of the Senators present concur; and he shall nominate, and by and with the Advice and Consent of the Senate, shall appoint Ambassadors, other public Ministers and Consuls . . . and all other Officers of the United States . . . .

The specifically enumerated presidential powers in foreign policy are concluded in Article II, section 3, with the statement that:

> he shall receive Ambassadors and other public Ministers; [and] he shall take Care that the Laws be faithfully executed . . . .

In some respects this linguistic outline has definitively answered separation of powers issues in foreign policy. No one doubts but that Congress may not constitutionally direct the President how to conduct tactical operations during wartime. The commander-in-chief power has, at least at its core, been clear as to that. Similarly, it has generally been accepted that the Article II, section 3 direction that the President "shall receive Ambassadors and other public Ministers" carries an exclusive implied presidential power to recognize foreign governments or nations on which Congress may not encroach. In many other respects, however, the sketchiness of the constitutional outline has, at least by itself, failed to resolve issues of separation of powers and, indeed, as Professor Corwin has observed: "the Constitution, considered only for its affirmative grants of power capable of affecting the issue, is an invitation to struggle for the privilege of directing American foreign policy."[18] In turn this lack of specificity in the Constitution concerning foreign policy has stimulated and enhanced the development and importance of competing constitutional theories about the respective roles of Congress and the President in foreign policy. Those supporting broad congressional authority have tended to ignore or downplay the Article II, section 1 general and unqualified grant to the President of "the executive Power"; have emphasized general congressional powers, as in the taxing and appropriations powers and the necessary and proper clause; have argued for broad implied powers from specific grants of legislative powers in

---

[18]*E. Corwin, The President: Office and Powers 1787-1957*, at 171 (4th rev. ed. 1957). This statement is sometimes erroneously taken for the overly broad proposition that there is no guidance in the Constitution concerning separation of powers in foreign policy.

Article I, section 8, or even general implied foreign affairs legislative power;[19] and

---

[19]Professor Louis Henkin, in his important work on *Foreign Affairs and the Constitution* enumerates a broad range of congressional powers in foreign policy. In this respect he says, "although explicitly the Constitution gives Congress only all legislative Powers herein granted, Congress, we know, has also an unenumerated foreign affairs power, the legislative derivative of the powers of the United States inherent in its sovereignty." *L. Henkin*, *supra* note 6, at 68. Professor Henkin also argues, by analogy from the growth in domestic reach of the commerce clause, that "[t]he Commerce Power, then, might be sufficient to support virtually any legislation that relates to foreign intercourse, *i.e.*, to foreign relations." *Id.* at 70.

For an analysis of the general authority of Congress and the President in foreign affairs from a perspective sympathetic to Congress, see L. Fisher, "Understanding the Role of Congress in Foreign Policy," 11 *George Mason U.L. Rev.* 153 (Fall 1988). As was also true of the Majority Report in the Iran-Contra affair ("Powers of Congress and the President in the Field of Foreign Policy" (Chapter 25), in *Report of the Congressional Committees Investigating the Iran-Contra Affair with Supplemental, Minority, and Additional Views, S. Rep. No.* 216 and *H.R. Rep.* No. 433, 100th Cong., 1st Sess. (Nov. 17, 1987)), this paper does not even mention the Article II, section 1 general grant of "[t]he executive Power" to the President. And while it is notably silent on any possible implied foreign affairs power in the Executive, it sweepingly argues that "Congress has extensive powers in foreign affairs, including not only the powers specifically enumerated in the Constitution but also those implied in the effective functioning of government." L. Fisher, *supra*, at 13.

For an even more recent analysis from a perspective sympathetic to Congress, see Schlesinger, "The Legislative-Executive Balance in International Affairs: The Intentions of the Framers," 12 *Wash. Q.* 99 (1989). Professor Schlesinger does point out that "Article II gave the president general executive power." *Id.* at 102. On an earlier occasion Professor Schlesinger took a different view more sympathetic to the power of the Presidency in foreign affairs--at least with respect to the deployment of military force. When President Truman came under criticism from conservative legislators for having committed United States forces to hostilities in Korea, Professor Schlesinger came to his defense. He denounced Senator Robert Taft's position that such a commitment required formal congressional authorization as "demonstrably irresponsible," and argued:

> From the day that President Jefferson ordered Commodore Dale and two-thirds of the American Navy into the Mediterranean to repel the Barbary pirates American Presidents have repeatedly committed American armed forces abroad without prior Congressional consultation or approval.
>
> In 1836 John Quincy Adams wrote:
>
> "However startled we may be at the idea that the Executive Chief Magistrate has

have stressed the advantages of congressional checks on executive power in a democratic government of checks and balances. Those supporting broad executive authority have stressed the unqualified grant of "the executive Power" to the President, and the contrast between this unqualified grant to the President and the Article I, section 1 qualified grant to Congress of the legislative Powers "herein granted"; have pointed out that under the theories of Locke, Montesquieu, and Blackstone known to the framers that the executive power included the foreign affairs power;[20] have argued that in matters of foreign policy where the general authority to represent the Nation is executive that congressional power should be narrowly construed (and thus certainly if the issue is one of interference with presidential foreign affairs power, no implied congressional foreign affairs powers, if any, or broadened commerce clause where the issue is competing state power, should be permitted to override presidential authority); have pointed out that the general grant of "the Executive Power" to the President derived from the New York Constitution, which unlike many of the other contemporary state constitutions had a strong Executive able to maintain its independence from the Legislature and that there had been widespread dissatisfaction with the weakness of the Executive under those other state constitutions;[21] have pointed out that the well-established principle

---

> the power of involving the nation in war, even without consulting Congress, an experience of fifty years has proved that in numberless cases he has and must have exercised that power * * *. Defensive war must necessarily be among the duties of the Executive Chief Magistrate."
>
> . . . .
>
> Until Senator Taft and his friends succeed in rewriting American history according to their own specifications these facts must stand as obstacles to their efforts to foist off their current political prejudices as eternal American verities.

Schlesinger, N.Y. Times, Jan. 9, 1951, "Letters to The Times" section, at 28, col. 6.

[20]Professor Quincy Wright observed in his classic study *The Control of American Foreign Relations* that "when the constitutional convention gave executive power to the President, the foreign relations power was the essential element in the grant." *Q. Wright, The Control of American Foreign Relations* 147 (1922).

[21]*See A. Sofaer, supra* note 8, at 17-19, 30. *See, e.g.*, on the early state constitutions and their contrast in the matter of executive authority with the constitutions of New York and Massachusetts, Howard, "The Renaissance of State Constitutional Law," in *National Association of Attorneys General, Emerging Issues in State Constitutional Law* 1, 2-3

of "unconstitutional conditions,"[22] as well as the *Myers* case, prohibit any blanket argument that anything Congress wishes to do can be done through the taxing and appropriations powers or the necessary and proper clause (indeed, they point out if these general grants were an adequate basis for any congressional action, there could be no separation of powers, or for that matter bill of rights guarantees); and have urged as policy grounds supporting this constitutional interpretation the functional attributes underlying executive foreign affairs authority, the need for the Nation to speak with one consistent voice in foreign affairs, and that the President is the only official in our democratic system elected by all the people of the United States.[23]

(Inaugural Issue: 1988).

[22]*See, e.g.*, as to the proposition that these general grants may not be used to infringe constitutional limitations McCray v. United States, 195 U.S. 27 (1904) (the taxing power); United States v. Butler, 297 U.S. 1 (1936) (the taxing power); Evans v. Gore, 253 U.S. 245 (1920) (the taxing power); United States v. Lovett, 328 U.S. 303 (1946) (the appropriations power); 9 Op. Att'y Gen. 462 (1860) (the appropriations power); 41 Op. Att'y Gen. 230 (1955) (the appropriations power); 41 Op. Att'y Gen. 507, 511 (1960).

See also on the limitations of the appropriations power, Turner, "The Power of the Purse: Controlling National Security Policy by Conditional Appropriations," *Atlantic Community Q.* 79 (Spring 1988).

[23]One of the most important and effective books making the case for broad presidential authority in foreign affairs is *R. Turner, Congress, the Constitution and Foreign Affairs* (University of Virginia Press, forthcoming 1989) [hereinafter *R. Turner, Congress*].

For a recent statement by the same author in the war powers setting, see Turner, "Restoring the `Rule of Law': Reflections on the War Powers Resolution at Fifteen," Prepared Testimony of Robert F. Turner Before the Senate Foreign Relations Special Subcomm. on War Powers (100 Cong., 2d Sess., Sept. 29, 1988). In concluding this testimony, Mr. Turner, a former Principal Deputy Assistant Secretary of State for Legislative and Intergovernmental Affairs, quotes a distinguished Harvard Law School Professor Charles Warren who wrote in 1930:

> Under our Constitution, each branch of the Government is designed to be a coordinate representative of the will of the people. . . . Defense by the Executive of his constitutional powers becomes in very truth, therefore, defense of popular rights--defense of power which the people granted him. . . . In maintaining his rights against a trespassing Congress, the President defends not himself, but popular government; he represents not himself, but the people.

In evaluating these competing models in constitutional theory it should be noted that at one time or another Hamilton, Madison and Jefferson all embraced the point that the general Article II grant of "the executive Power" to the President should be construed to mean that constitutional grants of authority to the Congress in associated areas are exceptions to be construed narrowly. Thus, in his first "Pacificus" letter of June 29, 1793, Alexander Hamilton wrote in defense of President Washington's neutrality proclamation:

> It will not be disputed that the management of the affairs of this country with foreign nations is confided to the Government of the United States.
>
> It can as little be disputed that a proclamation of neutrality, when a nation is at liberty to decline or avoid a war in which other nations are engaged, and means to do so, is a usual and a proper measure. Its main object is to prevent the nation's being responsible for acts done by its citizens, without the privity or connivance of the government, in contravention of the principles

---

Id. at 90 (quoting Warren, "Presidential Declarations of Independence," 10 *Boston U.L. Rev.* 1, 35 (1930)).

See also Turner, "The Constitution and the Iran-Contra Affair: Was Congress the Real Lawbreaker?," 11 *Houston J. Int'l L.* 83 (1988).

And for a presentation supporting Executive authority written by a thoughtful member of Congress with previous high level Executive branch experience who is currently serving as Secretary of Defense, see D. Cheney, "Congressional Overreaching in Foreign Policy" (Draft prepared for the American Enterprise Institute conference on "Foreign Policy and the Constitution," March 14-15, 1989).

> This essay is about patterns of Congressional overreaching during the years of the Reagan Administration. By choosing that subject, I do not mean to suggest that overreaching was limited to Capitol Hill. Anyone who followed the Iran-Contra affair knows that not to have been so. However, congressional aggrandizement does seem less generally understood, more systemic and more institutionally ingrained, than does its White House counterpart. Members of Congress may be asking for bipartisanship, but they have not given up what I would consider to be some of the more problematic aspects of their institutional self-understanding.

Id. at 2.

of neutrality; an object of the greatest moment to a country whose true interest lies in the preservation of peace.

The inquiry, then, is, what department of our government is the proper one to make a declaration of neutrality, when the engagements of the nation permit, and its interests require that it should be done?

A correct mind will discern at once, that it can belong neither to the legislative nor judicial department, and therefore of course must belong to the executive.

The legislative department is not the organ of intercourse between the United States and foreign nations. It is charged neither with making nor interpreting treaties. It is therefore not naturally that member of the government which is to pronounce on the existing condition of the nation with regard to foreign powers, or to admonish the citizens of their obligations and duties in consequence; still less is it charged with enforcing the observance of those obligations and duties.

It is equally obvious, that the act in question is foreign to the judiciary department. The province of that department is to decide the litigation in particular cases. It is indeed charged with the interpretations of treaties, but it exercises this function only where contending parties bring before it a specific controversy. It has no concern with pronouncing upon the external political relations of treaties between government and government. This position is too plain to need being insisted upon.

It must, then, of necessity belong to the executive department to exercise the function in question, when a proper case for it occurs.

It appears to be connected with that department in various capacities:--As the organ of intercourse between the nation and foreign nations; as the interpreter of the national treaties, in those cases in which the judiciary is not competent--that is, between government and government; as the power which is charged with the execution of the laws, of which treaties form a part; as that which is charged with the command and disposition of the public force.

This view of the subject is so natural and obvious, so analogous to general theory and practice, that no doubt can be entertained of its justness, unless to be deduced from particular provisions of the Constitution of the United States.

Let us see, then, if cause for such doubt is to be found there.

The second article of the Constitution of the United States, section first, establishes this general proposition, that "the executive power shall be vested in a President of the United States of America."

The same article, in a succeeding section, proceeds to delineate particular cases of executive power. It declares, among other things, that the President shall be commander-in-chief of the army and navy of the United States, and of the militia of the several States, when called into the actual service of the United States; that he shall have power, by and with the advice and consent of the Senate, to make treaties; that it shall be his duty to receive ambassadors and other public ministers, "and to take care that the laws be faithfully executed."

It would not consist with the rules of sound construction, to consider this enumeration of particular authorities as derogating from the more comprehensive grant in the general clause, further than as it may be coupled with express restrictions or limitations; as in regard to the co-operation of the Senate in the appointment of officers and the making of treaties; which are plainly qualifications of the general executive powers of appointing officers and making treaties. The difficulty of a complete enumeration of all the cases of executive authority would naturally dictate the use of general terms, and would render it improbable that a specification of certain particulars was designed as a substitute for those terms, when antecedently used. The different mode of expression employed in the Constitution, in regard to the two powers, the legislative and the executive, serves to confirm this inference. In the article which gives the legislative powers of the government, the expressions are: "All legislative powers herein granted shall be vested in a Congress of the United States." In that which grants the executive power, the expressions are: "The executive power shall be vested in a President of the United States."

The enumeration ought therefore to be considered as intended merely to specify the principle articles implied in the definition of executive power; leaving the rest to flow from the general grant of that power, interpreted in conformity with other parts of the Constitution, and with the principles of free government.

The general doctrine of our Constitution, then, is, that the executive power of the nation is vested in the President; subject only to the exceptions and qualifications which are expressed in the instrument.

Two of these have been already noticed: the participation of the Senate in the appointment of officers, and in the making of treaties. A third remains to be mentioned: the right of the Legislature "to declare war, and grant letters of marque and reprisal."

With these exceptions, the executive power of the United States is completely lodged in the President. This mode of construing the Constitution has indeed been recognized by Congress in formal acts, upon full consideration and debate; of which the power of removal from office is an important instance. It will follow, that if a proclamation of neutrality is merely an executive act, as, it is believed, has been shown, the step which has been taken by the President is liable to no just exception on the score of authority.

It may be said, that this inference would be just, if the power of declaring war had not been vested in the Legislature; but that this power naturally includes the right of judging whether the nation is or is not under obligations to make war.

The answer is, that, however true this position may be, it will not follow that the executive is in any case excluded from a similar right of judgment, in the execution of its own functions.

If, on the one hand, the Legislature have a right to declare war, it is on the other, the duty of the executive to preserve peace till the declaration is made; and in fulfilling this duty, it must necessarily possess a right of judging what is the nature of the obligations which the treaties of the country impose on the government; and when it has concluded that there is nothing in them inconsistent with neutrality, it becomes both its province and its duty to enforce the laws incident to that state of the nation. The executive is charged with the execution of all laws, the law of nations, as well as the municipal law, by which the former are recognized and adopted. It is consequently bound, by executing faithfully the laws of neutrality, when the country is in a neutral position, to avoid giving cause of war to foreign Powers.

This is the direct end of the proclamation of neutrality. It declares to the United States their situation with regard to the contending parties, and makes known to the community, that the laws incident to that state will be enforced. In doing this, it conforms to an established usage of nations, the operation of which, as before remarked, is to obviate a responsibility on the part of the whole society, for secret and unknown violations of the rights of any of the warring Powers by its citizens.

Those who object to the proclamation will readily admit, that it is the right and duty of the executive to interpret those articles of our treaties which give to France particular privileges, in order to the enforcement of them: but the necessary consequence of this is, that the executive must judge what are their proper limits; what rights are given to other nations, by our contracts with them; what rights the law of nature and nations gives, and our treaties permit, in respect to those countries with which we have none; in fine, what are the reciprocal rights and obligations of the United States, and of all and each of the Powers at war.

The right of the executive to receive ambassadors and other public ministers, may serve to illustrate the relative duties of the executive and legislative departments. This right includes that of judging, in the case of a revolution of government in a foreign country, whether the new rulers are competent organs of the national will, and ought to be recognized or not; which, where a treaty antecedently exists between the United States and such nation, involves the power of continuing or suspending its operation. For until the new government is acknowledged, the treaties between the nations, so far at least as regards public rights, are of course suspended.

This power of determining virtually upon the operation of national treaties, as a consequence of the power to receive public ministers, is an important instance of the right of the executive to decide upon the obligations of the country with regard to foreign nations. To apply it to the case of France, if there had been a treaty of alliance, offensive and defensive, between the United States and that country, the unqualified acknowledgment of the new government would have put the United States in a condition to become an associate in the war with France, and would have laid the Legislature under an obligation, if required, and there was otherwise no valid excuse, of exercising its power of declaring war.

This serves as an example of the right of the executive, in certain cases, to determine the condition of the nation, though it may, in its consequences, affect the exercise of the power of the Legislature to declare war. Nevertheless, the executive cannot thereby control the exercise of that power. The Legislature is still free to perform its duties, according to its own sense of them; though the executive, in the exercise of its constitutional powers, may establish an antecedent state of things, which ought to weigh in the legislative decisions.

The division of the executive power in the Constitution creates a concurrent authority in the cases to which it relates.

Hence, in the instance stated, treaties can only be made by the President and Senate jointly; but their activity may be continued or suspended by the President alone.

No objection has been made to the President's having acknowledged the republic of France, by the reception of its minister, without having consulted the Senate; though that body is connected with him in the making of treaties, and though the consequence of his act of reception is to give operation to those heretofore made with that country. But he is censured for having declared the United States to be in a state of peace and neutrality with regard to the Powers at war, because the right of changing that state, and declaring war, belongs to the Legislature.

It deserves to be remarked, that as the participation of the Senate in the making of treaties, and the power of the Legislature to declare war, are exceptions out of the general "executive power" vested in the President, they are to be construed strictly, and ought to be extended no further than is essential to their execution.

While, therefore, the Legislature can alone declare war, can alone actually transfer the nation from a state of peace to a state of hostility, it belongs to the "executive power" to do whatever else the law of nations, co-operating with the treaties of the country, enjoin in the intercourse of the United States with foreign Powers.

In this distribution of authority, the wisdom of our Constitution is manifested. It is the province and duty of the executive to preserve to the nation the blessings of peace. The Legislature alone can interrupt them by placing the nation in a state of war.

But though it has been thought advisable to vindicate the authority of the executive on this broad and comprehensive ground, it was not absolutely necessary to do so. That clause of the Constitution which makes it his duty to "take care that the laws be faithfully executed," might alone have been relied upon, and this simple process of argument pursued:

The President is the Constitutional executor of the laws. Our treaties, and the laws of nations, form a part of the law of the land. He who is to execute the laws must first judge for himself of their meaning. In order to the observance of that conduct which the laws of nations, combined with our treaties, prescribed to this country, in reference to the present war in Europe, it was necessary for the President to judge for himself, whether there was any thing in our treaties incompatible with an adherence to neutrality. Having decided that there was not, he had a right, and if in his opinion the interest of the nation required it, it was his duty as executor of the laws, to proclaim the neutrality of the nations, to exhort all persons to observe it, and to warn them of the penalties which would attend its non-observance.

The proclamation has been represented as enacting some new law. This is a view of it entirely erroneous. It only proclaims a fact, with regard to the existing state of the nation; informs the citizens of what the laws previously established require of them in that state, and notifies them that these laws will be put in execution against the infractors of them.

Pacificus.[24]

Madison, at the urging of Jefferson, responded to Hamilton, arguing principally that war powers and the treaty power were of their nature legislative and thus not

---

[24]Alexander Hamilton, "First *Pacificus* Letter 29 June 1793," *reprinted in 1 W. Goldsmith, The Growth of Presidential Power* 398, 400-04 (1974).

contained in the general grant of "the executive Power."[25] Four years earlier, however, Madison had endorsed the general proposition that at least for those powers included within the executive power, related congressional powers should be construed strictly. Thus, during the debate in Congress on establishing a Department of Foreign Affairs in 1789 Madison said:

> The doctrine . . . which seems to stand most in opposition to the principles I contend for, is, that the power to annul an appointment is, in the nature of things, incidental to the power which makes the appointment. I agree that if nothing more was said in the Constitution than that the President, by and with the advice and consent of the Senate, should appoint to office, there would be a great force in saying that the power of removal resulted by a natural implication from the power of appointing. But there is another part of the Constitution no less explicit than the one on which the gentleman's doctrine is founded; it is that part which

---

[25]See James Madison, "First *Helvidius* Letter August-September 1973," *reprinted in* 1 *W. Goldsmith, supra* note 24, at 405, 407-10. Madison's "Helvidius" position as it applies to the treaty power, of course, is not consistent with the Montesquieu theory or the British tradition, but it is consistent with the framers' pre-constitutional experience they may have been seeking to reject. Professor Corwin has written, "Blackstone, Locke, and Montesquieu were all in agreement in treating the direction of foreign relations as a branch of `executive,' . . . power." *E. Corwin, supra* note 18, at 416 n.1. Professor Quincy Wright referred to the writings of Montesquieu, Locke, and Blackstone as "the political Bibles of the constitutional fathers." *Q. Wright, supra* note 20, at 363. It should also be noted that even Albert Gallatin, Madison's close legislative ally, Jefferson's Secretary of the Treasury, and a strong advocate of legislative power in general, asserted that "[i]n every constitutional government the power of raising and granting money is vested in the legislative; that of making treaties, in the executive." Letter from Albert Gallatin to Mr. Everett, Jr., 1835, 2 *Gallatin's Writings* 479, quoted in 5 *J.B. Moore, Digest of International Law* 232 (1906). Finally, it might be noted with respect to Madison's "Helvidius" argument that the treaty power was not by its nature executive, that had the treaty-making power been perceived by the framers as essentially legislative in nature--particularly since this power had been exercised by the Continental Congress (along with the Commander-in-Chief power)--it is likely that it would have been vested in the legislature in Article I. Instead, the power "to make treaties"--subject to the condition that two-thirds of those senators present and voting consent to ratification--is vested by the Constitution in the President. The treaty power, of course, also appears in the same Article II, section 2, clause 2, as the appointment power Madison argues is executive.

> declares that the Executive power shall be vested in a President of the United States. The association of the Senate with the president in exercising that particular function, is an exception to this general rule; and exceptions to general rules, I conceive, are ever to be taken strictly.[26]

Less than a year later, another debate occurred regarding the appointment power. At issue was whether the Senate--which by the Constitution was given a veto over diplomatic appointments--had, as a result, the authority to determine the *grade* or *destination* of such an individual. Thomas Jefferson wrote a formal opinion on this issue, in which he reasoned:

> The Constitution has divided the powers of government into three branches, Legislative, Executive and Judiciary, lodging each with a distinct magistracy. The Legislature it has given completely to the Senate and House of representatives; it has declared that "the Executive powers shall be vested in the President," submitting only special articles of it to a negative by the Senate; and it has vested the Judiciary power in the courts of justice, with certain exceptions also in favor of the Senate.
>
> The transaction of business with foreign nations is Executive altogether. It belongs then to the head of that department, *except* as to such portions of it as are specially submitted to the Senate. *Exceptions* are to be construed strictly. . . .
>
> The Senate is not supposed by the Constitution to be acquainted with the concerns of the Executive department. It was not intended that these should be communicated to them; nor can they therefore be qualified to judge of the necessity which calls for a mission to any particular place; or of the particular grade, more or less marked, which special and secret circumstances may call for. All this is left to the President. They are only to see that no unfit person be employed.[27]

---

[26]J. Madison, *supra* note 11, at 496-97.

[27]*J. Boyd* (ed.), 16 *The Papers of Thomas Jefferson* 378-79 (1961) (emphasis in original).

Jefferson's memorandum was endorsed by President Washington and apparently shared with John Jay and Representative James Madison.[28] Three days later, Washington wrote in his diary:

> Had some conversation with Mr. Madison on the propriety of consulting the Senate on the places to which it would be necessary to send persons in the Diplomatic line, and Consuls; and with respect to the grade of the first--His opinion coincides with Mr. Jay's and Mr. Jefferson's--to wit--that they have no Constitutional right to interfere with either, and that it might be impolitic to draw it into a precedent, their powers extending no further than to an approbation or disapprobation of the person nominated by the President, all the rest being Executive and vested in the President by the Constitution."[29]

Jefferson was sent to meet with the relevant Senate committee members on May 24, 1790, and as a consequence--as recounted in Senator Maclay's *Diary*--"the Committee agreed to strike out the specific sum to be given to any foreign appointment, leaving it to the President to account, and appropriated 30,000 doll. generally for the purpose."[30]

Thus, while at least in his "Helvidius" letter Madison disagreed with the judgment of Hamilton, Jefferson and Gallatin[31] that the treaty power was in its nature executive, Madison, Hamilton and Jefferson all adopted the position that congressional powers which by their nature overlapped with the general grant of executive power in Article II, section 1, were to be strictly construed.

In assessing these competing constitutional theories of the foreign affairs power it should also be noted that scholars have generally taken the view that constitutional practice has more closely approximated the view of Hamilton, than

---

[28]*Id.* at n.380.

[29]*Quoted in id.*

[30]*Id.* at n.381.

[31]*See* the discussion in *supra* note 25.

that of Madison, in the "Pacificus-Helvidius" exchange.[32] Perhaps most importantly, what is certainly one of the most significant separation of powers cases yet to be decided by the Supreme Court, the case of Myers v. United States, decided in 1926, explicitly adopted the Madison, Hamilton and Jefferson view that grants of authority to Congress overlapping the general grant of "the executive Power" to the President are to be strictly construed. And in dictum the Court applied this doctrine to all of the blended powers in Article II, section 2, clause 2, ("the provisions of the second section of Article II") which, of course, includes the treaty power and thus adopts the Hamilton position in his "Pacificus" letter. Chief Justice Taft wrote in his opinion of the Court:

> The debates in the Constitutional Convention indicated an intention to create a strong Executive and after a controversial discussion the executive power of the Government was vested in one person and many of his important functions were specified so as to avoid the humiliating weakness of the Congress during the Revolution and under the Articles of Confederation. 1 Farrand, 66-97. . .
>
> The requirement of the second section of Article II that the Senate should advise and consent to the Presidential appointments, was to be strictly construed. The words of section 2, following the general grant of executive power under section 1, were either an enumeration and emphasis of specific functions of the Executive, not all inclusive, or were limitations upon the general grant of the executive power, and as such, being limitations, should not be enlarged beyond the words used. Madison, 1 Annals, 462, 263, 464. The executive power was given in general terms, strengthened by specific terms where emphasis was regarded as appropriate, and was limited by direct expressions where limitation was needed, and the fact that no express limit was placed on the power of removal by the Executive as convincing indication that none was intended. This is the same construction of Article II as

---

[32]For example, Professor William Goldsmith has written: "Historians have generally shied away from identifying the winner of this debate, but Hamilton's theory, with all of its dangers and pitfalls, has obviously been the theory and practice which has prevailed in this country, particularly in the modern period." 1 *W. Goldsmith, supra* note 24, at 404. *See also* the discussion in *id.* at 411-12.

that of Alexander Hamilton [in his Pacificus letter, quoted at length in this case]. . . .

A reference of the whole power of removal to general legislation by Congress is quite out of keeping with the plan of government devised by the framers of the Constitution. It could never have been intended to leave to Congress unlimited discretion to vary fundamentally the operation of the great independent executive branch of government and thus most seriously to weaken it. It would be a delegation by the Convention to Congress of the function of defining the primary boundaries of another of the three great divisions of government. The inclusion of removals of executive officers in the executive power vested in the President by Article II, according to its usual definition, and the implication of his power of removal of such officers from the provision of section 2 expressly recognizing in him the power of their appointment, are a much more natural and appropriate source of the removing power.

It is reasonable to suppose also that, had it been intended to give to Congress power to regulate or control removals in the manner suggested, it would have been included among the specifically enumerated legislative powers in Article I, or in the specified limitations on the executive power in Article II. The difference between the grant of legislative power under Article I to Congress, which is limited to powers therein enumerated, and the more general grant of the executive power to the President under Article II, is significant. The fact that the executive power is given in general terms strengthened by specific terms where emphasis is appropriate, and limited by direct expressions where limitation is needed and that no express limit is placed on the power of removal by the executive, is a convincing indication that none was intended. . . .

Our conclusion on the merits, sustained by the arguments before stated, is that Article II grants to the President the executive power of the Government, [and] . . . that the provisions of the second section of Article II, which blend action by the legislative branch, or by part of it, in the work of the executive, are limitations

to be strictly construed and not to be extended by implication. . .
[33]

Three other Supreme Court decisions are of particular importance in the debate about theoretical approaches to separation of powers in foreign policy. The first of these was the decision in *United States v. Curtiss-Wright Export Corp.* in 1936, frequently cited by advocates of broad presidential authority.[34] Since the *Curtiss-Wright* case dealt with the power of Congress to delegate authority to the President in the foreign affairs area, an area blending both the foreign affairs powers of Congress and the President, its holding, strictly construed, is of only limited significance. The importance of the case, however, is that Mr. Justice Sutherland's opinion, joined by six other justices, sets out both a general constitutional theory of the foreign affairs power as an inherent federal power and a broad endorsement of presidential authority in the realm of foreign affairs. In this later respect Sutherland writes:

> Not only, as we have shown, is the federal power over external affairs in origin and essential character different from that over internal affairs, but participation in the exercise of the power is significantly limited. In this vast external realm, with its important, complicated, delicate and manifold problems, the President alone has the power to speak or listen as a representative of the nation. He *makes* treaties with the advice and consent of the Senate; but he alone negotiates. Into the field of negotiation the Senate cannot intrude; and Congress itself is powerless to invade it. As Marshall said in his great argument of March 7, 1800, in the House of Representatives, "The President is the sole organ of the

---

[33]Myers v. United States, 272 U.S. 52, 116-118, 127-28, 151-52, 163-64 (1926).

[34]299 U.S. 304 (1936).
A thoughtful letter of September 21, 1987, from Congressman Henry J. Hyde to Senator George J. Mitchell, growing out of the separation of powers debate surrounding the Iran-Contra affair, discusses judicial and other precedents supporting a strong presidential role in the conduct of foreign policy and responds to recent arguments seeking to limit some of these authorities, such as the *Curtiss-Wright* case. Letter from the Honorable Henry J. Hyde to the Honorable George J. Mitchell (Sept. 21, 1987) (on file at the Center for Law and National Security, University of Virginia School of Law) (sixteen pages).

nation in its external relations, and its sole representative with foreign nations." Annals, 6th Cong., col. 613. The Senate Committee on Foreign Relations at a very early day in our history (February 15, 1816), reported to the Senate, among other things, as follows:

"The President is the constitutional representative of the United States with regard to foreign nations. He manages our concerns with foreign nations and must necessarily be most competent to determine when, how, and upon what subjects negotiation may be urged with the greatest prospect of success. For his conduct he is responsible to the Constitution. The committee consider this responsibility the surest pledge for the faithful discharge of his duty. They think the interference of the Senate in the direction of foreign negotiations calculated to diminish that responsibility and thereby to impair the best security for the national safety. The nature of transactions with foreign nations, moreover, requires caution and unity of design, and their success frequently depends on secrecy and dispatch." U.S. Senate, Reports, Committee on Foreign Relations, vol. 8, p. 24.

It is important to bear in mind that we are here dealing not alone with an authority vested in the President by an exertion of legislative power, but with such an authority plus the very delicate, plenary and exclusive power of the President as the sole organ of the federal government in the field of international relations--a power which does not require as a basis for its exercise an act of Congress, but which, of course, like every other governmental power, must be exercised in subordination to the applicable provisions of the Constitution. It is quite apparent that if, in the maintenance of our international relations, embarrassment--perhaps serious embarrassment--is to be avoided and success for our aims achieved, congressional legislation which is to be made effective through negotiation and inquiry within the international field must often accord to the President a degree of discretion and freedom from statutory restriction which would not be admissible were domestic affairs alone involved. Moreover, he, not Congress, has the better opportunity of knowing the conditions which prevail in foreign countries, and especially is this true in time of war. He has his confidential sources of information. He has his agents in the form of diplomatic, consular and other officials. Secrecy in respect of information gathered by them may be highly necessary, and the premature disclosure of it productive of harmful results. Indeed, so clearly is this true that the first President refused to accede to a request to lay before the House of Representatives the instructions, correspondence and documents relating to the negotiation of the Jay Treaty--a refusal the wisdom of which was recognized by the House itself and has never since been doubted. In his reply to the request, President Washington said:

"The nature of foreign negotiations requires caution, and their success must often depend on secrecy; and even when brought to a conclusion a full disclosure of all the measures, demands, or eventual concessions which may have been proposed or contemplated would be extremely impolitic; for this might have a pernicious influence on future negotiations, or produce immediate inconveniences, perhaps danger and mischief, in relation to other power. The necessity of such caution and secrecy was one cogent reason for vesting the power of making treaties in the President, with the advice and consent of the Senate, the principle on which that body was formed confining it to a small number of members. To admit, then, a right in the House of Representatives to demand and to have as a matter of course all the papers respecting a negotiation with a foreign power would be to establish a dangerous precedent." 1 Messages and Papers of the Presidents, p. 194.

The marked difference between foreign affairs and domestic affairs in this respect is recognized by both houses of Congress in the very form of their requisitions for information from the executive departments. In the case of every department except the Department of State, the resolution directs the official to furnish the information. In the case of the State Department, dealing with foreign affairs, the President is requested to furnish the information "if not incompatible with the public interest." A statement that to furnish the information is not compatible with the public interest rarely, if ever, is questioned.[35]

---

[35]United States v. Curtiss-Wright Export Corp., 299 U.S. 304, 319-21 (1936).

While in recent years some advocates of congressional power have sought to minimize the *Curtiss-Wright* case, and it is subject to some appropriate historical criticism,[36] sometimes in constitutional law a sweeping Supreme Court theory is as important if not more so than strict holding. As Professor Louis Henkin writes in *Foreign Affairs and the Constitution:* "[Justice Sutherland's] opinion, while containing far more than necessary to his decision, was joined by six other Justices, has been cited with approval in later cases, and remains authoritative doctrine."[37] Most recently, in its 1981 decision in *Haig v. Agee,*[38] the Supreme Court quoted with approval the following provision from the *Curtiss-Wright* case:

> In this vast external realm, with its important, complicated, delicate and manifold problems, the President alone has the power to speak or listen as a representative of the nation. . . . As Marshall said in his great argument of March 7, 1800, in the House of Representatives, "The President is the sole organ of the nation in its external relations, and its sole representative with foreign nations."[39]

The second decision is *Youngstown Sheet & Tube Co. v. Sawyer*[40] decided in 1952 and frequently cited by advocates of broad congressional authority. While the Court in *Youngstown* rejected President Truman's seizure of most of the steel mills in the United States because of labor unrest during the Korean War, the case is only peripherally, if at all, a foreign affairs case since the issue before the Court was one of a taking of private property in the United States without due process of law in violation of the fifth amendment, and the majority of the Court did not treat

---

[36]See the discussion, for example, of the *Curtiss-Wright* case in *L. Henkin, supra* note 6, at 19-26.

[37]*Id.* at 25-26. Indeed, the *Curtiss-Wright* case may be "the single most frequently cited case" concerning constitutional authority in the conduct of foreign policy. See Casper, "Constitutional Constraints on the Conduct of Foreign and Defense Policy: A Nonjudicial Model," 43 *U. Chi. L. Rev.* 463, 475 (1976).

[38]Haig v. Agee, 453 U.S. 280 (1981).

[39]453 U.S. at 291.

[40]343 U.S. 579 (1952).

the case as involving the President's foreign affairs power. The enduring significance of the case is not any on the merits judgment by the Court as to the parameters of separation of powers in foreign policy but rather a framework for analysis of separation of powers issues generally set out in the concurring opinion of Mr. Justice Jackson. Jackson set out a three part framework for analysis of challenges to presidential power in general as:

> 1. When the President acts pursuant to an express or implied authorization of Congress, his authority is at its maximum, for it includes all that he possesses in his own right plus all that Congress can delegate. . . .
>
> 2. When the President acts in absence of either a congressional grant or denial of authority, he can only rely upon his own independent powers, but there is a zone of twilight in which he and Congress may have concurrent authority, or in which its distribution is uncertain. . . . [and]
>
> 3. When the President takes measures incompatible with the expressed or implied will of Congress, his power is at its lowest ebb, for then he can rely only upon his own constitutional powers minus any constitutional powers of Congress over the matter. Counts can sustain exclusive presidential control in such a case only by disabling the Congress from acting upon the subject. . . .[41]

This intellectual framework set out in Justice Jackson's concurring opinion can be adapted to assessment of congressional as well as presidential power and remains a useful heuristic device for differentiating separation of powers issues and cases. It is embodied in the organization of Part V of this study. It should be emphasized, however, as Professor Henkin notes, "*Youngstown* has not been considered a 'foreign affairs case'."[42] Henkin went on to add:

> [T]he majority of the Supreme Court did not treat the case as involving the reach of his [the President's] foreign affairs power,

---

[41]Youngstown Sheet & Tube Co. v. Sawyer, 343 U.S. 579, 635-38 (1952) (Jackson, J., concurring).

[42]*L. Henkin, supra* note 6, at 341 n.11. It should also be noted that three justices dissented in the *Youngstown* case.

> and even the dissenting justices invoked only incidentally that power or the fact that the steel strike threatened important American foreign policy interests.[43]

Professor Henkin's judgment that *Youngstown* is not a real foreign affairs case finds support in the concurring opinion of Justice Rehnquist--joined by the Chief Justice and two other members of the Court--in *Goldwater v. Carter* where Rehnquist wrote:

> The present case differs in several important respects from Youngstown [citation omitted] . . . cited by petitioners as authority both for reaching the merits of this dispute and for reversing the Court of Appeals. In Youngstown, private litigants brought a suit contesting the President's authority under his war powers to seize the Nation's steel industry, an action of profound and demonstrable domestic impact. . . . Moreover, as in Curtiss-Wright, the effect of this action, as far as we can tell, is "entirely external to the United States, and [falls] within the category of foreign affairs. . . ."[44]

Similarly, in the 1981 decision in *Dames & Moore v. Regan*,[45] clearly a foreign affairs case, the Court cited the Justice Jackson classification as "analytically useful" but seemed to qualify it by also pointing out that:

> . . . we should be mindful of Justice Holmes' admonition, quoted by Justice Frankfurter in Youngstown . . . that "[t]he great ordinances of the Constitution do not establish and divide fields of black and white." . . . Justice Jackson himself recognized that his three categories represented "a somewhat over-simplified grouping," . . . and it is doubtless the case that executive action in any particular instance falls, not neatly in one of three pigeonholes, but rather at some point along a spectrum running from explicit

---

[43]*Id.*

[44]Goldwater v. Carter, 444 U.S. 996, 1004-05 (1979) (opinion of four members of the Court).

[45]Dames & Moore v. Regan, 453 U.S. 654 (1981).

> congressional authorization to explicit congressional prohibition. This is particularly true as respects cases such as the one before us, involving responses to international crises the nature of which Congress can hardly have been expected to anticipate in any detail.[46]

The third particularly important separation of powers case decided by the Supreme Court in addition to *Myers v. United States*, is the 1983 decision in *Immigration and Naturalization Service v. Chadha*.[47] In *Chadha* the Court struck down the so called "one house veto" as in violation of separation of powers rooted in the presentment and bicameral provisions of the Constitution. In doing so the Court demonstrated that importance of an issue, and even long-established congressional practice, does not preclude setting aside an assertion of congressional authority if in violation of separation of powers. And the Court stressed the importance to our constitutional scheme of vigorously maintaining the separation of powers. Thus, Justice Burger said in his opinion of the Court:

> We have recently noted that "[t]he principle of separation of powers was not simply an abstract generalization in the minds of the Framers: it was woven into the document that they drafted in Philadelphia in the summer of 1787." . . ;[48]

and

> The Constitution sought to divide the delegated powers of the new Federal Government into three defined categories, Legislative, Executive, and Judicial, to assure, as nearly as possible, that each Branch of government would confine itself to its assigned responsibility. The hydraulic pressure inherent within

---

[46]*Id.* at 669.

[47]Immigration and Naturalization Service v. Chadha, 462 U.S. 917 (1983).

[48]462 U.S. 946.

> each of the separate Branches to exceed the outer limits of its power, even to accomplish desirable objectives, must be resisted.[49]

Similarly, the Court cited with approval the language from the Myers case concerning the role of the President in providing a "national" perspective representative of all of the people:

> The Court also has observed that the Presentment Clauses serve the important purpose of assuring that a "national" perspective is grafted on the legislative process: "The President is a representative of the people just as the members of the Senate and of the House are, and it may be, at some times, on some subjects, that the President elected by all the people is rather more representative of them all than are the members of either body of the Legislative whose constituencies are local and not countrywide. . . ."[50]

And the Court cited Hamilton and Madison in pointing out that the framers were quite concerned lest Congress assume all powers and destroy checks and balances and that the principle of bicameralism was rooted in this fear:

> Hamilton argued that a Congress comprised of a single House was antithetical to the very purposes of the Constitution. Were the Nation to adopt a Constitution providing for only one legislative organ, he warned:
>
> > "[W]e shall finally accumulate, in a single body, all the most important prerogatives of sovereignty, and thus entail upon our posterity one of the most execrable forms of government that human infatuation ever contrived. Thus we should create in reality that very tyranny which the

---

[49]462 U.S. 951.

[50]462 U.S. 948.

> adversaries of the new constitution either are, or affect to be, solicitous to avert."...[51]

These observations are consistent with what many of the Framers expressed, none more cogently than Madison in pointing up the need to divide and disperse power in order to protect liberty:

> In republican government, the legislative authority necessarily predominates. The remedy for this inconveniency is to divide the legislature into different branches; and to render them, by different modes of election and different principles of action, as little connected with each other as the nature of their common functions and their common dependence on the society will admit." ...[52]

The Court also said that:

> policy arguments supporting even useful "political inventions" are subject to the demands of the Constitution which defines powers and, with respect to this subject, sets out just how those powers are to be exercised....[53]

and:

> when any Branch acts, it is presumptively exercising the power the Constitution has delegated to it....[54]

---

[51]462 U.S. 949. *See also* the important opinion of Mr. Justice Powell 462 U.S. 959, at 960-63.

[52]462 U.S. 950.

[53]462 U.S. 945. *See also* 462 U.S. at 944.

[54]462 U.S. 951.

Although not a foreign affairs case, the 1986 decision of the Supreme Court in the case of *Bowsher v. Synar*[55] illustrates the vitality of the separation of powers doctrine even when the issue at stake is of vital national interest. Thus, in *Bowsher* the Court struck down the so-called "reporting" provisions of the Gramm-Rudman-Hollings Balanced Budget and Emergency Deficit Control Act of 1985 on the grounds that the Act improperly assigned executive functions to execute the law to an agent of Congress, the Comptroller General. In an opinion for the five members of the Court Chief Justice Burger wrote:

> We noted recently that "[t]he Constitution sought to divide the delegated powers of the new Federal Government into three defined categories, Legislative, Executive, and Judicial." *INS v. Chadha,* 462 U.S. 919, 951, 103 S.Ct. 2764, 2784, 77 L.Ed.2d 317 (1983). The declared purpose of separating and dividing the powers of government, of course, was to "diffus[e] power the better to secure liberty." *Youngstown Sheet & Tube Co. v. Sawyer*, 343 U.S. 579, 635, 72 S.Ct. 863, 870, 96 L.Ed. 1153 (1952) (Jackson, J., concurring). Justice Jackson's words echo the famous warning of Montesquieu, quoted by James Madison in The Federalist No. 47, that "`there can be no liberty where the legislative and executive powers are united in the same person, or body of magistrates'. . . ." The Federalist No. 47, p. 325 (J. Cooke ed. 1961).
>
> Even a cursory examination of the Constitution reveals the influence of Montesquieu's thesis that checks and balances were the foundation of a structure of government that would protect liberty. The Framers provided a vigorous legislative branch and a separate and wholly independent executive branch, with each branch responsible ultimately to the people. The Framers also provided for a judicial branch equally independent with "[t]he judicial Power . . . extend[ing] to all Cases, in Law and Equity, arising under this Constitution, and the Laws of the United States." Art. III, Sec. 2.
>
> Other, more subtle, examples of separated powers are evident as well. Unlike parliamentary systems such as that of Great Britain, no person who is an officer of the United States may serve as a Member of the Congress. Art. I, Sec. 6. Moreover, unlike parliamentary systems, the President, under Article II, is responsible

[55]106 S.Ct. 3181 (1986). Justices White and Blackmun dissented in separate opinions.

not to the Congress but to the people, subject only to impeachment proceedings which are exercised by the two Houses as representatives of the people. Art. II, Sec. 4. And even in the impeachment of a President the presiding officer of the ultimate tribunal is not a member of the legislative branch, but the Chief Justice of the United States. Art. I, Sec. 3.

That this system of division and separation of powers produces conflicts, confusion, and discordance at times is inherent, but it was deliberately so structured to assure full, vigorous and open debate on the great issues affecting the people and to provide avenues for the operation of checks on the exercise of governmental power.

The Constitution does not contemplate an active role for Congress in the supervision of officers charged with the execution of the laws it enacts. The President appoints "Officers of the United States" with the "Advice and Consent of the Senate. . . ." Article II, Sec. 2. Once the appointment has been made and confirmed, however, the Constitution explicitly provides for removal of Officers of the United States by Congress only upon impeachment by the House of Representatives and conviction by the Senate. An impeachment by the House and trial by the Senate can rest only on "Treason, Bribery or other high Crimes and Misdemeanors." Article II, Sec. 4. A direct congressional role in the removal of officers charged with the execution of the laws beyond this limited one is inconsistent with separation of powers.

This was made clear in debate in the First Congress in 1789. When Congress considered an amendment to a bill establishing the Department of Foreign Affairs, the debate centered around whether the Congress "should recognize and declare the power of the President under the Constitution to remove the Secretary of Foreign Affairs without the advice and consent of the Senate." Myers, supra, 272 U.S., at 114, 47 S. Ct., at 24. James Madison urged rejection of a congressional role in the removal of Executive Branch officers, other than by impeachment, saying in debate:

> Perhaps there was no argument urged with more success, or more plausibly grounded against the Constitution, under which we are now deliberating, than that founded on the mingling of

> the Executive and Legislative branches of the Government in one body. It has been objected, that the Senate have too much of the Executive power even, by having a control over the President in the appointment to office. Now, shall we extend this connexion between the Legislative and Executive departments, which will strengthen the objection, and diminish the responsibility we have in the head of the Executive? 1 Annals of Cong. 380

Madison's position ultimately prevailed, and a congressional role in the removal process was rejected. This "Decision of 1789" provides "contemporaneous and weighty evidence" of the Constitution's meaning since many of the Members of the first Congress "had taken part in framing that instrument." *Marsh v. Chambers*, 463 U.S. 783, 790, 103 S.Ct. 3330, 3335, 77 L.Ed.2d 1019 (1983).3 [**3.** The First Congress included 20 members who had been delegates to the Philadelphia Convention:

IN THE SENATE

Richard Bassett (Delaware)	Rufus King (New York)
Pierce Butler (South Carolina)	John Langdon (New Hampshire)
Oliver Ellsworth (Connecticut)	Robert Morris (Pennsylvania)
William Few (Georgia)	William Paterson (New Jersey)
William Samuel Johnson (Connecticut)	George Read (Delaware)
	Caleb Strong (Massachusetts)

IN THE HOUSE

Abraham Baldwin (Georgia)	Nicholas Gilman (New Hampshire)
Daniel Carroll (Maryland)	James Madison (Virginia)
George Clymer (Pennsylvania)	Roger Sherman (Connecticut)
Thomas FitzSimons (Pennsylvania)	Hugh Williamson (North Carolina)
	Elbridge Gerry (Massachusetts)

This Court first directly addressed this issue in *Myers v. United States*, 272 U.S. 52, 47 S.Ct. 21, 71 L.Ed. 160 (1925). At issue in Myers was a statute providing that certain postmasters could be removed only "by and with the advice and consent of the Senate." The President removed one such postmaster without Senate approval, and a lawsuit ensued. Chief Justice Taft, writing for the Court, declared the statute unconstitutional on the ground that for Congress to "draw to itself, or to either branch of it, the power to remove or the right to participate in the exercise of that power . . . would be . . . to infringe the constitutional principle of the separation of governmental powers." *Id.*, at 161, 47 S.Ct., at 40.

A decade later, in *Humphrey's Executor v. United States*, 295 U.S. 602, 55 S.Ct. 869, 79 L.Ed. 1611 (1935), relied upon heavily by appellants, a Federal Trade Commissioner who had been removed by the President sought back pay. *Humphrey's Executor* involved an issue not presented either in the *Myers* case or in this case--i.e., the power of Congress to limit the President's powers of removal of a Federal Trade Commissioner. 295 U.S., at 630, 55 S.Ct., at 874-875. The relevant statute permitted removal "by the President," but only "for inefficiency, neglect of duty, or malfeasance in office." Justice Sutherland, speaking for the Court, upheld the statute, holding that "illimitable power of removal is not possessed by the President [with respect to Federal Trade Commissioners]." 295 U.S., at 628-629, 55 S.Ct., at 874. The Court distinguished *Myers*, reaffirming its holding that congressional participation in the removal of executive officers is unconstitutional. Justice Sutherland's opinion for the Court also underscored the crucial role of separated powers in our system:

> The fundamental necessity of maintaining each of the three general departments of government entirely free from the control or coercive influence, direct or indirect, of either of the others, has often been stressed and is hardly open to serious question. So much is implied in the very fact of the separation of the powers of these departments by the Constitution; and in the rule

> which recognizes their essential co-equality." 295 U.S., at 629-630, 55 S.Ct., at 874.

The Court reached a similar result in *Weiner v. United States*, 357 U.S. 349, 78 S.Ct. 1275, 2 L.Ed.2d 1377 (1958), concluding that, under *Humphrey's Executor*, the President did not have unrestrained removal authority over a member of the War Crimes Commission.

In light of these precedents, we conclude that Congress cannot reserve for itself the power of removal of an officer charged with the execution of the laws except by impeachment. To permit the execution of the laws to be vested in an officer answerable only to Congress would, in practical terms, reserve in Congress control over the execution of the laws. As the District Court observed, "Once an officer is appointed, it is only the authority that can remove him, and not the authority that appointed him, that he must fear and, in the performance of his functions, obey." 626 F.Supp., at 1401. The structure of the Constitution does not permit Congress to execute the laws; it follows that Congress cannot grant to an officer under its control what it does not possess.

Our decision in *INS v. Chadha*, 462 U.S. 919, 103 S.Ct. 2764, 77 L.Ed.2d 317 (1983), supports this conclusion. In *Chadha*, we struck down a one house "legislative veto" provision by which each House of Congress retained the power to reverse a decision Congress had expressly authorized the Attorney General to make:

> "Disagreement with the Attorney General's decision on Chadha's deportation--that is, Congress' decision to deport Chadha--no less than Congress' original choice to delegate to the Attorney General the authority to make that decision, involves determinations of policy that Congress can implement in only one way; bicameral passage followed by presentment to the President. Congress must abide by its delegation of authority until that delegation is legislatively

> altered or revoked." *Id.*, at 954-955, 103 S.Ct., at 2786.

To permit an officer controlled by Congress to execute the laws would be, in essence, to permit a congressional veto. Congress could simply remove, or threaten to remove, an officer for executing the laws in any fashion found to be unsatisfactory to Congress. This kind of congressional control over the execution of the laws, Chadha makes clear, is constitutionally impermissible.

The dangers of congressional usurpation of Executive Branch functions have long been recognized. "[T]he debates of the Constitutional Convention, and the Federalist Papers, are replete with expressions of fear that the Legislative Branch of the National Government will aggrandize itself at the expense of the other two branches." Buckley v. Valeo, 424 U.S. 1, 129, 96 S.Ct. 612, 687, 46 L.Ed.2d 659 (1976). Indeed, we also have observed only recently that "[t]he hydraulic pressure inherent within each of the separate Branches to exceed the outer limits of its power, even to accomplish desirable objectives, must be resisted." Chadha, 462 U.S., at 951, 103 S.Ct., at 2784.

. . . .

Congress of course initially determined the content of the Balanced Budget and Emergency Deficit Control Act; and undoubtedly the content of the Act determines the nature of the executive duty. However, as Chadha makes clear, once Congress makes its choice in enacting legislation, its participation ends. Congress can thereafter control the execution of its enactment only indirectly--by passing new legislation. Chadha, 462 U.S., at 958, 103 S.Ct., at 2787-2789. By placing the responsibility for execution of the Balanced Budget and Emergency Deficit Control Act in the hands of an officer who is subject to removal only by itself, Congress in effect has retained control over the execution of the Act and has intruded into the executive function. The Constitution does not permit such intrusion.

. . . .

We conclude the District Court correctly held that the powers vested in the Comptroller General under Sec. 251 violate the command of the Constitution that the Congress play no direct

> role in the execution of the laws. Accordingly, the judgment and order of the District Court are affirmed. . . .

And in a concurring opinion, joined by Justice Marshall, Justice Stevens wrote:

> I agree with the Court that the "Gramm-Rudman-Hollings" Act contains a constitutional infirmity so severe that the flawed provision may not stand. I disagree with the Court, however, on the reasons why the Constitution prohibits the Comptroller General from exercising the powers assigned to him by Sec. 251(b) and Sec. 251(c)(2) of the Act. It is not the dormant, carefully circumscribed congressional removal power that represents the primary constitutional evil. Nor do I agree with the conclusion of both the majority and the dissent that the analysis depends on a labeling of the functions assigned to the Comptroller General as "executive powers." *Ante*, at ----; *post*, at ---- -- ----. Rather, I am convinced that the Comptroller General must be characterized as an agent of Congress because of his longstanding statutory responsibilities; that the powers assigned to him under the Gramm-Rudman-Hollings Act require him to make policy that will bind the Nation; and that, when Congress, or a component or an agent of Congress, seeks to make policy that will bind the Nation, it must follow the procedures mandated by Article I of the Constitution--through passage by both Houses and presentment to the President. In short, Congress may not exercise its fundamental power to formulate national policy by delegating that power to one of its two Houses, to a legislative committee, or to an individual agent of the Congress such as the Speaker of the House of Representatives, the Sergeant at Arms of the Senate, or the Director of the Congressional Budget Office. *INS v. Chadha*, 462 U.S. 919, 103 S.Ct. 2764, 77 L.Ed.2d 317 (1983). That principle, I believe, is applicable to the Comptroller General. . . .

It should be noted that the majority of the Court focused on Congress improperly seeking to play a direct role in "the execution of the laws." The Stevens concurring opinion, however, focuses, as in *INS v. Chadha*, on the procedural concept that when Congress "seeks to make policy that will bind the nation, it must follow the procedures mandated by Article I of the Constitution--through passage by both Houses and presentment to the President."[56]

Similarly, while not a foreign policy case and reversed on appeal to the Supreme Court, it should also be noted that one Court of Appeals which recently addressed the constitutionality of the post-Watergate independent counsel law struck it down on separation of powers principles in a 2 to 1 divided opinion. The core of this decision rested on an accumulation of executive powers said to be violated, including the power to "take Care that the Laws be faithfully executed."[57] On June 29, 1988, however, in a 7-1 decision,[58] the Supreme Court upheld the constitutionality of the independent counsel law. The majority opinion by Chief Justice Rehnquist stressed that the case did "not involve an attempt by Congress itself to gain a role" and "[w]e observe first that this case does not involve an attempt by Congress to increase its own powers at the expense of the Executive Branch." Similarly, the majority opinion emphasized what it regarded as substantial continuing involvement by the Executive branch in the functioning of the independent counsel. Again, while not a case involving foreign affairs powers, with respect to separation of powers law it is significant that the Court addressed "the principle of separation of powers" as an independent inquiry. It is also significant, as pointed out by Judge Scalia in dissent, that the majority opinion did not discuss a presumption of constitutionality in the case since in separation of powers cases neither branch "can be presumed correct." Justice Scalia's dissent is also particularly relevant in reminding us that the phrase "we have `a government of Laws, and not of men'" comes from Article XXX of the Massachusetts Constitution of 1780, which provides in pertinent part:

---

[56]For an amplification of this approach to separation of powers theory more broadly, see H. Krent, "Separating the Strands in Separation of Powers Controversies" (a paper delivered at a faculty workshop at the University of Virginia School of Law, April 8, 1988). This paper has been published as Krent, "Separating the Strands in Separation of Powers Controversies," 74 *Va. L. Rev.* 1253 (1988) (*supra* note 8).

[57]*U.S. Court Upsets Law on Appointing Key Prosecutors*, N.Y. Times, Jan. 23, 1988, at 1, col. 6, and excerpts from the opinion, id. at 8. In re Sealed Case, 838 F.2d 476 (D.C. Dir. 1988).

[58]Alexia Morrison, Independent Counsel, Appellant v. Theodore B. Olson, Edward C. Schmults and Carol E. Dinkins, 56 *L. Week* 4835 (June 29, 1988).

> In the government of this commonwealth, the legislative department shall never exercise the executive and judicial powers, or either of them; the executive shall never exercise the legislative and judicial powers, or either of them; the judicial shall never exercise the legislative and executive powers, or either of them; to the end it may be a government of Laws, and not of men.

At least partly as a result of the relative rarity of Supreme Court decisions concerning separation of powers issues, the debate between competing theories of congressional and presidential authority in foreign affairs continues to rage. It is fueled not only by the failure of the Constitution to specifically address the full range of separation of powers issues but also by a rich 200 year history of constitutional practice in which both positions have been repeatedly taken by advocates of one or another policy. To some extent also arguments in the debate continue to be made based on ignorance of this rather esoteric--and not widely understood--area of constitutional law. For example, the still oft repeated argument that Congress can achieve any legislative purpose through the appropriations power even when it cannot directly legislate constitutionally is simply hubris. The only safe guide to navigating the shoals of separation of powers theory in foreign policy seems to be some modesty in understanding that many issues remain constitutionally debated and that the best guide is to insist on a careful delimitation of issues, with discrete exploration of answers for each.[59] The analysis in this study is intended to facilitate such a careful division of discrete issues in the overall "broad-narrow" debate.

b. The treaty power

The treaty power, as with other constitutionally established foreign affairs powers, is really a range of powers. These include--most broadly in assessing executive and congressional powers under the treaty power--the authority to

---

[59]Appropriate modesty in assessing constitutional claims by advocates of one or another branch is also suggested by the Supreme Court's language in *United States v. Nixon*, 418 U.S. 683 (1974), where the Court said: "[i]n the performance of assigned constitutional duties each branch of the Government must initially interpret the Constitution, and the interpretation of its powers by any branch is due great respect from the others." Id. at 703.

conclude international agreements,[60] the authority to interpret, implement and enforce international agreements, and the authority to terminate international agreements.[61] In turn, these powers can be subdivided into a range of more specific issues, including those resulting from an overlay of the Justice Jackson framework from the *Steel Seizure Case*. To be most useful and reliable, constitutional analysis should proceed by reference to the specific issues at stake. Accordingly, subsequent sections of this part will proceed to examine the specific treaty power issues raised in the "broad-narrow" debate. Just as such specific issues should be informed by the general constitutional framework and theory of separation of powers in foreign policy, however, so too they should be informed by the general constitutional theory of the treaty power within the broader context of separation of powers in foreign policy.[62] This section b., "the treaty power," will focus on this general constitutional theory of the treaty power.

The starting point for any analysis of the constitutional theory of the treaty power is the language of the Constitution. Article II, section 2, clause 2 of the Constitution provides that:

---

[60]*See generally* J.N. Moore, "Executive Agreements and Congressional Executive Relations," the Appendix to "Statement of John Norton Moore" (April 11, 1979) [hereinafter "Statement of John Norton Moore for Treaty Termination Hearings"], *in Treaty Termination: Hearings Before the Senate Comm. on Foreign Relations*, 96th Cong., 1st Sess. 400, 414 (1979) .

[61]On the authority to terminate international agreements *see generally* "Statement of John Norton Moore for Treaty Termination Hearings," *supra* note 60, at 400.

With respect to the House of Representatives and the treaty power, *see, e.g.*, Stone, "The House of Representatives and the Treaty-Making Power," 17 Ky. L.J. 216 (March 1929).

[62]As an interesting starting point in the constitutional debate about the treaty power, the reader might want to *compare* the paper by Dr. Louis Fisher writing from a congressional perspective and entitled "Constitutional Underpinnings of the Treaty Powers," *with* the paper by Robert F. Turner writing from an Executive branch perspective and also entitled "Constitutional Underpinnings of the Treaty Power." These papers were delivered March 19, 1989, at a conference on "Treaty Implementation and Interpretation Under the Constitution," at the Syracuse University College of Law. See *supra* note 1.

> [the President] shall have Power, by and with the Advice and Consent of the Senate, to make Treaties, provided two thirds of the Senators present concur . . . .

Article VI, clause 2 of the Constitution provides:

> This Constitution, and the Laws of the United States which shall be made in Pursuance thereof; and all Treaties made, or which shall be made, under the Authority of the United States, shall be the supreme Law of the Land . . . .

Article III, section 2 provides:

> The judicial Power shall extend to all Cases, in Law and Equity, arising under this Constitution, the Laws of the United States, and Treaties made, or which shall be made, under their Authority . . . .

And Article II, section 3 provides that:

> [the President] shall take Care that the Laws be faithfully executed . . . .[63]

The constitutional history of this treaty power language shows clearly that the framers rejected a treaty power vested either in the legislative branch alone or

---

[63]Article I, section 10 of the Constitution also provides:

> No State shall enter into any Treaty, Alliance, or Confederation . . . .
> . . . .
> No State shall, without the Consent of Congress . . . enter into any Agreement or Compact with another State, or with a foreign Power . . . .

And, of possible relevance particularly on the issue of Senate versus congressional authority over "domestic conditions," Article I, section 8 of the Constitution provides:

> To make all Laws which shall be necessary and proper for carrying into Execution the foregoing Powers, and all other Powers vested by this Constitution in the Government of the United States, or in any Department or Officer thereof . . . .

in the Senate alone.[64] Both the Pinckney plan and the Committee on Detail had assigned the power to make treaties exclusively to the Senate. The Brearley Committee, which dealt with unfinished business including the treaty power, changed this to the current language of the Constitution. As described by Abraham D. Sofaer, in his widely acclaimed book on *War, Foreign Affairs, and Constitutional Power*:

> Meanwhile, the Convention turned to the treaty power. The Committee on Detail had assigned this power exclusively to the Senate, which could adopt treaties by majority vote. This allocation operated in favor of the small states, and was inconsistent with practice under the Confederation, where nine of thirteen states had to approve treaties and where the Secretary of Foreign Affairs and other agents were used to handle negotiations. Dissatisfied rumblings were heard at various points against Senate control of treaties. Debate began in earnest on August 23, with an effort to allocate parts of the treaty power to branches other than the Senate. Madison observed "that the Senate represented the States alone, and that for this as well as other obvious reasons it was proper that the President should be an agent in treaties." His suggestion evoked no comment, apparently because of general agreement that a national spokesman and negotiator was necessary. Madison seems to have had more in mind for the President than simply to serve the Senate's will, as Congress's agents were expected to do under the Confederation. The President could represent the national interest--as opposed to the interests of individual states--and therefore would become an agent of the nation in treaty formulation, rather than of the Senate. Morris followed with a far more controversial effort to provide that, before any treaty would be "binding," it would have to be ratified by a law, passed by both houses of Congress. He received some distinguished support, but his motion failed.
>
> The treaty clause was eventually submitted to the Brearley Committee, which dealt with the matter along with other unfinishedbusiness, most notably the power of appointment. It recommended three important changes in the preexisting

[64]See *A. Sofaer, supra* note 8, at 26, 34-35.

> allocation: that the President be empowered to make treaties, with the "advice and consent" of the Senate; that the President make most important appointments, also subject to the "advice and consent" of the Senate; and that Senate approval in these matters be based on a two-thirds vote of the members present. The President would thereby be given the role of negotiating treaties, and also substantial capacity to control the executive departments and to distribute largesse. His treaties and nominations would be subject to Senate approval, however, by an extraordinary majority so as to enable a substantial minority of the states to block decisions felt to be detrimental to their interests.
>
> When the Brearley Committee's recommendation was reported to the Convention, James Wilson renewed the effort to require House concurrence to all treaties. Wilson argued that as treaties "are to have the operation of laws, they ought to have the sanction of laws also. The circumstance of secrecy in the business of treaties formed the only objection," he said, but this was outweighed by the necessity of the legislative sanction. John Sherman replied that "the necessity of secrecy in the case of treaties forbade a reference of them to the whole Legislature." Wilson's amendment was defeated, one state to ten.
>
> The Brearley Committee's proposal to require a two-thirds vote for treaty approval received intensive attention. Efforts were made: to except from the two-thirds requirement "treaties of peace," in order to facilitate an end to any conflict; to enable the Senate to adopt treaties of peace by a two-thirds vote even without the President's concurrence; and to eliminate entirely the two-thirds rule, requiring only majority approval. All these attempts ultimately failed, and the provision was included in the Constitution in virtually the committee's language.[65]

Thus, the framers seem to have entrusted the power to make treaties to the President, "with the Advice and Consent of the Senate" based on considerations of protecting the interests of the smaller states, promoting secrecy and dispatch in

---

[65]*Id.* at 34-35.

treaty negotiations and approval, and providing a check on Senate or presidential authority alone to conclude international agreements binding on the Nation.[66]

That the treaty power is lodged in Article II, concerning Executive authority under the Constitution, rather than Article I, concerning legislative authority, also suggests that the framers regarded it as primarily Executive in nature and not as a general legislative power.[67] Indeed, there is an interesting parallel between Article I containing the presentment clause and presidential veto power as a check on the legislative authority it grants and Article II containing the Senate "Advice and Consent" power as a check on the Executive's treaty authority it grants. Importantly, the treaty power is not contained in the Article I, section 8 enumeration of general legislative powers.[68]

---

[66]It might be noted that the treaty clause, as finally adopted, was similar to the basic outline suggested by Alexander Hamilton on June 18, 1787, "in which the chief executive,the Governor, would have `with the advice and approbation of the Senate the power of making all treaties.'" *Treaties and Other International Agreements: The Role of the United States Senate: A Study Prepared for the Senate Foreign Relations Comm. by the Congressional Research Service, Library of Congress,* 98th Cong., 2d Sess. 26 (Comm. Print June 1984) [hereinafter *Treaties and International Agreements Committee Print*] (quoting "Notes of Debates in the Federal Convention of 1787 reported by James Madison"). This report includes an interesting discussion of the constitutional history of the treaty clause. *See id.* at 25-28. It also says: "Thus, the power to make treaties, at first given to the Senate by the Committee of Detail, was transferred to the President by and with the advice and consent of the Senate." *Id.* at 28.

[67]In view of this action of the framers in lodging the treaty power in Article II, it is somewhat surprising that a theoretical debate could continue as to whether the treaty power is "primarily" legislative or executive *under the United States Constitution.*

[68]It has also been pointed out that under Article VI, clause 2 (the supremacy clause), treaties are treated separately from the general "Laws of the United States" and that in this category it is "Treaties made" that become binding under national law. *See* the discussion at the recent conference on "Treaty Implementation and Interpretation Under the Constitution," *supra* note 1, particularly the remarks by Professor Fred Morrison of the University of Minnesota Law School.

And, continuing with textual points about the treaty power, Dr. Louis Fisher of the Congressional Research Service, Library of Congress, also notes:

> With regard to the constitutional text, the treaty-making process is not divided into two stages that are exclusive and sequential: negotiation by

Early statements by the framers confirm that the treaty power was not conceived as a general legislative power and that the President had broad authority under the treaty power. Thus, John Jay wrote in *The Federalist* in March 1788 during the ratification debate:

> The power of making treaties is an important one, especially as it relates to war, peace and commerce; and it should not be delegated but in such a mode, and with such precautions, as will afford the highest security, that it will be exercised by men the best qualified for the purpose, and in the manner most conducive to the public good.
>
> . . . They who wish to commit the power under consideration to a popular assembly, composed of members constantly coming and going in quick succession, seem not to recollect that such a body must necessarily be inadequate to the attainment of those great objects, which require to be steadily contemplated in all their relations and circumstances, and which can only be approached and achieved by measures, which not only talents, but also exact information and often much time are necessary to concert and to execute.
>
> It seldom happens in the negotiation of treaties of whatever nature, but that perfect *secrecy* and immediate *dispatch* are sometimes requisite. There are cases where the most useful intelligence may be obtained, if the persons possessing it can be relieved from apprehensions of discovery. Those apprehensions will operate on those persons whether they are actuated by

---

> the President followed by Senate action. The President "makes" treaties, by and with the advice and consent of the Senate. The constitutional language for the treaty process is markedly different than for appointments, which does depend on exclusive and sequential stages. The Constitution provides that the President "shall nominate, and by [and] with the Advice and Consent of the Senate, shall appoint Ambassadors, other public Ministers and Consuls, Judges of the supreme Court, and all other Officers of the United States." Here the President's authority to nominate is set apart solely as an executive responsibility. No such division of authority is mandated by the treaty process.

Fisher, "Constitutional Underpinnings," *supra* note 1, at 2.

mercenary or friendly motives, and there doubtless are many of both descriptions, who would rely on the secrecy of the president, but who would not confide in that of the senate, and still less in that of a large popular assembly. The convention have done well therefore in so disposing of the power of making treaties, that although the president must in forming them act by the advice and consent of the senate, yet he will be able to manage the business of intelligence in such manner as prudence may suggest.

They who have turned their attention to the affairs of men, must have perceived that there are tides in them. Tides, very irregular in their duration, strength and direction, and seldom found to run twice exactly in the same manner or measure. To discern and to profit by these tides in national affairs, is the business of those who preside over them; and they who have had much experience on this head inform us, that there frequently are occasions when days, nay even when hours are precious. The loss of a battle, the death of a Prince, the removal of a minister, or other circumstances intervening to change the present posture and aspect of affairs, may turn the most favorable tide into a course opposite to our wishes. As in the field, so in the cabinet, there are moments to be seized as they pass, and they who preside in either, should be left in capacity to improve them. So often and so essentially have we heretofore suffered from the want of secrecy and dispatch, that the Constitution would have been inexcusably defective if no attention had been paid to those objects. Those matters which in negociations usually require the most secrecy and the most dispatch, are those preparatory and auxiliary measures which are not otherwise important in a national view, than as they tend to facilitate the attainment of the objects of the negociation. For these the president will find no difficulty to provide, and should any circumstance occur which requires the advice and consent of the senate, he may at any time convene them. Thus we see that the constitution provides that our negociations for treaties shall have every advantage which can be derived from talents, information, integrity, and deliberate investigations on the one hand, and from secrecy and dispatch on the other.

But to this plan as to most others that have ever appeared, objections are contrived and urged.

> Some are displeased with it, not on account of any errors or defects in it, but because as the treaties when made are to have the force of laws, they should be made only by men invested with legislative authority. These gentlemen seem not to consider that the judgments of our courts, and the commissions constitutionally given by our governor, are as valid and as binding on all persons whom they concern, as the laws passed by our legislature are. All constitutional acts of power, whether in the executive or in the judicial departments, have as much legal validity and obligation as if they proceeded from the Legislature, and therefore whatever name be given to the power of making treaties, or however obligatory they may be when made, certain it is that the people may with much propriety commit the power to a distinct body from the legislature, the executive or judicial. It surely does not follow that because they have given the power of making laws to the Legislature, and therefore they should likewise give them power to do every other act of sovereignty by which the citizens are to be bound and affected.[69]

---

[69]*The Federalist* No. 64, at 432-36 (J. Jay) (J. Cooke ed. 1961).

It has been noted that Jay's diplomatic experience makes his interpretation in *The Federalist* particularly important. Professor Arthur Bestor of the University of Washington writes:

> In this contribution to *The Federalist* Jay was of course examining the completed Constitution, not offering suggestions to those about to frame it. As an interpretation of the original intent of the document, Jay's essay is of the highest importance. His diplomatic experience--commencing with his appointment as minister to Spain in 1779; followed by his participation, as one of the commissioners, in the negotiation of peace with Great Britain; and continuing, from 1784 on, with his service as Secretary of the United States for the Department of Foreign Affairs--fitted him better than anyone else to judge the intended effect of the new Constitution both on the actual process of negotiation and on the character of the relationship that would have to be maintained between executive and legislative authorities.

Bestor, "Separation of Powers in the Domain of Foreign Affairs: The Intent of the Constitution Historically Examined," 5 *Seton Hall L. Rev.* 527, 621-22 (Spring 1974) (footnote omitted).

Alexander Hamilton wrote in *The Federalist* also in March of 1788:

> The essence of the legislative authority is to enact laws, or, in other words, to prescribe rules for the regulation of the society. While the execution of the laws, and the employment of the common strength, either for this purpose or for the common defence, seem to comprise all the functions of the executive magistrate. The power of making treaties is, plainly, neither the one nor the other. It relates neither to the execution of the subsisting laws, nor to the enaction of new ones; and still less to an exertion of the common strength. Its objects are CONTRACTS with foreign nations, which have the force of law, but derive it from the obligations of good faith. They are not rules prescribed by the sovereign to the subject, but agreements between sovereign and sovereign. The power in question seems therefore to form a distinct department, and to belong, properly, neither to the legislative nor to the executive. The qualities elsewhere detailed as indispensable in the management of foreign negotiations, point out the Executive as the most fit agent in those transactions; while the vast importance of the trust, and the operation of treaties as laws, plead strongly for the participation of the whole or a portion of the legislative body in the office of making them.[70]

---

[70]*The Federalist* No. 75, at 504-05 (A. Hamilton) (J. Cooke ed. 1961).

In arguing against the participation of the House of Representatives in the making of treaties, Hamilton wrote:

> The fluctuating, and taking its future increase into the account, the multitudinous composition of that body, forbid us to expect in it those qualities which are essential to the proper execution of such a trust. Accurate and comprehensive knowledge of foreign politics; a steady and systematic adherence to the same views; a nice and uniform sensibility to national character, decision, *secrecy* and dispatch; are incompatible with the genius of a body so variable and so numerous.

Id. at 507.

Treasury Secretary Hamilton wrote in his first letter in the famous "Pacificus-Helvidius" exchange with Madison over President Washington's proclamation of neutrality in the war between France and Great Britain:

> The Legislative Department is not the *organ* of intercourse between the UStates and foreign Nations. It is charged neither with *making* nor *interpreting* Treaties. It is therefore not naturally the Organ of the Government which is to pronounce the existing condition of the Nation, with regard to foreign Powers, or to admonish the Citizens of their obligations and duties as founded upon that condition of things. Still less is it charged with enforcing the execution and observance of these obligations and those duties.
>
> It is equally obvious that the act in question is foreign to the Judiciary Department of the Government. The province of that Department is to decide litigations in particular cases. It is indeed charged with the interpretation of treaties; but it exercises this function only in the litigated cases; that is where contending parties bring before it a specific controversy. It has no concern with pronouncing upon the external political relations of Treaties between Government and Government. This position is too plain to need being insisted upon.
>
> It must then of necessity belong to the Executive Department to exercise the function in Question--when a proper case for the exercise of it occurs.
>
> It appears to be connected with that department in various capacities, as the *organ* of intercourse between the Nation and foreign Nations--as the interpreter of the National Treaties in those cases in which the Judiciary is not competent, that is in the cases between Government and Government--as that Power, which is charged with the Execution of the Laws, of which Treaties form a part--as that Power which is charged with the command and application of the Public Force. . . .
>
> Hence in the case stated, though treaties can only be made by the President and Senate, their activity may be continued or suspended by the president alone.
>
> It deserves to be remarked, that as the participation of the senate in the making of Treaties and the power of the Legislature

> to declare war are exceptions out of the general "Executive Power" vested in the President, they are to be construed strictly--and ought to be extended no further than is essential to their execution.[71]

Similarly, Secretary of State Thomas Jefferson, a contemporary of great influence although not officially a constitutional framer, said in a legal opinion of April 24, 1790, prepared for President Washington:

> The Constitution has divided the powers of government into three branches, Legislative, Executive and Judiciary, lodging each with a distinct magistracy. The Legislative it has given completely to the Senate and House of representatives; it has declared that "the

---

[71]*H. Syrett*, 15 *The Papers of Alexander Hamilton* 33, 37, 38, 42 (1969) (italics in original). *But see* Dr. Louis Fisher's recent paper on the "Constitutional Underpinnings of the Treaty Powers," in which he declares on the basis of early practice of President Washington in seeking Senate advice on treaties and a brief excerpt by Alexander Hamilton in *The Federalist* No. 75 that "both Washington and Hamilton regarded the treaty power as more legislative than executive." See Fisher, "Constitutional Underpinnings," *supra* note 1, at 3. The excerpt from Hamilton as cited by Dr. Fisher in Dr. Fisher's own statement is: "Alexander Hamilton, in Federalist 75 . . . observed that the power of making treaties `will be found to partake more of the legislative than of the executive character, though it does not seem strictly to fall within the definition of either of them.'" *Id.* This statement weakly tilting in the legislative direction would hardly seem a match for the clear Hamiltonian statements to the contrary cited in text. Dr. Fisher also quotes an excerpt from a letter from President Washington to the Senate that: "In the appointment to offices, the agency of the Senate is purely executive, and they may be summoned to the President. In treaties, the agency is perhaps as much of a legislative nature and the business may possibly be referred to their deliberations in their legislative chamber." *Id.* (footnote omitted). To construe this letter as to whether the Senate "may possibly" have treaties referred to them in their legislative chamber and which uses the language "perhaps as much of a legislative nature" (emphasis added) in discussing what may well be the Senate treaty role (the referent here is at least as likely to the "agency of the Senate" as it is to the treaty power as a whole) does not, at least by itself, seem to support Dr. Fisher's view that "Washington regarded the treaty power as more legislative than executive." *Id.* Indeed, it may suggest the contrary by, among other factors, the issue even being considered of whether the Senate may be summoned to the President in carrying out its treaty advice and consent role. The reader should also compare this Washington excerpt quoted by Dr. Fisher with the 1796 Washington statement to the House quoted at note 162 *infra*.

> Executive powers shall be vested in the President," submitting only special articles of it to a negative by the Senate; and it has vested the Judiciary power in the courts of justice, with certain exceptions also in favor of the Senate.
>
> The transaction of business with foreign nations is Executive altogether. It belongs then to the head of that department, except as to such portions of it as are specially submitted to the Senate. *Exceptions* are to be construed strictly.[72]

Note that in this excerpt Jefferson refers to the Senate's role under Article II, which of course includes the Senate's role in the treaty power, as a "negative." He took the same view in his rules manual for the Senate specifically with respect to the Senate treaty role.[73] And of a conversation on July 10, 1793, with M. Genet, Jefferson said:

> He asked if they [Congress] were not the sovereign. I told him no, they were sovereign in making laws only, the executive was sovereign in executing them, and the judiciary in construing them where they related to their department. `But,' said he, `at least, Congress are bound to see that the treaties are observed.' I told him no, there were very few cases indeed arising out of treaties, which they could take notice of; that the President is to see that treaties are observed. `If he decides against the treaty, to whom is a nation to appeal?' I told him the Constitution had made the President the last appeal.[74]

On the other hand, as we have seen, James Madison, responding to Alexander Hamilton in the "Pacificus-Helvidius" exchange adopted the view that

---

[72]16 *J. Boyd, supra* note 27, at 378-79. Robert F. Turner points out that "Jefferson wrote in the margin of his file copy [of this memorandum]: `endorsed by Washington.'" See Turner, "Constitutional Underpinnings," supra note 1, at 14-15.

[73]*See T. Jefferson, A Manual of Parliamentary Practice for the Use of the Senate of the United States* §52, at 110 (3d ed. 1854).

[74]Thomas Jefferson, Secretary of State, Minutes of Conversation with M. Genet, *quoted in 4 J.B. Moore, supra* note 25, at 680-81.

the treaty power was more legislative than executive in nature, a view that, at least in so far as it asks the question under the United States Constitution, seems inconsistent with the lodging of the treaty power in Article II. Thus, Madison wrote:

> The substance of the first piece, sifted from its inconsistencies and its vague expressions, may be thrown into the following propositions:
>
> That the powers of declaring war and making treaties are, in their nature, executive powers:
>
> That being particularly vested by the constitution in other departments, they are to be considered as exceptions out of the general grant to the executive department:
>
> That being, as exceptions, to be construed strictly, the powers not strictly within them, remain with the executive.
>
> That the executive consequently, as the organ of intercourse with foreign nations, and the interpreter and executor of treaties, and the law of nations, is authorized to expound all articles of treaties, those involving questions of war and peace, as well as others;--to judge of the obligations of the United States to make war or not, under any *casus faederis* or eventual operation of the contract, relating to war; and to pronounce the state of things resulting from the obligations of the United States, as understood by the executive:
>
> That in particular the executive had authority to judge, whether in the case of the mutual guaranty between the United States and France, the former being bound by it to engage in the war:
>
> That the executive has, in pursuance of that authority, decided that the United States are not bound:--And . . .
>
> That its proclamation of the 22nd of April last, is to be taken as the effect and expression of that decision.
>
> The basis of the reasoning is, we perceive, the extraordinary doctrine, that the powers of making war, and treaties, are in their nature executive; and therefore comprehended in the general grant of executive power, where not especially and strictly excepted out of the grant.

Let us examine this doctrine: and that we may avoid the possibility of mistaking the writer, it shall be laid down in his own words; a precaution the more necessary, as scarce any thing else could outweigh the improbability, that so extravagant a tenet should be hazarded at so early a day, in the face of the public.

His words are--"Two of these [exceptions and qualifications to the executive powers] have been already noticed--the participation of the senate in the appointment of officers, and the making of treaties. A third remains to be mentioned--the right of the legislature to declare war, and grant letters of marque and reprisal."

Again--"It deserves to be remarked, that as the participation of the senate in the making of treaties, and the power of the legislature to declare war, are exceptions out of the general executive power, vested in the president; they are to be construed strictly, and ought to be extended not further than is essential to their execution."

If there be any countenance to these positions, it must be found either, first, in the writers of authority on public law; or, 2d, in the quality and operation of the powers to make war and treaties; or, 3d, in the constitution of the United States.

1. It would be of little use to enter far into the first source of information, not only because our own reason and our own constitution, are the best guides; but because a just analysis and discrimination of the powers of government, according to their executive, legislative, and judiciary qualities, are not to be expected in the works of the most received jurists, who wrote before a critical attention was paid to those objects, and with their eyes too much on monarchical governments, where all powers are confounded in the sovereignty of the prince. It will be found, however, I believe, that all of them, particularly Wolsius, Burlemaqui, and Vatel, speak of the powers to declare war, to conclude peace, and to form alliances, as among the highest acts of the sovereignty; of which the legislative power must at least be an integral and preeminent part.

Writers, such as Locke, and Montesquieu, who have discussed more the principles of liberty and the structure of government, lie under the same disadvantage, of having written before these subjects were illuminated by the events and discussions which distinguish a very recent period. Both of them, too, are evidently warped by a regard to the particular government of England, to which one of them owed allegiance; and the other professed an admiration bordering on idolatry. Montesquieu, however, has rather distinguished himself by enforcing the reasons and the importance of avoiding a confusion of the several powers of government, that by enumerating and defining the powers which belong to each particular class. And Locke, notwithstanding the early date of his work on civil government, and the example of his own government before his eyes, admits that the particular powers in question, which, after some of the writers on public law he calls federative, are really distinct from the executive, though almost always united with it, and hardly to be separated into distinct hands. Had he not lived under a monarchy, in which these powers were united; or had he written by the lamp which truth now presents to lawgivers, the last observation would probably never have dropped from his pen. But let us quit a field of research which is more likely to perplex than to decide, and bring the question to other tests of which it will be more easy to judge.

2. If we consult, for a moment, the nature and operation of the two powers to declare war and to make treaties, it will be impossible not to see, that they can never fall within a proper definition of executive powers. The natural province of the executive magistrate is to execute laws, as that of the legislature is to make laws. All his acts, therefore, properly executive, must presuppose the existence of the laws to be executed. A treaty is not an execution of laws: it does not presuppose the existence of laws. It is, on the contrary, to have itself the force of a law, and to be carried into execution, like all other laws, by the executive magistrate. To say then that the power of making treaties, which are confessedly laws, belongs naturally to the department which is to execute laws, is to say, that the executive department naturally includes a legislative power. In theory this is an absurdity--in practice a tyranny.

The power to declare war is subject to similar reasoning. A declaration that there shall be war, is not an execution of laws: it does not suppose pre-existing laws to be executed: it is not, in any respect, an act merely executive. It is, on the contrary, one of the most deliberate acts that can be performed; and when performed, has the effect of repealing all the laws operating in a state of peace so far as they are inconsistent with a state of war; and of enacting, as a rule for the executive, a new code adapted to the relation between the society and its foreign enemy. In like manner, a conclusion of peace *annuis* all the laws peculiar to a state of war, and revives the general laws incident to a state of peace.

These remarks will be strengthened by adding, that treaties, particularly treaties of peace, have sometimes the effect of changing not only the external laws of the society, but operate also on the internal code, which is purely municipal, and to which the legislative authority of the country is of itself competent to complete.

From this view of the subject it must be evident, that although the executive may be a convenient organ of preliminary communications with foreign governments, on the subjects of treaty or war; and the proper agent for carrying into execution the final determinations of the competent authority; yet it can have no pretensions, from the nature of the powers in question compared with the nature of the executive trust, to that essential agency which gives validity to such determinations.

It must be further evident, that if these powers be not in their nature purely legislative, they partake so much more of that, than of any other quality, that under a constitution leaving them to result to their most natural department, the legislature would be without a rival in its claim.

Another important inference to be noted is, that the powers of making war and treaty being substantially of a legislative, not an executive nature, the rule of interpreting exceptions strictly must narrow, instead of enlarging, executive pretensions on those subjects.

3. It remains to be inquired, whether there be any thing in the constitution itself, which shows, that the powers of making war and peace are considered as of an executive nature, and as comprehended within a general grant of executive power.

It will not be pretended, that this appears from any direct position to be founded in the instrument.

If it were deducible from any particular expressions, it may be presumed, that the publication would have saved us the trouble of the research.

Does the doctrine, then, result from the actual distribution of powers among the several branches of the government? or from any fair analogy between the powers of war and treaty, and the enumerated powers vested in the executive alone?

Let us examine:

In the general distribution of powers, we find that of declaring war expressly vested in the congress, where every other legislative power is declared to be vested; and without any other qualification than what is common to every other legislative act. The constitutional idea of this power would seem then clearly to be, that it is of a legislative and not an executive nature.

This conclusion becomes irresistible, when it is recollected, that the constitution cannot be supposed to have placed either any power legislative in its nature, entirely among executive powers, or any power executive in its nature, entirely among legislative powers, without charging the constitution, with that kind of intermixture and consolidation of different powers, which would violate a fundamental principle in the organization of free governments. If it were not unnecessary to enlarge on this topic here, it could be shown, that the constitution was originally vindicated, and has been constantly expounded, with a disavowal of any such intermixture.

The power of treaties is vested jointly in the president and in the senate, which is a branch of the legislature. From this arrangement merely, there can be no inference that would necessarily exclude the power from the executive class: since the senate is joined with the president in another power, that of appointing to offices, which, as far as relate to executive offices at least, is considered as of an executive nature. Yet on the other hand, there are sufficient indications that the power of treaties is regarded by the constitution as materially different from mere executive power, and as having more affinity to the legislative than to the executive character.

One circumstance indicating this, is the constitutional regulation under which the senate give their consent in the case of treaties. In all other cases, the consent of the body is expressed by a majority of voices. In this particular case, a concurrence of two-thirds at least is made necessary, as a substitute or compensation for the other branch of the legislature, which on certain occasions, could not be conveniently a party to the transaction.

But the conclusive circumstance is, that treaties, when formed according to the constitutional mode, are confessedly to have force and operation of laws, and are to be a rule for the courts in controversies between man and man, as much as any other laws. They are even emphatically declared by the constitution to be "the supreme law of the land."

So far the argument from the constitution is precisely in opposition to the doctrine. As little will be gained in its favour from a comparison of the two powers, with those particularly vested in the president alone.

As there are but few, it will be most satisfactory to review them one by one.

"The president shall be commander in chief of the army and navy of the United States, and of the militia when called into the actual service of the United States."

There can be no relation worth examining between this power and the general power of making treaties. And instead of being analogous to the power of declaring war, it affords a striking illustration of the incompatibility of the two powers in the same hands. Those who are to conduct a war cannot in the nature of things, be proper or safe judges, whether a war ought to be commenced, continued or concluded. They are barred from the latter functions by a great principle in free government, analogous to thatwhich separates the sword from the purse, or the power of executing from the power of enacting laws.

"He may require the opinion in writing of the principal officers in each of the executive departments upon any subject relating to the duties of their respective offices; and he shall have power to grant reprieves and pardons for offences against the United States, except in case of impeachment." These powers can have nothing to do with the subject.

"The president shall have power to fill up vacancies that may happen during the recess of the Senate, by granting commissions which shall expire at the end of the next session." The same remark is applicable to this power, as also to that of "receiving ambassadors, other public ministers, and consuls." The particular use attempted to be made of this last power will be considered in another place.

"He shall take care that the laws shall be faithfully executed, and shall commission all officers of the United States." To see the laws faithfully executed constitutes the essence of the executive authority. But what relation has it to the power of making treaties and war, that is, of determining what the laws shall be with regard to other nations? No other certainly than what subsists between the powers of executing and enacting laws; no other, consequently, than what forbids a coalition of the powers in the same department.

I pass over the few other specified functions assigned to the president, such as that of convening the legislature, etc., etc., which cannot be drawn into the present question.

It may be proper however to take notice of the power of removal from office, which appears to have been adjudged to the president by the laws establishing the executive departments; and which the writer has endeavoured to press into his service. To justify any favourable inference from this case, it must be shown, that the powers of war and treaties are of a kindred nature to the power of removal, or at least are equally within a grant of executive power. Nothing of this sort has been attempted, nor probably will be attempted. Nothing can in truth be clearer, than that no analogy, or shade of analogy, can be traced between a power in the supreme officer responsible for the faithful execution of the laws, to displace a subaltern officer employed in the execution of the laws; and a power to make treaties and to declare war, such as these have been found to be in their nature, their operation, and their consequences.

Thus it appears that by whatever standard we try this doctrine, it must be condemned as no less vicious in theory than it would be dangerous in practice. It is countenanced neither by the writers on law; nor by the nature of the powers themselves; nor byany general arrangements, or particular expressions, or plausible analogies, to be found in the constitution.

Whence then can the writer have borrowed it?

There is but one answer to this question.

The power of making treaties and the power of declaring war, are royal prerogatives in the British government, and are accordingly treated as executive prerogatives by British commentators.

We shall be the more confirmed in the necessity of this solution of the problem, by looking back to the area of the constitution, and satisfying ourselves that the writer could not have been misled by the doctrines maintained by our own commentators on our own government. That I may not ramble beyond prescribed limits, I shall content myself with an extract from a work which entered into a systematic explanation and defence of the constitution, and to which there has frequently been ascribed some influence in conciliating the public assent to the government in the form proposed. Three circumstances conspire in giving weight to this contemporary exposition. It was made at a time when no application to persons or measures could bias: the opinion given was not transiently mentioned, but formally and critically elucidated: it related to a point in the constitution which must consequently have been viewed as of importance in the public mind. The passage relates to the power of making treaties; that of declaring war, being arranged with such obvious propriety among the legislative powers, as to be passed over without particular discussion.

"Though several writers on the subject of government place that power [of making treaties] in the class of executive authorities, yet this is evidently an arbitrary disposition. For if we attend carefully to its operation, it will be found to partake more of the legislative than of the executive character, though it does not seem strictly to fall within the definition of either of them. The essence of the legislative authority, is to enact laws; or, in other words, to prescribe rules for the regulation of society: while the execution of the laws and the employment of the common strength, either for this purpose, or for the common defence, seem to comprise all the functions of the executive magistrate. The power of making treaties is plainly neither the one nor the other. It relates neither to the execution of the subsisting laws, nor to the enaction of new ones, and still less to an exertion of the common strength. Its objects are contracts with foreign nations, which have the force of law, but derive it from the obligations of good faith. They are not rules prescribed by the sovereign to the subject, but agreements betweensovereign and sovereign. The power in question seems therefore to form a distinct department, and to belong properly neither to the legislative nor to the executive. The qualities elsewhere detailed as indispensable in the management of foreign negotiations, point out the executive as the most fit agent in those transactions; whilst the vast importance of the trust, and the operation of treaties as laws, plead strongly for the participation of the whole or a part of the legislative body, in the office of the making them."--*Federalist*, p. 418. [No. 75, written by Mr. Hamilton. Footnote in Hunt's original.]

It will not fail to be remarked on this commentary, that whatever doubts may be started as to the correctness of its reasoning against the legislative nature of the power to make treaties; it is clear, consistent, and confident, in deciding that the power is plainly and evidently not an executive power.[75]

---

[75]Madison, "First *Helvidius* Letter," supra note 25, at 405-11. As previously discussed, this theoretical view of the treaty power does not seem to be the view of Montesquieu, Blackstone or Locke. Madison, as with other spokesmen in the heat of debate, may have been motivated by the debate in his characterization of the treaty power. Moreover, the treaty power, as such, of course, was not directly at stake in the neutrality proclamation that triggered the "Pacificus-Helvidius" exchange.

That Madison was presenting an adversary view of the issues in this "Helvidius" letter is further confirmed by his failure to note that the treaty power is lodged by the Constitution in Article II on the executive power rather than in Article I on the legislative power. Moreover, as the editor of *The Papers of James Madison* notes, James Madison "regarded Montesquieu highly as a political philosopher." Montesquieu, of course, included the foreign relations power as one of two types of Executive power. *See R. Rutland, Well Acquainted With Books: The Founding Framers of 1787,* at 56 (1987). And, Robert Wernick writes in his article describing Montesquieu as "The Godfather of the American Constitution":

> At the Convention, James Madison cited Montesquieu as his authority for insisting on the separation of the executive, legislative and judicial powers in the new government, forerunner of the celebrated system of checks and balances we use today. The man more than any other

Madison's views on the nature of the treaty power in his "Helvidius" letter should be read against the background of the Virginia Plan, based on a draft believed to be by Madison, (which contained no reference to the location of the power to make treaties and which may have thus assumed that the Treaty power was a legislative power) which was not adopted by the Convention,[76] Madison's proposal that treaties of peace should require assent of only a majority of the Senate which was not adopted by the Convention,[77] and Madison's later intervention in the debate over the

---

> responsible for our Constitution (SMITHSONIAN, September 1987), Madison also used the words of Chapter 6 [Montesquieu, *The Spirit of Laws,* book 10] as the text of his sermon on the separation-of-powers principle in his influential *Federalist* 47.
>
> . . . .
>
> Because Montesquieu had only limited faith in the goodness of human nature, he reasoned that anyone who possessed power would be likely to increase it, and the only way to stop him was by a system of rival powers, a view that the Founding Fathers, fearful alike of the tyranny by the many or the few, thoroughly subscribed to. "The oracle who is always consulted and cited on this subject," said Madison, "is the celebrated Montesquieu. If he be not the author of this invaluable precept in the science of politics, he has the merit at least of displaying and recommending it most effectually to the attention of mankind."

Wernick, *supra* note 9, at 193, 194-5.

[76]*See A. Sofaer, supra* note 8, at 26, 26-36; McDougal & Lans, "Treaties and Congressional-Executive or Presidential Agreements: Interchangeable Instruments of National Policy: II," 54 *Yale L.J.* 534, 538 (1945).

[77]McDougal & Lans, *supra* note 76, at 541. *See generally* on the historical origins of the treaty power, id. at 536-44.

In comparing the views on the treaty power expressed in the 1793 "Pacificus-Helvidius" debate between Hamilton and Madison, Robert F. Turner makes the following point:

> [A]s we get into a review of the debates which followed ratification of the Constitution--in particular the *Pacificus-Helvidius* debate of 1793 between Hamilton and Madison--we need to keep in mind that the treaty provisions of the Virginia Plan embraced by Madison (giving the congressionally selected executive(s) no role in treaty matters) was ultimately *rejected* in Philadelphia, while much of Hamilton's language [specifically on the

Committee on Detail draft to argue "that the president should be an agent in treaties" rather than having the treaty power lodged solely in the Senate.[78] It should also be noted that even Madison's "Helvidius" letter adopted the view that the Executive was "the proper agent for carrying into execution the final determinations of the competent authority,"[79] that "[t]he power of treaties is vested jointly in the president and in the senate,"[80] and that the President's power "[t]o see the laws faithfully executed constitutes the essence of the executive authority."[81] Moreover, Madison quotes at length Hamilton's statement in *The Federalist* No. 75 that includes the statements "the execution of the laws . . . seem to comprise all the functions of the executive magistrate" . . . "[i]ts [treaties] objects are contracts with foreign nations, which have the force of law, but derive it from the obligations of good faith. They are not rules prescribed by the sovereign to the subject, but agreements between sovereign and sovereign. . . ."[82] It should be further noted with respect to Madison's views of the treaty power in the "Pacificus-Helvidius" exchange that in any area in which Madison might concede an issue to be--or it were subsequently so held to be--inherently executive in its nature (as possibly interpretation of treaties under the concededly executive power to take care that the laws be faithfully executed) then the force of his argument would urge that any congressional powers in the area would be construed narrowly.[83] Finally, it should

treaty power] found its way into the final text.

Turner, "Constitutional Underpinnings," *supra* note 1, at 6.

[78]*A. Sofaer, supra* note 8, at 34. Sofaer says of this intervention by Madison: "Madison seems to have had more in mind for the President than simply to serve the Senate's will, as Congress's agents were expected to do under the Confederation." *Id.* at 34.

[79]1 *W. Goldsmith, supra* note 24, at 408.

[80] *Id.*

[81] *Id.* at 409.

[82] *Id.* at 410-11.

[83]Robert F. Turner has made this argument in a number of settings. *See generally R. Turner, Congress, supra* note 23.

be noted that Madison said on June 18, 1788, in addressing the Virginia Convention on the adoption of the Constitution:

> The exercise of the [treaty] power must be consistent with the object of the delegation.
>
> . . . The object of treaties is the regulation of intercourse with foreign nations and is external.[84]

State ratification convention debates are also of importance in understanding the meaning of the treaty power.[85] Some of the relevant debates, as appearing in Farrand's *The Records of the Federal Convention of 1787*, include the following. James Wilson defended against a charge in the Pennsylvania Convention that the Senate was given too much power in the proposed constitution by saying:

> I am not a blind admirer of this system. Some of the powers of the senators are not with me the favorite parts of it . . . . These additional powers, I believe, are, that of trying impeachments, that of concurring with the President in making treaties, and that of concurring in the appointment of officers. These are the powers that are stated as improper. It is fortunate, that in the exercise of every one of them, the Senate stands controlled; if it is that monster which it [is] said to be, it can only show its teeth, it is unable to bite or devour. With regard to impeachments, the senate can try none but such as will be brought before them by the house of representatives.

---

[84] 3 *J. Elliot, The Debates in the Several State Conventions on the Adoption of the Federal Constitution, as Recommended by the General Convention at Philadelphia, in 1787*, at 514 (2d ed. Philadelphia 1836) (reproduced 1937, J.B. Lippincott Co.).

[85]For example, James Madison said: "If we were to look, therefore, for the meaning of the instrument beyond the face of the instrument, we must look for it, not in the General Convention, which proposed, but in the State Conventions, which accepted and ratified the Constitution." 6 *G. Hunt* (ed.), *The Writings of James Madison* 272 (1906). The following examples from state ratification convention debates, Joseph Story's *Commentaries*, and this statement by Madison are set out in Turner, "Constitutional Underpinnings," *supra* note 1, at 10-13.

> The senate can make no treaties; they can approve of none unless the President of the United States lay it before them. With regard to the appointment of officers, the President must nominate before they can vote. So that if the powers of either branch are perverted, it must be with the approbation of some one of the other branches of government: thus checked on one side, they can do no one act of themselves.
>
> . . . Sir, I confess I wish the powers of the senate were not as they are. I think it would have been better if those powers had been distributed in other parts of the system.[86]

The following exchange took place on January 16, 1788 in the South Carolina Legislature:

> PIERCE BUTLER (one of the delegates of the Federal Convention) was one of a committee that drew up this clause, and would endeavor to recollect those reasons by which they were guided. It was at first proposed to vest the sole power of making peace or war in the Senate; but this was objected to as inimical to the genius of a republic, by destroying the necessary balance they were anxious to preserve. Some gentlemen were inclined to give this power to the President; but is was objected to, as throwing into his hands the influence of a monarch, having an opportunity of involving his country in a war whenever he wished to promote her destruction. The House of Representatives was then named; but an insurmountable objection was made to this proposition -- which was, that negotiations always required the greatest secrecy, which could not be expected in a large body. The honorable gentleman then gave a clear, concise opinion on the propriety of the proposed Constitution.
>
> Gen. CHARLES COTESWORTH PINCKNEY (one of the delegates of the Federal Convention) observed, that the honorable judge, from his great penetration, had hit upon one of those difficult points which for a long time occasioned much debate in the Convention. Indeed, this subject appeared to be of so much magnitude, that a committee

---

[86] 3 *M. Farrand* (ed.), *The Records of the Federal Convention of 1787*, at 162 (1911).

> consisting of one member from each state was appointed to consider and report upon it. His honorable friend (Major Butler) was on the committee for this state. Some members were for vesting the power for making treaties in the legislature; but the secrecy and despatch which are so frequently necessary in negotiations evinced the impropriety of vesting it there. The same reason showed the impropriety of placing it solely in the House of Representatives. A few members were desirous that the President alone might possess this power, and contended that it might safely be lodged with him, as he was to be responsible for his conduct, and therefore would not dare to make a treaty repugnant to the interest of his country; and from his situation he was more interested in making a good treaty than any other man in the United States. This doctrine General Pinckney said he could not acquiesce in. . . . At last it was agreed to give the President a power of proposing treaties, as he was the ostensible head of the Union, and to vest the Senate (where each state had an equal voice) with the power of agreeing or disagreeing to the terms proposed.[87]

And the following was said on July 28, 1788, during the debates in the North Carolina Convention:

> Mr. Davie. Mr. Chairman, although treaties are mere conventional acts between the contracting parties, yet, by the law of nations, they are the supreme law of the land to their respective citizens or subjects. All civilized nations have concurred in considering them as paramount to an ordinary act of legislation. . . .
>
> The power of making treaties has, in all countries and governments, been placed in the executive departments. This has not only been grounded on the necessity and reason arising from that degree of secrecy, design, and despatch, which is always necessary in negotiations between nations, but to prevent their being impeded, or carried into effect, by the violence, animosity, and heat of parties, which too often infect numerous bodies. Both of these reasons preponderated in the foundation of this part of the system. . . .

---

[87] 4 *J. Elliot, supra* note 84, at 263-65 (also in 3 *M. Farrand, supra* note 86, at 250-51).

> On the principle of the propriety of vesting this power in the executive department, it would seem that the whole power of making treaties ought to be left to the President, who, being elected by the people of the United States at large, will have their general interest at heart. But that jealousy of executive power which has shown itself so strongly in all the American governments, would not admit this improvement. . . .
>
> . . . I have only to add the principle upon which the General Convention went -- that the power of making treaties could nowhere be so safely lodged as in the President and Senate; and the extreme jealousy subsisting between some of the states would not admit of it elsewhere.[88]

Joseph Story's contemporary and influential *Commentaries on the Constitution of the United States* also emphasizes the executive nature of the treaty power:

> § 779. In the formation of treaties, secrecy and immediate despatch are generally requisite, and sometimes absolutely indispensable. Intelligence may often be obtained, and measures matured in secrecy, which could never be done, unless in the faith and confidence of profound secrecy. No man at all acquainted with diplomacy, but must have felt, that the success of negotiations as often depends upon their being unknown by the public, as upon their justice or their policy. Men will assume responsibility in private, and communicate information, and express opinions, which they would feel the greatest repugnance publicly to avow; and measures may be defeated by the intrigues and management of foreign powers, if they suspect them to be in progress, and understand their precise nature and extent. In this view the executive department is a far better depositary of the power, than congress would be. The delays incident to a large assembly; the differences of opinion; the time consumed in debate, and the utter impossibility of secrecy, all combine to render them unfitted for the purposes of diplomacy. And our own experience during the confederation abundantly demonstrated all the evils, which the theory would lead us to expect.

---

[88] 3 *M. Farrand, supra* note 86, at 347-49.

Besides; there are tides in national affairs, as well as in the affairs of private life. To discern and profit by them is the part of true political wisdom; and the loss of a week, or even of a day, may sometimes change the whole aspect of affairs, and render negotiations wholly nugatory, or indecisive. The loss of a battle, the death of a prince, the removal of a minister, the pressure or removal of fiscal embarrassments at the moment, and other circumstances, may change the whole posture of affairs, and ensure success, or defeat the best concerted project. The executive, having a constant eye upon foreign affairs, can promptly meet, and even anticipate such emergencies, and avail himself of all the advantages accruing from them; while a large assembly would be coldly deliberating on the chances of success, and the policy of opening negotiations. It is manifest, then, that congress would not be a suitable depositary of the power.

§ 780. The same difficulties would occur from confiding it exclusively to either branch of congress. Each is too numerous for prompt and immediate action, and secrecy. The matters in negotiations, which usually require these qualities in the highest degree, are the preparatory and auxiliary measures; and which are to be seized upon, as it were, in an instant. The president could easily arrange them. But the house, or the senate, if in session, could not act, until after great delays; and in the recess could not act at all. To have entrusted the power to either would have been to relinquish the benefits of the constitutional agency of the president in the conduct of foreign negotiations. It is true, that the branch so entrusted might have the option to employ the president in that capacity; but they would also have the option of refraining from it; and it cannot be disguised, that pique, or cabal, or personal or political hostility, might induce them to keep their pursuits at a distance from his inspection and participation. Nor could it be expected, that the president, as a mere ministerial agent of such branch, would enjoy the confidence and respect of foreign powers to the same extent, as he would, as the constitutional representative of the nation itself; and his interposition would of course have less efficacy and weight.

§ 781. On the other hand, considering the delicacy and extent of the power, it is too much to expect, that a free people would confide to a single magistrate, however respectable, the sole authority to act conclusively, as well as exclusively, upon the subject of

> treaties. In England, the power to make treaties is exclusively vested in the crown. But however proper it may be in a monarchy, there is no American statesman, but must feel, that such a prerogative in an American president would be inexpedient and dangerous. It would be inconsistent with that wholesome jealousy, which all republics ought to cherish of all depositaries of power; and which, experience teaches us, is the best security against the abuse of it. The check, which acts upon the mind from the consideration, that what is done is but preliminary, and requires the assent of other independent minds to give it a legal conclusiveness, is a restraint, which awakens caution, and compels to deliberation.
>
> § 782. The plan of the constitution is happily adapted to attain all just objects in relation to foreign negotiations. While it confides the power to the executive department, it guards it from serious abuse by placing it under the ultimate superintendence of a select body of high character and high responsibility. It is indeed clear to a demonstration, that this joint possession of the power affords a greater security for its just exercise, than the separate possession of it by either. The president is the immediate author and finisher of all treaties; and all the advantages, which can be derived from talents, information, integrity, and deliberate investigation on the one hand, and from secrecy and despatch on the other, are thus combined in the system. But no treaty, so formed, becomes binding upon the country, unless it receives the deliberate assent of two thirds of the senate. In that body all the states are equally represented; and, from the nature of the appointment and duration of the office, it may fairly be presumed at all times to contain a very large portion of talents, experience, political wisdom, and sincere patriotism, a spirit of liberality, and a deep devotion to all the substantial interests of the country. The consitutional check of requiring two thirds to confirm a treaty is, of itself, a sufficient guaranty against any wanton sacrifice of private rights, or any betrayal of public privileges.[89]

In addition to the "Pacificus-Helvidius" exchange, which was rooted more in a general debate about presidential and congressional authority in foreign affairs

---

[89] *J. Story, Commentaries on the Constitution of the United States* 554-57 (Cambridge 1833).

than in a specific treaty power issue, there have been at least four subsequent substantial debates about the treaty powers, as well as numerous more minor considerations of the issues during, for example, the course of private litigation. These four substantial debates were first the debate in the early 1950s about the Bricker Amendment, a proposed constitutional amendment which, in its principal form, sought to restrict the treaty power as a source of federal legislative authority to prevent international agreements from taking effect as domestic law without subsequent legislation and to restrict the President's authority to enter into executive agreements; second, the debate in the aftermath of the Vietnam War about the appropriate authority of the President to conclude executive agreements; third, the debate during the Carter Administration precipitated by presidential termination of the mutual defence treaty with Taiwan about the appropriate authority of the President to terminate international agreements; and, most recently, the debate about the appropriate authority of the President to interpret international agreements that has been precipitated by the "broad-narrow" dispute.[90] With the exception of the last, which is the subject of this study, none of these principal debates directly concerned the power of treaty interpretation. Moreover, in part because of the political question doctrine, none of these principal treaty power disputes has triggered Supreme Court decisions. Nevertheless, a succession of occasional Supreme Court decisions on the treaty power, as well as constitutional practice, have expanded our understanding of the theoretical underpinnings of that power.

---

[90] *See generally* on these first three episodes "Statement of John Norton Moore for Treaty Termination Hearings," *supra* note 60; and attached Appendix by J.N. Moore at 414. For a discussion of some of the legal issues presented by the Bricker Amendment and its legislative progeny, see Sutherland, "Restricting the Treaty Power," 65 *Harv. L. Rev.* 1305 (1952); Richberg, "The Bricker Amendment and the Treaty Power," 39 *Va. L. Rev.* 753 (1953); *American Bar Association Section of International and Comparative Law Committee on Constitutional Aspects of International Agreements, Report to Section of International and Comparative Law on Senate Joint Resolution 1 and the Knowland Substitute Amendment* (Aug. 24, 1953). There is also a lingering dispute about the authority of a self-executing treaty to dispose of or transfer federal property. In a two to one opinion growing out of a suit by members of the House of Representatives in the context of the Panama Canal Treaties, the Court of Appeals for the District of Columbia Circuit held that the property clause of the Constitution does not prohibit transfer of United States property to a foreign nation through a self-executing treaty. Edwards v. Carter, 580 F.2d 1055 (Ct. App. D.C. Cir. 1978). Judge MacKinnon filed a vigorous dissent. 580 F.2d at 1064-1103. For an indication that the dispute still lingers, see "XII. Additional Views of Senator Jesse Helms," in *The INF Treaty Report, supra* note 1, at 179, 240-46.

In the *Chinese Exclusion Case*[91] in 1899 the Supreme Court established the principle that a later act of Congress, passed within the constitutional legislative authority of the Congress, and clearly inconsistent with a prior treaty, will take precedence over the treaty obligation as a matter of United States domestic law as opposed to our international obligation which would remain unmodified. The Court said:

> [T]he act . . . was a constitutional exercise of legislative power, and . . . so far as it conflicted with existing treaties, it operated to that extent to abrogate them as part of the municipal law of the United States, though it could not have the effect of destroying their international obligation.[92]

It should be emphasized here that as a precondition to a later act of Congress taking effect over a treaty the Supreme Court found that the particular act was a "constitutional exercise of legislative power." Clearly under this precedent, as well as general principles of constitutional law, an unconstitutional legislative act, whether unconstitutional as a result of violation of the separation of powers or some other constitutional proscription, would have no such effect.

In *United States v. Schooner Peggy*[93] in 1801 the Supreme Court referred to a treaty in general terms as a contract or compact among nations. Thus, the Court said:

> It is certainly true that the execution of a contract between nations is to be demanded from, and, in the general, superintended by, the executive of each nation.[94]

---

[91]130 U.S. 581 (1899).

[92]130 U.S. 581, 581 (1899).

[93]5 U.S. (1 Cranch) 104 (1801).

[94]5 U.S. (1 Cranch) 104, 109.

This seems a general conceptual underpinning of the treaty power reflected in many Supreme Court decisions. Thus, in *The Amiable Isabella,*[95] decided in 1821, Justice Story wrote for the Court:

> In the first place, this Court does not possess any treaty-making power. . . . We are to find out the intention of the parties, by just rules of interpretation, applied to the subject-matter; and having found that, our duty is to follow it, so far as it goes, and to stop where that stops--whatever may be the imperfections or difficulties which it leaves behind. . . . It is a matter of negotiation between the Governments. . . .
>
> The same powers which have contracted, are alone competent to change or dispense with any formality. The doctrine of a performance cy pres, so just and appropriate in the civil concerns of private persons, belongs not to the solemn compacts of nations, so far as judicial tribunals are called upon to interpret or enforce them.[96]

In *Foster v. Neilson,* [97] decided in 1829, the Court said: "[a] treaty is, in its nature, a contract between two nations, not a legislative act."[98] In *Worcester v. Georgia,* [99] decided in 1832, Chief Justice Marshall wrote: "What is a treaty? The answer is, it is a compact formed between two nations or communities, having the right of self-government."[100] In the *Head Money Cases* in 1884[101] the Court said: "[a] treaty

[95]The Amiable Isabella, 19 U.S. (6 Wheat.) 1 (1821).

[96]*Id.* at 70, 72.

[97]27 U.S. (2 Pet.) 253 (1829).

[98]27 U.S. (2 Pet.) 253, 314.

[99]Worcester v. Georgia, 31 U.S. (6 Pet.) 515 (1832).

[100]*Id.* at 581.

[101]112 U.S. 580 (1884).

is primarily a compact between independent nations."[102] In *Whitney v. Robertson*[103] in 1888 the Court said: "[a] treaty is primarily a contract between two or more independent nations, and is so regarded by writers on public law."[104] And in the important treaty power case of *United States v. Belmont*[105] in 1937, which upheld the power of the President to enter into executive agreements incident to recognition of a foreign government, the Court said, citing *Altman & Co. v. United States*, 224 U.S. 583, 600: "[a] treaty signifies `a compact made between two or more independent nations with a view to the public welfare.'"[106] More recently, both the opinion of the Court and the dissenting opinion of Justice Stevens in the 1984 decision in *Trans World Airlines, Inc. v. Franklin Mint Corp.*[107] adopted this view. Thus, the opinion of the Court, delivered by Justice O'Connor, said: "A treaty is in the nature of a contract between nations."[108] And in dissenting, Justice Stevens said: "A treaty is essentially a contract between or among sovereign nations."[109] This line of cases strongly suggests that treaties are rooted in international agreement among nations rather than legislative act.

There are also several lines of Supreme Court cases suggesting that treaties are to be interpreted according to the intention of the parties or the principles of public international law, and that the scope of the treaty power is related to agreement among nations. Thus, concerning the standard for interpretation Justice Story wrote in the 1817 decision of *The Pizarro*:[110] "Indeed, in the language of the

---

[102]112 U.S. 580, 598.

[103]124 U.S. 190 (1888).

[104]124 U.S. 190, 194.

[105]301 U.S. 324 (1937).

[106]301 U.S. 324, 330.

[107]466 U.S. 243 (1984).

[108]466 U.S. 243, 253.

[109]466 U.S. 243, 262.

[110]The Pizarro, 15 U.S. (2 Wheat.) 227 (1817).

law of nations, which is always to be consulted in the interpretation of treaties. . . ."[111] Justice Field wrote for the Court in the 1890 decision of *Geofroy v. Riggs*: [112]

> . . . It is a general principle of construction with respect to treaties that they shall be liberally construed, so as to carry out the apparent intention of the parties to secure equality and reciprocity between them. As they are contracts between independent nations, in their construction words are to be taken in their ordinary meaning, as understood in the public law of nations, and not in any artificial or special sense impressed upon them by local law, unless such restricted sense is clearly intended. . . .[113]

In *Sullivan v. Kidd*,[114] decided in 1921, the Supreme Court said:

> Writers of authority agree that treaties are to be interpreted upon the principles which govern the interpretation of contracts in writing between individuals, and are to be executed in the utmost good faith, with a view to making effective the purposes of the high contracting parties; that all parts of a treaty are to receive a reasonable construction with a view to giving a fair operation to the whole.[115]

In *Jordan v. Tashiro*[116] in 1928 the Court said:

---

[111]15 U.S. at 246.

[112]Geofroy v. Riggs, 133 U.S. 258 (1890).

[113] *Id.* at 271-72.

[114]254 U.S. 433 (1921).

[115]254 U.S. 433, 439. *Accord* Tucker v. Alexandroff, 183 U.S. 424, 437 (1902); Hidalgo County Water Control and Improvement District No. 7 v. HEDRICK, 226 F.2d 1, 7 (Ct. App. 5th Cir. 1955).

[116]Jordan v. Tashiro, 278 U.S. 123 (1928).

> The principles which should control the diplomatic relations of nations, and the good faith of treaties as well require that their obligations should be liberally construed so as to effect the apparent intention of the parties and to secure equality and reciprocity between them.[117]

In *Santovicenzo v. Egan*,[118] decided in 1931, Chief Justice Hughes said for the Court:

> ... as treaties are contracts between independent nations, their words are to be taken in their ordinary meaning `as understood in the public law of nations.'[119]

And in *Factor v. Laubenheimer*,[120] decided in 1933, the Court said:

> . . . Considerations which should govern the diplomatic relations between nations, and the good faith of treaties, as well, require that their obligations should be liberally construed so as to effect the apparent intention of the parties to secure equality and reciprocity between them. . . . In ascertaining the meaning of a treaty we may look beyond its written words to the negotiations and diplomatic

---

[117]278 U.S. at 127. According to the *Restatement (Second) of the Foreign Relations Law of the United States,* even when the court interprets "an international agreement for the purpose of determining its effect as domestic law":

> The general rule obtains that the court is to be guided by the intention of the parties. . . .'" Dobrin v. Mallory S. S. Co., 298 Fed. 349, 351 (E.D.N.Y. 1924) [quoting Maiorano v. B. & O. R. R. Co., 216 Pa. 402, 406 (1907)].

Restatement (Second), supra note 185,§151 and reporters' note 1, at 462, 463.

[118]Santovicenzo v. Egan, 284 U.S. 30 (1931).

[119]284 U.S. at 40.

[120]Factor v. Laubenheimer, 290 U.S. 276 (1933). *Accord* Tucker v. Alexandroff, 183 U.S. 424, 437 (1902); Nielsen v. Johnson, 279 U.S. 47, 51 (1929).

correspondence of the contracting parties relating to the subject matter, and to their own practical construction of it. . . .[121]

With respect to the scope of the treaty power as rooted in negotiations and agreement Chief Justice Taney wrote in the 1840 case of *Holmes v. Jennison*:[122]

> The power to make treaties is given by the Constitution in general terms, without any description of the objects intended to be embraced by it; and, consequently, it was designed to include all those subjects, which in the ordinary intercourse of nations had usually been made subjects of negotiation and treaty. . . .[123]

In *Geofroy v. Riggs*[124] in 1890 the Court said:

> [t]hat the treaty power of the United States extends to all proper subjects of negotiation between our government and the governments of other nations, is clear. . . .[125]

In *re Ross*[126] in 1891 the Court said: "The treaty-making power vested in our government extends to all proper subjects of negotiation with foreign

---

[121]290 U.S. at 293, 295. *Accord* Air France v. Saks, 470 U.S. 392, 396 (1985). *See also* the line of Supreme Court cases using the history of relations or negotiations between the parties in interpreting treaties, *e.g.*, Kinkead v. United States, 150 U.S. 483 (1893); United States v. Texas, 162 U.S. 1 (1896); Terrace v. Thompson, 263 U.S. 197 (1923); Cook v. United States, 288 U.S. 102 (1933).

[122]Holmes v. Jennison, 39 U.S. (14 Pet.) 540 (1840).

[123]39 U.S. at 569-70.

[124]Geofroy v. Riggs, 133 U.S. 258 (1890).

[125]133 U.S. at 266.

[126]In *re Ross*, 140 U.S. 453 (1891).

governments."[127] In *Asakura v. Seattle*[128] in 1924 Justice Butler said for the Court: "The treaty-making power of the United States . . . does extend to all proper subjects of negotiation between our government and other nations."[129] And in the 1931 decision of *Santovicenzo v. Egan,*[130] Chief Justice Hughes said for the Court: "The treaty-making power is broad enough to cover all subjects that properly pertain to our foreign relations. . . ."[131]

In a 1955 opinion written jointly by the former International Court of Justice Judge Philip C. Jessup, who was then Hamilton Fish Professor of International Law and Diplomacy at Columbia, and then Associate Professor of Public Law at Columbia Oliver J. Lissitzyn, for the Power Authority of the State of New York in the important *Niagara Power* case,[132] after citing these lines of cases, Professors Jessup and Lissitzyn write:

> Additional confirmation of the principle that the operation of a treaty as the supreme law of the land cannot be dissociated from its existence as an agreement or contract between nations is found in the cases in which the Supreme Court has passed on contentions that certain treaties had been terminated. Although it is well established that a treaty may continue to exist as an international compact even when it has been superseded as the law of the land by an inconsistent Act of Congress, the converse is not true. There has been no case in which a treaty was held to operate as the law of the land after it has been found to have ceased to exist as an international agreement. CF., *e.g., Karnuth v. United States*, 279 U.S. 231 (1929); *Charlton*

---

[127] 140 U.S. at 463.

[128] Asakura v. Seattle, 265 U.S. 332 (1924).

[129] 265 U.S. at 341.

[130] Santovicenzo v. Egan, 284 U.S. 30 (1931).

[131] 284 U.S. at 40.

[132] *P. Jessup & O. Lissitzyn, Opinion of Philip C. Jessup and Oliver J. Lissitzyn With Respect to the United States Senate's Attempt to Repeal the Federal Power Act in its Relation to the Niagara Through the Use of the Treaty-Making Power* (Power Authority of the State of New York, Dec. 1955).

v. Kelly, 229 U.S. 447 (1913); Terlinden v. Ames, 184 U.S. 270 (1902); *Clark v. Allen*, 331 U.S. 503 (1947).[133]

These lines of cases together would seem to strongly suggest both that treaties are rooted in international agreement among nations rather than legislative act and that the appropriate standard for their interpretation and implementation is that of international law and mutuality of obligation between the parties. Indeed, this would also seem to be suggested by the constitutional divisions between the legislative power, given to the Senate and House together, subject to presidential veto, and the treaty power given to the President "by and with the Advice and Consent of the Senate."

Several other Supreme Court cases are useful in developing the constitutional theory of the treaty power insofar as it may be relevant to problems of treaty interpretation and implementation. In the case of New York Indians v. United States,[134] decided in 1898, the Court upheld a treaty with the New York Indians without applying a proviso not published with the treaty, despite the fact that the record of Senate consideration of the treaty apparently clearly indicated that the Senate had approved the treaty subject to the proviso. In disregarding the proviso the Court said that it would shock the conscience to put forth a treaty "as embodying the terms of an arrangement with a foreign power or an Indian tribe, a material provision of which is unknown to one of the contracting parties."[135] The Court also said there was no evidence that the proviso "ever received the sanction or approval of the President."[136] While this case involved an always unique setting of a treaty with an Indian tribe, the Court's language specifically said "with a foreign power or an Indian tribe" so certainly it contemplated a principle of general treaty applicability. If Senate action, as opposed to the actually concluded international agreement, were determinative under the Supremacy Clause, one would have expected the Court to uphold the proviso regardless of the actually concluded agreement. That the Court did the converse suggests that it regarded the actually

---

[133] *Id.* at 52.

[134] 170 U.S. 1 (1898).

[135] 170 US. 1, 23.

[136] 170 U.S. 1, 23.

concluded agreement, rather than Senate action--even very clear Senate action, as the legal basis for a treaty obligation.

A 1957 Court of Appeals decision similarly implying that an international agreement rather than Senate legislative action is the theoretical basis for the treaty power reached the Supreme Court only after the case had become moot and thus was not considered on the merits by the Court. But in this case of *Power Authority of the State of New York v. Federal Power Commission* (the *Niagara Reservation* case)[137] the United States Court of Appeals for the District of Columbia in anopinion by Judge Bazelon, while seemingly upholding a treaty, set aside a clear Senate reservation to the treaty on the grounds that "[i]t was merely an expression of domestic policy which the Senate attached to its consent" and "was not a counter-offer requiring Canadian acceptance before the treaty could become effective,"[138] and, as such, was beyond the power of the Senate to attach to the treaty as binding law. The dissent urged that:

> if the reservation was beyond the constitutional power of the Senate, it cannot be given effect. If it is beyond the power of the Senate, then not just the reservation falls, but the entire treaty. How can it be otherwise when the Senate has made it abundantly clear that without the reservation it would not have consented to the treaty?[139]

---

[137]247 F.2d 538 (D.C. Cir. 1957); *vacated as moot sub. nom.* in American Pub. Power Assn. v. Power Authority of the State of New York, 355 U.S. 64 (1957).

[138]247 F.2d 538, at 541.

[139] *Id.* at 546.

To a considerably lesser extent than with the so-called "legislative veto" struck down by the Supreme Court in the Chadha case despite a substantial use of the "legislative veto" in practice, there does seem at least recently to have grown up a limited practice of the Senate requiring Executive branch acceptance of "domestic conditions" as a condition of treaty acceptance. *See, e.g.*, the few examples collected in *The ABM Treaty Studies: Part II*, *supra* note 1, at 43-45. Examples given include certain Senate actions in connection with consideration of the SALT II Treaty and 1977 consideration of MontrealAviation Protocols 3 and 4. *Id.*

One example of an early "domestic condition" formally adopted as part of a Senate resolution advising ratification is that contained in paragraph four of the Resolution of Ratification to the 1882 Treaty of Peace, Amity, Commerce and Navigation between the United States and Korea. That "Senate resolution advising ratification" provides:

[Senate resolution advising ratification.]
IN EXECUTIVE SESSION,
SENATE OF THE UNITED STATES
January 9, 1883.

Resolved, (two thirds of the Senators present concurring,) That the Senate advise and consent to the ratification of the treaty of commerce and navigation between the United States and the Kingdom of Corea or Chosen, concluded on the 22nd of May 1882. Resolved, That it is the understanding of the Senate in agreeing to the foregoing resolution, that the clause, "Nor are they permitted to transport native produce from one open port to another open port," in Article VI of said treaty, it is not intended to prohibit and does not prohibit American ships from going from one open port to another open port in Corea or Chosen to receive Corean cargo for exportation, or to discharge foreign cargo, and

Resolved, That the President be requested to communicate the foregoing interpretation of said clause to the Corean or Chosen government on the exchange of ratifications of said treaty, as the sense in which the United States understand the same.

Resolved further, That the Senate in advising and consenting to the treaty mentioned in the foregoing resolutions does not admit or acquiesce in any right or constitutional power in the President to authorize or empower any person to negotiate treaties or carry on diplomatic negotiations with any foreign power, unless such person shall have been appointed for such purpose or clothed with such power by and with the advice and consent of the Senate, except in the case of a Secretary of State or diplomatic officer appointed by the President to fill a vacancy occurring during the recess of the Senate, and it makes the declaration in order that the means employed in the negotiation of said treaty be not drawn into precedent.

Resolved, That the Secretary communicate all the foregoing resolutions to the President.

Attest:

F. E. SHOBER, Acting Secretary.

"Corea," in 1 W. Malloy, *Treaties, Conventions, International Acts, Protocols and*

Agreements Between the United States of America and Other Powers 1776-1909, at 334, 340 (S. Doc. No. 357, 61st Cong., 2d Sess.) (1910). Robert E. Dalton, the Counselor on International Law to the Department of State, has written to the author of this study as follows about this condition and the reaction to it from the Executive:

> I am enclosing a copy of the Senate resolution of advice and consent to the 1882 Treaty of Peace, Amity, Commerce and Navigation between the United States and Korea as printed at Malloy 340.
>
> In accordance with paragraphs 2 and 3 of that resolution the President sought and obtained the agreement of Korea to the condition contained in paragraph 2.
>
> Paragraph 4 of the resolution [containing the "domestic conditions"] recites the Senate's attitude to the fact that Commodore Shufeldt, who had been appointed "Commissioner Plenipotentiary" for the negotiation of the treaty, had not been appointed for that purpose with its advice and consent. Nevertheless, the President appears -- properly in my view -- to have considered that provision not to have been part of the treaty. He did not include it in either the U.S. instrument of ratification exchanged with the Koreans or in the proclamation of the treaty, a copy of the pertinent part of which is also enclosed. My impression is that the paragraph 4 language was unusual for the nineteenth century.

Letter from Robert E. Dalton to John Norton Moore (Mar. 24, 1989). The pertinent part of the President's proclamation of the treaty, as discussed by Robert Dalton, provides:

> And whereas the Senate of the United States of America by their resolution of the ninth of January, one thousand eight hundred and eight-three (two-thirds of the Senators present concurring,) did advise and consent to the ratification of said Treaty subject to the condition following, viz:
>
> Resolved, that it is the understanding of the Senate in agreeing to the foregoing resolution, that the clause, "Nor are they permitted to transport native produce from one open port to another open port," in Article VI. of said treaty, is not intended to prohibit and does not prohibit American ships from going from one open port to another open port in Corea or Chosen to

---

> receive Corean cargo for exportation, or to discharge foreign cargo.
>
> And whereas, said treaty, has been duly ratified on both parts, subject to said condition, and the respective ratifications thereof exchanged.
>
> Now, therefore, be it known that I, Chester A. Arthur, President of the United States of America, have caused the said Convention to be made public, to the end that the same, and every clause and article thereof, may be observed and fulfilled with good faith by the United States and the citizens thereof.
>
> In witness whereof I have hereunto set my hand and caused the seal of the United States to be affixed. Done at the city of Washington this fourth day of June, in the year of our Lord one thousand eight hundred and eighty-three and of the Independence of the United States of America the one hundred and seventh
>
> CHESTER A. ARTHUR.
>
> By the President:
> FREDK. T. FRELINGHUYS
> Secretary of State.

"Treaty--Corea. May 22, 1882," 23 Stat. 720, 725 (1885). It is, of course, also common knowledge that the domestic condition attached to this Senate resolution does not reflect the established practice today on the subject.

The Senate Foreign Relations Committee Report on the SALT II Treaty, never formally adopted, explicitly divides possible committee action on advice and consent into three categories. Category I, which was said to be binding on the President, is clearly a category of "domestic conditions." Thus, it provides:

> *Category I*: provisions that do not directly involve formal notice to or agreement by the Soviet Union.

The SALT II Treaty: Report of the Senate Comm. on Foreign Relations, 96th Cong., 1st Sess. 28 (1979) (S. Exec. Rep. No. 14). This practice would seem to reflect the current position of the Senate Foreign Relations Committee on "domestic conditions." It is not

---

clear, however, whether even the Senate Foreign Relations Committee supports the position that "domestic conditions" or "declarations" are legally binding or whether they would simply have the effect of a "sense of the Senate" resolution. Thus, the 1984 report for the Senate Foreign Relations Committee, *Treaties and Other International Agreements: The Role of the United States Senate*, says:

> Declarations are statements of the Senate's position, opinion or intentions on matters relating to issues raised by the treaty in question, but not to its specific provisions. They are analogous to "sense of the Senate" resolutions. However, the President has on occasion interpreted such declarations as falling outside of the formal provisions to be incorporated in the "instruments" used in the ratification process.

Treaties and International Agreements Committee Print, supra note 66, at 110. Footnote ten to this description of "*Declarations*" says:

> [10] In the case of the 1976 Treaty of Friendship and Cooperation with Spain, the State Department did not include the text of a lengthy Senate declaration in the instruments of ratification. It defended its position on this point in a memorandum which appears in the 1976 Digest of United States Practice in International Law (Eleanor C. McDowell ed.), State Department Pub. 8908, November 1977, 215-17

.*Id.* at 110 n.10. The State Department memorandum referred to concludes with respect to declarations attached to the Senate resolution:

> The first three Senate declarations are statements of hope and expressions of opinion that have no bearing on the treaty. They are clearly not reservations or interpretations. They do not exclude, limit, or interpret the obligations of the Treaty, but rather are unrelated expressions that cannot bind Spain and thus cannot have international legal effect. Senate declarations (4) and (5) are related to the U.S. method of implementation of the treaty, but they are statements of domestic United States processes, and as such can have no application to Spain. Spain cannot be bound by a Senate statement with respect to U.S. domestic processes that have no bearing on the meaning of the treaty.

E. McDowell, Digest of United States Practice in International Law, 1976, at 216 (U.S. Dep't of State Pub. No. 8908, Sept. 1977) (quoting Dep't of State Memorandum of Aug.

This case seems to have pitted Professors Philip C. Jessup and Oliver J. Lissitzyn, who prepared a brief for the Power Authority agreeing with the view ultimately adopted by the Court of Appeals, with Professor Louis Henkin, who has disagreed and posed "several grounds for questioning the conclusion that the provision . . . is invalid."[140]

To the contrary, however, a recent opinion by Judge Harold H. Greene of the District Court for the District of Columbia in the *Rainbow Navigation* case,[141] madewithout full briefing of the views by opposing counsel or even citing of the earlier and apparently contradictory *Niagara Reservation* case in the Court of Appeals for the District of Columbia, and in a setting in which an initial Judge Greene opinion in the same case had become featured in the ongoing "treaty interpretation" debate spawned by the "broad-narrow" issue, upheld a Senate authority to at least formally and informally adopt "domestic conditions" incident to advice and consent to a treaty and seemed to regard Executive branch representations made in such a setting as obligatory. The *Rainbow Navigation* case, however, has been appealed by the Department of Justice, in part to request review of these issues in treaty interpretation and implementation.

Following the District Court decision in the *Rainbow Navigation* case, the Supreme Court had occasion to consider treaty interpretation again in the recent

---

4, 1976, Dep't of State File L/T).

[140] *See* Henkin, "The Treaty Makers and the Law Makers: The Niagara Reservation," 56 *Col. L. Rev.* 1151, 1181-82 (1956) [hereinafter Henkin, "Niagara Reservation"]; *L. Henkin, supra* note 6, at 134-36. *See also* Bishop, "Reservations to Treaties," 103 *Recueil Des Cours* 245, 317-22 (1961-II).

Irving Younger wrote in 1959 that this *Niagara Reservation* case rendered the legal effect of a Senate understanding "vague" which sought in 1930 to resolve in connection with the London Naval Treaty "[t]hat in ratifying said treaty the Senate does so with the distinct and explicit understanding that there are no secret files, documents, letters, understandings, or agreements which in any way . . . [modifies, adds to or takes away from the Treaty]." See Younger, *supra* note 12, at 755, 774-75.

[141]Rainbow Navigation v. Department of the Navy (Civil Action No. 88-0992, Nov. 15, 1988). This opinion of Judge Greene, together with his opinion in an earlier phase in this case and its interaction with the "treaty interpretation" debate, will be discussed more fully subsequently in this part.

United States v. Stuart [142] case decided February 28, 1989. In that case the Court did not directly cite the *Rainbow Navigation* case or address the issue of "domestic conditions" or the legal effect of Executive branch statements in such settings. In a footnote to Justice Brennan's majority opinion, however, the Court indicated--in opposition to the concurring opinion by Justice Scalia--that it was not improper in treaty interpretation to consult Senate "preratification" materials. The Court's opinion, however, in at least three separate places, seemed to adopt--consistent, as we have seen, with a long and unbroken line of Supreme Court decisions--"the intent of the Treaty parties" as the objective of treaty interpretation. And Justice Scalia's concurring opinion, which seemed to discuss Judge Harold H. Greene's opinion in the *Rainbow Navigation* case disapprovingly, also seemed to disapprove the general use of Senate preratification materials in treaty interpretation.

The case of *United States v. Pink,* [143] decided in 1942, is also relevant to the theory of the treaty power. This case, which like the earlier Belmont decision upheld the power of the President to conclude an executive agreement incident to the recognition power, specifically cited with approval in the treaty context the broadest language of the *Curtiss-Wright* decision. Thus, the Court said:

> Power to remove such obstacles to full recognition or settlement of claims of our nationals . . . certainly is a modest implied power of the President who is the "sole organ of the federal government in the field of international relations." *United States v. Curtiss-Wright*. . . . Effectiveness in handling the delicate problems of foreign relations requires no less. . . .[144]

In *Missouri v. Holland,* [145] a famous 1920 decision in which the Court held that valid treaties are binding on the States and that the scope of the treaty power is

---

[142]United States v. Stuart (No. 87-1064, Feb. 28, 1989). This case, and particularly arguments that can be made from the final sentence of this footnote 7 concerning the weight to be accorded the Senate preratification record in treaty interpretation, will be discussed more fully subsequently in this part.

[143]315 U.S. 203 (1942).

[144]315 U.S. 203, 229.

[145]252 U.S. 416 (1920).

not determined by the scope of the federal legislative power, the Court said in passing:

> Acts of Congress are the supreme law of the land only when made in pursuance of the Constitution, while treaties are declared to be so when made under the authority of the United States. It is open to question whether the authority of the United States means more than the formal acts prescribed to make the convention. We do not mean to imply that there are no qualifications to the treaty-making power; but they must be ascertained in a different way. . . .[146]

Reid v. Covert, [147] decided in 1957, made clear that a treaty, just as with legislation, may not violate the Constitution of the United States. In doing so the Court said:

> Article VI, the Supremacy Clause of the Constitution, declares:
>
> > "This Constitution, and the Laws of the United States which shall be made in Pursuance thereof; and all Treaties made, or which shall be made, under the Authority of the United States, shall be the supreme Law of the Land; . . . ."
>
> There is nothing in this language which intimates that treaties and laws enacted pursuant to them do not have to comply with the provisions of the Constitution. Nor is there anything in the debates which accompanied the drafting and ratification of the Constitution which even suggests such a result. These debates as well as the history that surrounds the adoption of the treaty provisionin Article VI make it clear that the reason treaties were not limited to those made in "pursuance" of the Constitution was so that agreements made by the United States under the Articles of Confederation, including the Important peace treaties which

---

[146]252 U.S. 416, 433.

[147]354 U.S. 1 (1957).

> concluded the Revolutionary War, would remain in effect. It would be manifestly contrary to the objectives of those who created the Constitution, as well as those who were responsible for the Bill of Rights--let alone alien to our entire constitutional history and tradition--to construe Article VI as permitting the United States to exercise power under an international agreement without observing constitutional prohibitions. In effect, such construction would permit amendment of that document in a manner not sanctioned by Article V. The prohibitions of the Constitution were designed to apply to all branches of the National Government and they cannot be nullified by the Executive or by the Executive and the Senate combined.[148]

It is clear that this constraint on the treaty power extends to the distribution of powers under the Constitution as well as to specific constitutionally protected private rights. The 1984 study for the Senate Foreign Relations Committee, *Treaties and Other International Agreements: The Role of the United States Senate*, says:

> *Separation of Powers and Rights under the Bill of Rights*.--
> As a general matter, an agreement cannot alter the constitutional distribution of powers or impair constitutionally protected rights.[149]

It should also be noted that in 1901 the Court held in *Fourteen Diamond Rings v. United States*,[150] that a resolution passed by the Senate by a vote of 26 to 22 virtually contemporaneous with Senate advice and consent to a treaty (according to the opinion of the Court eight days after "ratification" of the treaty and according to the concurring opinion the same day as the "ratification") and purporting to interpret the treaty "is absolutely without legal significance on the question before us."[151] The opinion of the Court said:

---

[148] 354 U.S. 1, 16-17.

[149] *Treaties and International Agreements Committee Print, supra* note 66, at 18.

[150] 183 U.S. 176 (1901). See also Jones v. Meehan, 175 U.S. 1 (1899).

[151] 183 U.S. 176, 180.

> We need not consider the force and effect of a resolution of this sort, if adopted by Congress. . . . It is enough that this was a joint resolution; that it was adopted by the Senate by a vote of 26 to 22, not two thirds of a quorum: and that it is absolutely without legal significance on the question before us. The meaning of the treaty cannot be controlled by subsequent explanations of some of those who may have voted to ratify it. What view the House might have taken as to the intention of the Senate in ratifying the treaty we are not informed, nor is it material; and if any implication from the action referred to could properly be indulged, it would seem to be that two thirds of a quorum of the Senate did not consent to the ratification on the grounds indicated.[152]

The Court thus declared as "absolutely without legal significance" a virtually contemporaneous indication by a Senate majority as to an interpretation to be given a just "ratified" treaty. Had the Senate action been the action of a Senate some years later after a dispute had arisen as to the meaning of a treaty it would be reasonably self-evident that it would not be legally binding or even of significant weight in assessing the intention of the original Senate. The Senate alone cannot take action (beyond the Senate) that is legally binding, and the after the fact views of a subsequent Senate (or legislature for that matter concerning the meaning of earlier legislation) are certainly of little weight as to the intention of an earlier Senate. The *Fourteen Diamond Rings* case, however, may be of considerably greater significance on matters of treaty interpretation than this unsurprising principle. For here the action by a Senate majority was virtually contemporaneous with treaty "ratification" and the opinion of the Court made a point of stressing that the vote on the Senate action was less than a two-thirds vote required for treaty advice and consent. That is, the Court was giving absolutely no weight to a virtually contemporaneous indication of Senate intent about the interpretation to be given a treaty expressed by a majority of the Senate in the absence of evidence that the particular interpretation was shared by the number of Senators voting for the treaty that would be necessary to meet the two-thirds advice and consent requirement. It should perhaps be pointed out in possibly limiting any such broad principle from the case, however, that the Court may have drawn an inference from the 22 votes cast against the interpretation that there was not a two-third majority sharing this interpretation. That is, the Court had before it specific evidence that could be used

---

[152]183 U.S. 176, 180.

to infer that two-thirds of the Senate did not support the interpretation of the treaty (although this does not follow as a matter of logic from the 26 to 22 vote on the resolution since there could have been other grounds to vote against it than the merits, and the Court itself here used the language "if any implication from theaction referred to could properly be indulged."). In any event, this case seems to imply that in a treaty interpretation case where the intention of the Senate may be relevant, the search for intention must be a search for the intention of an at least two thirds of a quorum voting for the treaty and necessary for advice and consent.

The concurring opinion of Mr. Justice Brown, while also specifically concurring in the reasons given in the opinion of the Court,[153] provides a further rich theoretical exploration of the underlying nature of the treaty power. Thus Justice Brown said:

> A treaty in its legal sense is defined by Bouvier as "a compact made between two or more independent nations with a view to the public welfare," (2 Law Dic. 1136,) and by Webster as "an agreement, league or contract between two or more nations or sovereigns, formally signed by commissioners properly authorized, and solemnly ratified by the sovereigns or the supreme power of each state." In its essence it is a contract. It differs from an ordinary contract only in being an agreement between independent states instead of private parties. *Foster v. Neilson*, 2 Pet. 253, 314; *Head Money Cases*, 112 U. S. 580. By the Constitution, (art. 2, sec. 2,) the President "shall have power, by and with the advice and consent of the Senate, to make treaties, provided two thirds of the Senators present concur." Obviously the treaty must contain the whole contract between the parties, and the power of the Senate is limited to a ratification of such terms as have already been agreed upon between the President, acting for the United States, and the commissioners of the other contracting power. The Senate has no right to ratify the treaty and introduce new terms into it, which shall be obligatory upon the other power, although it may refuse its ratification, or make such ratification conditional upon the adoption of amendments to the treaty. If, for instance, the treaty with Spain had contained a provision instating the inhabitants of the Philippines as citizens of the United States, the Senate might have refused to ratify it until this provision was stricken

[153] 183 U.S. 176, 182.

> out. But it could not, in my opinion, ratify the treaty and then adopt a resolution declaring it not to be its intention to admit the inhabitants of the Philippine Islands to the privileges of citizenship of the United States. Such resolution would be inoperative as an amendment to the treaty, since it had not received the assent of the President or the Spanish commissioners.
>
> Allusion was made to this question in the *New York Indians v. United States*, 170 U. S. 1, 21, wherein it appeared that, when atreaty with certain Indian tribes was laid before the Senate for ratification, several articles were stricken out, several others amended, a new article added, and a proviso adopted that the treaty should have no force or effect whatever, until the amendment had been submitted to the tribes, and they had given their free and voluntary assent thereto. This resolution, however, was not found in the original or in the published copy of the treaty, or in the proclamation of the President, which contained the treaty without the amendments. With reference to this the court observed: "The power to make treaties is vested by the Constitution in the President and the Senate, and, while this proviso was adopted by the Senate, there was no evidence that it ever received the sanction or approval of the President. It cannot be considered as a legislative act, since the power to legislate is vested in the President, Senate and House of Representatives. There is something, too, which shocks the conscience in the idea that a treaty can be put forth as embodying the terms of an arrangement with a foreign power or an Indian tribe, a material provision of which is unknown to one of the contracting parties, and is kept in the background to be used by the other only when the exigencies of a particular case may demand it. The proviso appears never to have been called to the attention of the tribes, who would naturally assume that the treaty embodied in the Presidential proclamation contained all the terms of the arrangement."
>
> In short, it seems to me entirely clear that this resolution cannot be considered a part of the treaty.[154]

Of particular importance it should be noted that Mr. Justice Brown is adopting a view that "the treaty must contain the whole contract between the parties, and the

[154] 183 U.S. 176, 182-84.

power of the Senate is limited to a ratification of such terms as have already been agreed upon between the President, acting for the United States, and the commissioners of the other contracting power." Under this view presumably there could not be an interpretation of a treaty apart from the meaning given by the treaty partners. Thus, Mr. Justice Brown is in his concurring opinion adding the additional ground for decision, not addressed in the opinion of the Court, that any interpretation of the Senate alone, even if unanimous, is ineffective absent evidence that the interpretation was also accepted by the President and the other party to the treaty. This stems at least in part from the nature of a treaty as a compact between nations and the role of the President in the treaty power.

The case of *Fourteen Diamond Rings* seems also to clearly establish that whatever the effect on interpretation of contemporaneous Senate action or subsequent full legislative action, the action of a subsequent Senate alone can have no significant legal effect (if indeed any effect at all as the case really says) on the interpretation of a treaty. It is likely that this same principle would even more strongly apply to a treaty issue other than the search for original interpretation since Senate action alone is neither that mandated by the Constitution for concluding treaties nor general legislative action for any purpose beyond the Senate itself. That is, a subsequent Senate alone has no treaty power. Similarly, as *Myers v. United States*[155] holds for the sister appointment power in Article II, section 2, clause 2, that two-thirds of a quorum of the Senate has a role to play in concluding agreements does not demonstrate that it has any other function with respect to treaties. Indeed, it would be anomalous in the extreme to adopt the view that treaties could only be interpreted, otherwise implemented or terminated by action of two-thirds of a quorum of a subsequent Senate.[156]

While the language of the Constitution says that the President "shall have Power, by and with the Advice and Consent of the Senate, to make treaties, provided two thirds of the Senators present concur," constitutional practice has interpreted this role as a Senate veto power. During the first administration of President Washington, the President twice formally sought the advice of the Senate on a proposed treaty with the Southern Indians. President Washington was dissatisfied with the performance of the Senate and apparently since then few

---

[155]272 U.S. 52 (1926).

[156]For a discussion of the full range of anomalies in adopting any such view, see "Statement of John Norton Moore for Treaty Termination Hearings," *supra* note 60, at 405-06.

presidents have sought the formal advice of the Senate as a whole, as opposed to the subsequent consent of the Senate or the advice or involvement of individual senators.[157] Professor Corwin writes of President Washington's effort to formally involve the Senate in giving "advice" on proposed treaties:

> The somber truth is that the conception of the Senate as a presidential council in the diplomatic field broke down the first time it was put to the test. . . .
>
> . . . .
>
> . . . [N]o President of the United States has since that day ever darkened the doors of the Senate for the purpose of personal consultation with it concerning the advisability of a desired negotiation.[158]

---

[157]See *A. Rovine, Digest of United States Practice in International Law*, 1973, at 173-74 (U.S. Dep't of State Pub. No. 8756, July 1974). See also *E. Corwin, supra* note 18, at 209-10.

[158]*E. Corwin, supra* note 18, at 209-10. *See also J. Rogers, World Policing and the Constitution* 22 (1945). *See also L. Henkin, supra* note 6, at 132-33.

The pattern of constitutional practice concerning participation in negotiation of treaties is summarized by Professor Phillip R. Trimble in a forthcoming commentary in the *University of Pennsylvania Law Review*:

> [T]he original understanding of the Treaty Power, which envisioned Senate consultation prior to the negotiation or conclusion of treaties, was quickly reinterpretated [sic] in an informal manner. In 1789, in connection with an upcoming negotiation, President Washington went before the Senate and asked its advice on a series of specific negotiating questions. The Senate postponed consideration of all but one such question to a second session. The procedure was unsatisfactory both to the President and the Senate, and was abandoned. Even the practice initiated by President Washington of seeking written advice on particular negotiating questions was abandoned by Washington before the end of his first administration. Because Washington presided at the Constitutional Convention and most Senators participated in some formal way in the Constitution's preparation or ratification, the early experience would seem to reflect the original understanding.
>
> The original understanding of the Senate's role in treaty-making, however, continued to change over time in light of experience. "By 1816 the practice had become established that the Senate's formal participation in treaty-making was to approve, approve with conditions, or disapprove treaties after they had been

Arthur W. Rovine, who served as one of the Department of State's principal treaty affairs officers, wrote in the 1973 *Digest of United States Practice in International Law* in response to a proposal, S. Res. 99, that would have expressed the sense of the Senate that "the President is required to consider the Senate as a Council of Advice with respect to the negotiation of treaties":

> Over the nearly 200 years of practice under our Constitution, there has been only one occasion on which any President has attempted to utilize the Senate as a formal council of advice with respect to the negotiation of a treaty. That attempt, by President Washington in the first year of his first administration, resulted in delay and discord. The experience demonstrated to the satisfaction of Washington and, apparently, all successive Presidents that such a role for the Senate in the actual course of negotiations would be unwise and impractical. (See Corwin, *The President: Office and Powers* 257-258 (3rd ed.)).
>
> At the same time, Presidents have recognized the wisdom of holding adequate consultations during the course of negotiations to ensure that agreements were not negotiated which were unlikely to

---

> negotiated by the President or his representative." The lesson is that the original entrenched meaning of a constitutional term can be changed, even over a relatively short period of time, by subsequent history. Moreover, the process consisted of executive initiative and senatorial acquiescence. An attempt in 1973 by Senator Hartke to reaffirm the "historic" role of the Senate in treaty-making by constituting it as a council of advice for that purpose came to naught in the face of executive constitutional objections.[45]

Trimble, "The Constitutional Common Law of Treaty Interpretation: A Reply to the Formalists," 137 *U. Penn. L. Rev.* 1461, 1473-74 (forthcoming May 1989) (quoted from page proofs subject to final editing) (footnotes 42-44 omitted). Footnote 45 to this excerpt provides:

> S. Res. 99, 119 CONG. REC. 7274-5 (1973), was opposed by the Department of State on the grounds that the consistent practice since Washington had been to consult but not to use the Senate as a "Council of Advise." DIGEST OF UNITED STATES PRACTICE IN INTERNATIONAL LAW 172-76 (A. Rovine ed. 1973)

Id. at 1474 n.45.

gain the approval of the Senate by the required two-thirds majority. This point was quite clearly demonstrated in the course of President Wilson's experience with the League of Nations Charter, of which no President can remain oblivious.

The practice of the Executive Branch regarding the conduct of negotiations not only has been consistent over the years but finds strong support in the Constitution as interpreted by the Supreme Court. In 1936, the Court set forth its view in the clearest possible terms, stating that in the "vast external realm" of foreign affairs

> "the President alone has the power to speak or listen as a representative of the nation. He makes treaties with the advice and consent of the Senate; but he alone negotiates. Into the field of negotiation the Senate cannot intrude; and Congress itself is powerless to invade it." (*U.S. v. Curtiss-Wright Corporation*, 299 U.S. 304, 319 (1936)).[159]

---

[159]*A. Rovine, supra* note 157, at 172-74.

An article written by William W. Dewhurst of the Florida Bar and printed in 1921 by the Senate concedes that the exclusive authority of the President to negotiate treaties is widely accepted and "may now be the law by custom established" but he argues for a Senate role in the negotiation of treaties based largely on his assessment of original intent. In beginning his article he cites a letter from the Chairman of the Senate Foreign Relations Committee to the President which "admits, `as of course,' that the committee `was aware that negotiations are wholly in the hands of the Executive.'" *See* Dewhurst, "Is the President the Sole Negotiator of Treaties?--An Article on the Respective Powers of the Senate and of the President in the Negotiation of Treaties," 67th Cong., 1st Sess. 3, 7 (Senate Doc. No. 9, May 3, 1921, presented by Mr. Brondegee).

A 1920 monograph by Professor Ralston Hayden on *The Senate and Treaties 1789-1817* has an interesting discussion of early Senate practice in relation to treaties and the rapid evolution in practice from Senate involvement in pre-treaty advice to the Senate role conceived largely as post-treaty consent. *See R. Hayden, The Senate and Treaties 1789-1817* (1920).

An early treatise on treaties, apparently undertaken at the suggestion of John Bassett Moore, contains the following description of the power of the President to negotiate treaties under the Constitution:

> To the President is entrusted the exclusive power of communication with foreign states. "The President is the sole organ of the nation in its external relations, and its sole representative with foreign nations." [citing John Marshall, in the House of

One reason for this non-use of the Senate in a formal advice mode, no doubt, is the substantial expansion in the size of the Senate over that known to the framers. The first Senate of the United States had 22 members and the first House of Representatives (which the framers thought too large to share the treaty power) had only 59 members.[160] The present Senate, of course, has 100 members, considerably larger than the size of the original House deemed too large by the framers to share the treaty power. The role played in the framing of the treaty power by this issue of size is developed by McDougal and Lans in their seminal article on "Treaties and Congressional-Executive or Presidential Agreements":

> Twice the Pennsylvania delegates proposed that the House be associated with the Senate in the ratification of treaties; both times the proposal was defeated, with their state casting the only affirmative ballot. While it was subsequently stated that exclusion of the House was necessary to retain the adherence of the small states

---

> Representatives, March 7, 1800 Annals, 6th Cong., 613]. Accordingly, with him resides the right of determining finally on all negotiations to be conducted with foreign powers. . . .

S. Crandall, Treaties: Their Making and Enforcement 93 (2d ed. 1916).

[160]*See A. Sofaer, supra* note 8, at 61.

In a recent paper on "Constitutional Underpinnings of the Treaty Powers," Dr. Louis Fisher of the Congressional Research Service, Library of Congress, points out that this increase in the size of the Senate prompted the House of Representatives in 1945 to support a constitutional amendment to provide for treaty consent by both Houses. Dr. Fisher writes:

> Jay's logic was less compelling after the Seventeenth Amendment subjected Senators to popular election. Jay had also argued that the small size of the Senate permitted greater secrecy and dispatch than the House. But by 1859 the Senate had grown from twenty-six members to sixty-six, or larger than the original House membership of sixty-five. These changes prompted the House in 1945 to adopt a resolution, passed by the margin of 288 to 88, to amend the Constitution to provide for treaty ratification by a majority of both Houses. Not unexpectedly, the Senate never acted on the bill.

Fisher, "Constitutional Underpinnings," *supra* note 1, at 8 (footnote omitted).

to the union, relatively few suggestions of this character were made at the Convention itself. However, the debates at both the Philadelphia and the state conventions, as well as the subsequent comments of delegates, clearly reveal that the compelling reason for exclusion of the House was the belief that it was not suited to participate in the task then contemplated for the Senate, that of *participating equally with the President in the detailed negotiation of treaties*. As a sheer question of expediency, it was felt that the House was too large to maintain the secrecy and dispatch deemed requisite in negotiation. This point was emphasized by Washington, by Hamilton and Jay in *The Federalist*, and by a great number of delegates to the conventions. Thus Major Pierce Butler, who had been a member of the South Carolina contingent at the Philadelphia gathering, declared at his state's ratifying convention:

> "The House of Representatives was then named; but an insurmountable objection was made to this proposition--which was, that *negotiations* always required the greatest secrecy, which could not be expected in a large body."

Another decisive reason for exclusion of the House, stemming from the delegates' general distrust of democracy, was that the Representatives were to be elected by direct suffrage, whereas the President was to be chosen by the Electoral College and the Senate was to be chosen by the state legislatures, and was expected by some to become a "second House of Lords."[161]

---

[161]McDougal & Lans, *supra* note 76, at 539-40.

Under the Articles of Confederation "the sole and exclusive right and power to make treaties [was] vested in Congress." *S. Crandall, supra* note 159, at 24. This included control over negotiations. Id. at 25-27. Indeed, under the Articles of Confederation Congress had actually drawn up negotiating instructions for the Jay-Gardoqui negotiations (*S. Bemis, A Diplomatic History of the United States* 78-80 (rev. ed. 1942)) and had established and instructed a commission for negotiating treaties of commerce (*S. Bemis,supra*, at 65-84 (1936)). But the cumbersomeness of detailed congressional control quickly began to lead to recognition of the need to entrust greater power to the negotiator. *S. Crandall, supra* note 159, at 26-27.

McDougal and Lans also point out that President "Washington stated in a message to the House of Representatives in 1796: `The necessity of such caution and secrecy was one cogent reason for vesting the power of making treaties in the President, with the advice and consent of the Senate . . . .'"[162]

With respect to the "consent" portion of the Senate role in advice and consent, there is considerable authority that the nature of the role is a "veto" or "negative," although it is clear that the Senate can attach to its consent reservations, amendments or understandings concerning the international obligation. Thus, Thomas Jefferson wrote in the "Treaties" section of his *Manual of Parliamentary Practice for the Use of the Senate*:

> *By the Constitution of the United States, this department of legislation is confided to two branches only of the ordinary legislature; the President originating, and the Senate having a negative.*[163]

As we have seen, Mr. Justice Brown, concurring in the Fourteen Diamond Rings case in 1901 said of the Senate role in "consent" to treaties:

> [T]he power of the Senate is limited to a ratification of such terms as have already been agreed upon between the President, acting for the United States, and the commissioners of the other contracting power. The Senate has no right to ratify the treaty and introduce new terms into it, which shall be obligatory upon the other power, although it may refuse its ratification, or make such ratification conditional upon the adoption of amendments to the treaty.[164]

Modern constitutional scholars have also taken this view. Professor Louis Henkin has written:

---

[162]McDougal & Lans, *supra* note 76, at 539 n.26.

[163]*T. Jefferson, A Manual of Parliamentary Practice for the Use of the Senate of the United States* 169 (2d ed. 1812) (italics in original).

[164]183 U.S. 176, 183 (1901).

> Rooted in an English system where the treaty power was in the executive and the legislative power in the Parliament, the constitutional arrangement created a hybrid system giving one house of Congress, the less numerous house, an advisory and veto power in the promulgation of treaties. . . .[165]

Professor Quincy Wright, one of the most important American scholars on constitutional issues in foreign policy as well as on international law, says in his seminal work on *The Control of American Foreign Relations*:

> We conclude that the power of making international agreements is largely vested in the President. The states' power in this respect is practically nil. Though the Senate has an absolute veto on treaties, and Congress may suggest the opening of negotiations, may authorize executive agreements and may refuse to execute treaties, yet the real initiative, the negotiation and the final decision to ratify are all at the discretion of the President.[166]

And again:

> [T]hese powers have been distributed among independent organs. Is there a single principle underlying this distribution? We believe there is. The President initiates, controls and concludes, checked by the possibility of a Senate veto on permanent international agreements . . . .
>
> For meeting the ordinary responsibilities and exercising the ordinary powers of states in the family of nations, guided by international law, the President alone is competent, and his powers, being in the main derived from the Constitution itself, he is not

---

[165]Henkin, "Niagara Reservation," supra note 140, at 1151, 1170. For a discussion of the legal controversies as to the Senate role in attaching conditions other than those modifying the international obligations of a treaty, see *L. Henkin, supra* note 6, at 134-36.

[166]*Q. Wright, supra* note 20, at 261-62.

> subject to the detailed direction of Congress, as he is in exercising his powers in domestic administration.[167]

Similarly, Professor Edward S. Corwin, another giant in the field of American constitutional law, writes in his classic treatise:

> In short, the Senate's role in treaty making is nowadays simply the power of saying whether a proposed treaty shall be ratified or not, the act of ratification being the President's. Its power is that of *veto*, which may be exercised outright, or conditionally upon the nonacceptance by the President or the other government or governments concerned of such amendments or reservations as it chooses to stipulate . . . .[168]

And Florence Ellinwood Allen, a Judge of the United States Court of Appeals for the Sixth Circuit, writes in her 1952 monograph on the treaty power:

> [T]he framing of treaties is a wholly executive function. The treaties, so far as form is concerned, are presented to the Senate as an accomplished fact. The Senate may reject them *in toto*, make reservations, or reject separate articles; but the changes that it proposes do not become effective until they are accepted by the country with which the treaty is made.[169]

It is also significant that the 1984 study for the Senate Foreign Relations Committee on *Treaties and Other International Agreements: The Role of the United States Senate* entitles a section "The Senate's Treaty Veto," which states that "[t]he Senate has used its veto sparingly," and that "[t]he Senate's treaty power is one of

---

[167] *Id.* at 335-36.

[168] *E. Corwin, supra* note 18, at 211.

[169] *F. Allen, The Treaty as an Instrument of Legislation* 6 (1952).

the few legislative vetoes that has been recognized as permissible by the Supreme Court."[170]

In examining the fundamental theory of the treaty power it should also be noted that it is settled practice under United States constitutional law that only self-executing treaties may be directly enforced by the Courts under the supremacy clause without implementing action under national law. As Chief Justice Marshall wrote in *Foster v. Neilson* in 1829:

> . . . But when the terms of the stipulation import a contract, when either of the parties engages to perform a particular act, the treaty addresses itself to the political, not the judicial department; and the legislature must execute the contract before it can become a rule for the Court.[171]

It is likely that most, if not all, arms control treaties would be regarded by the courts as non-self-executing.[172] It should be noted that to the extent a treaty is not self-executing, the theoretical argument for their "legislative" nature because of their directly affecting national law is further diminished.

In examining the theory of the treaty power it is also relevant to note that constitutional practice, the writings of publicists, and on some of these issues an occasional judicial decision have established that the President and Congress acting together have authority to enter into any international agreement (that is the congressional-executive agreement power is the functional equivalent of the treaty power), the President has authority to conclude a presidential agreement solely on presidential authority on any subject within his independent authority (and most, if not all, of this very small category of agreements fall within an area of exclusive presidential authority as to which Congress could not encroach), and that, at least

---

[170]*Treaties and International Agreements Committee Print, supra* note 66, at 14, 15.

[171]Foster v. Neilson, 27 U.S. (2 Pet.) 253, 314 (1829). *See also* Head Money Cases, 112 U.S. 580, 598 (1884). *See generally L. Henkin, supra* note 6, at 156-61.

[172]This has been the decision with respect to the United Nations Charter. *But for* a recent argument, not in an arms control setting, urging that the category of non-self-executing treaties should be restricted, see J. Paust, "Self-Executing Treaties," 82 *Am. J. Int'l L.* 760 (1988).

absent contrary congressional direction, the President may terminate treaties.[173] There is some question whether treaties may be terminated by congressional action without presidential approval, although it is probable that such action if directed to passing inconsistent legislation within the regular constitutional powers of the Congress to legislate would take effect as domestic law. Unilateral action by the Congress, of course, could not alter the international obligations of the United States under a treaty. In connection with this general issue of the authority, if any, of Congress to terminate treaties it should be recalled that Hamilton urged in his first "Pacificus" letter that "treaties can only be made by the President and Senate jointly; but their activity may be continued or suspended by the President alone."[174] According to Charles Warren, a former Assistant Attorney-General of the United States, President Wilson ignored an act of Congress directing:

> the President to notify all foreign countries of the termination, after due notice, of all treaty restrictions upon the right of the United States to impose discriminating customs duties on imports on foreign vessels. President Wilson did not veto this act; but he announced officially, through the Secretary of State (September 24, 1920), that he intended to disregard the provisions of this section, on the ground that Congress had no right to control the President's power and discretion as to treaty matters. "The action sought to be imposed upon the Executive," he said "would amount to nothing less than the breach or violation of said treaties which are thirty-two in number. . . . The President . . . does not deem the direction contained . . . an exercise of any constitutional power possessed by the Congress." President Harding and President Coolidge later took the same position.[175]

And Professor Louis Henkin has written, after exploring the issue of congressional authority: "[i]f issues as to who has power to terminate treaties arise again . . . it

---

[173] *See generally* "Statement of John Norton Moore for Treaty Termination Hearings," *supra* note 60; and the "Appendix" to *id.* at 400, 414.

[174] Hamilton, "First Pacificus Letter," supra note 24, at 403.

[175] Warren, "Presidential Declarations of Independence," 10 *Boston U.L. Rev.* 1, 33 (1930).

seems unlikely that Congress will successfully assert the power."[176] In the recent case of *Goldwater v. Carter*,[177] decided by the Supreme Court in 1979, a number of senators and congressmen sought declaratory and injunctive relief to prevent President Carter from terminating the mutual defense treaty with the Republic of China (Taiwan). A divided Court directed that the case be dismissed, primarily on ripeness and political question grounds, although in his dissenting opinion Justice Brennan indicated that he would have affirmed the Court of Appeals decision for the President on the grounds that the treaty termination in this case was within the President's exclusive recognition power.[178] The practical effect of the Court of Appeals and Supreme Court decisions was to vindicate the President's action in terminating the treaty.

As the *Goldwater v. Carter* decision illustrates, the courts are likely to continue to regard many disputes between the President and the Congress incident to ongoing foreign policy issues as not ripe for review or lacking in standing of plaintiffs or as non-justiciable political questions.[179]

---

[176] *L. Henkin, supra* note 6, at 170.

[177] 444 U.S. 996 (1979).

[178] 444 U.S. 996, 1007.

[179] *See generally* on the political question doctrine in foreign affairs cases, *J.N. Moore,Indo-China, supra* note 17, chapter XIII.

For a recent example having the practical effect of vindicating a presidential action in foreign affairs, see Dole v. Carter, 569 F.2d 1109 (Ct. App. 10th Cir. 1977). In a per curiam decision the Court of Appeals wrote:

> The action of the President is to return to the people of Hungary property which belongs to them. The situation is one which "uniquely demand[s] single-voiced statement of the Government's views." Baker v. Carr, 369 U.S. at 211, 82 S.Ct. at 707. We are aware of no "judicially discoverable and manageable standards for resolving [the issue]." We have no way of ascertaining the interest of the United States, or of its people, in the controversy. The President has decided that our foreign relations are best served by the return of the crown. We decline to enter into any controversy relating to distinctions which may be drawn between executive agreements and treaties. We say only that on the facts before us we find no justiciable controversy.

Id. at 1110 (paragraph number omitted).

The opinion of Mr. Justice Brennan, writing for the Court in the 1962 case of *Baker v. Carr*, 369 U.S. 186 (1962), contains the classic discussion of the "political question" doctrine. In that opinion, the Supreme Court said the following of relevance to potential treaty power political question issues:

> We have said that "In determining whether a question falls within [the political question] category, the appro[p]riateness under our system of government of attributing finality to the action of the political departments and also the lack of satisfactory criteria for a judicial determination are dominant considerations." *Coleman v. Miller*, 307 U. S. 433, 454-455. The nonjusticiability of a political question is primarily a function of the separation of powers. Much confusion results from the capacity of the "political question" label to obscure the need for case-by-case inquiry. Deciding whether a matter has in any measure been committed by the Constitution to another branch of government, or whether the action of that branch exceeds whatever authority has been committed, is itself a delicate exercise in constitutional interpretation, and is a responsibility of this Court as ultimate interpreter of the Constitution. To demonstrate this requires no less than to analyze representative cases and to infer from them the analytical threads that make up the political question doctrine. We shall then show that none of those threads catches this case.
>
> *Foreign relations*: There are sweeping statements to the effect that all questions touching foreign relations are political questions.[31] [[31] *E.g.*, "The conduct of the foreign relations of our Government is committed by the Constitution to the Executive and Legislative-'the political'--Departments of the Government, and the propriety of what may be done in the exercise of this political power is not subject to judicial inquiry ordecision." *Oetjen v. Central Leather Co.*, 246 U. S. 297, 302.] Not only does resolution of such issues frequently turn on standards that defy judicial application, or involve the exercise of a discretion demonstrably committed to the executive or legislature;[32] [[32] See *Doe v. Braden*, 16 How. 635, 657; *Taylor v. Morton*, 23 Fed. Cas., No. 13,799 (C. C. D. Mass.) (Mr. Justice Curtis), affirmed, 2 Black 481.] but many such questions uniquely demand single-voiced statement of the Government's views.[33] [[33] See *Doe v. Braden*, 16 How. 635, 657.] Yet it is error to suppose that every case or controversy which touches foreign relations lies beyond judicial cognizance. Our cases in this field seem invariably to show a discriminating analysis of the particular question posed, in terms of the history of its management by the political branches, of its susceptibility to judicial handling in the light of its nature and posture in the specific case, and of the possible consequences of judicial action. For example, though a court will not ordinarily inquire whether a treaty has been terminated, since on that question "governmental action . . . must be regarded as of controlling importance," if there has been no

In understanding the theory of the treaty power it should also be noted that when the issue is interpretation of treaties, the President relies not only on his authority under the treaty power and his general Article II grant of "[t]he executive Power" and any included or implied foreign affairs power as well as his other grants of foreign affairs authority and associated implied powers, such as the Commander-in-Chief and receiving Ambassadors powers but, perhaps most importantly, his explicit grant of authority in Article II, section 3 to "take Care that the Laws be faithfully executed." As has been seen, both Hamilton and Madison in the "Pacificus-Helvidius" exchange emphasized that this power, which would certainly include the authority to interpret treaties made by Article VI the "Supreme Law of the Land," is a core executive, as opposed to legislative, power. Thus, whatever general powers the President has in concluding and terminating international treaties and agreements, he may have substantially greater authority in the area of treaty interpretation. And whatever general power the Congress has in this area, it may have less authority if the issue is interpretation. Again, as has been seen, Hamilton in his first "Pacificus" letter expressly stated that the legislative department is not charged with interpreting treaties.[180]

In the matter of interpreting and implementing treaties in general, a long line of Supreme Court decisions has given great weight and generally deferred to the actions of the political departments of the government.[181] Because of the combined foreign affairs and execute the laws powers of the President, the courts would seem

---

> conclusive "governmental action" then a court can construe a treaty and may find it provides the answer. Compare *Terlinden v. Ames*, 184 U. S. 270, 285, with *Society for the Propagation of the Gospel in Foreign Parts v. New Haven*, 8 Wheat. 464, 492-495.[34] [34. And see *Clark v. Allen*, 331 U. S. 503.] Though a court will not undertake to construe a treaty in a manner inconsistent with a subsequent federal statute, no similar hesitancy obtains if the asserted clash is with state law. Compare *Whitney v. Robertson*, 124 U. S. 190, with *Kolovrat v. Oregon*, 366 U. S. 187.

369 U.S. 186, 210-12 (Mr. Justice Brennan, Opinion of the Court).

[180]Hamilton, "First *Pacificus* Letter," *supra* note 24, at 400.

[181] *See, e.g.*, Ware v. Hylton, 3 U.S. (3 Dal.) 199, 261 (1796); United States v. Schooner Peggy, 5 U.S. (1 Cranch) 104, 109 (1801); Doe v. Braden, 57 U.S. (16 How.) 635, 657 (1853); Whitney v. Robertson, 124 U.S. 190, 195 (1887); Charlton v. Kelly, 229 U.S. 447, 468, 474-76 (1913); Sullivan v. Kidd, 254 U.S. 433, 442 (1921).

particularly likely to defer--if indeed they do not even have an affirmative obligation to defer to the Executive on matters of interpretation--in settings of non-self-executing treaties not creating rights under domestic law. In this respect the dictum in the 1801 decision of the Supreme Court in *United States v. Schooner Peggy*[182] may be illustrative: "[i]t is certainly true that the execution of a contract between nations is to be demanded from, and, in general, superintended by, the executive of each nation. . . ."[183]

This discussion of the general theoretical underpinnings of the treaty power might be summarized in part with the following observations.

First, there are a number of factors suggesting that once ratified the authority of a treaty and its status under the Supremacy Clause in national law stems more from the international agreement itself than from Senate action as a legislative act. A considerable line of Supreme Court decisions refers to a treaty as a compact or contract between nations. Indeed, in the 1829 case of *Foster v. Neilson* the Supreme Court said: "A treaty is, in its nature, a contract between two nations, not a legislative act." Similarly, a substantial line of Supreme Court decisions refers to international law or mutuality of obligations between the parties as the appropriate standard for interpretation of a treaty and another substantial line of such cases roots the scope of the treaty power in matters of negotiations among nations. Professors Jessup and Lissitzyn, among the foremost international lawyers our nation has produced, have given a joint opinion in the *Niagara Reservation case* "that the operation of a treaty as the supreme law of the land cannot be dissociated from its existence as an agreement or contract between nations." The Senate "consent" power has been described as a "veto" or "negative," including in a statement by Thomas Jefferson in his *Manual of Parliamentary Practice for the Use of the Senate*. Mr. Justice Brown, concurring in the *Fourteen Diamond Rings* case, has written:"[t]he Senate has no right to ratify the treaty and introduce new terms into it. . . ." The Supreme Court in the *New York Indians v. United States* case held that a Senate proviso adopted as a condition of Senate consent to a treaty but not published with the treaty nor apparently conveyed to the other party was not binding and could not "be considered as a legislative act, since the power to legislate is vested in the President, Senate and House of Representatives." Hamilton wrote in *The Federalist* No. 75 and his statement was incorporated by James Madison in his first "Helvidius" letter that: "[i]ts [treaties] objects are contracts with foreign

---

[182]5 U.S. (1 Cranch) 104 (1801).

[183]5 U.S. (1 Cranch) 104, 109.

nations, which have the force of law, but derive it from the obligations of good faith. They are not rules prescribed by the sovereign to the subject, but agreement between sovereign and sovereign. . . ." Similarly, it can be inferred from the distinction in the Constitution between the normal legislative power, lodged in both houses of Congress subject to a qualified presidential veto, and the treaty power, lodged in the President with the advice and consent of the Senate, that the treaty power is other than a power to legislate but rather is rooted in a power to conclude an international agreement with another nation. And the Supremacy Clause talks separately about both "Laws" and "Treaties." Thus again arguably the authority of a treaty under the Supremacy Clause stems from its status as a "treaty" or international compact rather than as a "law." Finally, while vacated as moot by the Supreme Court, a 1957 opinion of Judge Bazelon writing for the United States Court of Appeals for the District of Columbia Circuit upheld a treaty while setting aside a clear Senate reservation to the treaty on the grounds that "[i]t was merely an expression of domestic policy which the Senate attached to its consent" and, as such, was beyond the power of the Senate. Apparently, only the sweeping recent District Court opinion of Judge Harold H. Greene, apparently made without full argumentation of these issues or even citing of the *Niagara Reservation* decision in the Court of Appeals--and *itself* currently on appeal, seems to provide primary authority that the Senate has any legislative authority under its treaty advice and consent role.

Second, the President would seem to have broad authority under a number of constitutional grants of power to interpret treaties. These include powers under his general Article II "executive Power," the included or inferred foreign affairs power of the President, powers incident to or implied from specific grants of authority to the President in foreign affairs such as the treaty power, the commander-in-chief power and the power to receive ambassadors and, perhaps most importantly, the duty to "take Care that the Laws be faithfully executed." This latter power, which certainly includes the power to interpret international obligations, has been described by both Madison and Hamilton as the essence of the executive role. The President also seems to have broad general authority in the implementation and termination of treaties, at least in the absence of contrary direction by the Congress.

Third, actions of a subsequent Senate, acting alone, are of only limited, if any, authority concerning interpretation of an earlier Senate consented treaty. Indeed, the Supreme Court has held in the *Fourteen Diamond Rings* case that even a virtually contemporaneous but later Senate interpretation of a treaty was "absolutely without legal significance." *A fortiori*, it is likely that actions of a subsequent Senate, acting alone, are of no authority concerning any other treaty function of conclusion, implementation or termination. The Senate role in the treaty power is a "consent" role to conclusion of a negotiated treaty by a two-thirds vote of Senators present and constituting a quorum. There is little, if any, significant primary constitutional authority that it constitutes general legislative power to deal comprehensively with treaties, as seems at least implicit in some positions in the current debates and in Judge Harold H. Greene's recent opinion in the *Rainbow Navigation* case. Indeed, even the position that the Senate has a general "legislative" power to adopt implementing "domestic conditions" incident to its advice and consent function seems contradicted by language of the Supreme Court in the *New York Indians* case and by the opinion of Judge Bazelon in the *Niagara Reservation* case and could also do violence to the recognized House role in participating in implementing legislation where necessary.

Fourth, the power of Congress as a whole to conclude executive-congressional agreements with the President is clear and seems at least the legal (but not the political) functional equivalent of the treaty power. Congress also can pass subsequent legislation that will supercede treaty obligations as domestic law provided they are within the constitutional powers of the Congress to legislate and Congress clearly manifests its intention contrary to the prior treaty obligation. It is, however, unclear to what extent, if at all, a Congress may direct the President to interpret or terminate international agreements in opposition to a prior contrary decision of the Executive.

Finally, for a variety of reasons, courts are likely to be cautious about playing a major role in resolving differences between Congress and the President concerning treaty interpretation or implementation. These reasons include the "passive virtues" of ripeness, standing and political question and, at least in the route of private right involvement, also the doctrines of non-self-executing treaties and the tendency to defer to the political branches in matters of treaty interpretation, implementation and termination. While it is not constitutionally inevitable that the courts will not become actively involved in such cases,[184] the recent case of

[184]For example, Professor Herbert Wechsler's concept of "political question" would require the Court to resolve cases concerning constitutional disputes between the branches. *See* Wechsler, "Toward Neutral Principles of Constitutional Law," 73 *Harv. L. Rev.* 1 (1959). This, however, is not the "political question" doctrine adopted by the Supreme Court in the landmark decision of *Baker v. Carr*, 369 U.S. 217 (1962). Similarly, Justice Powell's concurring opinion in *Goldwater v. Carter*, 444 U.S. 996, 997 (1979), rejected the view that the issue in the case could never be considered by the Court. Rather Justice Powell emphasized that if in this case Congress "by appropriate formal action had

Goldwater v. Carter illustrates that judicial restraint in this area, at least at the Supreme Court level, continues to be robust.

2. Presidential authority to interpret treaties in the absence of congressional action

This section will examine the authority of the President (or appropriate executive branch officials) to interpret treaties in the absence of congressional action to interpret such treaties. It does not address the standard of interpretation nor the authority of a subsequent Senate or Congress to interpret a treaty advised and consented by a prior Senate. These latter issues are the subject of later sections.

Presidential authority to interpret a treaty stems not only from the general Article II executive power and any powers implied from specific constitutional grants of foreign affairs powers, including the treaty and Commander-in-Chief powers, but also the specific Article II, section 3 power, indeed duty, that the President "shall take Care that the Laws be faithfully executed." This specific power was consistently regarded by the framers as executive in its nature, thus suggesting that the specific grant would be interpreted broadly and, quite probably, as Hamilton, Jefferson and Madison all suggested, that any inconsistent congressional powers would be interpreted narrowly.

Because of the relatively clear constitutional basis for presidential authority to interpret treaties, at least in the absence of subsequent congressional or judicial efforts at interpretation, there seems no constitutional doubt that the President (and appropriate executive branch officials acting with presidential authority) has such authority, at least in the first instance, to interpret treaties. Thus, the *Restatement (Second) of the Foreign Relations Law of the United States* says:

§ 149. Authority to Interpret as to International Effect

> **The President of the United States, or an appropriate official acting under his authority, has the authority to determine the interpretation of an international**

---

challenged the President's authority" then "it would be the duty of this Court to resolve the issue." *Id.* at 1002. *See also*, adopting a view different than that of Wechsler, Scharpf,"Judicial Review and the Political Question: A Functional Analysis," 75 *Yale L.J.* 517 (1966).

> **agreement to be asserted by the United States in the conduct of its foreign relations.**[185]

The comment to this section says:

> a. *Power of the President over foreign affairs.* Only the President, or an official authorized to act for him, can speak officially for the United States as to the position taken by the United States in the conduct of its foreign relations concerning the meaning of an international agreement. This exclusive authority is based on Article II of the Constitution from which the power of the President over foreign affairs is derived.[186]

The recent *Revised Restatement* combines rules concerning authority to interpret as to international effect (the old section 149) and authority to interpret as domestic law (the old section 150) and provides:

> §326. AUTHORITY TO INTERPRET INTERNATIONAL AGREEMENTS: LAW OF THE UNITED STATES
>
> (1) The President has authority to determine the interpretation of an international agreement to be asserted by the United States in its relations with other states.
>
> (2) Courts in the United States have final authority to interpret an international agreement for purposes of applying it as law in the United States, but will give great weight to an interpretation made by the Executive Branch.[187]

The comment to this part begins:

---

[185] *American Law Institute, Restatement (Second)* of the Foreign Relations Law of the United States, §149, at 460 (1965) [hereinafter *Restatement (Second)*].

[186] *Id.* comment *a.*

[187] *American Law Institute, Restatement (Revised) of the Foreign Relations Law of the United States,* §326, at 109 (Tent. Draft No. 6, Vol. 2, April 12, 1985) [hereinafter *1985 Revised Restatement*].

> a. Presidential authority to interpret. The President has authority to interpret international agreements for the purpose of U.S. foreign relations since he is the "sole organ" of the United States in its international relations and is responsible for carrying out agreements with other nations.[188]

While the Restatements have in various respects been criticized, and they should not be relied on as unfailing authorities, there seems no indication that presidential authority to interpret treaties in the first instance is not at least as broad as reported in the Restatements. Thus, Professor Louis Henkin writes in his important Foreign Affairs and the Constitution:

> The obligation and authority to implement or enforce a treaty involve also the obligation and authority to interpret what the treaty requires. For international purposes, no doubt, the President determines the United States position as to the meaning of a treaty.* Domestically, too, since the President has usually the principal, often the sole, responsibility to execute a treaty the treaty means what he says it means.[189]

---

[188]*Id.* comment a, at 109. This comment then says: "The Senate, whose consent is necessary before the United States can conclude a treaty, has no part in the implementation of the treaty after it is made, but understandings expressed by the Senate in the process of giving its advice and consent have to be respected." *Id.* Since this comment raises issues that are the subject of the next sections of this study, it, and related *Restatement* comments, will be addressed in these next sections.

[189]*L. Henkin, supra* note 6, at 167. Professor Henkin includes a footnote * which says: "[s]ubject to any `understanding' imposed by the Senate in its consent to ratification. . . ." This issue, involving the standard for interpretation, is dealt with in the next section of this study. And Professor Henkin goes on to discuss the roles of Congress and the courts in treaty interpretation which is dealt with in the part appearing in section V(B)(5) of this study.

Similarly, the courts seem to agree that the Executive will, at least in the first instance, have authority to interpret treaties. In the *United States v. Schooner Peggy* case,[190] decided in 1801, the Supreme Court said:

> It is certainly true that the execution of a contract between nations is to be demanded from, and, in the general, superintended by, the executive of each nation. . . .[191]

And a recent unanimous decision of the United States Court of Appeals for the District of Columbia Circuit in the 1983 case of *Collins v. Weinberger* [192] noted:

> No treaty can determine all its own applications. Interpretation, classification and implementation are always necessary, and it is the executive branch, in agreement with the other party to the treaty, which bears primary responsibility for these functions. Courts should defer to such executive actions provided they are not inconsistent with or outside the scope of the treaty.[193]

There also seems no constitutional obligation for the President to consult with the Senate or the Congress in his treaty interpretation power, even though in some cases it may be a wise practice politically. Thus, Professor Kevin C. Kennedy writes in a recent article in the *American Journal of International Law*:

> . . . there appears to be no constitutional requirement that the President consult with the Senate on matters of treaty interpretation.
> . . .
>
> As a threshold question, is the President obligated to consult with the Senate on a matter of treaty interpretation? Considering that the

---

[190]United States v. Schooner Peggy, 5 U.S. (1 Cranch) 104 (1801). *See also* Charlton v. Kelly, 229 U.S. 447 (1913).

[191]5 U.S. at 109.

[192]Collins v. Weinberger, 707 F.2d 1518 (1983).

[193]707 F.2d at 1522.

> President is responsible under his foreign affairs powers for carrying out treaty obligations, the President ordinarily would appear to have no constitutional duty to consult with the Senate on such matters--although failure to do so could be political suicide.[194]

The conclusion that there is no constitutional obligation for the President to consult the Senate on matters of treaty interpretation is clearly correct. Nothing in the Constitution explicitly gives the Senate any role in issuing treaty interpretations as to prior treaties, and such a role certainly does not follow as a matter of logic from the power to advise and consent to the making of treaties. Would any such power be one exercisable only by a two-thirds Senate majority of senators present as is required for Senate advice and consent in the making of treaties? In any event, in this area the Supreme Court decision in the *Fourteen Diamond Rings* case would seem clearly on point. A subsequent Senate simply has no role, acting alone, in giving a legally binding interpretation of a treaty approved by a prior Senate.[195] There is likewise no reason to believe that the President must constitutionally consult with Congress before interpreting a treaty. Neither the executive power nor the power to take care that the laws be faithfully executed contain any suggestion that they are exercisable only after consultation with Congress. And, as we have seen, since treaty interpretation is part of the core executive authority to implement and enforce the law, as well as the President's role as spokesman of the nation in foreign affairs, those powers are likely to be interpreted broadly.

There is also an important policy consideration suggesting that any general requirement that as a matter of law--as opposed to appropriate political prudence in cases of unusual political significance--the Executive must consult with Congress or the Senate before interpreting the treaty obligations of the United States would be unworkable. The foreign policy of the United States is, as a practical matter, executed in a complex process including hundreds of daily decisions embodied in cable traffic from the Department of State and numerous decisions made within United States delegations to international organizations, conferences and elsewhere. Many of such decisions may involve interpretations of treaty obligations as, for example, the decision to vote for or against a Security Council resolution condemning the actions of a member state as in violation of the Charter. To require

---

[194]Kennedy, "Treaty Interpretation by the Executive Branch: The ABM Treaty and `Star Wars' Testing and Development," 80 *Am. J. Int'l L.* 854, 871, 876 (1986).

[195]See Fourteen Diamond Rings v. United States, 183 U.S. 176 (1901).

Senate or congressional consultation whenever an issue of treaty interpretation arises in this process would be virtually unworkable and, more importantly, could work a massive transfer of the executive power to conduct the day to day foreign policy of the United States and the executive power to "take Care that the Laws be faithfully executed."

In summary, whatever the political constraints and prudential realities, the President (and executive branch officials operating with presidential authority) has clear authority in the first instance to interpret treaties and there is no constitutional obligation in doing so to first consult with the Senate or the Congress.[196]

3. Relevance and weight of the record of Senate consideration of a treaty for interpretation of that treaty

The most contentious legal issue under national law in the "broad-narrow" debate has been, in its broadest terms, the relevance and weight to be accorded an informal record of Senate consideration of a treaty for interpretation of that treaty (and particularly in this setting the legal effect of Executive branch statements to the Senate). This issue has divided some members of Congress from Executive branch spokesmen and has divided the Congress itself. In many respects this issue is a case of first impression in American constitutional theory and practice and it is not surprising that it would generate a variety of strongly held views. One potent source of confusion, however, is that the issue has frequently been oversimplified as a single issue when, in fact, it poses at least three interrelated but separate major sets of issues. Indeed, as will be seen, this tripartite division is simply a first level of complexity. These are first, the threshold questions as to the goal of treaty interpretation under national law. That is, what is the appropriate standard for treaty interpretation? Is there a single standard that coincides with the international legal

---

[196]This does not mean, of course, that a president could amend a treaty under the guise of interpretation in a setting not reasonably presenting an interpretation issue. The substantial constitutional authority of the Executive in this area, however, suggests that an Executive branch determination that an issue is a proper subject of interpretation is, in the words of the Supreme Court in *United States v. Nixon*, "due great respect from the . . . [other branches]." United States v. Nixon, 418 U.S. 683, 703 (1974). Moreover, as will be seen in section V(B)(7) of this study, there is a well established body of case law that Executive branch determinations concerning treaty interpretation are accorded "great weight," as indeed is also reflected in section 326(2) of the *Revised Restatement* set out above.

standard and focuses on the agreement between the treaty parties or a dual standard that would apply the international standard for assessing the United States international legal obligation and a second standard rooted in the history of Senate consideration of the treaty that would become binding on the United States as national law whenever there were differences with the international legal obligation? In most settings this issue could also be thought of as the legal effect under national law of any informal Senate condition not formally attached to a treaty and communicated to the other treaty party (or the legal effect of such an Executive branch statement made to the Senate during Senate consideration for advice and consent). Second, under either unitary or dual standard--but particularly under any dual standard--what is the relevance and weight to be accorded a range of elements, such as committee hearings, committee reports, statements of witnesses, statements of Executive branch officials, and floor statements of individual members of the Senate in the process of Senate consideration of a treaty? This is an issue analogous to that of the weight to be accorded different elements in legislative history as an extrinsic aid to interpretation. And finally, at least in major groupings of issues, there are questions of the level of generality in posing the issue of Senate purpose or intent. A central component of this issue is ascertaining and handling the intent of Congress in settings involving potential differences between national and international legal obligations. A subcomponent is, in turn, what would be the effect of an error in Senate understanding of the international legal obligations created by a treaty which could, of course, result from either an error of the Executive branch, the Senate, or both, as to the meaning of a treaty? In such a setting not, of course, involving a formal Senate amendment, reservation or understanding which by definition is formally communicated to the other treaty party and would normally merge Senate intent and international obligations, is the most meaningful statement of Senate purpose that the Senate would have intended to bind the United States even if another party were not bound or that, as in all treaties, it contemplated mutuality and reciprocity of obligation? How would any such issue be resolved if a Senate had contemporaneously expressed its belief that the treaty it was consenting to created reciprocal obligations and had strongly supported equality of obligation in general?

Surprisingly, the first of these three issues--and the most directly constitutional--has been addressed in only the most sweeping terms, largely obscuring the core constitutional issue, the second has been generally oversimplified, and the third has been generally overlooked. The sections that follow will address each of these three issues in turn and will then offer an interrelated synthesis.

a. Threshold questions as to the goal of treaty interpretation under national law: the problem of unitary or dual standards for interpretation

Because of the considerable confusion surrounding the largely implicit debate about this issue, it may be useful at the outset to review what this first threshold issue is and is not. It *is* the issue of whether generally there will be a single standard for treaty interpretation in the foreign policy of the United States coincident with the standard used for establishing the international legal obligations of the United States and its treaty partners or whether the United States will be generally obligated to apply a dual standard in treaty interpretation composed of the international standard as restricted or enlarged by the informal record of Senate advice and consent (or even as restricted or enlarged by Executive branch statements to the Senate) where this record indicates Senate intent (or the Executive statement) varies from the result that would be reached under the international standard. To somewhat oversimplify a complex issue, is the bottom line for treaty interpretation under national law the mutual obligations of the parties under the treaty or the informally expressed intent of the Senate or an Executive statement during the process of advice and consent? The issue is *not*, except perhaps in rare settings as in the *New York Indians* [197] case, whether formally adopted Senate amendments, reservations, understandings, or provisos are binding. Because normally such formal Senate actions during advice and consent are made known to the other treaty partners they would normally create a congruence between Senate intent and international obligation.[198] Rather, the general issue of unitary or dual standard is presented by a range of informal elements in the history of Senate advice and consent of a particular treaty (including centrally for some in the debate, Executive branch statements made to the Senate during the process of advice and consent) that are not communicated in an internationally binding manner to the other treaty partners.

Similarly, the issue is *not* most usefully whether the record of Senate non-formal action in consideration of a treaty is entitled to no weight. Footnote seven

---

[197]New York Indians v. United States, 170 U.S. 1 (1898).

[198] *See generally* Vienna Convention on the Law of Treaties, *opened for signature* May 23, 1969, Articles 19-23, with respect to the international effect and procedure of reservations.

of the recent opinion of the Supreme Court in the case of *United States v. Stuart* would seem to make clear that "reliance on the Senate's preratification debates and reports [is not] improper" in treaty interpretation.[199] The issue is whether, absent communication to the other party in a form sufficient to create an internationally binding obligation, the record of non-formal Senate action is to receive the weight normally accorded such a national record, along with all the other permissible indicators in treaty interpretation, pursuant to the legal standard rooted in agreement between the parties,[200] or whether the record of informal Senate action is to be an *exclusive* standard under national law overriding whatever indicators or interpretation from such indicators in settings of variance between the international standard, such as, for example, the negotiating record, and the record of informal Senate action. It should be recalled in this connection that the view of the United States Department of State, widely accepted within the international legal community, is that Articles 31-33 of the Vienna Convention on the Law of Treaties

---

[199]United States v. Stuart, (No. 87-1064, Feb. 28, 1989), 12 n.7. *But see* the separate concurring opinions of Justices Kennedy and O'Connor and Justice Scalia. There is, as Justice Scalia's opinion illustrates, at least a lingering dispute even on this issue. Thus, Justice Scalia, concurring in the *Stuart* case, seemed to reject reliance on Senate preratification materials in treaty interpretation, and at a recent conference on "Treaty Implementation and Interpretation Under the Constitution," *supra* note 1, John Oldham McGinnis, the Deputy Assistant Attorney General in the Office of Legal Counsel of the Department of Justice, seemed to reject any weight for such materials unless related to some Executive branch representation.

For a recent comment supporting the use of Senate history in treaty interpretation and seeming to assume, as does the author of this study, that the issue in the *Stuart* case was the permissibility of the use of such materials in treaty interpretation, see Vagts, "Senate Materials and Treaty Interpretation: Some Research Hints for the Supreme Court," 83 *Am. J. Int'l L.* 546 (1989). After citing a series of Supreme Court decisions examining such history, Professor Vagts writes:

> One hopes that counsel will continue to research and cite Senate history in argumentation concerning the meaning of treaties, a practice of long standing that sometimes, but not always, produces illuminating guidance.

Id. at 550.

[200]*See generally* Articles 31-33 of the Vienna Convention on the Law of Treaties, *supra* note 198, and the earlier discussion in part II of this study, with respect to the international legal standard for treaty interpretation.

generally reflect customary international law in their rules of treaty interpretation. Under this framework, if the international standard were the rule of decision, the record of Senate non-formal action in consideration of a treaty not formally communicated to the other party would, for example, be one possible factor in considering "[a] special meaning . . . given to a term" by the parties under Article 31, or one factor under Article 32 as a supplementary means of interpretation concerning "the preparatory work of the treaty and the circumstances of its conclusion." This is in sharp contrast to the *exclusive* weight to be accorded such a non-formal record or Executive branch statement for purposes of national law even when in conflict with the overall record otherwise, as would be the standard if this issue were decided under what will be termed in this study a "dual" approach as opposed to the "single" international standard.

The issue is *not* whether a President has an obligation, at least implicit in our democratic form of government, to work with the Senate in good faith in facilitating the important Senate role in treaty advice and consent. Certainly a President should seek to provide the Senate with the best judgment of the Executive branch as to the meaning of a treaty presented for advice and consent.[201] To the extent that the Executive branch is aware at the time of ratification of a Senate interpretation that may vary from the international agreement it generally should both alert the Senate, and if the Senate continues its interpretation, require a formal reservation, or at the least convey the Senate interpretation to the other treaty parties at the time of United States ratification or adherence.[202] And certainly a deliberate effort by a President

---

[201]For this reason this study recommends the practice of generally submitting a carefully prepared article-by-article legal analysis and a summary negotiating history with each treaty submitted to the Senate for advice and consent.

[202]See section 314 of the 1985 *Revised Restatement of the Foreign Relations Law of the United States* which provides:

> §314. RESERVATIONS AND UNDERSTANDINGS: LAW OF THE UNITED STATES
>
> (1) When the Senate of the United States gives its advice and consent to a treaty subject to the United States entering a reservation, the President, if he makes the treaty, must include the reservation in the instrument of ratification or accession, or otherwise make it clear that the adherence of the United States is subject to the reservation.
>
> (2) When the Senate gives its advice and consent to a treaty on the

or his spokesmen to mislead or defraud a Senate as to the meaning of a treaty during Senate consideration of advice and consent to that treaty would be reprehensible. Indeed, it may also be criminally punishable under existing laws punishing intentional misrepresentations to Congress. And, it might, if egregious enough, be grounds for impeachment under Article I, sections 2 and 3 of the Constitution.[203]

> basis of a particular understanding of its meaning, the President, if he makes the treaty, must do so on the basis of the Senate's understanding.

1985 Revised Restatement, *supra* note 187, §314, at 80. *See also* the commentary to this section, particulary comment d, at 82. To the extent that this provision addresses the central issue of this section it will be discussed more fully below.

[203]There may also be an issue of estoppel operative in such or similar settings. Assistant Attorney General Cooper concluded in a memorandum of April 9, 1987, to Abraham D. Sofaer on "Relevance of Senate Ratification History to Treaty Interpretation":

> [I]n a case in which the statements by the executive branch amount to a formal representation by the President concerning the meaning of a particular treaty provision, the ratification record may be conclusive. If, for example, the ratification record unequivocally shows that the President presented the treaty to the Senate based on specific official representations regarding the meaning of an ambiguous provision, that the Senate regarded that understanding as important to its consent, and that the Senate relied on the representations made by the executive branch in approving the treaty (and thus in refraining from attaching a formal reservation setting forth the understanding), we believe the President, would, in effect be estopped from taking a contrary position in his subsequent interpretation of the treaty, just as he would be bound by a formal reservation or understanding passed by the Senate to the same effect. . . . Obviously, a President could not negotiate a treaty with other nations on the basis of one understanding of its import, submit the treaty to the Senate on a wholly different understanding, and then, in implementing the treaty, rely solely on the understanding he had reached with the other parties. Similarly, he could not reach a secret agreement with the other party that substantially modifies the obligations and authorities created by the text of the treaty submitted to the Senate, and then seek to use the secret agreement as a basis for actions inconsistent with the text of the treaty. Such results would essentially eviscerate the Senate's constitutional advice and consent role, because it would deprive the Senate of a fair opportunity to determine whether, or with what conditions, the treaty should become the "supreme

---

> Law of the Land." Accordingly, in such extreme cases, we have little doubt that, as a matter of domestic law, the courts would construe the treaty as presented to and accepted by the Senate, even if as a matter of international law the treaty might have a different meaning.

Cooper, "Memorandum to Abraham D. Sofaer," *supra* note 1, at 14-15. Assistant Attorney General Cooper cited no case in support of this proposition in which a domestic court had held that a treaty would be interpreted at odds with the international meaning of the treaty, although he did cite a case concerning domestic legislation and one where a court had not followed the Executive's view of the international obligations created by a treaty.

As discussed below, even this seemingly fair "estoppel" position may present a more complex constitutional and policy issue than discussed by Mr. Cooper in this brief reference. One such sub-issue would be simply whether a treaty can ever create domestic law apart from its international obligation. A second sub-issue would be whether the consequence of such a setting would be simply to void the treaty under domestic law, as opposed to estopping the Nation (not just the Presidency) to the erroneous Executive branch statement. Similarly, there could also be substantial questions whether a subsequent President should always be "estopped" by actions of a prior President or whether any estoppel would be limited to settings of intentional misstatement as opposed to mere mistake or oversight. Perhaps most importantly, as will be examined subsequently in this section, such an estoppel could be estopping a prior Senate to a treaty it would not have accepted had it been aware that the purported obligation was not internationally binding on the other party. That is, is such an estoppel working against the President, the prior ratifying Senate, both, or, more meaningfully, the Nation in possibly creating a gap between it and the other parties' obligations under the treaty? The most general issue posed by this problem is whether altering the nation's international obligations is ever a constitutionally permissible or desirable remedy for Executive branch failure in informing the Senate about the meaning of a treaty.

This set of issues will be explored more fully in section V(B)(4) below.

It might be noted that in a letter to the Editor of the *Wall Street Journal* on March 15, 1988, Senator Sam Nunn responded to a February 22, 1988, *Wall Street Journal* "Opinion Editorial" by Robert F. Turner, "Beware the Tyranny of the Senate," that criticized the Byrd-Nunn approach to treaty interpretation, solely by invoking part of the above "estoppel" quotation from Assistant Attorney General Charles Cooper. In terms considerably more deferential to a legal opinion from a high level Executive branch official than accorded to Judge Sofaer's "broad" interpretation, Senator Nunn said:

> Assistant Attorney General Cooper has earned a reputation as a zealous advocate for the prerogatives of the executive branch. It is most unlikely that the Justice Department would have reached this conclusion if the

> administration viewed the opinion, in Mr. Turner's words, as to "concede ultimate authority to the Senate to `interpret' treaties." Rather, this statement by the assistant attorney general reflects an accurate and faithful reading of the constitutional role of the Senate in this important area.

Senate's Role in Treaty Process, Letter to the Editor from Senator Sam Nunn, Wall St. J., Mar. 15, 1988, at 35, col. 1, 2.

Whether or not Assistant Attorney General Cooper's "estoppel" argument is fully correct (and ignoring whether the Byrd-Nunn three principles are congruent with the Cooper position as quoted), this reliance by Senator Nunn on the legal opinion of one high level Executive branch spokesman, but challenge to that of another, illustrates a fundamental point. Ultimately, the authority of any Executive branch legal opinion--or that of a member of Congress--depends in substantial measure on its correctness under the law. As such, it should not be the fact of a legal opinion from these sources but rather the strength of the underlying reasons supporting it which is of primary relevance. This latter proposition, of course, does not fully reflect the nuance of a sophisticated jurisprudential appraisal concerning the authoritative effect of opinions by Executive branch officials within the scope of their official duties (and particularly as to such legal opinions that through time become widely accepted), but it is a fundamental tenet of a government of laws.

The "Opinion Editorial" by Robert F. Turner to which Senator Nunn was responding, provided as follows:

> The effort by Sens. Sam Nunn and Robert Byrd to hold the INF Treaty "hostage" until the president agrees to surrender his constitutional powers to interpret the nation's international treaty obligations brings to mind Thomas Jefferson's observation that the nation must be wary of the "tyranny of the Legislatures."
>
> This is but the latest round in a continuing assault on the Constitution that dates back nearly two decades. When the Supreme Court in 1983 struck down by implication the "legislative veto" provisions in several hundred laws--including the controversial 1973 War Powers Resolution--because they infringed upon the independent constitutional power vested by the people in the president, Congress essentially thumbed its nose at the high court. A recent survey by a Library of Congress scholar identified more than 100 "legislative vetoes" that have been enacted into law since the mechanism was held to be unconstitutional.
>
> Now Senate Democratic leaders--particularly Sens. Nunn and Byrd--have reportedly informed Secretary of State George Shultz in an angry letter that they will hold up Senate consideration of the INF Treaty if the

president refuses to concede ultimate authority to the Senate to "interpret" treaties. In essence, they are telling the president that his effort to reduce nuclear armaments and enhance the prospects for world peace will be held hostage if he refuses to acquiesce to further encroachments upon his constitutional powers.

'Executive Altogether'

The senators misunderstand the constitutional separation of powers regarding the making, interpretation and implementation of treaties, and they misunderstand the process of determining international treaty obligations. As a matter of settled constitutional law, the Senate neither "makes" nor "ratifies" treaties. The Senate possesses what Jefferson, in the first Senate Rules Manual, characterized as a "negative" (i.e., veto) over a treaty negotiated by the president or his agent. More recently, such respected constitutional scholars as Edwin Corwin have also described this Senate power as a "veto."

In 1790, Jefferson wrote: "The transaction of business with foreign nations is executive altogether. It belongs then to the head of that department, except as to such portions of it as are specially submitted to the Senate. Exceptions are to be construed strictly." In his first Pacificus letter in June 1793, Alexander Hamilton described the president as "the interpreter of the National Treaties in those cases in which the Judiciary is not competent, that is in the cases between Government and Government."

When two weeks later, French Minister "Citizen Genet" threatened to appeal President Washington's interpretation of a treaty to Congress, Jefferson responded that "there were very few cases indeed arising out of treaties, which [Congress] could take notice of; that the President is to see that treaties are observed." Genet inquired: "If he decides against the treaty, to whom is a nation to appeal?" In his subsequent account of the exchange, Jefferson wrote: "I told him the Constitution had made the President the last appeal."

As early as 1801, in *U.S. v. Schooner Peggy*, the Supreme Court said: "The execution of a treaty between nations is to be demanded from, and, in general, superintended by, the executive of each nation. . . ." More recently, the president's constitutional pre-eminence in this field has been recognized by the Second Restatement of Foreign Relations Law (1972), which states in Section 149: "The President of the United States, or an appropriate official acting under his authority, has the authority to determine the interpretation of an international agreement to be asserted by the United States in the conduct of its foreign relations."

A treaty is a compact between (or among) nations. Its meaning is to be found by determining the genuine shared expectations of the parties. This is done by looking at the text of the treaty and any supplementary documents agreed to by both parties; and if this proves indecisive, by considering supplementary means of interpretation such as the preparatory works or negotiating history to the agreement.

The senators are certainly right when they argue that the president may not ratify a treaty other than the one to which the Senate gave its consent (including any formal Senate amendments, reservations and declarations). But that has to do with the text and not the interpretive nuances of the agreement and associated documents.

Sens. Nunn and Byrd are alleging that every statement made by administrative witnesses (some of whom may have had little direct involvement in the negotiations themselves) becomes binding upon the U.S., and it is the subjective understanding of the Senate that establishes the true "meaning" of the treaty--even if subsequent developments establish that a particular statement inadvertently did not reflect the actual agreement made by the two parties. In reality, statements made in internal national ratification processes are properly given very little weight in the business of interpreting treaties.

Consider, for a moment, the logical consequences of the senators' viewpoint. By the doctrine of reciprocity, the terms of the treaty are expected to be applied equally to all parties to the treaty (unless the treaty clearly provides otherwise).

If the Senate claims that statements made either by senators or by administration witnesses during hearings are primary factors in determining the international meaning of the treaty, it must be prepared to accept as binding any interpretation put forward during consideration of the treaty by the Supreme Soviet. By Sen. Nunn's doctrine--which does not require that the Senate's "understanding" or "interpretation" of a treaty be communicated to the other party--the U.S. could be held to strained interpretations agreed upon in secret by another state's legislature long after the Senate itself had consented to the ratification of the treaty.

The constitutional role of the Senate is an important but limited one. The Senate has a veto over a treaty negotiated by the president or his agent. By longstanding practice the Senate may also propose changes to a treaty. However, as a matter of international law the Senate does not actually "amend" or modify the treaty itself--rather, it technically refuses to consent to the treaty that has been submitted while notifying the

---

president in advance that he has its consent to "make" a treaty that incorporates the terms set forth in the Senate's resolution.

In such an instance, the president may attempt to renegotiate the treaty to incorporate the Senate's conditions--and, if accepted by the other party, the Senate's terms become a part of the treaty. However, the president has complete discretion after the Senate has given its consent--conditioned or otherwise--to decide whether to proceed with the ratification of the treaty.

For the Senate to exceed its proper constitutional role in the treaty process--as proposed by Sens Nunn and Byrd--not only would be another unlawful act, but in practical terms could create a confusing and even dangerous situation. First, there is the problem of establishing precisely what "meaning" each senator understood concerning every provision of every treaty at the time the Senate gave its consent to ratification. (From my observation, most senators do not attend treaty hearings, read committee reports on treaties, or even personally examine the texts of most proposed treaties before they are called upon to vote.) Further, many difficult questions of interpretation occur because of developments unforeseen by both the negotiators and the Senate at the time it gave its consent.

Even if those problems could be resolved, the Nunn-Byrd proposal would be a bad idea. If the president were legally required to follow the Senate's "understanding" of the meaning of a treaty during subsequent disputes, three possible results could occur:

. If the Senate properly understood the meaning of the treaty and its interpretation coincided with the shared expectations of the parties in light of all of the evidence, the "Nunn-Byrd" rule would have no effect on the treaty's meaning.

. If the Senate erred--either out of its own ignorance or as a result of a mistake by an executive branch witness--and underestimated the extent of the true U.S. obligation, forcing the president to follow this "interpretation" would make the U.S. an international lawbreaker.

. If, on the other hand (as may be the present situation), the Senate inadvertently overestimated the actual obligations of the treaty, the Nunn-Byrd rule would result in the U.S. being bound to a more restrictive course of action than would apply to the other party to the treaty. In a matter as critically important as an arms-control treaty with Moscow, that is hardly a result to be welcomed. It is, furthermore, in conflict with the expressed views of the Senate that approved ratification of the ABM Treaty in 1972. That year the Senate approved a joint resolution (signed into law as P.L. 92-448) that included a provision known as the Jackson Amendment. It

The issue is *not* the power of Congress to override the treaty obligations of the United States under national (but not international) law by subsequent passage of clearly inconsistent legislation. As has been seen under section (B)(1)(b) of this part, it is settled law that an otherwise constitutionally valid act of Congress passed subsequent to a treaty and clearly conflicting with it will take precedence over the treaty for purposes of national law.[204] The issue of whether Congress as a whole may constitutionally pass a law solely for the purpose of treaty interpretation will be dealt with in section (B)(4) of this part.

Conversely, the issue is *not* whether or to what extent an uncommunicated informal Senate record in considering advice and consent can alter the international legal obligations of the United States. Generally such a record will not alter the international legal obligations of the United States except at the margin and operating, if at all, under the normal international law rules for interpretation of

---

> formally requested the president in future arms-control negotiations to seek a treaty that would not place greater force limits on the U.S. than on the Soviet Union.
>
> **Domestic Implications**
>
> Even were there no constitutional difficulties with the Nunn-Byrd approach, it would thus still be bad policy. Nor would the senators wish to see their "theory" followed to its reasonable conclusion. If the most authoritative interpretation of a treaty is that understood by the Senate at the time it decides not to exercise its "veto," would it not follow that the controlling interpretation of domestic laws ought to be the understanding of the president as he decides not to exercise his "veto" over the proposed statute?
>
> As important as the INF Treaty is in promoting international peace and stability, it is certainly less important than the Constitution. As the late Harvard Law Prof. Charles Warren observed: "In maintaining his rights against a trespassing Congress, the president defends not himself, but popular government; he represents not himself, but the people."

Turner, *Beware the Tyranny of the Senate*, Wall St. J., Feb. 22, 1988, at 20, cols. 2-6.

[204] *See e.g.*, The Chinese Exclusion Case, 130 U.S. 581 (1889).

treaties.[205] Rather the issue is the standard to be applied under national law in treaty interpretation and specifically whether there is any separate national standard that could override, as a matter of national law, the international standard for treaty interpretation when in conflict with it.

And, at least in this study, the issue centrally addressed is not the legal effect under national law of Executive branch statements to the Senate made during the process of Senate advice and consent, or formal or informal Senate conditions accompanying Senate advice and consent, either of which solely concerns issues of national law or policy in implementing a treaty rather than interpretation of an international agreement. This latter setting of the validity of what might be called "domestic conditions" does not centrally concern treaty interpretation in the foreign policy of the United States and for a variety of reasons may present different policy considerations in its resolution. Indeed, it is possible that the failure to differentiate this "domestic conditions" setting from that of the effect under national law of treaty interpretation per se may be a contributing factor in the overall level of disagreement about these issues. It should also be noted, however, that if there is no general Senate "legislative" authority incident to the Senate advice and consent role, then it would seem highly likely that a "dual" approach, dependent by definition on a separate legal effect under national law, also would be invalid. The converse, however, is not necessarily true and thus the issues should be kept separate.[206]

---

[205]Again, *see* Articles 31-33 of the Vienna Convention on the Law of Treaties, supra note 198. And, for more complex and sophisticated possibilities for internal procedures having an effect on international obligations, see Articles 46-48 of the Vienna Convention, *id.*

Specifically with respect to the Soviet view of ratification documents, Thomas K. Longstreth, John E. Pike and John B. Rhinelander write in their 1985 monograph on *The Impact of U.S. and Soviet Ballistic Missile Defense Programs on the ABM Treaty*, that concerning a definition of "development" submitted for the record by Ambassador Smith during Senate advice and consent hearings on the ABM Treaty: "Privately, the Soviets have indicated they are under no obligation to comment on documents prepared for U.S. ratification purposes." Longstreth, Pike & Rhinelander, *The Impact of U.S. and Soviet Ballistic Missile Defense Programs on the ABM Treaty* 26 (March 1985).

[206]One important way in which the "domestic conditions" issue presents a different policy setting is that where such conditions are consistent with an international agreement, then, whether or not one or another lawful property option in treaty implementation is binding under national law does not affect United States adherence to its international

---

obligations. The core issue centrally addressed in this study, however, if it has any legal effect, *always* results in a discrepancy between the national and international legal obligations of the United States. While this study does not centrally address this "domestic conditions" setting, and urges that this issue should be intellectually understood as a separate issue presenting different policies, it does not mean to imply that answers are clear even with respect to the "domestic conditions" setting.

A central issue in holding Executive branch statements or Senate informal--or even formal--understandings concerning "domestic conditions" as legally binding under national law concerns whether such actions are "legislative" actions rather than treaties, and, if so, whether they would be required to be adopted pursuant to the affirmative action of both houses of Congress and presentment to the President. Presumably this issue would, in turn, raise not only issues in exegesis of the text of the Constitution, but also policy issues as to whether our national constitutive process should function in such settings through more broadly based domestic law making than simply actions of the Senate alone or statements of Executive branch officials, whether or not even reflecting a cleared Executive branch position, or whether an exception to this general "legislative" mode is appropriate for adjustments surrounding treaties. If so, how broad should such an exception be? Would it even encompass full domestic implementing "legislation" as a Senate condition pursuant to the treaty power? If so, what would this do to the role of the House of Representatives in the legislative process? If not, where would the line be drawn and on what constitutional basis? Settings in which purported "domestic conditions" were inconsistent with a treaty they were presumably accompanying would also raise some of the same issues presented by the "core" issue addressed in this study.

While this study does not primarily focus on this issue of the legal effect of formal or informal "domestic conditions," the earlier review of the theoretical nature of the treaty power in this study is also certainly relevant to this issue. As to more or less direct primary authority, it should be noted that a recent District Court opinion by Judge Harold H. Greene in the *Rainbow Navigation* case would seem, in a setting where the issues were not really briefed, to support the binding nature of such informal "domestic conditions" and Executive branch statements concerning such "domestic conditions." On the other hand, a prior Court of Appeals decision in the *Niagra Reservation* case and in the same circuit has declared such a "domestic condition" invalid, and the language and theory of the Supreme Court in the *New York Indians* case would seem incompatible with adoption of such conditions through the normal legislative process. Moreover, the *Rainbow Navigation* case has been appealed. These decisions will be cited and discussed in full later in this study.

Policy considerations at stake in the "domestic conditions" issue include, on the one hand, whether exclusively national law should be made only with the protective integrity of the full legislative process, including action by *both* houses and an opportunity for meaningful presentment to the President, and whether any looser "legislative" process for

---

such conditions would invite abuse in Senate consideration of treaties, and on the other hand, whether Senate consideration of treaties might be facilitated by a looser "legislative" process incident to the Senate advice and consent function. One difficulty that proponents of such a "legislative" process may have is that once it is conceded that the Senate has "legislative" authority incident to its treaty advice and consent power, what, if anything, would be the limits of such authority? At a recent conference on these issues at the Syracuse University College of Law in March of 1989, the author of this study posed the question to Professor David A. Koplow, who seems to support such a "legislative" power incident to the Senate advice and consent process, whether such a Senate power would support full implementing legislation through a Senate condition. Professor Koplow answered that in his judgement it would. Such an answer, however, reveals both the theoretical difficulty in limiting the authority once it is conceded as incidental to the Senate advice and consent process, and it illustrates the drastic effect such a doctrine could have on the constitutional legislative role of the House of Representatives. Needless to say, of course, such a power would also be inconsistent with the established practice that implementing legislation is submitted to the normal legislative process. In this connection, Professor Ivan M. Stone reminds us in his article on "The House of Representatives and the Treaty-Making Power," that during the House debate on the Jay Treaty in 1796:

> Mr. Madison presented a logical and studied contention against the encroachment of the treaty-making power on the prerogatives of the Legislature. The House should be careful, he asserted, to avoid intrusions on the powers of the other departments, but it should also be alert to guard its own powers against aggression. He held it to be important and decisive that "if the Treaty power alone could perform any one act for which the authority of Congress is required by the Constitution, it may perform every act for which the authority of that part of the Government is required." As regards the power of the purse, the Treaty power could not be considered as paramount to that of Congress. Ours is a Government of checks and balances, and it is not unreasonable "to lean towards a construction that would limit and control the Treaty-making power, rather than towards one that would make it omnipotent." The latter construction Madison held to be "utterly inadmissible."

Stone, *supra* note 61, at 225. Professor Stone also reminds us of the classic "constitutional dilemma" under the treaty power as to whether the House of Representatives is morally or legally bound to pass implementing legislation for ratified treaties. *Id.* at 230-43. Would at least one reasonable basis for protecting the "legislative" power of the Congress as a whole in construing the treaty power be to prohibit unilateral adoption of "domestic conditions" by the Senate and to restrict the treaty power to approving international agreements? In considering the role of the House of Representatives, it further might be recalled that Senator Dick Clark, on January 10, 1977, introduced S. Res. 24, entitled the

---

"Treaty Powers Resolution," which would have used the Senate's role in budget authorization for implementing measures to control which agreements are submitted to the Senate as treaties. This measure was opposed in a letter of June 27, 1977, from the Chairman of the House Committee on International Relations to Secretary of State Vance. Chairman Clement J. Zablocki said in this letter that "the House is likely to resent exclusion and work its will on the agreement in any event, using the vehicle of the implementing legislation if necessary." And he termed S. Res. 24 as "seriously out of step with the times and potentially divisive." J. Boyd, *Digest of United States Practice in International Law 1977*, at 413-18, 413-14, 415 (U.S. Dep't of State Pub. No. 8960, Jan 1979).

Another constitutional issue concerning the underpinnings of any general Senate authority to adopt legally binding--as opposed to politically significant--"domestic conditions" incident to the Senate's advice and consent power may be suggested by the well-established constitutional doctrine of the impermissibility of "unconstitutional conditions." Clearly, the Senate could not attach a "domestic condition" violative of the Bill of Rights to approval of a treaty simply on the theory that if the Senate has the authority to adopt or reject a treaty it has the authority to approve subject to any condition it wishes. This line of reasoning, after all, is rejected under the doctrine of "unconstitutional conditions" even for the appropriations power jointly exercised by both houses. Yet, if such an approach cannot bypass the Bill of Rights, how can it bypass the bicameralism and presentment clauses and seek to legislate legally binding "domestic conditions" by action of the Senate alone (or even a statement in a Senate committee report or a statement from an Executive branch witness)? In this respect, it might be noted that concluding that the Senate has no such authority would still provide the Senate flexibility to adopt such conditions as politically significant conditions, as opposed to legally binding conditions, as seems to be the assumption underlying some Senate practice. Moreover, it should be noted that it would always seem within Senate power to refuse to provide advice and consent to a treaty until prior passage of appropriate implementing legislation passed in the normal legislative process and containing whatever constitutionally permissible "domestic conditions" were sought by the Senate. There is, however, a serious constitutional process question, in a system of checks and balances, as to whether it is appropriate to permit the Senate, acting alone, to enact "domestic conditions" incident to advice and consent to treaties. And this is particularly so if such legally binding conditions are asserted to be legislatively established *even without formal Senate action or simply by committee reports or Executive branch statements,* as seems to be the implication of Judge Harold H. Greene's decision in the *Rainbow Navigation* case.

As one further point, and one that is rooted in the text of the Constitution, it might also be noted that *the Senate advice and consent power* in Article II, section 2, is to give advice and consent to the making of treaties, not to their implementation or execution. In contrast, *Congress*, rather than the Senate acting alone, is given power under the necessary and proper clause in Article I, section 8 "[t]o make all Laws which shall be necessary and proper for carrying into Execution the foregoing Powers, and all other Powers vested by this Constitution in the Government of the United States or in any Department or Offices thereof." Are "domestic conditions" primarily a power incident to the *making* of treaties (which by a long line of Supreme Court decisions are agreements or compacts among nations) or primarily a power "*for carrying into Execution*" treaties under domestic law once such treaties are made? For a brief explanation of House prerogatives in the treaty context, see section "II. House Prerogatives" in Fisher, "Constitutional Underpinnings," *supra* note 1, at 7-11.

Professor Henkin writes in *Foreign Affairs and the Constitution*, in broad but cautious support of the constitutionality of "domestic conditions":

> If the Senate can give or withhold consent it can also give its consent on condition that changes be made. Or, one might say, the Senate withholds consent from the treaty presented to it but indicates what revised treaty will earn its consent, and gives it in advance to a treaty as so revised. (Of course, the President might decide not to "make" the treaty that is satisfactory to the Senate.)[21] [21. see note 15, and text at note 22, this chapter. A reservation by another party, entered after the Senate had consented to the original treaty, presents the United States with a modified treaty and requires new consent. Such later reservations have in the past often (not always) been submitted for Senate consent. See, *e.g.*, the Treaty with France 1800, 1 MALLOY, TREATIES 496; HAYDEN, TREATIES 124. See generally CRANDALL, TREATIES 86-89; 5 MOORE, DIGEST 207. See MILLER, RESERVATIONS TO TREATIES 11-14 (1919). The principle has been reaffirmed recently by the Department of State in 60 AM.J.INT'L L. 562 (1966), but in fact foreign reservations have apparently not been submitted for Senate consent in many years. Perhaps that is because reservations by others after ratification by the United States are likely to occur in respect of multilateral treaties, and have not affected U.S. rights or obligations in ways deemed of major importance; perhaps, in these cases, the Executive concluded that, knowing the practice, the Senate had waived the need for its consent. Or that he could accept these modification of his own authority. See Chapter VI.]
>
> The Senate has sometimes imposed conditions that seek not modification of the international obligations of the treaty but some control of its effect in the United States.* [*Some speak of Senate "amendments" to describe reservations that seek a chance in the treaty obligations as distinguished from other conditions.] In an extended and unedifying controversy with several Presidents, the Senate consented to United States adherence to general arbitration conventions only on condition that any specific submission to arbitration thereafter also obtain the consent of the Senate. [22] [22. See 36 Stat. 2199, 2240 (1909), 35 Stat. 1960 (1908); MALLOY,

---

TREATIES 814, 2247. Presidents resisted these reservations. See CRANDALL, TREATIES 98-99. See HOLT 204 *et seq.*, 230 *et seq.*,; WRIGHT 109-10; 1 WILLOUGHBY 541-43.] The Senate has sometimes insisted that a treaty should not take effect, or that action shall not be taken under it by United States officials, without prior approval of Congress. [23] [23. Particularly as to treaties which affect the revenue, *e.g.,* Treaty with Great Britain concerning Canada, 10 Stat. 1089, 1092 (1854); Treaty with Hawaii, 19 Stat. 625, 627 (1875); Treaty with Mexico, 24 Stat. 987, 988 (1883); Commercial Convention with Cuba, 33 Stat. 2136, 2143 (1903). See 2A HINDS, PRECEDENTS OF THE HOUSE OF REPRESENTATIVES § §1531-33, at 994-1002 (1907); 1 WILLOUGHBY, 558-60; S.DOC. NO. 47, 57th Cong., 2d Sess. (1902), reprinted in 2 HINDS, *supra* at 1001-02; see also United States v. American Sugar Co., 202 U.S. 563 (1906), where the Supreme Court gave effect to the Senate's reservation that the Cuba Convention should not take effect until it had been approved by Congress. Compare 42 Stat. 1946, 1949 (1921). And see the Niagra reservation, discussed at pp. 134-135. The reservations to the Treaty of Versailles included several designed to ensure for Congress a major role in the implementation of the treaty. See Wright, *Validity of the Proposed Reservations to the Peace Treaty*, 20 COLUM.L.REV. 121, 125, 126, 138-42 (1920). One reservation would have authorized denunciation of the treaty by concurrent resolution of Congress (without Presidential assent). See Chapter IV, p.121.] There are reservations requiring the President to perform some domestic act. [24] [24. The Senate Reservation to the Reciprocal Military Service Convention with Great Britain, June 3, 1918, 40 Stat. 1620, required the President, before ratifying the Convention, to issue a general certificate exempting from military service citizens of the United States in Great Britain who were outside the ages of military service specified in the laws of the United States. He complied in substance by an exchange of diplomatic notes. See S.EXEC.DOC. NO. 5 presented as H.R.DOC. NO. 1220, 65th Cong., 2d Sess. 2, 7 (1918). In consenting to a treaty with Korea in 1883, the Senate resolved that it "does not admit or acquiesce" in any assertion of a right "to negotiate treaties or carry on diplomatic negotiations" other than by persons confirmed by the Senate. MALLOY, TREATIES 340. The Senate has lost that one. Some of the Senate reservations to the Treaty of Versailles would have enhanced the powers of some organs of the federal government and limited the authority of others. See Wright, *Validity of the Proposed Reservations to the Peace Treaty*, 20 COLUM.L.REV. 121, 123-24 (1920).] On several occasions the Senate provided that nothing in the treaty shall enhance the powers of the President; in a recent instance the Senate expressed its intent also that nothing in the treaty shall add to, or subtract from, the reach of the powers of Congress. [25] [25. See the previous note. Compare a recent, far-reaching expression by the Senate in consenting to ratification of the Convention on the Organization for Economic Cooperation and Development:

"...with the interpretation and explanation of the intent of the Senate that nothing in the convention, or the advice and consent of the Senate to the ratification thereof, confers any power on the Executive to bind the United States in substantive matters beyond what the Executive now has, or to bind the United States without compliance with applicable procedures imposed by domestic law, or confers any power on the Congress to take action in fields previously beyond the authority of Congress, or limits Congress in the exercise of any power it now has." 107 CONG.REC. 4149 (1961); [1961] 12 U.S.T. 1728, 1751, T.I.A.S. NO. 4891. Compare analogous Congressional "reservations," Chapter IV, pp.120-21.]

The legal effect of such "reservations" has been seriously debated in only one instance, involving a treaty with Canada to divide the waters of the Niagara River. In the United States there were divisions of opinion and interest as to the regime that should govern the exploitation of our share of the waters. Had the treaty been ratified without more, these waters would have been subject to general federal legislation governing waters belonging to the United States for which no special provision was made. In consenting to ratification of the treaty, the Senate resolved that the United States reserves the right to provide for redevelopment of its share of the waters by act of Congress, and no such redevelopment should be undertaken until specifically authorized by Act of Congress. Both the United States and Canada treated this provision like other reservations; the President asked Canada to accept it and Canada--though somewhat mystified--did.[26] [26. See Uses of the Waters of the Niagara River, Convention Between the United States of America and Canada, Feb. 27, 1950, [1950] 1 U.S.T. 694 T.I.A.S. NO. 2130. See generally Henkin, *The Treaty Makers and the Law Makers: The Niagra Reservation*, 56 COLUM.L.REV. 1151, 1154-58 (1956) [hereinafter cited as Henkin, *Niagra*]. The relevant portions of the treaty and the diplomatic exchanges are quoted there.]

Some who wished to see the treaty come into effect without the Senate's limitation argued that the reservation had no legal effect: it was not a proper treaty provision since it contained no element of international obligation. [27] [27. See, *e.g.*, the Memorandum of Law by Thomas F. Moore, Jr., counsel for the Power Authority of the State of New York, reproduced in N.Y. Times, Oct. 29, 1955, at 9, col. 1.] That objection, of course, does not relate to the Senate's part in the treaty-making process; it would apply as well if the same provision had been inserted by the negotiators in the original treaty. (I discuss that objection below).* [*See pp.143, 160-61.] But the arguments failed to consider the effect of the Senate proviso as a condition to its consent. If the Senate gave its consent only on condition that the United States share of the waters should await disposition by Congress, the treaty could take effect only subject to that condition. If the Senate's condition did not operate to prevent the treaty from coming into effect, it is questionable whether the President had authority to ratify the treaty until Congress adopted the implementing legislation called for by the Senate, and whether his ratification in disregard of the Senate's condition was constitutionally effective. [28] [28. See Henkin, *Niagara* 1176-81. For this reason (and others, see pp.160-61) I believe that the Court of Appeals for the District of Columbia erred in refusing to give effect to the Senate "reservation." The court's judgement was vacated by the Supreme Court when the issue became moot because Congress adopted the legislation called for by the Senate. See Power Authority v. Federal Power Comm'n, 247 F. 2d 538 (D.C.Cir. 1957), vacated and remanded with directions to dismiss as moot, *sub nom.*, American Public Power Ass'n v. Power Authority, 355 U.S. 64 (1957). New York Indians v. United States, 170 U.S. 1 (1898) is different. There the Supreme Court refused to let the President's non-compliance with the Senate's requirements (which the Court said were perhaps only directory and not mandatory) defeat the claim of the Indians under the treaty. The rights of Indians, moreover, are different. *Cf.* Squire v. Capoeman, 351, U.S. 1, 6, 7 (1956); United States v. Shoshone Tribe, 304 U.S. 111, 117 (1938).] Similarly, when the Senate gives consent to a treaty on condition that officers appointed by the President pursuant to the treaty shall be appointed only with Senate approval, the President who proceeds to ratify the treaty has been deemed obligated to conform to the condition. [29] [29. Compare note 24, this chapter. A very different condition couched as an understanding (p.135 above) was that appended by the Senate in consenting to the London Treaty, 73 CONG.REC. 378 (1930): [beginning of quote] *Resolved further*, That in ratifying said treaty the Senate does so with the distinct and explicit understanding that there are no secret files, documents, letters, understandings, or agreements which in any way, directly or indirectly, modify, change, add to, or take away from any of the stipulations, agreements, or statements in said treaty; and that the Senate ratifies said treaty with the distinct and explicit understanding that, excepting the agreement brought about through the exchange of notes between the Governments of the United States, Great Britain, and Japan having reference to Article XIX, there is no agreement, secret or otherwise, expressed or implied, between any of the parties to said treaty as to any construction that shall hereafter be given to any statement or provision contained therein. [end of quote] This "understanding" does not amend or interpret the treaty, nor does it require any action. Presumably it serves to deny Senate consent to any secret agreed construction that might exist. Perhaps, even the Senate's consent would not be effective if a secret understanding in fact existed, and the President could not proceed to ratify.]

A different question is whether the Senate can impose conditions unrelated to the treaty itself. While the Senate has never attempted to do so, one may ask hypothetically whether, say, it can tell the President that it will consent to a treaty only if he dismisses his Secretary of State. Perhaps such conditions were not contemplated, perhaps the Senate that made them would be abusing its power, and

---

> indeed it seems incredible that a Senate would put such a condition, at least formally and publicly. But since the Senate can withhold its consent for no reason, perhaps it can withhold it for any reason, and a President may have to buy that consent at whatever price and in whatever form the Senate asked. It would be particularly difficult to conclude that when the Senate imposes a condition which is not "proper," the President can disregard the condition, treat the Senate's consent as unconditional, and proceed to ratify the treaty.

L. Henkin, supra note 6 at 134-36, 379-81 nn.21-29.

This discussion by Professor Henkin seems largely premised on the assumption that: "[i]f the Senate can give or withhold consent it can also give its consent on condition . . . ." *Id.* at 134. But Professor Henkin does not discuss the doctrine of "unconstitutional conditions" and whether any such "domestic conditions" would be unconstitutional "legislative" actions not adopted pursuant to the bicameralism and formal presentment clauses. Nor does he cite any real judicial authority for "domestic conditions." As has been seen, the *New York Indians* and *Niagara Reservation* cases discussed by Professor Henkin seem to support an opposite conclusion that there may be no "domestic conditions" authority in the Senate acting alone. But Professor Henkin gives only his *condition* argument in a question-begging conclusion: "I believe that the Court of Appeals for the District of Columbia [in the *Niagara Reservation* case] erred in refusing to give effect to the Senate 'reservation.'" *Id.* at 380 n.28. Moreover, Professor Henkin's description of the Supreme Court decision in *United States v. American Sugar Co.,* 202 U.S. 563 (1906), seems misleading in the context of authority for "domestic conditions." Professor Henkin says of this case: "where the Supreme Court gave effect to the Senate's reservation that the Cuba Convention should not take effect until it had been approved by Congress." *Id.* at 379 n.23. But the *American Sugar Company* case is in two major respects *not* a Senate "domestic conditions" case. First, the Senate amendment in question was "ratified and approved by Cuba" and became part of the *internationally binding obligation* between the two nations when the treaty went into force. As such, it was *not* a "domestic condition" but rather an international condition accepted by both parties and establishing an obviously internationally relevant common time of entry into force of the treaty for both parties. And second, the Court had before it implementing legislation passed by both houses of Congress, not solely a Senate imposed "domestic condition." The Court, in upholding the amendment said: "It was open to Cuba to reject the amendment; it was open to Cuba to reject the legislation. If she chose to accept both they become her contracts." 202 U.S. 563, 577 (1906). It might also be noted that in this case the Solicitor General arguing on behalf of the United States said:

> Even if the approval of Congress and the action of the President were not strictly in accordance with the terms of the treaty, no one but Cuba could take

Finally, the issue is *not* the closely related issues to be dealt with in sections (B)(3)(b) and (B)(3)(c) of this part concerning the weight to be given elements of "legislative" history as extrinsic aids to interpretation or the appropriate level of generality in seeking to pose the issue of a general understanding or intention of the Senate. Both of these issues do become considerably more important if a dual approach standard, as opposed to a unitary standard, is constitutionally permissible and the second of these issues *only* exists, at least as a matter of national law, in that setting.

> exception. The interpretation and enforcement of such treaty stipulations are for the determination of the political departments of the Government, and courts will respect their decision. *Foster v. Neilson*, 2 Pet. 253; *The Cherokee Tobacco*, 11 Wall. 616; *Whitney v. Robertson*, 124 U.S. 190; *Botiller v. Dominguez*, 130 U.S. 238; *Fong Yue Ting v. United States* 149 U.S. 698. Cuba has concurred in the action of this Government, and the arrangement was essentially reciprocal. Both the United States and Cuba have put this treaty into effect on the same day to operate prospectively, and there is nothing to indicate that the two governments are not perfectly satisfied that the true intent of the treaty has been observed. The argument, reiterated by our opponents, that one party to the agreement has undertaken to modify it without consulting the other party, is simply disproved by the facts.

Id. at 568-69. In short, there seems no known Court of Appeals or Supreme Court authority for a right to enact "domestic conditions" incident to approval of treaties, much less enactment of such conditions without formal vote solely by legislative history or Executive branch statement.

While the author of this study regards the "domestic conditions" issue as a somewhat separate issue from the core issue addressed in this part as to the international meaning of a treaty (under national law), on balance existing case law, though sparse, seems to suggest, contrary to the now appealed recent District Court opinion of Judge Harold H. Greene in the *Rainbow Navigation* case, that there may be no legislative authority in the Senate alone to enact legally binding "domestic conditions" incident to the treaty advice and consent process--and particularly to do so via informal "legislative" history with no formal Senate "domestic condition" to interpret through such history. If there is not, then *a fortiori* it is highly likely that there can be no "dual" approach to treaty interpretation under the Constitution. Constitutional checks and balances can be inefficient and cumbersome but, as the *Chadha* decision of the Supreme Court illustrates, they are a fundamental mainstay of our great democracy.

Before proceeding to an examination of the legal merits of the "unitary" and "dual" standard positions it may be useful to review a representative sample of positions taken at least implicitly on this issue during the "broad-narrow" debate.

Thus, on the one hand, Senator Joseph R. Biden, Jr., stated on March 11, 1987, in introducing his "ABM Treaty Interpretation Resolution":

> [A]ction to implement the "reinterpretation" without formal acceptance by the Senate would provoke a constitutional crisis. . . . For the Executive branch to act on its "reinterpretation" would represent a severe challenge to the Constitution's delineation for the treaty power. . . .
>
> . . . as eminent constitutional scholars have affirmed and as the Resolution [the ABM Treaty Interpretation Resolution] expressly states, "during the period in which a treaty is in force, the meaning of that treaty is what the Senate understands the treaty to mean when it gives its advice and consent, a meaning which is informed by reference to expressions of intent by the Senate as well as Senate acquiescence in any interpretation communicated by the Senate." And, to the extent such meaning is clear, "anything not transmitted to the Senate, including the negotiating record, is not relevant to the meaning of the treaty."[207]

Apart from the assumptions in this position of relevance to other sections of this part, it seems to embody an assumption that a "dual" standard of interpretation is constitutionally not only permissible but required. Similarly, the majority report of the Senate Foreign Relations Committee on *The ABM Treaty Interpretation Resolution* seems to embody a similar view. That report states in a section entitled "Evaluation of the Legal Adviser's Theory":

> The Committee recognizes the difficulty of the Legal Adviser's task in trying to justify a scheme by which the Senate's original understanding of a treaty may be regarded as irrelevant to its subsequent interpretation. The Legal Adviser's effort to do [sic] has

---

[207]Biden, "The Constitution and the ABM Treaty," *reprinted as* "Prepared Statement of Senator Joseph R. Biden, Jr.," introducing " the ABM Treaty Interpretation Resolution" (March 11, 1987) in *The ABM Treaty and the Constitution*, *supra* note 1, at 252, 262.

necessarily required a confused cobbling of arguments from constitutional and international law.

(a) Source of Meaning.--The Legal Adviser's principal premise is the equivocal assertion that a treaty's meaning derives from communications between the parties. This is true--under international law. But it is not true under United States law.

Under U.S. domestic law the governing rules are, by definition, those of the United States Constitution. The Constitution permits the incorporation into U.S. law of some principles of international law, but there is none that it *requires* be incorporated. Moreover, there is no requirement under international law that a nation give domestic force to the norms of international law. Consequently, the Legal Adviser's analysis, grounded as it is on international law, is entirely misdirected in shedding light on the requirements of treaty interpretation mandated by the Constitution.

Constitutionally, the President is required to respect the Senate's conditions when the Chief Executive ratifies a treaty following Senate advice and consent. The President cannot cause the United States to become a party to a treaty to which the Senate has not given its advice and consent. Nor can he cause the United States to become a party to a treaty different from the one to which the Senate has given its advice and consent. Thus, if the United States is to adhere to a given treaty, it can adhere only to the treaty concerning which a "meeting of the minds" has occured between the President and the Senate.

(b) Role of Senate.--In the implementation of this constitutional principle, the particular form of the Senate's understanding is not relevant. The Legal Adviser argues that the Senate knows how formally to condition its consent to a treaty and it knows how expressly to direct the President to respect such a condition, and that in the absence of either the President is free to disregard the Senate's understanding. But this assertion leads to absurdity.

Under the Sofaer theory, it matters not how fundamental the issue, or how clear and oft-expressed the Senate's understanding. If, for example, the text of a treaty appears to mean X, if the President personally assures the Senate that a treaty means X, if the Secretary of State and other executive branch spokesmen solemnly reiterate this assurance in hearings, if the report of the Foreign Relations Committee repeats that interpretation, and if 100 Senators take the Senate floor to state that their understanding is identical, a President would still, if guided by the Sofaer theory, feel free to ignore his earlier assurance and to disregard the Senate's understanding in bringing the treaty into force or in interpreting it later--unless the Senate had taken the bizarre step of *formally* conditioning its acceptance on its own extensive, elaborately worded, perhaps treaty-length rendering of interpretation X. According to the Sofaer theory, the President and his successors are not compelled constitutionally to honor the apparent meaning of a treaty text and the interpretation presented to the Senate during ratification proceedings.

Applying this theory to the ABM Treaty, Judge Sofaer hypothesizes that President Nixon--through negligence or inadvertence--brought into force a version of the ABM Treaty altogether different from the one described to the Senate by his representatives, that this was constitutionally permissible, and that the Reagan Administration has simply, years later, acted to correct an enormous misunderstanding. In the Committee's considered opinion, this is nonsense.

First, the U.S. "negotiating record" provides no serious evidence of the slightest divergence between the private understandings and public representations of the ABM Treaty negotiators. Based upon a review of that record by Committee members and staff, the Committee agrees with Senator Nunn that the "preponderance of evidence in the negotiating record supports the Senate's original understanding of the treaty--that is, the Traditional Interpretation," and concludes that Mr. Sofaer has engaged in an elaborate effort to rewrite history.

Second, contrary to Mr. Sofaer's contentions, a President's failure to respect the Senate's original understanding of the treaty, however manifested, would represent a grievous breach of his constitutional obligations. Professor Louis Henkin affirmed the President's obligation to respect implicit as well as explicit Senate understandings:

> It seems to be suggested . . . that if the Senate does not make its understanding a condition of its

> consent, how the Senate interpreted a treaty is essentially irrelevant. That is not correct. In my view, if the Senate's understanding is clear, the President can make the treaty only in accordance with that understanding, whether or not that understanding is expressed as a condition of consent. Indeed, if there is any reason to doubt that the Senate's understanding is shared by the other party or parties to the treaty, or if it appears that the Senate's understanding might somehow differ from what the treaty might be held to mean as a matter of international law, the President is bound to communicate the Senate's understanding as being the understanding of the United States when he make [sic] the treaty.

Professor Laurence Tribe added as follows:

> [Mr. Sofaer] presumes that the President unilaterally "makes" treaties with foreign nations which the Senate subsequently is asked to ratify. The Constitution provides otherwise. The President has the power to "make treaties" only "by and with the Advice and Consent of the Senate . . . provided two-thirds of the Senators present concur.["] No treaty is "made" until the Senate has given its consent. This is how a treaty becomes part of "the supreme Law of the Land."
>
> Under the Legal Adviser's model, the meaning of the ABM treaty is to be gleaned not by examination of what the President and the *Senate* agreed upon, but by examination of what the President and the *Soviets* agreed upon--regardless of what the President may or may not have told the Senate about what he had negotiated. *This is tantamount to saying that President Nixon made the ABM treaty the supreme law of the United States with the advice and consent of the Soviet Union.*

> Obviously, the ABM treaty that became law in 1972 was the ABM treaty, accompanied by various formal submissions, to which the Senate gave its consent. The Executive may not now unveil a hitherto secret record of negotiations or understandings to defend an interpretation of the law inconsistent with what the Senate was led to believe it was accepting. To allow such a ply would be to allow the Executive to make treaties *without* the advice and consent of the Senate. Nothing in the Legal Adviser's analysis makes this position plausible.

The absurdity of the assertion that the President must respect only formally-expressed Senate understandings was underscored by Professor Abram Chayes, who served as the State Department Legal Adviser under President Kennedy. What, he asked, is the Senate "to do when, as in the case of the ABM Treaty, there is no dispute about the meaning of the text and no wish to change the meaning?":

> The very absence of reservations or understandings itself confirms that the Senate understood the treaty to be susceptible of only one interpretation--the one that emerges from the plain meaning of the text and was confirmed by representatives of the Executive at the time of ratification. What is important about [the] ratification history of this Treaty is that it shows there was no issue of interpretation. Everyone agreed.

Under traditional U.S. practice, the Senate has used conditions--reservations, understandings, declarations, amendments, and the like--as a means of clarifying or altering the legal rights and obligations to be established by the treaty. However, if the text of a treaty is clear to the Senate, and if there is no disposition to alter the obligations entailed by the treaty, there is no reason for the Senate to append formal conditions to its resolution authorizing ratification.

> Consequently, the Legal Adviser's model would impose upon the Senate a requirement to perform practical acts of fundamental illogic: to express formal conditions concerning provisions of agreements about which there is no disagreement. And if the Senate failed to do so, those very matters--about which genuine consensus exists--would be most subject to subsequent "reinterpretation" by the President![208]

And in concluding the majority report states:

> The Committee can find no evidence to contradict the conclusion that the Reagan Administration's "reinterpretation" of the ABM Treaty constitutes the most flagrant abuse of the Constitution's treaty power in 200 years of American history.[209]

On the other hand, Senator Malcolm Wallop made a statement on the Senate floor on April 8, 1987, in which he said:

> . . . I cite the Senate's historical practice because a treaty was then, at it is now, in essence a contract between or among nations. It was inevitable that the custom was accepted in both the Senate and in international law that the deliberations upon the treaty within the Senate's committees or other internal deliberations of that body could not affect the nature of the contract between or among nations. Only the ratification of amendments or reservations together with the treaty could affect that nature. . . .[210]

---

[208]*The ABM Treaty Interpretation Resolution, supra* note 1, at 55-58. *See also id.* at 37-53, 58-62, in further developing this position. *And see* the excerpting of portions of this report and additional views of Senators Helms, Pressler, and Trible in "The ABM Treaty Interpretation Resolution," 82 *AM. J. Int'l L.* 151 (1988).

[209]*The ABM Treaty Interpretation Resolution, supra* note 1, at 66.

[210]Statement by Senator Malcolm Wallop on the ABM Treaty Negotiating Record, Wednesday, April 8, 1987.

Similarly, Senator Richard G. Lugar stated in his prepared statement introducing the Senate Foreign Relations Committee hearings on the constitutional aspects of the "broad-narrow" issue:

> The initial panel in this hearing is to address a very important aspect of the current debate about the interpretation of the ABM Treaty--namely, the proper standards under international and domestic law for the interpretation of treaties, and the Senate role in the treaty-making process.
>
> My understanding of the current state of the law is that, where the text of a treaty is not clear on its face, there are several sources of material that are relevant to determining the proper interpretation of the treaty. These include the negotiating record, the subsequent practice of the parties, and the record of the ratification proceedings.
>
> It is natural for Senate committees to have a particular interest in the record of the Senate ratification proceedings, since they embody the Senate's role in the treaty-making process. It is very important, however, that we keep in proper perspective the relative significance of those proceedings in the overall process of interpreting a treaty.
>
> The Senate does have the ability to attach conditions to its advice and consent to a treaty in its resolution of ratification, and the President has an obligation to adhere to them if they are within constitutional bounds. Beyond that, the Senate has a right to expect that the President will give appropriate weight to any understandings expressed during Senate proceedings, just as is the case for material in the legislative record of a statute.
>
> We should not forget, however, that a treaty is first and foremost an agreement between the governments which are party to it, and the basic object of the treaty interpretation is to determine what those parties intended the treaty to mean. The Senate's ratification proceedings may shed light on what one of the parties understood the treaty to mean, but statements made during internal ratification proceedings cannot bind any other party.
>
> In my view, the Resolution introduced by Chairman Biden does not give a fully accurate portrayal of these principles. It treats the process of treaty interpretation as though it were simply a matter

of determining what the Senate understood the treaty to mean during ratification. It says that the negotiating record is not relevant to the meaning of the treaty if the Senate's understanding is clear, and it even says that one may only refer to the text if there is no evidence as to what the Senate intended.

> All of this would, of course, come as an unpleasant surprise to other treaty partners, who are not bound under international law by what is said in our ratification proceedings, and who have every right to rely on what they actually negotiated with us. For our part, the United States would never accept the assertion by another country that it would disregard the treaty text and the record of its negotiation, in favor of the understanding of the treaty stated in its own internal ratification proceedings.
>
> The Biden resolution purports only to speak to what is required under the U.S. Constitution. Without agreeing with what the resolution says on this point, it simply does not provide us in any event with an adequate basis on which to make a sensible judgement on how to interpret a treaty. The purpose of a treaty is to establish mutual rights and obligations with a foreign government, in this case the Soviet Union. It does us no good whatsoever to attempt to impose limitations on the President based on what may have been stated during Senate proceedings, if the other party will not be bound by those limitations.
>
> Therefore I would oppose the Biden resolution. I think we should focus our attention on determining whether the Administration's views on the ABM Treaty are correct and sensible, taking into account all factors that are relevant under the law.[211]

Senator Ernest F. Hollings' prepared statement in testimony during these same hearings said:

> Senator Nunn bases his conclusions supporting the restrictive interpretation of the ABM Treaty almost exclusively on the Senate ratification proceedings. Such proceedings have the least probative utility for judging a treaty's meaning when the Senate fails

[211]"Prepared Statement of Senator Richard G. Lugar," in *The ABM Treaty and the Constitution, supra* note 1, at 435-37.

to make any such interpretation a part of its resolution of ratification, and especially when the treaty's wording is susceptible to objective interpretation and the negotiation record is clear. Rather than focusing on the ratification proceedings, he should have weighted the evidence of the Treaty text and the negotiation record in the first instance. Had that evidence offered up a convincing meaning, as it does, the ratification proceedings need only be referred to for consistency or deviation from the understanding of the Parties. . . . Even then, that record could not provide a basis for binding the Soviets to an understanding of which they were not formally informed. . . .

But Senator Nunn's legal analysis is backward; no one can seriously contend that the negotiation process in an arms control treaty is of lesser probative value that the ratification process. The second day Senator Nunn made a brief presentation of the actions of the parties subsequent to the Treaty and, almost as an afterthought, the third day he touched on the negotiation record, again quoting sources that have little probative value (his classified study of that record is still not available). I must state categorically to my colleagues that in an arms control treaty, the negotiation process cannot be disregarded and, indeed, often governs the result. You cannot get the true meaning or understand the content of any of our arms control treaties without a reference to the negotiation process. The Soviets accept this and have recently done so. Particularly is this true of the ABM Treaty. . . .

The Senate ratification proceedings cannot be used to prove the circumstances surrounding the Parties' understanding of the "context in which the written words were used." They can only give tentative indications of one Party's unilateral intentions, the least element of a last resort consideration. The President's critics attribute--erroneously--the far greatest weight to this element.

In no case can one sovereign nation be bound by the unilateral statements of another. There is no reason for the Soviets to accept these unilateral interpretations as an "instrument which was made by one or more parties in connection with the conclusion of the treaty and accepted by the other parties as an instrument related to the treaty." (Vienna Convention on the Law of Treaties, Article 31.) Even if a unilateral statement to the Senate were clear, it could not

> be considered an "instrument related to the treaty," and in any case it was not "accepted by the other parties."
>
> A claim is made by the President's critics (page S2981, Congressional Record, March 11, 1987) that a Soviet citizen was present during Senate hearings on the treaty; further, that his failure to speak binds the Soviets to the views being discussed--erroneously cast by Senator Nunn as "restrictive" views. It is the ultimate naivete to claim that Moscow was bound by its silence to something heard by some Soviet official in an internal U.S. forum. Taking this point one step further, why would a Soviet official object to a unilateral decision by the U.S. to abide by a provision not required by a Treaty? Obviously, it's to the Soviet's advantage and to our detriment. . . .[212]

And the minority report to the Senate Foreign Relations Committee report on *The ABM Treaty Interpretation Resolution* containing the additional views of Senators Helms, Pressler, and Trible says:

> Where the Senate as a body does not condition its advice and consent to ratification upon an amendment to the treaty, reservation, or qualification of the resolution of ratification, the internal deliberations of a Senate committee may have only a supplementary, probative value in ascertaining the meaning of the terms of a treaty, if the meaning of the terms in the treaty instruments, as supplemented by the generally more pertinent preparatory work on the treaty, remains unclear. Internal Senate deliberations may be utilized as supplementary means of interpretation, per Article 32 of the Vienna Convention.
>
> When the terms of a treaty are explained by a report of a committee of the Senate, the report of the committee is neither binding on the United States nor on other parties but it may constitute a supplementary means of ascertaining the agreement of the parties. . . .
>
> By passing a "clean" resolution of ratification, the Senate had no reason to and did not instruct the President to communicate

---

[212]"Prepared Statement of Senator Ernest F. Hollings," in *The ABM Treaty and the Constitution, supra* note 1, at 442, 448, 450, 459-60.

> any particular interpretation of the obligations under the treaty respecting future-type OPP ABM systems. Even had the Senate acted as a body to qualify its consent to ratification, which it did not, the failure to communicate that qualification to the President, and from the President to the other treaty party, would have the effect of deleting the qualification from the treaty obligations.
>
> It was, in 1972, settled law that a proviso adopted by the Senate to qualify a treaty, if excluded from the instruments of ratification, and not communicated to the other treaty party, will have no legal effect on the other treaty party. This is still settled law today.[213]

These statements seem, at least implicitly, to support a unitary approach to the question of the standard for interpreting a treaty. That is, the single appropriate standard is the international standard and we look to that standard to ascertain, simultaneously for both national and international law, the weight, if any, to be accorded Senate internal deliberations not leading to formally communicated amendments, reservations, provisos or understandings and, of course, the ultimate interpretation of the treaty.

Even though this issue has not always been explicitly joined in the "broad-narrow" debate it is central to the opposing positions. As such, it may be helpful to more fully present the arguments for both constitutional positions and then to assess which seems the stronger. In doing so it should be understood that in many respects this is a case of first impression under the American constitutional system and that some modesty in degree of conviction might be in order, as opposed to rhetoric about a "constitutional crisis."

arguments for "dual" standards

constitutional theory

[213]"Additional Views of Senators Helms, Pressler, and Trible," entitled "The Anti-Ballistic Missile Treaty of 1972: Treaty Formation and Interpretation Under the U.S. Constitution," in *The ABM Treaty Interpretation Resolution*, *supra* note 1, at 89, 94-95 (paragraph numbers omitted) (emphasis in original).

The principal underlying theoretical argument for the constitutional correctness of the "dual" standards approach seems of be that since treaties are only made "by and with the Advice and Consent of the Senate" the only treaty that can be made is that understood and consented to by the Senate. In the language of the recent report of the Senate Foreign Relations Committee on *The ABM Treaty Interpretation Resolution*:

> Constitutionally, the President is required to respect the Senate's conditions when the Chief Executive ratifies a treaty following Senate advice and consent. The President cannot cause the United States to become a party to a treaty to which the Senate has not given its advice and consent. Nor can he cause the United States to become a party to a treaty different from the one to which the Senate has given its advice and consent. Thus, if the United States is to adhere to a given treaty, it can adhere only to the treaty concerning which a "meeting of the minds" has occurred between the President and the Senate.[214]

primary authorities

Proponents of the "dual" standards approach seem not yet to have found or cited any Supreme Court decision adopting the "dual" approach. Supreme Court cases, of course, are of particular importance on constitutional issues. Nor do such proponents seem yet to have found any primary legal authority even analogously supporting the "dual" approach in a setting of divergence between the international meaning of a treaty and an informal Senate understanding or Executive branch representation. It should be understood, however, that the apparent scarcity of clear primary authority for this approach is, by itself, not determinative. In many respects this issue seems to be a case of first impression and there are two recent opinions, including a 1989 decision of the Supreme Court, that lend analogous support to the "dual" approach.

One recent District Court case that does lend support to the "dual" approach, and which itself seems to have both drawn upon and in turn been featured in the "broad-narrow" treaty debate, is the 1988 case of *Rainbow Navigation, Inc. v.*

---

[214]*The ABM Treaty Interpretation Resolution, supra* note 1, at 56.

Department of the Navy,[215] currently on appeal. This case involved a suit by Rainbow Navigation against the Department of the Navy growing out of implementation of the September 24, 1986, "Treaty Between the United States and Iceland to Facilitate Their Defense Relationship" and against a background of protracted litigation between the parties.

In a decision on May 17, 1988, granting a preliminary injunction for Rainbow Navigation, Judge Harold H. Greene found that the treaty was self-executing and that the "construction . . . [of the treaty] by the Navy is contrary to the ordinary meaning of the language." In that setting he wrote, of relevance for the "dual" approach:

> Perhaps even more significant than the treaty language are the representations made by Executive Branch officials to the United States Senate in connection with the ratification proceedings. These statements, discussed below, clearly support the interpretation that rights would vest without further legislation, for the officials represented to the Senate that if ratified, the treaty would protect the existing U.S.-flag presence on the United States-Iceland route.
>
> Thus, at the hearings on ratification of the treaty, the Honorable Edward J. Derwinski, Counselor of the Department of State, with Rear Admiral Walter T. Piotti, Jr., Commander of the Military Sealift Command, at his side, assured the Senate that he agreed with the statement by American maritime organizations of which the following paragraph is a part:

---

[215]Rainbow Navigation, Inc. v. Department of the Navy, Civil Action No. 88-0992 (HHG) (D.D.C. Nov. 15, 1988) (merits) (699 F. Supp. 339 (D.D.C. 1988)). Rainbow Navigation, Inc. v. Department of the Navy, 686 F. Supp. 354 (D.D.C. 1988) (preliminary injunction); 783 F.2d 1072 (D.C. Cir. 1986); 620 F. Supp. 534 (D.D.C. 1985).

For an analysis of the *Rainbow Navigation* case supporting its importance for the "dual" approach after the May 17 decision and before that of November 15, see R. Earle & D. Koplow, *Analysis: Of Arms Pacts and Ocean Routes: Sofaer Doctrine on Rocks*, Legal Times, Aug. 22, 1988, at 14-15. ("Now a judge has spoken: It may be convenient for presidents to reinterpret ratified treaties to conform to a political agenda--but it's also against the law." Id. at 14.) This comment was apparently written before an appeal was filed by the Justice Department in the *Rainbow Navigation* case.

> The Administration must further assure that the Treaty, if ratified, will be implemented in such a fashion that the existing United States-flag service in the Iceland trade will not be disadvantaged. In other words, the United States-flag presence and the maritime employment will be maintained just as if the 1904 Act were fully in effect in the Iceland trade.

Similarly, on the question as to how the treaty would affect Rainbow, the only U.S.-flag carrier on that route, Senator Mathias asked and Mr. Derwinski replied:

> SENATOR MATHIAS: What about the current American flag carrier? Are there any plans in effect to save harmless the current cargo carrier that is now carrying supplies to the [U.S.] military base in Iceland?
>
> DERWINSKI: My understanding is that the current carrier has been involved in a number of discussions with appropriate authorities, and despite the fact that we could not provide, obviously, within the treaty for specific protection for an entity, we did have in mind at all times the need *to protect the interests of the current carrier* (emphasis added).

Relying in part upon these representations, the Senate Foreign Relations Committee recommended that the Senate ratify the treaty. In fact, the Committee stated in its report to the full Senate that advice and consent were being conditioned upon three assurances given by the Departments of State and Defense, one of them being that

> the treaty will be implemented in such a way that the existing United States-flag service in the Iceland trade would not be disadvantaged as a result of the Treaty. The Committee received these assurances

> at its hearing and recommends advice and consent on that basis only.

Two days after the Committee Report was issued, and on the day the Treaty was ratified, Senator Pell repeated this condition of ratification on the Senate floor.

This history clearly shows that the Senate was concerned about protecting the interests of the current American carrier; that to give meaning to that concern, it intended the treaty to provide that protection without further requirements; and that the Executive Branch agreed.[216]

And in a footnote Judge Greene wrote:

> **17.** The Department of Justice disavowed in court the representations made by the Navy and the Department of State to the Senate during treaty ratification proceedings as merely "precatory" and "non-binding." Hearing on Rainbow's motion for a temporary restraining order, April 15, 1988. This position is disturbing since it undercuts the foundation upon which Senate ratification was based, at least in part. As Professor Henkin recently testified:
>
> > The President can only make a treaty that means what the Senate understood the treaty to mean when the Senate gave its consent . . . The Senate's understanding of the treaty to which it[s] consent is binding on the President. He can make the treaty only as so understood. He cannot make the treaty and insist that it means something else . . . the Constitution clearly implies that it is what the Senate understands the treaty to mean--that is what the treaty means for purposes of its consent.
>
> The ABM Treaty Interpretation Resolution, Report of the Committee on Foreign Relations United States Senate, S.Rep. No. 164, 100th Cong., 1st Sess. 49 (1987). *See also* Restatement (Second) Foreign

---

[216]686 F. Supp. at 357-58 (footnotes omitted).

> Relations Law of the United States (Revised), Tentative Draft No. 6 (1985), §314, comment d and §314(2).[217]

Finally, in concluding Judge Greene wrote:

> The Court understands that Iceland is a staunch ally of the United States, and it sympathizes with the efforts of our government to satisfy the demands of that nation. But this may not be done at the expense of one of the few remaining American-flag vessels of our merchant marine and the few remaining American seamen who have found employment there. More particularly, this may not be done in violation of American law, of the language and purpose of a treaty, and of the solemn representations made to the United States Senate in connection with the ratification of that treaty.[218]

It should be noted that this was *not* a case in which Judge Greene found a discrepancy between the international meaning of the treaty and either an informal Senate understanding or an Executive branch representation to the Senate during advice and consent. Rather, both the Executive branch representations to the Senate and the even stronger indications of concern expressed "informally" within the Senate process supported his conclusion from the Treaty language on both interpretation issues as to whether the Treaty was self-executing and whether it contemplated only a single competition for maritime cargo. It should also be noted, as will be discussed subsequently, that the only authority cited by Judge Greene as supporting his relevant statements were the secondary authorities of Professor Henkin testifying on the ABM Treaty Interpretation Resolution and a tentative draft of section 314 of the *Restatement of the Foreign Relations Law of the United States* whose Chief Reporter was Professor Henkin. And it should be noted that this case involved not only an Executive branch representation as to implementation of the Treaty but one which was made by the chief United States negotiator of the Treaty and which was reflected in the Senate Foreign Relations Committee report in the strong language: "The Committee received these assurances at its hearing and

---

[217]686 F. Supp. at 357 n.17.

[218]686 F. Supp. at 361.

recommends advice and consent on that basis only."[219] Finally, it should be noted that the Executive branch representations *and* Senate informal record seemed to principally concern assurances concerning *domestic implementation* of the Treaty rather than specific treaty interpretations.

Coming during the debate on the INF Treaty interpretation condition and on the eve of the vote on that condition, Judge Greene's decision, which had already been influenced by the "broad-narrow" debate, itself became a talking point in that debate. Thus, the *New York Times* editorialized on May 25, 1988:

> The Treaty and Its Enemies
>
> For a while, it looked as though several willful men could derail the Euromissile treaty and President Reagan's wish to make the treaty a centerpiece of his summit meeting in Moscow next week. Two of them are Jesse Helms and Gordon Humphrey, Republican Senators who have been trying to obstruct ratification with one niggling amendment after another.
>
> Their obstructionism now seems to have been swept away, leaving just one willful man blocking fulfillment of President Reagan's wish: President Reagan.
>
> If only he would now agree to a simple, honorable proposition - that the Administration means what it says to the Senate - the treaty will be his.
>
> This final obstacle arises from the Administration's devotion to Star Wars. Wanting to conduct tests prohibited by the Antiballistic Missile Treaty when it was presented to the Senate under President Nixon, the Reagan Administration hit on a novel idea: reinterpret the treaty. The State Department's legal adviser, Abraham Sofaer, obliged with an opinion saying that what an Administration tells the Senate about a treaty's meaning is not necessarily binding.
>
> This expedient assault on the Senate's treaty responsibilities understandably offended the Foreign Relations Committee. It approved this treaty to eliminate Soviet and U.S. missiles with ranges of 300 to 3,400 miles and attached only one condition: Testimony to the Senate on the treaty's meaning is indeed binding.

---

[219] 686 F. Supp. at 358.

> The need for such explicit reassurance was shown anew in a little-noticed Federal court case decided last week that demonstrated the Administration's determination to revise treaties as it wishes. In this case, it tried to reinterpret an obscure treaty concerning Iceland; Judge Harold Greene told a Justice Department attorney, "You are taking the same position that the State Department is taking on the [Euromissile] treaty, that whatever is said to the Senate doesn't mean anything." The judge held that reinterpretations may not violate "the solemn representations" made to the Senate.
>
> Unless the Administration is willing to reassure the Senate as to the integrity of its role in treaty-making, the ratification Mr. Reagan seeks is unlikely. But once reassurance is given, ratification will follow swiftly and overwhelmingly.
>
> The United States has not ratified an arms control treaty for 16 years. This treaty richly warrants ratification. It requires the Soviet Union to destroy missiles that can carry four times as many nuclear warheads as the missiles to be destroyed by the U.S. It is the most thoroughly examined, exhaustively detailed arms control pact in history.
>
> Mr. Reagan can win rousing Senate backing for this sound treaty, and add the final seal of approval in Moscow, just as he hopes. He need only agree that when his Administration tells the Senate what the treaty means, it means what it says.[220]

And the next day the decision was placed in the *Congressional Record* by supporters and opponents alike of the INF Treaty condition and invoked in the debate in support of that condition.[221] Thus, Senator Nunn said as part of a more general argument in support of the INF Treaty condition:

> Now that the treaty interpretation condition has performed its service and brought us to the point where timely Senate consent is virtually assured, there are some who have suggested that we

---

[220] *The Treaty and Its Enemies*, N.Y. Times, May 25, 1988, at A26, col. 1 (editorial desk, late city final ed.).

[221] *See* 134 *Cong. Rec.* S6756-58, S6772-90 (daily ed. May 26, 1988).

should strip it from the resolution of ratification and rely on the good faith of the executive branch. Should anyone doubt that the Sofaer doctrine is alive and well, they need only consider the position that the executive branch has taken in a case entitled Rainbow Navigation, Inc. versus Department of the Navy, decided only last week in the District Court for the District of Columbia.

The *Rainbow Navigation* case involved a 1986 treaty between the United States and Iceland regarding allocation of shipping rights. An American carrier, Rainbow Navigation, alleged that the Navy planned to administer the rights in a manner that would prejudice the interests of American shipping protected by the treaty, and a preliminary injunction was granted by Judge Harold Greene.

In the course of his opinion, Judge Greene noted that the administration had expressly testified on the issue in question:

> Perhaps even more significant than the treaty language are the representations made by Executive Branch officials to the United States Senate in connection with the ratification proceedings. These statements * * * clearly support the interpretation that rights would vest without further legislation, for the officials represented to the Senate that if ratified, the treaty would protect the existing U.S. flag presence on the United States-Iceland route.

Judge Greene noted that during the litigation, the administration "disavowed in court the representations made by the Navy and the Department of State to the Senate during treaty ratification proceedings as merely `precatory' and `nonbinding.'"

When you tell the court that your testimony before the Senate Foreign Relations Committee on a treaty is merely precatory and nonbinding, you have indeed undermined not only the Senate as an institution but the whole treaty ratification process as set forth in the U.S. Constitution. So this is not a trivial matter.

The executive branch's position in the Rainbow Navigation case illustrates very well the administration's utter contempt for the ratification process.

This was not an ancient treaty or an agreement negotiated by a different administration. This was a case in which the current administration found it convenient to disavow its own testimony less than 2 years after it was presented to the Senate.

What is particularly damning about the Rainbow Navigation case is the fact that the administration's testimony to the Senate on the Iceland treaty was, in the now-famous words of the Culvahouse letter, "clearly intended, generally understood, and relied upon by the Senate in its advice and consent to ratification" and hence binding on the President "as a matter of domestic law." As Judge Greene noted in his opinion:

> Relying on these representations, the Senate Foreign Relations Committee recommended that the Senate ratify the treaty. In fact, the committee stated in its report to the full Senate that advice and consent were being conditioned upon * * * assurances given by the Departments of State and Defense * * *.

By adopting a position in the Rainbow Navigation case that deviates even from the statements made by the administration in the Culvahouse letter, the administration has made it very clear to us that we obviously cannot rely on letters or memos as the basis for precluding reinterpretation of the INF Treaty by a future administration.

This Justice Department simply has no sense of shame. At the very height of the controversy over treaty interpretation, it has had no compunction about telling a Federal court that when the executive branch represents the meaning of a treaty to the Senate, it can say whatever it wants and then disavow it shortly after ratification. Without a treaty interpretation provision, we have nothing to prevent the executive branch from walking away from its INF testimony in less than a year. It is essential that we condition our consent to the treaty upon the agreement of the executive branch

> to abide by the meaning of the treaty as presented to us in our hearings.
>
> Without a treaty interpretation provision, we have nothing to prevent the executive branch from walking away from its testimony on INF in less than a year. I do not think that is going to happen, but certainly this provision would ensure that it does not happen.
>
> In the future this amendment, which has bipartisan support, will be deemed to have set forth not a new law, not something that is new, not a new constitutional principle, but rather a reaffirmation of what the law of the land and the Constitution of the United States have provided for all of these years.
>
> This is not a new departure. It is really unfortunate that we are even having to deal with it because it is so clearly based on history, based on the U.S. Constitution, based on the laws of the land, based on the role of the Senate as an institution, and based on pure common sense and comity between the executive branch and the Senate as an institution.[222]

When the case next came before Judge Greene for a decision on the merits he seemed to pick up on these issues of the effect of Executive branch representations and informal Senate understandings and to give them greater prominence in his decision for *Rainbow Navigation*. Thus, in his decision on the merits of November 15, 1988, he wrote:

> In order to understand the current phase of the dispute between the parties, it is necessary to discuss the proceedings in the United States Senate in connection with the ratification of the Icelandic treaty.
>
> The first question to be considered in that connection is a legal one -- what is the effect of representations made by the Executive Branch to the Senate? Although when this litigation was before the Court last Spring the government took the position that the representations made in connection with the treaty ratification proceedings were merely "precatory" and "non-binding," Rainbow III, supra, 686 F. Supp. at 357 n.17, this apparently is no longer the

[222] 134 Cong. Rec. S6774-75 (daily ed. May 26, 1988) (statement of Sen. Nunn).

government's view. The Court rejected that position, and the government now appears to disavow it, stating that

> . . . authoritative Executive branch representations concerning the meaning of a Treaty which form part of the basis upon which the Senate gives advice and consent are entitled to be accorded binding weight as a matter of domestic constitutional law, and the Executive branch fully accepts that it is bound by such statements . . . .

Defendants' Reply Brief and Opposition to Plaintiff's Cross-Motion for Summary Judgment at 2 n.2.

This Court has no doubt about the obligation of the Executive Branch to stand behind the representations made by its officials to the Senate committee having jurisdiction, and to comply with the conditions attached, formally or informally, by the Senate as part of its ratification. Any other rule would undermine the authority of the Senate under Article 2 section 2 of the Constitution to concur or to fail to concur in treaties made by the Chief Executive. If, following ratification, the Executive could unilaterally change the meaning of a treaty as it had been presented to the Senate, the careful consideration the Senate gives to treaty language, purposes, and effect, would stand in constant peril of nullification by reinterpretation by Executive officials, high or low.

It is appropriate, then, to consider exactly what representations were made by the Executive Branch witnesses regarding the meaning and effect of the Iceland treaty, and what conditions or understandings were arrived at as part of the ratification process.

The principal Executive Branch witnesses who testified before the Senate Committee on Foreign Relations on the Icelandic treaty were the Hon. Edward J. Derwinski, Counselor of the Department of State, and Rear Admiral Walter T. Piotti, Jr., Commander of the Navy's Military Sealift Command. Senator Mathias asked the witnesses about the "current American flag carrier," i.e., Rainbow, and whether any plans were in effect to "save harmless the current cargo carrier." Mr. Derwinski replied to this query with two assurances: (1) that carrier has been involved in a number of discussions with appropriate authorities, and (2) although the Department obviously could not provide in the treaty for specific protection for an entity, "we did have in mind at all time the need to protect the interests of the current carrier" (emphasis added).

While this language suggests that Rainbow had been a party to discussions regarding the appropriate way of implementing the treaty (and by inference that there was agreement with the plans made with respect thereto), and that the Department was mindful of the need "to protect the interests" of Rainbow and to "save [it] harmless," these assurances were apparently not deemed to be sufficiently airtight by Rainbow and those who were supporting its cause.

Accordingly, language was included in the Senate Report which recommended ratification of the treaty to make more explicit the requirement that Rainbow was to be protected, as follows:

> [T]he committee recommends that the Senate advise and consent only with the assurances of the Departments of State and Defense that . . . the treaty will be implemented in such a way that the existing United States-flag service in the Iceland trade would not be disadvantaged as a result of the treaty. The Committee received those assurances at its hearing, and recommends advice and consent on that basis only.
>
> The Committee understands and expects that the economic viability of the United States-flag service will be maintained as if the 1904 Act were fully in effect in the Iceland trade.

S. Rep. No. 27, 99th Cong., 2d Sess. 2 (1986). at 3.

This was not a unilateral Senate declaration; Mr. Derwinski, the principal Administration witness, testified: "I have seen the language which is proposed for your committee report, yes, sir. And I have absolutely no objections to it."

> The Court concludes that, insofar as the United States government is concerned, the treaty includes two undertakings: first, that the existing United States-flag service in the Iceland trade would not be disadvantaged as a result of the treaty; and second, that the economic viability of that service will be maintained just as if the 1904 Act were fully in effect. The issue before the Court is whether the method chosen by the Navy in the proposed RFP for implementing the treaty is consistent with these undertakings.[223]

In five significant footnotes Judge Greene wrote:

> [15] The same position has also been rejected by eminent authorities in other contexts. See The ABM Treaty Interpretation Resolution, Report of the Committee on Foreign Relations, United States Senate, S. Rep. No. 164 (100th Cong., 1st Sess. 49 (citing testimony of Prof. Henkin) (1987). See also, Restatement (Second) Foreign Relations Law of the United States (Revised), Tentative Draft No. 6 (1985), §314 (comment d and §314(2); and see also, 134 Cong. Rec. S6774-75 (daily ed. May 26, 1988) (statement of Sen. Nunn) (government's position in Rainbow that treaty testimony is nonbinding "undermined not only the Senate as an institution but the whole treaty ratification process as set forth in the U.S. Constitution").
>
> [16] However, on this issue as on the issue of the requirement of a single competition (see notes 11 and 12, supra), the government's position is still either shifting or equivocal. Thus, the government has observed that Executive statements should be given binding weight only when they were "authoritatively and explicitly communicated to the Senate by the Executive and were part of the basis on which the Senate granted its consent . . . ." Further, referring to Mr. Derwinski's "save harmless" statement (see p. 11, infra), the government asserts that his statement "imposes no binding obligations on the government" (emphasis added). Defendants' Reply Brief to Intervenor Eimskip's Response at 2 n.1. These

[223]Civil Action No. 88-0992 (HHG) (U.S. District Court for the District of Columbia, Nov. 15, 1988) at 8-14 (footnotes omitted).

assertions appear to be crafted to construct yet another avenue of retreat from commitments made to the Senate.

As indicated below, Counselor Derwinski and Admiral Piotti represented the Executive Branch before the Senate Committee on Foreign Relations. It would be seriously misleading to the Senate and disruptive of the constitutional ratification process if it were to be accepted that some representations made to that legislative body by witnesses such as these were deemed authoritative but not others, depending upon a subsequent decision of members of the Executive Branch.

[17] As indicated below, the Senate Committee on Foreign Relations recommended advice and consent to the Icelandic treaty only on the basis of the Executive assurances made regarding Rainbow.

[18] The Senate Committee on Foreign Relations has stated in connection with the debate over the ABM treaty, the Executive's unilateral reinterpretation of treaties "assaults the Constitution's allocation of the treaty power," "disparages the Constitution's requirement that the President take care that the laws be faithfully executed" and "denigrates the central precept of international order -- the principle that treaty obligations are to be carried out in good faith." Senate Committee on Foreign Relations, The ABM Treaty Interpretation Resolution, S. Rep. No. 164, 100th Cong., 1st Sess. 47 (1987).

[23] Senator Pell reiterated during the floor debate that the Executive had "assured the Committee that the Treaty will be implemented in such a way that the existing Icelandic trade would not be disadvantaged." 132 Cong. Rec. S15661 (daily ed. October 8, 1986).[224]

And Judge Greene concluded in general terms about the case:

[224] *Id.* at 9 nn.15-18, 13 n.23.

This case presents a sorry saga of duplicity. What is particularly mystifying about its history is why the government, acting through the Departments of the Navy and Justice, persists with iron determination to put out of business a small American maritime carrier in order to please foreign shipping interests, and why this is being done at a time when America's merchant marine has been decimated and most of its merchant seamen have lost their jobs to those working on foreign flag vessels.

As the above recitation of events demonstrates, this governmental effort has proceeded systematically now for over three years, buttressed by false sworn statements, and notwithstanding law, regulation, treaty obligation, and solemn undertaking. As a consequence of this effort, a small American corporation has had to fight for its life and the livelihood of its sailors, no doubt at great and potentially crippling expense, again and again and yet twice again. The arrogance of power has seldom been displayed in more telling fashion.

Much has been said and written in recent years, some of it well justified, about the intrusion of the Judiciary into areas of policy-making that are properly reserved to the political branches of government. But the courts legitimately can and must perform the function of calling a halt when governmental officials, in the name of Executive prerogative, oppress citizens in violation of law, regulation, and plain fair dealing. Certainly the courts have an obligation to provide the protective umbrella of the law when, as here, either for foreign policy advantage or simply out of pique at resistance by means of litigation, the Executive denies to a small American company the rights granted to it, as to all citizens, under law.

Oliver Wendell Holmes, one of our most distinguished jurists, said sixty years ago certain governmental action injurious to citizens would not be countenanced "while this Court sits." That principle, which has been invoked several times since then in other cases involving the protection of citizens' rights, is still alive, and not merely at the level of the Supreme Court.

> A permanent injunction prohibiting implementation of the latest set of measures adopted by the Navy is being issued contemporaneously herewith.[225]

Because Judge Greene directly addressed and gave prominence to several central tenets of the "dual" approach as incorporated in the INF Treaty condition, this District Court decision--currently on appeal--lends significant support to that approach. Thus, he said:

> This Court has no doubt about the obligation of the Executive Branch to stand behind the representations made by its officials to the Senate committee having jurisdiction, and to comply with the conditions attached, formally or informally, by the Senate as part of its ratification. Any other rule would undermine the authority of the Senate under Article 2 section 2 of the Constitution to concur or to fail to concur in treaties made by the Chief Executive.[226]

This sweeping language, however, should be placed in overall context in which Judge Greene had earlier held that the language of the Treaty and the Executive branch representations were consistent, his note 17 to this language reflecting the report of the Foreign Relations Committee on the Treaty that "the Senate Committee on Foreign Relations recommended advice and consent to the Icelandic treaty only on the basis of the Executive assurances made regarding Rainbow," and the seeming focus of the case on domestic implementation of the Treaty rather than any treaty dispute with Iceland.

The second judicial authority arguably lending at least analogous support to the "dual" approach is footnote 7 in the opinion of the Supreme Court in the recent case of *United States v. Stuart*.[227] The *Stuart* case involved whether there was any bar under either domestic law or the 1942 Convention Respecting Double Taxation between the United States and Canada for the Internal Revenue Service to honor a Canadian request for information under the 1942 Convention without first

---

[225] *Id.* at 28-30 (footnotes omitted).

[226] *Id.* at 10 (footnote 17 omitted).

[227] United States v. Stuart (U.S. Supreme Court, No. 87-1064, Feb. 28, 1989).

determining that Revenue Canada's investigation had not reached a stage analogous to a Justice Department referral by the IRS. The Court held that there was no bar to honoring the Canadian request for information either under domestic legislation or under the treaty. There was no hint in the case of any underlying dispute between Canada and the United States over the interpretation of the treaty nor was there any evidence that the proper international interpretation was inconsistent with either an informal Senate understanding or an Executive branch statement to the Senate during the preratification process. Indeed, the Court pointed out that: "The Senate Committee on Foreign Relations did not hold hearings on the Convention prior to its ratification in 1942, and the Committee Report did not even mention the provisions for exchange of information."[228] The Court, however, did discuss the sketchy preratification (treaty history) record in the Senate, saying: "The sole reference to these provisions during the brief floor debate in the Senate contained no hint that the 1942 Convention was intended to incorporate domestic restrictions on the issuance of summonses by the IRS in connection with American tax investigations, such as the limitation later codified in §7602(c)."[229] In a footnote 7 to this use of "treaty history" materials, the Court defended the permissibility of its reliance on preratification materials as one element in treaty interpretation. It said:

> Contrary to JUSTICE SCALIA'S suggestion, see post, at 8, the Solicitor General relied on the preratification Senate debate in his brief, see Brief for United States 29, and n. 11, pointing out that the only reference to intergovernmental exchanges of information came in the following colloquy:
>
> "Mr. TAFT . . .
>
> "In other words, if an American citizen were using a Canadian bank deposit to evade income taxation, I think the convention would permit the United States Government to ask the Canadian Government to obtain information from its own bank and furnish it to this Government in connection with the enforcement of our internal-revenue laws.
>
> "Mr. GEORGE. It does provide for exchange of information, as the Senator from Ohio points out." 88 Cong. Rec. 4714 (1942).

---

228 *Id.* at 12 (Brennan, J., Opinion of the Court).

229 *Id.* at 12.

Nor is reliance on the Senate's preratification debates and reports improper. As JUSTICE SCALIA acknowledges, the American Law Institute's most recent Restatement counsels consideration of such materials. See Restatement (Third) of the Foreign Relations Law of the United States§314, Comment *d* (1987) ("indication that . . . the Senate ascribed a particular meaning to the treaty is relevant"); *id.*,§325, Reporter's Note 5 ("A court . . . is required to take into account . . . (i) Committee reports, debates, and other indications of meaning that the legislative branch has attached to an agreement . . ."). Consultation of these materials is eminently reasonable. *Pace* JUSTICE SCALIA, reviewing preratification Senate debates and reports is not akin to "determining the meaning of a bilateral contract between two corporations on the basis of what the Board of Directors of one of them thought it meant when authorizing the Chief Executive Officer to conclude it." *Post*, at 4. Senate debates do not occur behind closed doors, out of earshot of proposed treaty partners, nor are preratification Senate reports kept under seal. Both are public statements. They therefore bear no resemblance to the private deliberations of a Board of Directors prior to the Board's decision whether to authorize the Chief Executive Officer to sign an agreement. Insofar as the contract analogy is apt, the better comparison is to a meeting of the Board whose minutes and position papers the other corporation's Board and Chief Executive Officer are invited to peruse. It is hornbook contract law that the proper construction of an agreement is that given by one of the parties when "that party had no reason to know of any different meaning attached by the other, and the other had reason to know the meaning attached by the first party." Restatement (Second) of Contracts§201(2)(b) (1981). See also E. Farnsworth, Contracts 487-488 (1982). A treaty's negotiating history, which JUSTICE SCALIA suggests would be a better interpretive guide than preratification Senate materials, see *post*, at 4, would in fact be a worse indicator of a treaty's meaning, for that history is rarely a matter of public record available to the Senate when it decides to grant or withhold its consent.[230]

[230] *Id.* at 12 n.7.

The thrust of this footnote is clearly to defend the proposition that reliance on Senate preratification materials is not improper. As has been seen, this is *not* the core issue in the "dual" versus "unitary" debate about the proper approach to treaty interpretation under the Constitution. Nevertheless, it can be argued that the footnote lends at least analogous support to the "dual" approach by citing section 314 of the *Restatement (Third)* and by saying in the last sentence of the footnote: "A treaty's negotiating history, which JUSTICE SCALIA suggests would be a better interpretive guide than preratification Senate materials, . . . would in fact be a worse indicator of a treaty's meaning, for that history is rarely a matter of public record available to the Senate when it decides to grant or withhold its consent."

While the limitations on any effect of this footnote at least arguably in support of the "dual" approach will be discussed more fully in the section of this part on "rebuttal of arguments for the 'dual' approach," it should be noted here that in addition to its principal thrust as simply supporting the separate issue that reliance on Senate preratification materials is not improper in treaty interpretation cases, several other factors also limit the legal effect of this footnote. These include that any broader effect for this footnote could at most be dictum since, as has been seen, there was no evidence in the case of any difference between the appropriate international interpretation of the treaty and either an informal Senate understanding or an Executive branch statement, and that three justices either demurred on or disagreed with the footnote, pointing out in two separate concurring opinions either that the issue was not ripe for decision in this case or that it had not been briefed and argued before the Court.[231] Even more importantly, the opinion of the six justices embodying footnote 7 seems in at least two places in the opinion to embody a standard of treaty interpretation rooted in the intent of the parties[232] and the opinion explicitly endorses reliance on subsequent practice of the parties which, by

---

[231]See the separate concurring (in part) opinions of Justices Kennedy and O'Connor. "I agree with JUSTICE SCALIA that we should not reach, either in a direct or an implicit way, the question whether Senate debates or ratification are authoritative or even helpful in determining what the signatories to a treaty intended. That determination should be reserved until we confront a case where the language of the treaty itself does not yield a clear answer to the question before us." *Id.* (Kennedy & O'Connor, JJ., concurring). And the separate opinion concurring in the judgment of the Court, by Justice Scalia, both suggests that the issue is not ripe for decision in the *Stuart* case and that preratification Senate materials should not be relied on in treaty interpretation. *Id.* (Scalia, J., concurring).

[232] *See* the opinion of the Court, *id.* at 11, 14-15.

definition, could not be before a Senate during consideration for advice and consent.[233] These premises would not seem consistent with an approach that it is solely the intent of the Senate or a statement by an Executive branch official to the Senate that would be controlling on treaty interpretation.

secondary authorities

The principal secondary authority on which the "dual" approach might be inferred seems to be the revised *Restatement of the Foreign Relations Law of the United States,*[234] which, as finalized, became the *Restatement (Third).*[235] Section 314(2) of the *Revised Restatement* provides:

> When the Senate gives its advice and consent to a treaty on the basis of a particular understanding of its meaning, the President, if he makes the treaty, must do so on the basis of the Senate's understanding.[236]

Comment d to this section provides:

> A treaty ratified (or acceded to) by the United States with a statement of understanding becomes effective in domestic law (§131) subject to that understanding. If no such statement is made, indication in the record that the Senate ascribed a particular meaning to the treaty is relevant to the interpretation of the treaty by a United States court in much the same way that the legislative history of a statute is relevant to its interpretation. See §325, Reporters' Note 5.
>
> Although the Senate's resolution of consent may contain no statement of understanding, there may be such statements in the

---

[233] *See* the opinion of the Court, *id.* at 14-15.

[234] *1985 Revised Restatement, supra* note 187.

[235] *American Law Institute,* 1 *Restatement of the Law Third, The Foreign Relations Law of the United States* (1987) [hereinafter *Restatement (Third)*].

[236] *1985 Revised Restatement, supra* note 187, §314, at 80.

> report of the Senate Foreign Relations Committee or in the Senate debates. In such case, the President must decide whether they represent a general understanding by the Senate and if he finds that they do, must respect them in good faith.[237]

Reporters' Note 5 to section 325, "Interpretation of International Agreements," of the *Restatement (Third)* provides:

> Use of domestic sources. In determining the effect of an international agreement as domestic law, a court or agency of the United States is required to take into account national materials relating to the formation of an international agreement which an international body, such as the International Court of Justice, might not consider. These may include:
>
> (i) Committee reports, debates, and any other indications of the meaning that the legislative branch has attached to an international agreement in cases where the agreement, as a matter of internal law, requires the assent of the Senate or of Congress. See §314, Comment b, as to the obligation of the President with respect to qualifications upon such assent.
>
> (ii) The history of the negotiations leading to the agreement, including unilateral statements of understanding not included in the President's proclamation or otherwise communicated to the other party, and, probably, internal official correspondence and position papers prepared for the use of the United States delegation to the negotiation that produced the agreement. Although internationally some of this evidence of intention may not be given great weight it may be necessary for domestic courts to consider it in view of the weight to be given to executive interpretations of an agreement under §326(2).[238]

Arguably the second paragraph of comment d, as set out above, embodies a "dual" approach in which the President is bound to apply an understanding of the Senate even if contained only in informal Senate records not communicated to the other

---

[237] *Id.* comment d, at 82.

[238] *1985 Revised Restatement, supra* note 187, §325, reporters' note 5, at 107-8.

treaty party if the President decides that it "represent[s] a general understanding by the Senate."

The *Restatement (Third)* provides in principal relevant part:

> **(2) When the Senate gives its advice and consent to a treaty on the basis of a particular understanding of its meaning, the President, if he makes the treaty, must do so on the basis of the Senate's understanding.**
>
> . . . .
>
> d. *Understandings*. A treaty that is ratified or acceded to by the United States with a statement of understanding becomes effective in domestic law (§ 111) subject to that understanding. If no such statement is made, indication that the President or the Senate ascribed a particular meaning to the treaty is relevant to the interpretation of the treaty by a United States court in much the same way that the legislative history of a statute is relevant to its interpretation. See §325, Reporters' Note 5; §326, Reporters' Note 2.
>
> Although the Senate's resolution of consent may contain no statement of understanding, there may be such statements in the report of the Senate Foreign Relations Committee or in the Senate debates. In that event, the President must decide whether they represent a general understanding by the Senate and, if he finds that they do, must respect them in good faith.[239]

And Reporters' Note 5 to section 325, "Interpretation of International Agreement," of the *Restatement (Third)* provides:

> *Use of domestic sources*. A court or agency of the United States is required to take into account United States materials relating to the formation of an international agreement that might not be considered by an international body such as the International Court of Justice. These may include:

---

[239] *Restatement (Third), supra* note 235, §314(2) and comment *d*, at 186, 188.

(i) Committee reports, debates, and any other indications of the meaning that the legislative branch has attached to an agreement which, as a matter of internal law, requires the assent of the Senate or of Congress. See §314, Comment b, as to the obligation of the President with respect to qualifications upon such assent.

(ii) The history of the negotiations leading to the agreement, including unilateral statements of understanding not included in the President's proclamation or otherwise communicated to the other party, and, probably, internal official correspondence and position papers prepared for use of the United States delegation to the negotiation. Some of this evidence of intention may not be given great weight internationally, but domestic courts may have to consider it in view of the weight to be given to Executive interpretations of an agreement. See §326(2).[240]

Professors Louis Henkin of the Columbia Law School and Laurence Tribe and Abram Chayes of the Harvard Law School also seem to have made statements in the context of the recent Senate hearings on *The ABM Treaty Interpretation Resolution* at least strongly suggestive of the "dual" standard approach.

Thus, Professor Henkin is quoted in the majority report of the Senate Foreign Relations Committee as affirming:

> In my view, if the Senate's understanding is clear, the President can make the treaty only in accordance with that understanding, whether or not that understanding is expressed as a condition of consent. Indeed, if there is any reason to doubt that the Senate's understanding is shared by the other party or parties to the treaty, or if it appears that the Senate's understanding might somehow differ from what the treaty might be held to mean as a matter of international law, the President is bound to communicate the Senate's understanding as being the understanding of the United States when he make [sic] the treaty.[241]

---

[240] *Id.* §325, reporters' note 5, at 201.

[241] *The ABM Treaty Interpretation Resolution, supra* note 1, at 57. Professor Richard B. Bilder of the University of Wisconsin School of Law seems to support this Henkin view.

Professor Laurence Tribe is quoted by the majority report as saying:

> [Mr. Sofaer] presumes that the President unilaterally "makes" treaties with foreign nations which the Senate subsequently is asked to ratify. The Constitution provides otherwise. The President has the power to "make treaties" only "by and with the Advice and Consent of the Senate . . . provided two-thirds of the Senators present concur.["] No treaty is "made" until the Senate has given its consent. This is how a treaty becomes part of "the supreme Law of the Land."
>
> Under the Legal Adviser's model, the meaning of the ABM Treaty is to be gleaned not by examination of what the President and the Senate agreed upon, but by examination of what the President and the Soviets agreed upon--regardless of what the President may or may not have told the Senate about what he had negotiated. This is tantamount to saying that President Nixon made the ABM treaty the supreme law of the United States with the advice and consent of the Soviet Union.[242]

And the majority report says of Professor Chayes' views:

> The absurdity of the assertion that the President must respect only formally-expressed Senate understandings was underscored by Professor Abram Chayes, who served as the State Department Legal Adviser under President Kennedy. What, he asked, is the Senate "to do when, as in the case of the ABM Treaty, there is no dispute about the meaning of the text and no wish to change the meaning?":
>
>> The very absence of reservations or understandings itself confirms that the Senate understood the treaty to be susceptible of only one interpretation--the one that emerges from the plain meaning of the text and was confirmed by

---

See his letter of May 3, 1987, to Senators Claiborne Pell and Joseph R. Biden *reprinted in The ABM Treaty and the Constitution, supra* note 1, at 542, 543-44.

[242]*The ABM Treaty Interpretation Resolution, supra* note 1, at 57.

> representatives of the Executive at the time of ratification. What is important about [the] ratification history of this Treaty is that it shows there was no issue of interpretation. Everyone agreed.[243]

Professor Henkin's statement is particularly important since he is one of the country's most recognized experts in constitutional aspects of foreign policy. Moreover, since 1979 he has been the Chief Reporter for the *Revised Restatement of the Foreign Relations Law of the United States*. It should perhaps be noted that Professor Henkin's recently expressed view, although including a technically different issue, is consistent with his earlier expressed position solicitous of the prerogative of the Senate in the treaty power as expressed in his article on the Niagara Reservation dispute. The issue in the Niagara dispute involved the legal effect of a Senate reservation in the Niagara River treaty with Canada concerning a prohibition on redevelopment of the United States side of such waters without a specific subsequent authorization by Congress. Professor Henkin published an article on this issue in 1956 raising questions about arguments for the Power Authority of the State of New York that had challenged the reservation as an invalid effort at domestic legislation by the Senate[244] exceeding the treaty power. In the article, Professor Henkin seemed to support the reservation as valid and broadly suggested ". . . we would ask for argument to support the proposition that there can be an effective treaty if the Senate's condition, whatever its character, is disregarded."[245]

As has been seen, Professor Louis Henkin, now University Professor Emeritus and Special Service Professor of Law at Columbia University School of Law, has been a principal proponent of the "dual" approach, including serving as Chief Reporter of the *Restatement (Third)* which constitutes the principal legal

---

[243]*Id.* at 58.

[244]Henkin, "Niagara Reservation," *supra* note 140, at 1151.

[245]*Id.* at 1181. *See also L. Henkin, supra* note 6, at 134-36, where Professor Henkin reiterates his views on the *Niagara Reservation* case without alerting the reader to the decision of the Court of Appeals in that case contrary to the views expressed by Professor Henkin. In fairness to Professor Henkin the Court of Appeals decision was vacated as moot by the Supreme Court.

authority for that approach. In a recent essay entitled "Treaties in a Constitutional Democracy,"[246] Professor Henkin writes as follows in support of that approach:

> Some implications of the procedure prescribed by the Constitution are not disputed. The President can negotiate or not, can heed or disregard Senate advice if, whenever, and however given. The Senate can offer any advice, and can refuse consent for any reason or no reason; it can consent on conditions.[15] [15. Contrary to common parlance, the Senate cannot enter reservations to or amend a treaty; in effect, it refuses consent to the text as it is, while declaring that it will consent if the text is changed as indicated. This may be done ordinarily by amendment by the parties (in the case of a bilateral treaty) or by reservation by the United States (in adhering to a multilateral treaty). *See infra* page 415.] The President can make (bind the United States to) the treaty if the Senate has consented to it; he cannot make the treaty without Senate consent.
>
> One implication of the constitutional requirement of Senate consent seems obvious but it surfaced -- and was confirmed -- only recently in the tempest surrounding the ABM treaty. At stake was a politically important difference between a "narrow" and a "broad" interpretation of that treaty, between a construction that would permit and one that would forbid steps towards a Strategic Defense Initiative ("Star Wars") program. But the underlying constitutional issue, though novel, was small, and the area of disagreement, though generating much heat, was comparatively narrow.
>
> All were agreed that the President can make a treaty only if the Senate has consented to it. Therefore, the President can make only the treaty to which the Senate consents. Generally, the Senate consents to what the text of the treaty provides, as reasonably interpreted. But if there is any ambiguity, the treaty to which the Senate consents is, inevitably, the treaty as the Senate understands it. However, all were not agreed upon what would constitute binding evidence of the Senate's understanding.
>
> The Senate has often explicitly declared its understanding of the meaning of a possibly-ambiguous treaty provision by an express

---

[246]Henkin, *supra* note 7, at 406.

"understanding" in its resolution of consent. If the Senate declares its understanding, the President must honor it: the treaty as so understood is the treaty to which the Senate consents. The President communicates to the other party (or parties) the Senate's understanding of the treaty as constituting the United States' understanding of it, and, unless the other parties reject it, that becomes the meaning of the treaty.

In the case of the ABM Treaty, the Senate's understanding of the provision later in issue was not formally declared. But it was in fact clear (and I think not seriously disputed) that the Senate had understood the treaty to be more rather than less restrictive, less rather than more permissive. For a time, the Executive Branch appeared to take the position that if the Senate's understanding of a treaty was not formally declared it was of no effect and need not govern the meaning of the treaty for the United States later.[16] [16. There appears to have been also an issue as to the Senate's reliance on informal Executive communications. The Executive Branch insisted, in effect, that the Senate must accept what the President formally communicates and not form any understandings on the basis of informal communications from individuals in the Executive Branch. There is something to be said for the view that ordinarily the Senate should not rely on views or communications of individual officials. But the Senate gave its consent to the treaty as it understood it, no matter how or from whom it obtained that understanding.] That view, I think, is mistaken: whether or not the Senate expressed an understanding, what the Senate in fact thought the treaty meant is the treaty to which the Senate consented.[17] [17. *See* United States v. Stuart, 109 S. Ct. 1183, 1192 n.7 (1989), in which the Supreme Court invoked the RESTATEMENT (THIRD) FOREIGN RELATIONS LAW OF THE UNITED STATES §314, comment *d* & §325, reporters' note 5 (1987), and looked to the record of Senate preratification materials as a guide to interpreting the treaty in question.] The Executive Branch challenge to that view was untenable, and the Executive may itself have abandoned it, but not without leaving severe political bruises.

The ABM confrontation was unprecedented, but perhaps an inevitable consequence of our unique, complex treaty process involving independent, powerful, constitutionally-based institutions.

The controversy involved a major security treaty, concluded after long negotiations that were heavily shrouded; the subject of the treaty -- arms control generally, and the particular treaty under negotiation -- was esoteric and one as to which the Executive and the Senate were both ambivalent, and both internally divided. Both President and Senate had been uneasy over making a commitment; both were distrustful of the USSR; and the Senate and the Executive did not trust each other fully. As to the particular treaty, a later President, less-than-wholly sympathetic to the treaty and eager to relax its restraints, was tempted to revise an earlier President's undertakings to which the Senate had consented. But the present majority of the Senate continued to favor the treaty and resisted a new interpretation which it disfavored. Above all, the Senate was determined to vindicate its earlier consent and to preserve the integrity of its consent power.[18] [18. The President does not have to make a treaty even after the Senate gives its consent and the President can terminate a treaty that has been made. *See infra* note 39. But if a treaty has been made and has not been terminated, the Senate is entitled to resist a Presidential interpretation of a treaty that renders it effectively a treaty other than the one to which the Senate had consented. The Senate was not asserting a power to interpret a treaty at a later time. Once a treaty is made, the Senate has no special authority in relation to it. The President later interprets the treaty for purposes of executing it. Congress -- both Houses -- interpret the treaty for legislative purposes. Courts may interpret it for their purposes. The Supreme Court's interpretation of a treaty made in deciding a case or controversy is authoritative for purposes of U.S. law and is binding on all courts as well as on the political branches.]

The controversy surrounding the interpretation of the ABM Treaty highlights larger consequences of our treaty process and of the separation of powers. In the United States, all branches of the government are bound by the text of a treaty made by the United States as the Senate understood it. Presumably, the United States must pursue that interpretation also for international purposes. But the international system -- including international courts and arbitral tribunals -- is not bound by the subtleties of United States treaty procedure, and by internal interpretations that are not expressed,

> adopted, and communicated to the other parties to the treaty. The international system, then, may come to an interpretation of a treaty different from the one the Senate tacitly assumed. If that happens and is established, the international interpretation of the treaty may later become the meaning within the United States as well, a consequence of the "slippage" between internal and international law in our modified dualist system.[247]

Most recently, an additional secondary authority from which the "dual" approach might be inferred is an article by Professor David A. Koplow to be published in the *University of Pennsylvania Law Review* and entitled: "Constitutional Bait and Switch: Executive Reinterpretation and Arms Control Treaties."[248] While not fully focusing on the constitutional issue discussed in this study as the "dual" versus "unitary" approaches, Professor Koplow clearly endorses the legal conclusion that informal Senate understandings are legally binding. He writes:

> Despite [the] practical problem of establishing the existence and terms of a Senate understanding that is not written into the resolution of ratification, there is no conceptual difficulty in assessing its legal status, once such a subtle understanding has been shown to exist. That is, the Senate's understandings and conditions -- however they are evidenced -- are fully binding upon the President once the treaty is "made". The Senate's view of the treaty -- whether explicit or implicit -- becomes a part of the treaty, and the president cannot proceed to ratification on any other terms.[249]

---

[247]*Id.* at 413-15.

[248]Koplow Draft, *supra* note 1.

For the views of three Senior-Attorney Advisors in the Office of Policy Development, United States Department of Justice, critical of Professor Koplow's approach, the position of the *Restatement (Third)*, and the "dual" approach to treaty interpretation in general, see the forthcoming commentary: Block, Casey & Rivkin, "The Senate's Pie-in-the-Sky Treaty Interpretation Power and the Quest for Legislative Supremacy," 137 *U. Penn. L. Rev.* 1481 (forthcoming May 1989) (reviewed from page proofs subject to final editing).

[249]Koplow Draft, *supra* note 1, at 90 (footnote omitted).

The only authority cited by Professor Koplow in a footnote to this conclusion is section 314 of the *Restatement (Third)* discussed above, and the recent testimony of Professor Louis Henkin, the Chief Reporter of the *Restatement*, in *The ABM Treaty Interpretation Resolution* hearings. This same footnote also cites the statement of Abraham D. Sofaer made during these same hearings as authority to the contrary for the proposition that: "`When [the Senate] gives its advice and consent to a treaty, it is to the treaty that was made, irrespective of the explanations it is provided.'"[250] In developing this position Professor Koplow seems to reject any rigid notion of "estoppel" from Executive branch statements to the Senate or that such statements are, of their own weight, legally "authoritative" or binding, and, similar to the *Restatement* view, he roots any binding legal effect of an informal Senate understanding in "whether the Senate did, in fact, have a coherent view of this point." Thus, he writes:

> The point here is *not* that the president or a successor should be "estopped" from asserting a contrary interpretation at a later time. Rather, it is that the president's representations, having been accepted by the Senate, have contributed to the growth of a particular understanding or interpretation that has become affixed in law to the treaty text. Executive presentations regarding a recently-concluded treaty will ordinarily be especially compelling upon the Senate, and especially likely to generate a shared, albeit perhaps inexplicit, understanding or interpretation -- but the key inquiry remains simply whether the Senate did, in fact, have a coherent view of this point. Whether this view was instigated by the executive or by other sources is therefore of lesser importance.[251]

Moreover, Professor Koplow's analysis concedes the difficulty in accurate assessment of Senate understanding from the record of legislative history. He writes:

> There is, of course, a substantial problem of proof in assessing the more tacit forms of Senate understandings. Obviously,

---

[250]*Id.* at 90 n.225 (quoting *The ABM Treaty and the Constitution, supra* note 1, at 130 (statement of A. Sofaer)).

[251]*Id.* at 95 (footnotes omitted) (emphasis in original).

> it is easier to be confident about "what the Senate wanted" when the entire body has gone on record, with an up-or-down vote, on the question of including a particular provision in the resolution of ratification. Conversely, report language, floor colloquies, and the like, are often more ambiguous expressions of intent, and subsequent analysts may question the degree to which the Senate as a whole subscribed to the views of any few leaders. Most problematic of all will be the effort to draw inferences from Senate silence -- when does the absence of any expression on point indicate that the Senate shared an understanding so basic that no elaboration was required, and when does it signify, instead, that the Senate simply had no considered view of the subject?[252]

And again he cautions that not every informal discussion or Executive branch statement will give rise to a binding Senate understanding:

> Conversely, it will be more legitimate for a subsequent administration to rebut an original interpretation when conditions suggest that the earlier statements did not create a common Senate understanding: if the issue was covered only sparingly and obliquely; if administration witnesses were inconsistent on point; if the original interpretation was sponsored only by relatively junior, or relatively uninformed authorities, especially when speaking "off the cuff", (as in impromptu oral responses to spontaneous questions) rather than pursuant to detailed, coordinated executive branch instructions.[253]

Professor Koplow then goes on to recommend a balancing of "eight factors" for determining when an interpretation "should be considered legally binding."[254] Notably he does not discuss where he finds these "eight factors" in the Constitution or any constitutional theory of the issues. More importantly, however, since he explicitly takes the view that "no one of [these factors] could ordinarily be

---

[252]*Id.* at 88-89 (footnotes omitted).

[253]*Id.* at 122-23 (footnote omitted).

[254]*Id.* at 117-28.

dispositive by itself,"[255] and his "eight factors" include two relating to an informal Senate understanding or Executive branch statement, his own analysis would seem to be inconsistent with adoption of the "dual" approach that an informal Senate understanding or Executive branch statement is *ipso facto* binding under national law.[256] Indeed, that six out of his eight factors relate to the international effect or meaning of the treaty illustrates his recognition of the importance of the international effect or meaning in legal determination as to treaty interpretation under national law. These factors as suggested by Professor Koplow are:

> 1. *What did the Senate say about the particular issue at the time of providing its advice and consent to the treaty?* . . .
>
> . . . .
>
> 2. *What was said to the Senate, creating an understanding of the treaty, prior to ratification?* . . .
>
> . . . .
>
> 3. *What has been the attitude of the other party to the competing interpretations of the treaty?* . . .
>
> 4. *How much support is there in the treaty text and record for the two interpretations?* . . .
>
> 5. *What is the record of "subsequent practice" of the treaty parties?* . . .
>
> 6. *How different is the new interpretation from the old?* . . .

---

[255]Id. at 117.

[256]Professor Koplow describes his approach as:

> This section of the article, therefore, attempts to define "entrenchment," to describe the circumstances under which an interpretation of a treaty should be considered legally binding. The discussion proceeds by listing eight factors, no one of which could ordinarily be dispositive by itself, but all of which may have a bearing upon a particular case. The task of the analyst, therefore, is to collect the relevant data and balance these eight elements against each other. Whenever the executive proffers a treaty reinterpretation, its legitimacy and its ability to oust a prior interpretation of the treaty can be analyzed in this way.

Koplow Draft, *supra* note 1, at 117-18.

7. *Does the new interpretation purport to create new obligations, or to release old ones?* . . . [and]

8. *Are there any changed circumstances that affect the treaty?*[257]

While some of these "factors" are factors used in interpretation under the Vienna Convention on the Law of Treaties, just as this list seems not reflective of any constitutional theory rooted in either a "dual" or "unitary" view of treaty interpretation under the Constitution, so too it is not simply rooted in the international legal standard for treaty interpretation as embodied in the Vienna Convention. Professor Koplow seems to be suggesting a pragmatic balancing of national and international factors as legally determinative of treaty interpretation issues under national law rather than simply supporting either "dual" or "unitary" approaches.

policy arguments supporting the "dual" approach

A "dual" standards approach can be seen as supporting several important policies in the treaty making process. Thus, it would arguably most effectively protect the meaningfulness of the Senate role in the treaty process. The President would have a powerful incentive to provide maximum information to the Senate--and to get it right--during Senate consideration of a treaty. Moreover, abuse of the process by a President not proceeding in good faith with a Senate would have a ready remedy. Finally, the Senate might be more relaxed about not seeking formal reservations or understandings or having access to an entire negotiating record. This latter concern does seem to have been heightened in the Senate as a result of the "broad-narrow" debate.[258]

---

[257] *Id.* at 118-27.

[258] Paradoxically, Senate nervousness in at least initially seeking the full negotiating record of the INF Treaty can be seen at least in part as a form of pragmatic recognition that the majority report of the Senate Foreign Relations Committee, based on the "dual" approach, would not necessarily govern future treaty interpretations. This, of course, then led to the INF Treaty interpretation condition.

The policy arguments supporting the "dual" approach are summarized effectively in a speech delivered by former Senator and Secretary of State Edmund S. Muskie at Cornell on September 17, 1987:

> . . . The quest for constitutional harmony is too important for a temporary assertion of superior numbers in Congress or preemptive maneuvers by the executive.
>
> A case in point is the serious disagreement that has arisen over the treaty powers. The controversy over interpretation of the Antiballistic Missile Treaty of 1972 has raised profound issues. While the argument over the treaty is rooted in differences over strategic policy, its import reaches far beyond matters of strategic defense. Some suggest that it has degenerated into a squabble among lawyers, but no squabble has ever contained more potential for altering the constitutional balance between Senate and president.
>
> This is not the place to review those arguments in detail, but a few observations are in order. The assertion by some that the executive branch is not bound by treaty interpretations presented to the Senate in support of ratification is constitutional anathema. Not only would that principle render meaningless the role assigned to the Senate by the Constitution, such a rule would contradict the central tenets of limited government operating under law--for in some sense the law would be unknowable to senators and citizens alike.
>
> At the same time, the practical consequences of such a stand would emasculate American diplomacy. Senator Sam Nunn has made clear that that view would force the Senate to demand the entire negotiating record of any proposed treaty. For if the Senate cannot rely on executive interpretations of the agreement, it must determine for itself what undertakings were made to the treaty's other parties. That prospect could stifle the negotiations and very likely eliminate the treaty-making process as we have known it.
>
> That radical revision of historic practice is no more desirable to the executive than to the legislative branch. Common sense and constitutional values both argue against the extreme claims that have crept into the debate over the Antiballistic Missile Treaty.
>
> Secretary of state Shultz struck the right theme when he stressed that trust is the coin of the realm. If we lose sight of that cardinal truth, we doom ourselves to constant quarrels and political

> paralysis. For a congress cannot cooperate with an executive whose words it cannot trust, and a president cannot confide in a congress that violates his confidence. The sad experience of recent years is not a verdict on the impossibility of legislative-executive accommodation. It is an object lesson in the obligation of each branch to warrant the other's trust. . . .[259]

In a recent article in *Foreign Affairs* on "Foreign Affairs and the Constitution,"[260] Professor Louis Henkin, University Professor, Columbia University, also seems to support a "dual" approach, as well as implicitly passing

---

[259]Edmund S. Muskie, "The Chains of Liberty: Congress, President, and American Security," delivered at Cornell for the University's bicentennial celebration for the U.S. Constitution on September 17, 1987.

And in a "Commentary" published in a recent issue of the *Virginia Journal of International Law*, and adapted from a speech delivered at the University of Virginia School of Law in April 1988, former Senator Muskie writes:

> The administration's reinterpretation stands logic on its head. How can a treaty of *unlimited* duration, intended to ban "a defense of the territory" of each country apply only to ABM systems and components available during the period of negotiations. How can the Senate solemnly consent to ratify a treaty based on one administration's explanation of U.S. obligations only to have another assert that the treaty's central provisions meant no such thing? Is it any wonder that the Senate has not allowed its constitutional role to be subverted in this way?
>
> . . . .
>
> While the Reagan administration's treaty reinterpretation -- as well as the Congress' resistance to it -- have not hurt our negotiating position, they have hurt our standing around the world. Other nations expect us to live by our word and to carry out faithfully our solemn treaty obligations, not to play word games over mutually binding obligations that have been observed for a decade and a half.

Muskie, "Congress and National Security," 28 Va. J. Int'l L. 949, 960 (1988).

[260]Henkin, "Foreign Affairs and the Constitution," Foreign Aff. 284 (Winter 1987/88) [hereinafter Henkin, "Foreign Affairs article"].

on the factual issues concerning the record in Senate consideration of the "broad-narrow" issue,[261] when he says:

> The Senate's consent to a treaty is constitutionally necessary, and for that purpose the Senate is entitled to know what the treaty means; often it will insist on articulating explicit understandings as to what it means. When, as has recently happened in respect of the ABM treaty, the executive branch later seeks to interpret a treaty to an effect different from what it had told the Senate in seeking its consent, the executive would seem to be violating the constitutional conception. Surely such attempts by the executive invite the Senate in the future to probe ambiguities and to express understanding with nearly paranoid scrupulousness, from fear not only of what other states may make of a treaty but of what the future executive branch will make of it. The president must be candid; the senate must restrain itself.[262]

This same policy concern is emphasized by Senator Joseph R. Biden, Jr., Chairman of the Senate Judiciary Committee, and John B. Ritch, III, Deputy Director of the Senate Foreign Relations Committee, in a forthcoming commentary in the *University of Pennsylvania Law Review*. They write:

> [A]s a matter of practicality, the Sofaer Doctrine threatened paralysis in American treaty-making -- since the Senate's only recourse would be to attach elaborate and numerous conditions to treaties in order to ensure that its understanding became an integral and explicit part of a treaty's ratification documents.[263]

---

[261]Professor Henkin gives no supporting argumentation in support of his implicit factual conclusions concerning Senate consideration of the "broad-narrow" issue.

[262]Henkin, "Foreign Affairs article," *supra* note 260, at 305.

[263]Biden & Ritch, "The Treaty Power: Upholding a Constitutional Partnership," 137 *U. Penn. L. Rev.* 1529, 1538-39 (forthcoming May 1989) (quoted from page proofs subject to final editing).

Similarly, in a meeting with the author on July 7, 1989, Mr. Robert G. Bell, Professional Staff Member for the Arms Control Observer Group of the Senate Armed Services Committee, developed this policy argument as it applies to what he terms a "means test" of a shared understanding that must be clearly intended, generally understood and relied upon by the Senate, in addition to having been authoritatively communicated. He pointed out that the Senate had held approximately 40 hearings on the INF Treaty and that the committee staff had prepared an analysis of some 139 issues under the Treaty. If the Senate could not rely on authoritative representations by Executive branch spokesman as to the answers on these issues, then it would be necessary to have an "amen chorus" in which the Senate would be forced to affirm in each case that the authoritative Executive branch communication was clearly intended, generally understood and relied upon by the Senate in its advice and consent to ratification. He indicates that even such a "means test" (which, of course, is a test reflecting the "dual" approach) would cause the important Senate advice and consent process to sink of its own weight.

rebuttal of arguments for the "unitary" approach

In addition to arguing that the United States "can adhere only to the treaty concerning which a `meeting of the minds' has occurred between the President and the Senate,"[264] and that this principle extends to informal "legislative" history expressions of Senate intention as well as formal reservations or understandings,[265] the majority report of the Senate Committee on Foreign Relations on *The ABM Treaty Interpretation Resolution* also seeks to rebut two policy arguments supporting the unitary approach.[266] Thus, in response to the policy argument that a "dual" approach would result in an unworkable obligation of states, including the United States, to monitor the internal constitutional processes of all other states ratifying or adhering to international agreements, the majority report says:

---

[264]*The ABM Treaty Interpretation Resolution, supra* note 1, at 55-56.

[265]*Id.* at 56-59.

[266]*Id.* at 59-61.

> -- First, few other nations have a bifurcated approval procedure comparable to that of the United States; legislative approval of treaties is the exception, not the rule. . . .
>
> -- Second, for prudential reasons the State Department does in fact already monitor certain states' ratification proceedings, particularly on key agreements. . . .
>
> -- Third, the United States has, as a matter of past practice, regarded its own ratification proceedings as having international significance. . . .
>
> -- Finally, it is quite reasonable to expect--indeed, disingenuous to pretend otherwise--that other nations are sufficiently interested and capable to monitor U.S. ratification proceedings. . . .
>
> . . . .
>
> In sum, it is simply not accurate to contend that a new or unrealistic surveillance "duty" would be imposed on the U.S. Government or other governments by the requirement that ratification proceedings be regarded as centrally relevant to the meaning of treaties.[267]

And in responding to the policy argument that the "dual" approach could serve as an additional process of divergence between the international obligations of the United States and its obligations under domestic law, and particularly that it "could bind the United States more strictly under its own constitutional law than it--and the other party--are bound by international law"[268] the majority report says:

> The Legal Adviser implies that the problem of reconciling two intersecting systems--domestic and international--is one created by those who wish to assert the relevance of the Senate's role in the treaty ratification process. In fact, the problem of harmony--to the limited degree it exists--inheres in the very existence of two separate

---

[267]*Id.* at 59-60.

[268]*Id.* at 60.

> but interactive systems. To achieve harmony between the two is, as experience demonstrates, generally possible. But harmony is not the only interest at stake. Surely the interest of the United States in preserving the integrity of its domestic legal order is far weightier. Certainly harmony should not be sought by dispensing with clear imperatives of the Constitution.
>
> In any case, the practical reality is that problematical instances are extremely rare . . . .[269]

In his recent manuscript for the *University of Pennsylvania Law Review,* Professor David A. Koplow also presents a policy argument in rebuttal of the view "that strict `mutuality of obligations' is an inherent and vital aspect of international agreements, and that any asymmetry in parties' commitments is somehow indicative of impropriety or folly."[270] Thus he writes:

> It is sometimes asserted that strict "mutuality of obligations" is an inherent and vital aspect of international agreements, and that any asymmetry in parties' commitments is somehow indicative of impropriety or folly. In fact, however, this mirror-imaging of treaties may be the exception, rather than the rule, and it is, in any case, wholly unnecessary as a matter of law.
>
> Although reciprocity and "equal security" are important political aspects of most arms control accords, there are several reasons why a treaty regime may impose asymmetrical obligations upon its parties. First, the negotiated terms of the treaty itself may create differing requirements for the participants. Even when the parties are of equal bargaining power, they may agree, for example, to retain stockpiles of armaments that are unequal in numbers but otherwise equivalent in power; they may similarly find it expedient to agree on unequal reductions in arms in order to reach lower, equal ceilings.
>
> Second, there may be ambiguities or gaps in the treaty's coverage, and the parties may lawfully move unilaterally in different directions under it. Each party will retain control over its own

---

[269]*Id.* at 60-61.

[270]Koplow Draft, *supra* note 1, at 99.

military forces, and will implement the treaty in its own interests -- and the parties may accordingly take different actions that are associated with the items covered by the treaty. For example, the INF Treaty eliminates intermediate-range and shorter-range missiles, but leaves each party free to take its own course regarding aircraft and very-short range missiles. The parties may well react differently to this opportunity, in ways that nonetheless have implications for the security relationship contemplated by the Treaty.

Third, the domestic processes leading to treaty ratification may impose different obligations on the various parties. "Category I" understandings, for example, are of internal legal effect only, but they may nonetheless create for any one country new law governing areas close to the treaty, and having an international importance. Subsequent enactments, too, can create dissimilar arrangements among treaty powers.

Finally, there is a sense in which treaties are inherently "non-mutual". An international obligation, even one which on its face is purely symmetric, will take its place inside the network of domestic law that characterizes each of its parties. Since these legal systems vary so much, and the two domestic legal environments into which the treaty will move are so dissimilar, the effects of the treaty may be different in noteworthy ways, too.

As between the United States and the Soviet Union, for example, the legal surroundings of any new treaty will be starkly different. The U.S. implementation of any treaty will be affected by the limitations of the Bill of Rights, the environmental protection legislation, the laws regarding occupational health and safety, and the internal revenue code, to cite a few conspicuous examples. While none of these sources of law might directly conflict with the treaty, each may subtly shape its implementation, resulting in an alignment of government powers and privileges somewhat different from that available to the Soviet government inside its own territory and legal system.

For example, a treaty might afford the parties identical rights to destroy excess missiles by explosive means, yet the U.S. environmental protection laws might effectively forbid such actions inside this country, creating a *de facto* asymmetry where the negotiators contemplated none. Similarly, U.S. constitutional restrictions upon the conduct of government searches and seizures might impact upon the ability to conduct on-site inspections inside the United States, even if no parallel limitations appeared for the Soviet Union.

These inherently non-mutual factors mean that whenever an arms control treaty is concluded, it is quickly transformed into two treaties, one governing the U.S. and a very similar, but subtly different one restricting the U.S.S.R. The fundamental obligations under international law remain symmetric, but the governments' respective abilities to take advantage of the permissions, and to implement the restrictions, under their differing domestic law, will quickly diverge.

The U.S. will, of course, have a political interest in the domestic implementation of the treaty inside the U.S.S.R., and *vice versa*. But neither will have a lawful claim to intervene in the other's internal processes, and each will be free to alter its own domestic law, as it sees fit, so long as the international obligations are met. One nation's domestic arrangements may well constrain it more than the other party's law constrains its sovereign, but this anomaly is a matter of municipal, not international law, and it is by no means necessarily indicative of any failure of the treaty regime.

It may be poor politics, or poor international strategy, for the United States to tolerate any gross disjunction between the treaty-as-domestic-law that constrains the United States and the (corollary, but presumably less restrictive) treaty-as-domestic-law that constrains the U.S.S.R. However, the possibility of such a disparity is an inevitable by-product of the Constitution's structure of a separation of powers. As long as there is a two-step process for treaty-making, with the legislature putting its own stamp of approval and understanding upon a document negotiated by the executive, the opportunities will always exist for subtle slippages between the moment of negotiation and the moment of ratification, shattering the illusion of mutuality.[271]

---

[271]*Id.* at 99-106 (footnotes omitted). It might be noted of relevance to the "broad-narrow" interpretation dispute that in talking of areas of ambiguity in treaty interpretation, Professor Koplow acknowledges in his arguments set out in text that: "there may be ambiguities or gaps in the treaty's coverage, and the parties may lawfully move unilaterally

Professor Koplow then goes on to offer a rebuttal of the argument for the "unitary" view of an increased monitoring burden in monitoring national legislative processes. Thus, he writes:

> Another red herring, associated with the argument for mutuality, is the claim that if the ratification process is considered an effective device for making law, then treaty negotiators would suddenly be forced to assume a major new burden of monitoring each other's legislative process. The Legal Adviser has asserted that if a state's domestic advice and consent phase has international significance, then U.S. diplomats would be required to devote considerable additional energy to scrutinizing in detail the progress of a treaty through other nations' domestic ratification processes, and would also bear a burden to ensure that all other treaty parties were being equally attentive in studying the events leading to the U.S. ratification.
>
> The short answer to this illusion is a return to the previous observation of the distinction between the international and the domestic law-making operations of a treaty. That is, one country's advice and consent process cannot impose legal burdens upon the other state -- only a mutually-accepted negotiated agreement can accomplish that. So neither side has an *obligation* to monitor the other's domestic processes. On the other hand, each country will ordinarily have a profound political interest in discovering what its negotiating partner is contemplating, especially in areas that are intimately connected with an arms control treaty. So while the advice and consent process does make domestic law for the United States, it is law that -- insofar as it varies from the obligations assumed by both parties in the negotiations -- is binding only upon this country. The U.S.S.R. will, in all likelihood, continue to monitor these developments closely, but will not be constrained by them.[272]

---

in different directions under it." *Id.* at 101.

[272] *Id.* at 107-08 (footnotes omitted).

arguments for a "unitary" standard

---

constitutional theory

There are several theoretical arguments serving as constitutional underpinnings of the "unitary" approach.

First, the treaty power is a power to make international agreements. It is not a general legislative power to make laws, apart from the underlying international agreement, that would be binding under domestic law. When the framers bestowed the general legislative power it was bestowed on the Congress as a whole and the President was given a qualified veto. As a majority of the Supreme Court recently reminded us in the 1983 *Chadha* decision, the framers carefully established the legislative power to require concurrence of two separately established houses of Congress and a qualified veto in the President.[273] They emphasized why in a system of checks and balances such a power should not simply be entrusted to a single house. In this carefully constructed framework the treaty power was entrusted to the President "by and with the Advice and Consent of the Senate" to make treaties, and not to create a general legislative power apart from the underlying international agreement. And certainly the framers did not intend that the record of informal "legislative" history of the Senate alone, as embodied in the "dual" approach, could create binding rights, privileges, powers and immunities under United States national law apart from the underlying international agreement. It should also be recalled in this connection that both Article III, section 2, the judiciary article, and Article VI, the supremacy clause, differentiate between "laws of the United States" and "Treaties," and it is not informal Senate proceedings that are made binding domestically but "all Treaties made, or which shall be made, under the Authority of the United States." This first constitutional objection to the "dual" approach is developed by Michael H. Mobbs, a former Assistant Director for Strategic Programs of the Arms Control and Disarmament Agency, and David B. Rivkin, Jr., an attorney with Baker & McKenzie, in a recent "Commentary" in the *Washington Times*:

> . . . under the Supremacy Clause of the Constitution, a treaty generates binding domestic obligations only to the extent of the

---

[273]Immigration and Naturalization Service v. Chadha, 462 U.S. 917, 948-50 (1983).

international obligations assumed by the treaty parties. A Senate understanding or an interpretation not agreed to by the other treaty party, even if embraced by the sitting president, is no more than a private side-deal between the president and the Senate. As such, it is not legally binding on anyone.

The Democratic leadership's position amounts to an assertion that the Senate may constitutionally create domestic law by the device of squeezing understandings out of the administration during the treaty hearings--even though those understandings are not in the Senate's resolution of advice and consent but are at most derivable from the Senate debate on the treaty--and may bind the president and his successors to that understanding even though the other treaty party never agreed to it.

The Democratic leadership's approach would lead to the unacceptable result that the Senate could introduce new terms into a treaty and force the United States to honor them, even though the other country never agreed to those terms and was not bound by them.

Indeed, under this approach the Senate could obtain such a result simply by sprinkling the record with speeches embracing the purported Senate understanding, and getting the administration, eager for swift ratification, to embrace it. This would amount to unilateral senatorial treaty-making by ambush, and to usurpation by the Senate of the legislative power vested jointly in the House of Representatives and the Senate.

As Justice Brown wrote in the famous 1901 Supreme Court decision on the Fourteen Diamond Rings, "the power of the Senate is limited to ratification of such terms as have already been agreed upon between the president . . . and the other contracting power. The Senate has no right to ratify the treaty and introduce new terms into it . . . although it may refuse its ratification, or make such ratification conditional upon the adoption of amendments to the treaty." . . .[274]

Second, in the overall constitutional framework the Senate role in the treaty process is similar to that of the President in the legislative process, a form of veto.

---

[274]Michael Mobbs & David Rivkin, Jr., *Cloud on the INF Horizon*, Wash. Times, Feb. 15, 1988, at D1, col. 1, D2.

It is not a power to affirmatively legislate apart from the underlying international agreement. As we have seen, in his *Manual of Parliamentary Practice for the Use of the Senate*, Thomas Jefferson characterized the Senate role in the treaty making process as a "negative." It is particularly difficult to conceptualize under such a role how any action of the Senate, let alone informal "legislative" history, could create a binding legal obligation under domestic law not required by the underlying international agreement.

Third, there is an important grouping of arguments which share in common objections to the level of generality with which the principal theoretical underpinning of the "dual" approach is advanced; that is, the argument that the President can only make the treaty "concerning which a `meeting of the minds' has occurred between the President and the Senate."[275] Certainly any President should proceed in good faith only to ratify a treaty consented to by the Senate, should seek to ensure that other treaty parties are bound by any Senate adopted amendments, reservations or understanding and should proceed in good faith to raise with the Senate and the other treaty parties any Senate understanding, formal or informal, which he believes inconsistent with the treaty obligations. But this overly general theoretical formula obscures, in several respects, rather than sharpens, the real issues. Thus, what happens under this formula if for some reason, through mistake, failure to focus on an issue or some other, a President does in good faith conclude an agreement which it later turns out means something different than what the Senate--and perhaps even the President--understood. That is, in many, if not virtually all, real world settings the issue will be one of failure to focus carefully on a relatively obscure part of an agreement or a mistake of fact or law becoming known only *after* an agreement has been concluded. In this setting the theoretical argument made for the "dual" approach obscures rather than clarifies at least two important issues. Thus, why would the legal result of any such setting be to bind the United States to the erroneous interpretation, not contained in the agreement, as opposed to declaring the treaty void altogether in its domestic affect? That is, if a President did conclude a treaty that in its real international legal effect went beyond the "meeting of minds between the President and the Senate" and as this theoretical basis says, the President cannot make such a treaty, why isn't the treaty simply void?[276] More importantly, isn't the real issue here not the good faith standard we

---

[275] *The ABM Treaty Interpretation Resolution*, *supra* note 1, at 56.

[276]It should be recalled that the dissent by Judge Bastian in the *Niagara Reservation* case argued that if the reservation were invalid then the treaty itself must be invalid. See 247 F.2d 538, 544, 546 (Judge Bastian, dissenting). Thus, he

expect of any President in carefully following the Senate intent as he ratifies a treaty, but rather in a setting subsequently arising where there is a divergence between either the Senate or the Senate-President understanding of the meaning of a treaty and what may turn out to be its real international meaning. The case of such settings, which are likely to be infrequent, will be settings of good faith failure to address adequately an issue considered peripheral, even if important, or settings of good faith mistake of law. In such settings is there anything in the Constitution that requires that the United States adhere to a mistaken legal interpretation even when the other party is not bound or, as may be suggested more strongly by this general theory, treat the treaty as void under domestic law even when it as a whole is viewed as important to continue the treaty regime? That is, the real issue here is the constitutional requirement in dealing with settings of mistake as to the legal interpretation of an already concluded treaty. The general theory advanced for the "dual" approach both obscures this issue and contains no necessary internal guidance as to why an approach freezing the United States to an obligation not shared by other treaty parties is constitutionally required over an approach that would declare the treaty void or an approach that would in such settings follow the international obligation. Related to this objection rooted in the level of generality of the conceptual underpinning of the "dual" approach is the issue that will be addressed subsequently in this part. If, in fact the result of the "dual" approach were to hold the United States to an obligation not shared by the other party, would such a result really carry out the intention of the ratifying Senate which, by definition, believed the other party bound? In many, if not most, settings it clearly would not do so. Yet if the core of this approach is to protect the Senate prerogative does it do so, or undercut that intent in many, if not most settings by enforcing a provision unilaterally against the United States which the Senate believed binding on both parties? There is also a significant issue in United States treaty ratification practice not automatically answered by the general argument cited for the "dual" approach. That is, whether Senate execution of its veto power is to be carried out through

---

said:

> [I]f the reservation was beyond the constitutional power of the Senate, it cannot be given effect. If it is beyond the power of the Senate, then not just the reservation falls, but the entire treaty. How can it be otherwise when the Senate has made it abundantly clear that without the reservation it would not have consented to the treaty?

Id. at 546.

formal conditions when we wish to ensure a domestic impact that could vary from an international obligation as opposed to informal considerations in "legislative" history that would be relevant for treaty interpretation but not considered *ipso facto* binding under domestic law. It is not clear that there is anything in the language of the Constitution, much less the general theoretical underpinning cited for the "dual" approach, that would compel the conclusion that informal "legislative" history is to have the legal effect of ipso facto creating a domestic obligation not contained in the treaty or a formal Senate condition. Indeed, when combined with the first two theoretical underpinnings for the "unitary" approach this issue might well be resolved for the requirement that some formal action is required. Finally, the general argument cited for the "dual" approach does not, of itself, identify how Senate action alone could generate a domestically binding legal effect or whether it is assumed this will result only in settings in which the President joins in the Senate understanding, and if the latter is assumed, this, of course, adds an additional dimension beyond enumeration of the record of Senate consideration.

Finally, several related theoretical questions concerning the constitutional underpinnings of the "dual" approach in relation to the constitutional limits of the treaty power itself might also be noted. First, the treaty power itself is probably not a plenary legislative authority, but is rather probably a power in general terms to enter into international agreements on any subject which is genuinely a "`matter[] of international concern,'"[277] or "properly the subject of international negotiations,"[278] or "any matter which is properly the subject of negotiation with a foreign country."[279] Since, however, if the "dual" approach has any meaning in interpretation of international agreements it results solely in creation of domestic law--not international law--and indeed even domestic law always at variance with the underlying international agreement being interpreted, is it not *ipso facto* always purely a matter of domestic law not within even the outermost parameters of the treaty power? Second, this same theoretical question applies to the general category of "domestic conditions." That is, by definition "domestic conditions" affect *only* domestic law and not the treaty to which they may be attached. How then do such conditions even fall within the outermost parameters of the treaty power?

---

[277]*Treaties and International Agreements Committee Print, supra* note 66, at 64 (quoting remarks of C.E. Hughes in 23 Am. Soc. Int'l L. Proc. 194 (1929)).

[278]*Id.* at 17, 64.

[279]Geofroy v. Riggs, 133 U.S. 258, 267 (1890) (this is also quoted in *Treaties and International Agreements Committee Print, supra* note 66, at 61).

There is also a potential theoretical constitutional problem in treating informal treaty history as law-making in settings where it is not reviewed to ascertain the intention of an underlying legal instrument formally adopted pursuant to the treaty process. That is, legislative history is resorted to--despite all its associated problems--to ascertain "legislative" intent surrounding some legal instrument adopted pursuant to formal constitutional processes. Legislative history alone, without passage by the legislature of an underlying legal instrument being interpreted, certainly is not law-creating. To apply this comparison initially to the generic category of "domestic conditions," how can "domestic conditions" be created by "legislative" or "treaty" history alone, no matter how clear, absent formal adoption of an underlying condition to be interpreted? Judge Harold H. Greene's decision in the *Rainbow Navigation* case at least arguably does exactly this? For the "treaty" history in that case seems to have been created by Executive branch statements, congressional statements, and a report of the Senate Foreign Relations Committee with no underlying formally adopted "domestic condition" to be interpreted. And by their very nature, "domestic conditions" are not an interpretation of the treaty--embodying an international agreement. And if this absence of a formally adopted underlying legal prescription to be interpreted is a bar to informal adoption of "domestic conditions" in settings lacking a formally adopted underlying condition, then would it not also be a constitutional bar to the "dual" approach? For the essence of that approach--indeed its very legal meaning--is to create domestic law known or assumed to be at variance with the underlying formal prescription to be interpreted. Moreover, the "dual" approach does not seek to apply "treaty" history for the purpose of ascertaining the legal meaning of the formal instrument as an international agreement, but rather to create domestic law under some theory of policing the integrity of the Senate role in the treaty process. In turn, how is such a purpose within the treaty power; and, in any event, how can it be achieved by informal "treaty" history without an underlying formally adopted condition which it is interpreting? It might be noted that the general constitutional issue addressed by this part of the study is sometimes posed as raising the question "at what point does a `reinterpretation' of a treaty represent an amendment--or a new treaty?"[280] The answer to this question--which the author of this study believes is

---

[280]*See, e.g., T. Franck & M. Glennon, Foreign Relations and National Security Law: Cases, Materials and Simulations* 419 (1987).

In their recent book, Franck and Glennon include the following "Introductory Note" to a section on "Interpretation or Amendment? The ABM Treaty Controversy":

not a particularly illuminating question in understanding the real issues--seems reasonably clear, at least for the legal purpose of ascertaining Executive branch authority to interpret treaties. [The legal realists have taught us that legal answers may vary depending on why a question is asked, so some caution in answering such a general question is always in order.] The answer is that it would seem always to be at that point where an interpretation is *not* a legally correct interpretation of an underlying agreement as ascertained pursuant to normal rules of interpretation of international agreements and in a process in which interpretations of the Executive are entitled to "great weight." But this in turn highlights that contrary to the normal intent in raising this issue in the "broad-narrow" debate--to question Executive

---

INTRODUCTORY NOTE

On March 11, 1987, the Senate Foreign Relations Committee and the Senate Judiciary Committee began a series of joint hearings on the effort of the Reagan Administration to reinterpret the 1972 ABM Treaty. The Treaty traditionally had been accorded a "narrow" interpretation, pursuant to which the development and testing of certain elements of the Strategic Defense Initiative (also known as "SDI," or "Star Wars") would have been prohibited. The new interpretation would have allowed greater development and testing. In response, Senator Joseph Biden introduced Senate Resolution 167, which reasserted the propriety of the narrow interpretation and made certain findings concerning pertinent constitutional principles. It is the dispute concerning these principles, rather than the dispute concerning the merits of the narrow versus the broad interpretation, that the following materials address. Three central issues emerge. First, at what point does a "reinterpretation" of a treaty represent an amendment--or a new treaty? Second, in resolving this issue, what weight is to be accorded the negotiating record of a treaty--and what difference does it make that that record was not transmitted to the Senate at the time it approved the treaty? Third, when the negotiating record is not transmitted (most are not), what weight is to be accorded the Senate's implicit understanding concerning the meaning of a treaty--to be gleaned, for example, from statements made by Senators during committee hearings or on the Senate floor--as opposed to *explicit* Senate understandings, such as actual reservations made by the Senate upon its consent to a treaty? As this book went to press, controversy concerning these questions continued.

Id. at 418-19.

authority in adopting the "broad" interpretation--the "dual" interpretation will, if it means anything, always amount to an "amendment--or a new treaty" for purposes of national law. Yet the question is not asked: How can purely national "treaty" history create an amendment to a treaty or a new treaty (for purposes of national law), and particularly absent an underlying formally adopted "domestic condition" seeking to alter the correct international legal meaning of the treaty?

Similarly, a forthcoming commentary by Senator Sam Nunn in the University of Pennsylvania Law Review[281] says in concluding:

> As previously noted, however, more was at stake in this long struggle than the Senate's constitutional powers and responsibilities. For had the precedent been established that the original meaning of a treaty could be unilaterally changed by a future President, our Nation's reliability as a negotiating partner could have been called into question, with destructive consequences for the conduct of U.S. foreign policy. Professor Koplow's article will help ensure that these lessons are not forgotten.[282]

But apparently no president has asserted a power to unilaterally change "the original meaning of a treaty" in the sense in which it would call into question "our Nation's reliability as a negotiating partner," that is, the meaning of the treaty between the parties as established pursuant to normal international legal principles. In this respect, the "broad" interpretation is either right or wrong under recognized principles of the international law of treaty interpretation, *but it does not involve a claim to a new presidential power*. Indeed, presidential authority to interpret treaties is hornbook law, and the power to "take Care that the Laws be faithfully executed" is an Article II, section 3 constitutional *obligation* of the presidency. In contrast, however, it would seem to be the Senate, through the theory of the "dual" interpretation of treaties, that *would* be claiming a power to unilaterally change "the original meaning of a treaty" in that sense of relevance for "our Nation's reliability as a negotiating partner." For if the "dual" theory is meaningful at all, its effect is precisely to require under national law that the Nation either violate its treaty

---

[281]Nunn, "A Common-Sense Definition of `Common Understanding,'" 137 *U. Penn. L. Rev.* 1523 (forthcoming May 1989) (reviewed from page proofs subject to final editing).

[282]*Id.* at 1527 (quoted from page proofs subject to final editing).

obligations or adhere to obligations not accepted in the international agreement by other parties *whatever the correct original international legal meaning.*

primary authorities

While, with one possible exception, there are no primary authorities squarely addressing the core "dual" versus "unitary" approach issue, there are a number of cases strongly supporting the principal theoretical underpinnings of the "unitary" approach. The one exception, which can be read to have rejected the "dual" approach, at least as a blanket theoretical requirement, is the 1898 decision of the Supreme Court in *New York Indians v. United States*.[283] As we have seen, that case held that a Senate proviso adopted as a condition of Senate consent to a treaty but not published with the treaty nor apparently conveyed to the other party was not binding and could not "be considered as a legislative act, since the power to legislate is vested in the President, Senate and House of Representatives."[284] The Indian treaty cases as a group have sometimes been said to present special considerations which might alter their precedental effect for treaties as a whole. Nevertheless, in this case the agreement with the New York Indians was treated by the Court as taking effect under the treaty power and it did so pursuant to the treaty obligation despite a clearly expressed and formally adopted Senate proviso held not to be controlling. And while an Indian treaty case, the setting was particularly strong for the "dual" approach since it involved a formal Senate condition rather than informal legislative history, yet the Court did not even hold this uncommunicated formal condition binding. It should also be noted that the setting presents what is likely to be the principal real-world setting of dealing with the consequences of mistake in an already concluded agreement.

In addition to the Supreme Court decision in the *New York Indians* case there is a substantial body of cases supporting the principal theoretical underpinnings of the "unitary" approach. Thus, as we have seen in the general discussion of the treaty power, a considerable line of Supreme Court decisions refers to a treaty as a compact or contract between nations. For example, in the 1829 case of *Foster v. Neilson* [285] the Supreme Court said: "[a] treaty is, in its

[283]170 U.S. 1 (1989).

[284]170 U.S. 1, at 23.

[285]27 U.S. (2 Pet.) 253 (1829).

nature, a contract between two nations, not a legislative act."[286] Similarly, as has been discussed, a substantial line of Supreme Court decisions refers to international law or mutuality of obligation between the parties as the appropriate standard for interpretation of a treaty and another substantial line of such cases roots the scope of the treaty power in matters of negotiation among nations. Again, as we have seen, Mr. Justice Brown, concurring in the *Fourteen Diamond Rings* case in 1901 said of the Senate role in "consent" to treaties:

> . . . the power of the Senate is limited to a ratification of such terms as have already been agreed upon between the President, acting for the United States, and the commissioners of the other contracting power. The Senate has no right to ratify the treaty and introduce new terms into it, which shall be obligatory upon the other power, although it may refuse its ratification, or make such ratification conditional upon the adoption of amendments to the treaty.[287]

While vacated by the Supreme court "upon the ground that the cause is moot," a 1957 opinion of Judge Bazelon, writing for the United States Court of Appeals for the District of Columbia Circuit in the famous *Niagara Reservation* case,[288] upheld a treaty with Canada about the waters of the Niagara river while setting aside a clear Senate reservation to the treaty on the grounds that "[i]t was merely an expression of domestic policy which the Senate attached to its consent" and, as such, was beyond the power of the Senate.[289] In addition to the fact that this decision was vacated as moot by the Supreme Court,[290] a decision that the Senate has no power to set domestic conditions incident to a treaty is not necessarily the

---

[286] 27 U.S. (2 Pet.) 253, 314.

[287] 183 U.S. 176, 183 (1901). *Accord F. Allen*, supra note 169, at 6.

[288] Power Authority of the State of New York v. Federal Power Commission, 247 F.2d 538 (D.C. Cir. 1957); *vacated as moot sub. nom.* in American Pub. Power Assn. v. Power Authority of the State of New York, 355 U.S. 64 (1957).

[289] 247 F.2d 538, 541 (D.C. Cir. 1957).

[290] A decision by the Supreme Court to vacate a Court of Appeals decision as moot does not indicate agreement or disagreement by the Court with the merits of the decision.

same as a decision that the Senate has no power to create a domestic legal obligation going beyond the international agreement if related to the matter of interpretation of that agreement. Nevertheless, this decision lends some real-world support to the "unitary" approach since it demonstrates that at least one thoughtful court had rejected a Senate condition perceived as having legal effect apart from the underlying international legal obligation. Moreover, it was decided with the benefit of considerable theoretical discussion about the nature of the treaty power and its roots in international agreement in a ninety-six page opinion written by Professors Philip C. Jessup and Oliver J. Lissitzyn of the Columbia University School of Law.[291]

While reversed on other grounds, mooting a direct conflict between unitary and dual approaches, a 1984 decision of the United States Claims Court in *Coplin v. United States*[292] seemed clearly to reject a "dual" approach and to take the position that informal expressions of Senate intent not included in the instrument of ratification and communicated to the other treaty party could have no legal effect. This position was adopted where the legal issue was one principally of domestic legal concern as to the liability of a United States citizen for United States federal income tax. Thus, a unanimous Court said:

> . . . [A]ll three branches of our government have taken the position that even the clearest expression of legislative intent cannot change the legal effect of an international agreement to which the Senate has given its approval. In *Fourteen Diamond Rings v. United States*, 183 U.S. 176, 179-80, 22 S.Ct. 59, 60-61, 46 L.Ed. 138 (1901), the Court held that a Senate Resolution that had not been brought to the attention of Spain, the other signatory to the treaty, was "absolutely without legal significance." Charles Evans Hughes, in his letter to the Senate of 1919, considered this proposition as black letter law: "The adoption of resolutions by the Senate setting forth its views will not affect the obligations of the covenant if it is in fact ratified without reservations which constitute part of the instrument of ratification." 58 Cong.Rec. 3302 (1919).

---

[291]*Opinion of Philip C. Jessup and Oliver J. Lissitzyn, supra* note 113.

[292]Coplin v. United States, 6 Cl. Ct. 115 (1984), *rev'd on other grounds*, 761 F.2d 688 (Fed. Cir. 1985), aff'd, 107 S. Ct. 247 (1986). *See also* Harris v. United States, 768 F.2d 1240 (11th Cir. 1985), *vacated*, 107 S. Ct. 450 (1986).

The Senate thoroughly considered the same issue during the deliberations over the Kellogg-Briand Peace Treaty of August 27, 1928. See 70 Cong.Rec. 1655 *et seq*. (1929). After considerable debate, the Senate concluded that a legislative report not mentioned or included in the resolution of ratification could not modify or amend the treaty in any way. See id. at 1730. This view was accepted by the Department of State and related to other signatories of the treaty. Telegram from Secretary of State Kellogg to Ambassador to Great Britain (Jan. 17, 1929) & Telegram from Secretary Kellogg to Ambassador to France (Jan. 18, 1929), cited in 5 Hackworth, *Digest* 153.

The State Department has consistently taken this view. For example, on May 24, 1907, Secretary of State Root wrote Dominican Republic Minister Joubert concerning the effect of a resolution adopted by the Dominican Congress in approving a convention with the United States. Secretary Root requested that the resolution--which explained the Dominican Congress' interpretation of the convention--not be included in the instrument of ratification because to do so might change the legal effect of the treaty, making it impossible for our President to accept the ratification. On the other hand, Secretary Root took the position that if the legislative report was not attached to the ratification documents, it could have no legal effect on the relationship between the parties, even though the United States was fully aware of it. Letter from Secretary of State Root to Dominican Minister Joubert (May 24, 1907), *cited in* 5 Hackworth, *Digest* 125-26.

There are important policies behind the refusal to give legal effect to expressions of intent that are not contained in the ratification documents and thereby made part of the formal agreement between the parties. Unless such statements are included in the ratification instruments, it is impossible to determine whether the confirming body (here the Senate) assented to the proposed interpretations. *See Fourteen Diamond Rings*, 183 U.S. at 180, 22 S.Ct. at 61. Here, for example, the Committee Report, which reflects the State Department's section-by-section analyses, was voted upon by the members of the Foreign Relations Committee but not by the full Senate. Even if one were persuaded that the Foreign Relations Committee accepted all of the State Department's analyses, there is no assurance that two-thirds of the full Senate would have.

As the Court of Claims cautioned in *Hart*, "[t]o legislate by committee report would raise a [serious] constitutional problem." 585 F.2d 1025, 218 Ct.Cl. at 222. In addition, where the document is not part of the ratification protocol, there is no assurance that the President has given his approval to it. *See New York Indians v. United States*, 170 U.S. 1, 23, 18, S.Ct. 531, 536, 42 L.Ed. 927 (1897).

Perhaps most important, foreign governments dealing with us must rely upon the official instruments of ratification as an expression of the full intent of the government of the United States, precisely as we expect from foreign governments. The Supreme Court confronted this very issue in *New York Indians* where the United States relied upon a provision in the resolution of ratification not included in the President's proclamation ratifying the treaty. The Court held the resolution to be of no effect, stating as follows:

> There is something . . . which shocks the conscience in the idea that a treaty can be put forth as embodying the terms of an arrangement with a foreign power or an Indian tribe, a material provision of which is unknown to one of the contracting parties, and is kept in the background to be used by the other only when the exigencies of a particular case may demand it.

Id. More recently, Professor Bishop stated the same proposition in more general terms:

> The fundamental basis remains, that no state is bound in international law without its consent to the treaty. This is the starting point for the law of treaties, and likewise for our international law rules dealing with reservations.

Bishop, 103 Receuil des Cours 255.

The Senate managed to attach a multitude of reservations, understandings and other modifications to the treaties with Panama as a condition for giving its advice and consent. Each of those

> instruments was approved by two-thirds of the Senate, presented by the President and accepted by Panama. It would be entirely inappropriate--and inconsistent with the established policy of the United States--to now modify the agreement on the basis of views expressed in committee and never approved by the Senate or presented to Panama for its concurrence or rejection. *See New York Indians*, 170 U.S. at 22-23, 18 S.Ct. at 536.[293]

It should also be noted in the *Coplin* case that the court examined a negotiating record, in detail, including materials not presented to the Senate,[294] in seeking to ascertain "the intention of the two governments"[295] as the appropriate standard for treaty interpretation. Indeed, of particular importance, the opinion of the United States Court of Appeals in the Federal Circuit, reversing the Claims Court, did so in part on the confirming evidence of a diplomatic note of February 25, 1985, from "the Panamanian Foreign Minister in which he confirmed that the Panamanian Foreign Ministry shared the United States' view"[296] of the treaty. This note was not available to the Claims Court and, of course, could not have been available to the consenting Senate. Thus, a grounds on which the Court of Appeals confirmed a treaty interpretation reversing the Claims Court--and on which two members of the Court seemed to principally rely--focused on understanding of the interpretation between the parties, and the Court explicitly permitted in evidence a diplomatic note as to the intent of the other treaty party not available to the consenting Senate. Nothing in this Court of Appeals reversal suggests that it is only the intent of the consenting Senate or material submitted to the Senate that is relevant to treaty interpretation. In fact, the opinion of the Court of Appeals written by Judge Bissell confirmed in reversing that the standard for treaty interpretation was the intent of the treaty parties:

---

[293]6 Cl. Ct. 115, at 144-45. *See also* the discussion of the court, id. at 139-42.

[294]6 Cl. Ct. 115, at 128-35.

[295]6 Cl. Ct. 115, at 126. *See* the court's discussion of the appropriate standard, *id.* at 125-27.

[296]761 F.2d 688, at 691.

> The court's "role is limited to giving effect to the intent of the Treaty parties" . . . treaties must be construed to enforce intent of contracting parties. . . .[297]

No judge in additional or concurring views disputed this point.

There is also a line of cases implicitly supporting the "unitary" approach by adopting an interpretive standard rooted in the international agreement even if the interpretive evidence of that agreement was not necessarily before the Senate. Thus, the decision of the Supreme Court in the 1985 case of *Air France v. Saks*[298] referred extensively to the *travaux preparatoires* of the Warsaw Convention and specifically it looked to the French text of that Convention even though it pointed out that the official American translation of the text was before the Senate when it ratified the Convention. Thus the Court said: "We look to the French legal meaning for guidance as to these expectations [the shared expectations of the contracting parties] because the Warsaw Convention was drafted in French by continental jurists."[299] Similarly, in 1967 in *Block v. Compagnie Nationale Air France*,[300] the United States Court of Appeals for the Fifth Circuit declared that "[t]he binding meaning of the terms [of the Warsaw Convention] is the French legal meaning,"[301] even though it simultaneously noted that "the text that was read to the Senate, and to which the resolution of ratification was directed, was a text in English originally published in a Treaty Information Bulletin of the Department of State."[302] And, of course, the 50 year pattern of subsequent practice considered by the Supreme Court in, among other cases, the 1984 decision in *Trans World Airlines, Inc. v. Franklin Mint Corp.*,[303] clearly took into account information not before the Senate when it gave

---

[297] 761 F.2d 688, at 691-92.

[298] 470 U.S. 392 (1985).

[299] 470 U.S. 392, 399 (and *compare with* 397).

[300] 386 F.2d 323 (1967).

[301] 386 F.2d 323, 330.

[302] 386 F.2d 323, 330 n.19.

[303] 466 U.S. 243 (1984).

its advice and consent to the Warsaw Convention in 1934.[304] These cases simply

---

[304]466 U.S. 243, 255-60.

In *Day v. Trans World Airlines, Inc.*, decided in 1975, the United States Court of Appeals for the Second Circuit said the following in relying on a pattern of subsequent conduct of the treaty parties clearly going beyond what was before the Senate:

> Those called upon to construe a treaty should, in the words of Judge Clark, strive to "give the specific words of a treaty a meaning consistent with the genuine shared expectations of the contracting parties." *Maximov v. United States*, 299 F.2d 565, 568 (2d Cir. 1962), *aff'd* 373 U.S. 49, 83 S.Ct. 1054, 10 L.Ed.2d 184 (1963). These expectations can, of course, change over time. Conditions and new methods may arise not present at the precise moment of drafting. For a court to view a treaty as frozen in the year of its creation is scarcely more justifiable than to regard the Constitutional clock as forever stopped in 1787. Justice Holme's counsel concerning Constitutional construction, set forth in his opinion in *Missouri v. Holland*, 252 U.S. 416, 433, 40 S.Ct. 382, 383, 64 L.Ed. 641 (1920), applies with equal force to the task of treaty interpretation:
>
>> [W]hen we are dealing with words that also are a constituent act . . we must realize that they have called into life a being the development of which could not have been foreseen completely by the most gifted of its begetters.
>
> The conduct of the parties subsequent to ratification of a treaty may, thus, be relevant in ascertaining the proper construction to accord the treaty's various provisions. *See Pigeon River Improvement Slide & Boom Co. v. Cox*, 291 U.S. 138, 158-63, 54 S.Ct. 361, 78 L.Ed. 695 (1934); *Husserl v. Swiss Air Transport Co., supra*; Harvard Research, Article 19; M. McDougal, H. Lasswell and J. Miller, The Interpretation of Agreements and World Public Order 56, 58 (1967); II. C. Hyde, International Law 72 (1922); Vienna Convention Art. 31(3).

Day v. Trans World Airlines, Inc., 528 F.2d 31, 35-36 (1975). This dynamic view of the "genuine shared expectations of the contracting parties" as a standard to be applied through time would not seem consistent with a view that the meaning of a treaty is frozen as it is presented to the Senate. Moreover, such a view would not more dramatically illustrate, because specifically adverting to differences in material before the Senate and interpretive materials rooted in the international agreement relied on by the Court, a widespread--indeed hornbook--practice in interpreting treaties to look to the materials rooted in the international agreement, such as comparative language texts, negotiating history, and subsequent conduct, without inquiring whether such materials were also before the Senate.[305]

It can also be argued by analogy to a well established principle of United States constitutional law that since under the "dual" approach any finding--if the approach is meaningful--would be departing from an international agreement based only on an "informal" Senate understanding, if even that, then such a finding would not be "clearly expressed," as required for a departure from a treaty under national law, and that, indeed, the most meaningful way to police this standard that such an intent be "clearly expressed" would be to require formal rather than informal Senate action. The well established principle, of course, reflecting important national support for the rule of law in international affairs, is that legislative repeal of a treaty requires a clearly expressed legislative intent. As recently stated by the Supreme Court in *Trans World Airlines, Inc. v. Franklin Mint Corp.*:[306]

> There is, first, a firm and obviously sound canon of construction against finding implicit repeal of a treaty in ambiguous congressional action. "A treaty will not be deemed to have been abrogated or modified by a later statute unless such purpose on the

---

only seem more consistent with the international legal standard for treaty interpretation reflected in the Vienna Convention on the Law of Treaties, but would also seem more consistent with the United States-U.S.S.R. arms control practice of considering interpretive issues within the Standing Consultative Commission, treaty review conferences and other subsequent practice settings. Would the "dual" approach suggest that such subsequently agreed interpretations--some in settings such as the SCC that remain secret--could not be binding under national law because not before the Senate during consideration of advice and consent?

[305]*See, e.g.*, the authorities collected note 411 *infra.*

The "dual" approach could also inhibit the natural instincts of courts to look to legislative history and patterns of practice in relation to multilateral treaties in seeking to promote uniform interpretation. See Block v. Compagnie Nationale Air France, 386 F.2d 323, 337-38 (1967).

[306]466 U.S. 243 (1984).

part of Congress has been clearly expressed." *Cook v. United States*, 288 U. S. 102, 120 (1933).[307]

But if this is the rule where the subsequent congressional action is rooted in a clear legislative power of both houses acting together with presentment to the President, why shouldn't it also apply even more strongly to a setting where action is solely that of the Senate or simply a statement by an Executive branch official? There is, of course, a simple method to ensure such clear expression of intent to alter an international meaning in the treaty advice and consent setting, and that is through a requirement of formal action, *i.e.*, a Senate adopted amendment or understanding. At the least this principle should establish a high standard of "clear expression" of intent by a Senate--and possibly even one of adverting to a change in a treaty regime--in a "dual" approach standard rooted solely in informal action or a statement by an Executive branch official during the advice and consent process.[308]

Finally, the opinion of the Court in the 1983 *Chadha* decision stressed the framers' intent, and specifically quoted Hamilton and Madison, with respect to the decision that the legislative power under the Constitution should be shared between two houses of Congress with a qualified veto in the President, rather than entrusted to a single house. This certainly heightens the question whether a "dual" approach would conceptually be regarded as embodying a "legislative" power to create a domestic obligation going beyond the international obligation which by its "legislative" nature could only be undertaken by both houses of Congress and the President rather than, at least theoretically, the Senate alone.

---

[307]466 U.S. 243, 252.

[308]It can also be urged that the "dual" approach, giving binding weight to informal Senate understandings even if inconsistent with the underlying treaty, can be inconsistent with the general approach that supplemental means of interpretation are not to be consulted when the language of a treaty is clear. *See* Hidalgo County Water Control and Improvement District No. 7 v. Hedrick, 226 F.2d 1, 8 (Ct. App. 5th Cir. 1955) (dictum).

secondary authorities

Many secondary authorities lend support to the treaty power as an agreement between nations, not a legislative act.[309] For example, Judge Florence Ellinwood Allen writes in her 1952 study of the treaty power:

> When the founding fathers made the treaty the supreme law of the land, little mention was made of the inherent distinction between treaty and statute, and none of the fact that requisites for negotiating a compact and for passing a law are inherently different. Since the treaty is a contract, it is often initiated by an offer made by one government to another or to several other governments, which is accepted. In other words, it is a prerequisite to the treaty that there be a "meeting of the minds" between two or more states. The statute is enacted by the legislature of one single state, and the consent or agreement of another country is neither sought nor required. Being a contract, the treaty as a practical matter, had to be negotiated by the executive--in our country, the President. This conformed to the fact that the treaty is a compact between sovereigns.[310]

Similarly, Professor Norman J. Singer writes in Sands Fourth Edition of Sutherland Statutory Construction:

> . . . The prevailing concept of the nature and function of a treaty is that of a contract between nations in which the principals promise how they will conduct their respective sovereign affairs on matters which affect their mutual interests and relationships. . . .[311]

---

[309]The reader should at this point also review the authorities cited earlier in this part, including such authorities as Corwin and Wright, for the proposition that the Senate role in the treaty process is a veto.

[310]*F. Allen*, *supra* note 169, at 6-7.

[311]1A *Sutherland Statutory Construction,* § 32.01, at 539 (Sands 4th ed., N. Singer ed. 1985 rev.) [hereinafter *Sutherland Stat. Const.*].

> A treaty is in its nature a contract between two nations, not a Legislative act.[312]

And Judge Allen, as we have seen, indicates that, consistent with the veto nature of the Senate role in the treaty power, proposed Senate changes in a treaty become effective only when accepted by the other treaty partner:

> . . . the framing of treaties is a wholly executive function. The treaties, so far as form is concerned, are presented to the Senate as an accomplished fact. The Senate may reject them *in toto*, make reservations, or reject separate articles; but the changes that it proposes do not become effective until they are accepted by the country with which the treaty is made.[313]

Perhaps the most important secondary authority lending support to the "unitary" approach is a detailed opinion by Professors Philip C. Jessup and Oliver J. Lissitzyn written in support of the position of the Power Authority of the State of New York in the much fought over *Niagara Reservation* case already discussed.[314] While not directly confronting the "dual" versus "unitary" issue in all its possible dimensions, this opinion did squarely relate to one such dimension, whether the Senate can attach a treaty condition operative only under domestic law, and it did address at length and adopt the most important theoretical consideration underlying the "unitary" approach; that is, the conclusion that the treaty power by its nature is a compact or contract between nations and not a legislative power going beyond the underlying agreement. Paradoxically, Professor Philip C. Jessup, who became a judge of the International Court of Justice and was one of the United States' most distinguished international lawyers, was then holding a chair at Columbia subsequently held by Professor Louis Henkin (Hamilton Fish Professor of International Law and Diplomacy) whose testimony on the "ABM Treaty Interpretation Resolution" was interpreted by the majority of the Senate Foreign Relations Committee in favor of the "dual" approach. As has previously been discussed, although vacated as moot by the Supreme Court, the Court of Appeals in the *Niagara Reservation* case decided for the Jessup-Lissitzyn view as set out in

---

[312]*Id.* at 541.

[313]*F. Allen, supra* note 169, at 6.

[314]*Opinion of Philip C. Jessup and Oliver J. Lissitzyn, supra* note 132.

these distinguished lawyers' "opinion" and not the Henkin view, as expressed by Professor Henkin in his 1956 article[315] before the decision of the Court of Appeals in 1957. That is, although subsequently vacated by the Supreme Court as moot, the Court of Appeals decision in the *Niagara Reservation* case had accepted the theoretical underpinnings of the Jessup-Lissitzyn view rather than the Henkin view. There seems no judicial decision, even one vacated as moot, that has accepted the Henkin view other than the opinion of Judge Harold H. Greene in the Rainbow Navigation case that is currently on appeal.

The Jessup-Lissitzyn opinion is a detailed ninety-six printed page exploration of the Niagara reservation issue with special attention to the theoretical underpinnings of the treaty power. Anyone pursuing the general "dual" versus "unitary" issue is urged to read it in full as it contains a detailed discussion of relevant Supreme Court and secondary authorities with respect to the nature of the treaty power and reservations. Pertinent conclusions supporting the constitutional underpinnings of the "unitary" approach, made after this detailed examination of the authorities include the following:

> . . . it is clear that "treaties" was a word that had to be understood by the United States with reference to the expectations of the other nations and, consequently, with reference to international usage. It was not a term that could have a significance peculiar to the United States alone. Subsequent decisions of the courts confirm the view that the meaning of the term "treaty" and the interpretation of particular treaties were understood to be governed by international usage and international law. . . .[316]
>
> This examination of the origins of the provisions of the Constitution concerning treaties shows that inherent in the concept and term "treaty" as used in those provisions is the notion of negotiation and agreement with another nation or state (or an entity similar to a state in some important respects, as in the case of Indian tribes) on a matter of concern to that nation or state, and that this notion is primarily derived from, and must be understood with reference to, international usage. . . .[317]

---

[315]Henkin, "Niagara Reservation," *supra* note 140, at 1151.

[316]*Opinion of Philip C. Jessup and Oliver J. Lissitzyn, supra* note 132, at 41.

[317]*Id.* at 41-42.

> As shown above, the framers of the constitution provided for two categories of cases in which they realized that federal law-making would be necessary. One category embraced the usual necessities of any nation in passing laws to govern its own internal life. The other category embraced those situations where a foreign or international aspect required special measures to protect the country from possible dangers and to permit it to discharge the obligations, as it reaped the benefits, of intercourse with the rest of the world. For the first category, the Constitution provided the legislative procedure of action by the two Houses of Congress with the concurrence of the President except where a veto may be overridden by a special vote. For the second category, the Constitution provided the treaty-making process, giving the Executive the initiative in international negotiations but requiring the concurrence of the Senate in the manner specified. Either of the two procedures, properly exercised in its own field, results in establishing the law of the land. . . .[318]

Professors Jessup and Lissitzyn include in their "Conclusions" the following:

> 9. A "treaty," as that term is used in the Constitution, is an international contract which either creates rights and duties as between two or more nations, or modifies or abrogates pre-existing rights and duties in the relations of nations, or confirms and recognizes with binding effect an existing international legal situation;
>
> 10. A declaration by one party must modify the legal effect of a treaty on the relations between the parties in order to constitute a reservation to a treaty;
>
> 11. The so-called "reservation" to the 1950 Niagara Treaty does not have these requisite characteristics of a treaty or of a reservation and can not legally be considered as a treaty or part of a treaty;

---

[318] *Id.* at 91.

> 12. The inclusion of the "reservation" in the ratification of the Treaty was a mere colorable use of the treaty-making power and therefore derives no legal validity from the Constitution; . . . .[319]

The *Niagara Reservation* case has prompted at least one other writer to question the legal effect of a Senate resolution made on ratifying the 1930 London Naval Agreement and concerning an understanding that there were no secret agreements related to the treaty. Thus Irving Younger writes in a 1959 article in the *University of Pittsburgh Law Review* on "Congressional Investigations and Executive Secrecy: A Study in the Separation of Powers":

> It would be rash to assert that the President always wins his fight with Congress, for we do not have complete records of the innumerable working compromises by which Congress got the information it wanted. However, where the clash between them is overt, history suggests that the President does not lose. He may select his weapons from a veritable political arsenal. Congress enjoys no such advantage: the best it can do is memorialize and resolve, in the vain hope that the voters are heedful. One instance will suffice. On July 21, 1930, the Senate ratified the London agreement on Naval Forces. Fearful of secret provisions, and powerless to compel presidential disclosure whether any existed, the Senate resolved as follows:
>
>> That in ratifying said treaty the Senate does so with the distinct and explicit understanding that there are no secret files, documents, letters, understandings,

---

[319]*Id.* at 96. Of related interest in the Jessup-Lissitzyn "Opinion" the authors write:

> It may be well to note here that in construing the nature and effect of the "reservation" the Supreme Court would feel free to inquire into its legislative history and into the correspondence and negotiations between the United States and Canada, since the Court has not hesitated to resort to preparatory work in the interpretation of treaties . . . and to legislative history in the interpretation of statutes. . . .

Id. at 90-91.

> or agreements which in any way, directly or indirectly, modify, change, add to, or take away from any of the stipulations, agreements, or statements in said treaty and that the Senate ratifies said treaty with the distinct and explicit understanding that . . . there is no agreement, specific or otherwise, expressed or implied, between any of the parties to said treaty as to any construction that shall hereafter be given to any statement or provision contained therein.

> The legal effect of such an understanding is vague; [citing the *Niagara Reservation* case] its political effect is probably nil.[320]

In the context of the "broad-narrow" dispute at least one attorney has squarely recognized the "dual" versus "unitary" issue[321] and has unequivocally

---

[320]Younger, *supra* note 12, at 755, 774-75.

[321]The author of this study has also generally discussed the "dual" versus "unitary" issue with five of the country's most prominent foreign relations law scholars, all of whom, at least in general terms, seem to support the "unitary" approach. These scholars are L.F.E. Goldie, Sterling Professor of Law and Director of International Legal Studies at Syracuse University; Monroe Leigh, a former State Department Legal Adviser and a past President of the American Society of International Law; Professor Myres McDougal, a former Sterling Professor of Law at Yale and a past President of the American Society of International Law and of the Association of American Law Schools; Eugene V. Rostow, formerly Under Secretary of State for Political Affairs, Director of the U.S. Arms Control and Disarmament Agency, and Dean of the Yale Law School; and Robert F. Turner, a former Deputy Assistant Secretary of State for Congressional Relations and prolific author on separation of powers in foreign policy. In addition, at a discussion of separation of powers issues June 23, 1988, before the Los Angeles Bar Association, Professor Thomas M. Franck of the New York University School of Law seemed to take the view, not fully developed, that the Senate had gone too far with the INF Treaty interpretation condition. Robert F. Turner has now specifically rejected the "dual" approach in a recent paper presented at the conference on "Treaty Implementation and Interpretation Under the Constitution" on March 10, 1989, at the Syracuse University College of Law, *supra* note 1. *See also* the papers

supported the correctness of the "unitary" approach. Thus, David B. Rivkin, Jr., an attorney with the Washington office of Baker & McKenzie and an author on defense and foreign policy issues, has recently written:

> In ascertaining U.S. domestic legal obligations under the ABM Treaty, it is of the utmost importance that it is the broad, and not the restrictive, interpretation that correctly describes the U.S.--Soviet agreement. Under the U.S. Constitution, a ratified treaty becomes the "law of the land," but only to the extent of its binding international obligations. There is only one instance in which U.S. international and domestic legal obligations may diverge; the United States may be bound internationally pursuant to a properly signed treaty, yet, the same treaty may have no domestic legal force, if it is not self-executing, and Congress never passes the enabling legislation. At the same time, *it would be improper to construe any treaty to give it greater impact domestically than internationally*, since "extra" domestic obligations would not constitute the "law of the land." In fact, the only way in which such obligations can ever become legally binding, is if they could be tied to one of Congress's constitutional powers, and be independently enacted into law by both houses of Congress. This obviously did not happen following the ABM Treaty ratification.[322]

Similarly, William R. Harris, an international lawyer and senior staff member of the RAND Corporation, in a prepared statement of February 26, 1987, for the Subcommittee on Arms Control, International Security and Science of the House Committee on Foreign Affairs wrote:

> What if the Senate could be shown to have relied upon a scope for Article V of the ABM Treaty beyond the scope derived from the

---

presented at this conference by Professor Fred L. Morrison of the University of Minnesota Law School and Mr. Robert E. Dalton, Counselor on International Law with the Office of the Legal Adviser in the Department of State.

[322]Rivkin, "The Flaws in Senator Nunn's Interpretation of the ABM Treaty," (International Security Papers No. 3, Center for Peace and Freedom). *See also* Rivkin, "Sam Nunn and the ABM Treaty," in the National Security Record of the Heritage Foundation.

> treaty instruments or the negotiating record? A mistake of law, however widely shared, would not expand the duties under the ABM Treaty, unless the Senate expressed those restrictions in a reservation to the treaty, and the Soviet Union acquiesced in those additional restrictions. This the Senate did not do.[323]

While not specifically indicating that this statement was intended to address the domestic legal effect of any "mistake of law" as well as the international legal effect, to the extent that it was so intended it would at least implicitly embrace at least one parameter of the "unitary" approach.

In a forthcoming commentary to be published during 1989 in the *University of Pennsylvania Law Review*, three Senior-Attorney Advisors in the Office of Policy Development, United States Department of Justice, squarely reject the "dual" approach.[324] During a twenty-eight page exploration of the general issue they write:

> [T]reaties have no independent domestic legal status separate from their status as international agreements; there are not two sets of obligations, one domestic and one international.[325]

And:

> The treaty-making process is not an independent means of domestic lawmaking, elevating part of the treaty-making process not actually included verbatim in the text of the treaty, such as testimony, to the

---

[323]Prepared Statement of William R. Harris entitled "The ABM Treaty as a Framework for Strategic Defense Programs and Arms Control Negotiations," *reprinted in Review of ABM Treaty Interpretation Dispute and SDI: Hearing Before the Subcomm. on Arms Control, International Security and Science of the House Comm. on Foreign Affairs*, 100th Cong., 1st Sess. 103 (Feb. 26, 1987) [hereinafter *Review of ABM Treaty Interpretation Dispute and SDI Hearing*].

[324]Block, Casey & Rivkin, *supra* note 248, at 1481.

[325]*Id.* at 1495 (quoted from page proofs subject to final editing) (footnote omitted).

> level of law. It does not allow the President and the Senate to circumvent the House of Representatives.[326]

In support of their rejection of the "dual" approach and, along the way, the position of the *Restatement (Third)* on the issue, as well as that of Professor Koplow in his forthcoming article in the *University of Pennsylvania Law Review,* they write:

> Arguing *reductio ad absurdum*, the key point of why the treaty-making process cannot be used to increase the purely domestic legal obligations of the United States also can be illustrated by demonstrating the profoundly unconstitutional results of such an arrangement. First, the "two treaty" argument would lead to the unacceptable result that the Senate could introduce new terms into a treaty and make those terms binding on the President, even though the other treaty party never agreed to those terms. Indeed, under this approach the Senate could obtain such a result merely by sprinkling the ratification record with floor speeches, hearing testimony and the like, on the basis of which one could argue later that the ratification debate supported the purported Senate understanding at issue. . . .
>
> . . . .
>
> Second, such an approach would make a mockery of the constitutional principles governing the enactment of legislation. . .
>
> . . . .
>
> . . . Indeed, it is ironic that modern day "ultra-whigs," masquerading as defenders of legislative power, seem prepared to flout the fundamental principle of American republicanism -- that the only valid laws are those properly enacted by Congress, in the exercise of its enumerated powers, and brought before the President, who either acquiesces or vetoes the legislation.
>
> If the Senate Foreign Relations Committee is to be believed, however, the Senate alone could make legislation by tacking on any provisions it wished to a treaty or by inserting an "understanding" into the ratification debate that effectively added new provisions to the treaty, albeit purely of domestic import. Under such a scheme the Senate could completely cut the House of Representatives from the legislative process. For that matter, the President himself could use such a scheme as a ruse for bypassing the House with legislation

[326] *Id*. at 1497.

> that he expected to win Senate approval but that was unlikely to pass muster in the House. It is interesting to speculate, for example, what the reaction of congressional Democrats would have been had President Reagan decided, for example, to conclude a treaty with Honduras containing an extra domestic provision permitting the United States Government to support the Nicaraguan Democratic Resistance. In fact, one easily can envision a treaty loaded like a Christmas tree with all sorts of domestic provisions -- something akin to the regrettably popular omnibus continuing budget resolutions that sweep everything into their vortex. The profoundly unconstitutional nature of such arrangements should be self-evident.[327]

And they summarize the law of treaty interpretation as follows:

> [T]he law with regard to treaty interpretation is clear and straightforward: (1) only the President may definitively interpret the meaning of a treaty as a matter of international law; (2) the President can construe the treaty as a matter of domestic law, but only the courts may definitively interpret its meaning as a matter of domestic law in the context of specific cases and controversies; (3) the Senate has no authority to interpret a treaty, once it is ratified, as a matter of either international or domestic law; (4) if the Senate's resolution of advice and consent states a particular understanding of an as yet unratified treaty, the President may ratify the treaty subject to that understanding only, and the treaty will take effect only if the other treaty party accepts that understanding; (5) where, however, the Senate resolution contains no understanding, but the record of Senate deliberations establishes that the Senate attaches a particular meaning to the as yet unratified treaty, the President has the discretion to decide what, if any, international legal effect the Senate intended its record to have and to take appropriate action, or no action; (6) a Senate understanding not contained in the Senate's resolution of advice and consent and not formally accepted by the

---

[327]*Id.* at 1498, 1499-1501 (footnotes omitted).

> other high contracting party is not controlling in the interpretation of the treaty as a matter of either international or domestic law.[328]

The "Additional Views of Senators Helms, Pressler, and Trible" to the report of the Senate Foreign Relations Committee on *The ABM Treaty Interpretation* Resolution also seem at least implicitly to adopt the "unitary" approach. Thus their "Additional Views" states:

> Where the Senate as a body does not condition its advice and consent to ratification upon an amendment to the treaty, reservation, or qualification of the resolution of ratification, the internal deliberations of a Senate committee may have only a supplementary, probative value in ascertaining the meaning of the terms of a treaty, if the meaning of the terms in the treaty instruments, as supplemented by the generally more pertinent preparatory work on the treaty, remains unclear. Internal Senate deliberations may be utilized as supplementary means of interpretation, per Article 32 of the Vienna Convention.
>
> When the terms of a treaty are explained by a report of a committee of the Senate, the report of the committee is neither binding on the United States nor on other parties, but it may constitute a supplementary means of ascertaining the agreement of the parties.[329]

With the exception of the possible "estoppel" hypothesized in a setting of "formal representation by the President concerning the meaning of a particular treaty provision" and presumably based as much or more on the law of estoppel as on the law of treaties,[330] the April 9, 1987, Justice Department memorandum from the Office of Legal Counsel on "Relevance of Senate Ratification History to Treaty Interpretation" seems also implicitly to proceed largely on the "unitary" approach

---

[328]*Id.* at 1492.

[329]"Additional Views of Senators Helms, Pressler, and Trible," *supra* note 213, at 89, 94 (paragraph numbers omitted).

[330]For a brief discussion of this issue, see *supra* note 203. For a fuller discussion, see section (B)(4) of this part.

and certainly contains language reenforcing the "veto" underpinning of the "unitary" approach as well as otherwise supporting that approach. Thus, it says:

> In determining the weight to be assigned to that record, it should be observed that, conceptually, the constitutional division of treaty-making responsibility is essentially the reverse of the division of law-making authority. Congress initially agrees upon and enacts the language of domestic legislation, while the President reserves the right to determine whether that legislation will go into effect (subject, of course, to the override of any veto). Treaties, however, are proposed and negotiated by the President, subject to the approval or disapproval of the Senate. Given this conceptual framework, it is clear that the portions of the treaty ratification record that should be accorded more weight as to the treaty's meaning are the representations of the executive--the draftsman, in effect, of the treaty. Statements by individual senators, or even groups of senators, are certainly entitled to no more consideration--and perhaps less--than the limited weight such statements are given in the interpretation of domestic legislation when they are not confirmed by the legislation's sponsor in colloquy or otherwise. . . .[331]
>
> The more difficult question is what relevance, if any, the President must give to less formal, contemporaneous indications of the Senate's understanding of the treaty--*i.e.*, statements in committee reports, hearings, and debates, which may reflect an understanding of certain treaty provisions by some senators, but which were not embodied in any formal understanding or condition approved by the entire Senate. With the not insubstantial exception of representations made or confirmed by the executive branch (see below), we believe such statements have only limited probative value and therefore are entitled to little weight in subsequent interpretations of the treaty.
>
> . . . [I]t must be observed that a treaty is fundamentally a "contract between or among sovereign nations," and the primary responsibility--whether of the executive or the courts--is "to give the specific words of the treaty a meaning consistent with the shared expectations of the contracting parties." Air France v. Saks, 470 U.S. 392, 399 (1985). See generally *Foster*

[331]Cooper, "Memorandum to Abraham D. Sofaer," *supra* note 1, at 2.

> *& Elam v. Neilson*, 27 U.S. (2 Pet.) 253, 314 (1830) ("A treaty is in its nature a contract between two nations, not a legislative act."). . . .[332]
>
> . . . the constitutional role of the Senate is limited to approval or disapproval of the treaty, much as the President's constitutional role in enacting domestic legislation is limited to his veto power. The Senate may, if it chooses, amend or interpret the treaty by attaching explicit conditions to its consent, which are then transmitted to, and either accepted or rejected by, the other parties. Absent such conditions, the Senate does not participate in setting the terms of the agreement between the parties, and therefore statements made by senators, whether individually in hearings and debates or collectively in committee reports, should be accorded little weight unless confirmed by the Executive. We note that even in the case of domestic legislation, where Congress--rather than the President and other foreign governments--directly shapes the operative language, "[r]eliance on legislative history in divining the intent of Congress is . . . a step to be taken cautiously." . . .
>
> Indeed, profound foreign policy implications would be raised if the United States were to supplement or alter treaty obligations to foreign governments based on statements made by members of the Senate during its consideration of the treaty that were not communicated to those governments in the form of express conditions. . . . We can well imagine that the United States would be deeply disturbed if the Soviet Union resolved ambiguities in a treaty by reference to deliberations in a Soviet legislative body charged with consenting to its ratification. . . .[333]

Several examples in United States practice also seem to lend greater support, at least implicitly, to the "unitary" approach than the "dual" approach. Thus, a message of July 30, 1923, from Secretary of State Hughes to Ambassador Houghton seems to fall in this category. As described in Hackworth's *Digest*:

> In a diplomatic interchange concerning the question whether the Treaty of Berlin automatically gave the United States rights accorded by the Treaty of Versailles, Germany referred to statements made by Senator Lodge in debate in the Senate upon the Treaty of Berlin. Concerning this Secretary Hughes wrote the Ambassador to Germany:

---

[332]*Id.* at 8.

[333]*Id.* at 9-10.

> Should occasion arise, you may orally explain to the German Foreign Office that expressions of opinion as to the meaning of the treaty of August 25, 1921, such as those to which the Foreign Office refers, occurring in general debate, cannot be regarded as affecting the interpretation of that treaty.[334]

Similarly, a series of "Answers to Questions for the Record on the Legal Status of the SALT II Documents Transmitted to the Senate" prepared by the State Department Legal Adviser Herbert J. Hansell provided:

> Q. (c) If the Senate were to add a simple policy statement--in the form, say, of a "declaration"--to its resolution of ratification, would the President feel constrained, constitutionally, to transmit that statement, as a part of the instrument of ratification, to the Soviet Union?
>
> A. The U.S. instrument of ratification will include any statements or conditions concerning the Treaty documents which are incorporated in the Senate's resolution of ratification.
>
> Q. (d) Suppose the statement were made in a simple Senate resolution adopted at the same time as the resolution of ratification; would the content of that resolution be transmitted to the Soviet Union?
>
> A. If the Senate were to adopt a separate resolution--in addition to its resolution of ratification--there would be no legal requirement that the content of that resolution be transmitted to the Soviet Union. However, if the Senate wished to adopt such a procedure, the Administration would be pleased to consult in this regard.
>
> Q. (e) If such a resolution were adopted which set forth the Senate's understanding or interpretation concerning various Treaty provisions, what would be its legal force and effect?
>
> A. Statements of understanding or interpretation not included in the Senate's resolution of ratification and the U.S. instrument of ratification accepted by the Soviet Union would not be legally binding *per se*. However, if

---

[334] 5 *G. Hackworth, Digest of International Law* 262 (U.S. Dep't of State Pub. No. 1927, 1943).

> provided to the Soviet Union prior to the exchange of instruments of ratification, and not contradicted by the Soviets, they would constitute persuasive evidence of the manner in which the Parties interpret the Treaty.[335]

Certainly there is no hint of a "dual" approach in this response conveyed to the Senate in answer to questions posed for the record by the Chairman of the Senate Foreign Relations Committee.

Perhaps the most important example in United States practice supporting the "unitary" approach is the position of Secretary of State Kellogg expressed in telegrams to the Ambassadors to Great Britain and France that an interpretative report filed by the Senate Foreign Relations Committee during Senate consideration of the Kellogg-Briand pact "had no legal effect whatsoever upon the treaty." As described by Green Hackworth, the Legal Adviser of the Department of State, in 1943:

> When the Senate gave its advice and consent to the ratification of the Kellogg-Briand peace pact signed at Paris, August 27, 1928, the Foreign Relations Committee filed a report containing its interpretations of the treaty. The report was not put before the Senate for vote and was not included or mentioned in the resolution of ratification. It concluded with the following statement:
>
>> This report is made solely for the purpose of putting upon record what your committee understands to be the true interpretation of the treaty, and not in any sense for the purpose or with the design of modifying or changing the treaty in any way or effectuating a reservation or reservations to the same.
>
> For a statement that the report of the Senate Committee had no legal effect whatsoever upon the treaty, see Secretary Kellogg to the Ambassador to Great Britain, telegram 12, Jan. 17, 1929, MS. Department of State, file 711.0012 Anti-War/622; Mr. Kellogg to the Ambassador to France, telegram 25, Jan. 18, 1929, *ibid.* /623.

---

[335]"Answers to Questions for the Record on the Legal Status of the SALT II Documents Transmitted to the Senate" *reprinted in M. Nash, Digest of United States Practice in International Law, 1979*, at 697, 710, 713-14 (U.S. Dep't of State Pub. No. 9374, 1983).

See also discussion in the Senate of the legal effect of such a report, Cong. Rec., vol. 70, pt. 2, pp. 1655 et seq.[336]

---

[336]5 *G. Hackworth, supra* note 334, at 152-53 (citations omitted).

See also the "Report of the Senate Committee on Foreign Relations on the Multilateral or Kellogg-Briand Treaty, January 14, 1929," *reprinted in Disarmament and Security: A Collection of Documents 1919-55, Subcommittee on Disarmament Pursuant to Senate Resolution 93, and Continued by Senate Resolution 185, Eighty-fourth Congress,* 84th Cong., 2d Sess. 665-66 (Comm. Print for Senate Comm. on Foreign Relations, 1956).

The Senate discussion of the Kellogg-Briand pact included the following statements:

> In my opinion there is no reason for reservations or amendments to the treaty. So far as I am concerned, I shall be glad to vote for it without any change in its phraseology or any explanatory notes or reservations. The Senator from Connecticut [Mr. BINGHAM] has insisted that the Committee on Foreign Relations submit a report in the nature of an interpretation of the treaty, or at any rate as an explanation of their views as to what the treaty means. Mr. President, I have respect for the members of that committee, but their interpretation of the treaty, I submit, should not be controlling upon Senators. If the treaty is ambiguous and uncertain, then it should perhaps be amended or, at any rate, ambiguities should be removed by explanatory reservations. Where an instrument is clear and unambiguous, then interpretations are not needed. The duty rests upon Senators to determine as best they can the meaning of measures presented for their consideration. The responsibility rests upon them for their action. It might not be regarded as a valid excuse if a Senator were to say, "I relied upon the statements of some other Senator as to the meaning of a measure or a treaty, and finding the interpretation to be wrong I seek immunity from criticism." Of course, the Senate should be advised with respect to an important document such as this treaty is in regard to all matters pertinent and germane. Whatever information that bears upon the treaty they are entitled to possess. Indeed, it is their duty to secure all available information, and having secured it and acquainted themselves with the treaty, the responsibility rests upon them when they vote upon the question of its ratification.

70 *Cong. Rec.* 1721 (1929) (statement of Sen. King). And:

The original January 18, 1929, cable from Secretary Kellogg to the American Embassy in France, as referred to by Hackworth in this analysis, provides:

TELEGRAM SENT

Department of State

Washington,
January 18, 1929.
[10 am]

I desire now to address myself very briefly to some of the objections which have been raised by the technical hairsplitters--and, of course, we are bound to have technicians in a great body like this, and it is well that we should go into minute detail in undertaking to understand the effects of a legal document like this.

It is my understanding, not only as to treaties but as to contracts, even so limited as between individuals, that in the interpretation of a contract, the correspondence and conversations leading up to the consummation of the agreement are competent evidence in determining what the contract means, if there should arise a controversy over its interpretation.

What does this treaty obligate the United States to do? No more than it obligates any other nation to do, because, as developed a few days ago in a colloquy between the distinguished Senator from Idaho [Mr. BORAH] and myself, this treaty can not mean one thing for one nation and another thing for another nation. If it is a multilateral treaty, that means, in my judgment, that it is alike to all nations, is the same to all of them. There is no nation that signs it or that adheres to it that can adhere to the benefits that accrue under the treaty, and, at the same time, deny or renounce whatever obligations may accrue under it. In interpreting this treaty in that light, even assuming that the interpretation of this treaty given by the distinguished Secretary of State for Foreign Affairs of Great Britain in the explanatory note which he saw fit to send to our country as the agent of Great Britain, as it reflects Great Britain's attitude, is the correct interpretation--and I think it is a correct interpretation--it can not mean that for Great Britain and something else for the United States, or France, or Italy, or any other country in the world.

70 *Cong. Rec.* 1455 (1929) (statement by Sen. Barkley).

AMEMBASSY

Paris (France).

[25]

Evidently the press entirely misunderstand the effect of the report of the Foreign Relations Committee. The treaty was ratified by the Senate without any interpretation, reservation or condition. The report of the Senate Committee has no legal effect whatever. It is the same as any report of any of the committees of Congress. It is not attached to the treaty or the ratification. In other words the ratification was without any condition.

KELLOGG.[337]

Similarly, in 1974 when the Senate Foreign Relations Committee recommended Senate consent to the 1925 Geneva Protocol on chemical and bacteriological methods of warfare, it did so explicitly on the basis of a written question and answer from the Director of the Arms Control and Disarmament Agency which adopted the view that simultaneous Executive branch assurances given to the Senate that the Administration would renounce, as a matter of national policy, the first use in war of herbicides and riot control agents (with certain limited exceptions), would not bind the Administration as a matter of "formal legal impediment." Thus, the Senate Foreign Relations Committee, which viewed the constraints on herbicides and riot control agents as stemming from an interpretation of the Treaty itself (as opposed to the Executive branch view of the Treaty that its obligations did not so extend), stated the following in its report:

> Among the questions posed by the Committee to Dr. Ikle in connection with his December 10 testimony, all of which form a part of the legislative history of the Senate's action, the Committee attaches particular importance to the following:

---

[337]Secretary of State Kellogg to the Ambassador to France, telegram 25, Jan. 18, 1929, MS. Dept. of State, File 111.0012 Anti-War/623. This copy was obtained from State Department files and officially declassified on April 28, 1989. The file containing the telegram to the Ambassador to Great Britain, as discussed by Hackworth, is missing from State Department files.

> Question. Assuming the Senate were to give its advice and consent to ratification on the grounds proposed by the Administration, what legal impediment would there be to subsequent Presidential decisions broadening the permissible uses of herbicides and riot control agents?
>
> Answer. There would be no formal legal impediment to such a decision. However, the policy which was presented to the Committee will be inextricably linked with the history of Senate consent to ratification of the Protocol with its consent dependent upon its observance. If a future administration should change this policy without Senate consent whether in practice or by a formal policy change, it would be inconsistent with the history of the ratification, and could have extremely grave political repercussions and as a result is extremely unlikely to happen.
>
> On the basis of this and other Executive Branch assurances and explanations reflected in the hearing record, the Committee recommends that the Senate give its prompt advice and consent to ratification of the Geneva Protocol of 1925.[338]

Rather than challenging the view of the Director of the Arms Control and Disarmament Agency that the Executive branch assurances given to the Senate as part of the process of Senate advice and consent would create no "formal legal impediment" to a contrary subsequent presidential decision, the Report of the Senate Foreign Relations Committee said that "the Committee attaches particular importance" to the question and answer exchange.

On September 25, 1979, during a Senate Foreign Relations Committee hearing on SALT I compliance, Sidney Graybeal, a principal ABM negotiator, commented on the effect of Executive branch presentations to the Congress in the following terms:

> What about Soviet compliance with the agreement "as presented to Congress"?

---

[338] *Senate Comm. on Foreign Relations, The Geneva Protocol of 1925, S. Exec. Rep. No.* 35, 93rd Cong., 2d Sess. 5 (1974). The Senate went on to approve a resolution of advice and consent 90-0. *See* 120 *Cong. Rec.* 40,068 (1974).

> The language of the agreement, the agreed statements and the common understandings reflect what could be negotiated and what is binding on the two parties.
>
> Presentations to Congress can help explain the language and how it was derived, but they should not change the meaning of the language or the scope of the provisions of the agreement.[339]

And during a 1985 hearing before the Senate Foreign Relations Committee on genocide, the Departments of State and Justice replied in pertinent part in response to written questions from Senator Helms about the legal effects of an understanding attached to the resolution of ratification for the Genocide Convention that "[t]he scope of the obligation accepted by the United States is the obligation set forth in the instrument of ratification."[340]

policy arguments supporting the "unitary" approach

A considerable number of policy arguments support the "unitary" approach.

First, under the unitary approach Senate ratification history will not serve to create discrepancies between the Nation's international and domestic legal obligations. While the record of Senate ratification consideration will be taken into account and accorded weight pursuant to the international standard for treaty interpretation, the interpretation then reached will be identical under both international and national law. In contrast, the dual approach may require that the United States adopt an interpretation under national law either in violation of its international legal obligation or an additional unilateral obligation not assumed by the other treaty party. To argue that such an eventuality will rarely occur misses the point since by definition it will *always* occur *in every setting in which the "dual" versus "unitary" approach is relevant*. For the issue, of course, does not arise when

[339]*Briefing on SALT I Compliance: Hearing Before the Senate Comm. on Foreign Relations,* 96th Cong., 1st Sess. 13 (1979) (statement of Sidney Graybeal).

[340]*See Crime of Genocide: Hearing Before the Senate Comm. on Foreign Relations,* 99th Cong., 1st Sess. 172 (1985). For a compilation of United States treaty practice generally supporting this view, see *The ABM Treaty Studies: Part II, supra* note 1, at 29-42.

national and international legal interpretations are identical. Adoption of a rule which, whenever relevant, would require the United States either to violate its international treaty obligations or to unilaterally assume a non-reciprocated legal obligation would impose a substantial cost on the United States in its agreement-making process. To illustrate the potential cost of the "dual" approach for effectiveness in United States foreign policy the following summary of the logical possibilities might be helpful:

* If the uncommunicated Senate understanding agrees with the actual meaning of the treaty, it would have no effect and the "unitary-dual approach" issue would not arise.

* If the uncommunicated Senate understanding supported a conclusion that the United States had a lesser obligation than that actually imposed by the treaty--and compelled the Executive branch to violate the terms of the treaty by adhering to the Senate interpretation--the United states would be in violation of its international legal obligations. This uncommunicated understanding would almost certainly have no effect on the rights of the other party to the treaty. (A contrary view could cede to the Supreme Soviet or Politburo the power to "interpret" U.S. treaty obligations for our government.)

* If the uncommunicated Senate understanding supported a conclusion that the United States has a greater obligation than the treaty actually imposes, the result would be to handicap the United States Government and to hold it to a higher standard of conduct than it and its treaty partner had agreed to accept during negotiations. In the critical area of arms control, this could be dangerously destabilizing and, as illustrated by the Jackson Amendment, is unlikely to reflect a general Senate intention were it informed accurately of the treaty obligations.

It should also be noted in this connection that the legal effect of the "dual" approach in imposing this cost on United States foreign policy would be imposed not by legislation approved by the normal legislative route, as in a clearly manifest subsequent act of Congress taking precedence over a prior and clearly inconsistent treaty, nor even necessarily a clear statement approved by two-thirds of the Senate, but rather would be inferred from the "legislative" history of Senate ratification consideration.

Second, the core circumstance in which the "dual" versus "unitary" issue is likely to arise is one in which an issue was only peripherally considered during the ratification process and/or one on which there is a subsequently discovered mistake of fact or law. To adopt an approach in such a setting that would require the United States under national law either to void a treaty (and thus in most settings be in violation of our international legal obligations) or to adopt an interpretation either in violation of the treaty or unilaterally imposing a non-reciprocal legal obligation, rather than serving to protect the Senate intent, could, and perhaps even in most cases would, grotesquely subvert the intent of the original ratifying Senate. Would the original ratifying Senate have chosen to void a treaty over a mistake concerning a peripheral issue? Would it have insisted on an interpretation if it knew either that such an interpretation would put the Nation in violation of its legal obligations or cause the Nation to unilaterally adopt an obligation not binding on the other treaty party? And if these latter questions are the real issues as to intent of the original Senate does the "legislative" history relied on provide answers not only as to what the Senate thought but what it would have thought had it known the true circumstance of a gap between its interpretation and the international legal obligations of the Nation as created by the treaty? That is, the "dual" approach, rather than serving to protect the integrity of the Senate role, could, and perhaps most frequently would, by ignoring the core settings of only peripheral attention and mistake in which the issue arises, distort Senate intent and undermine the integrity of the ratification process. This issue will be more fully discussed as an issue apart from the "dual" versus "unitary" approach issue later in this part.

Third, it would seem as likely, if not more likely, that the legal result of a "dual" approach would be, not the adoption of the particular legal interpretation of the Senate, but the voiding of the treaty as a whole. If this were the legal effect then United States constitutional processes would have been interpreted to require an anomalous setting of voiding national treaty obligations, no matter how important the treaty, whenever there is any mistake, no matter how peripheral. And why would not the voiding of a treaty be at least as likely an outcome under the theoretical underpinnings of the "dual" approach? If, when a "Senate's understanding is clear, the President can make the treaty only in accordance with that understanding" then why, when a President does ratify a treaty inconsistent with that understanding, isn't the treaty void under national law rather than in force with the interpretation not "made" with the other treaty partner? Indeed, doesn't the problem of mistake previously discussed as well as the general difficulty in perceiving materiality of particular conditions within the overall treaty strongly suggest that under the theoretical underpinnings of the "dual" approach this would be the legal effect rather than declaring the treaty in force with the obligation not agreed by the other party? If this were the legal effect, the foreign policy costs to the United States would be greatly magnified.

Fourth, to the extent that the "dual" approach is supported as creating binding domestic legal obligations inconsistent with or not embedded in the Nation's treaty obligations solely on the basis of the "legislative history" of Senate advice and consent proceedings then, at least in some settings, it would seem inconsistent with the constitutional structure of shared power. That is relying solely on the Senate "legislative history" involves neither the check of another house nor even necessarily the President. Yet even the treaty power clearly is a shared power--that is the President "shall have Power, by and with the Advice and Consent of the Senate, to make treaties." It is unexplained how the "dual" approach could result in a binding obligation under national law not necessarily even rooted in participation by the President.[341] Moreover, if, as many authorities have said, the

---

[341]As a theoretical matter the "dual" approach could perhaps answer this objection, at least in part, by narrowing its approach to settings where the legislative history clearly shows both the President and Senate shared a common understanding. A core issue would remain even under this objection, however, as to whether the President's participation in the making of treaties under the Constitution is satisfied simply by his views expressed to the Senate or depends also on conclusion with another nation of an international agreement containing particular obligations.

In a draft opinion editorial of February 10, 1988, opposing what he terms the "Nunn-Byrd approach" to treaty interpretation,
Robert F. Turner, a former Principal Deputy Assistant Secretary of State for Legislative and Intergovernmental Affairs, raises an interesting additional policy issue concerning the interplay between "vetos," interpretation of statutes and treaties, and the respective roles of Congress and the President.

Thus he writes:

> Even were there no constitutional difficulties with the Nunn-Byrd approach, it would thus still be bad policy. Nor would the Senators wish to see their "theory" followed to its reasonable conclusion. If the most authoritative interpretation of a treaty (which, under the Constitution, is a part of the supreme "law" of the land) is that understood by the Senate at the time it decides not to exercise its "veto," would it not follow that we have erred in past years in giving "legislative intent" primary emphasis in interpreting domestic statutes? Surely, henceforth, we can count on the good Senators to acknowledge that the controlling interpretation of domestic laws ought to be

Senate role in the treaty process is that of a "negative" or "veto" within the concept of checks and balances, then how could it affirmatively create a national legal obligation apart from the underlying treaty? Would such an affirmative law-creating authority be consistent with the Senate limited "veto" role under separation of powers? Arguably also the treaty power, as an exception to the checks and balances of the ordinary legislative process, should not be interpreted as creating any legislative power under national law apart from the underlying international legal obligation. In this connection, it should be recalled that proposals to expand--or since disputed at least to clarify--Senate authority in declaring the relation under national law between a treaty and prior legislation were a part of the controversial Bricker Amendment not adopted and now generally considered as a dangerous proposal that the Nation was fortunate to have escaped. Any such expansion of authority, of course, in some settings at least, comes at the expense of the normal legislative process and the authority of the House of Representatives. As Professor Covey Oliver wrote in 1957 in an editorial comment considering not only the Bricker Amendment but also the *Niagara Reservation* case:

> There is, however, another question, one which does not seem within the ambit of the current litigation [in the Niagara Reservation case]. It is the question of the respective roles of the Senate and the House of Representatives in the law-making process, where under the Constitution (now or as amended) the Senate has a treaty function which the House does not have, but where the House can never legislate alone. There is an interesting parallel between the assumptions of the Senate in the case of the Niagara reservation and Section 2 of Senate Joint Resolution 3 [The Bricker Amendment]. The latter formulation for Constitutional change gives the Senate the power to prevent a self-executing treaty from superseding a prior inconsistent Act of Congress; it also permits the Senate to do just the opposite and by two-thirds vote provide that a treaty shall have self-executing legislative effect.

---

the understanding of the President as he decides not to exercise his "veto" over the proposed statute.

Robert F. Turner, "The Nunn-Byrd INF Rift and the Constitution" (draft opinion editorial of Feb. 10, 1988, on file at the Center for Law and National Security, University of Virginia School of Law). This draft subsequently became the *Wall Street Journal* "Opinion Editorial" of February 22, 1988, responded to by Senator Nunn on March 15, 1988. *See supra* note 203.

We know from precedent and practices of treaty negotiators that treaties as signed do not always make it entirely clear whether they are intended to be self-executing or not; hence the "grammar test" of the United States Supreme Court. Heretofore instances in which the Senate by reservation has attempted to decide the issue have been rare. The role of the courts has become well established.

Should the Senate by virtue of Constitutional amendment be given a clear power to do that which is uncertain and disputed, namely, the competence to determine as between a prior bicameral act and its own unicameral act as to which is the law? Certainly the amendment would generally resolve in favor of Senate power what is now at issue for a narrower situation in the litigation between the State Power Authority and the Federal Power Commission.

Despite the lack of any concrete evidence that the House of Representatives does concern itself about the steady increase of Senate power *de facto* throughout the field of lawmaking--an increase sometimes almost as much at the expense of executive power as of the legislative power of the "popular" branch of the national legislature--the policy question, and it is a big one, remains for decision: How much actual legislative power is it wise to lodge in one House at the expense of the other, either by constitutional change or by toleration?[342]

Fifth, to the extent that the "dual" approach were adopted and were through time to alter the current international legal rules for treaty interpretation, the United States could have a substantially enhanced monitoring role in ensuring that other nations had not adopted, anywhere in their internal ratification processes no matter how informal, an interpretation inconsistent with that of the United States. Such a rule as a matter of general international law would, even more importantly, serve to reduce the certainty and predictability of international treaty obligations.[343]

---

[342]Oliver, "Editorial Comment: Treaties, the Senate, and the Constitution: Some Current Questions," 51 *Am. J. Int'l L.* 606, 609-10 (1957).

[343]Such a rule could have a particularly chaotic effect with respect to the network of relationships created under multilateral agreements.

In his exchange with Senator Sam Nunn on the "broad-narrow" issue in the *Washington Quarterly*, Judge Abraham D. Sofaer, the State Department Legal Adviser, makes the following points with respect to the legal effect of a record of uncommunicated informal Senate deliberations or actions during advise and consent hearings, and problems in enhancing the monitoring burden if uncommunicated

---

indications from the informal record of ratification proceedings were regarded as binding:

> The legal significance of this record is far from authoritative. The Senate has enormous power over the meaning of a treaty, but that power is most effectively exercised by the adoption of amendments, conditions, reservations, or understandings. When such actions are communicated by the president to the other party to a treaty, they become part of the treaty itself, or of the context in which a treaty is construed. Absent such actions, the ratification process has little if any significance as to the treaty's meaning under international law. The Senate has repeatedly evidenced awareness of this principle by qualifying its grant of advice and consent in appropriate and formal measures. A Senate Foreign Relations Committee Staff Memorandum of 1977, *The Role of the Senate in Treaty Ratification*, makes the point, in distinguishing between a treaty's international and its domestic effect, that committee reports are "purely domestic documents and of no concern to [the] other party."
>
> Senator Nunn goes so far as to suggest that binding understandings can be conveyed to the Soviets through statements made at a Senate committee hearing, where a Soviet official is in the hearing room, if the Soviets thereafter remain silent. This suggestion has no basis in international law or practice, and when such an argument was made by U.S. negotiators in 1981, the Soviets rejected it, pointing out that U.S. deliberations were an internal matter to which the Soviets had no duty to respond, and that the Soviets were bound only by the letter of the agreement involved. Senator Nunn's theory would require the United States to monitor foreign ratification proceedings to know precisely the extent of its obligations, an untenable result.

A. Sofaer, "The ABM Treaty: Legal Analysis in the Political Cauldron," *Wash. Q.* 59, 70-71 (Autumn 1987).

Modern international law seems to reflect a rule that internal violations of national requirements regarding competence to conclude treaties will not vitiate treaty obligations unless the violation of national requirements "was manifest and concerned a rule of its internal law of fundamental importance." *See*, as evidence of customary international law, Articles 23, 27, and 46 of the Vienna Convention on the Law of Treaties, *supra* note 198. In this choice the modern law opts for the rule of law internationally and to relieve governments of any burden of following the internal handling of treaties by other national governments. Thus, the

International Law Commission said in 1966 in its commentary to proposed Article 43 of the Vienna Convention on the Law of Treaties, after reviewing the decisions of international tribunals and state practice, both found supportive of its proposed article 43 (which became Article 46 in the Convention) adopting this view, that:

> [w]hen a treaty has been made subject to ratification, acceptance or approval, the negotiating States would seem to have done all that can reasonably be demanded of them in the way of taking account of each other's constitutional requirements. It would scarcely be reasonable to expect each Government subsequently to follow the internal handling of the treaty by each of the other Governments, while any questioning on constitutional grounds of the internal handling of the treaty by another Government would certainly be regarded as an inadmissible interference in its affairs.

and:

> [t]he great majority of the Governments which have commented on this article have indicated their approval of the position taken up by the Commission on this problem: namely, that a violation of a provision of internal law regarding competence to conclude treaties may not be invoked as invalidating consent unless that violation was manifest. . . .

"Report of the International Law Commission on the work of the second part of its seventeenth session," U.N. Doc. A/6309/Rev.1, *reprinted in* [1966] 2 Y.B. *Int'l L. Comm'n* 169, 240-42, 241-42, U.N. Doc. A/CN.4/SER.A/1966/Add.1 [hereinafter "1966 Reports of the Commission"]. The Commission also gave as a second policy reason in support of this view that: "the majority of the diplomatic incidents in which States have invoked their constitutional requirements as a ground of invalidity have been cases in which for quite other reasons they have desired to escape from their obligations under the treaty." *Id.* at 242.

In a 1967 book on *Modern Trends in Treaty Law*, Kaye Holloway provides a survey of national constitutions with respect to requirements for the conclusion of treaties. *See K. Holloway, Modern Trends in Treaty Law* 151-237 (1967). The book also summarizes the "major schools of thought" concerning the interrelation between these national requirements for agreement effectiveness and the international requirements for agreement effectiveness as:

> Against the background of the opinion of writers, cited and analysed

Certainly, we wish to encourage the parties to communicate with one another the elements of an agreement. For this reason it seems highly unlikely that the international legal system would adopt a rule that informal indicators of intent during national internal ratification processes would be *ipso facto* binding in the process of treaty interpretation. Thus, as a practical matter it seems likely that the "dual" approach presents a central policy dilemma for the United States under the first policy reason discussed, that of enhanced discrepancy between national and international obligations, rather than any increased monitoring burden concerning the international obligation. It is possible, however, that even if the general international rule were not affected, if the United States followed an approach under national law giving conclusive effect to internal ratification history, that an international tribunal might hold that any other nation could reciprocally invoke that principle against the United States thus effectively imposing an expanded, and quite possibly impractical, monitoring burden on the United States.

There is yet another but related way in which if a "dual" approach were to be adopted by the United States and were through time--by demonstration effect of an important international actor--to alter the current international legal rules for treaty interpretation, that it could serve to reduce the certainty and predictability of treaty

---

> above, it is not surprising that Sir Gerald Fitzmaurice, who has viewed the problem from the standpoint of the practice of States on the international plane, has held with singular consistency that the only logical consequence of the propositions put forward by thevarious schools of thought is: States cannot be held in general to have knowledge of each other's constitutional laws; a State which purports to be bound by an international obligation "must be presumed to have complied with its own internal constitutional requirements. . . ."

Id. at 149. And concludes:

> Having rendered, it is hoped, justice to various trends of legal thinking on the issue of the effect of constitutional requirements, it is submitted that in spite of apparent divergence and some confusion there seems to be a fairly wide consensus that constitutional provisions are neither a decisive factor nor even relevant, and that any consideration of their international relevance raises insoluble difficulties, hence the various doctrinal constructions to circumvent these. . . .

Id. at 149-50.

obligations. For an approach conditioning effectively observable treaty obligations on internal ratification processes not always easily understood by others, could provide a convenient--and potentially huge--loophole for nations to break unwanted treaties by invoking internal rules. This risk, in fact, was one of the main reasons the International Law Commission rejected a broad rule for taking into account internal constitutional requirements as a grounds for treaty invalidity. Certainly as a Nation concerned with enhancing the rule of law in international affairs, we should not adopt an internal rule concerning treaty implementation that could through time encourage diminished adherence to solemn international obligations.

Sixth, to the extent that the "dual" approach did not alter the general international law rule of interpretation, the United States would not have available as a substantial defense in international interpretation of its obligations that an informal Senate understanding, not communicated to the other party, released the United States from an obligation understood during negotiations between the parties. The "dual" approach, however, might well more strongly tilt disputed international interpretation decisions against the United States in settings in which the other party can point out that the particular interpretation is binding under United States national law. That is, in international litigation the United States would have available to support its interpretation only the single international standard. Yet our adversaries in such disputes could draw not only on the international standard but, at least with considerable potential psychological effect, on the second "ratification record" track inherent in the "dual" approach.[344]

Seventh, a strong argument can be made that the Senate role in the ratification process will be strengthened, not weakened, by a rule that places a premium on the Senate as a whole acting through formal amendment, reservation, or understanding rather than placing reliance on more ambiguous "legislative" history. As will be

---

[344]In this connection, it is not clear that anyone even knows all of the legal consequences that would follow from declaring a separate meaning of a treaty under "national law" pursuant to the "dual" approach. Would it mean, for example, that in international adjudication the United States could not even itself assert an internationally binding meaning of a treaty favorable to the United States position if inconsistent with an informal Senate understanding (with all of the uncertainty surrounding how such an informal understanding is established) or even a clearly erroneous Executive branch statement to the Senate? If so, the "dual" approach would always mean that our adversaries in international adjudication could prevail on either the internal Senate advice and consent record or the international interpretive record, while the United States could only prevail on the international interpretive record.

subsequently discussed in this part, interpreting "legislative" history and particularly "treaty" ratification history is a frequently uncertain process. A rule that encourages the Senate to formally adopt its views on issues felt to be important both greatly enhances its ability to ensure that points of importance will be agreed by the other treaty parties (which is the most important effect of Senate action and its only clear opportunity to participate in the making of the international legal obligation) and ensures that its intent is both an intent of a two-thirds majority of the Senate and will be so understood as such. Should not any Senate consideration in the international and domestic obligation-making process be clearly understood by all members of the Senate, the President, and the other treaty parties, as such? To do so strongly suggests enhancing reliance on the formal process of amendment, reservation, or understanding rather than informal legislative history. Nor should this be an overwhelming burden for the Senate in consideration of treaties. Robert Dalton, the Counselor on International Law to the Department of State, points out that the Senate considers only an average of roughly twelve treaties per year.[345] Moreover, a byproduct of the effort to make Executive branch statements to the Senate ipso facto binding may be to create in the Senate itself a relaxation of its own duty to independently examine issues of interpretation presented incident to the advice and consent process. That this is not simply a theoretical prospect is suggested by the language of the Senate Foreign Relations Committee report on the INF Treaty as the Committee struggled to decide how to handle the INF Treaty "negotiating record" made available to it at the request of Senator Nunn. Thus the committee report says:

> Now that the INF Treaty "negotiating record" has been made available to the Senate, the status of these documents requires resolution. In the Committee's view, that resolution would not have been satisfactorily achieved by any stipulation in the resolution of ratification declaring that the Senate had scrutinized the "record" and satisfied itself that the "record" was in harmony with the formal Executive branch presentation of the Treaty. Such an approach could entail three significant problems:
>
> (a) institutionally, it could imply that such scrutiny is important to the Senate's examination of treaties and thus should be institutionalized;

---

[345]Statement by Robert Dalton, "Treaty Implementation and Interpretation Under the Constitution" conference, *supra* note 1.

(b) retroactively, it could imply that such scrutiny should have been exercised in the past; and

(c) specifically, with regard to the INF Treaty, it could leave open the question of what is to be done if, in the future, there is an assertion--for example, by a subsequent Administration--that notwithstanding the Senate's perception of harmony there was an inconsistency between the "record" and the Executive presentation.

Accordingly, the Committee believes that no formal finding concerning the contents of the INF Treaty "negotiating record" would be wise. In the Committee's judgment, the status of this "record" is established by the basic principles affirmed in the Biden Condition. If U.S. treaty interpretation is to be based upon the shared understanding of the Senate and the Executive at the time of ratification, and if the common understanding is reflected in authoritative Executive branch statements made in seeking Senate consent to ratification, then sources of interpretation which appear at variance must be subordinated to those authoritative statements.

In sum, although internal Executive memoranda and other negotiating materials may have been available to members of the Senate, some of whom have sought to assure themselves that this "record" is consistent with the Administration's formal presentation, the clear corollary of the constitutional principles cited in the Biden Condition is that such documents need not have been examined for consistency and should not be deemed material to U.S. interpretation of the INF Treaty insofar as they are inconsistent with the Executive branch's formal presentation of the INF Treaty.[346]

It is particularly striking that this discussion, referring to "U.S. treaty interpretation," seems completely preoccupied with what is--under the "dual" approach supported by the committee report--only a treaty interpretation binding under national law. Surely the duty of the Senate, as that of the Executive branch, should be primarily focused on the international obligation. And in that important dimension to declare that negotiating materials made available to the Senate "should not be deemed material to U.S. interpretation of the INF Treaty insofar as they are

---

[346] *The INF Treaty Report, supra* note 1, at 101.

inconsistent with the Executive branch's formal presentation of the INF Treaty," when Executive branch statements to the Senate clearly do not *ipso facto* prevail internationally over the treaty negotiating record, is for the Senate to ignore one of its most important obligations: to ensure that it understands and concurs in the treaty that will become internationally binding on the United States. Indeed, this point is made in the "Additional Views of Senator Helms" in *The INF Treaty Report*:

> A final worrisome problem found in the majority view on treaty interpretation is that "authoritative testimony" when clarifying ambi[g]uities, drafting errors, or omissions in the Treaty serves to obviate the need for the Senate to adopt clarifying amendments, reservations, understandings, or declarations. While this may be true insofar as regards those few aspects of the Treaty which have strictly domestic application in the United States, it is decidedly untrue with respect to the meaning of the international obligations undertaken.
>
> Simply because the Executive and the Senate have a "common understanding" of an international obligation does not mean that the other contracting state has the same understanding *nor does it bind it.* The *only* method of *ensuring* that our *internal* "common understanding" extends to the other sovereign (unless it is patently clear in the Treaty text or on the face of the negotiating record) is to adopt amendments, reservations, understandings, or declarations (depending on the scope and nature of the problem to be corrected) and to secure the assent (for amendments and some understandings) or the acquiescence (for reservations and declarations) of the other sovereign by incorporation of such provision either in the Treaty text or in the ratification instruments exchanged.
>
> The Senate should therefore avoid the temptation to forget that not just domestic law but an *international contract* as well is being forged during treatymaking and that "authoritative testimony" while good enough for domestic purposes is generally not sufficient to tie down the behavior of another nation, especially when that nation is the Soviet Union from which at best every sharp practice possible can be expected.
>
> The Senate, therefore, cannot assume, as the majority view implies, that the "authoritative testimony" received by the Senate will serve as any means whatsoever to bind Russia and must take

> those steps necessary to ensure that there is a meeting of the minds of the *contracting parties* and not just of the minds of the Senate and the President.[347]

Eighth, at least one observer has suggested that a "dual" approach could enhance incentives to negotiating vagueness and deception on the part of our arms control treaty partners. Thus, William R. Harris of the RAND Corporation testified before the Senate Foreign Relations Committee on February 18, 1988:

> The second disadvantage of a peremptory status for testimony before the Senate or interpretations in a Senate report is that, once the Soviet Union's diplomats see a new vehicle to bind the United States without binding the Soviet government, there will be even greater incentives for Soviet negotiating deception than already exist. If U.S. negotiators can be convinced that the treaty instruments accomplish a mutual limit, and they later testify to that effect before the Senate, then by a rule of peremptory validity for testimony before the Senate, the United States will be restricted while the Soviet Union may have greater latitude.[348]

To this observation it might be added that on any issues testified to but not previously clearly pinned down with the U.S.S.R. or other treaty partner, the "binding" testimony of United States officials could, under the "dual" approach, reduce the costs or even create an incentive for that party to maintain ambiguity on the issue or possibly even to adopt an opposite interpretation while knowing that the United States would remain constrained under national law to the testified to interpretation regardless of their actions.

Ninth, as has been seen, the United States Supreme Court has evolved a practice, consistent with the Vienna Convention on the Law of Treaties, to take

---

[347]"XII. Additional Views of Senator Jesse Helms" in *The INF Treaty Report, supra* note 1, at 179, 250-51.

Surely, rather than being ignored, areas of inconsistency known to the Senate should be of great concern to it as it provides advice and consent on treaties.

[348]Harris, "Clarifying Legal Obligations, Facilitating Verification Measures, and Strengthening Incentives For Arms Control Compliance: What Can the Senate Do?," Prepared Statement of William R. Harris Before the Senate Committee on Foreign Relations, Feb. 18, 1988, at 13.

account of subsequent practice of the parties in treaty interpretation settings. If, however, informal "advice and consent process history" or Executive branch statements can be binding under national law regardless of the appropriate construction of a treaty under international law, then this flexibility in using subsequent practice in treaty interpretation could be eroded. This would also follow from any approach that stresses that all evidence usable in treaty interpretation must have been before a consenting Senate. A genius of the common law, however, is that principles evolved through case by case adjudication frequently reflect greater merit in serving the needs of the real world than principles adduced from *a priori* theorizing. As such, this existing flexible practice of the Supreme Court, fully consistent with the international practice, may reflect greater wisdom in treaty interpretation than a rule mandating a "dual" approach and reflecting little, if any, judicial experience.[349]

Tenth, an approach weighting a record of informal Senate consideration or declaring any statements made by Executive branch spokesmen during such consideration as "authoritative" or "binding" could place a substantial--and quite possibly unworkable--additional burden on the Executive branch in its day-to-day application of treaties in the ongoing foreign policy process. Issues of treaty interpretation arise in a myriad of ways in the day-to-day conduct of United States foreign policy, including clearance of hundreds of cables to embassies, preparation of instructions to delegations, examination of options in United States foreign policy, consideration of issues concerning a broad agenda within international organizations, and diplomatic discussions around the world. In a forthcoming commentary in the *University of Pennsylvania Law Review*, Professor Phillip R.

---

[349]One paradox of the "dual" approach within the "broad-narrow" debate is that many of the principal supporters of the "dual" approach also heavily weight "subsequent practice" within the "broad-narrow" interpretation dispute. They seem not to have addressed how the underpinnings of a "dual" approach would undercut reliance on "subsequent practice" within a national process of treaty interpretation. An illustration of this paradox is contained in the largely contradictory findings in Section 2 of S. Res. 167 that on the one hand says "the meaning [of a treaty] is to be determined in light of what the Senate understands the treaty to mean when it gives its advice and consent" and "the Senate's understanding of a treaty cannot be informed by matter of which it is not aware, such as private statements made during the negotiations that were not communicated to the Senate," and on the other hand says "any subsequent practice between the parties in the application of the treaty is to be taken into account in interpreting the treaty."

Trimble says that "treaty interpretation . . . is an integral part of the day-to-day conduct of foreign relations that is the heart of the President's executive function."[350] The pervasive importance of ongoing interpretation of law, international and national, as the President carries out his constitutional responsibilities, is also discussed by Professor Eugene V. Rostow, a former Dean of the Yale Law School, Under Secretary of State, and Director of the Arms Control and Disarmament Agency, in a forthcoming comment on Professor David Koplow's article in the *University of Pennsylvania Law Review*. Professor Rostow writes in opposition to Professor Koplow's analysis and the *Restatement (Third)* position:

> The phenomenon of Presidential interpretation and reinterpretation of treaties is not "previously unknown," as Koplow states. It occurs daily in every nook and cranny of the law. When the President sends instructions to representatives of the United States at the United Nations Security Council and at international conferences on dozens if not hundreds of subjects ranging from telecommunication and aviation to fisheries and the law of war, he is interpreting and reinterpreting treaties as he "faithfully executes" the law. Similar interpretations and reinterpretations are made by the Executive Branch in carrying out domestic statutes of all kinds: the Internal Revenue Code, for example. This process of change and development is inherent in the growth of the law. Sometimes the changes are incremental and interstitial. Sometimes they are considerable. They are in fact inevitable as law confronts life every day of the week. Laws evolve around the broad policy purposes sought by their progenitors. But the progenitors can never freeze the law into a static pattern, nor anticipate exactly how it should be applied in all future circumstances. Nor can it be assumed that every lawmaker voted for the reasons advanced by one or a number of his

---

[350]Trimble, *supra* note 158, at 1479 (quoted from page proofs subject to final editing). In this commentary Professor Trimble writes in full:

> Although treaty interpretation p[l]ays a less important role in the grand scheme of United States foreign policy, it is an integral part of the day-to-day conduct of foreign relations that is the heart of the President's executive function.

Id.

or her colleagues in debate, or by representatives of the Executive Branch in testimony before committees.[351]

If informal Senate consideration of a treaty or any associated Executive branch statements to the Senate are automatically binding, then in each treaty interpretation setting the Executive branch must either exhaustively review the informal record of Senate consideration, including all statements by Executive branch spokesmen, or risk violation of the law. In contrast, an approach relying on conditions, formal or informal, shared with the other treaty partners would reduce any such burden. One would normally expect any such internationally shared conditions to be collected with the text of the treaty and United States action on it, in contrast with the potentially hidden law associated with the "dual" approach. Indeed, that the emphasis on informal record or "authoritative" Executive branch statements requires reliance on comparatively less visible law contradicts an important jurisprudential tenet of any good legal system; that is, that a legal system should promulgate law clearly and eschew hidden law. Yet the "dual" approach not only reduces the visibility of law for our treaty partners but also for our own national foreign policy process. This policy consideration is, of course, a matter of degree since interpretation will always be a complex process and the use of legislative history--and, for treaties, negotiating history--is commonplace in settings of ambiguity. But it is significant that the "dual" approach would add to the burden and complexity of treaty interpretation and would probably reduce the visibility of "law" as opposed to the "unitary" approach.

Eleventh, as has been seen, the general real-world effect of the "dual" approach is to create a treaty interpretation binding solely under national law. Absent communication to the other treaty party or parties, or some manifest defect in domestic approval procedures available to the other parties, the informal understanding or Executive branch statement to the Senate cannot alter the underlying international legal obligations created by the treaty. But even if the Senate has authority to "legislate" domestic conditions incident to treaty advice and consent, an issue as to which there is considerable doubt, is it appropriate that such domestic conditions be adopted in settings where the Senate believes it is simply approving an international obligation, as opposed to setting out a "domestic condition" not mutually binding under the treaty? That is, if there is any authority to "legislate" domestic conditions, should it not at least be confined to settings

---

[351]E. Rostow, "The Reinterpretation Debate and Constitutional Law," 137 *U. Penn. L. Rev.* 1451, 1457 (forthcoming May 1989) (quoted from page proofs subject to final editing).

where the Senate knows that it is doing so? Would not such a requirement better protect the integrity of the Senate approval process as opposed to an approach that would have the Senate adopt a purely "domestic condition" unilaterally binding the United States under domestic law without even knowing that it was doing so? This, of course, is simply another way of expressing the paradox that the "dual" approach can in any event never restore the original intent of a consenting Senate that by definition believed that it was consenting to an *international* right, privilege, power, or immunity.

Twelfth, a "dual" approach to treaty interpretation under the United States Constitution could complicate the ability of the United States to accept binding third party resolution of international disputes. For if an informal Senate understanding or Executive branch statement not communicated to another treaty party can be binding under national law, then the United States might be able to comply with findings to the contrary under international law by an international dispute settlement body such as the International Court of Justice only through an act of Congress or a new international agreement. That would mean that an already difficult process in use of international adjudication could be made even more difficult by requiring a new treaty or specific act of Congress to accept binding international adjudication. Absent such a prior national law altering event, a potential partner of the United States in international adjudication could have only reduced confidence that a treaty interpretation going against the United States in international adjudication would be implemented by the United States. Professor David A. Koplow, who seems to support the "dual" approach, at least in some settings, cites this problem as a real concern in his recent article to be published in the *University of Pennsylvania Law Review*.[352] Koplow writes:

> The final suggestion of this article is a type of "counterpoint" to its main thrust, and a warning about a rather different kind of possible future danger -- one that is latent in too-tight restrictions upon treaty interpretation. As noted, treaties have implications as both domestic and international law -- and these may conflict. For municipal purposes, the official United States interpretation is dispositive -- any understandings or interpretations that are read into the treaty at the time of ratification will be law of the land, binding upon all three branches, and subject to change only through the law-making process.

[352]Koplow Draft, *supra* note 1.

For international purposes, however, the United States may not have the last word. Although no arms control treaties currently provide for independent international adjudication other types of important international agreements do commit the United States to binding arbitration or to other neutral adjudication. In these instances, the international tribunal, when presented with an issue of treaty interpretation, will weigh the competing views offered by the parties, and determine authoritatively what the treaty means in the international context.

If the ruling goes against the United States, this country will have the power (although not the "right") to decide whether to comply with the order of the international proceeding and take actions necessary to conform to the new authoritative position, or, conversely, to stand in violation of it. This choice may be a difficult one, and many factors will impinge upon it. But it would not serve U.S. interests to be preemptively locked in to the position that the United States will never change its position or interpretation without amending the treaty.

The Byrd Amendment to the INF Treaty resolution of ratification is unclear on this point. It provides that "the United States shall not agree to or adopt an interpretation different from [the current executive-legislative understanding of the treaty] except pursuant to Senate advice and consent to a subsequent treaty or protocol, or the enactment of a statute." Under this language, could the United States reliably submit disputes to binding international adjudication? Does the language require that, whenever the United States' interpretation is rejected, this country will resist the authoritative international interpretation, unless the other party agrees to renegotiate the treaty (and give up in diplomacy a victory it just won in litigation) or new domestic U.S. law is created to effectuate the new ruling?

Knee-jerk unilateralism in foreign affairs is not a sound device for aiding the establishment of a viable network of international law and order. The Byrd Amendment, on its face, does not require this hostility toward international law, but neither does it seem to contemplate any expansion of the sphere within which international adjudication can be effective. Perhaps any such developments are a long way off, at least in the sphere of arms control and national security, but it seems appropriate to note that

> over-vigilance in entrenching a particular interpretation into U.S. law may not be fully consistent with a willingness to join the international community in enhancing the role of binding international dispute resolution.[353]

International adjudication has had its problems in recent years, but if the United States were to adopt an internal rule of constitutional law significantly complicating the process of resort to binding third party dispute settlement through international adjudication--or any other mode of binding third party dispute resolution--it would certainly not encourage more mature development of the rule of law internationally.

Thirteenth, even if a "dual" approach would not, through time, alter the general international law rule of treaty interpretation, the "dual" approach could have a chilling effect on potential United States treaty partners. For such treaty partners would be interested not solely in protecting their international legal rights, but in ensuring that the United States effectively implemented its treaty obligations in the real world. And the "dual" approach could be yet another potential hurdle in such effective implementation.

Finally, the "unitary" approach is supported by a substantial policy underpinning of the constitutional framers as they addressed the new nation's treaty commitments. That is, one of their motivations was to create a mechanism that would reduce the internal difficulties experienced under the Articles of Confederation in ensuring adherence to the Nation's treaty obligations. They believed that it was important for the Nation to take its treaty obligations seriously and to seek to structure internal processes to enhance observance of those obligations. This, of course, reflects both pragmatic underpinnings that to be taken seriously a nation must respect its international obligations, and elements of fairness and honor that the Nation should deal fairly and honorably in its relations with other nations. Both of these objectives are supported by the "unitary" approach and are harmed by the "dual" approach. Under the "unitary" approach there is a single standard for treaty interpretation and that standard coincides with the Nation's international obligations. In contrast, under the "dual" approach the Nation can be compelled under national law to be in violation of its international obligations without the checks inherent in the normal legislative process of clearly manifest

---

[353]*Id.* at 141-44 (footnotes omitted). This policy problem was also cited as a reason to reject a "dual" approach by at least one international lawyer participating in the recent conference on "Treaty Implementation and Interpretation Under the Constitution" held at the Syracuse University College of Law on March 10-11, 1989, *supra* note 1.

action by both houses of Congress and participation of the President through the qualified veto for so serious a step. Similarly, under the "unitary" approach the Nation would not establish internal ratification processes which would reserve the potential for not complying with treaty obligations though proceedings not communicated to other treaty partners. That is, under the "unitary" approach the Nation would directly affect international obligations only through amendments, reservations or understandings, formal or otherwise, that had been communicated to the other party. Not coincidentally, this also reflects the standard for international behavior generally adopted in international law both at the time of the framers and today as reflected in the Vienna Convention. In contrast, the "dual" approach would establish internal ratification processes capable of affecting the Nation's performance under its treaties without advance communication to the other treaty parties. Some of these underlying policies supporting the framers' consideration of the Nation's handling of its treaty obligations and supporting the "unitary" approach were clearly articulated by the Supreme Court in the New York *Indians* case.[354] As has been discussed, in that case the Supreme Court applied a treaty with the New York Indians while rejecting a formally passed Senate proviso to the treaty clearly affecting the international obligation when the evidence suggested that the proviso had never been communicated to the Indians. In so doing the Court said as one ground for this decision:

> There is something, too, which shocks the conscience in the idea that a treaty can be put forth as embodying the terms of an arrangement with a foreign power or an Indian tribe, a material provision of which is unknown to one of the contracting parties, and is kept in the background to be used by the other only when the exigencies of a particular case may demand it.[355]

It is quite possible, if not probable, that the constitutional framers also would have been shocked at the proposition that the treaty ratification processes which they were creating would subsequently be urged by proponents of the "dual" approach

---

[354]New York Indians v. United States, 170 U.S. 1 (1898).

[355]170 U.S. 1, 23 (1898) (Mr. Justice Brown in the Opinion of the Court).

as capable of creating national meanings of treaties on the basis of informal--and internationally considered internal--unilateral uncommunicated events.[356]

It should be noted that these fourteen principal policy arguments for the "unitary" approach are not simply costs imposed on the Presidency, in an issue sometimes erroneously conceptualized as simply between the Presidency and the Congress, but are costs imposed on the Nation as a whole in its foreign policy, on the constitutional system of checks and balances for creating binding national legal obligations, and on the integrity and effectiveness of the Senate role in the treaty advice and consent process.[357]

rebuttal of arguments for the "dual" approach

In a system awash with courts it is difficult to categorically state that no primary authority exists for any view. To date, however, except for sweeping dictum (at least with respect to the "core" issue of a discrepancy between the international meaning of a treaty and either an informal Senate understanding or an Executive branch representation) in a recent federal District Court decision now on appeal and a footnote in a recent Supreme Court decision for the proposition that reliance on the record of Senate preratification history is not improper in treaty interpretation, no proponent of the "dual" approach seems to have cited any such authority for that approach, including even cases analogously supporting the approach. In contrast, as has been seen, there is at least strong analogous authority for the "unitary" approach stemming from several lines of Supreme Court cases.

In view of the substantial reliance on the recent opinions of Judge Harold H. Greene in the *Rainbow Navigation* case by some supporters of the "dual" approach (or at least supporters of elements of that approach recently embodied within the INF Treaty condition), it may be useful to summarize why that District Court case does not constitute a square holding for the "dual" approach on the core issue principally addressed by this study. In any event, of course, that case is now on appeal.

---

[356]Deliberate, clear decision pursuant to the normal legislative process to depart from prior treaty obligations is, of course, a separate issue, as is the normal role of domestic courts in the treaty interpretation process.

[357]This is also an important reason why arguments rooted in "estoppel" against the Presidency in such settings are more difficult than they may first appear.

First, on any characterization, the *Rainbow Navigation* case does not present an issue of choice between an Executive branch statement to the Senate or an informal Senate understanding on the one hand and the meaning of an agreement internationally on the other. For Judge Greene clearly interpreted the international agreement as supporting the position of Rainbow Navigation, quite apart from any Executive branch statement or Senate understanding. Thus, he said on the treaty interpretation issues presented: "The language of the treaty itself suggests that it was intended to operate of its own force upon ratification";[358] "[t]he language of the MOU is straightforward and unmistakable . . .";[359] "[t]he language of the MOU--which the Court finds to be unambiguous in its support of Rainbow's position . . .";[360] and "[t]he construction . . . [of the Treaty] adopted by the Navy is contrary to the ordinary meaning of the language . . . ."[361] That is, *Rainbow Navigation* is a case where the deciding judge believes that Executive branch statements and Senate understandings are consistent with--and *not* departing from--the international obligation.

Second, the issue in this case, at least insofar as it invokes the evidence relied on by the court of Executive branch statements to the Senate or a Senate informal understanding, seems principally one of treaty implementation under national law, that is a "domestic condition" setting, rather than a treaty interpretation dispute. Thus, the key exchange relied on between Senator Mathias and Edward J. Derwinski does not specifically address either treaty interpretation issue before the court but rather provides--particularly in view of the question asked--what at least arguably could be interpreted as a general assurance of protection for the current carrier during treaty implementation:

> SENATOR MATHIAS: What about the current American flag carrier? Are there any plans in effect to save harmless the *current cargo carrier* that is now carrying supplies to the [U.S.] military base in Iceland?

---

[358]686 F. Supp. 354, 357 (1988).

[359]*Id.* at 359 (footnotes omitted).

[360]*Id.* at 360.

[361]*Id.* at 361.

> DERWINSKI: My understanding is that the current carrier has been involved in a number of discussions with appropriate authorities, and despite the fact that we could not provide, obviously, within the treaty for specific protection for an entity, we did have in mind at all times the need to *protect the interests of the current carrier* (emphasis added).[362]

And similarly the specific language in the Senate Foreign Relations Committee on the Treaty unmistakably concerns domestic issues including implementation of the Treaty. It provides in relevant part:

> Consequently, the committee recommends that the Senate advise and consent to ratification only with the assurances of the Departments of State and Defense that: (1) the treaty would not be understood as, or appear to be a precedent for, similar weakening of the 1904 Cargo Preference Act in other trades; (2) the administration is committed to the overall integrity and vigorous enforcement of the 1904 act; and (3) the treaty will be implemented in such a way that the existing United States-flag service in the Iceland trade would not be disadvantaged as a result of the treaty. The committee received these assurances at its hearing, and recommends advice and consent on that basis only.
>
> The committee understands and expects that the economic viability of the United States-flag service will be maintained just as if the 1904 act were fully in effect in the Iceland trade. The committee further understands that the Department of Defense will withdraw its rulemaking proposal at 51 Fed. Feg. [sic] 27016 (July 28, 1986), a proposal which purported to interpret the "excessive or otherwise unreasonable" provision in the 1904 act, but which would have, in effect, given the Secretary of the Navy the discretion to waive the act at any time.[363]

---

[362] 686 F. Supp. 354, 358.

[363] *Treaty Between the United States and Iceland to Facilitate Their Defense Relationship: Report Submitted by Mr. Lugar, Senate Comm. on Foreign Relations, S. Exec. Rep. No.* 27, 99th Cong., 2d Sess. 3 (Oct. 8, 1986).

Nothing in this language, which is the language Counselor Derwinski is also quoted by the court as not objecting to,[364] addresses either of the specific treaty interpretation issues, and its thrust is unmistakably that of a "domestic condition." Similarly, Senator Pell's floor statement on the Treaty, also relied on by Judge Greene says:

> Mr. President, the Committee on Foreign Relations reported the treaty between the United States of America and the Republic of Iceland to facilitate their defense relationship this afternoon at its weekly business meeting and recommended that the Senate give its advice and consent to ratification. Obviously with the Government of Iceland planning to serve as the gracious host of this weekend's presummit meeting between President Reagan and General Secretary Gorbachev it is particularly appropriate that the United States ratify this treaty with Iceland in order to remove a source of friction which has existed between our two countries since 1984.
>
> This agreement supersedes United States cargo preference laws for military cargos to Iceland only. Instead, it will permit both United States and Icelandic shippers to bid competitively for the right to carry such cargo between the United States and Iceland. This agreement was carefully crafted to ensure that the treaty does not appear to establish a precedent for the weakening of the 1904 Cargo Preference Act--an act which is preceived [sic] to be a very important protection for the United States cargo industry. The administration has committed itself to the overall integrity of the 1904 act, and assured the committee that the treaty will be implemented in such a way that the existing United States-flag service in the Iceland trade would not be disadvantaged.
>
> I believe that the treaty is in the interest of the United States and Iceland. I am pleased that President Reagan will be able to personnally [sic] deliver the good news of Senate action on this matter to the Government of Iceland. I urge my colleagues to give their advise and consent to ratification.[365]

---

[364]Civil Action No. 88-0992 (HHG) (D.D.C. Nov. 15, 1988), at 13.

[365]132 *Cong. Rec.* S15660 (daily ed. Oct. 8, 1986) (statement of Sen. Pell).

Senator Pell, as well as the Senate Foreign Relations Committee report, both even speak explicitly in terms of language of implementation: "the treaty will be implemented in such a way . . . ."[366] Apparently no statement of any Executive branch witness or any member of Congress or other "informal" indicator cited by Judge Greene specifically addresses either of the treaty interpretation conditions also before the court. Quite simply, then, the *Rainbow Navigation* case, whether or not reflecting the law of the land in settings of "domestic conditions," is, insofar as it involves the legal effect of Executive branch statements or informal Senate conditions as cited by Judge Greene, principally a "domestic conditions" case rather than the core "dual" versus "unitary" issue principally addressed by this study.

It is interesting to note in this connection that the domestic condition in question either was intended to be politically binding only or it was an intentional exercise of what is essentially a "legislative" power to make binding national law by *informal legislative history*. For the principal issue here was not use of legislative history to address an uncertain interpretive issue under either national or international law. Rather, the condition, which principally concerned domestic options under the treaty, and was made explicit in the Senate Foreign Relations Committee report, was not presented to the Senate as part of the Resolution of Ratification, and thus, if intended to create binding law was intended to do so *solely by informal legislative history* as opposed to formal action by even a single house of Congress.

Third, in its inability to cite a single judicial decision for its sweeping conclusions, the decision actually reveals the legal weakness of the position espoused. As has been seen, Judge Greene cites in support of his position only the new *Restatement* (which itself cites no authority for its position), Professor Henkin (the Reporter for the same *Restatement*) testifying on the ABM Treaty Interpretation Resolution, and a statement of Senator Nunn, who in turn, as we have seen, cited Judge Greene's opinion on the Senate floor.

Fourth, on constitutional issues a single District Court decision is of only limited authority. Such a decision is, unlike a Court of Appeals or Supreme Court decision, that of a single judge. Moreover, typically the issues may be argued and considered less fully at the District Court level. Specifically, in the *Rainbow Navigation* case the issues concerning the effect of informal Senate conditions and Executive branch statements do not seem to have been fully argued by opposing counsel and, as a comparison with the legal analysis of opposing positions in this

---

[366]*See also* "the statement by American maritime organizations" with which Counselor Derwinski is reported by Judge Greene as assuring the Senate he agreed. 686 F. Supp. 354, 358.

study suggests, consideration of the issues by Judge Harold H. Greene was perfunctory. Indeed, apparently not even the obviously relevant Supreme Court decision in the *New York Indians* case nor the opinion of Judge Bazelon in the *Niagara Reservation* case was discussed or cited in the opinion. In this connection it should also be noted that footnote 7 in the opinion of the Supreme Court in the recent Stuart case[367] did not rely for authority on the *Rainbow Navigation* case, and that, in contrast, the concurring opinion of Judge Scalia which does cite Rainbow Navigation, and which rejects footnote 7, would at least sharply limit its broad dictum.[368]

Fifth, it should also be noted with respect to the decision in the *Rainbow Navigation* case that on March 6, 1989, the Department of Justice filed an appeal in the United States Court of Appeals for the District of Columbia Circuit.[369] The "Appellants' Statement of Issues To Be Raised On Appeal" from the Appellants' Docketing Statement includes the following:

> 8. Whether the challenged procurement decisions in this case involve a clear and prejudicial violation of applicable law.
>
> (a) Do the terms of the Treaty and related MOU require: (i) that Rainbow (as opposed to U.S.-flag carriers in general) never be "disadvantaged" in the future procurement of transportation services for carriage of U.S. military cargo to Iceland; (ii) that Rainbow's "economic viability" be preserved in perpetuity; and/or (iii) that the Navy "hold" Rainbow "harmless" forever.
>
> (b) What degree of weight (if any) in the context of treaty interpretation must be accorded statements by representatives

---

[367]United States v. Stuart (U.S. Supreme Court, No. 87-1064, Feb. 28, 1989), at 12 n.7 (Brennan, J., Opinion of the Court).

[368]*See id.* at concurring opinion of Justice Scalia.

[369]Appellants' Docketing Statement (Rainbow Navigation v. Department of the Navy, Case Nos. 89-5019, 5020 (D.C. Cir.)), including "Appellants' Statement of Issues To Be Raised On Appeal," enclosed in letter from John P. Schnitker, U.S. Department of Justice, to Constance L. Dupre, Clerk, U.S. Court of Appeals for the District of Columbia Circuit (March 6, 1989).

of the Executive Branch during the treaty ratification process before the United States Senate.

(c) If Executive Branch "representations" made during the Senate ratification process have determinative weight in subsequent interpretation of the terms of a treaty, were any such "representations" made here.

(d) Do the Executive Branch "representations" (if any) made during the Senate ratification of the Treaty and related MOU require: (i) that Rainbow (as opposed to U.S.-flag carriers in general) never be "disadvantaged" in the future procurement of transportation services for carriage of U.S. military cargo to Iceland; (ii) that Rainbow's "economic viability" be preserved in perpetuity; and/or (iii) that the Navy "hold" Rainbow "harmless" forever.

(e) Notwithstanding the plain terms of the Treaty and MOU, do any Executive Branch "representations" to the Senate during the treaty ratification process create any additional rights in U.S.-flag carriers in general, or any particular carrier such as Rainbow, beyond: (i) the right to compete with Icelandic carriers in accordance with the terms of the Treaty and related MOU for 65% or 35% of the trade; and (2) the promise of a continued U.S.-flag presence in the trade.

(f) In particular, do any such Executive Branch "representations" give Rainbow:

(i) an unfettered, carrier-specific right to freedom from any "disadvantage" or "harm" to its economic interests in implementation of the Treaty and related MOU.

(ii) a right to exclusive, carrier-specific competitive advantages and protection for as long as its remains in the Icelandic trade, irrespective of whether other U.S. carriers wish to compete in that trade.

(iii) a right to an exclusive, carrier-specific guarantee of "economic viability," including measures (such as, *inter alia*, a time charter) designed to ensure that Rainbow suffers no revenue shortfall because of implementation of the Treaty and related MOU.

(g) Whether any "disadvantage" or lack of "economic viability" to Rainbow in the challenged procurement(s) is directly attributable to the terms of the Treaty and related MOU, which permits Icelandic carriers to directly compete with U.S.-flag carriers in the provision of transportation services for carriage of U.S. military cargo to Iceland, rather than the terms and conditions of the Navy's various Requests for Proposals (RFP).

9. Whether the terms and conditions of the Navy's 1988 Request for Proposals (RFP) or the RFP *sua sponte* proposed by the Navy to the district court in June, 1988 for procurement of transportation services for carriage of U.S. military cargo to Iceland have a rational basis and/or involve a clear and prejudicial violation of applicable law.

(b) Whether the terms of the Treaty and MOU and/or any Executive Branch "representations" to the Senate require that the Navy procure excess transportation capacity at taxpayer expense, which it does [sic "not" ?] need and cannot possibly use.

. . . .

11. Whether the U.S.-flag carriers in the Icelandic trade in general, or any particular U.S. carrier such as Rainbow, are legally entitled to continue receiving all of the benefits and protections of the 1904 Cargo Preference Act, notwithstanding the entry into force of the Treaty and related MOU.

(a) Specifically, whether, notwithstanding the terms of the Treaty and related MOU, the Navy is obligated to apply the Cargo Preference Act as if it were still fully in effect in the Icelandic trade, or whether the Navy should be allowed reasonable discretion to apply that Act only to the extent it is consistent with the terms of the Treaty and related MOU.

> 12. Whether the terms of the Treaty -- as distinguished from the MOU -- require a single competition between U.S.-flag carriers and Icelandic carriers for the provision of transportation services for carriage of U.S. military cargo to Iceland.
>
> 13. Whether the district court erred in its conclusion that the Navy's conduct toward Rainbow demonstrated "bad faith," a specific intent to destroy plaintiff's "economic viability" and to "disadvantage" plaintiff in the Icelandic trade.
>
> 14. Whether the district court's injunction in this case unconstitutionally infringes upon the authority of the President to negotiate treaties.
>
> 15. Whether the district court's injunction unconstitutionally infringes upon and frustrates the exercise of the President's constitutional and Treaty-based authority to negotiate, conclude and implement amendments to the MOU which the Secretary of States deems appropriate and consistent with the terms of the Treaty.[370]

Of particular importance, it should be noted that point 8(b) of the "Appellants' Statement of Issues" poses the question:

> (b) What degree of weight (if any) in the context of treaty interpretation must be accorded statements of representatives of the Executive Branch during the treaty ratification process before the United States Senate.[371]

It is, of course, possible that the *Rainbow Navigation* case ultimately will result in a Supreme Court decision on this issue.

While not directly cutting to its authority in support of the "dual" approach, a number of other points should be noted about the *Rainbow Navigation* case in the overall "broad-narrow" constitutional-national law dispute. First, the evidence relied on by the court with respect to an informal Senate understanding concerning domestic implementation includes repeated statements by Counselor Derwinski, the

---

[370]*Id.*, "Appellants' Statement of Issues To Be Raised On Appeal" at i-iv.

[371]*Id.* at i.

chief negotiator of the Treaty, and specific language in the report of the Foreign Relations Committee that: "The committee received these assurances at its hearing, and recommends advice and consent on that basis only." Second, the evidence goes beyond a single statement by an Executive branch official and includes not only the proviso in the committee report that was before the Senate but also a roughly equivalent statement by a senior member of the Senate Foreign Relations Committee made on the Senate floor immediately before the vote on the resolution of ratification.[372] Third, there is apparently nothing in the record that is cited from any source even leaning to a contrary conclusion on the domestic implementation assurances, whatever their precise meaning.[373]

---

[372]*See* 132 *Cong. Rec.* S15660 (daily ed. Oct. 8, 1986) (statement of Sen. Pell).

[373]Of peripheral significance it might be noted that the case seems to reflect strong feelings by Judge Greene against actions of the Navy in this case, reflected in language such as: "The present effort is as disingenuous as the other two." 686 F. Supp. 354, 361. "Once again, the Secretary's determination and the sworn statements of his military and civilian subordinates were false." Civil Action No. 88-0992 (HHG) (D.D.C. Nov. 15, 1988), at 4. "This case presents a sorry saga of duplicity." *Id.* at 28. "The arrogance of power has seldom been displayed in more telling fashion." *Id.* at 29. And to get an overall flavor of the battle between Judge Greene and the Navy as perceived by the Judge:

> This case, which involves shipping between the United States and Iceland, is now before this Court for the fourth time in three years. On the first three occasions, the Court concluded that the government's legal position was erroneous, its factual statements at odds with the facts, or both. As discussed below, with every negative ruling, the government devised yet new and different means for eliminating the plaintiff from the United States-Iceland trade. The Court now holds that the Executive's latest action has no more validity than its three previous efforts.

Id. at 1. It might also be noted that these underlying constitutional issues seem to have been only peripherally briefed by opposing counsel, although plaintiff's counsel did clearly invoke the issue of effect of Executive branch statements and Senate action.

Finally, it might be noted that the issues concerning Executive branch statements and informal Senate conditions became more prominent in Judge Greene's opinion on the merits that was written after his opinion in the *Rainbow Navigation* case at

Finally, it might be noted that in his first May 17, 1988, opinion Judge Greene included two footnotes on the standards for treaty interpretation that provided in full:

> **25.** An MOU is an international executive agreement which must be interpreted according to the principles applicable to treaties. *Air Canada v. U.S. Department of Transportation*, 843 F.2d 1483, 1486 (D.C.Cir.1988). The general rule in interpreting treaties is:
>
> > The clear import of treaty language controls unless "application of the words of the treaty according to their obvious meaning effects a result inconsistent with the intent or expectations of its signatories."
>
> *Sumitomo Shoji America, Inc. v. Avagliano*, 457 U.S. 176, 180, 102 S.Ct. 2374, 2377, 72 L.Ed.2d 765 (1982), *quoting Maximov v. United States*, 373 U.S. 49, 54, 83 S.Ct. 1054, 1057, 10 L.Ed.2d 184 (1963).
>
> **26.** "An international agreement is to be interpreted in good faith in accordance with the ordinary meaning to be given to its terms in their context and in the light of its objects and purpose." Restatement of the Law (Second) Foreign Relations Law of the United States (Revised), Tentative Draft No. 6 (1985), § 325(1). This same rule of interpretation is prescribed by the Vienna Convention of the Law of Treaties Article 31(1). S.Exec.L. 92d Cong., 1st Sess. (1971), 8 I.L.M. 679. As the State Department has noted, "the Convention is already recognized as the authoritative guide to current treaty law and practice." *Id.*[374]

---

the preliminary injunction stage was cited on the Senate floor during the debate on the INF Treaty condition and entered into the *Congressional Record.*

Indeed, apart from conditions of domestic implementation, Judge Greene's November 15, 1988, opinion on the merits seems barely to address any issues of treaty interpretation as were addressed in his May 17, 1988, opinion.

[374]686 F. Supp. 354, 359 nn.25-26 (D.D.C. 1988).

Quite apart from the opinion of Judge Harold H. Greene in the *Rainbow Navigation* case itself, that opinion is only an opinion by a single District Court judge and is seemingly in conflict with an opinion of the higher Court of Appeals in the *Niagara Reservation* case and at least the theory of the Supreme Court in the *New York Indians* case. That is, as a federal District Court opinion, Judge Greene's opinion in *Rainbow Navigation* must be read in the context of conflicting opinions. Particularly if inconsistent with the decision of a higher court of appeals, or indeed, of the Supreme Court itself, it would seem of only limited authority, if any at all.

Similarly, it may be useful to review more specifically why footnote 7 in the opinion of the Court (six Justices joining) in the recent case of *United States v. Stuart*[375] is of only peripheral relevance, if that, in support of a "dual" approach.

First, as has been seen, the thrust of footnote 7 is simply to support the proposition--not at issue in the "dual" versus "unitary" approach--that it is not improper to *use* preratification Senate materials in treaty interpretation. Indeed, footnote 7 refers four times to this issue. Thus, it says: "Nor is *reliance* on the Senate's preratification debates and reports improper"; "[a]s JUSTICE SCALIA acknowledges, the American Law Institute's most recent *Restatement* counsels *consideration* of such materials"; and "[*c*]*onsultation* of these materials is eminently reasonable"; and again, ". . . *reviewing* preratification Senate debates and reports . . . ."[376] Moreover, in quoting the *Restatement* section 314, comment d, the Court quotes only that part of comment d which seems to stand for the proposition that Senate preratification materials may be relevant in treaty interpretation. Specifically and importantly it *does not* quote the controversial paragraph which constitutes the principal authority of any kind for the "dual" approach. It should be recalled that this paragraph *not quoted* provides:

> Although the Senate's resolution of consent may contain no statement of understanding, there may be such statements in the report of the Senate Foreign Relations Committee or in the Senate debates. In that event, the President must decide whether they represent a general understanding by the Senate and, if he finds that they do, must respect them in good faith.[377]

---

[375]United States v. Stuart (U.S. Supreme Court, No. 87-1064, Feb. 28, 1989).

[376]*Id.* at 12 n.7 (Brennan, J., Opinion of the Court) (emphasis added).

[377]*Restatement (Third), supra* note 235,§ 314, comment d, at 188.

Since the Court quoted from the immediately preceding paragraph of section 314, comment *d*, it could easily have quoted this paragraph if it felt that were the issue before the Court and that it was addressing in the footnote rather than simply the issue of whether it is not improper to use Senate preratification materials in a genuine search for the intention of the two parties. That it did not do so, coupled with its repeated description of the issue as such use, suggests that footnote 7 was intended to address the use issue rather than the "dual" versus "unitary" constitutional issue.

Second, the standard repeatedly used by the Court for treaty interpretation was the intention of the treaty parties. That, of course, is the standard underlying the "unitary" approach. Thus, in only a brief treatment of the treaty interpretation issues the Court looked to the intent of the treaty parties on three separate occasions and it was implicit on a fourth occasion. In beginning the analysis of the treaty interpretation issue the Court quoted from the *Sumitomo* and *Maximov* cases that "`[t]he clear import of treaty language controls unless "application of the words of the treaty according to their obvious meaning effects a result inconsistent with the intent or expectations of its signatories."'"[378] And again the Court wrote: "Nontextual sources that often assist us in `giving effect to the intent of the Treaty parties,' such as a treaty's ratification history and its subsequent operation, further fail to sustain respondents' claim."[379] And in reviewing the subsequent practice of the treaty parties the Court wrote: "The practice of treaty signatories counts as evidence of the treaty's proper interpretation, since their conduct generally evinces their understanding of the agreement they signed."[380] Finally, the Court implied this same standard when it wrote that "a treaty should generally be `construe[d] . . . liberally to give effect to the purpose which animates it.'"[381]

---

[378]United States v. Stuart (U.S. Supreme Court, No. 87-1064, Feb. 28, 1989) (Brennan, J., Opinion of the Court) at 11.

[379]*Id.* at 12 (citation omitted).

[380]*Id.* at 14-15.

[381]*Id.* at 14.

It might also be noted that the Court's reliance on "[t]he clear import of treaty language" implies that such clear language would prevail even over a clearly expressed informal Senate understanding to the contrary, unless that clear understanding were to effect "a result inconsistent with the intent or expectations of its signatories." *Id.* at 11.

Third, as has just been seen, the Court reviewed, as one aid to interpretation, the subsequent practice of the treaty signatories.[382] Such practice, by definition, cannot be before a Senate during its consideration of a treaty, and its underpinning is the intention of the treaty parties, not the intention of the Senate or statements by Executive branch officials to the Senate during treaty consideration.

Fourth, in reviewing the preratification Senate treaty history, such as committee hearings, committee reports, floor debate and the President's message accompanying transmittal, the Court specifically began the paragraph with a sentence clearly indicating that "[n]ontextual sources that often assist us in `giving effect to the intent of the Treaty parties,' such as a treaty's ratification history and its subsequent operation, further fail to sustain respondents' claim."[383] This introductory sentence makes clear that the purpose of the Court in turning to Senate preratification history was to "assist in `giving effect to the intent of the Treaty parties.'" That is precisely the purpose for reviewing preratification history under the "unitary" approach.

Fifth, the Court also specifically said in its opinion that "`[a]lthough not conclusive, the meaning attributed to treaty provisions by the Government agencies charged with their negotiation and enforcement is entitled to great weight.'"[384] This, as will be reviewed subsequently in this study, is hornbook law and would seem to weight the views of Executive agencies in treaty interpretation.

Sixth, the "dual" versus "unitary" issues apparently were not briefed by the parties or argued before the Court. The *Stuart* case is in major respects a strange case to be seriously addressing important constitutional issues in treaty interpretation, suggesting that the Court may not have believed that it was doing so. Thus, potential serious constitutional issues seem not to have been seriously argued, and, factually, the only reference even to a single floor colloquy and a letter to the Senate during Senate consideration of the 1942 Convention seems to be in a short footnote in the "Brief for the United States."[385] John O. McGinnis, the Deputy

---

[382]*Id.* at 14-15.

[383]*Id.* at 12 (citation omitted).

[384]*Id.* at 15.

[385]"Brief for the United States," at 29 n.11, United States v. Stuart (U.S. Supreme Court, No. 87-1064, decided Feb. 28, 1989). This footnote provides:

> [11] The following colloquy took place on the floor of the Senate during the

Assistant Attorney General to the Department of Justice, has indicated to the author that "the issue of their relevance ["preratification deliberations"] was obviously not fully briefed."[386] Indeed, the concurring in part opinion of Justices Kennedy and O'Connor disagreed even with addressing the peripheral issue of "whether Senate debates on ratification are authoritative or even helpful in determining what the signatories to a treaty intended" because they felt the issue not ripe for decision in this case.[387] The complete opinion of Justices Kennedy and O'Connor said:

> It is quite unnecessary for the resolution of this case to explore or discuss the Senate proceedings that led to ratification of the 1942 Convention Respecting Double Taxation; for, as the court

---

debate on ratification of the 1942 Convention (88 Cong. Rec. 4714 (1942)):

> Mr. Taft. In other words, if an American citizen were using a Canadian bank deposit to evade income taxation, I think the [treaty] would permit the United States Government to ask the Canadian Government to obtain information from its own bank and furnish it to this Government in connection with the enforcement of our internal-revenue laws.
>
> Mr. George. It does provide for exchange of information, as the Senator from Ohio points out.

See also *United States v. A.L. Burbank & Co.*, 525 F.2d at 17 n.7. The same view is expressed in a letter from the Acting Secretary of State that accompanied the Convention when it was presented to the Senate for ratification. S. Exec. Doc. B, 77th Cong., 2d Sess. 1, 2, 4-5 (1942), *reprinted in* Joint Comm. on Int. Rev. Tax., 77th Cong., 2d Sess., 1 *Legislative History of United States Tax Conventions* 445, 448-449 (1962).

Id.

[386]Letter from John O. McGinnis to John Norton Moore (Mar. 21, 1989).

[387]Opinion of Justices Kennedy and O'Connor concurring in part and concurring in the judgment, United States v. Stuart (U.S. Supreme Court, No. 87-1064, Feb. 28, 1989). Note also even that Justices Kennedy and O'Connor cite the issue as one of the effect of Senate ratification debates "in determining what the signatories to a treaty intended." *Id.*

> unanimously agrees, the text of the Treaty is quite sufficient to decide the issue before us. The intent of the Treaty's signatories is manifest from the language of the document itself. I agree with JUSTICE SCALIA that we should not reach, either in a direct or an implicit way, the question whether Senate debates on ratification are authoritative or even helpful in determining what the signatories to a treaty intended. That determination should be reserved until we confront a case where the language of the treaty itself does not yield a clear answer to the question before us. For these reasons I join the judgment of the Court and all but Part II-C of the Court's opinion.[388]

One of the principal reasons dictum is accorded less weight than holding is that frequently the underlying issues may not have been fully presented to the Court. That clearly seems to be the case here. Compare, for example, the discussion of the issue--and the serious debate surrounding it--contained in this study with the virtual nontreatment of the issue in the opinion of the Court.[389]

Seventh, while footnote 7 centrally addresses the issue of the appropriateness in consideration of preratification Senate history in treaty interpretation, and as such does not address the "dual" versus "unitary" constitutional issue, much less whether an Executive branch statement to the Senate is *ipso facto* binding, Justice Scalia's concurring opinion does suggest that at least one member of the Court squarely rejects the "dual" approach. While the first part of the Scalia opinion focuses

---

[388]*Id.*

[389]There is a hint in the concurring opinion of Justice Scalia that the Brennan opinion may have been hunting broader game: "It can hardly have escaped the Court's attention that the role of Senate understanding in the treaty ratification process has recently been the subject of some considerable dispute between the Senate and the Executive." Opinion of Justice Scalia, concurring, United States v. Stuart (U.S. Supreme Court, No. 87-1064, Feb. 28, 1989), at 6. While it cannot be known what motivated footnote 7, and it should be assumed--as that footnote says four times--that it was simply addressing the issue that it was not improper to use preratification Senate materials in treaty interpretation, if and to the extent that the Court were hunting broader game, one can question the appropriateness of even peripherally approaching a major and complex constitutional issue in separation of powers without a briefing of the issue, argumentation, or even an understanding by the parties that such an issue may be involved in the case or discussion by the Court of the principal constitutional and legal issues involved.

generally on the debate concerning text versus nontextual materials in interpretation, the second part of his opinion seems to reject the use of Senate preratification materials at all in treaty interpretation, much less a view that would make informal expressions of Senate intent controlling.[390] And in doing so Justice Scalia seems to reject both the new *Restatement* position (which he notes "refers to not a single case, of this or any other United States court, that has employed the practice")[391] and

---

[390]Concurring opinion of Justice Scalia, *id.*

[391]*Id.* at 6.

Of related interest, it might be noted that the Associated Press reported on August 6, 1989, that Justice Byron R. White said at the 1989 American Bar Association annual convention in urging that Congress write laws clearly:

> "the Statute as it is written, it is said, is what Congress enacted, not statements in hearings, not discussion of statutory terms contained in committee reports and not statements on the floor," . . . .
>
> . . . .
>
> The debate over how statutes should be interpreted "is extremely important since it involves how the courts may best carry out the will of Congress," he said.
>
> White suggested, among other things, that Congress make it clear when it plans to supersede state law.

Justice White Urges Clearly Written Laws, Wash. Post, at A16, cols. 1-2 (final edition). The fuller, early edition article on Justice White's remarks provides in full:

> Congress could make the Supreme Court's job easier by writing laws clearly, eliminating the need for time-consuming court interpretations, Justice Byron R. White told the American Bar Association's convention Friday.
>
> In the past 50 years, courts trying to determine congressional intent have looked at the legislative history of laws as well as the wording of the statutes, White said. Such history includes committee hearings and reports, floor debates and conference committee actions.
>
> White said a nearly 100-year-old high court decision, *Holy Trinity Church v. United States*, which allowed the interpretation of even a clear statute based on legislative history, "barely" survived the Supreme Court's last session.
>
> In their interpretations, the courts begin with the statutory language,

the discussion of the issues in Judge Harold Greene's decisions in *Rainbow Navigation*. Justice Scalia's opinion provides in full:

> I concur only in the judgment of the Court because I believe that the text of Articles XIX and XXI of the Convention Respecting Double Taxation, Mar. 4, 1942, United States-Canada, 56 Stat. 1405-1406, T. S. No. 983, is completely dispositive of petitioners' claim under the agreement. The Court apparently agrees. See *ante*, at 10-12. Given that the treaty's language resolves the issue presented, there is no necessity of looking further to discover "the intent of the Treaty parties," *ante*, at 12, and special reason to avoid the particular materials that the Court unnecessarily consults.
>
> I
>
> Of course, no one can be opposed to giving effect to "the intent of the Treaty parties." The critical question, however, is whether that is more reliably and predictably achieved by a rule of

---

which if thought clearly to reflect legislative intent, is followed, he said.

However, "most statutory cases involve not plain, but ambiguous language, and in these cases resort to legislative history has been the usual course," White said. "This is often a very large undertaking, taking hours and hours of effort by judges, law clerks and librarians, to say nothing of the time lawyers spend and charge for seeking to present the materials that the judiciary has indicated are relevant to decision."

With the complexity of subjects considered by courts, more people, including Justice Antonin Scalia, advocate a return to interpreting statutes based almost wholly on the legislation's text, White said.

"The statute as it is written, it is said, is what Congress enacted, not statements in hearings, not discussion of statutory terms contained in committee reports and not statements on the floor," said White, who was appointed to the court by President John F. Kennedy in 1962.

The debate over how statutes should be interpreted "is extremely important since it involves how the courts may best carry out the will of Congress," White said, adding that in some cases Congress may be vague on purpose, to force court decisions.

Justice White Urges Clearly Written Laws, Wash. Post, at A5, cols. 1-3.

construction which credits, when it is clear, the contracting sovereigns' carefully framed and solemnly ratified expression of those intentions and expectations, or rather one which sets judges in various jurisdictions at large to ignore that clear expression and discern a "genuine" contrary intent elsewhere. To ask that question is to answer it.

One can readily understand the appeal of making the additional argument that the plain language of a treaty (which is conclusive) does indeed effectuate the genuine intent as shown elsewhere--just as one can understand the appeal, in statutory cases, of pointing out that what the statute provides (which is conclusive) happens to be sound social policy. But using every string to one's bow in this fashion has unfortunate implications. ("It would be wrong; and besides, it wouldn't work.") Here the implication is that, *had* the extrinsic evidence contradicted the plain language of the treaty it would govern. That is indeed what we mistakenly said in the earlier case that the Court cites as authority for its approach. In *Sumitomo Shoji America, Inc. v. Avagliano*, 457 U. S. 176 (1982), we stated that "`[t]he clear import of treaty language controls unless `application of the words of the treaty according to their obvious meaning effects a result inconsistent with the intent or expectations of its signatories.' . . . *Maximov v. United States*, 373 U. S. 49, 54 (1963)." The authority quoted for that proposition in fact does not support it. In *Maximov*, confronted with an argument appealing to the "intent or expectations" of the signatories, we responded that "[t]he immediate and compelling answer to this contention is that . . . the language of the Convention itself not only fails to support the petitioner's view, but is contrary to it." *Maximov v. United States*, 373 U. S. 49, 54 (1963). We then continued: "Moreover, it is *particularly* inappropriate for a court to sanction a deviation from the clear import of a solemn treaty . . . when, as here, there is no indication that application of the words of the treaty according to their obvious meaning effects a result inconsistent with the intent or expectations of its signatories." *Ibid.* (emphasis added). The import of the highlighted adverb is, of course, that it would be inappropriate to sanction a deviation from clear text *even if there were* indications of contrary intent. Our *Sumitomo* dictum separated the last clause of this quotation from its context to support precisely the opposite of what it said. Regrettably, that passage from *Sumitomo* is already being quoted by lower courts as "[t]he general rule in interpreting treaties." *Rainbow Navigation, Inc. v. Department of Navy*, 686 F. Supp. 354, 359, n. 25 (DC 1988).

Notwithstanding the *Sumitomo* dictum to which the Court alludes, our traditional rule of treaty construction is that an agreement's language is the best evidence of its purpose and its parties' intent. In *Rocca v. Thompson*, 223 U. S. 317 (1912), it was urged upon us that a treaty granting consuls the right "to intervene in the possession, administration, and judicial liquidation of the estate of the deceased" also granted them the right to administer the property of the deceased, since that would effectuate the treaty's "objects and purposes." We conducted no separate inquiry into the intent or expectations of the signatories beyond those expressed in the text, but said simply:

> "[T]reaties are the subject of careful consideration before they are entered into, and are drawn by persons competent to express their meaning and to choose apt words in which to embody the purposes of the high contracting parties. Had it been the intention to commit the administration of estates of citizens of one country, dying in another, exclusively to the consul of the foreign nation, it would have been very easy to have declared that purpose in unmistakable terms." Id., at 332.

That is the governing principle of interpretation. Only when a treaty provision is ambiguous have we found it appropriate to give authoritative effect to extra-textual materials. See, e. g., *Air France v. Saks*, 470 U. S. 392, 400 (1985); *Nielsen v. Johnson*, 279 U. S. 47, 52 (1929).

II

Even, however, if one generally regards the use of preratification extrinsic materials to confirm an unambiguous text as an innocuous practice, there is special reason to object to that superfluous reference in the present case. What is distinctive here is the nature of the extra-textual materials to which the Court unnecessarily refers. To discover Canada's and the United States' "intent and expectations," the Court looks solely to the United States Senate floor debates that preceded the President's ratification of the treaty. *Ante*, at 12-13 and nn. 7-8. The use of such materials is unprecedented. Even where the terms of the treaty are ambiguous, and resort to preratification materials is therefore appropriate, I have been unable to discover a single case in which this Court has consulted the Senate debate, committee hearings or committee reports. It would be no more appropriate for me than it is for the Court, to use the present case as the occasion for pronouncing upon the legitimacy of using such materials, but it is permissible to suggest some of the arguments against it. Using preratification Senate materials, it may be said, is rather like determining the meaning of a bilateral contract between two corporations on the basis of what the Board of Directors of one of them thought it meant when authorizing the Chief Executive Officer to conclude it. The question before us in a treaty case is what the two or more sovereigns agreed to, rather than what a single one of them, or the legislature of a single one of them, thought it agreed to. And to answer that question accurately, it can reasonably be said, whatever extra-textual materials are consulted must be materials that reflect the mutual agreement (for example, the negotiating history) rather than a unilateral understanding. Thus, we have declined to give effect, not merely to Senate debates and committee reports, but even to an explicit condition of ratification adopted by the full Senate, when the President failed to include that in his ratification. We said:

> "The power to make treaties is vested by the Constitution in the President and Senate, and, while this proviso was adopted by the Senate, there is no evidence that it ever received the sanction or approval of the President. It cannot be considered as a legislative act, since the power to legislate is vested in the President, Senate and House of Representatives. There is something, too, which shocks the conscience in the idea that a treaty can be put forth as embodying the terms of an arrangement with a foreign power or an Indian tribe, a material provision of which is unknown to one of

> the contracting parties, and is kept in the background to be used by the other only when the exigencies of a particular case may demand it." *New York Indians v. United States*, 170 U. S. 1, 23 (1898).

Of course the Senate has unquestioned power to enforce its own understanding of treaties. It may, in the form of a resolution, give its consent on the basis of conditions. If these are agreed to by the President and accepted by the other contracting parties, they become part of the treaty and of the law of the United States, see *Northwestern Bands of Shoshone Indians v. United States*, 324 U. S. 335, 351-352 (1945); see also Restatement (Third) of Foreign Relations Law of the United States§ 314 (1987). If they are not agreed to by the President, his only constitutionally permissible course is to decline to ratify the treaty, and his ratification without the conditions would presumably provide the basis for impeachment. Moreover, if Congress does not like the interpretation that a treaty has been given by the courts or by the President, it may abrogate or amend it as a matter of internal law by simply enacting inconsistent legislation. *La Abra Silver Mining Co. v. United States*, 175 U. S. 423, 460 (1899); *Edye v. Robertson (Head Money Cases)*, 112 U. S. 580, 599 (1884). But it is a far cry from all of this to say that the meaning of a treaty can be determined, not by a reservation attached to the President's ratification at the instance of the Senate, nor even by formal resolution of the Senate unmentioned in the President's ratification, but by legislative history of the sort that we have become accustomed to using for purpose of determining the meaning of domestic legislation.

The American Law Institute's Restatement of the Foreign Relations Law of United States would permit the courts to refer to materials of the sort at issue here. See Restatement (Third) of the Foreign Relations Law of the United States § 314, Comment *d* (1986); *id.*,§ 325, Reporter's Note 5. But despite the title of the work, this must be regarded as a proposal for change rather than a restatement of existing doctrine, since the commentary refers to not a single case, of this or any other United States court, that has employed the practice. The current version of the Restatement provides no explanation for (or even acknowledgment of) this curiosity. An explanation was provided in the Proposed Official Draft of the Second Restatement, which is of some interest:

> "There is virtually no precise decisional authority on this matter, probably because of the domestic interpretative rule, stated in§ 155, that executive interpretations of international agreements are given great weight by courts in the United States or because, as explained in Comment a to this Section, the courts wish to avoid if possible creating disharmony between the international and the domestic meanings of international agreements." Restatement of the Foreign Relations Law of the United States§ 154, Comment b(ii) (Prop. Off. Draft 1962).

This is not the case in which to commit ourselves to an approach that significantly reduces what has hitherto been the President's role in the interpretation of treaties, and commits the United States to a form of interpretation plainly out of step with international practice.

It can hardly have escaped the Court's attention that the role of Senate understanding in the treaty ratification process has recently been the subject of some considerable dispute between the Senate and the Executive. See Washington Post, Mar. 19, 1988, p. A11, col. 1 (discussing disagreement on the importance to be accorded to Senate understanding of the Anti-Ballistic Missile Treaty at the time of advice and consent to the President's ratification); Washington Post, Feb. 17, 1988, p. A17, col. 1 (same); Washington Post, Feb. 6, 1988, p. A1, col. 6 (same). The first (and, as far as I am aware, the only) federal decisions relying upon pre-ratification Senate materials for the interpretation of a treaty were issued by the District Court for the District of Columbia, in successive phases of the same controversy, last May, see *Rainbow Navigation, Inc. v. Department of Navy*, 686 F. Supp. 354 (1988), and last November, see *Rainbow Navigation, Inc. v. Department of Navy*, 699 F. Supp. 339 (1988). In the first of those cases, the court rejected the Government's contention that its representations to the Senate regarding the meaning of a treaty are not binding as to the treaty's interpretation. See 686 F. Supp., at 357-358, n. 17.* [*The court relied in part

> upon testimony--reproduced in The ABM Treaty Interpretation Resolution, Report of the Committee on Foreign Relations United States Senate, S. Rep. No. 100-164, p. 49 (1987)--by none other than the reporter for the Restatement of Foreign Relations Law, Professor Louis Henkin. Thus, by self-exertion, so to speak, there is now at least one case that the Restatement *almost* restates. The qualifier is needed because, as I discuss later in text, even that case does not go as far as the Restatement (and the Court's opinion today) would do.] In the second of them, the Government conceded that "authoritative Executive branch representations concerning the meaning of a Treaty which form part of the basis upon which the Senate gives advice and consent are entitled to be accorded binding weight as a matter of domestic constitutional law, and the Executive branch fully accepts that it is bound by such statements." 699 F. Supp., at 343 (quoting Defendants' Reply Brief and Opposition to Plaintiff's Cross-Motion for Summary Judgment 2, n. 2.). It is not clear that this latest position taken by the Government in District Court is correct, or would even be the position taken before us by the Solicitor General. It is even less clear, however, assuming that position to be correct, that Senate understandings which are *not* the product of Executive representations in the advice-and-consent hearings should have any relevance. It is odd, to say the least, that in the present case, where the language of the treaty is clear, where the role of Senate reports and debates has not even been argued, and where the Solicitor General has not been requested to give us the benefit of his views on that subject, we should reach out to use such materials for the first time in two centuries of treaty construction.[392]

If Senate preratification debates cannot even be *used* in treaty interpretation then certainly they could not be controlling in opposition to the intention of the treaty parties.

Finally, several other points should be noted about the *Stuart* case. First, whatever its peripheral relevance in support of the "dual" approach, the *Stuart* case provides no authority for the proposition, now apparently ensconced in the INF Treaty condition, that Executive branch statements to the Senate are *ipso facto* binding in treaty interpretation regardless of the meaning ascertained under normal

---

[392]United States v. Stuart (U.S. Supreme Court, No. 87-1064, Feb. 28, 1989) (Scalia, J., concurring).

international law rules or whether a Senate even shared an informal understanding on the issue. Second, it should be noted that in considering Senate preratification or "treaty history" materials the Court looked to a broad range of indicators including the President's transmittal message, hearings, committee reports, floor debates, and the President's proclamation on signature. Third, it should be noted that the final sentence of footnote 7, which is the sentence arguably most strongly supporting a "dual" approach, is in its factual premise questionable and in its arguable implicit theory inconsistent with the thrust of the Court's opinion. That sentence provides:

> A treaty's negotiating history, which JUSTICE SCALIA suggests would be a better interpretive guide than preratification Senate materials, see *post*, at 4, would in fact be a worse indicator of a treaty's meaning, for that history is rarely a matter of public record available to the Senate when it decides to grant or withhold its consent.[393]

But the premise that a negotiating history is not available to the Senate--which, in fairness the Court qualifies by adding "rarely" and "a matter of public record" before its main thrust of "available to the Senate when it decides to grant or withhold its consent"--is in several respects misleading. Historically, the Senate has in a number of cases throughout the Nation's history had before it some or all of the negotiating history. Senate consideration of the INF Treaty is the latest example. Moreover, it may well be that the Senate can request the full negotiating record and thus it is available to it in any treaty consideration. And the premise is also misleading in ignoring settings of clear notification by the Executive to the Senate during consideration of a treaty that the negotiating record will be used in future interpretation disputes. This, of course, was the case in Senate consideration of the 1972 ABM Treaty. Furthermore, it is also relevant that at least prior to 1919 during a period when the normal Senate practice was to consider treaties in executive session, apparently such consideration did not produce a public record of Senate deliberations that would be available to a subsequent decision-maker in the interpretive process. Thus, during the constitutionally formative period of the treaty power, the normal mode of Senate consideration itself did not produce a public record as thought of today. Turning to its arguably implicit theory, and any such theory's inconsistence with the thrust of the Court's opinion on treaty interpretation, it can be argued that implicit in a sentence saying that a treaty's negotiating history

---

[393]Opinion of Justice Brennan writing for the Court, *id.* at 13 n.7.

would be a worse indicator of a treaty's meaning than preratification Senate materials because the former would be rarely available to the Senate, is a theory that it is the intent of the Senate that is controlling rather than the intent of the parties. But, as has been seen, on at least three occasions in its opinion the Court looks to the intent of the parties as the criteria for treaty determination and it expressly relies on subsequent practice of the parties, which by definition, could not be "available to the Senate when it decides to grant or withhold its consent." By this footnote 7 last sentence test, of course, such subsequent practice also would be a "worse indicator" yet the Court considers it and does not say that it is a worse indicator. And, of course, if subsequent practice materials not available to the Senate can be considered, why not the treaty negotiating history? Both are relevant precisely because of the light they shed on the intent of the parties as opposed necessarily to the intent of the Senate. Most importantly, it is simply inconsistent for the Court to repeatedly adopt a standard for treaty interpretation in its opinion that looks to ascertaining the intent of the parties, and then in the last sentence of a footnote to argue that materials historically--and under the recognized international law standard for treaty interpretation--given far greater weight (and properly so) in ascertaining treaty intent are a less good indicator of that intent of the parties than Senate preratification history. This suggests that rather than reading a sweeping constitutional theory into this footnote last sentence by implication, the Court may rather have been principally making the point in this sentence that the record of negotiating history is not always available whereas in contrast the Senate preratification record is--at least since 1919--always available.

As previously discussed, the principal secondary authority cited for the "dual" approach is the recently revised *Restatement of the Foreign Relations Law of the United States*, particularly the second paragraph of comment d to section 314. There are several factors, however, suggesting that the revised *Restatement* contributes only minimal, if any, authority to the general "dual" approach. At the outset, it should be understood that the *Restatements* as a whole are not binding legislation or judicial authority but rather are the work product of the private American Law Institute and particularly within that voluntary association may be heavily influenced by the work of the principal "reporters." The *Restatements* as a whole, including the *Restatements of the Foreign Relations Law of the United States*, have on many issues made a significant contribution to development of the law by clarifying and systematizing the law. Nevertheless, they are notoriously controversial in the academic community for the frequent oversimplifications of the law which such an exercise inevitably makes. The revised *Restatement of the Foreign Relations Law*, has among such *Restatements* generated at least its share of controversy. Ultimately the *Restatements* are only as authoritative as the underlying authorities cited and the strength of the analysis given in support of a position. Thus, it is important to note first that on this issue of a "dual" approach the revised *Restatement* cites no authority whatsoever, primary or secondary.[394] Second, it should be noted that the revised *Restatement* consideration of the "dual" versus "unitary" approach never explicitly addresses that core issue and, as such, cannot be of much weight on it. Thus, while the second paragraph of comment *d* above says that the President has an obligation to respect a "general understanding by the Senate" even if not formally adopted, this comment does not specifically advert to a setting where the understanding may not have been communicated to the other party and where there is consequently a potential divergence between United States international and national obligations. And where such a divergence is at least implicit in the setting, as in Reporters' Note 5 to section 325 set out above, the revised *Restatement* merely says that treaty "legislative history" materials should be "taken into account" or "considered" by a domestic court interpreting the treaty rather than that they are ipso facto conclusive as seems required by the "dual" approach. Third, the immediate predecessor *Restatement*, the *Restatement (Second) of the Foreign Relations Law of the United States*, as revised and published in 1965 clearly adopts the position that informal indicators from Senate treaty consideration are *not ipso facto* effective under national law but are simply to be taken into account "as that of the record of legislative history on the interpretation of a statute." Section 135 of the *Restatement (Second)* provides:

§ 135. Effect of Statement of Understanding as Domestic Law

---

[394]A draft of the *Restatement (Second)* candidly noted the lack of decisional authority on these issues in section 154, comment *b*, "Domestic criteria that are not material internationally":

> There is virtually no precise decisional authority on this matter, probably because of the domestic interpretative rule, stated in § 155, that executive interpretations of international agreements are given great weight by courts in the United States or because, as explained in Comment a to this Section, the courts wish to avoid if possible creating disharmony between the international and the domestic meanings of international agreements.

American Law Institute, Restatement of the Foreign Relations Law of the United States, § 154, comment b, at 555 (Prop. Off. Draft 1962) [hereinafter *1962 Restatement Draft*].

> **(1) If a statement of understanding as to the meaning of a treaty is either attached at signature by the United States or is included in the instrument of ratification by the United States either because required by the Senate resolution of advice and consent or to reflect a particular meaning that the Senate ascribed to the treaty in giving its advice and consent, the treaty and the understanding become effective as domestic law under the rule stated in§141.**
>
> **(2) In the absence of a statement of understanding as described in Subsection (1), an indication from the record of the Senate's consideration of the treaty that the Senate ascribed a particular meaning to the treaty has the same bearing on the interpretation of the treaty as domestic law as that of the record of legislative history on the interpretation of a statute.**[395]

And comment b to this section says:

> *Interpretative effect of meaning attributed by Senate.* If the Senate does not insert an understanding in its resolution of advice and consent and the President does not feel that it is necessary to do so in the instrument of ratification, conclusions based upon the deliberations of the Senate are not controlling in the interpretation of the treaty as the domestic law of the United States. Under Supreme Court precedents discussed in § 151, Reporters' Note 1, courts in the United States, in interpreting an international agreement, take into account manifestations of intention made during the course of its formation. In the case of a treaty, the deliberations and action of the Senate are a necessary phase of such formation. Moreover, it is clear from Senate practice that the Senate gives its advice and consent in the expectation that its understanding, whether or not included in the

---

[395] *Restatement (Second), supra* note 185, § 135, at 422.

> resolution of advice and consent, will be taken into account in determining the effect of the treaty as domestic law.[396]

Thus, the immediate predecessor *Restatement* clearly adopted the position that informal indications from the record of Senate intent, as opposed to formal statements of understanding either attached at signature or included in the instrument of ratification, would not *ipso facto* become "effective as domestic law" but rather would only be "taken into account." Moreover, the comment to this section makes it clear that informal "conclusions based upon the deliberations of the Senate are not controlling in the interpretation of the treaty as the domestic law of the United States."[397] The revised *Restatement* cites no authority for departing from this view.[398] Finally, it should be noted that the Chief Reporter of the revised

---

[396]*Id.* comment *b*, at 422-23.

[397]It might also be noted that a draft of the *Restatement (Second)* pointed out:

> If the Senate does not insert its understanding in its resolution of advice and consent . . . it should never have more than an interpretative significance. Where Senate action in giving its consent is thus ambiguous, the courts should be left free to interpret the Senate's intent with respect to the internal effect of the "understanding". Even as so restricted, the situation is one that creates possibilities for serious variance between domestic effect and international effect. Hence, considerations of policy support a limited, interpretative effect to this manifestation of Senate intent.

1962 Restatement Draft, supra note 394, § 138, comment b, at 505.

[398]A draft student note entitled "'Spontaneous Generation' in the Restatement (Third) of Foreign Relations Law: The Error of Allowing Informal Senate Understandings to Govern Treaty Interpretation," concludes in rejecting the *Restatement (Third)* approach:

> Obviously, the President should not lie to the Senate about the meaning of a treaty, nor should he seek to exploit ambiguities to circumvent the clear intent of the Senate or U.S. treaty partners in ratifying or signing a treaty. It does not follow, however, that any rule preventing such abuse is desirable. The Third Restatement view on informal Senate understanding addresses a critical problem in constitutional law, but its suggested solution--proclaimed

Restatement is Professor Henkin, whose views on an analogous issue in the *Niagara Reservation* case were rejected in 1957 by Judge Bazelon writing for the Court of Appeals for the District of Columbia Circuit[399] and apparently were opposed by his senior colleagues at Columbia, Professors Jessup and Lissitzyn.

Professor Louis Henkin's view, given in testimony before the Senate Foreign Relations Committee considering the "ABM Treaty Interpretation Resolution," as excerpted in the majority report of the Senate Foreign Relations Committee as a basis for its adoption of the "dual" approach is:

> It seems to be suggested . . . that if the Senate does not make its understanding a condition of its consent, how the Senate interpreted a treaty is essentially irrelevant. That is not correct. In my view, if the Senate's understanding is clear, the President can make the treaty only in accordance with that understanding, whether or not that understanding is expressed as a condition of consent.

> without precedent, echoed by the Senate, and incorporated without analysis by the courts--is unnecessary and has serious, undesirable consequences.
>
> Trumpeted as a way to hold the Executive to his word to the Senate, this doctrine is not in fact required to restrain the President's discretion in interpreting treaties for the U.S. First, evidence of Senate understandings will be taken into account in interpreting treaties. Second, both the Senate and the treaty partners of the United States have means at their disposal to influence the President's interpretation of a treaty. These means, moreover, have the considerable benefit of decreasing the likelihood of the Executive facing inconsistent treaty obligations internationally and domestically. The discretion to interpret treaties and to determine the obligations the U.S. faces abroad and which it asserts against other nations is a fundamental part of the foreign relations power and should be granted to the Executive subject to the internal, political controls already in place.

"Spontaneous Generation' in the Restatement (Third) of Foreign Relations Law: The Error of Allowing Informal Senate Understandings to Govern Treaty Interpretation," at 52 (Unpublished Draft Note of April 8, 1989, authored by Michael Coe).

[399]This case, as has been discussed, was subsequently vacated as moot by the Supreme Court. *See* Power Authority v. Federal Power Commission, 247 F.2d 538 (D.C. Cir. 1957); *vacated as moot sub. nom.* in American Pub. Power Assn. v. Power Authority of the State of New York, 355 U.S. 64 (1957).

> Indeed, if there is any reason to doubt that the Senate's understanding is shared by the other party or parties to the treaty, or if it appears that the Senate's understanding might somehow differ from what the treaty might be held to mean as a matter of international law, the President is bound to communicate the Senate's understanding as being the understanding of the United States when he make [sic] the treaty.[400]

As has been seen, the issue separating the "dual" verses "unitary" approach is not whether the record of Senate consideration is irrelevant. Nor is it that, whatever the precise nature of the obligation, when a President is aware that a generally held Senate understanding, even if informal, is inconsistent with the treaty interpretation of the other treaty party that the President should insist on treating the issue as an amendment, reservation or formal understanding and should not only communicate the Senate's understanding but should seek a modality that ensures the other party will be bound by the understanding. The issue, rather, is whether when a President (or in most cases a former President) has concluded an international agreement without awareness of a difference between an informal Senate understanding and the interpretation accepted by the other party that is internationally binding, is such a treaty void, in effect pursuant to the Senate informal understanding as national law and the international obligation as international law, or in effect under both national and international law pursuant to the international obligation. It is simply the garden variety logical fallacy known as a *non sequitur* [401] to conclude from this Henkin statement on one issue the answer to another, as the majority report seems to. And even if, as we have seen, it were concluded that a President's or prior President's failure to "make the treaty only in accordance with" the Senate's informal understanding produces some legal consequence, it is not clear from this view why that consequence is that the treaty goes into effect under national law pursuant to the informal Senate understanding as opposed to a legal consequence that the treaty as a whole is simply void under national law, or some other legal consequence.

With respect to the recent views of Professor Louis Henkin, as has been seen his essay in the Spring 1989 issue of the *Michigan Journal of International Law*

---

[400]*The ABM Treaty Interpretation Resolution, supra* note 1, at 57 (quoting Professor Louis Henkin).

[401]*See generally* on logical fallacies *S. Barker, The Elements of Logic* 174-211 (1965).

reaffirms his support for the "dual" approach. Thus, he writes: "[W]hether or not the Senate expressed an understanding, what the Senate in fact thought the treaty meant is the treaty to which the Senate consented."[402] Strikingly, however, this essay cites only the *Restatement (Third)* and footnote 7 in the *Stuart* case (which Professor Henkin notes "invoked" the *Restatement (Third)*, but which he fails to note did not quote the controversial paragraph in comment d that seems to constitute the principal authority for the "dual" approach) as authority for this view. Moreover, Professor Henkin offers virtually no constitutional or policy arguments in support of this view. Indeed, his discussion seems to concede that at least the constitutional text is "not wholly clear." Thus, he writes:

> The constitutional provision conferring power to make treaties is brief:
>
> > [The President] shall have Power, by and with the Advice and Consent of the Senate, to make Treaties, provided two thirds of the Senators present concur. . . .[9] [9. U.S. CONST. art II, § 2, cl. 2.]
>
> The text seems simple and clear, but even clear constitutional text is not wholly clear. Notably, we have "advice and consent," a historic phrase that has entered our daily language; but what is "advice," when and by whom is it to be given, and must it be heeded? Consent has proved clear enough, but not crystal clear: may consent be conditional, and what kinds of conditions may the Senate impose? And what is a treaty? May the President make other agreements without Senate consent?[403]

Moreover, while supporting the "dual" interpretation in general, Professor Henkin seems to suggest that the INF Treaty interpretation condition is not a legally binding "condition of consent but only an expression of the Senate's view of the Constitution." He writes:

---

[402]Henkin, *supra* note 7, at 414.

[403]*Id.* at 408-09. While Professor Henkin properly goes on to develop constitutional practice as an important source of much constitutional law of the treaty power, he cites no example of constitutional practice, other than the "broad-narrow" debate, concerning the "dual" versus "unitary" issue.

> In my view the constitutional principle declared by the Senate [attached to the INF Treaty] is sound and its implications for treaty interpretation unexceptionable. But its title as a condition is dubious. The President, eager to make the treaty, accepted the Senate's consent subject to the Senate's "condition," but issued a statement declaring the condition to be "improper." Proper or not, such conditions are not very significant except as a salvo in President-Senate warfare in the conduct of their shared treaty power. Attaching a constitutional principle as a "condition" of consent to a treaty does not bind future Presidents to that principle. A future President might not agree that there is such a constitutional principle. The principle may not bind even the President who ratified that particular treaty. The principle is not really a condition of consent but only an expression of the Senate's view of the Constitution. The Senate's view may be disputed by the President and must stand or fall on its merits.
>
> Non-amending conditions sometimes reflect distrust between the United States and the other party to the treaty, or Senate mistrust of the Executive (or of later Executives). Sometimes such conditions are blows in larger battles with the President. They reflect and inevitably aggravate friction in the treaty process and beyond, another consequence of our bifurcated treaty procedure.[404]

Perhaps most tellingly, Professor Henkin does not come to grips with a central problem of the "dual" approach even under his theory that it is rooted in a Senate condition to consent. That is, if "what the Senate in fact thought the treaty meant is the treaty to which the Senate consented,"[405] then how can a treaty be legally binding under national law *if* in fact it turns out that the treaty meant something else--either more or less restrictive? This, of course, reflects a central dilemma of the "dual" approach that such an approach makes a difference *only* if there is a difference between what a Senate understood and the internationally binding meaning of the treaty. Yet clearly the Senate not only had an understanding of a particular meaning *but also* believed it was the meaning internationally agreed between the parties in the treaty unless it adopted a "domestic condition" making clear it conditioned approval on a particular interpretation whether or not

---

[404]*Id.* at 417.

[405]*Id.* at 414.

internationally binding under the treaty. *That* is the treaty "to which the Senate consented," *not one* with a particular meaning either in violation of the treaty itself or more restrictive than the treaty. Where, then, does a "dual" approach get its constitutional authority when by definition whenever it would make a difference it would not enforce the full understanding of the Senate both as to meaning and that *the treaty* had that meaning. And, how, then, does the "dual" approach protect the integrity of a Senate understanding better than a "unitary" approach? Finally, it is ironic that Professor Henkin makes an argument for the supremacy of treaties over United States statutes[406] while apparently not adverting to the fact that the "dual" approach would subordinate the international treaty obligations of the Nation not just to legislation enacted by both houses of Congress after presentment to the President, nor even to domestic conditions unilaterally but formally adopted by the Senate, but rather to *informal* indicators of intent *of but one house*. Moreover, in doing so, apparently this approach also would not even apply the well-recognized principle of national law, intended to protect the international legal obligations of the United States, that a later United States statute will not set aside a prior treaty obligation unless the contradicting congressional intent is clearly manifest.

With respect to the testimony of Professor Laurence H. Tribe,[407]

---

[406]Professor Henkin writes:

> [T]here is evidence . . . that, in general, the Framers assumed that the United States -- all the Branches -- would respect the Law of Nations, including treaty obligations. Certainly, there is an argument for the supremacy of international law and treaties in our jurisprudence, subject to the Constitution.

Id. at 426.

[407]*See* "Statement of Laurence H. Tribe, Ralph S. Tyler, Jr., Professor of Constitutional Law, Harvard University, Cambridge, MA," and "Prepared Statement of Laurence H. Tribe," in *The ABM Treaty and the Constitution, supra* note 1, at 83 and 412 respectively.

In evaluating Professor Tribe's arguments it may be relevant to note that in his text on *American Constitutional Law* he says, in part, of the President's authority concerning treaties:

> Taken together with the command of Article II, Sec. 3, that the President "shall take Care that the Laws be faithfully executed," these constitutional provisions have come to be regarded as explicit textual manifestations of the

cited by the majority report as authority for its adoption of the "dual" approach, the reasons given by Tribe seem either question begging or clearly erroneous, perhaps in significant measure because of a too great reliance on an analogy between the legislative process and the treaty process. Thus, the argument that "[n]o treaty is `made' until the Senate has given its consent,"[408] is simply wordsmithing. That is, of course, under the Constitution the President has the "Power, by and with the Advice and Consent of the Senate, to make treaties." But this truism contains no guidance as to the legal effect of a ratified treaty under national law when subsequently there is found to be a discrepancy between an informal Senate understanding and the treaty as internationally binding. Indeed, if one were to continue the wordsmithing game presumably since the Senate did not give its

---

> inherent presidential power to administer, if not necessarily to formulate, the foreign policy of the United States. Although influenced (often decisively) by congressional action or constitutional restraint, the President thus has exclusive responsibility for . . . negotiating, administering, and terminating treaties or executive agreements . . . and generally for applying the foreign policy of the United States. . . .

L. Tribe, American Constitutional Law 164-65 (1978). And he further notes:

> Presidential exercise of the treaty-making power is limited not only by the procedural requirements of article II, Sec. 2, but also by substantive constitutional restrictions. First, the Constitution may well import at least the core of the Framers' conception of what a treaty is. Thomas Jefferson, in his *Manual of Parliamentary Practice* prepared for the United States Senate, wrote that a treaty "must concern the foreign-nation party to the contract, or it would be a mere nullity. . . ." The Supreme Court, in dictum, has embraced Jefferson's view as a constitutional limitation: a treaty must deal with questions: "properly the subject of negotiations with a foreign country." With global interdependence reaching across an ever broadening spectrum of issues, however, this seems unlikely to prove a serious limitation. . . .

Id. at 169. As has been seen, the Jeffersonian view of the nature of a treaty is, of course, one of the underpinnings of the "unitary" approach.

[408]*The ABM Treaty Interpretation Resolution, supra* note 1, at 57 (quoting Professor Laurence Tribe).

consent to the treaty in all its particulars the treaty was simply never "made" and thus must be non-existent or void under domestic law. It is absurd to believe from such wordsmithing, which can as easily be run for different legal conclusions, that one has revealed a constitutional requirement that whenever any discrepancy arises between an informal Senate understanding of a treaty and its subsequent international legal interpretation that the treaty becomes void under domestic law or that it enters into force under domestic law pursuant to the informal, but mistaken, Senate understanding. Professor Tribe also seems to engage in a generous amount of hyperbole when he poses the issue as:

> [u]nder the Legal Adviser's model, the meaning of the ABM treaty is to be gleaned not by examination of what the President and the Senate agreed upon, but by examination of what the President and the Soviets agreed upon--regardless of what the President may or may not have told the Senate about what he had negotiated. *This is tantamount to saying that President Nixon made the ABM treaty the supreme law of the United States with the advice and consent of the Soviet Union.*[409]

Whatever Professor Tribe's interpretation of the Legal Adviser's view, a fairer and fuller characterization of the "unitary" view would be that the meaning of the ABM Treaty is to be found through application of the normal international rules of interpretation as applied to the agreement negotiated between the Executive branch and the Soviet Union as modified by any formal or informal Senate action during the United States ratification process communicated to the Soviet Union as part of or along with the instrument of ratification (or withholding of ratification), and taking into account as relevant under the general international rules of treaty interpretation any uncommunicated informal general Senate understanding on the Treaty. Certainly this is not remotely equivalent to saying that "President Nixon made the ABM treaty the supreme law of the United States with the advice and consent of the Soviet Union." Professor Tribe seems to commit a more serious sin than wordsmithing when he says in his prepared statement for the ABM Treaty interpretation resolution hearings:

> Whatever one's view as to the proper place of legislative history that is theoretically public but practically unavailable, there can be but one answer to the question of what place an indisputably

[409]*The ABM Treaty Interpretation Resolution, supra* note 1, at 57.

> secret negotiating history can have in the meaning of any law -- whether domestic legislation passed by Congress and signed by the President or passed by a two-thirds vote over his veto, or a treaty negotiated by the President and consented to by a two-thirds vote of the Senate. Such secret histories cannot be taken into account because they were not part of the record on which the legally decisive votes were taken.[410]

But unlike the legislative setting where the requisite intent is that of the legislature, the Supreme Court and other federal courts have repeatedly held in the treaty setting, where they have looked to the intent of the treaty parties, that treaty negotiating histories, subsequent conduct, and foreign language texts of a treaty may be used in treaty interpretation, and they have done so without inquiring whether such histories, conduct, or texts were "part of the record on which the legally decisive votes" of Senate advice and consent were taken.[411] Indeed, this is

---

[410]"Prepared Statement of Laurence H. Tribe," *supra* note 407, at 412, 416.

Professor Michael J. Glennon, who indicates that he served as a consultant to the Senate Foreign Relations and Judiciary Committees on the treaty interpretation resolution, adopts the view that an untransmitted negotiating record is not part of legislative history and can be taken into account only when not inconsistent with the Senate's understanding of a treaty's meaning. Thus, in a recent article he writes:

> Although Senate Resolution 167 does not expressly address the issue, it would permit a secret negotiating record, not transmitted to the Senate when it approved a treaty, to be taken into account when that record is not inconsistent with the Senate's understanding of a treaty's meaning. However, that would be disallowed when the Senate understood otherwise, as reflected in the treaty's legislative history. Then, the Senate's understanding would control, as indeed it should. Legislative intent is reflected by legislative history, and an untransmitted negotiating record by definition is not part of the legislative history.

Glennon, "Interpreting `Interpretation': The President, the Senate, and When Treaty Interpretation Becomes Treaty Making," 20 *U. Cal. Davis* 913, 917 (1987).

[411]*See, e.g.*, Factor v. Laubenheimer, 290 U.S. 276, 293-96, 300 (1933); Trans World Airlines, Inc. v. Franklin Mint Corp. et al, 466 U.S. 243, 259 (and dissent of Justice Stevens at 266-270) (1984) (negotiating history); *Air France v. Saks*, 470

a hornbook proposition of United States foreign relations law even as applied to

U.S. 392, 399-400 (1985) (French text, negotiating history and subsequent conduct); O'Connor v. United States, 107 S.Ct. 347, 351, 352 (1986) (subsequent conduct and negotiating history); Block v. Compagnie Nationale Air France, 386 F.2d 323, 330, 336-48 (1967) (French text of treaty, negotiating history and subsequent conduct); Day v. Trans World Airlines, Inc., 528 F.2d 31, 34-35, 35-36 (Ct. App. 2d Cir. 1975) (negotiating history and subsequent conduct). In *Air France v. Saks* a unanimous Court (Justice Powell not participating) looked to the governing text of the Warsaw Convention in the French language while noting that there was an "official American translation . . . which was before the Senate when it ratified the Convention." 470 U.S. at 397 n.2. The Court also said: "[I]t is our responsibility to give the specific words of the treaty a meaning consistent with the shared expectations of the contracting parties. We look to the French legal meaning for guidance as to these expectations because the Warsaw Convention was drafted in French by continental jurists." 470 U.S. at 399 (citation omitted). And the Court said quoting the *Choctaw Nation* case: "`[T]reaties are construed more liberally than private agreements, and to ascertain their meaning we may look beyond the written words to the history of the treaty, the negotiations, and the practical construction adopted by the parties.'" 470 U.S. at 396 (citation omitted). Similarly, in *Trans World Airlines, Inc. v. Franklin Mint*, both the opinion of the Supreme Court and the dissenting opinion of Justice Stevens relied on negotiating history even in a setting in which the Court knew, as pointed out by Justice Stevens, that "[t]he President submitted the Convention to the Senate in 1934, which gave its advice and consent by voice vote without committee hearings, committee reports, or floor debate." 466 U.S. 273 (dissenting opinion of Justice Stevens). Thus, it seems highly unlikely that the negotiating history in question had been before the Senate. And, in *Block v. Compagnie Nationale Air France*, the Fifth Circuit Court of Appeals relied on a French text of a convention while simultaneously pointing out that "the text that was read to the Senate, and to which the resolution of ratification was directed, was a text in English originally published in a Treaty Information Bulletin of the Department of State in March 1934." 386 F.2d 330 n.19. The opinion of Mr. Justice Brennan, writing for the Supreme Court in the recent case of *United States v. Stuart*, also expressly relies on subsequent practice, as well as the meaning attributed to treaty provisions by government agencies charged with their negotiation and enforcement, without inquiring whether such materials were before a consenting Senate. Indeed, they almost certainly were not. As such, in this respect the text of the opinion itself would seem to sharply limit the effect of the final sentence of footnote 7 which might be argued to support theTribe view. *See* United States v. Stuart (No. 87-1064, Feb. 28, 1989) at 14-15, 12 n.7.

unilateral negotiating records. It may be instructive in this respect to examine the *Restatement (Second)* and more recent *Revised Restatements of the Foreign Relations Law of the United States*. Thus, the *Restatement (Second)*, as revised and published in 1965, says:

> Position papers of delegations, conference records kept by delegations for their own use, and stenographic transcripts made by the secretariat, if not made available by the secretariat or the host state, will usually be excluded, although as indicated in § 151, national courts for domestic purposes may resort to the state's own records of the negotiation.[412]

---

[412]*Restatement (Second), supra* note 185, § 147, comment d, at 452, 453.
It might also be noted that the classic Harvard Research in International Law concluded "that the United States Supreme Court frequently takes preparatory work into consideration when interpreting a treaty, and places considerable reliance thereupon as evidence of the actual design of the contracting parties." Harvard Research in International Law, "Law of Treaties," 29 *Am. J. Int'l L. Supp.* 653, 965 (1935) [hereinafter "Harvard Research on Treaties"]. The full discussion of Supreme Court practice by the "Harvard Research" is:

> It may be noted, in addition to what has been already considered, that the United States Supreme Court frequently takes preparatory work into consideration when interpreting a treaty, and places considerable reliance thereupon as evidence of the actual design of the contracting parties. See Cook v. United States (1933), 288 U. S. 102; *Terrace v. Thompson* (1923), 263 U. S. 197; *Kinkead v. United States* (1893), 150 U. S. 483. See also *United States v. Texas* (1896), 162 U. S. 1; *Jordan v. Tashiro* (1928), 278 U. S. 123; *Nielsen v. Johnson* (1929), 279 U. S. 47; *Todok v. Union State Bank* (1930), 281 U. S. 449; *Factor v. Laubenheimer* (1933), 290 U. S. 276. Chang, on the basis of a study of the cases, declares that the Supreme Court relies frequently on the evidence of prior negotiations, that it has not attempted to appraise the relative probative value of deductions drawn from the text itself and evidence furnished by such prior negotiations, and that it has shown no preference for one form of evidence over the other. "The Court," he says, "in ascertaining the design of the contracting parties has followed a simple method of using all possible sources of evidence at its disposal." *The Interpretation of Treaties by Judicial Tribunals* (1933), pp. 131-139.

And the draft *Revised Restatement* says:

> Use of domestic sources. In determining the effect of an international agreement as domestic law, a court or agency of the United States is required to take into account national materials relating to the formation of an international agreement which an international body, such as the International Court of Justice, might not consider. These may include:
>
> . . . .
>
> (ii) The history of the negotiations leading to the agreement, including unilateral statements of understanding not included in the President's proclamation or otherwise communicated to the other party, and, probably, internal official correspondence and position papers prepared for the use of the United States delegation to the negotiation that produced the agreement. Although internationally some of this evidence of intention may not be given great weight it may be necessary for domestic courts to consider it in view of the weight to be given to executive interpretations of an agreement under § 326(2).[413]

It seems particularly unrealistic in view of the President's undoubted role in treaty interpretation to seek to exclude Executive branch records as to the negotiated meaning of a treaty. The implications of such a rule for carrying out arms control agreements could be particularly harmful if rigidly interpreted. Among other problems such a rule could introduce greater uncertainty as to the meaning of arms control agreements and could make impossible the normal operations of fora such as the Standing Consultative Commission (SCC) in secretly working out agreed interpretations of a treaty's meaning. Moreover, in the alternative, a practice of routinely submitting all negotiating records to the Senate in full along with the agreement to receive advice and consent or an SCC agreed interpretation could have an undesirable chilling effect on an already difficult negotiating context. In connection with Professor Tribe's argument that a "secret negotiating history" can have no role in treaty interpretation unless before the Senate at the time of advice and consent it should also be noted that specifically in the ABM Treaty context Secretary of State Rogers fully informed the Senate that:

Id.

[413] *1985 Revised Restatement, supra* note 187, § 325, reporters' note 5, at 107-08.

> [if] questions of interpretation arise in the future, we certainly will go back and look at the memoranda because there wasn't a complete transcript kept of the plenary sessions. . . .[414]

It seems probable that Professor Tribe's testimony concerning the impermissibility of using a negotiating record not part of the Senate record of advice and consent, which is almost certainly wrong as a matter of law, may be one factor in the recent Senate request for the full INF negotiating record.[415]

With respect to the arguments of Professor Abram Chayes cited by the majority report as a basis for adopting the "dual" approach, his statement that "[t]he very absence of reservations or understandings itself confirms that the Senate understood the treaty to be susceptible of only one interpretation" does not follow from the premise and is yet another *non sequitur*. That is, one possible interpretation of an absence of formal reservations or understandings is, as Chayes suggests, that there is no dispute as to meaning or substance. But other equally plausible explanations, inconsistent with Professor Chayes conclusion, are that an issue has not been significantly addressed, or is considered peripheral, or both. And the Chayes "paradox" underlying this example of what is the Senate to do when there is no dispute about the meaning of the text exists to some extent under both "dual" and "unitary" approaches. That is, even under the "dual" approach, if there is no record of Senate consideration, formal or informal, the same "paradox" is

---

[414]*See* the Sofaer April 10 memorandum at page 16.

[415]Even the legal memorandum entitled "Principles of Treaty-Making and Interpretation," rooted in the "dual" approach and included as the first item in an Appendix to the Senate Foreign Relations Committee report on the INF Treaty, substantially qualifies this view of Professor Tribe. It provides:

> This principle does not imply that an untransmitted negotiating record is in all circumstances irrelevant to treaty interpretation. A negotiating record not placed before the Senate at the time of its consent proceedings might conceivably have some bearing on the meaning of a treaty in the event that no meeting of the minds occurred between the President and the Senate with respect to a given issue. In such circumstances, the import of the negotiating record would not displace that of other indicia of the treaty-makers' intent.

"Principles of Treaty-Making and Interpretation" in *The INF Treaty Report, supra* note 1, at 437, 440.

present. As this illustrates, to some extent this "paradox" is nothing more than a normal feature of any law making process relying on language to convey meaning. Law makers do not address all possible interpretations, particularly those they consider reasonably clear from the language by whatever the mechanism considered necessary to legally clarify the issue. But the inevitable price is the occasional (or even more frequent) interpretive dispute when they fail to focus on an issue that becomes important. It should also be noted that both "dual" and "unitary" approaches start from the same treaty language, particularly under the Vienna Convention standards of interpretation, in interpreting the meaning of a treaty considered by the Senate. As we have seen, and as the Chayes "paradox" suggests, it may be true that with respect to national law, the "unitary" approach places a greater burden on the Senate to adopt views felt important in the form of formal amendments, reservations or understandings, but the difference is one of degree and not kind; and, more importantly, if a Senate is concerned, as it properly should be, with the binding obligations being created internationally for the United States, this burden is not at all lessened under the "dual" approach. More importantly, there is a shadow "paradox" not discussed in the Chayes "paradox" that is the flip side of the issue. If a process is one of making an international agreement, why should one party be bound by the uncommunicated, and possibly different, interpretive assumptions of another? And if the other party is not to be bound why should either party regard the agreement as binding? Most settings in which the language of the treaty seems clear will probably result in no differences between the parties. But when differences do arise it hardly seems persuasive to argue that there could be no interpretive differences because the issue was considered so clear as not to be mutually addressed. And just as it may be true that the "unitary" approach places a greater burden on the Senate under national law to clarify important issues as amendments, reservations or understandings, it also, for the very same reason, maximizes the Senate role in the international agreement making process by encouraging formal action on an issue in a form that will be communicated to the other treaty party and become incorporated in the agreement. Moreover, it can also be argued that the "unitary" approach may even lessen the Senate's burden overall, because under that approach it must be concerned only with the international obligations and is not simultaneously potentially creating a separate set of independent obligations under national law.

It may also be useful in examining the arguments for the "dual" approach from the perspective of the "unitary" approach to briefly review the arguments of the majority report of the Senate Foreign Relations Committee on *The ABM Treaty Interpretation Resolution* in rejecting the "monitoring" and "mutuality of obligation" policy arguments supporting the "unitary" approach.[416]

Thus, as we have seen, the majority report says in rebutting the "monitoring" argument:

> In his testimony, Mr. Sofaer argued that if ratification proceedings were to be seen as relevant to a treaty's meaning, the United States would have to send trained personnel to monitor other treaty signatories' ratification proceedings. But this worry is unnecessary.
>
> -- First, few other nations have a bifurcated approval procedure comparable to that of the United States; legislative approval of treaties is the exception, not the rule. Even in such parliamentary democracies as the United Kingdom, Australia, and India, there is no constitutional requirement for legislative aproval [sic] of treaties. This should not be surprising; in unitary, parliamentary governments, the "executive" which negotiates treaties is, after all, a part of the legislature.
>
> -- Second, for prudential reasons the State Department does in fact already monitor certain states' ratification proceedings, particularly on key agreements. A recent example concerns the Panama Canal Treaties. During and following Senate consideration, the Foreign Relations Committee was kept thoroughly briefed by the Executive concerning legislative developments in Panama that might bear on the rights and obligations imposed by those Treaties. Indeed, certain Senators who opposed the Treaties alluded to Panamanian legislative events in contending that Panama was interpreting the Treaties in an unacceptable manner.
>
> -- Third, the United States has, as a matter of past practice, regarded its own ratification proceedings as having international significance. In three of the six contentious cases in which the United States has appeared in the International Court of Justice, the State Department's

---

[416]*The ABM Treaty Interpretation Resolution, supra* note 1, at 59-61.

Legal Adviser has relied on the record of Senate ratification proceedings in urging a particular interpretation of a treaty. In those cases, the Legal Adviser has found ratification proceedings highly relevant--indeed authoritative--on the question of treaty meaning.

-- Finally, it is quite reasonable to expect--indeed, disingenuous to pretend otherwise--that other nations are sufficiently interested and capable to monitor U.S. ratification proceedings. Can anyone seriously believe that the Soviets have remained studiously oblivious to Senate proceedings with regard to arms control? The Committee is well aware of the contrary; Soviet diplomats are diligent in the extreme in monitoring deliberations of the Senate, most particularly on matters pertaining to U.S.-Soviet relations. Moreover, in the words of Professor Tribe:

> [S]urely it is not asking too much of the Soviets--who evidently know every word whispered behind the locked and guarded doors of the American Embassy--to keep abreast of the *public* exchanges between the American Executive and the American Senate during the process of advice and consent. The Soviets come to the negotiating table well aware that the treaty they would make must satisfy the Senate as well as the Executive, because those two institutions *together* speak for the United States under the Constitution. Who can doubt that the Soviets followed the American ratification of the ABM Treaty very closely indeed? To advocate presidential power to deceive the Senate is bad enough; to do so on the basis of Soviet stupidity is sheer folly.

In sum, it is simply not accurate to contend that a new or unrealistic surveillance "duty" would be imposed on the U.S. Government or other governments by the requirement that ratification proceedings be regarded as centrally relevant to the meaning of treaties. Indeed, until the "reinterpretation" initiative

> brought forth the Legal Adviser's extraordinary theory, their relevance had never been questioned.[417]

At the outset it should be noted that this listing omits what may well be the strongest argument *for* the majority position; that is whatever the United States does in adopting a "dual" or "unitary" position is unlikely, at least in the short run, to change the well entrenched international law rule that internal uncommunicated treaty ratification records are not centrally relevant to the international legal interpretation of treaties unless a "violation of a provision of . . . internal law regarding competence to conclude treaties . . . was manifest and concerned a rule of its internal law of fundamental importance."[418] Conversely, it is probably current international law that internal ratification records may be considered--that is, are at least relevant--in the international interpretation of treaties but would, of course, in the framework of Articles 31 and 32 of the Vienna Convention be considered along with many other frequently more important factors.[419] Thus, arguably even if the United States were to adopt a "dual" approach it would not be subjected in international fora to an increased need to monitor others' internal processes over current needs but rather its own uncommunicated internal processes unless manifest, meaning under the Vienna Convention "objectively evident to any State conducting itself in the matter in accordance with normal practice and in good faith,"[420] would not serve to release the United States from its international obligations. There is, however, a possibility that should the United States adopt a "dual" approach an international court might hold that other nations could reciprocally invoke the doctrine against us and there would also be some possibility that our practice could begin through time to erode the general international legal rule. If either of these events occurred, monitoring needs might indeed be enhanced by the "dual"

---

[417]*Id.* at 59-60.

[418]*See* as evidence of customary international law the Vienna Convention on the Law of Treaties, *supra* note 198, Articles 23, 27, and 46.

[419]Ratification records may, however, be "relevant" to treaty interpretation under the standards of Articles 31 and 32. See Articles 31 and 32 of the Vienna Convention, *supra* note 198.

[420]*Id.* Article 46(2). Professor Koplow, as previously noted, seems to understand this as a central point in rebutting an overly broad "monitoring" argument more clearly than the majority report of the Senate Foreign Relations Committee. *See* Koplow Draft, *supra* note 1, at 107-08.

approach. The listing of factors that was set out in the majority report does accurately illustrate that internal ratification records are relevant to treaty interpretation, both practically and, at least in some settings, legally.[421] But this is true under both "dual" and "unitary" approaches and nothing on the list suggests that such uncommunicated internal processes not involving manifest defects in internal procedures for concluding treaties would be regarded as ipso facto conclusive indicators for treaty interpretation regardless of the shared expectations of the parties, as may be the case under the "dual" approach. Most importantly, this discussion of the issue focused on "monitoring" needs misses the most important policy issue embedded in the "monitoring" argument. That is, is it wise for the United States to adopt an internal rule that would be inconsistent with the thrust of international law that international agreements to be binding should result from communicated and shared expectations? Most international lawyers would support the thrust of modern treaty law that seeks to enhance openness and communication between the parties in reaching international agreements. "Monitoring" needs are only one undesirable symptom of a broader concern that parties reach their treaty obligations through clear communication and adhere to those mutually agreed obligations. In that setting it is probably desirable to continue to narrow arguments for varying mutually agreed treaty obligations based on uncommunicated internal processes. Finally, it should be noted that the concluding statement of this argument postulating "that ratification proceedings be regarded as centrally relevant to the meaning of treaties" and stating that "their relevance had never been questioned" is simply inaccurate if, as would be required for the argument to have meaning in the "dual" versus "unitary" approach debate, it is uncommunicated ratification proceedings that are intended. As has just been discussed, it is to the contrary clear under international law that uncommunicated internal ratification proceedings are in most settings not centrally relevant to the meaning of treaties. And while probably correct under treaty interpretation law that such records are relevant in treaty interpretation in a variety of settings, as we have seen, Hackworth reports at least one important diplomatic interchange in which the United States Secretary of State instructed our Ambassador to Germany to:

> explain to the German Foreign Office that expressions of opinion

---

[421]It would seem obvious that in international litigation parties whose interpretive positions are supported by internal uncommunicated records of either side will advance such records. Courts, in turn, might give such records greater weight against the party in whose internal processes they were made than against the party to whom they were never communicated.

> as to the meaning of the treaty of August 25, 1921, such as those to which the Foreign Office refers, occurring in general debate, cannot be regarded as affecting the interpretation of that treaty.[422]

In rebutting the "mutuality of obligation" argument the majority report says:

> The overarching specter posited by the Legal Adviser is of a procedure which could bind the United States more strictly under its own constitutional law than it--and the other party--are bound by international law. In short, he posits an absence of mutuality of obligation through excessive concern for constitutional niceties.
>
> The Committee recognizes that the intersection of constitutional and international law raises a variety of "iffy" questions. Suppose, for example, that the negotiating record of a treaty and the subsequent, consistent practice of the parties support interpretation X and the text and ratification proceedings support interpretation Y; what interpretation should apply? This and other questions make for wonderful law school "hypotheticals," although the likelihood is minimal that most such examples would actually occur.
>
> This is not to ignore the very real possibility that a disparity in domestic and international obligations could actually arise. The best example is an agreement entered into in technical violation of a nation's domestic law. Under international law, such an agreement can be binding internationally notwithstanding the domestic violation. Indeed, such an agreement is binding internationally unless the agreement violates a "fundamental rule" of domestic law and that violation is "manifest." Because the domestic law is contravened, the agreement is invalid domestically, but binding internationally.
>
> The Legal Adviser implies that the problem of reconciling two intersecting systems--domestic and international--is one created by those who wish to assert the relevance of the Senate's role in the treaty ratification process. In fact, the problem of harmony--to the limited degree it exists--inheres in the very existence of two separate but interactive systems. To achieve harmony between the two is, as experience demonstrates, generally

---

[422] 5 *G. Hackworth, supra* note 334, at 262.

> possible. But harmony is not the only interest at stake. Surely the interest of the United States in preserving the integrity of its domestic legal order is far weightier. Certainly harmony should not be sought by dispensing with clear imperatives of the Constitution.
>
> In any case, the practical reality is that problematic instances are extremely rare and--directly to the point--that the ABM Treaty is not, on the basis of relevant circumstances, such an instance. With the ABM Treaty, the only issue is whether the text, the ratification record, and the subsequent practice should control when all support the same interpretation. The Committee has no doubt that the answer is emphatically yes.[423]

From the perspective of the "unitary" approach this discussion is wholly inadequate in meeting the variety of "mutuality of obligation" issues supporting the "unitary" approach. First, the issue is not fairly met by arguing that the ABM Treaty is not an agreement with a different interpretation resulting under international and national law. Some proponents of both "broad" and "narrow" approaches have taken the position that both national ratification records and the international interpretive standard support their position. But only proponents of the "narrow" position have asserted the additional argument that if the informal Senate ratification record is clear in indicating a general Senate understanding for the "narrow" interpretation (or even if Executive branch statements were made presenting that interpretation) that this would be binding under national law regardless of the interpretation that would result from application of the international standard. This is the issue raising, among other factors to be subsequently discussed in this part, the "dual" versus "unitary" approach. Similarly, the mutuality issues are not fairly engaged by the question begging statement, which is certainly accurate if the "dual" approach were a "clear imperative of the Constitution" that "[c]ertainly harmony should not be sought by dispensing with clear imperatives of the Constitution." The central defect of this discussion is not to candidly recognize that the core of the difference between the "unitary" and "dual" approaches is whether the Nation will have a treaty ratification process that may, in some settings, lead to differences between our treaty obligations under national and international law. However rarely such instances may occur they will *always* be presented in settings concerning "dual" versus "unitary" approaches because *that is the central difference between these approaches*. As such, it is

---

[423]*The ABM Treaty Interpretation Resolution, supra* note 1, at 60-61.

simply not meaningful to discuss this issue as rarely occurring or stemming from "the very existence of two separate but interactive systems." (What a wonderful, obfuscatory turn of phrase!) It is not necessary at this point to repeat the policy arguments involving "mutuality of obligations" as set out earlier under the discussion of policy arguments supporting the "unitary" approach, particularly policy arguments one, six, eight, twelve, thirteen and fourteen, but it should be observed that the brief discussion of this issue in the majority report largely simply ignores these important issues related to the undesirability of the Nation adopting a rule which would lead to a double standard of treaty obligation for the Nation and which would, at least in some settings, fail to treat other nations fairly by giving conclusive effect to uncommunicated indicia of understanding.[424]

---

[424]In a 1987 essay, Professor Michael J. Glennon, who indicates that he served as a consultant to the Senate Foreign Relations and Judiciary Committees on the treaty interpretation resolution, refers to this need for the Nation not to have a treaty ratification process leading to differences between our treaty obligations under national and international law as a "tidiness interest" or a concern "about mere orderliness." Thus, he writes:

> [D]uring the dispute concerning interpretation of the ABM Treaty, the State Department Legal Adviser, Abraham Sofaer, repeatedly cautioned the Senate against endorsing a principle that would "[deprive] our nation of the benefits of mutuality of obligation in its treaty relations." "The United States," the Legal Adviser testified, "would be put at a significant disadvantage if the President is subject to stricter constraints, as a result of internal understandings of the Senate, than those which apply to other parties." It is important, he appeared to suggest, that the Senate not endorse a principle that could result in one obligation for the United States and another for a treaty partner.
>
> Surely all nations have a tidiness interest; it ill behooves a nation that takes law seriously to skirt juridical schizophrenia by readily permitting itself to undertake dissonant domestic and international obligations. Yet the Legal Adviser seemed to assume wrongly that the possibility of disparity was some novel idea propounded by a few Senators, rather than a contingency inherent in the nature of the relationship between the two legal systems. Moreover, he seemed to assume wrongly that the interest in harmony between the two legal regimes is the only interest at stake. Surely a far greater interest is involved: surely the interest of every state -- and the United States in particular -- in preserving the integrity of the domestic legal order must prevail over concerns about mere orderliness.

Glennon, *supra* note 410, at 914-15 (footnotes omitted). His analysis, of course, also seems to assume that "the domestic legal order" of the United States requires the "dual"

Similarly, the arguments advanced by Professor David A. Koplow in the manuscript for his soon to be published article in the *University of Pennsylvania Law Review* as to why a departure from "strict `mutuality of obligations'"[425] in treaties should not be regarded as a serious policy objection[426] completely miss the point (and, of course, as a result completely miss the strength of the policy underpinnings supporting the "unitary" approach). No one has ever doubted, per the examples given by Professor Koplow, that nations can intentionally negotiate asymmetrical obligations, that parties retain freedom of action where not bound by a treaty's coverage, and that treaties may be lawfully implemented under differing national laws in ways consistent with the treaty obligation but which nevertheless reflect differing requirements of national law. But this is not *remotely* the same as a rule of national law requiring either that the United States violate its international treaty obligations or be unilaterally bound in a setting in which mutuality of obligation was intended as part of the negotiating bargain. Indeed, to not focus on this latter real issue, which is a core policy dilemma underlying the "dual" versus "unitary" debate, as opposed to the undoubted and largely irrelevant truisms presented by Professor Koplow, would in a setting of the most important arms control obligations of the Nation seem little short of incredible. The real policy concerns, among others, are whether a bargained for international treaty obligation will be binding on the United States or whether an effort to obtain a reciprocally binding treaty commitment will be unilaterally binding on the United States even if not internationally binding on the other treaty party. They are not the obvious and trivial realities that parties may bargain for asymmetrical obligations and be free to implement different choices where not mutually bound otherwise. And in settings of critical arms control obligations these real policy concerns can be of fundamental importance to the Nation.

The policy argument, which is a mainstay of the "dual" approach and the effort to declare Executive branch statements *ipso facto* binding, that without such an approach there would be no way to police the integrity of the Senate ratification

---

approach. For this assumption he cites no judicial authority. He does, however, cite comment d to section 314 of the *1985 Revised Restatement* concerning the effect of informal general understandings by the Senate in the process of giving advice and consent. Glennon, *supra* note 410, at 918.

[425]Koplow Draft, *supra* note 1, at 99.

[426]*Id.* at 99-106. And see the arguments by Professor Koplow set out in text at *supra* note 271 of this study.

process against executive abuse proves too much. For there are in fact a variety of powerful remedies available to protect the integrity of the process. First, intentional misrepresentation to the Congress is punishable as a crime. Indeed, this is widely thought of as a core "lesson" of the Iran-Contra affair and the indictment of Lieutenant Colonel Oliver North. In this respect, for example, section 1001 of the *United States Code* provides:

> Whoever, in any matter within the jurisdiction of any department or agency of the United States knowingly and willfully falsifies, conceals or covers up by any trick, scheme, or device a material fact, or makes any false, fictitious or fraudulent statements or representations, or makes or uses any false writing or document knowing the same to contain any false, fictitious or fraudulent statement or entry, shall be fined not more than $10,000 or imprisoned not more than five years, or both.[427]

And section 1505 provides in relevant part:

> Whoever corruptly, or by threats or force, or by any threatening letter or communication influences, obstructs, or impedes or endeavors to influence, obstruct, or impede the due and proper administration of the law under which any pending proceeding is being had before any department or agency of the United States, or the due and proper exercise of the power of inquiry under which any inquiry or investigation is being had by either House, or any committee of either House or any joint committee of the Congress--
>
> Shall be fined not more than $5,000 or imprisoned not more than five years, or both.[428]

Second, at least in any setting in which the Congress was responding to intentional Executive branch misrepresentation to a Senate during consideration of a treaty for advice and consent--and was not simply seeking to overrule a prior Executive branch interpretation of a treaty made pursuant to the President's duty to "take Care that the Laws be faithfully executed"--the Congress would seem to have broad

---

[427] 18 U.S.C. § 1001 (1982).

[428] 18 U.S.C. § 1505 (1982).

legislative authority to remedy the situation. Third, treaty articles or provisions kept secret from the Senate could not be included in the Senate resolution of ratification and, as such, would not have received Senate advice and consent. Fourth, if an intentional misrepresentation to the Senate were sufficiently central as to vitiate the Senate consent as a whole it is quite possible that a court would be prepared to treat the entire advice and consent as fraudulently induced and thus void, and to treat the treaty as of no legal effect under national law. Fifth, the Congress has broad investigative powers relevant to the execution of its constitutional authority and such powers have the potential to require clear public accountability and major political embarrassment for any such intentional misrepresentation to the Senate about the meaning of a treaty. Sixth, the Senate and the Congress as a whole have a myriad of real-world powers to ensure that their views on major national issues are considered. This includes for the Senate, of course, consideration of a regular stream of treaties, and for the Congress, consideration of a regular stream of authorizing and appropriating measures across a wide range of issues.[429] Finally, in egregious cases of intentional presidential misrepresentation of a treaty to a Senate during its consideration for advice and consent, a president might be impeached and convicted pursuant to Article I, sections 2 and 3 of the Constitution. In this connection it might also be noted that there is not the slightest indication on the "broad-narrow" issue that the problem arose through intentional misrepresentation nor, to date, has anyone in the debate cited a *single* example in United States treaty history of such intentional presidential misrepresentation of the meaning of a treaty during Senate advice and consent. In a forthcoming commentary in the *University of Pennsylvania Law Review*, three Senior-Attorney Advisors in the Office of Policy Development of the Department of Justice write the following with respect to the policy argument made for the "dual" theory that without such a theory the President "could mislead the Senate . . . and obtain advice

---

[429]In a recent essay on the treaty power, Professor Louis Henkin, a principal supporter of the "dual" approach, includes the following discussion of response mechanisms for a Senate unhappy with use of executive agreement form:

> Periodically, the Senate bristles at an executive agreement, and sometimes threatens to use its political weapons, both treaty and not-treaty related, e.g., its power to hold up confirmation of the President's appointments. The Senate also has weapons as part of the legislature, to "punish" the Executive by adopting or not adopting laws or withholding appropriations.

Henkin, "Treaties in a Constitutional Democracy," *supra* note 7, at 419.

and consent under false pretenses":[430]

> The chances of a President deliberately misleading the Senate regarding the meaning of a treaty are little short of fantastic. The very openness of the process, the number of people involved in the negotiation and ratification of a treaty, not to mention the attitude of the other party, make such a scenario virtually impossible. Indeed, the present controversy was not sparked by charges that either President Nixon or President Reagan misled the Senate regarding the interpretation of the ABM treaty. The issue arose from unforeseen changes of circumstance and technology, some less than precise treaty language (reflecting the failure of the parties in 1972 to agree on the issue), and an honest difference of opinion on whether America should be defended against nuclear attack.[431]

That is, the "horrible" invoked in this central policy argument for the "dual" approach may be largely an "imaginary horrible." Similarly, it might be noted that despite the lingering dispute between the Executive branch and many members of the Senate about the appropriate interpretation of the 1972 ABM Treaty, as well as about the underlying constitutional and other legal issues of treaty interpretation, the Senate Foreign Relations Committee took the view within its *INF Treaty Report* that the ABM Treaty interpretation issue--as opposed to the underlying constitutional issue--was "being adequately addressed elsewhere." And its discussion of how this issue was being "adequately addressed" did not rely on the committee adopted interpretation being *ipso facto* binding under national law on the basis of an informal Senate understanding or "binding" Executive branch statement to the Senate. Rather, the committee report said:

> In 1987, the Foreign Relations Committee devoted considerable time and attention to the ABM Treaty dispute in both of these dimensions: factual and constitutional. Having done so, the Committee found no reason, while considering the INF Treaty, to debate again the overall validity of the Administration's

---

[430]Block, Casey & Rivkin, *supra* note 248, at 1505 (quoted from page proofs subject to final editing).

[431]*Id.*

> assertion of a "broad" interpretation of the ABM Treaty as opposed to the traditional "narrow" interpretation. Indeed, in the Committee's view, that issue is being adequately addressed elsewhere:
>
> -- First, as to U.S. defense policy in pursuing the development and testing of ABM systems, that issue is now being addressed through the normal give-and-take of the U.S. *defense budget process*. By means of an amendment to the FY 1988-89 DoD authorization, Congress has employed the power of the purse to assert its view, and similar amendments in the future will succeed or fail on the basis of policy debate.
>
> -- Second, and even more to the point, it has become patently clear that what is permitted by the ABM Treaty will ultimately be decided by *superpower negotiation*. Such negotiation is virtually inevitable--and the need for it is now part of the Reagan Administration's own position--because the United States, as a precondition of agreeing to major reductions in strategic offensive arms, will be required by self interest to achieve its own clear and detailed understanding of which kinds of Soviet ABM systems to anticipate in the future strategic environment. Any Treaty amendment would, of course, be subject to Senate advice and consent.
>
> In sum, the future of U.S. policy with regard to ABM systems, and U.S. participation in the ABM Treaty, will be addressed in the budget process and in negotiations with the Soviet Union. The Committee was unanimous in believing that its action on the INF Treaty required no resolution of the "broad-versus-narrow" ABM Treaty debate.[432]

It should again be noted in response to this core policy argument for the "dual" approach, that in any event it is a remedy which itself seems likely, at least more often than not, to frustrate the intent of a consenting Senate rather than to protect

---

[432]*The INF Treaty Report, supra* note 1, at 88-89 (footnote omitted).

that intent. For the Senate typically would *not* have intended to create obligations binding on the United States only and not reciprocally binding on the other treaty party.

Finally, one point in rebuttal to the argument that under a "unitary" approach the Senate would be required to obtain the full negotiating record should be noted. Under the "unitary" approach the United States is bound to the international legal obligation. Under the "dual" approach the United States is bound to informal Senate understandings as a matter of national law regardless of the obligations of the Nation or the lack of reciprocity on the part of the other treaty partners. Why is it that the Senate should be less concerned with creating unilateral advantages for American treaty partners or violating American treaty obligations than for holding to its own erroneous assumptions at the time of treaty ratification? How is it that such an approach better serves the goal of adherence to the rule of law in the Nation's treaty making process? That is, under either approach--however we jiggle which side of the policy equation should be the greater concern for the Senate--the Senate has an interest in the accurate reporting of the negotiating record and in ensuring that its understandings are internationally binding. And that interest is even better served, not necessarily by reviewing the full negotiating record, but by insisting where important on formal conditions that must be approved by the other treaty partners as a condition of ratification by the United States.

Similarly, the policy argument that the substantial range of issues in Senate consideration of complex treaties (more than 139 in the INF Treaty) would require an "amen chorus" to meet the terms of a "means test" (this is a term that has been used by some in the debate for a standard that an Executive branch statement was not just "authoritatively communicated" but also resulted in a shared understanding that was clearly intended, generally understood and relied upon by the Senate in its advice and consent to ratification), if any such were adopted under a "dual" approach, seems to greatly oversimplify the issue. As has been seen, under the "dual" approach (including a "dual" approach with a "means test") the advice and consent process would be establishing national law overriding any inconsistent international legal obligations or privileges created by the same treaty. While declaring "authoritative" Executive branch statements made during this process by themselves binding in this sense would ensure adherence under national law to those statements, it *would not* ensure that those statements were part of a *treaty obligation of the United States*. But that is the core of the treaty making process, advising and consenting to a treaty, not a legislative exercise in national law making. And there is simply no substitute for a Senate which wants to meaningfully protect itself that a meaning *is the correct international legal meaning under the treaty it is considering* than for that Senate to fully explore issues which particularly concern it and where there is doubt to attach a formal reservation or understanding which, in time, will become part of the treaty obligation. Moreover, the exercise in law making implicitly suggested in this policy argument is a process apparently previously unknown under the Constitution, in which *any* "authoritative" Executive branch statement would of itself create binding national law apparently apart from any necessary showing of a rational nexus between the statement and an understanding shared by an at least two-thirds majority of the Senate (much less of a majority of both houses with presentment to the President). Even if less cumbersome, as was also argued and rejected in the *Chadha* case for the congressional veto, how can such an approach set aside the critical law making processes under the Constitution? It might also be noted that this problem of an "amen chorus" arises as a practical matter only under a variant of the "dual" approach. Since such a chorus would not necessarily alter the correct interpretation of a treaty there would be less incentive to build an *informal* record on each issue if the "unitary" approach were adopted. That is, in any "dual" approach which takes seriously some nexus rooted in an understanding of an at least two-thirds majority of a Senate voting for advice and consent (as opposed to an extraordinary law making approach holding "authoritative" Executive branch statements ipso facto binding) then the process could produce this "amen chorus." This policy argument then--under real world constitutional options which do not provide for Senate advice and consent solely by Executive branch statement--may even become an argument against the "dual" approach. Perhaps most importantly, the specter of collapse of the process if the Senate is required to focus on issues that are important to it seems to substantially overstate the case. It is inherent in the law making process that to have an effect a legislative body must focus on the issue. And do we seriously want to suggest any other kind of law making process--particularly in a setting where any *law making* effect apart from the underlying treaty would, by definition, be inconsistent with the treaty and could even violate the international obligations of the United States? No one has suggested that Executive branch statements made during the normal legislative process are ipso facto binding; yet that process seems to function normally. Nor apparently had anyone suggested the "dual" approach in United States treaty interpretation history until Professor Henkin and the *Restatement (Third)*, as amplified in the "broad-narrow" debate. Yet the treaty process was not in collapse as a result.

synthesis of arguments for the "dual" and "unitary" approaches

---

As has been observed, the "dual" versus "unitary" approach issue is in many respects an issue of first impression in the constitutional system of the United States. Significant arguments can and have been made for both positions during the ABM "broad-narrow" interpretation debate, although it is striking how little the underlying conceptual issue has been clearly addressed.

Despite strong arguments on both sides, on balance the weight of authority, constitutional theory and policy argument leans for the "unitary" approach. At least one Supreme Court decision, the *New York Indians* case,[433] has held that even formally adopted Senate action will not affect a treaty obligation of the United States unless communicated to the other treaty party, and a long line of Supreme Court decisions on the treaty power root that power in a contract or compact between nations. Similarly, the decision of the Court of Appeals for the District of Columbia Circuit in the 1957 *Niagara Reservation* case,[434] although subsequently vacated as moot, set aside a clear Senate reservation on the grounds that it related solely to domestic matters and was not a Senate counter-offer to the other treaty partner, and it did so after opposing arguments on the theoretical issues by Professor Louis Henkin, who, in a major law review article, seemed to support the Senate authority, and his then colleagues at Columbia, Professors Jessup and Lissitzyn, who opposed the Senate authority in a ninety-six page opinion for the position of the Power Authority of the State of New York. Moreover, Mr. Justice Brown, concurring in the 1901 Supreme Court decision in the *Fourteen Diamond Rings* case[435] wrote clearly that "the power of the Senate is limited to a ratification of such terms as have already been agreed upon between the President, acting for the United States, and the commissioners of the other contracting power."[436] Citing this case, among other authorities, the United States Claims Court decision in *Coplin v. United States,* [437] decided in 1984 and reversed on other grounds in 1985, seemed clearly to reject a "dual" approach and argued that only matters included in an instrument of ratification and communicated to another government could affect the

---

[433]New York Indians v. United States, 170 U.S. 1 (1898).

[434]Power Authority of the State of New York v. Federal Power Commission, 247 F.2d 538 (D.C. Cir. 1957); *vacated as moot sub. nom.* in American Pub. Power Assn. v. Power Authority of the State of New York, 355 U.S. 64 (1957).

[435]183 U.S. 176 (1901).

[436]183 U.S. 176, 183.

[437]Coplin v. United States, 6 Cl. Ct. 115 (1984), *rev'd on other grounds*, 761 F.2d 688 (Fed. Cir. 1985).

legal meaning of a treaty. And as we have seen in the theoretical discussion of the treaty power, there are yet other indicators, such as the conception of the Senate treaty role as a veto or negative, that support a conclusion that the "unitary" approach is constitutionally correct in rooting the treaty power in the international agreement rather than legislative act. In contrast, there seems little, if any, relevant primary authority supporting the "dual" approach and the theoretical "case" for that approach seems considerably weaker than that for the "unitary" approach. Neither the recent opinion of Judge Harold H. Greene of the District Court for the District of Columbia in the *Rainbow Navigation* case--now on appeal--nor footnote 7 in Mr. Justice Brennan's opinion for the Court in the recent *Stuart* case, which at least arguably lend analogous support to the "dual" approach, addresses a setting of an interpretation dispute with a different meaning under the normal international law standard for treaty interpretation on the one hand and an informal Senate understanding or Executive branch statement to the Senate on the other. In both cases the evidence of treaty intent from all sources seemed congruent. Moreover, *Rainbow Navigation* seems principally a case concerning the legal effect of "domestic conditions" or Executive branch statements concerning such "domestic conditions" and on that issue is a single District Court decision now on appeal and seemingly at odds with a higher Court of Appeals ruling in the *Niagara Reservation* case (and the theory of the Supreme Court in the *New York Indians* case). And footnote 7 in the Stuart case deals principally with the proposition that Senate preratification materials may be considered in seeking to ascertain the intention of the treaty parties. Indeed, to the extent that it is a decision directly on point it suggests merely that at least one Justice of the Supreme Court would reject the "dual" approach since Justice Scalia's rejection of even the use of Senate preratification history would necessarily preclude such materials being given controlling weight. Finally, on balance the policy arguments supporting the "unitary" approach seem stronger than those supporting the "dual" approach, particularly those rooted in "mutuality of obligation" generally, fair communication to our treaty partners, maintenance of checks and balances within the overall constitutional framework, protecting the ability of the Nation to effectively participate in international adjudication, and interrelations with the problem of mistake in protecting the integrity of the Senate ratification process. It is particularly important to note, in an issue sometimes erroneously conceptualized as simply between the Presidency and the Congress, that the stakes go far beyond any such rivalry and are ultimately rooted in the interests of the Nation as a whole in an effective and fair foreign policy, the strength of its constitutional system of checks and balances for creating binding legal obligations, and in the integrity and effectiveness of the Senate role in the treaty advice and consent process.

That the "unitary" approach is, on balance, stronger than the "dual" approach as a matter of constitutional law and policy does not mean that Presidents should ignore the important role of the Senate in the advice and consent process. Joint steps that can be taken to support the Senate role and overall effectiveness of American foreign policy relating to the treaty ratification process include: transmitting a carefully drawn article-by-article legal analysis and, possibly also, summary negotiating history at least with every major treaty submitted to the Senate for advice and consent (and such analyses should carefully avoid making claims not clearly supported by the language and negotiating history or other interpretive indications); not discouraging the Senate from considering important issues on which there is any legal uncertainty as formal amendments, reservations and understandings (this, of course, does not mean that the Executive branch would not be free to support or oppose such formal actions on the merits); reviewing the informal record of Senate consideration with a view to formally communicating to the treaty partners at the time of ratification any informal understandings reflecting a general understanding of two-thirds of the Senate and that might be legally uncertain with respect to the underlying agreement; and continuing to support the proposition that the informal record of Senate consideration is relevant to treaty interpretation within the overall international interpretive framework. And, of course, the Executive branch should always candidly inform the Senate of all rights, privileges, powers and immunities of which it is aware arising under a proposed treaty and should proceed diligently and in complete good faith in its dealings with the Senate. It is doubtful, however, whether routinely conveying a full negotiating record to the Senate is, on balance, helpful to the Nation's treaty ratification processes. And it is doubtful whether efforts to identify an "authoritative" Executive view, except, of course, to identify as such those individuals speaking for an administration, could constitutionally bind the Nation in the event of an honest mistake or overlooked issue. This latter effort is highly likely to be inconsistent with the Constitution in some settings involving a discrepancy between the views expressed and the international obligation, or the views expressed and a preponderance of other evidence as to Senate intent from the informal Senate record of consideration, at least when such discrepancy arose because of an honest mistake or overlooked issue and it obscures the real policy issues at stake, including important policies in protecting the integrity of the Senate advice and consent process itself.

b. Questions of the relevance and weight to be accorded a range of elements in the process of Senate consideration: the problem of legislative

(or treaty) history as an extrinsic aid to interpretation

Overall determination as to the relevance and weight to be accorded the record of Senate consideration of a treaty for interpretation of that treaty depends as a first stage complexity on interaction among three principal sub-issues. These are first, the threshold question, just discussed, as to the goal of treaty interpretation under national law: the problem of "unitary" or "dual" standards for interpretation; second, questions of the relevance and weight to be accorded a range of elements in the process of Senate consideration: the problem of legislative (or treaty) history as an extrinsic aid to interpretation (including an important threshold question as to the overall goal or standard of "treaty history" interpretation); and third, questions of the level of generality in posing the issue of Senate purpose or intent: the problem of appropriate breadth of context and/or mistaken interpretation in Senate consideration for advice and consent. This part will discuss the second of these issues. Before doing so, however, it should be noted that this issue may be relevant regardless of the proper answer to the first of these issues. That is, if the appropriate standard for treaty interpretation under national law is the "unitary" standard which incorporates the international law standard for interpretation, then to whatever extent the informal record of Senate consideration is relevant as an aid to interpretation under that international standard, at least some of the rules, standards, and policies for assessing the weight to be accorded the elements of the informal Senate "treaty history" record may be of at least some relevance in assessing the weight to be accorded any such elements of "treaty history" within the parameters of the overall international rule of interpretation. And if the appropriate standard for treaty interpretation under national law is the "dual" standard, then the international interpretive process would apply these rules, standards, and policies, as above, while the national interpretive process would look squarely to these rules, standards, and policies for assessing the overall effect of "treaty history" events in assessing Senate purpose or intent for purposes of national law. It should thus be emphasized that even if, indeed particularly if, the "dual" standard were the appropriate constitutional standard, as this study concludes it is not, then it is not simply any statement in Senate hearings that produces a legally meaningful record of informal Senate intent, but rather the law of legislative (or treaty) history as an aid to interpretation must be carefully reviewed for guidance in assessing any particular record. As with the "unitary-dual" standard issue, surprisingly little attention has been given to the "treaty history" issue within the "broad-narrow" debate, although this issue has received greater focus than the other two elements in assessing overall relevance and weight of a Senate record of treaty consideration.

the overall goal of "treaty history" interpretation

In appraising a record of Senate consideration of a treaty for purposes of subsequent interpretation of a treaty other than under the international standard it is obviously not appropriate to conclude that the goal of assessing Senate "treaty history" is to determine whether any single member or small group of the Senate believed in a particular interpretation. Rather, while events indicating the interpretation of any individual senator or groups of senators may be suggestive as to the interpretation of two-thirds of the members of the Senate supporting an action, the goal for appraisal of national law under any "dual" approach must be an interpretation shared by the at least *two-thirds of the members of the Senate present voting for advice and consent to the treaty.* This does not mean that there must be evidence that each of these senators adverted to the issue and believed a particular interpretation correct, but rather that the evidence from the interpretative record as a whole reasonably suggests that a two-thirds majority of the Senate voting for advice and consent adverted to the issue and believed a particular interpretation correct. The authority under the Constitution of the Senate in giving consent to a treaty is an authority exercised only by two-thirds of the Senate supporting a particular action, not an authority exercised by individual senators, committees of the Senate, or senators voting against the two-thirds majority.

This conclusion as to the goal of assessing Senate "treaty history" is not only inherent in the treaty power as set out in Article II, section 2, clause 2 of the Constitution, but also seems inherent in the theory of the treaty power as developed by the Supreme Court. Thus, the opinion of Chief Justice Fuller for the Court in the 1901 *Fourteen Diamond Rings* [438] case was rooted in the premise that the Senate acts in treaty advice and consent through a two-thirds majority and not through the actions of individual senators or groups of senators less than a two-thirds majority. His opinion stressed as the bottom line in rejecting the actions of a subsequent Senate seeking to interpret a treaty consented to by a prior Senate, that "it would seem to be that two thirds of a quorum of the Senate did not consent to the ratification on the grounds indicated."[439] Although less clearly spelled out, this conclusion also seems to be supported by the 1985 tentative draft of the *Revised*

---

[438]Fourteen Diamond Rings, Emil J. Pepke, Claimant v. United States, 183 U.S. 176 (1901). *See also* Coplin v. United States, 6 Cl.Ct. 115 (1984), *rev'd on other grounds*, 761 F.2d 688, at 145, (Fed. Cir. 1985), explicitly adopting a two-thirds standard.

[439]183 U.S. 176, 180.

Restatement of the Foreign Relations Law of the United States which says in comment d to section 314:

> Although the Senate's resolution of consent may contain no statement of understanding, there may be such statements in the report of the Senate Foreign Relations Committee or in the Senate debates. In such case, the President must decide *whether they represent a general understanding by the Senate* and if he finds that they do, must respect them in good faith.[440]

This initial goal of treaty interpretation other than under the international standard, that is to be legally effective an interpretation must at least be shared by two-thirds of the members of the Senate voting for advice and consent to the treaty, in turn implies the principal relevant policies in interpretation of events in "treaty history." That is, individual statements or other events are more or less important as they more or less strongly lend support to a conclusion about whether or not a two-thirds majority of the Senate voting for advice and consent shared a particular interpretation. Inherent strengths or weaknesses in individual indicators in enabling fair conclusion about the views of two-thirds of the Senate will be important in assessing the weight to be accorded any such indicators. Since there are formidable weaknesses in concluding general legislative intent from most "legislative history" events, substantial care is in order when relying on such "legislative history" as an extrinsic aid in interpretation. Mr. Justice Holmes summarized this need for caution when he wrote that basing "speculations about the purposes or construction of a

---

[440] *1985 Revised Restatement, supra* note 187, § 314, comment d, at 82 (emphasis added). It should be noted that this draft made an important change in Tentative Draft No. 1 of April 1, 1980, in this respect which provided simply:

> Although the Senate's resolution of consent may contain no statement of understanding, there may be such statements in the report of the Senate Foreign Relations Committee or in the Senate debates. In such case, the President must nonetheless respect such understanding, in accordance with subsection (2).

American Law Institute, Restatement (Revised) of the Foreign Relations Law of the United States, § 323, comment b, at 132, 133 (Tent. Draft No. 1, April 1, 1980) [hereinafter *1980 Revised Restatement*].

As has been seen, the comment in main text set out above was adopted with only minor, and seemingly not material stylistic changes, in the *Restatement (Third). See* comment *d* set out in text at *supra* note 239.

statute upon the vicissitudes of its passage" is a delicate business.[441]

Caution in using legislative history as an extrinsic aid to interpretation is also suggested by the general policy that laws be knowable by those who must rely on them. As stated in *Sutherland Statutory Construction*:

> Consideration of fairness weighs on the side of reading the materials of legislative history from the vantage point of the public or those affected by the law. The maxim that people are held to know the law becomes unfair concerning portions of the law which are essentially undiscoverable. Basing decisions of statutory interpretation on historical events that are, practically speaking, obscured from the awareness of persons not directly involved in the legislative process has the character of enforcing secret law.[442]

Yet an additional policy may also be relevant to the interpretation of "treaty history." That is, in order to support congruence between United States treaty obligations and domestic law, it may be appropriate that in settings where ambiguity remains *after* reviewing all indicators, that such ambiguity should be resolved in favor of the internationally correct interpretation. This principle is well established in construing subsequent acts of Congress as not to be in conflict with prior treaty obligations unless Congress clearly so intended.[443] This principle, to the

---

[441]*See* De Sloov`ere, "Extrinsic Aids in the Interpretation of Statutes," *reprinted in* 3 *Sutherland Stat. Const., supra* note 311, at 721, 738. De Sloov`ere added the context of this quote.

[442]2A *Sutherland Stat. Const., supra* note 311, § 48.02, at 284.
While this policy would seem to apply to Senate consideration of a treaty, as well as regular legislation, it may, as has been discussed, not be as achievable in considering background negotiating records when the "lawmaking" process is essentially an agreement between two nations.

[443]*See, e.g.*, Whitney v. Robertson, 124 U.S. 190, 194 (1888) ("[w]hen the two relate to the same subject, the courts will always endeavor to construe them so as to give effect to both, if that can be done without violating the language of either. . . ."); The Chinese Exclusion Case, 130 U.S. 581, 600 (1889) ("[i]t will not be presumed that the legislative department of the government will lightly pass laws which are in conflict with the treaties of the country. . . ."). For an important recent application of this principle, see United States v. Palestine Liberation Org., No. 88 Civ. 1962. slip op. at 35 (S.D.N.Y. June 29, 1988). And for a recent discussion of this case and this principle, see Reisman, "An

extent applicable, would seem to have its chief effect under a "dual" interpretive approach that can reach a national interpretation at odds with an international interpretation. It would not necessarily be irrelevant, however, in assessing the weight to be accorded ambiguous "treaty history" under the "unitary" approach, although under such an approach any relevance would seem to go to the relation between other indicators of treaty intent and ambiguous Senate "treaty history" as an indicator in making a single internationally and nationally binding interpretation.

One potentially significant possibility should also be noted in appraising the overall goal or guiding requirement to be met through a search of legislative or "treaty" history if the position of the *Restatement (Third)*, as discussed previously, were to be adopted. The *Restatement (Third)*, and Judge Abraham D. Sofaer, the Legal Adviser of the Department of State, in a forthcoming commentary in the *University of Pennsylvania Law Review*,[444] use language of a particular understanding "on the basis" of which the Senate gave its advice and consent. If, however, the *Restatement (Third)* position that informal Senate understandings concerning treaty interpretation can create binding obligations under national law is rooted in the proposition espoused by Professor Henkin that the Senate has the general authority to condition its advice and consent as it sees fit, then the overall requirement under the *Restatement (Third)* approach may be that to become binding under national law an informal understanding must not only be "generally held by the Senate," but also must be generally held by the Senate *as a condition* or "on the basis" *of which the Senate gave its advice and consent*. That is, under the *Restatement (Third)* approach, possibly *both* requirements of *intent as to a particular interpretation* and *intent to condition acceptance of a treaty on that interpretation*, that is, to give advice and consent "on the basis of" that interpretation, must be met. Presumably, under such a view, *both* requirements would be ascertained "in much the same way that the legislative history of a statute is relevant to its interpretation."[445] Thus, lacking evidence from legislative or "treaty" history providing a rational nexus for a reasonable conclusion that an at least two-thirds majority of a Senate consenting to advice and consent intended its

---

International Farce: The Sad Case of the PLO Mission," 14 *Yale J. Int'l L.* 412, 429-32 (1989).

[444]Sofaer, "Treaty Interpretation: A Comment," 137 *U. Penn. L. Rev.* 1437, 1441-42 (forthcoming May 1989) (reviewed from page proofs subject to final editing).

[445]*Id.* at 1441 (quoting the Restatement (Third), § 314, comment d) (quoted from page proofs subject to final editing).

advice and consent to be so *conditioned*, the key element of conditionality may not be met even if there were sufficient evidence of Senate intent concerning a particular interpretation. In this connection, an issue of weight to be accorded elements in overall "treaty" history also may become of potential significance. By definition, settings of informal Senate understandings as to "conditions" are settings where no relevant formal conditions are included in a Senate resolution of ratification. Under the *Restatement (Third)* approach, however, what weight should be accorded in the "treaty" history process to the fact that the resolution of ratification was formally adopted by the Senate *without such a condition*? Would such an official act in the treaty approval process, which certainly has as high a visibility to the Senate as a whole as virtually anything in that process, require a "strong," "clear," "manifest," or some other showing to overcome? Note that the "treaty" history issue here is *not* an interpretation of an unclear condition in a resolution of ratification, but is rather a finding of Senate conditional approval from informal expressions of treaty meaning in a setting in which the formal and officially adopted resolution of ratification *has no such condition*.

Importantly, it should be noted that from the perspective of at least one knowledgeable congressional staff participant in the "broad-narrow" debate, the national law dimensions of that debate no longer principally concern what has been termed in this study "the goal of treaty interpretation under national law," or the "dual" versus "unitary" approach, but rather focus on the standard or test for ascertaining when "authoritative" Executive branch statements made during the advice and consent process would create binding national law. In a meeting with the author on July 7, 1989, Mr. Robert G. Bell, Professional Staff Member for the Arms Control Observer Group of the Senate Committee on Armed Services, seemed to imply that the remaining debate really focuses on whether the test is that set out in the "Byrd-Biden" condition, which he supports; the Specter amendment to the INF Treaty rejected by an over two-thirds vote of the Senate on May 27, 1988, that

> [s]uch common understanding means a shared interpretation which is both authoritatively communicated to the Senate by the Executive and clearly intended, generally understood and relied upon by the State [sic "Senate"?] in its advice and consent to ratification;[446]

or the statement in the June 10, 1988, message to the Senate from President Reagan that "Executive statements should be given binding weight only when they were

[446]134 *Cong. Rec.* S6884 (daily ed. May 27, 1988) (Amendment No. 2328).

authoritatively communicated to the Senate by the Executive and were part of the basis on which the Senate granted its advice and consent to ratification."[447] It is interesting to note in connection with this position that the standards or tests rejected seem to be those generally rooted in the *Restatement (Third)*, which is the principal legal authority for the "dual" approach accepted as the starting point for this view. That is, the *Restatement (Third)* seems to suggest that to be binding any informal condition must be "a general understanding by the Senate," and, further, that the Senate gave its consent "on the basis of" the understanding.[448] Moreover, since Professor Henkin, whose views provide the principal intellectual underpinning for the "dual" approach, was the Chief Reporter of the Restatement (Third), it is not clear how the "Byrd-Biden" test could reflect his views on this point if viewed as rejecting the Restatement (Third) qualifications on the "dual" approach. Further, even the April 9, 1987, "estoppel" position of then Assistant Attorney General Charles Cooper, also cited by Mr. Robert G. Bell in support of this "Byrd-Biden" condition, contains substantial qualifying language. Thus, in the principal relied on part it says:

> If . . . the ratification record *unequivocally shows* that the President presented the treaty to the Senate based on *specific, official representations regarding the meaning of an ambiguous provision, that the Senate regarded that understanding as important to its consent, and that the Senate relied on the representations made by the executive branch in approving the treaty (and thus in refraining from attaching a formal reservation setting forth the understanding),* we believe the President would, in effect, be estopped from taking a contrary position in his subsequent interpretation of the treaty, just as he would be bound by a formal reservation or understanding passed by the Senate to the same effect.[449]

It remains a mystery as to what constitutional legal basis or other legal authority [perhaps with the exception of Judge Harold H. Greene's opinion in *Rainbow*

---

[447]Letter from President Ronald Reagan to the Senate of the United States (June 10, 1988).

[448]*Restatement (Third), supra* note 235, § 314, comment d, and § 314(2).

[449]Cooper, "Memorandum to Abraham D. Sofaer," *supra* note 1 (emphasis added).

Navigation--now on appeal] supports the view that an "authoritative" statement by an Executive branch official is *ipso facto* legally binding without more, and how any approach could achieve this effect under the Constitution absent a rational nexus between the action said to be *ipso facto* binding and a reasonable conclusion that in a particular context it reflected the position of an at least two-thirds majority of a Senate present consenting to advice and consent. If, as one possible basis for the "Byrd-Biden" condition, "authoritative" Executive branch representations are advanced as always *ipso facto* binding because they are argued to reflect a judgement that more likely than not--and regardless of context--they will reflect a position of an at least two-thirds majority of a Senate, then--without addressing the reasonableness of these assumptions--why would the Specter amendment approach be an anathema to this position?

It should be noted that in the discussion that follows attention will first be given to issues of "legislative history." Subsequently, the important question will be addressed as to how, if at all, the process of "treaty history" does and should vary from "legislative history."

"legislative history" as an extrinsic aid to interpretation

The law has struggled for years to develop an authoritative and policy responsive approach to statutory interpretation. The subject has been repeatedly engaged as a fundamental issue of jurisprudence. While it is difficult to generalize about such a complex issue, in general United States law has evolved from a "classic" or English position which sometimes completely denied the relevance of "legislative history" and generally exhibited extreme skepticism toward the relevance of most such history to a more liberal position permitting the "taking into account" of all such history but only weighing it consistent with any real world effect it has in demonstrating a *general* legislative intent or purpose.[450] Whatever the approach, it should be born in mind that the principal underlying policy reasons both for considering and for limiting the effect of such consideration remain unchanged. That is, while we seek to give effect generally to the purpose or intent of the legislature, we also want to ensure that it is a *general* legislative intent and not simply that of some witnesses or members of the legislature and we seek to be fair to those who may be affected by the law but unaware of the interstices of the

[450]*See generally, e.g.*, the classic writings on statutory interpretation collected in *Sutherland Stat. Const.*, *supra* note 311, pt. 5 (vols. 2A-3A).

record. It is these underlying policies that provide guidance as we assess the impact as an extrinsic aid to interpretation of statements by witnesses and legislative members in hearings, committee reports, floor debates, statements by principal sponsors, and closely related legislative acts.

assessing the relevance and weight of recurrent common events in "legislative" history

---

Some of the principal recurrent common events in legislative history sought to be used as extrinsic aids to interpretation are statements by witnesses and legislative members during committee hearings, committee reports, statements made during legislative debate, statements by principal sponsors or committee persons in charge of the legislative act, statements by opponents, records of textual changes, closely related legislative acts, and relevant executive messages. Principal considerations applicable to each are as follows:

statements by witnesses and legislative members during committee hearings

At least in construing acts of Congress, statements by witnesses and legislative members during committee hearings may be "taken into account." On the other hand, unless reflecting a statement of a principal sponsor, a recommendation for an amendment subsequently made, or some similar special circumstance, such statements are of only limited relevance in demonstrating a *general* legislative intent. Militating for weighting such statements, at least Congress keeps a record of such hearings and statements, these records may have been known to legislators not present at the hearing, and they at least suggest how witnesses or certain members of Congress may interpret the act. Militating against any substantial weight for such indicators are factors including that the records of such hearings are frequently voluminous and even published after the legislation is passed so that it is probably the norm that most legislators on most legislation would not be familiar in detail with such hearings at the time they voted for an act, that such statements would not necessarily have been subjected to full opportunity for discussion or rebuttal, that witnesses are not legislators and do not necessarily reflect the intent of the legislature, and that the views of a majority of legislators, or even a majority of committee members, are not necessarily reflected in such hearings.

In her important monograph on *Legislative History* Gwendolyn B. Folsom says flatly: "Congressional Committee hearings are of limited utility as an aid to statutory construction."[451] The 1985 revision of *Sutherland Statutory Construction* reasonably summarizes the net effect of statements by witnesses and legislative members at committee hearings as:

> Statements in the committee report concerning the purpose or nature of the proposed law are used by courts to determine legislative intent. Courts are hesitant to resort to similar statements made by committee members or other persons at the committee's hearings. . . .
>
> In Congress official verbatum records of Committee hearings are kept. They are printed and distributed to members of the legislature and the public. In the Federal courts statements of members of the committee or of interested parties at the hearing have been considered as aids in determining the legislative intent. Because records of committee hearings are distributed to members of Congress, it is assumed they had knowledge of these statements and of the evils described. Passage of the proposed bill is evidence of their intent to remedy these evils. The use of such statements is justified on the ground that it is felt the committee intent is the legislative intent. The probative force of particular entries may not be great because of the length of many of these records. . . .
>
> Statements of the draftsman of a proposed bill concerning his understanding of its nature and effect, made at the committee hearings, have been accepted in the federal courts as indicative of the legislative intent. If the bill or a portion of it remains unchanged, it is reasonably assumed that the legislature adopted the view of the draftsman. Similarly, if the legislature adopts an amendment urged by a witness, it may be assumed that the intent voiced was adopted by the legislature.
>
> Generally statements made by others at the committee hearings concerning the nature and effect of a bill are not accorded any weight. . . .[452]

The footnote to this last sentence in *Sutherland* contains the further

---

[451]G. Folsom, *Legislative History: Research for the Interpretation of Laws* 37 (2d printing 1973).

[452]2A *Sutherland Stat. Const., supra* note 311, § 48.10, at 318-19.

statement, citing *Turner v. Prod*, 707 F.2d 1109 (Ct. App. 9th Cir. 1983), "[t]estimony of witnesses before congressional committees prior to the passage of legislation generally constitutes only weak evidence of legislative intent."[453]

committee reports

Committee reports, at least if prepared and distributed to members of the legislative body prior to adoption of an act, generally have considerable weight in interpretation.[454] Such reports are likely at least to reflect the views of a majority of the committee, and if distributed prior to legislative action, are much more likely to have been known to more members of the legislative body. Thus, while not necessarily conclusive, they are likely to be accorded substantial weight. *Sutherland* summarizes this effect of committee reports as:

> The report of the standing committee in each house of the

---

[453]*Id.* at 321 n.11.

[454]Within the regular legislative process one of the most important committee reports is, of course, the conference report reflecting interpretations and understandings reviewed by both houses. Thus, the United States General Accounting Office's "Principles of Federal Appropriations Law" says: "A conference report is generally viewed as the most authoritative single source of legislative history." See United States General Accounting Office, Office of the General Counsel, *Principles of Federal Appropriations Law* 2-47 (1st ed. June 1982).
The report of a principal committee seems to rank just below a conference report (which, of course, does not exist in the process of Senate consideration of a treaty for advice and consent as opposed to the legislative process). See, e.g., Garcia v. United States, 469 U.S. 70 (1984):

> In surveying legislative history we have repeatedly stated that the authoritative source for finding the Legislature's intent lies in the Committee Reports on the bill, which "represen[t] the considered and collective understanding of those Congressmen involved in drafting and studying proposed legislation." *Zuber v. Allen*, 396 U. S. 168, 186 (1969). We have eschewed reliance on the passing comments of one Member, *Weinberger v. Rossi*, 456 U. S. 25, 35 (1982), and casual statements from the floor debates. . . . Committee Reports are "more authoritative" than comments from the floor, and we expressed a similar preference in *Zuber* . . .

469 U.S. 70, 76.

> legislature which investigated the desirability of the statute under consideration is often used as a source for determining the intent of the legislature. . . . Although not decisive, the intent of the legislature as revealed by the committee report is highly persuasive. . . . There is a division of authority as to which should prevail in the event of a conflict between what is indicated by committee reports and the contemporaneous and practical construction given to the act by those charged with its administration. . . .
>
> Increasingly, courts have turned to reports of standing committees for aid in interpretation. . . .[455]

Silence or ambiguity in a principal committee report may also be significant. A footnote to this same section in *Sutherland* on effect of committee reports states: in a committee report on a significant issue is important because most members of Congress are likely to consult the committee report in order to gain an understanding of the purpose and effect of a bill before they cast their votes."[456] Arguably in a setting of only weak interpretive indicators from "legislative history," the fact that a principal committee report was silent or ambiguous on an issue may suggest that a majority of the legislative body was also silent or ambiguous on the issue. That is, in such a setting, the substantial weight to be accorded a committee report would be supportive of a conclusion that a majority had no intent on the issue.

statements made during legislative debate

Statements by individual legislators during legislative debate who are neither committee persons presenting the legislative act nor sponsors of the act are generally accorded little weight in interpretation. As an indication of at least one legislator's views they are properly entitled to some weight but they are of little probative value in determining a *general* legislative intent. As with statements of legislators and witnesses before committee hearings, it is not known whether other legislators agreed with such statements or, in many cases, whether many or any other legislators were even aware of them. There is also a general awareness that not all legislators speak all the time with knowledge or authority about legislative

---

[455] 2A *Sutherland Stat. Const., supra* note 311, § 48.06, at 308-09.

[456] *Id.* at 311 n.3.

intent. Moreover, as we will see in a subsequent section, there is a special skepticism directed at the statements of legislative opponents of a measure since it is felt that at least sometimes they may not reflect a majority view and may seek to magnify the reach of what they view as defects.[457] There is also a special problem in using general debate statements printed in the *Congressional Record* prior to March 1978--which of course, is the case in the "broad-narrow" issue.[458] For prior to that date members were permitted to extensively edit remarks or even to insert speeches never made on the floor with no indication that such remarks or speeches were not made on the floor. Since that date, such remarks or speeches not made on the floor must be marked with a bullet. A substantial and consistent pattern of floor statements, however, with no contrary indication in the record, would at least be entitled to some, if not significant, weight in searching for a general intent.

Sutherland, perhaps somewhat too strictly, summarizes these general points about the weight to be accorded statements of individual legislators during legislative debate as:

> [s]tatements by individual members of the legislature about the meaning of provisions in a bill, made during the general debate on the bill following presentation by a standing committee, are generally held not to be admissible as aids in construing the statute. Legislative debates are "expressive of the views and motives of individual members, and hence may not be resorted to, in ascertaining the meaning and purpose of the lawmaking body," and ". . . it is impossible to determine with certainty what construction

---

[457]Gwendolyn B. Folsom says of the views of opponents:

> The views of opponents in debates and minority reports, since they may tend to overstate the reach of the provision opposed, are given little probative effect as against the stated views, or even silence, of proponents.

G. Folsom, supra note 451, at 35.

[458]See Wald, "Some Observations on the Use of Legislative History in the 1981 Supreme Court Term," reprinted in *3 Sutherland Stat. Const., supra* note 311, at 791, 798. (Patricia M. Wald was Circuit Judge, United States Court of Appeals for the District of Columbia and formerly was Assistant Attorney General for Legislative Affairs). *See also G. Folsom, supra* note 451, at 36. "Statements of individual members of Congress inserted in the *Congressional Record* after passage of an act have been given no effect since they could represent only the personal views of those members." *Id.* at 36.

> was put upon an act by the members of the legislative body that passed it by resorting to the speeches of individual members thereof. Those who did not speak may not have agreed with those who did; and those who spoke might differ from each other. . . ."
>
> As further reason for discounting the value of statements made in floor debate, it has been noted "in the course of oral argument on the Senate floor, the choice of words by a Senator is not always accurate or exact."
>
> The traditional view ruled out consideration of legislative debates under any circumstance. This rule has been modified to permit consideration of explanatory statements by the sponsor of a bill, or by the member of the standing committee who is in charge of its presentation to the legislative house and leads the debate. Now the federal courts hold that statements by any members during legislative debates may be considered in the interpretation about the meaning of an ambiguous provision. . . . Statements of legislators made during legislative discourse but not in the context of debate are given very little weight.
>
> If legislative intention is the standard of decision on a question of statutory construction, it can be argued that any legislator's remarks which would shed light on the meaning of those words should be admitted. Although generally entitled to little probative weight, the value of such remarks could be left to depend upon how well informed their author appeared to be and how well he seemed to represent the views of his colleagues. There is support for this approach to the problem.[459]

In an annotated version of remarks delivered in 1982 at the Eighth Circuit Judicial Conference, Judge Patricia M. Wald of the United States Court of Appeals for the District of Columbia and a former Assistant Attorney General for Legislative Affairs summarized the effect of legislative debate as:

> [t]he value of floor debate varies. Statements of sponsors or managers of legislation are worthy of weight, but ad lib comments by marginal participants are not.[460]

---

[459]2A *Sutherland Stat. Const., supra* note 311, § 48.13, at 329-30.

[460]Wald, *supra* note 458, at 791, 797.

Statements subsequent to legislative action by members or former members of the legislature as to past legislative intent are generally entitled to little or no weight.[461] This, of course, reflects the risk, among others, that such statements may be affected by particular disputes.

statements by principal sponsors or committee persons in charge of the legislative act

As an exception to the general rule that statements by individual legislators are entitled to only minor weight in interpretation, statements made by principal sponsors or committee persons in charge of a legislative act may be entitled to substantial weight.[462] This reflects both the special knowledge that such members may have and, perhaps even more importantly, that their colleagues may be aware of and give greater attention to their statements. Gwendolyn Folsom, in her monograph on *Legislative History*, ranks statements of sponsors of proposed legislation as "[n]ext in importance to committee reports"[463] as an aid to interpretation. Sutherland cautions, however, that:

> [s]tatements by sponsors must be evaluated cautiously for two reasons. The first reason is that in actual practice the legislator who is identified as the sponsor of a bill often assumes that role at the instance of some private party who is interested in passage of the bill. The "sponsor" in fact knows no more about the bill than anyone else. Second, where the sponsor does have specific knowledge of the bill, his statements may sacrifice complete candor to partisan interest in enactment of the bill.[464]

statements by opponents

A number of scholars indicate that statements of legislative opponents of

---

[461]*See* 2A *Sutherland Stat. Const., supra* note 311, § 48.16. *See also G. Folsom, supra* note 451, at 31.

[462]*See* 2A *Sutherland Stat. Const., supra* note 311, § § 48.14-15.

[463]G. Folsom, *supra* note 451, at 34.

[464]2A *Sutherland Stat. Const., supra* note 311, § 48.15, at 337.

a measure should be treated with special caution in interpretation. This seems rooted in a general concern that opponents may be tempted to exaggerate the reach of provisions which they regard as undesirable. Thus, Gwendolyn B. Folsom writes in her 1973 monograph on *Legislative History*:

> The views of opponents in debates and minority reports, since they may tend to overstate the reach of the provision opposed, are given little probative effect as against the stated views, or even silence, of proponents.[465]

Folsom cites four Supreme Court decisions for this proposition.[466] She then adds:

> They may, however, be relevant and useful particularly when the proponents do not respond to a specific objection. They may also add cumulative effect where both sides agree on the purpose and effect of a proposed provision.[467]

Similarly, Professor Otto J. Hetzel writes:

> [T]he remarks of those speaking in clear opposition to a measure generally are not appropriate sources for interpreting the meaning of a provision unless the comments arise during a colloquy with one whose commitment is accorded weight by the members voting for the measure.[468]

---

[465]*G. Folsom, supra* note 451, at 35.

[466]*Id.* at 35 n.63. The cases cited are National Woodwork Mfrs. Assn. v. NLRB, 386 U.S. 612, 639-40 (1967); NLRB v. Fruit & Vegetable Packers, 377 U.S. 58, 66 (1964); Mastro Plastics Corp. v. NLRM, 350 U.S. 270, 288 (1956); Schwegmann Bros. v. Calvert Distillers Corp., 341 U.S. 384, 394-95 (1951).

[467]*G. Folsom, supra* note 451, at 35-36.

[468]Hetzel, "Instilling Legislative Interpretation Skills in the Classroom and the Courtroom," 48 *Pittsburgh L. Rev.* 663, 685 (1987).

record of textual changes

There is substantial evidence that courts pay particular attention to the record of any textual changes as they are made during the legislative process. In an essay on *Dealing With Statutes*, derived from a lecture in the prestigious James S. Carpentier Lectures at Columbia, James Willard Hurst puts this second only to committee reports as a useful interpretive source. He writes:

> Most influential are the reports of the legislative committees that considered the bill that became the statute. It is an appropriate emphasis, because the committee is normally the workplace in which members have hammered out the particular content of the measure. Probably next in consequence are inferences to be drawn from comparing the original text of a bill with amendments made in course of passage.[469]

closely related legislative acts

Statutes dealing with the same subject matter as the one being construed may also be used as a significant extrinsic aid to interpretation. Such statutes may shed light on an overall intent or purpose of a legislature. They are particularly significant if closely rooted in the same subject matter and passed at the same session of the legislature. *Sutherland* discusses this rule, often referred to as "statutes in pari materia" as:

> Other statutes dealing with the same subject as the one being construed--commonly referred to as statutes in pari materia--comprise another form of extrinsic aid useful in deciding questions of interpretation. . . .
>
> Statutes can be interpreted to be in pari materia from either the perspective of the legislature (legislative intent) or the meaning to the public. . . .[470]
>
> When a legislature enacts a provision, it has available all the other provisions relating to the same subject matter whether in the same statute or in a separate act. Experience indicates that a

---

[469] *J. Hurst, Dealing With Statutes* 42 (1982).

[470] 2A *Sutherland Stat. Const., supra* note 311, § 51.01, at 449.

legislature does not deliberately enact inconsistent provisions when it is cognizant of them both, without expressly recognizing the inconsistency. The critical question concerns how reasonable it is to assume that legislators and members of the public know the provisions of other acts on the same subject when they consider the meaning of the act to be construed. . . . This principle that such statutes should be construed in pari materia is a restatement of the presumption against the implied repeal of statutes. . . .[471]

It is assumed that whenever the legislature enacts a provision it has in mind previous statutes relating to the same subject matter. . . .

Provisions in one act which are omitted in another on the same subject matter will be applied when the purposes of the two acts are consistent. . . .

. . . If there is an irreconcilable conflict between the new provision and the prior statutes, the new provision will control as it is the later expression of the legislature. . . .[472]

. . . The guiding principle, however, is that if it is natural and reasonable to think that the understanding of members of the legislature or persons to be affected by a statute, be influenced by another statute, then a court called upon to construe the act in question should also allow its understanding to be similarly influenced. . . .

To be in pari materia, statutes need not have been enacted simultaneously or refer to one another. However, the rule that statutes in pari materia should be construed together has the greatest probative force, in the case of statutes relating to the same subject matter passed at the same session of the legislature, especially if they were passed or approved or take effect on the same day, or in the case where the later of two or more statutes relating to the same subject matter refers to the earlier. . . .[473]

relevant executive messages

---

[471]*Id.* § 51.01, at 450-51.

[472]*Id.* § 51.02, at 453-54.

[473]*Id.* § 51.03, at 468-69.

Relevant executive messages come in at least two principal forms. First, those involved with the recommendation of the legislative measure and its presentment to the legislature, and second, messages or statements accompanying executive signing or veto. The first is clearly part of legislative history but is, of course, subject to the weakness of all such materials that it is not direct proof that it reflects a general legislative intent. Its strength, at least for materials formally submitted at the outset to the legislative body, is that there is a higher likelihood that it will be carefully prepared and known to a more substantial body of the legislature. The second, at least if it is in a signing message, is necessarily made after legislative consideration and thus could not have influenced the intention or purpose of the legislature. Gwendolyn B. Folsom says of this latter category of executive messages:

> [M]essages or statements of the Executive accompanying approval of an action, while sometimes used as indicating legislative intent, are perhaps more properly considered as contemporaneous executive construction rather than as a part of the legislative history proper.[474]

brief overview summary of important general principles in assessing "legislative history"

The modern view is to consider most indicia of "legislative history" but to do so with caution and sensitivity as to the strengths and weaknesses of the indicators put forth for a particular interpretation. The most significant indicators seems to be committee reports, record of textual changes during enactment, statements of principal sponsors, and legislative actions in pari materia. Where present, it is probable that important executive messages delivered to the legislative body as a whole would also be viewed as a significant indicator. On the other hand, statements of witnesses and legislative members during hearings, general statements made during legislative debate, and statements of opponents of a measure are all of limited utility. Actions of the Executive accompanying veto or approval may be of even more limited significance and statements made by legislators subsequently in a post-enactment time frame are given little, if any, weight. In this overall process, rigid "canons" of construction are likely to be of little significance as repeatedly

---

[474] *G. Folsom, supra* note 451, at 39-40.

demonstrated by some of the Nation's best thinkers in jurisprudence.[475] A better guide is the significance of the material, including its strengths and weaknesses, in suggesting general legislative focus and agreement on a particular issue. And certainly no rigid "canon" of construction should survive as an overriding "legally binding" norm regardless of context, such as the proposed effect for any Executive branch statements, which does not reflect a rational nexus between the event and the conclusion that it at least more reasonably than not suggests that a two-thirds majority of a Senate voting for advice and consent adverted to the issue and believed a particular interpretation correct.

This general overview, and the caution necessary in using any materials from "legislative history" to demonstrate general legislative purpose or intent, is summarized by James Willard Hurst as follows:

> . . . The twentieth-century approach is to be prepared and willing to give weight to particular legislative history, to the pattern of succession of statutes in a given field, to the bearing of general sectors of legislation on particular acts, and to the course of practical construction of legislation by officials charged with putting it in operation.
>
> Most influential are the reports of the legislative committees that considered the bill that became the statute. It is an appropriate emphasis, because the committee is normally the workplace in which members have hammered out the particular content of the measure. Probably next in consequence are inferences to be drawn from comparing the original text of a bill with amendments made in course of passage. . . .
>
> Courts are cautious in using materials from legislative history other than committee reports or the record of changes in the text of bills. Material beyond these points is likely to present sharper questions of credibility. Legislative hearings may produce detailed comments on pending bills, but typically these come from positions of one interest or another and must be discounted accordingly. . . . Congress of course produces the Congressional Record. Debate there preserved is often fragmentary, subject to members' off-floor "amendment" of their remarks, and blurred by

---

[475]*See, e.g.*, Llewellyn, "Remarks on the Theory of Appellate Decision and the Rules or Canons About How Statutes Are to be Construed, 3 *Vand. L. Rev.* 395 (1950); *K. Llewellyn, The Common Law Tradition* (1960).

> diversity of views which may go without ordered challenge or review. Thus it is not surprising to hear a Supreme Court opinion warning that "In construing laws we have been extremely wary of testimony before committee hearings and in debates on the floor of Congress save for precise analyses of statutory phrases by the sponsor of the proposed laws."
>
> Out of such concerns the Supreme Court--more by what it has done than through closely articulated doctrine--has indicated cautionary limits on reaching far into evidence from legislative hearings or debates. Where the Court has invoked material from hearings, most often it has been in defining the general purpose of a measure rather than its meaning in detail. . . .
>
> In using recorded debate, the Court has distinguished between what was said on the floor by specialists on the pending bill or provision--members of the committee which considered the bill, members in charge of allocating the time limited for discussion under a rule of the chamber, or sponsor --and what was said by members who had no such special connection with shaping the measure. The Court will give weight to what the specialist members said, either on general purpose or on detailed content of the bill. But it is unlikely to regard isolated statements by generalist members, especially on matters of detailed meaning; probably the generalists' statements will have influence only when they make a fairly consistent pattern identifying the broad purposes of the proposal. Judges are not invariably this cautious and sometimes press reliance on legislative history to a point that elicits objections from colleagues. On the whole, however, the decisions approach the matter with common sense appraisal of the credibility of the material.[476]

Professor Eric Lane, who has served as counsel to the New York State Senate Democrats from 1981-1987, also echoes this caution in dealing with "legislative history."

> The use of direct references to vehicles of legislative communications other than statutes, commonly referred to as legislative history, is equally problematic. Aside from a

---

[476] *J. Hurst, supra* note 469, at 42-44.

constitutional concern about reliance on non-enacted language in determining statutory meaning, a court must concern itself with the difficult task of measuring the reliability of any such communication. To determine the reliability of a particular item of legislative history, an interpreter must ascertain the relationship between the provision under interpretation and the item of legislative history, whether the item was intended to be evidence of legislative intent, and whether the legislative body focused, even constructively, on this item as reflecting legislative intent. Very few items of legislative history satisfy these standards of reliability.

One item of legislative history that generally satisfies these standards is a joint resolution of the legislative body on a particular provision which is in dispute. . . .

Inalterably excluded from any list of potentially reliable items of legislative history are postenactment statements of any character. These statements are never the object of legislative attention and are always tempered by the political context that evolves subsequent to the time in which the dispute over the statute arose.

All other items of legislative history must be approached cautiously, with a presumption of unreliability. I am tempted to suggest that Professor Dickerson is entirely correct when he argues that "interpretative materials . . . are slovenly prepared and, even when carefully prepared by professionals, have almost no reliability. Their total elimination therefore would be a net benefit." However, if approached on a case by case basis, other exceptions exist. For example, the floor comments of a bill's principal sponsor on the meaning of a particular provision are generally reliable, unless otherwise contradicted. Explanations found in committee reports, particularly on complex bill provisions, may also be reliable depending on the accepted function of committee reports in the particular legislative body. In Congress, for example, where there is an inordinate focus on the committee as the legislative working arm and consequentially on committee reports, it may be argued that these reports are, at least constructively, made before the entire legislative body. . . .

Other than the two items of legislative history discussed above, it is difficult to perceive, at least in New York, any other items of legislative history that reliably reflects legislative intent. Judge Mikva has made a similar observation from the perspective of the legislative process of the United States Congress:

> Because the committee reports frequently are used in the legislative arena for political horsetrading, individual ego trips, it's too easy for a chairman who's trying to resist an amendment to say, "Well, look we'll put it in the report. Don't worry about it." And, unfortunately, those reports are then viewed by the courts as gospel. . . . I used to wince when I would hear a member of Congress get up and say, "Now for the purpose of making legislative history, I want to utter the following remarks." It happens all the time and unfortunately some judges treat those remarks with special credibility.[477]

issues concerning differences in interpreting "treaty history" from that of "legislative history"

This part will review issues concerning what changes, if any, should be made in interpreting "treaty history" as opposed to legislative history. It should initially be noted that if the "unitary" standard, discussed above, is correct for treaty interpretation then, unlike statutes, treaties will be interpreted pursuant to the international standard for treaty interpretation. At present this means that the informal record of Senate consideration of a treaty will be only one factor in treaty interpretation[478] and, if not formally communicated to other treaty parties, would normally receive less weight than any subsequent practice or negotiating record. This part will not review the "dual versus unitary" standard issue, however, but it will inquire whether, within whatever weight is to be accorded an informal record of Senate treaty consideration pursuant to either "dual" or "unitary" approach, what are the differences, if any, in considering "treaty history" as opposed to "legislative

---

[477]Lane, "Legislative Process and Its Judicial Renderings: A Study in Contrast," 48 *Pittsburgh L. Rev.* 639, 658-59 (1987).

[478]*See, e.g.,* Vienna Convention on the Law of Treaties, *supra* note 198, Articles 31, 32.

history." This issue also is largely an issue of first impression with little direct primary authority perhaps largely because courts have looked to the international agreement and its history with respect to treaty interpretation.

First, it should be noted that there are likely to be differences, possibly major differences, stemming from a variety of differences between treaties and legislative acts, such as that treaties are in the first instance at least negotiated by the Executive, treaties are normally sent to the Senate with a statement of general purpose and interpretation from the President and Secretary of State and possibly even an article by article analysis, frequently a principal negotiator testifies as to the general purpose and meaning of the treaty, treaties must be approved by a two-thirds majority of the Senate rather than a simple majority of both houses, and treaties are agreements between nations and the Senate role has been generally conceptualized as primarily a "negative" or check on adoption of the agreement. Thus *Sutherland* says:

> Although the ordinary rules of construction which apply to statutes and other written instruments are also relevant in the interpretation of international and interstate agreements, their application is conditioned by special circumstances of the process by which such agreements are brought into being. . . .[479]

Second, at minimum the weight to be accorded particular indicators in "legislative history" is likely to be altered by more substantially weighting statements from the Executive to the Senate as a whole and the testimony of principal Executive branch witnesses, particularly the chief negotiator, which can be expected to be particularly authoritative and probably also more available to the Senate as a whole. By analogy these are in part at least serving a role of committee reports--although perhaps even more important and authoritative--and that of principal committee persons or sponsors. Conversely, statements in legislative hearings, at least by non-experts on the treaty, and non-expert general debate, are likely to have at least somewhat--if not greatly--reduced weight in the overall interpretive process of seeking to ascertain whether two-thirds of the Senate focused on a particular issue and adopted a common interpretation. Assistant Attorney General Charles J. Cooper made this point in his memorandum of April 9, 1987, on "Relevance of Senate Ratification History to Treaty Interpretation":

---

[479] 1A *Sutherland Stat. Const., supra* note 311, § 32.09, at 558-59.

> In determining the weight to be assigned to that record, it should be observed that, conceptually, the constitutional division of treaty-making responsibility is essentially the reverse of the division of law-making authority. Congress initially agrees upon and enacts the language of domestic legislation, while the President reserves the right to determine whether that legislation will go into effect (subject, of course, to the override of any veto). Treaties, however, are proposed and negotiated by the President, subject to the approval or disapproval of the Senate. Given this conceptual framework, it is clear that the portions of the treaty ratification record that should be accorded more weight as to the treaty's meaning are the representations of the executive--the draftsman, in effect, of the treaty. Statements by individual senators, or even groups of senators, are certainly entitled to no more consideration--and perhaps less--than the limited weight such statements are given in the interpretation of domestic legislation when they are not confirmed by the legislation's sponsor in colloquy or otherwise.[480]

Pursuant to this general theoretical observation Assistant Attorney General Cooper concludes that little weight should be given statements in committee reports, hearings, and debates in treaty interpretation:

> The more difficult question is what relevance, if any, the President must give to less formal, contemporaneous indications of the Senate's understanding of the treaty--*i.e.*, statements in committee reports, hearings, and debates, which may reflect an understanding of certain treaty provisions by some senators, but which were not embodied in any formal understanding or condition approved by the entire Senate. With the not insubstantial exception of representations made or confirmed by the executive branch . . . we believe such statements have only limited probative value and therefore are entitled to little weight in subsequent interpretations of the treaty.[481]

In the footnote to this statement Cooper says:

---

[480]Cooper, "Memorandum to Abraham D. Sofaer," *supra* note 1, at 2.

[481]*Id.* at 8.

> We note that while a few courts have alluded to the record the Senate creates in advising and consenting to the ratification of treaties, none has advanced a comprehensive theory of what weight should be given to particular portions of the ratification record and none, to our knowledge, has specifically relied on representations in the Senate record to support a particular construction of a treaty.[482]

Subsequently, Cooper addresses the weight to be given an Executive branch statement about a treaty and says:

> . . . consistent with the President's role as the nation's exclusive negotiator of treaties with foreign governments, we believe that statements made to the Senate by the executive branch during the ratification debates are relevant in much the same way that contemporaneous statements by congressional draftsmen or sponsors of domestic legislation are relevant to any subsequent interpretation of the statute. . . .[483]
>
> The weight to be given to an interpretive statement made by an executive branch official to the Senate during the ratification process will likely depend upon such factors as the formality of the statement, the identity and position of the executive branch official making the statement, the level of attention and interest focused on the meaning of the relevant treaty provision, and the consistency with which members of the executive branch adhered at the time to the view of the treaty provision reflected in the statement. All of these factors affect the degree to which the Senate could reasonably have relied upon the statement and, in turn, the weight that courts will attach to it. At one extreme, a single statement made by a middle-level executive branch official in response to a question at a hearing would not be regarded as definitive. . . .[484]

---

[482]*Id.* at 8 n.16.

[483]*Id.* at 11.

[484]*Id.* at 13.

Similarly, consistent with the uniqueness of the treaty process, as opposed to a legislative act, there may be differences stemming also from the Senate's own rules and procedures. For example, Assistant Attorney General Cooper also reminds us that:

> [a]lthough jurisdiction to review treaties is vested solely in the Foreign Relations Committee, see Rule 25, Standing Rules of the Senate, Sen. Doc. No. 99-13, 99th Cong., 1st Sess. (1985), upon occasion other committees have asserted an interest in the subject matter of the treaty, even though they have no jurisdiction to make formal recommendations. . . .[485]

And the 1984 report for the Senate Foreign Relations Committee (*Treaties and Other International Agreements: The Role of the United States Senate*) says that "the Foreign Relations Committee has had exclusive jurisdiction over treaties--as presently recognized in Rule 25."[486] According to this report:

> Since its creation in 1816, the Foreign Relations Committee has had exclusive jurisdiction over treaties--as presently recognized in Rule 25. From time to time other Senate committees have sought referral of particular treaties without success. The most notable recent example was the effort by the Senate Armed Services Committee to obtain joint or sequential referral of the SALT II Treaty. However, there have been various occasions on which other Senate committees have conducted hearings on the issues raised by particular treaties even when they did not formally have jurisdiction to make recommendations to the Senate. In the case of SALT II, for example, the Armed Services Committee held extensive hearings on the "military implications" of the treaty, similar to the parallel hearings it held in 1963 on the Nuclear Test Ban Treaty, in 1969 on the Nuclear Non-Proliferation Treaty and in 1978 on the Panama Canal Treaties. Armed Services even took a vote on the SALT II Treaty and prepared an extensive report in opposition to Senate approval, although Senate Majority Leader Byrd did not permit it to be filed until the end of the

---

[485]*Id.* at 5 n.9.

[486]*Treaties and International Agreements Committee Print, supra* note 66, at 106.

> Ninety-sixth Congress, almost a year later. Other Senate and House committees have occasionally held hearings and prepared reports on treaties of particular concern to them. Sometimes the Foreign Relations Committee has invited members of other committees to participate in its hearings relating to treaties of obvious interest to such committees. The NATO Treaty was one example; SALT II was another.[487]

To summarize this second point, while there seems to be little primary authority on point or even direct theoretical discussion in the secondary literature, it would seem highly likely from the principles underlying an analysis of "legislative history" that the substantial differences between the legislative process and the treaty process will, at minimum, result in changes in weightings in indicators of general Senate intent where, within the overall standard of treaty interpretation, the record of Senate informal consideration is entitled to some weight in the overall interpretive process. These changes in weightings are likely to include significant weight attached to formal submissions accompanying the treaty at the time of executive submission of the treaty to the Senate, significant weight attached to the views of knowledgeable principal Executive branch witnesses, particularly the principal treaty negotiator, and possibly, if not probably, at least some reduction in the already minor weight accorded statements in committee hearings and floor debate. Committee reports would be likely to retain significance, although their effect and that of committee hearings and spokesmen, would also reflect the Senate's rule that only the Foreign Relations Committee has jurisdiction to make formal recommendations.

It is also possible that courts may give less weight in general to legislative history in interpreting the meaning of a treaty as a result of concern about the international dimensions of a treaty. Thus, in a 1984 Claims Court decision in *Coplin v. United States*,[488] reversed on other grounds in 1985, a unanimous Claims Court rejected an argument as to the meaning of a treaty even in the face of an assurance from the State Department Legal Adviser that a Senator's concern would be dealt with and language appearing in the report of the Senate Foreign Relations Committee. The court said:

---

[487]*Id.* at 106-07 (footnotes omitted).

[488]Coplin v. United States, 6 Cl. Ct. 115 (1984), *rev'd on other grounds*, 761 F.2d 688 (Fed. Cir. 1985).

Article XV of the Implementation Agreement exempted Commission employees only from Panamanian taxation and not from United States taxation. Defendant cites in support of its proposition the colloquy between Senator Stone and the State Department's Legal Adviser, Mr. Hansell, *see* p. 138 *supra*, and the Report of the Senate Foreign Relations Committee, which incorporated the State Department's section-by-section analysis.

Even in the case of purely domestic legislation, "[r]eliance on legislative history in divining the intent of Congress is . . . a step to be taken cautiously." *Piper v. Chris-Craft Industries, Inc.*, 430 U.S. 1, 26, 97 S.Ct. 926, 941, 51 L.Ed.2d 124 (1977); *see Hart v. United States*, 585 F.2d 1025, 218 Ct.Cl. 212, 221-31 (1978). That caution must be even greater where the document in question grows out of sensitive negotiations with a foreign government whose intentions and views can only be expressed through treaty language and other documents attached to the ratification process.

It should first be noted that the legislative history cited by defendant is not as compelling as it would have the court believe. The most one can say about the conversation between Senator Stone and Mr. Hansell is that one member of the Senate Foreign Relations Committee may have been persuaded by the position taken by the Executive Branch; there is no indication that any other members of the Committee shared those views. "[O]rdinarily even the contemporaneous remarks of a single legislator . . . are not controlling in analyzing legislative history." *Consumer Products Safety Commission*, 447 U.S. at 118, 100 S.Ct. at 2061. The Committee Report merely recites the interpretation offered by the State Department without elaboration or discussion. Of course, there was no reason the Committee should have questioned the interpretation offered by the Executive Branch. The issue, on its face, appeared to be merely one of domestic tax law; the negotiating transcripts, which place the matter in a wholly different light, were still classified and there is no indication that they were presented to or examined by the Committee.[489]

---

[489] 6 Cl. Ct. 115, at 144.

And, it is further possible to argue that informal indicators of Senate intent are entitled only to a dramatically altered weighting from that of such indicators in "legislative history." As we have seen, at least Gwendolyn B. Folsom feels that executive messages accompanying presidential approval of an action should perhaps more properly be viewed as "contemporaneous executive construction" rather than part of "legislative history." If the Senate "veto" role in the treaty process is analogous to that of the President in the legislative process, then, it can be asked whether informal indications of Senate intent should be entitled to greater weight than executive messages accompanying a presidential signing of a bill. At least within a "unitary" approach this position would seem in most settings to produce differences of nuance more than major substance. Within a "dual" approach, however, it could affect an outcome dramatically in moving toward a result similar to one that might be achieved under a "unitary" approach. Perhaps the existence of this issue might, at least in part, be considered another factor militating for a "unitary" approach.

Finally, one of the most important issues concerning potential differences in interpretive effect between "treaty history" and "legislative history" concerns the overall guide or standard if the "dual" approach were adopted in treaty interpretation and informal Senate "understandings" or "conditions" were accorded binding weight under national law even where inconsistent with the international legal meaning of the treaty being interpreted. In such settings, as has been seen, there is an issue as to whether to become binding under national law an informal understanding must not only represent a general understanding of the Senate, but also must be generally held *by the Senate as a condition or "on the basis of" which the Senate gave its advice and consent. The Restatement (Third)* seems simply ambiguous in its reference to advice and consent "on the basis of a particular understanding." Does this mean simply that an informal understanding must represent a general understanding of the Senate as to a particular meaning? Or does it mean that an informal understanding must represent a general understanding by the Senate both *as to a particular meaning* and *that advice and consent was being conditioned on such a meaning*? If any Senate authority to depart from the international meaning of a treaty as negotiated between the parties comes from any authority of the Senate to *condition* its consent, then at least arguably the latter standard may be required. That is, the Senate must have intended to condition its consent to the treaty "on the basis of a particular understanding of its meaning." Moreover, since the legal effect of this *Restatement (Third)* approach, if any, is not that of an *understanding* but rather *is* that of *a condition* binding solely under national law, why should not the standard for any such legal effect be that *of* a condition? Further, if this standard requiring an intent to *condition* a treaty were combined with the general law of legislative interpretation that an intention of Congress must be clear to justify interpreting a later legislative enactment as inconsistent with a prior treaty obligation of the United States, then it could be urged that for the same policy reasons in protecting the rule of law in the international relations of the United States, any such general Senate understanding to be binding apart from the treaty it is interpreting must include a clear understanding that a treaty is being conditioned on a particular meaning as binding under national law *whether or not inconsistent with the treaty obligations of the United States under the treaty being considered*. Such a standard would serve much the same function in seeking to protect the rule of law in any binding informal interpretive "understandings" as is served by the important rule of United States constitutional practice requiring clear congressional intent in a later enactment to override a prior treaty obligation of the United States. And it would in fact require the legislative process to focus on the full implications of its actions to achieve a binding legal effect under national law potentially inconsistent with the treaty it was considering. Similarly, as has been seen, under a *Restatement (Third)* "dual" approach to treaty interpretation, if the standard includes evidence of Senate intent to *condition* treaty advice and consent, what weight should be accorded in the "treaty history" process to the fact that the resolution of ratification was formally adopted by the Senate *without such a condition*? Would any such official act in the treaty approval process, which certainly has as high a visibility to the Senate as a whole as virtually anything in that process, require a "strong," "clear," "manifest," or some other showing to overcome? Whatever the precise standard of interpretation under the *Restatement (Third)* "dual" interpretation approach--or more importantly, any such an approach under the Constitution if constitutionally permissible--these questions focus on yet additional complexities in any such "dual" approach. For it is *certainly* possible for a Senate to even generally share a particular understanding as to the meaning of a treaty without generally intending that such a meaning would be binding under national law regardless of the international legal meaning of the treaty or that the treaty was conditioned on such a meaning becoming binding under national law if inconsistent with the treaty. Indeed, it is not clear that these latter intentions would ever realistically reflect intent of an at least two-thirds majority of the Senate under normal circumstances in considering consent to a treaty. And an *absence* in the formal resolution of ratification of any condition may be relevant in assessing overall Senate intent on this issue.

It might further be noted at this point that one of the current issues most focused on in the continuing debate about treaty implementation stemming from the "broad-narrow" debate relates broadly to the issue of the standard or test for treaty interpretation generally under the *Restatement (Third)* or "dual" approach. Principal standards focused on seem to concern the meaning, significance, or legitimacy of tests such as authoritatively communicated Executive branch statements as "part of the basis on which the Senate granted its advice and consent to ratification,"[490] or "authoritatively communicated to the Senate by the Executive and clearly intended, generally understood and relied upon by the Senate in its advice and consent to ratification";[491] "the understanding involved not only must be generally held by the Senate, but must be an understanding `on the basis' of which the Senate gave its advice and consent";[492] "[w]hen the Senate gives its advice and consent to a treaty on the basis of a particular understanding of its meaning" and "the President must decide whether they represent a general understanding by the Senate";[493] and:

> such common understanding is based on:
>
> (A) First, the text of the Treaty and the provisions of this resolution of ratification; and
>
> (B) Second, the authoritative representations which were provided by the President and his representatives to the Senate and its Committees, in seeking Senate consent to ratification, insofar as such representations were directed to the meaning and legal effect of the text of the Treaty . . . .[494]

In assessing these, or other standards as developed in this study or elsewhere, it is submitted that the basis for any such standards of treaty interpretation under national law must be the Constitution of the United States and, where relevant, the law and jurisprudence related generally to rationally ascertaining legislative intent from legislative or treaty history. No such standard which fails to trace its roots to

---

[490]Letter from President Ronald Reagan to the Senate of the United States (June 10, 1988).

[491]Letter from Arthur B. Culvahouse, Jr., Counsel to the President, to The Honorable Richard D. Lugar, U.S. Senator (March 17, 1988).

[492]Sofaer, *supra* note 444, at 1441-42 1989) (quoted from page proofs subject to final editing).

[493]*Restatement (Third), supra* note 235, § 314(2) and comment *d*.

[494]134 *Cong. Rec*. S6724 (daily ed. May 26, 1988) (Amendment No. 2305) (the "INF Treaty interpretation condition" or "Byrd amendment").

these sources is likely to genuinely reflect the rule of law. Moreover, to the extent that any such standards reflect or assume a "dual" approach to treaty interpretation under the constitution, they may be incomplete or inappropriate if such an approach is not the correct standard of treaty interpretation under the Constitution, as this study concludes is likely the law. Indeed, it may be useful to remind the reader at this point of the principal range of constitutional issues and requirements underlying legal appraisal of any such tests lest the current debate about a precise test mislead as to the full range of constitutional and other national law issues presented by any such tests. These include:

1. Is there *any* constitutional authority for *the Senate* (as opposed to the Congress as a whole) *to legislate domestic conditions* (that is, conditions with legally binding effect under, and purely under, national law as opposed to a potentially still important political effect or posing alterations or clarifications for legal adoption as part of the treaty with another nation) incident to giving advice and consent to treaties? If so, *what is the scope of any such Senate authority to legislate legally binding domestic conditions* apart from the underlying treaty? Would any such authority extend to creating a legally binding effect of the treaty under domestic law inconsistent with the treaty itself?

2. If there is any such authority to formally adopt purely domestic conditions (and particularly conditions inconsistent with the underlying treaty as ratified), *can any such conditions be adopted purely by "legislative or treaty history" absent any formally adopted condition to interpret?*

3. If there is any authority to adopt purely domestic conditions and to do so even by informal "treaty history" absent any formally adopted condition to interpret, *if the issue is simply one of treaty interpretation under the Constitution, is the correct approach the "unitary" approach or the "dual" approach?* (That is, is the interpretive standard the meaning as agreed between the parties or an informal understanding of the Senate

whenever it may vary from the meaning as agreed between the parties?)

4. If there is authority to adopt domestic conditions or interpretations binding under national law even by purely informal "treaty history" and even when inconsistent with a ratified treaty serving as the basis for any Senate authority in relation to the treaty, is the standard under such a "dual" approach for creating a legally binding effect under national law *any* "authoritative" (with all the associated semantic interpretation issues surrounding this phrase) Executive branch statement, or *any* statement in the record, or rather that the evidence from the interpretative record as a whole reasonably suggests that a two-thirds majority of the Senate voting for advice and consent adverted to the issue and believed a particular interpretation correct, or some other standard? That is, must there be a rational nexus between the evidence as a whole and the actions of the constitutionally qualified majority for Senate advice and consent? (*The Restatement (Third)* uses language here of "a general understanding by the Senate.")

5. Under any "dual" approach, in assessing evidence of Senate intent as to a particular interpretive meaning in considering a domestic legal effect apart from the treaty, how would evidence that the Senate attached importance to reciprocity of obligation and believed that the treaty obligation was reciprocal be integrated into assessment of legal effect?

6. When the asserted legal effect of Senate action under a "dual" approach is to make a treaty interpretation binding under domestic law in a manner not based on the underlying treaty, that is, to achieve the legal effect of a domestic condition, must any such "general understanding" reflecting the actions of the constitutionally qualified majority for Senate advice and consent--or any other requirement--stemming from point

four above, reflect solely an understanding as to the "correct" interpretation of the treaty or *also* that *the Senate intends that such an interpretation be made a condition of treaty approval and become binding under national law whatever the correct international interpretation?* (That is, possibly in the language of the *Restatement (Third)*, must the Senate advice and consent be "on the basis of a particular understanding of its meaning"? If such an additional understanding must also be present to create a legally binding condition under national law that would prevail under national law over the international legal meaning of a treaty adopted simultaneously by the Senate, what is the effect or weight in assessing overall "treaty history" to be accorded the fact that no relevant formal condition was adopted by the Senate?

7. How would the general rule of interpretation that subsequent legislative action even of the full Congress should prevail in national law over the treaty obligations of the Nation only where an intention is clearly manifest to do so, apply in answering questions under points two, three, four, five and six above. That is, how would this important principle in interpretation of actions even of the full Congress and intended to assist the Nation in adhering to the rule of law internationally apply in settings where it is asserted that mere informal "treaty history" or Executive branch statements during the process of Senate advice and consent should prevail in national law over the international legal obligations of the Nation? Should a process be encouraged either that there is no such effect, preferably by clear adoption of the "unitary" approach, or by requiring only formal conditions, or at least by a requirement that any such condition should be clear as a condition--not just an understanding as to meaning--intended as such, by a Senate giving advice and consent?

8. Finally, in settings in which there is an existing interpretation of a treaty by the Executive branch, what effect will be given to the well established principle that

the interpretation given by the Executive branch is entitled to "great weight"?

summary of the relevance and weight
to be accorded elements of "treaty history"
within the process of Senate advice and consent

This summary as to the relevance and weight to be accorded elements of "treaty history" within the process of Senate advice and consent provides guidance for ascertaining Senate purpose and intent as that is properly weighted within the overall standard of treaty interpretation.[495] It is clear that individual members or committees of the Senate have no independent role in advice and consent of treaties apart from the Senate itself in which they serve. The appropriate goal of "treaty history" interpretation, then, would seem to be a conclusion that an interpretation is shared by the at least two-thirds of the members of the Senate who voted for advice and consent. This does not mean that there must be evidence that each of these senators adverted to the issue and believed a particular interpretation correct, but rather that the evidence from the interpretative record as a whole more reasonably than not suggests that a two-thirds majority of the Senate voting for advice and consent adverted to the issue and believed a particular interpretation correct. In addition, while this study will not go beyond the goal or standard just suggested, it would also seem reasonable--if not constitutionally required under any "dual" approach--that if an informal Senate understanding is to have the legally binding effect under national law of a *condition* (if *any such conditions* are constitutionally permissible as binding *legal* obligations) that it must also meet the

---

[495]The 1984 report for the Senate Foreign Relations Committee, *Treaties and Other International Agreements: The Role of the United States Senate*, says with respect to "the basic document of U.S. `legislative history' on particular treaties":

> The Senate Foreign Relations Committee report, along with the President's initial "Letter of Transmittal," becomes the basic document of U.S. "legislative history" on particular treaties since the negotiating records of the executive branch are generally unavailable to the public--and even to Congress itself. Although the Senate floor debate on a treaty may also provide interpretive guidance, the usual practice on non-controversial treaties is for the Chairman and Ranking Minority Member to make brief statements summarizing rather than supplementing the Committee report.

Treaties and International Agreements Committee Print, supra note 66, at 108.

standard for a condition: that is, that the Senate itself also intended it as a condition to treaty advice and consent--or at least intended it to take effect as legally binding under national law independent of the underlying treaty obligation--and that the record more reasonably than not also suggests this conclusion. Indicators from "treaty history" are relevant to these goals insofar as they reasonably suggest or fail to suggest such conclusions. General principles from "legislative history" practice, as affected by principal differences between the legislative process and the treaty process, suggest the following with respect to the relevance and weight to be accorded the principal such indicators. Formal Executive branch submissions accompanying a treaty to the Senate are entitled to significant weight; testimony from principal Executive branch spokesmen, particularly the actual negotiators of the agreement, during such initial Senate consideration is significant; Senate committee reports, particularly those of the Senate Foreign Relations Committee, are significant; discussions concerning any formal changes in the treaty made at least in part during the advice and consent process, are significant; relatively contemporaneous legislative acts involving a focus on the same subject matter may be significant; statements made by an expert legislative "sponsor" of the treaty, if any, are significant; statements made during hearings or general floor debate, particularly those by treaty opponents, are entitled to little weight unless confirming a general pattern of Senate intent; and subsequent testimony or statements from former or current legislators as to the intent of a former Senate are entitled to only marginal, if any, weight. In considering the totality of relevant indicators it is permissible to consider as a factor that many, or all, principal indicators entitled to significant weight either did not address an issue or addressed it ambiguously. Such a factor is relevant to reaching a conclusion as to whether a two-thirds majority of the Senate shared a conclusion about a particular interpretation.

c. Questions of the level of generality in posing the issue of Senate purpose or intent: the problem of appropriate breadth of context and/or mistaken interpretation in Senate consideration for advice and consent

A third general issue concerning the relevance and weight to be accorded the record of Senate consideration of a treaty for interpretation of that treaty concerns questions of the level of generality in posing the issue of Senate purpose or intent. This grouping of questions can also be conceptualized as the problem of appropriate breadth of context and/or mistaken interpretation in Senate consideration for advice and consent. It focuses on settings in which there may be a mistaken interpretation generally held by the Senate as to an appropriate interpretation of an international obligation embodied in the treaty. In such a setting it asks is it appropriate in the search for Senate purpose or intent solely to focus on the then accepted interpretation or, if there is reason to believe that the consenting Senate was or would have been concerned about United States breach of its treaty obligations, or about undertaking a unilateral obligation not binding on the other party, or about vigorously pursuing an activity up to international treaty limits, is it more appropriate to broaden the context and ask what that Senate intended concerning the interpretation issue in light of that interpretation not being congruent with the international obligation or other Senate expectations? Actually, this complicated issue poses two separate but related issues. The first asks if there is evidence from the record of Senate consideration that the Senate opposed the United States assuming a treaty obligation unilaterally--that is an obligation that was not reciprocally binding on both parties--or that it wished the United States to vigorously take action in a particular area up to the international treaty limits, should not such evidence be at least as important in an overall search for Senate intent as the narrower context alone of Senate belief in a particular interpretation? Note that this first sense of the issue is solely one of whether the actual full context of Senate consideration or only a partial context is to be taken into account in the search for Senate purpose or intent. This sense does *not* ask what would the Senate have intended *if* it had known that an interpretation were mistaken, but rather, given the known conflicting intentions *actually* held by the Senate which should prevail; the belief that a particular interpretation was correct or the intent that the United States not be unilaterally bound to obligations and/or that the United States vigorously pursue activities up to internationally permitted limits? The second sense of the issue asks, either in a setting with a component of conflicting Senate intent as the context is broadened as above, or in a setting with no evidence of such intent, whether the appropriate standard of Senate intent is simply the Senate belief that a particular interpretation was correct--without accurate information that it was incorrect--or the broader question if the Senate had known that an interpretation were incorrect and thus not binding on the other side (or in violation of an international obligation binding on the United States) would it have intended to unilaterally bind the United States or to violate international law? This combined issue seems not to have been significantly addressed within the "broad-narrow" dispute yet seems potentially important in clarifying the relevance and weight to be accorded the Senate process of informal consideration. Indeed, it is an issue focused squarely on maintaining the integrity of the Senate advise and consent process as a whole.

On the one hand, in support of a position that the context should not be broadened, it can be argued that it is essentially unknowable what a particular Senate would have intended if it had known that the interpretation it generally held was not consistent with the international obligations of the United States created by a treaty. It can also be argued, at least under the "dual" approach, that whatever the mistake the action of the Senate was binding.

On the other hand, in support of a position that the full context should be considered, if the context demonstrates that the Senate would almost certainly have rejected assuming a unilateral United States obligation not binding on the other treaty party or unilaterally restricting particular actions which it wished to promote to the maximum extent consistent with the international treaty obligation, then it would seem bizarre to ascribe an intent to a Senate that it would have been shocked by. That is, if there is evidence in the legislative record, as strong as or stronger than that concerning any understanding about a particular interpretation, which suggests that the Senate rejected lack of reciprocity of obligation, or was particularly interested in pursuing a particular course of action to the extent permitted by the treaty, then one simply has a conflict between Senate purpose and intent on several dimensions of an overall issue. Not to consider the full context could, thus, subvert rather than carry out the intent of the Senate. The arguments for narrowing the context do not seem to even address this first sense of the issue. And, going beyond this more cautious position one can in the second sense ask whether it is ever a reasonable interpretation of general intent of two-thirds of the Senate present during advice and consent proceedings, absent an affirmative "treaty history" record clearly demonstrating such an intent, that the Senate intended to adopt as binding on the United States a particular treaty interpretation either in violation of the United States' international legal obligations or unilaterally binding only the United States and not the other treaty partner *under the very treaty it was considering*. Under either approach for broadening the context, if from the full context one believes that the Senate intent was not to adopt an interpretation either inconsistent with United States international treaty obligations nor imposing a unilateral obligation on the United States, then it is simply question begging to argue that the supposed Senate intent based on a narrower context was "binding." Moreover, the question of assessing the Senate intent in overall context is arguably no different in theory than that of assessing its intent on the narrow issue. Indeed, arguably the effort to assess Senate intent must always be to assess that intent in its full context; anything else would violate the very principles supporting a search for such intent. That is, either there is a commitment to fully explore Senate intent in relation to all of the particulars of an issue or there is a substantial risk that real

Senate intent will not be served. The alternative of exploring the full context is also somewhat analogously supported by the principle of legislative interpretation that any ambiguity in a latter statute will be interpreted consistent with the prior United States treaty obligations and only a clear congressional intent to override a prior treaty obligation will be permitted to do so. That is, by analogy, if a Senate intent, particularly one to impose a unilateral obligation on the United States, is to be found, should not such a finding require affirmative or even clear or manifest evidence of an intent to be bound whatever the international legal obligation? Similarly, it should be noted of analogous relevance that an established principle of interpretation permits correction of legislative errors and omissions if the true meaning of a provision appears from the entire enactment.[496] Earl T. Crawford describes this as "simply making the strict letter of a statute yield to the obvious intent of the legislators."[497] But if the mistaken letter of a statute can be made to yield to the intent of the legislature why cannot and should not mistaken Senate assumptions as to a particular meaning be made to yield to an even more important expression of Senate intent and purpose on a more centrally addressed policy issue? In both cases the guiding principle would seem to be to carry out the real intention of the legislators. An approach that does not do this should be rejected.

It might also be recalled that Judge Learned Hand has hypothesized the task of legislative interpretation as "the proliferation of purpose."[498] What could be more central in such a task than recognizing there may indeed be more than one legislative purpose (or a clash between a mistaken intent and a purpose) and that selecting the one the legislature (or Senate) would have considered the most important is not only relevant, but indeed essential, in such settings.

In assessing the possible positions on this grouping of issues it should be noted that they largely disappear under a "unitary" approach in which the international obligation under a treaty is congruent with the national obligation. While there seems little, if any, direct authority on this issue, on balance the position permitting examination of full context seems stronger on policy grounds. Certainly this seems the better position in settings where there is evidence of affirmative Senate intent in the first sense that obligations assumed should be reciprocal and/or that the United States should vigorously pursue a particular

---

[496]*See E. Crawford, The Construction of Statutes* 348-49 (1940).

[497]*Id.* at 349.

[498]From an article by Felix Frankfurter, "Some Reflections on the Reading of Statutes," *reprinted in 3 Sutherland Stat. Const., supra* note 311, at 265, 268.

program up to the internationally permitted treaty limits. This seems the position more likely to effectuate the real-world intent of the approving Senate as well as minimizing settings in which the United States would either be in violation of its legal obligations or assuming treaty obligations unilaterally that were not binding on its treaty partners. That this set of issues does not arise as a significant issue under the "unitary" approach further seems to support such an approach.

d. A synthesis concerning relevance and weight of the record of Senate consideration

The broad issue of relevance and weight of a record of Senate consideration of a treaty for interpretation of a treaty is really composed as a first stage of complexity of at least three separate but related issues. First, is the goal of such interpretation the meaning of the treaty as internationally binding and as determined pursuant to the international law of treaty interpretation (the "unitary" standard) or a meaning ascribed to the Senate from an informal record of consideration (or an Executive branch spokesman) even if not congruent with the treaty and, as such, either in violation of United States treaty obligations or unilaterally imposing on the United States an obligation not reciprocally binding on the other treaty party or parties (the "dual" standard)? Second, what are the relevance and weight to be accorded a range of events in Senate "treaty history" consideration of a treaty (including an issue as to the overall goal or standard in such consideration) under either of the alternatives under issue one--but particularly under any "dual" standard? For example, what weight should be accorded a subsidiary witness at a committee hearing or a floor statement by a general member of the Senate? How should such indicators be weighted in comparison to non-treatment of an issue in Executive branch transmittal papers or committee reports or intimations to the contrary from principal Executive branch witnesses? Finally, what is the appropriate level of generality in posing the issue of Senate intent? In the first sense of this issue, should affirmative evidence that the Senate was concerned generally to promote reciprocity in such treaty matters and/or that it was concerned to vigorously pursue a program up to internationally permitted treaty limits be weighted at least as much as a mistaken view as to what the international obligation was? If not, would not such a Senate in fact be shocked and offended to learn that it had been interpreted as having an intent contrary to these expectations? And, in the second sense of this issue, even where there is no such affirmative evidence of broader Senate intent should any Senate be interpreted as intending a particular interpretation of a treaty at odds with the real international obligation in the absence of affirmative evidence of such an intent including evidence that lack of congruence with the international obligation was regarded as unimportant? Another way of posing this second sense of the issue is to ask is not the real issue the one posed by the real world with all of its full context: that is what would the Senate have intended if it had been aware that the interpretation it believed accurate was not congruent with the Nation's international legal obligations under the treaty?

Although these issues are in many respects issues of first impression in United States constitutional and treaty interpretation law, and arguments about them may be made for a variety of positions, the view on the first issue most strongly supported by law and policy seems to be the "unitary" approach. As to the second issue there is a substantial body of "legislative history" law and policy that at least sets minimum requirements for judging a particular record of "treaty history" evidence, although the fact that it is "treaty" history and not "legislative" history being interpreted may alter the weight of such evidence in relation to other such evidence, particularly with respect to the relative weight to be accorded Executive branch and congressional branch representations. That *minimum* requirement with respect to the overall goal of assessing Senate "treaty history" would seem to be in interpretive settings other than assessing the internationally binding interpretation that the evidence from the interpretive record as a whole reasonably suggests that a two-thirds majority of the Senate voting for advice and consent believed a particular interpretation correct. Moreover, as has been seen, it at least can be argued that this overall *minimum* requirement for assessing Senate treaty history under any "dual" approach should be increased by a similar requirement for any such approach that the Senate gave its advice and consent "on the basis of the Senate's understanding" and intended the particular interpretation as a *condition* of advice and consent whatever the appropriate international legal interpretation of the treaty. And it can further be argued that the interpretive principle requiring that any interpretation of a congressional action which holds that the action is inconsistent with the treaty obligations of the United States must reflect a clear congressional intention, also requires a clear or manifest Senate intent to depart from the international treaty standard in such an interpretive setting. Despite the considerable strength of the case for these additional requirements, this study will apply only the minimum requirement in assessing the "broad-narrow" issue. And, as to the third issue, it would seem that the better view is always to consider the full context of Senate intent in the search for genuine intent. Particularly in settings where there is strong evidence that a Senate intended that United States treaty obligations should be reciprocal or that the Nation should vigorously pursue a particular program up to internationally binding treaty limits it would seem bizarre to ascribe a Senate intent to follow what might be a peripheral, mistakenly assumed treaty obligation while ignoring the broader Senate intent clearly focused on as a principal Senate purpose.

It should be noted that for the view on this general issue expressed in the majority report of the Senate Foreign Relations Committee on *The ABM Treaty Interpretation Resolution*[499] to prevail--that is that the "narrow" interpretation would be directly binding under United States national law whatever the interpretation of the ABM Treaty under international law and without any subsequent congressional action on the issue--the following assumptions would in combination and at minimum all be required:

1. that the "dual" approach is constitutionally correct rather than the "unitary" approach to treaty interpretation under national law;

2. that the relevance and weight to be accorded the full range of elements in the Senate "treaty history" of consideration of the ABM Treaty reasonably support a conclusion that at least two-thirds of the Senate approved the treaty on the informal understanding that the "narrow" interpretation was correct--or that any Executive branch statement to the Senate conveying a particular meaning is legally binding regardless of context; and that

3. there is no balancing evidence of Senate intent on broader issues of reciprocity or vigorous national performance up to treaty limits on "broad-narrow" issues or the only relevant context as to Senate intent is the narrow context as to the specific meaning disregarding the issue of mistake or broader context of Senate intent.

4. Issues of estoppel arising from the advice and consent process

It is possible, although as yet apparently without clearly applicable precedent, that some representations in some settings by the Executive branch during the advice and consent process may create binding obligations under national

---

[499] *The ABM Treaty Interpretation Resolution, supra* note 1, at 55-62.

law pursuant to the principle of "estoppel"[500] rather than the interpretive process, regardless of the appropriate international legal interpretation of a treaty. As will be examined, however, such settings, if any, are likely to be confined to an extremely narrow range of circumstances and are not lightly to be presumed.

Within the context of general debate triggered by the "broad-narrow" issue, the April 9, 1987, memorandum by Assistant Attorney General Charles J. Cooper on the "Relevance of Senate Ratification History to Treaty Interpretation"[501] contains the following relevant language concerning this possible basis for national legal effect of a treaty:

> In general . . . less formal statements made by the executive branch before the Senate (such as the one described in the preceding hypothetical) will be but one source of relevant evidence to be considered in interpreting an ambiguous treaty provision.
>
> In contrast, in a case in which the statements by the executive branch amount to a formal representation by the President concerning the meaning of a particular treaty provision, the ratification record may be conclusive. If, for example, the ratification record unequivocally shows that the President presented the treaty to the Senate based on specific, official representations regarding the meaning of an ambiguous provision, that the Senate regarded that understanding as important to its consent, and that the Senate relied on the representations made by the executive branch in approving the treaty (and thus in refraining from attaching a formal reservation setting forth the understanding), we believe the President would, in effect, be estopped from taking a contrary position in his subsequent interpretation of the treaty, just as he would be bound by a formal reservation or understanding passed by the Senate to the same effect. See generally *United States v. Vogel Fertilizer Co.*, 455 U.S. at 31 (refusing to uphold current Treasury Department interpretation in light of evidence that the Treasury Department

---

[500]This is a doctrine known traditionally as "estoppel by conduct," "equitable estoppel," or simply "estoppel." *See generally, e.g., M. Bigelow, A Treatise on the Law of Estoppel and Its Application in Practice* 431-503 (2d ed. 1876); *W.P. Keeton,* ed., *Prosser and Keeton on the Law of Torts* 733-36 (5th ed. 1984).

[501]Cooper, "Memorandum to Abraham D. Sofaer," *supra* note 1.

> proposed and presented the legislation to Congress on a different understanding). Obviously, a President could not negotiate a treaty with other nations on the basis of one understanding of its import, submit the treaty to the Senate on a wholly different understanding, and then, in implementing the treaty, rely solely on the understanding he had reached with the other parties. Similarly, he could not reach a secret agreement with the other party that substantially modifies the obligations and authorities created by the text of the treaty submitted to the Senate, and then seek to use the secret agreement as a basis for actions inconsistent with the text of the treaty. Such results would essentially eviscerate the Senate's constitutional advice and consent role, because it would deprive the Senate of a fair opportunity to determine whether, or with what conditions, the treaty should become the "supreme Law of the Land." Accordingly, in such extreme cases, we have little doubt that, as a matter of domestic law, the courts would construe the treaty as presented to and accepted by the Senate, even if as a matter of international law the treaty might have a different meaning.[502]

As emphasized in the introduction to section (B)(3) of this part, it would, of course, be completely inappropriate--indeed shockingly wrong--for a President to intentionally falsify the meaning of a treaty or conceal a secret meaning during Senate consideration of advice and consent to a treaty. The issue of when and if Executive branch representations to the Senate during the advice and consent process would create an "estoppel" that would bind the United States either to breach its treaty obligations or to adopt an obligation unilaterally not binding on the other party, however, is complex, uncertain, and strongly suggestive, as Assistant Attorney General Cooper implies, that such "estoppel," if any, could arise in only a narrow category of cases. It is particularly questionable whether any such "estoppel" would or should arise in a setting of honest mistake as to an issue viewed as minor by the consenting Senate, a setting in which an issue was only incidentally addressed by subordinate Executive branch officials or occurs in a "treaty history" record of mixed signals as to meaning, or in a setting which even may suggest that a principal Executive branch statement in question may have resulted from a process akin to "leading the witnesses" by a member of the Senate pressing a witness during questioning, or in a setting in which "treaty history" fails to demonstrate that a two-

[502] *Id.* at 13-15.

thirds majority of the Senate relied on the representation in consenting to the treaty, or in a setting in which there is significant evidence that the Senate regarded it as important either that the United States not assume unilateral obligations not binding on the other party or that the country pursue a vigorous program up to permitted international treaty limits.

The classic doctrine of "estoppel by conduct" or "equitable estoppel" is described by Melville M. Bigelow in his early classic treatise on estoppel as:

> all of the following elements must be present in order to an estoppel by conduct:--
>
> 1. There must have been a representation or a concealment of *material* facts.
>
> 2. The representation must have been made with *knowledge* of the facts.
>
> 3. The party to whom it was made must have been *ignorant of the truth* of the matter.
>
> 4. It must have been made with the *intention* that the other party should act upon it.
>
> 5. The other party must have been *induced to act upon it.*[503]

Bigelow also says in elaborating on these elements of the classic doctrine that:

> The representation, in order to work an estoppel, must generally be a statement of *fact*. It can rarely happen that the statement of a proposition of law will conclude the party making it from denying its correctness, except where it is understood to mean nothing but a simple statement of fact.[504]

And:

---

[503]*M. Bigelow, supra* note 500, at 437 (emphasis in original).

[504]*Id.* at 438 (emphasis in original).

> the general rule being that *fraud* is necessary to the existence of an estoppel by conduct. . . . [I]t is in general a defence to the estoppel claimed that the representation was made under a mistake; . . . .[505]

And:

> It is also well established that, in order to the estoppel, there must have been knowledge, actual or constructive, by the party making the representation, that the other party intended at the time to act upon it.[506]

And:

> But, unless the representation is acted upon, the estoppel cannot arise. And it seems that it must be exclusively acted upon; at all events, there can be no estoppel where the party claiming one is obliged to inquire for the existence of other facts, and to rely upon them also in acting.[507]

Contrary to Bigelow, the modern law of estoppel does not seem to require that a representation be made with knowledge of its falsity,[508] although such a factor would likely make a finding of estoppel more probable. Similarly, it is probable that the modern doctrine could apply in some settings of misrepresentation of law as well as fact.[509] Most importantly, however, the doctrine of "estoppel" achieved its principal application in disputes between private parties and there is substantial added uncertainty as to applicability to government action,[510] much less its

---

[505] *Id.* at 467 (emphasis in original). But see id. at 471.

[506] *Id.* at 476.

[507] *Id.* at 492-93 (emphasis in original) (footnote numbers omitted).

[508] *W. Keeton, supra* note 500, at 734.

[509] *See, e.g.* the setting addressed in *Heckler v. Community Health Services*, 467 U.S. 51 (1984).

[510] On the general subject of estoppel of government *see, e.g.*, Heckler v. Community Health Services, 467 U.S. 51 (1984); Walrath, "Recent Developments in Administrative

applicability between branches of the government. Lower courts have frequently estopped the government in protecting private parties but to date the Supreme Court, while leaving the issue open as a general proposition of law, has not yet found an estoppel against the government. The most recent of these Supreme Court decisions not finding an estoppel but leaving the issue open is *Heckler v. Community Health Services*,[511] decided in 1984. Justice Rehnquist was joined by the Chief Justice in a concurring opinion in *Heckler* in which they pointed out:

> In none of these cases have we ever held the Government to be estopped by the representations or conduct of its agents. In INS v. Hibi . . . we noted that it is still an open question whether, in some future case, "affirmative misconduct" on the part of the Government might be grounds for an estoppel. . . .
>
> I agree with the Court that there is no need to decide in this case whether there are circumstances under which the Government may be estopped, but I think that the Court's treatment of that question . . . gives an impression of hospitality towards claims of estoppel against the Government which our decided cases simply do not warrant. . . .
>
> We do not write on a clean slate in this field, and our cases have left open the possibility of estoppel against the Government only in a rather narrow possible range of circumstances. . . .[512]

Even when estoppel against government is permitted there is some authority restricting it to settings of "proprietary" rather than "sovereign capacity" governmental actions.[513]

Law: Liability of Administrative Agencies and Officials: Estopping the Federal Government: Still Waiting for the Right Case," 53 *Geo. Wash. L. Rev.* 191 (1984); Raven-Hansen, "Regulatory Estoppel: When Agencies Break Their Own `Laws,'" 64 *Tex. L. Rev.* 1 (1985); M. Gillett, "Equitable Estoppel Is Alive and Well in Government Contracts" (Unpublished monograph March 1976 in the University of Virginia Law Library).

[511]467 U.S. 51 (1984).

[512]Heckler v. Community Health Services, 467 U.S. 51, 67-68 (1984) (Concurring opinion of Justice Rehnquist joined by the Chief Justice).

[513]See M. Gillett, *supra* note 510, at 10.

One principal concern underlying the caution in applying estoppel generally to governmental action is the concern that so doing could, at least in some settings, bypass the normal constitutional processes for the making of laws. That is, in the language of the Court in *Heckler*: "When the Government is unable to enforce the law because the conduct of its agents has given rise to an estoppel, the interest of the citizenry as a whole in obedience to the rule of law is undermined."[514]

In addition to the substantial added uncertainties of the doctrine of estoppel as it is sought to be applied to governmental actions, there is yet further uncertainty in seeking to apply it between branches of the government. The only case cited by Assistant Attorney General Cooper even analogously supporting estoppel against the Executive in an inter-branch setting was the 1981 Supreme Court decision in *United States v. Vogel Fertilizer Co.*[515] But Vogel was a dispute not between two branches but between the Federal Government and a private party, involved a matter of legislative, not treaty, interpretation, and the Court did not invoke estoppel but rather conducted a standard analysis of "legislative history" in which it said it attached "great weight" to a Treasury Department "General Explanation" of an amendment it had initially suggested to Congress.[516] This, as we have seen, would be consistent with normal rules for the use of "legislative history" as an extrinsic aid in statutory construction. Thus, while the *Vogel* decision may be suggestive of weight to be attached to formal Executive branch statements made to Congress in settings in which the Executive branch participated in drafting a measure, it is less directly on point for the process of treaty interpretation and a hypothetical intra-branch dispute.

In exploring the doctrine of "estoppel," if any, from Executive branch statements to the Senate in the treaty advice and consent process a number of issues would seem particularly relevant.

First, it should be understood that by definition the consequence of operation of the principle of estoppel in the "treaty history" setting will be a divergence between national and international legal obligations so that the United States will either be in violation of its international legal obligations or will be held unilaterally to an obligation not binding on the other treaty party or parties. In such a setting the issue of whether the United States can make law not congruent with its

---

[514]Heckler v. Community Health Services, 467 U.S. 51, 60 (1984).

[515]United States v. Vogel Fertilizer Co., 455 U.S. 16, 31 (1982).

[516]455 U.S. 16, at 31. The Court's analysis of legislative history runs from pages 26-32 in its opinion.

international obligation through the treaty process again reappears. Indeed, this is the counterpart of the constitutional processes concern in the general area of "estoppel of government." In addition, it should be noted that any "estoppel" in such a setting would be operating in a meaningful sense against not only the Nation as a whole, but also the Senate, as well, of course, as the Executive. That is, in an "estoppel" setting, by definition the Senate would not be consenting to exactly what it intended but rather to an interpretation it believed correct but which--contrary to its normal expectation--it did not know was either in violation of the Nation's international legal obligation or created a unilateral obligation on the United States that was not binding on the other treaty party. This setting in which any "estoppel" claim must--virtually inevitably--arise[517] poses a substantial constitutional issue and one which seems considerably more formidable to recognizing any "estoppel" than that arising in the general "estoppel of government" setting. For if, as previously discussed, a "unitary" approach is constitutionally required in treaty interpretation under national law, then any operation of the doctrine of "estoppel" would be violating this constitutional requirement and making treaty law without an international agreement to support it in a setting in which the Senate itself--whose interest is presumably being protected by the estoppel--would be being "estopped" into a treaty violation or unilateral action quite contrary to any reasonable expectation it may have had that this was an interpretation of an international agreement *and* the "estoppel" cost would be borne by the Nation as a whole in its foreign relations with other nations. That is, unlike the usual "estoppel of government" setting, here the "estoppel" runs against--not the general legislative power but--rather the treaty power rooted in international agreement, its consequences are almost inevitably also to "estop" the party intended to be protected, it does not operate simply to make a private party whole in a quasi-tort or contract setting, and it would work to estop the Nation as a whole in its foreign relations even though the estoppel does not run in favor of the foreign nation. Given the great caution with which the Supreme Court has approached the general issue of "estoppel of government" it is not at all clear that the Court would uphold as constitutional any doctrine of estoppel against the Executive branch arising from the treaty advice and consent process.

Second, this issue of any "estoppel" working at least partially against a Senate, as well as against the Executive branch, becomes particularly acute if the "treaty history" record contains evidence suggesting that the Senate opposed non-

---

[517]Only the extraordinary--and perhaps even inevitably imaginary--setting of a "treaty history" record clearly and affirmatively showing that the Senate supported a particular interpretation whether or not binding on the other treaty party would lessen this dilemma.

reciprocal obligations binding on the United States or sought vigorous implementation of programs up to the limits permitted by the international treaty obligation. In such a setting, as previously explored in the last section of this paper on the treaty interpretation issue, the intent of the Senate clearly could be damaged more by applying an "estoppel" than not so applying it. Moreover, since the normal expectation of a Senate is that interpretations presented are, except in settings of reasonable mistake, the internationally binding interpretation, would not it usually be as likely that any "estoppel" approach would subvert the intent of the Senate as that it would support it, at least in the absence of an affirmative record of Senate intent that congruence with the international obligation is not regarded as importantly as a particular interpretation?

Third, should any doctrine of "estoppel" in such treaty interpretation settings be reserved for settings where, as required by the classic doctrine, the Executive branch representation was knowingly false? Certainly the setting of intentional misrepresentation or concealment from a Senate during the advice and consent process is the setting of greatest concern--though perhaps largely an imaginary horrible in the real world. And why should honest mistake in the interpretation of a complex international agreement--a mistaken interpretation by definition shared by both the Executive branch and the Senate--bind the United States under its own domestic law regardless of the correct international legal interpretation? Or suppose the interpretation was the best the Executive branch could reasonably do at the time but subsequently a different interpretation was made by an international arbitral body or Court whose decision was binding on the United States? Would the United States then be bound under domestic law to disregard the binding international judgment? These questions suggest that application of this doctrine to settings other than intentional misrepresentation to the Senate might be quite unwise.

Fourth, under the usual requirements of any doctrine of estoppel, to be applicable the "treaty history" would need to show at least reasonably clearly that the Executive branch presentation as a whole presented the interpretation to the Senate with the understanding that the Senate would act on it, and that a two-thirds majority of the Senate consented to the treaty on the reasonable understanding that the interpretation was correct and material. Thus, issues from the record such as the level of spokesman or indication from the Executive branch, whether the Executive branch record of presentation on the issue was mixed or ambiguous overall, whether made in Executive branch submission of the treaty to the Senate or in testimony of principal Executive branch witnesses or rather made only by subsidiary Executive branch spokesmen, whether the Executive branch representations were written or oral,[518] whether subsequently incorporated into committee reports, whether made only during hearings, whether intended that the Senate would rely on the presentation as one of expert knowledge on the issue, whether the issue was significant or obscure to the Senate in its overall consideration of the treaty, and whether a two thirds majority of the Senate was aware of and relied on the presentation in giving consent to the treaty, all these and other "treaty history" relevance and weight issues would be relevant. To the extent that the overall "treaty history" context casts doubt either that the Executive branch clearly presented an authoritative presentation to the Senate or that the Senate relied on it in giving consent, then the doctrine of estoppel would not seem applicable under normal estoppel rules even if the doctrine is applicable to an inter-branch treaty interpretation dispute.

Fifth, what Senate is entitled to raise any "estoppel" and how would it do it? The Supreme Court has clearly held that only the consenting Senate, not a subsequent Senate, is entitled to make a "treaty history" record relevant in the interpretation process. Does estoppel automatically occur from certain settings or must it be invoked as in actions between private parties and indeed even between private parties and the government? If it must be invoked can it be invoked by a subsequent Senate that may not fully reflect the concerns of the consenting Senate? If invocation is necessary how is it done--by a majority or two-thirds vote of a Senate?

Similarly, should a subsequent Executive branch administration that discovers either a mistake or misrepresentation in the presentation of a prior administration on a treaty be "estopped" by the actions of that prior administration? Or should it be encouraged to come forward with the knowledge of the correct interpretation by a rule that would permit change in interpretation? If it is not so encouraged do we not in effect reward fraud or misrepresentations and discourage "whistle blowing" in important settings? If a subsequent administration is to be "estopped," on what grounds is the conduct of that subsequent administration "affirmative misconduct" as suggested by the Supreme Court might be a requirement for general "estoppel of the government"? Should any such rules of intra-branch "estoppel" apply between branches regardless of changes in those branches? In what non-treaty settings might such principles of "estoppel" estop the Senate or Congress in relations with subsequent Executive branch administrations if any general law of intra-branch "estoppel" is to be created? If the doctrine works only against the Executive branch and not against the Senate or Congress why is it

---

[518]See the majority opinion discussions of this issue in Heckler v. Community Health Services, 467 U.S. 51, 65 (1984).

so limited? It is not, of course, necessary to answer all of these questions to determine that in some settings a doctrine of "estoppel" may apply against some Executive branch representations in the treaty setting. Nevertheless, these questions fairly pose a range of major additional complexities in invoking any such doctrine.

Finally, it is not clear that "estoppel" to a particular interpretation is necessarily the only or best remedy against either mistaken or even intentional Executive branch misrepresentation. As one powerful remedy, intentional misrepresentation to Congress may be punishable as a crime. Congress also retains the authority to investigate and publicize error or intentional wrongdoing and in many settings to enact general subsequent domestic law provisions, that as a matter of national law, can prevail over prior inconsistent national treaty obligations. Certainly the investigative route contains substantial potential for checking abuse while not creating a divergence between national and international obligations. Yet another more drastic possibility, which in some settings might even be more supportive of the overall intent of the original Senate, might be to void the treaty as a whole under national law. In settings of gross intentional misrepresentation a President still in power could be impeached. In short, it is clear that "estoppel" as well as a "dual" approach to treaty interpretation--as previously discussed in rebuttal of arguments for the "dual" approach--is not the only remedy to protect against Executive branch error or abuse and even if an "estoppel" setting arises which would not estop the consenting Senate as meaningfully as the Executive, such a setting may pose the option of voiding the treaty under domestic law as well as "estopping" the treaty in force with the mistaken interpretation.

On balance, it is unclear whether and to what extent there is any doctrine of "estoppel" that would operate to freeze into national law--whatever the international legal obligation--an interpretation of a treaty mistakenly or even intentionally misrepresented by the Executive branch in the process of Senate advice and consent. On the one hand, in favor of such a doctrine in the treaty advice and consent setting, there is a well-established if somewhat vague general doctrine of estoppel in Anglo-American law. It can also be argued that such a doctrine would be helpful, at least in settings of intentional misrepresentation or omission, in policing the integrity of the advice and consent process. On the other hand, there are serious concerns, including constitutional concerns, raised by any such doctrine. These include, among others, potentially making national treaty law outside the international agreement process and particularly, in some settings at least, risking "estopping" a prior Senate to an unintended overall conclusion. The opinion of the Supreme Court in the 1984 *Heckler* case implies at least a heavy burden in generally seeking to invoke estoppel in a governmental setting.[519] Certainly, any such doctrine would require a setting in which it is clear from the "treaty history" record that the Executive branch authoritatively presented a particular interpretation to the Senate and that a two-thirds majority of the Senate reasonably relied on the representation in providing consent to the treaty. Thus, an oral statement in a committee hearing by a subsidiary Executive branch witness with no similar representation by principal witnesses or treaty negotiators, no written presentation in transmission documents, and no incorporation in committee reports, would seem virtually certain not to raise any "estoppel." Similarly, it is unclear, and probably unlikely, that any such doctrine would be applied to a setting of honest mistake by subsidiary Executive branch witnesses or perhaps even to that of honest mistake by any Executive branch witness. And it is at least unclear whether it would be applied to a subsequent administration, charged, as was its predecessor, to take care that the laws be faithfully executed, to "estop" it by the mistake or misrepresentation of a prior administration. It should also be noted that even if, indeed particularly if, an international misrepresentation were made to the Senate, why would the Senate want a doctrine to freeze such a misrepresentation as national law? Is not this exactly the kind of setting where we would want flexibility to reopen an issue as elsewhere occurs in such settings? Perhaps most importantly, invocation of this doctrine, if any, should only be with sensitivity to the fundamental dilemma that the intent of the prior Senate may be as violated by estoppel into a setting of breach of treaty obligation or unilateral compliance as by altering what it may have believed to be a particular treaty interpretation and that the price of "estoppel" would be paid by the Nation as a whole in its conduct of foreign policy.

5. The authority of a subsequent Senate or Congress to interpret a treaty consented to by a prior Senate

The authority of a subsequent Senate or Congress to interpret a treaty consented to by a prior Senate is really two principal issues. First, what is the authority, if any, of a subsequent Senate or Senate committee? And second, what is the authority, if any, of a subsequent Congress? These will be addressed in turn.

a. The authority of a subsequent Senate or Senate committee

[519]Heckler v. Community Health Services, 467 U.S. 51, 61 (1984) (". . . however heavy the burden might be when an estoppel is asserted against the government. . . .").

It is a settled proposition of constitutional law that a subsequent Senate, acting alone, has no authority to give an interpretation of the previously consented to treaty obligations of the United States. *A fortiori*, a subsidiary unit of a subsequent Senate, such as a Senate committee, also can have no such authority.

As a matter of constitutional theory, as we have seen, the Senate power in the treaty process seems to be primarily a qualified negative or "veto" over United States adoption of a treaty. It is probably not a general legislative power with respect to treaties; much less is it a general judicial power to interpret the laws in cases or controversies or a general executive power to "take Care that the Laws be faithfully executed."[520] Not surprisingly, it seems to be settled law today that a subsequent Senate has no role or authority in interpretation of a treaty approved by a prior Senate.

The 1901 Supreme Court decision in *Fourteen Diamond Rings v. United States*[521] is strongly suggestive that a subsequent Senate has no authority in interpreting a treaty consented to by a prior Senate. While the Senate vote in question in this case was not a two-thirds vote, the majority opinion said in terms that would always seem to rule out an interpretive role by a subsequent Senate that "[t]he meaning of the treaty cannot be controlled by subsequent explanations of some of those who may have voted to ratify it."[522]

The 1985 American Law Institute *Revised Restatement of the Foreign Relations Law of the United States* provides in comment a to section 326 "Authority to Interpret International Agreements: Law of the United States":

> The Senate, whose consent is necessary before the United States can conclude a treaty, has no part in the implementation of the treaty after it is made . . . .[523]

And Reporters' Note 1 to this section says:

---

[520]For the limitations on the Senate role in the appointments process, see the analogous case of Myers v. United States, 272 U.S. 52 (1926).

[521]Fourteen Diamond Rings v. United States, 183 U.S. 176 (1901).

[522]183 U.S. 176, at 180.

[523]*1985 Revised Restatement, supra* note 187, § 326, comment a, at 109.

> Subsequent Senate interpretation. In Fourteen Diamond Rings v. United States, 183 U.S. 176, 180 (1901), the Court ignored a later Senate resolution purporting to clarify the status of the Philippines as to customs duties under the treaty of peace between the United States and Spain. It said: "[t]he meaning of the treaty cannot be controlled by subsequent explanations of some of those who may have voted to ratify it."[524]

Similarly, Professor Louis Henkin writes in his important book on *Foreign Relations and the Constitution*:

> Once the Senate has consented, the President is free to make (or not to make) the treaty and the Senate has no further authority in respect of it. Attempts by the Senate to withdraw, modify or interpret its consent after a treaty is ratified have no legal weight; nor has the Senate any authoritative voice in interpreting a treaty or in terminating it.[525]

This issue seems to be settled constitutional law today with no significant contrary authority.[526] If, of course, a subsequent Senate has no authority to give an interpretation of a treaty consented to by a prior Senate, *a fortiori* a subsidiary unit of such a Senate, such as the Senate Foreign Relations Committee or any other Senate committee, could have no such authority. Indeed, since the action of a Senate committee is always below the threshold of a two-thirds Senate majority, the *Fourteen Diamond Rings* decision would seem even more squarely applicable to any such committee action. This holding would also seem squarely applicable to any subsequent effort by individual members of the previously consenting Senate to seek to interpret a treaty, whether through subsequent testimony, subsequent letters or subsequent petitions.

---

[524]*Id.* reporters' note 1, at 111.

[525]*L. Henkin, supra* note 6, at 136.

[526]The majority report of the Senate Foreign Relations Committee also seems to concede that a subsequent Senate has no authority, acting alone, to interpret a treaty consented to by a prior Senate. *See The ABM Treaty Interpretation Resolution, supra* note 1, at 46, 52.

b. The authority of a subsequent Congress

While it is settled constitutional law that a subsequent Senate, or Senate committee, has no authority to interpret a treaty consented to by a prior Senate, there is no controlling authority and the issue remains unclear as to whether a subsequent Congress may interpret a treaty consented to by a prior Senate in opposition to a prior interpretation by the Executive branch.

Initially, it should be noted that the issue is not whether a subsequent Congress can pass general legislation clearly inconsistent with a prior treaty and thereby supersede the treaty as a matter of domestic law without, of course, altering the international legal obligation. As we have seen, that is settled constitutional law and is not an interpretation of a treaty. Rather, it is a recognition of congressional legislative power to override any inconsistent treaty obligation whatever its meaning. Again, as we have seen, even in such settings the courts will require a clear expression of congressional intent to take action inconsistent with the international legal obligation before interpreting subsequent legislation as inconsistent with the international treaty obligation. Similarly, the issue is not the undoubted necessity of Congress in enacting general implementing legislation or subsequent general legislation to consider in doing so the meaning of the treaty.[527] Rather, the issue is whether Congress can take legislative action specifically for the purpose of compelling a particular interpretation of a treaty under national law (it can, of course, not affect the Nation's international legal obligation) in a setting in which a dispute or disagreement has arisen as to the meaning of the treaty. Pursuant to the *Steel Seizure* framework it may also be useful to ask whether Congress may act in such settings when it either acts with the President, or where the President has not acted, or finally when the President (or the courts) has given a different interpretation of the treaty.

On the one hand, in favor of an argument that Congress possesses broad authority extending even to legislative action for the specific purpose of compelling a treaty interpretation under national law in a setting of disputed meaning, it can be pointed out that Congress has, among other enumerated powers in foreign policy, power "[t]o regulate Commerce with foreign Nations" and power "[t]o define . . . Offenses against the Law of Nations." It also exercises the appropriation power and any powers reasonably implied from its enumerated powers or "necessary and proper for carrying into Execution the foregoing Powers, and all other Powers

---

[527]Even in this setting, however, the constitutional issue is not clear as to the authority of Congress to disregard an interpretation of a treaty as made within their respective spheres of competence by the courts or the President.

vested by this Constitution in the Government of the United States, or in any Department or Officer thereof." Moreover, if Congress has undoubted constitutional authority to supersede a prior treaty if clearly intended by subsequent legislation, it may be difficult to separate such settings of general legislative intent from interventions solely for the purpose of interpreting a treaty or resolving a treaty interpretation dispute under national law. It can also be argued that Congress ought to have such authority as an additional check on the Executive branch. In support of the proposition that Congress would have constitutional authority to compel a particular treaty interpretation under national law, at least if the law were carefully crafted, Mr. Lloyd N. Cutler was asked by the Subcommittee on Arms Control, International Security and Science of the House Committee on Foreign Affairs "to testify concerning the constitutional power of Congress to enact a statute or joint resolution that would . . . require the Executive Branch not to engage in any action that would violate a stated interpretation of the ABM Treaty with the Soviet Union." In a brief prepared statement delivered on February 26, 1987, in hearings before the Committee, Mr. Cutler, who served as Counsel to President Carter during 1979-80, stated flatly: "In my opinion, such a law would be constitutional."[528] Raising a possible concern with respect to interference with the President's power to take care that the laws be faithfully executed, however, Cutler said in concluding his analysis:

> In order to avoid the constitutional question of whether Congress would be invading the President's executive power to interpret the meaning of a treaty, it would be preferable for the law to be drafted so as to bar the specified actions whether or not they violate the terms of the ABM treaty.[529]

On the other hand, in favor of an argument that Congress does not have authority to take action specifically for the purpose of interpreting a treaty under national law, or at least may not do so when either the President or the courts have given a treaty a contrary interpretation while acting within their constitutional authority in treaty interpretation, it can be argued both that Congress has no such

---

[528]"Statement of Hon. Lloyd N. Cutler," in *Review of ABM Treaty Interpretation Dispute and SDI Hearing, supra* note 323, at 16, 19-23, 20. Mr. Cutler's legal analysis of this issue covered only 3 paragraphs and discussed no arguments that might be posed against his conclusion.

[529]*Id.* at 21.

authority within its enumerated or reasonably implied powers, and that interpretation of the laws is exclusively a judicial and executive function within their respective constitutional roles. Moreover, arguably whatever added legislative authority Congress may receive from United States adherence to a treaty in its implementing role for that treaty cannot exceed the international obligations of the treaty itself. And from a policy standpoint it can be argued both that Congress is structured as a political body and not as an appropriate body for making dispassionate analysis of the interpretation of laws or resolution of particular interpretation disputes, and that any such congressional authority would undermine the respective judicial and executive roles in resolution of interpretation disputes.[530]

While there seems no controlling authority resolving this issue of separation-of-powers law,[531] a number of statements or legal principles are relevant to its consideration.

Thus, it should be noted that, as we have seen, in his first "Pacificus" letter of June 29, 1793, Alexander Hamilton wrote:

---

[530]The 1984 report for the Senate Foreign Relations Committee, *Treaties and Other International Agreements: The Role of the United States Senate*, seems to concede that the Congress plays no role in interpretation of an agreement as its provisions are carried out. Thus, in a section on "Implementation and Oversight" it omits any discussion of a congressional role in "Interpretation" of treaties. This section says:

> The executive branch has the primary responsibility for carrying out treaties and ascertaining that other parties fulfill their obligations. However, there are many elements in the phase that begins when treaties and other international agreements enter into force, and in some of these Congress plays a role.
>
> . . . .
>
> *Interpretation.*--The executive branch interprets the requirements of an agreement as it carries out its provisions. U.S. courts may also interpret a treaty's effect as domestic law in appropriate cases.

Treaties and International Agreements Committee Print, supra note 66, at 13 (paragraph number omitted).

[531]Of peripheral authority compare United States v. Navarre, 173 U.S. 77 (1899); *with* Jones v. Meehan, 175 U.S. 1 (1899).

In *Jones v. Meehan*, Mr. Justice Gray, writing for the Court, said: "The construction of treaties is the peculiar province of the judiciary; and, except in cases purely political, Congress has no constitutional power to settle the rights under a treaty, or to affect titles already granted by the treaty itself. . . ." 175 U.S. 1, 32 (1899).

> The legislative department is not the organ of intercourse between the United States and foreign nations. It is charged neither with making nor interpreting treaties. . . .
>
> The province of . . . [the judiciary] department is to decide the litigation in particular cases. It is indeed charged with the interpretations of treaties, but it exercises this function only where contending parties bring before it a specific controversy. It has no concern with pronouncing upon the external political relations of treaties between government and government. This position is too plain to need being insisted upon.
>
> It must, then, of necessity belong to the executive department to exercise the function in question, when a proper case for its occurs . . . as the organ of intercourse between the nation and foreign nations; as the interpreter of the national treaties, in those cases in which the judiciary is not competent--that is, between government and government; as the power which is charged with the execution of the laws, of which treaties form a part; . . . .[532]

Similarly, as we have seen, Secretary of State Thomas Jefferson said of a conversation on July 10, 1793, with M. Genet:

> He asked if they [Congress] were not the sovereign. I told him no, they were sovereign in making laws only, the executive was sovereign in executing them, and the judiciary in construing them where they related to their department. `But,' said he, `at least, Congress are bound to see that the treaties are observed.' I told him no, there were very few cases indeed arising out of treaties, which they could take notice of; that the President is to see that treaties are observed. `If he decides against the treaty, to whom is a nation to appeal?' I told him the Constitution had made the President the last appeal.[533]

The power of the President in this area of treaty interpretation includes not only his general foreign affairs power (whatever the source), but also his Article II,

---

[532]Hamilton, "First *Pacificus* Letter," supra note 24, at 398, 400.

[533]Jefferson, Minutes of Conversation with M. Genet, *supra* note 74, at 680-81.

section 3 enumerated Executive power to "take Care that the Laws be faithfully executed." Moreover, in an interpretation dispute concerning the meaning of an arms control treaty it is possible, if not probable, that the President would obtain significant additional authority from the Article II, section 2 "Commander in Chief" power. It should also be noted in ascertaining the constitutional boundary in this area that, as we have seen, at least Hamilton and Jefferson argued that the authority of Congress in the area of foreign policy was an exception out of the general Article II executive authority of the President and should be construed narrowly. Even Madison supported this argument as it related to clear areas of Executive authority, such as the President's power to "take Care that the laws be faithfully executed." And, as we have seen, that Congress has a general appropriations power does not, under the well established constitutional doctrine of "unconstitutional conditions," serve as a basis of congressional authority if its actions would otherwise breach the constitutional principle of separation of powers. Arguably also, whatever treaty power has been given to Congress as a whole has been given to the Senate, yet a subsequent Senate, as we have seen, has no power to interpret prior treaties.

Of further relevance it should be noted that, at least to the extent that Congress's power to pass implementing legislation is exclusively rooted in a prior treaty, it is questionable whether its authority could go beyond the limits of the international agreement created by the treaty. Thus, Professor Henkin writes: "Presumably a treaty must be valid and binding under international law to support legislation as necessary and proper to implement it."[534]

Professor Henkin also argues that it is doubtful whether Congress has authority to terminate treaties: "[i]f issues as to who has power to terminate treaties arise again . . . it seems unlikely that Congress will successfully assert the power."[535] Yet if there is doubt as to whether Congress can terminate a treaty, by what authority would it alter; that is terminate or add to, a treaty in the process of national interpretation if it cannot internationally alter the treaty meaning? And if it seeks to add to a treaty through interpretation would not this be the "making" of treaties entrusted to the Executive branch with qualified Senate consent? Charles Warren tells us that President Hayes denied the power of Congress to modify an existing treaty, whether adding or deleting to it, even when he felt that Congress did clearly have the authority to terminate treaties:

---

[534]*L. Henkin, supra* note 6, at 408 n.105.

[535]*Id.* at 170. *See generally* the discussion in *id.* at 167-71.

> Congress, in 1879, passed a Chinese immigration restriction bill, one provision of which directed the President to abrogate certain articles of the Burlingame Treaty of 1869. Hayes, in vetoing this bill (March 1, 1879), gave among other grounds, the following. While he admitted that the authority of Congress to terminate a treaty was free from controversy, yet since the bill did not abrogate the entire treaty but simply a part of it, "as the power of modifying an existing treaty, whether by adding or striking out provisions, is a part of the treaty making power under the Constitution, its exercise is not competent for Congress."[536]

Professor Louis Henkin's general discussion of conflicts between Congress and the President in the foreign affairs area from exercise of the President's obligation to execute the laws is also relevant:

> Early Presidents claimed that the constitutional provision that "He shall take Care that the Laws be faithfully executed" gave them discretion not to execute encroachments that, in their view, were unconstitutional, and in foreign affairs a President might raise the particular objection that Congress was invading his domain. . . .
>
> . . . Presidential authority not to execute some Congressional mandates would have to be found in some other constitutional power: the argument might be that Congress cannot impose foreign policy on the President and the President's "primacy" in foreign relations gives him special discretion as to whether and how to execute laws relating to foreign affairs. . . . The issue of principle remains unresolved.[537]

---

[536]Warren, *supra* note 175, at 1, 27-28.

[537]*L. Henkin, supra* note 6, at 110-11.

One possible analogy might be noted here. If Congress has authority to exercise the appropriations power conditioned in a manner intended *solely* to block or reverse a particular Executive branch interpretation of a treaty made in the exercise of the President's constitutional duty to "take Care that the Laws be faithfully executed," then would Congress also have authority to exercise the appropriations power conditioned on the Supreme Court reviewing only certain laws or issues, or controlling the results of particular cases or interpretations in the exercise of its "judicial Power"?

See generally for a review of limits on legislative power to interfere with the continuing jurisdiction of the courts--and particularly legislative efforts to decide the merits of a case

Of further note, it is not impossible that a constitutional test of congressional power to interpret a treaty would even turn on whether Congress were seeking to interpret a provision of the treaty for some purpose of domestic implementation of the treaty or whether its purpose was to assert a correct international interpretation binding on the President in United States foreign policy as well as under national law. Such a test might arguably be rooted, at least partially, in the general foreign affairs power of the President.

That Congress itself may have doubts as to the limits of its authority concerning interventions with respect to presidential implementation of arms control

---

under the guise of limiting jurisdiction--*Ex Parte McCardle* 74 U.S. (7 Wall.) 506 (1869); United States v. Klein, 80 U.S. (13 Wall.) 128 (1871); State v. Fleming, 26 Tenn. (7 Humph.) 152 (1846); DeChastellux v. Fairchild, 15 Pa. 18 (1850); 1 *R. Rotunda, J. Nowak & J.N. Young, Treatise on Constitutional Law: Substance and Procedure* § 2.10, at 66-71 (1986). According to Professors Rotunda, Nowak and Young:

> [T]here is no evidence that the framers intended that the exceptions clause give Congress the power to control the results of particular cases. Analogously then, Congress may not use the power to restrict the federal courts' jurisdiction in order to control the results of particular cases and achieve the result forbidden by a proper interpretation of the exceptions clause.

Id. at 69. And they write of the important *Klein* decision:

> The decision in *Klein* strongly supports the contention that Congress must exercise its power to limit jurisdiction in a manner consistent with constitutional limitations and the independence of the judiciary. Any jurisdictional limitation must be neutral; that is, Congress may not decide the merits of a case under the guise of limiting jurisdiction. And, Congress' power under the exceptions clause is subject, like other congressional powers, to the limitations expressed in the Constitution, including the limitations found in the Bill of Rights. Thus Congress could not exercise its exceptions power so as to violate the fifth amendment due process clause or other Constitutional limits.

Id. at 70-71 (footnote omitted). *See also id.* § 2.11, at 71-81.

See also the discussion of the limits of congressional power to control jurisdiction of the federal courts in *E. Barrett & W. Cohen, Constitutional Law: Cases and Materials* 36-42 (7th ed. 1985). Professors Barrett and Cohen write: "The *McCardle* case is the only example of a result-oriented restriction on the Supreme Court's appellate jurisdiction sustained by the Supreme Court." *Id.* at 41. *And see* the discussion in *J. Barron & C.T. Dienes, Constitutional Law: Principles and Policy* 18-31 (2d ed. 1982).

treaties seems suggested by section 903 of the National Defense Authorization Act for Fiscal Year 1989. Section 903 declares:

> **SEC. 903. SENSE OF CONGRESS CONCERNING ROLE OF CONGRESS IN ARMS CONTROL AND DEFENSE POLICIES**
>
> It is the sense of Congress--
>
> (1) that Congress, in exercising its authority under the Constitution "to raise and support Armies" and "provide and maintain Navies" and, in the case of the Senate, to advise and consent to the ratification of treaties, has a role to play in formulating arms control and defense policies of the United States, but
>
> (2) that Congress, in exercising that authority, should not usurp, undermine, or interfere with the authority of the President under the Constitution to negotiate and implement treaties, especially in the case of treaties which affect arms control and defense policies of the United States.[538]

Finally, it might be noted that even in the area of interpretation of general legislation, the general pronouncements of a later Congress as to the meaning of a prior congressional enactment are not generally conclusive.[539] A principal reason seems to be that to make such general expressions of a subsequent Congress binding, as opposed to merely persuasive, would be to undercut the role of the interpreting branch.

---

[538]National Defense Authorization Act, Fiscal Year 1989, Pub. L. No. 100-456, § 903, 102 Stat. 2031 (Sept. 29, 1988).

[539]*See, e.g.*, Teamsters v. United States, 431 U.S. 324, 354 n.39 (1977); E. Crawford, supra note 496, at 404-406; Kennedy, *supra* note 194, at 873 ("The Supreme Court has stated that the views of a subsequent Congress as to the meaning of a given statute cannot override the unmistakable intent of the enacting one; it is the intent of the enacting Congress that controls." *Id.* at 873).

The above considerations are not set out to establish conclusively the proposition that a subsequent Congress does or does not have authority specifically to interpret an international treaty in settings either where the courts or the President have or have not given a conflicting interpretation. They do suggest, at minimum, however, that it is far from clear whether even Congress as a whole, as opposed to the Senate acting alone, has constitutional authority to specifically interpret a treaty to resolve an international public law dispute that has arisen about interpretation, and particularly whether it has such authority when the President previously has made a conflicting interpretation.

6. presidential and congressional authority concerning suspension or termination of a treaty in whole or in part in response to prior breach of agreement

a. Presidential authority in the absence of congressional action

As previously discussed, there has been an ongoing debate as to whether the President has the authority, acting alone, generally to terminate a treaty.[540] I have testified elsewhere to what I believe is both the majority and constitutionally better position that the President does have such authority.[541] This is also the position adopted by both the Restatement (Second) of the Foreign Relations Law of the United States and the 1980 and 1985 revisions of this Restatement.[542] Whatever the answer with respect to treaty termination generally, however, there is very substantial authority for the proposition that the President has authority, acting alone, to suspend or terminate a treaty in whole or in part in response to prior breach of agreement.

First, it should be noted that suspension or termination of a treaty in response to prior breach of agreement, as discussed in Part IV of this study, would

---

[540]*See e.g.*, Goldwater v. Carter, 444 U.S. 996 (1979); "Statement of John Norton Moore for Treaty Termination Hearings," *supra* note 60, at 400-426.

[541]"Statement of John Norton Moore for Treaty Termination Hearings," *supra* note 60, at 406-08.

[542]*1985 Revised Restatement, supra* note 187, § 339, at 155-60 (339-1 to 339-6). *But see, e.g., T. Jefferson, Manual of Parliamentary Practice, supra* note 163, § 52.

seem inherently an action within the President's explicit Article II, section 3 authority, indeed obligation, to "take Care that the Laws [including Treaties made under the Authority of the United States] be faithfully executed." This explicit authority would be added to any general authority the President would have in this area such as the Article II, section 1 general "executive Power" or the general presidential role as the sole representative of the Nation in foreign affairs.

Second, the general diplomatic practice of the United States records examples where the President, acting alone, has suspended or terminated a treaty in whole or in part in response to prior breach of agreement. One relatively recent example is the United States cessation of minesweeping operations in North Vietnamese ports in response to prior North Vietnamese breach of the Paris Accords.[543]

Third, with respect to the closely analogous authority of the President to waive a prior breach of treaty, Attorney Adviser Furman wrote in a memorandum of November 15, 1954, to State Department Legal Adviser Herman Phleger:

> It seems clear at least that, as a practical matter, the President has the "power" to remain silent in the face of the breach of a treaty. The Executive Branch is necessarily the exclusive agent of this Government in its dealings with foreign States. Should the Executive Branch fail to take action when a treaty is breached, or should the action taken be less than effective, the Congress and the Senate have only limited means at their disposal with which to force a change in policy. For example, while a subsequent Act of Congress could terminate the effectiveness of the treaty as the internal law of the United States, this action would not serve by itself to terminate the treaty as an international obligation of the United States and of the other party.
>
> The Supreme Court recognized the power of the President to waive the breach of a treaty in *Charlton v. Kelly* [229 U.S. 447 (1913)]. . . .
>
> I conclude that the answer to your question on whether the President has the power to waive the breach of a treaty is that the

---

[543]*See* the United States diplomatic note to Vietnam dated April 20, 1973, discussed in *A. Rovine, supra* note 157, at 479, 472. For a discussion generally of the termination power, not limited to responses to prior breach, but also citing a category of termination on presidential authority, see 14 *M. Whiteman, Digest of International Law* 460, 462 (U.S. Dep't of State Pub. No. 8547, 1970).

> President does have such power, although this power would presumably be exercised only in the light of the circumstances of the particular case, including anticipated Congressional reactions, and in the light of the general assumption that the President may modify a treaty only by the conclusion, with the consent of the Senate, of another treaty.[544]

Fourth, the Department of Justice adopted the position in 1941 that the President did not need approval of Congress or the Senate to declare a treaty "inoperative or suspended." Acting Attorney General Biddle said with respect to the International Load Line Convention:

> The convention may be declared inoperative or suspended by the President. A declaration by the President to that effect would validly render the convention inoperative or suspended, as the case may be. Attention to the observance of treaties is an executive responsibility. Jefferson to Genet, 4 Moore, Digest Int. L. 680-681 (1906). It is not proposed that the United States denounce the convention under article 25 . . . , nor that it be otherwise abrogated. Consequently action by the Senate or by the Congress is not required. . . . The facts which bring into operation the right to declare the convention inoperative or suspended, are within the knowledge of and can be promptly and adequately appraised by the Executive department; and it is proper that the President, as "the sole organ of the nation in its external relations," should speak for the nation in announcing action which international law clearly permits. See United States v. Curtiss-Wright . . . See also Charlton v. Kelly, 229 U.S. 447 (1913).[545]

Finally, with respect to secondary authorities, the 1965 *Restatement (Second) of the Foreign Relations Law of the United States*, together with the 1980 and 1985 proposed revisions leading to the *Restatement (Third)*, all adopt the position that the President has authority, acting alone, to suspend an agreement in

---

[544]Memorandum from Attorney Adviser Furman to Legal Adviser Phleger (U.S. Dep't of State, Office of the Legal Adviser, Nov. 15, 1954), *quoted in 14 M. Whiteman, supra* note 543, at 477-78.

[545]*Quoted in 5 G. Hackworth, supra* note 334, at 338-39.

whole or part in response to a prior breach.[546] Section 163 of the *Restatement (Second)* provides in pertinent part:

> **§ 163. Authority to Modify, Suspend, or Terminate**
>
> **(1) Under the law of the United States, the President or a person acting under his authority, has, with respect to an international agreement to which the United States is a party, the authority to**
>
> . . . .
>
> **(b) make the determination of conditions that establish that the agreement may be suspended or terminated under the rule stated in § 158** [Violation of Agreement] **because of its violation by another party** . . .
>
> **(c) elect in a particular case not to suspend or terminate the agreement when the United States may do so under the rule stated in § 158 because of violation of the agreement** . . . .
>
> **(2) The modification, suspension, or termination of an international agreement to which the United States is a party, by the consent of the parties under the rule stated in § 156, is subject to the same rules as apply to the making of an international agreement as stated in § § 117-121.**[547]

Comment *a* to this section provides:

> The rules stated in this Section are based on the authority of the President to conduct the foreign relations of the United States as

---

[546]*Restatement (Second), supra* note 185, § 163, at 493-96; 1980 *Revised Restatement, supra* note 440, § 352, at 191-95; 1985 *Revised Restatement, supra* note 187, § 339, at 155-160 (339-1 to 339-6).

[547]*Restatement (Second), supra* note 185, § 163, at 493.

> part of the executive power vested in him by Article II, Section 1 of the Constitution. This authority is normally exercised in his name by the Secretary of State, and references to the President in this Section include the Secretary or other members of the executive branch acting under the authority of the President.[548]

Comment *c* provides:

> *Determination of conditions calling for suspension or termination.* The application of the rule stated in § 158, which permits a party to an international agreement to suspend or terminate it with respect to another party that violates the agreement, calls for a determination that the agreement has in fact been violated. This is a matter for the President to determine as the person authorized to conduct the foreign relations of the United States and having the necessary knowledge on which to base the determination.[549]

Comment *d* provides of analogous relevance:

> *Waiver of violation of agreement.* Whether or not a right of the United States under an international agreement shall be enforced at all in a particular case is a matter for the President to decide. This is not to say that he may surrender a right of the United States under an international agreement to which it is a party or that, for example, he could forego the claim of the United States to the right so often and for such a period of time that the United States would be estopped by laches from claiming it. But in each particular case in which there is a violation of a right of the United States under one of its agreements, it is the responsibility of the President to decide, not only in the light of the legal issue as such but also in the light of all other circumstances, including considerations of policy, whether it shall be enforced at all.[550]

---

[548] *Id.* comment *a*, at 493.

[549] *Id.* comment *c*, at 494.

[550] *Id.* comment *d*, at 495.

And comment *e* provides:

> *Modification, suspension, or termination by new agreement.* To agree to modify, suspend, or terminate an agreement is in effect to make a new agreement. Hence all the rules concerning authority to make international agreements in § § 117-121 apply to their modification, suspension, or termination by agreement of the parties.[551]

And in the language of section 339 of the 1985 proposed revision leading to the *Restatement (Third)*:

> § 339. AUTHORITY TO MODIFY, SUSPEND OR TERMINATE INTERNATIONAL AGREEMENT: LAW OF THE UNITED STATES
>
> Under the Law of the United States, the President has the power to
>
> (a) take the action necessary to suspend or terminate an agreement in accordance with its terms;
> (b) make the determination that would justify the United States in terminating or suspending an agreement because of its violation by another party or because of supervening events and proceed to terminate or suspend the agreement on behalf of the United States; or
> (c) elect in a particular case not to suspend or terminate an agreement.[552]

Comment a to this section provides:

> The Constitution does not expressly allocate to the President authority to terminate or suspend an international agreement on behalf of the United States. The rules stated in this section are

---

[551] *Id.* comment *e*, at 495.

[552] *1985 Revised Restatement, supra* note 187, § 339, at 155 (underlining in original).

> based on the established constitutional authority of the President to conduct the foreign relations of the United States.[553]

And the Reporters' Notes to this section say:

> The President's authority to terminate or suspend international agreements is implied in his office as it has developed over almost two centuries. In United States v. Curtiss-Wright Export Corp., 299 U.S. 304 (1936), the Court recognized the "very delicate, plenary and exclusive power of the President as the sole organ of the federal government in the field of international relations, a power which does not require as a basis for its exercise an act of Congress." A power so characterized, it would appear, includes the authority to make a decision on behalf of the United States to terminate a treaty when it no longer serves the national interest, when it is out of date, or when the other side has breached it.[554]

The new *Restatement (Third)*, based closely on the 1985 proposed revision, provides in section 339:

> **§ 339. Authority to Suspend or Terminate International Agreement: Law of the United States**
>
> **Under the law of the United States, the President has the power**
>
> **(a) to suspend or terminate an agreement in accordance with its terms;**
>
> **(b) to make the determination that would justify the United States in terminating or suspending an agreement because of its violation by another party or because of supervening events, and to proceed to terminate or suspend**

---

[553]*Id.* comment a, at 155.

[554]*Id.* reporters' note 1, at 156-57 (339-2 to 339-3).

the agreement on behalf of the United States; or

(c) to elect in a particular case not to suspend or terminate an agreement.[555]

With minor wording changes the *Restatement (Third)* also embraces the excerpts from comment a and the Reporters' Notes to the 1985 proposed revision set out above.[556]

Similarly, Professor Louis Henkin writes in his *Foreign Affairs and the Constitution*:

> If there is a breach of a treaty by the other party, it is the President not the courts who will decide whether the United States will denounce the treaty, consider itself liberated from its obligations, or seek other relief or none at all.[557]

And again in the footnote to this statement:

> Put another way, breach by a foreign government may render a treaty voidable at the option of the United States to be exercised by the President; if he chooses not to void it, the courts will give it effect. . . .[558]

It seems virtually certain constitutionally that, at least in the absence of congressional action, the President has authority, acting alone, to suspend a treaty in whole or in part for prior material breach of agreement. While it could be argued, as does a comment to the 1980 and 1985 revisions of the *Restatement* in respect to

---

[555]*Restatement (Third), supra* note 235, § 339, at 226.

[556]*Id.* at 226-27.

[557]*L. Henkin, supra* note 6, at 170-71.

[558]*Id.* at 419 n.138.

treaty termination,[559] that "Congress ([and] not the Senate alone) might claim a voice in the termination of a treaty where termination might create serious danger of war" "in view of the authority of Congress" to declare war, it might also be

---

[559]*1980 Revised Restatement, supra* note 440, § 352, comment a, at 192, 193; *1985 Revised Restatement, supra* note 187, § 339, comment a, at 155, 156 (339-1, 339-2). This comment in the 1980 and 1985 revisions specifically speaks only of "termination" not "suspension for material breach." Its vague language of "might claim a voice" does not specifically address whether congressional action would be required in advance in any such settings. Moreover, the *Restatement (Second)* contained no such comment which is not supported by citation to judicial authority in the revisions.

The opinion of Justice Iredell in *Ware v. Hylton*, 3 U.S. (3 Dall.) 199, 256, at 260, 261 (1796), says in dictum that the authority to declare a treaty broken "must be grounded on the solemn declaration of Congress alone, (to whom, I conceive, the authority is entrusted)," *id.* at 260, and elsewhere in dictum:

> If Congress, therefore, (who, I conceive, alone have such authority under our Government) shall make such a declaration, in any case like the present, I shall deem it my duty to regard the treaty as void, and then to forbear any share in executing it as a Judge.

Id. at 261. These statements, which were solely his own and not those of other Justices, however, were not only dictum but also were merely setting out the reasons he had given in support of his judgment in the Circuit Court as he was not voting in the Supreme Court decision. *See id.* at 256 n.*. Moreover, the theoretical reasons given by Justice Iredell for his view seem patently erroneous in stemming from his apparent belief that sovereign authority to declare a treaty terminated must be rooted either in the treaty power clause or the declaration of war clause. *See id.*, the discussion at page 259. It should be noted that the case involved neither a termination or suspension by either Congress or the President and was, at core, an issue of treaty law prevailing over a state statute.

A 1987 student note in the *Harvard Law Review* adopted the position that "[a]ny reciprocal violation authorized solely by the president may trigger constitutional concerns because it contravenes both the treaty obligations and the law of the United States without congressional approval." This student note then went on incorrectly to cite *Youngstown Sheet & Tube Co. v. Sawyer* and *Coplin v. United States*, discussed earlier in this study, as authority for this proposition. It was apparently not aware of any of the authority to the contrary, including the Henkin treatise or the Restatement, on this point. *See* Note, "Legal Models of Arms Control: Past, Present, and Future," 100 Harv. L. Rev. 1326, 1338, 1338 n.64 (1987). Professor Abram Chayes of the Harvard Law School, without citing any authority for his view, also seemed to adopt a position similar to that discussed in the student note above at a panel debate on the "broad-narrow" issue chaired by the author of this study at an Annual Meeting of the American Society of International Law.

argued in most such cases, and certainly those involving prior breach of arms control treaties, that the President has even greater authority to suspend for material breach in such settings in view of his "Commander-in-Chief" power. In any event, there would seem to be a pretty clear requirement of imminent war to overcome the normal rule even if Congress "might claim a voice" in any such settings, which is certainly not clear. It is also revealing that on this point the Restatement (Third) adds the word "perhaps" in this comment before the phrase "claim a voice," thus recognizing the uncertainty in the proposition.[560]

b. Congressional authority

As we have seen, it is clear that, at least absent congressional action, the President has authority to suspend a treaty in whole or in part in response to prior breach of agreement. It is considerably less clear whether this authority is exclusive. That is, would Congress have authority to direct suspension of a treaty for prior breach over the veto of a President or would Congress have authority to direct a President not to suspend in response to prior breach, again over the veto of the President? As yet another variant, could a Senate, in the case of a treaty, or a Congress, in the case of a congressional-executive agreement, condition consent to a particular agreement on Senate or congressional consent to any future suspension? Finally, would answers to one or more of these questions turn on the nature of the agreement? That is, might the answer differ with respect to commercial treaties, arms control treaties, or treaties incident to recognition or conduct of hostilities? While arguments are available for a variety of answers to these questions, the reality is that our constitutional system has for the most part not yet provided definitive answers. Nevertheless, it may be useful to examine a rough outline of available arguments and to explore those settings where there may be strong indications of an answer.

On the one hand, arguments for a broad congressional role could include arguments for congressional authority stemming from specific delegated authority such as the power "[t]o regulate Commerce with foreign Nations" and the power "[t]o define and punish . . . Offenses against the Law of Nations," from broadly implied powers from these specific enumerated powers, from general congressional powers as in the appropriations power and the necessary and proper clause, and from policy arguments as to the need for congressional checks on presidential power. In addition, with respect to conditions on Senate approval of treaties or congressional authorization of congressional-executive agreements, authority can

---

[560] *Restatement (Third), supra* note 235, § 339, comment a, at 227.

be argued to flow respectively from the Senate's role in providing advice and consent to treaties and in the Congress's role in conditioning delegated authority. On these latter points comment a to section 339 to the 1985 revision of the *Restatement of the Foreign Relations Law of the United States* says:

> If the United States Senate, in giving consent to a treaty, declared that it did so on condition that the President shall not terminate the treaty without the consent of Congress or of the Senate, or that he shall do so only in accordance with some other procedure, that condition would presumably be binding on the President if he proceeded to make the treaty. § 303, Comment d. Congress could impose such a condition in authorizing the President to conclude an executive agreement that depended on Congressional authority.[561]

Comment d to section 303, as cited in the above comment says in pertinent part:

> The Senate has often given its consent subject to conditions. Often the Senate consents only on a particular understanding of the meaning of the treaty, or on condition that the United States obtain a modification in the terms of the treaty or enter a reservation to it. The Senate may also give its consent on conditions that do not require change in the substance of the treaty but relate to its domestic application, e.g., that the treaty shall not be self-executing; or that agreements or appointments made in implementation of the treaty shall require Senate consent.
>
> There is no accepted doctrine indicating limits on the price the Senate can exact as the condition for its consent. Surely, it ought not to impose a condition that has no relation to the treaty before it, for example a requirement that the President accept the Senate's view on some constitutional principle, or dismiss or appoint some cabinet officer. But a condition relating to the treaty before it and having plausible relation to its adoption or

[561] *1985 Revised Restatement, supra* note 187, § 339, comment a, at 155-56 (339-1 to 339-2).

implemention [sic] is presumably not improper and if the President proceeds to make the treaty he is bound by the condition.[562]

Reporters' Note 4 to section 303 of the 1985 *Revised Restatement* also says in full:

> Senate conditions of domestic import. A condition imposed by the Senate in its consent to a treaty, that does not seek to modify the treaty and is solely of domestic import, is not part of the treaty when it comes into effect and does not partake of its character as "supreme Law of the Land." § 131(1) and Comment d. It was once assumed, therefore, that a Senate proviso that a treaty shall not take effect for the United States until Congress adopts implementing legislation, not being part of the treaty, was not law of the land and could not have the force of law necessary to prevent the agreement from taking effect as law in the United States. See Power Authority v. Federal Power Commission, 247 F.2d 538 (D.C. Cir. 1957), vacated and remanded with instructions to dismiss as moot, 355 U.S. 64 (1957). The effectiveness of such a Senate proviso, however, does not depend on its becoming law of the land as part of the treaty. The proviso finds support in the Senate's constitutional authority to grant or withhold consent of a treaty, or to grant its consent subject to a condition. The authority to impose such conditions implies that they must be given effect in the constitutional system. See Henkin, "The Treaty Makers and the Law Makers: The Niagara Power Reservation," 56 Colum. L. Rev. 1151 (1956).
>
> The Senate has not made a practice of attaching conditions that are unrelated to the treaty before it. If, hypothetically, the Senate were to do so, or were to attach a condition invading the President's constitutional powers, for example, his power of appointment, the condition would not be effective and the President would have to decide from all the circumstances whether

[562] *1985 Revised Restatement, supra* note 187, § 303, comment d, at 30-31 (303-3 to 303-4) (citations omitted).

Note particularly the admonition in this comment that "[the Senate] ought not to impose a condition that has no relation to the treaty before it, for example a requirement that the President accept the Senate's view on some constitutional principle." *Id.*

he could assume that the Senate would have given its consent without the condition.[563]

It should be noted that all of these comments in the 1985 Revised Restatement embody the constitutional theory of its Chief Reporter, Professor Louis Henkin, that Senate conditions of domestic effect in granting consent to a treaty must be given effect. As we have seen in the earlier discussion of the "unitary" and "dual" approaches to treaty interpretation, this theory is, at minimum, highly controversial. Indeed, Reporters' Note 4 is particularly revealing in dismissing as a view "once assumed" the *Niagara Reservation* case that held counter to Professor Henkin's theory, while citing as the only authority for it an article by Professor Henkin that was not persuasive to the D.C. Court of Appeals in that case. Even more revealingly, Reporters' Note 4 concedes that such domestic conditions are not "supreme Law of the Land" and then develops a rather strained and question begging theory why despite this "[t]he authority to impose such conditions implies that they must be given effect in the constitutional system." This 1985 *Revision* then must spend some time trying to draw the line against the potential linkage abuse inherent in this approach. Whatever the merits of this theory, as explored more fully earlier in this study, it should be noted that Reporters' Note 4 does concede that a condition invading "the President's constitutional powers . . . would not be effective."

With respect to arguments for a broad executive authority in this area, such arguments can draw on the unqualified Article II, section 1 grant of "the executive Power" to the President, the broad general authority of the President as the executor and spokesman of the Nation in foreign affairs, the President's explicit authority, and indeed duty, from Article II, section 3, to "take Care that the Laws be faithfully executed," a variety of explicit foreign affairs related powers such as the "Commander in Chief" power and the power to participate in the making of treaties, and arguments, as we have seen previously, made by Hamilton, that in foreign affairs congressional authority should be "construed strictly, and ought to be extended no further than is essential to their execution." In addition, it can be pointed out that the only judicial decision to date, other than the *Rainbow Navigation* case currently on appeal, squarely considering the legal effect of Senate conditions of domestic import in consenting to treaties, the *Niagara Reservation* case, while subsequently dismissed as moot, declined to give legal effect to such a domestic condition. And at least the language and theory of the Supreme Court in the *New York Indians* case would seem to cast doubt on the constitutionality of even

[563]*Id.* reporters' note 4, at 37-38 (303-10 to 303-11).

formally adopted "domestic conditions." As a matter of constitutional theory it should be noted that *if* determinations as to prior breach and subsequent suspension in response are considered an exercise of an exclusive presidential power to "take Care that the Laws be faithfully executed" as applied to treaties, then such power would be exclusive with respect to all treaties. If, however, this is not held to be a basis for exclusive presidential authority in dealing with breach and responsive suspension, then individual categories of treaties may still fall within exclusive presidential authority with respect to issues of breach and suspension, as, for example, a treaty concerning recognition or conduct of hostilities and, arguably, an arms control treaty.

In further support of broad executive authority in dealing with suspension for prior breach of treaties, Alexander Hamilton's statement in his first "Pacificus" letter should be noted. There Hamilton wrote: "[T]reaties can only be made by the President and Senate jointly; but their activity may be continued or suspended by the President alone."[564] And, of course, as we have seen, Secretary of State Thomas Jefferson is recorded as having said to M. Genet in the summer of 1793:

> He asked if they [Congress] were not the sovereign. I told him no, they were sovereign in making laws only, the executive was sovereign in executing them, and the judiciary in construing them where they related to their department. 'But,' said he, 'at least, Congress are bound to see that the treaties are observed.' I told him no, there were very few cases indeed arising out of treaties, which they could take notice of; that the President is to see that treaties are observed. 'If he decides against the treaty, to whom is a nation to appeal?' I told him the Constitution had made the President the last appeal.[565]

It should also be noted that section 339 of the 1985 *Revised Restatement* uses the unqualified language:

> the President has the power to
>
> . . . .
>
> . . . make the determination that would justify the United States in terminating or suspending an agreement because of its

---

[564]Hamilton, "First *Pacificus* Letter," *supra* note 24, at 403.

[565]Jefferson, Minutes of Conversation with M. Genet, *supra* note 74, at 680-81.

violation by another party or because of supervening events and proceed to terminate or suspend the agreement on behalf of the United States . . . .[566]

Since the 1985 *Revised Restatement* does in commentary discuss a limited congressional role "where termination might create serious danger of war" or where the Senate or Congress had imposed a condition concerning suspension or termination at time of authorization of the agreement, then it also might be interpreted as general authority for the proposition that in other settings presidential authority in this area is exclusive.

Finally, in support of broad executive authority in the area of suspension in whole or in part for prior breach of agreement, it should be noted that to whatever extent presidential authority in this area is exclusive, whether in all cases stemming from the power to "take Care that the Laws be faithfully executed," or in individual cases stemming from individual subject matter areas of exclusive presidential authority, then under the well established doctrine discussed earlier of "unconstitutional conditions," the area of exclusive authority cannot be constitutionally invaded by Congress in the exercise of its appropriations power.

In summary, it is unclear under current United States constitutional law whether, and to what extent, Congress has authority to override presidential actions concerning suspension of treaties in whole or in part for prior breach of agreement. At minimum, some treaties may so clearly involve substantive areas considered exclusively presidential that Congress would have no authority concerning suspension for prior breach. More broadly and importantly, it is simply unclear whether the President's authority to execute the laws gives the President an exclusive authority concerning suspension in whole or in part for prior breach in all treaty settings.

Although not of direct relevance to the constitutional issue in this area, one further sentence in comment a to section 339 of the 1985 *Revised Restatement* is significant in addressing the general issue of the presidential and congressional roles in dealing with treaties. That is:

> If Congress enacts legislation that makes it impossible for the United States to carry out its obligations under an international

[566] *1985 Revised Restatement, supra* note 187, § 339, at 155 (339-1).

agreement . . . the President should take steps to terminate the agreement.[567]

While intended to protect the integrity of United States treaty obligations, it is less clear than suggested by this cryptic sentence whether there is any such legal obligation binding on the President or whether it would always make good policy sense to terminate such treaties. The implications of such a sentence for any "dual" approach to treaty interpretation could be huge. Would it mean that in every case where a "dual" approach finds the Senate did not accept one or more of the international treaty obligations created by the agreement that the President should always terminate the agreement? This would be almost the functional equivalent of saying that under the "dual" approach we really require United States withdrawal from a treaty whenever there is a legal obligation binding under the treaty but not known to the Senate, for whatever the reason or however minor the discrepancy. This example illustrates yet again a significant theoretical and policy problem with a "dual" approach to treaty interpretation.

This sentence also poses a broader issue of presidential responsibility in response to some forms of hypothetical congressional involvement with the treaty obligations of the United States when such involvement creates a discrepancy between national law requirements mandated by the Congress and our Nation's international legal obligations. If, at least in some settings a President might wish to terminate a treaty when congressional constraints make it impossible to perform, might he also, at least in some settings where mutuality of obligations are important or even critical--as in most arms control agreements--wish to terminate a treaty when congressional constraints impose serious unilateral obligations on the United States not reciprocally binding on the other treaty party. Again, such a result is theoretically possible under a "dual" approach to treaty interpretation as well as through certain kinds of congressional national law constraints.[568]

---

[567]*Id.* comment a, at 155, 156 (339-1, 339-2).

[568]While not directly posing this issue, it can be argued that the at least partially congressionally imposed unilateral United States decision not to deploy one fixed land-based ABM site as permitted by the ABM Treaty, even though the Soviet Union did deploy, has the potential to erode support for the agreement through time as the agreement is then perceived, accurately or inaccurately, as non-reciprocal and possibly as giving certain pragmatic advantages to the Soviet Union in testing and development.

7. Weight to be accorded Executive branch actions interpreting or implementing a treaty

As discussed in previous sections of this study, it is clear that the President has authority to interpret treaties, at least in the absence of congressional action. It is also clear that a subsequent Senate, Senate committee, or individual member of the Senate, has no authority to interpret a treaty consented to by a prior Senate and that the authority of Congress, if any, to interpret a treaty solely as a matter of establishing the correct interpretation of the treaty that the United States should regard as binding in its international relations is unclear. If, of course, Congress has no authority to so interpret a treaty, then, except for the appropriate role for judicial interpretation, presidential authority in the interpretation of treaties is exclusive. Whether in addition to executive authority to interpret international agreements there is a judicial role alone (of some scope), or judicial and congressional roles (of some scope), the importance of the presidential role in interpretation of international agreements suggests that a presidential interpretation should be accorded substantial weight. This section will explore the well established doctrine that a treaty interpretation by the Executive branch is entitled to "great weight." In some respects, the issue of weight to be accorded executive treaty interpretations may also be relevant to the broader issue of whether Congress has any authority to interpret a treaty solely as a matter of establishing the correct interpretation of the treaty that the United States should regard as binding in its international relations--particularly in a setting where the President has made a prior contrary interpretation.

There is a well established body of case law supporting the proposition that courts will give "great weight" to the interpretation given by the Executive branch to a treaty.[569] In summarizing this doctrine, the 1965 *Restatement of the Law (Second) of the Foreign Relations Law of the United States* says in section 152:

> **§ 152. Weight Given by Courts to Executive Interpretation of International Agreements**
>
> **In interpreting an international agreement for the purpose of determining its effect as domestic law, a court in the United States gives great weight to an interpretation made by the executive branch in exercising the authority described in § 149** [Authority to Interpret as to International Effect].[570]

Comment *a* to this section says:

> The judiciary, when interpreting an international agreement, must take into account the fact that every international agreement to which the United States is a party and which becomes involved in domestic litigation has two aspects: (i) its international aspect, which is not the charge of the courts under the Constitution, and

---

[569]*See, e.g.*, Sullivan v. Kidd, 254 U.S. 433, 438-42 (1920); Factor v. Laubenheimer, 290 U.S. 276, 294-95 (1933); Kolovrat v. Oregon, 366 U.S. 187, 194 (1961); Corliss v. United States, 567 F.Supp. 162 (W.D. Ark., 1983).

This recognized principle of law that courts will give "great weight" to the interpretation given by the Executive branch to a treaty seems considerably stronger even than the analogous principle of considerable deference to Executive branch interpretations of statutes. *See, e.g.*, Japan Whaling Association v. American Cetacean Society, 54 U.S.L.W. 4929, 4932 (1986); Chevron U.S.A. v. Natural Resources Defense Council, 467 U.S. 837, 843 (1984). *See also* Collins v. Weinberger, 707 F.2d 1518 (1983):

> No treaty can determine all its own applications. Interpretation, clarification and implementation are always necessary, and it is the executive branch, in agreement with the other party to the treaty, which bears primary responsibility for these functions. Courts should defer to such executive actions provided they are not inconsistent with or outside the scope of the treaty.

Id. at 1522 (Wilkey, Circuit Judge, District of Columbia, Opinion for the Court).

[570]*Restatement (Second), supra* note 185, § 152, at 465.

> (ii) its internal aspect as the law of the case before the court. No instance has been found in which an interpretation of an international agreement of which the Supreme Court has approved has resulted in serious difficulties being created for the executive branch in its conduct of the foreign relations of the United States.[571]

The Reporters' Note to this section also points out that:

> [t]he principle of judicial abstention [the "political question" doctrine] has been applied to, among others, the following types of questions arising in litigation involving international agreements:
>
> . . . .
>
> (d) *Whether a foreign power has violated a treaty with the United States and the effect thereof.* Taylor v. Morton, 23 Fed. Cas. 784 (No. 13799) (C.C.D. Mass. 1855); Head Money Cases, 112 U.S. 580, 597 (1884); Whitney v. Robertson, 124 U.S. 190, 193 (1888); Chinese Exclusion Case, 130 U.S. 581, 600 (1889).[572]

The 1985 proposed *Revised Restatement of the Foreign Relations Law of the United States* says in section 326:

> (1) The President has authority to determine the interpretation of an international agreement to be asserted by the United States in its relations with other states.
>
> (2) Courts in the United States have final authority to interpret an international agreement for purposes of applying it as law in the United States, but will give great weight to an interpretation made by the Executive Branch.[573]

Comment b to this section says:

---

[571]*Id.* comment *a*, at 465.

[572]*Id.* reporters' note, at 467.

[573]*1985 Revised Restatement, supra* note 187, § 326, at 109 (326-1).

> In exercising the authority stated in Subsection (1), the President has to take into account interpretations of the courts of the United States. But the President in some cases may decide to adopt a different interpretation vis-à-vis other states in order not to put the United States in violation of the agreement as a matter of international law. On the other hand, courts in the United States give "great weight" to interpretations of an agreement by the President in his conduct of U.S. foreign relations. Subsection (2).
>
> Presidential interpretations are important also insofar as international agreements are law of the United States. § 131. The President "shall take Care that the Laws be faithfully executed." U.S. Constitution, Article II, section 3. Execution of international agreements as domestic law will often require interpretation of the agreement, and the President will determine what the agreement means in the first instance. The courts, however, have the final say as to the meaning of an international agreement insofar as it is law of the United States applicable to cases and controversies before the courts.[574]

Reporters' Note 2 to this section says:

> The Supreme Court has given great weight to the interpretation of an agreement by the executive branch. In fact it has increasingly taken to inviting the Solicitor General to file amicus briefs giving the views of the executive branch in cases involving interpretation. . . . Courts are more likely to defer to an executive interpretation already made in diplomatic negotiation with other countries (on the ground that the United States should speak with one voice) than to one adopted by the Executive in relation to a case before the courts, especially where individual rights or interests are involved.[575]

And Reporters' Note 4 to this section adds:

> Courts give "particular weight" to Executive views on customary international law (§ 132(3)), and "great weight" to executive

---

[574]*Id.* comment b, at 109-10 (326-1 to 326-2).

[575]*Id.* reporters' note 2, at 111-12 (326-10 to 326-11) (citations omitted).

> interpretations of international agreements. Different formulations in the two contexts may not be significant, but "great weight" in this Section has the authority of the Supreme Court of the United States.[576]

Similarly, Professor Louis Henkin writes in *Foreign Affairs and the Constitution*:

> The obligation and authority to implement or enforce a treaty involve also the obligation and authority to interpret what the treaty requires. For international purposes, no doubt, the President determines the United States position as to the meaning of a treaty* [*Subject to any "understanding" imposed by the Senate in its consent to ratification. . . .]. Domestically, too, since the President has usually the principal, often the sole, responsibility to execute a treaty, the treaty means what he says it means. But Congress, too, has occasion to interpret a treaty when it considers implementing legislation or other legislation on the same subject; the courts also interpret treaties in cases before them. Both Congress and the courts have claimed the right to interpret a treaty independently, even while admitting that the Executive's interpretation is entitled to "great weight." It could happen, then, that Congress and the courts would in effect apply treaty provisions different from those that bind the United States internationally--another cost of the separation of powers.[577]

And the 1984 study for the Senate Committee on Foreign Relations, *Treaties and Other International Agreements: The Role of the United States Senate*, says:

---

[576]*Id.* reporters' note 4, at 113 (326-5). The *Restatement (Third)* is virtually identical and provides:

> Courts give "particular weight" to Executive views on customary international law (§ 112, Comment *c*), and "great weight" to Executive interpretations of international agreements. These different formulations may not be significant, but the term "great weight" used in this section has the authority of the Supreme Court of the United States.

Restatement (Third), supra note 235, § 326, reporters' note 4, at 204.

[577]L. Henkin, *supra* note 6, at 167.

> [W]hen interpreting a treaty under *domestic* law, U.S. Courts include as criteria indications of U.S. intent in making the agreement as well as the executive branch's interpretation of the agreement's meaning. United States courts generally assign "great weight" to such executive branch interpretation of an international agreement. Thus, for example, in 1933, the U.S. Supreme Court in deciding whether a particular offense was extraditable under the extradition convention with Great Britain of 1899, noted the treaty's construction by the executive branch as a factor to be considered in reaching its decision to extradite the appellant. The U.S. Supreme Court noted similarly in 1961 that "While courts interpret treaties for themselves, the meaning given them by the departments of government particularly charged with their negotiation and enforcement is given great weight."[578]

On this point that Executive branch interpretations of treaties are entitled to "great weight," both the majority and minority reports of the Senate Foreign Relations Committee on *The ABM Treaty Interpretation Resolution* agree. Thus, the majority report says: "The President's interpretation of a treaty is entitled to great weight in United States law . . . ."[579] And the "Additional Views of Senator Helms" says:

> No special preference is given under international law to the interpretations of a treaty made by governmental authorities of either party. In applying the provisions of a treaty for purposes of domestic law, however, U.S. courts will typically give great weight to any reasonable interpretation articulated by the U.S. Executive Branch. As explained in Part II, this results both from the normal deference given to Executive agencies in interpreting Federal statutes, and from the special deference given to the President in the interpretation of treaties as an aspect of conducting the Nation's foreign affairs. While longstanding interpretations by the

---

[578] *Treaties and International Agreements Committee Print, supra* note 66, at 136 (footnotes omitted).

[579] *The ABM Treaty Interpretation Resolution, supra* note 1, at 39 (majority report). The majority report goes on to propose a test for confining this presidential authority, however, as embodied in subparagraph (A) of section 2, paragraph 2 of proposed S. Res. 167.

> Executive Branch must be accorded great weight, the Supreme Court has also accorded great weight to an interpretation even though it had not been previously maintained by the Executive Branch.[580]

It seems clear that, at minimum, an interpretation of a treaty by the Executive branch is entitled to "great weight" before both the courts and the Congress. It is also arguable from this same body of authority, although perhaps with some strain, that when the issue is solely the meaning of a treaty in the international relations of the United States, as opposed to domestic applications of the treaty, the President is or ought to be the sole voice of the United States both with respect to cases before the courts as well as the Congress and that in such a setting the executive interpretation would be conclusive.[581] On balance, however, the broader issue of the role of Congress in interpreting a treaty consented to by a prior Senate remains, as discussed previously, unclear. It should, in conclusion, also be noted as suggested in the 1965 *Restatement (Second) of the Foreign Relations Law of the United States* that Executive branch determinations as to whether a foreign nation has violated a treaty and the legal effect of such a violation may be treated as "political questions" by the courts.

---

[580]"Additional Views of Mr. Helms," in *The ABM Treaty Interpretation Resolution, supra* note 1, at 68, 87.

[581]*See also* the opinion of the Court in the *Head Money Cases*, 112 U.S. 580, at 598-99 (1884), which seems to suggest a distinction in judicial consideration between a treaty's effect as an international compact ("with all this the judicial courts have nothing to do and can give no redress") and its effect in conferring private rights under national law ("[a] treaty, then, is a law of the land as an act of Congress is, whenever its provisions prescribe a rule by which the rights of the private citizen or subject may be determined.") *And see* the opinion of the Court in *United States v. Schooner Peggy*, 5 U.S. (1 Cranch) 104, at 109-10 (1801) ("It is certainly true that the execution of a contract between nations is to be demanded from, and, in the general, superintended by, the executive of each nation. . . ." *Id.* at 109). *But see* "Statement of Arthur W. Rovine, Esq., Baker & McKenzie, New York, NY, Former Assistant Legal Adviser For Treaty Affairs, Department of State," in *The ABM Treaty and the Constitution, supra* note 1, at 192, 194, with respect to the role of the courts as ultimate arbiter. Rovine does agree, however, that "the courts of this country normally accord great deference to the manner in which the Executive interprets a treaty." *Id.* at 194.

8. Other potentially relevant national laws and a possible obligation of any administration to make known, at least to Congress, what it comes to believe may be a mistaken interpretation of an arms control agreement

The principal source of authority concerning the national law of treaty implementation and respective executive and congressional authority with respect to such implementation is, of course, the Constitution of the United States. Several other national laws, however, may also be relevant.

The first of these is section 33 of the 1961 Arms Control and Disarmament Act which provides:

> The Director is authorized and directed to prepare for the President, the Secretary of State, and the heads of such other government agencies, as the President may determine, recommendations concerning United States arms control and disarmament policy: Provided, however, That no action shall be taken under this or any other law that will obligate the United States to disarm or to reduce or to limit the Armed Forces or armaments of the United States, except pursuant to the treaty making power of the President under the Constitution or unless authorized by further affirmative legislation by the Congress of the United States.[582]

The proviso to this section reflects a clear intent of Congress that the United States will not undertake obligations "to disarm or to reduce or to limit the Armed Forces or armaments of the United States," except pursuant to treaty or further affirmative legislation by Congress. Presumably Congress seeks in this provision to prevent limiting obligations on United States forces unless carefully resulting from Senate consideration in the treaty process or affirmative legislation by the Congress. While an argument can also be made to the contrary,[583] it can be argued from this

[582]Arms Control and Disarmament Act of 1961, Pub. L. No. 87-297, § 33, 75 Stat. 631 (1961), 22 U.S.C. § 2573.

[583]The principal argument to the contrary would be in a setting where the Senate or Congress believed a particular limiting interpretation was a correct international interpretation of the agreement, even though it did not know the other side was not bound, and thus it could be argued Congress or the Senate had already assented. But the "assent"

provision that if a subsequent administration finds a mistaken interpretation of an arms control treaty limiting United States forces unilaterally, that it has an obligation to Congress to make the mistake known and to not implement the unilateral restriction absent subsequent Senate or congressional assent. Indeed, it can also be argued that, quite apart from this provision, there should be an obligation on any administration to promptly reveal, at least to Congress, what it comes to believe to be a mistaken interpretation of an arms control or other treaty.

The second potentially relevant national law, other than the Constitution, is Public Law 92-448 of September 30, 1972, the Joint Resolution approving and authorizing the President to accept the Salt Interim Agreement. That Resolution provides in full:

SALT AGREEMENT
PUBLIC LAW 92-448; 86 STAT. 746

[H. J. Res. 1227]

Joint Resolution approval and authorization for the President of the United States to accept an Interim Agreement between the United States of America and the Union of Soviet Socialist Republics on Certain Measures With Respect to the Limitation of Strategic Offensive Arms.

Be it resolved by the Senate and House of Representatives of the United States of America in Congress assembled, That:

The Congress hereby endorses those portions of the Declaration of Basic Principles of Mutual Relations Between the United States of America and the Union of Soviet Socialist Republics signed by President Nixon and General Secretary Brezhnev at Moscow on May 29, 1972, which relate to the dangers of military confrontation and which read as follows:

"The United States of America and the Union of Soviet Socialist Republics attach major importance to preventing the

---

given is certainly flawed in such a setting of congressional or Senate misinformation on a point of fundamental importance about the other side being bound by the same restriction.

development of situations capable of causing a dangerous exacerbation of their relations . . ." and "will do their utmost to avoid military confrontations and to prevent the outbreak of nuclear war" and "will always exercise restraint in their mutual relations," and "on outstanding issues will conduct" their discussions and negotiations "in a spirit of reciprocity, mutual accommodation and mutual benefit," and

"Both sides recognize that efforts to obtain unilateral advantage at the expense of the other, directly or indirectly, are inconsistent with these objectives," and

"The prerequisites for maintaining and strengthening peaceful relations between the United States of America and the Union of Soviet Socialist Republics are the recognition of the security interests of the parties based on the principle of equality and the renunciation of the use or threat of force.".

SEC. 2. The President is hereby authorized to approve on behalf of the United States the interim agreement between the United States of America and the Union of Soviet Socialist Republics on certain measures with respect to the limitation of strategic offensive arms, and the protocal [sic] related thereto, signed at Moscow on May 26, 1972, by Richard Nixon, President of the United States of America and Leonid I. Brezhnev, General Secretary of the Central Committee of the Communist Part of the Soviet Union.

SEC. 3. The Government and the people of the United States ardently desire a stable international strategic balance that maintains peace and deters aggression. The Congress supports the stated policy of the United States that, were a more complete strategic offensive arms agreement not achieved within the five years of the interim agreement, and were the survivability of the strategic deterrent forces of the United States to be threatened as a result of such failure, this could jeopardize the supreme national interests of the United States; the Congress recognizes the difficulty of maintaining a stable strategic balance in a period of rapidly developing technology; the Congress recognizes the principle of United States-Soviet Union equality reflected in the antiballistic missile treaty, and urges and requests the President to seek a future treaty that, inter alia, would not limit the United States to levels of intercontinental strategic forces inferior to the limits provided for the Soviet Union; and the Congress considers that the success of these agreements and the attainment of more permanent and comprehensive agreements are dependent upon the maintenance under present world conditions of a vigorous research and development and modernization program as required by a prudent strategic posture.

SEC. 4. The Congress hereby commends the President for having successfully concluded agreements with the Soviet Union limiting the production and deployment of antiballistic missiles and certain strategic offensive armaments, and it supports the announced intention of the President to seek further limits on the production and deployment of strategic armaments at future Strategic Arms Limitation Talks. At the same time, the Senate takes cognizance of the fact that agreements to limit the further escalation of the arms race are only preliminary steps, however important, toward the attainment of world stability and national security. The Congress therefore urges the President to seek at the earliest practicable moment Strategic Arms Reduction Talks (SART) with the Soviet Union, the People's Republic of China, and other countries, and simultaneously to work toward reductions in conventional armaments, in order to bring about agreements for mutual decreases in the production and development of weapons of mass destruction so as to eliminate the threat of large-scale devastation and the ever-mounting costs of arms production and weapons modernization, thereby freeing world resources for constructive, peaceful use.

SEC. 5. Pursuant to paragraph six of the Declaration of Principles of Nixon and Brezhnev on May 29, 1972, which states that the United States and the Union of Soviet Socialist Republics: "will continue to make special efforts to limit strategic armaments. Whenever possible, they will conclude concrete agreements aimed at achieving these purposes"; Congress considers that the success of the interim agreement and the attainment of more permanent and comprehensive agreements are dependent upon the preservation of longstanding United States policy that neither the Soviet Union nor the United States should seek unilateral advantage by developing a first strike potential.

Approved September 30, 1972.[584]

This joint resolution was passed subsequent to and virtually contemporaneous with Senate consent to the 1972 ABM Treaty which was given on August 3, 1972. And in it, Congress explicitly "recognizes the principle of United States-Soviet Union equality reflected in the antiballistic missile treaty" and states that it "considers that the success of these agreements and the attainment of more permanent and comprehensive agreements are dependent upon the maintenance under present world conditions of a vigorous research and development and modernization program as required by a prudent strategic posture." It is a reasonable inference that these provisions of section 3, stemming from the so-called "Jackson Amendment" to Senate Joint Resolution 241 on the Interim Strategic Offensive Arms Agreement, embody concerns as to which Congress--and particularly the Senate--felt strongly. These certainly include the concern that important arms control agreements be reciprocally limiting and that a vigorous research and development program proceed up to treaty limits. Thus, as will subsequently be discussed, this contemporaneous legislative provision will be relevant under well-recognized principles of interpretation in seeking to ascertain the overall intent of the Senate in consenting to the 1972 ABM Treaty. The existence of this provision, however, would further seem to heighten the obligation of any administration to promptly at least share with Congress any interpretation of the 1972 ABM Treaty which it believes may have been mistaken and which, if not corrected in United States practice, could lead to a lack of reciprocity between United States and Soviet practices under the agreement, and particularly if it would also unilaterally inhibit a United States development program.[585]

C. An Overview History of Congressional Consideration of the "Broad-Narrow" Issue

This section will review in turn a summary overview of congressional consideration of the "broad-narrow" issue during initial consideration of the 1972

---

[584]Pub. L. No. 92-448, 86 Stat. 746 (Sept. 30, 1972).

[585]Arguably, the legal effect of this contemporaneous provision could be even greater. For example, could it be viewed as an implicit congressional direction to follow a "unitary" approach in interpreting the 1972 ABM Treaty that would not result in a discrepancy between the international obligations under the treaty and national law obligations even if such approach were not constitutionally required?

ABM Treaty, as previously developed in detail in section (III)(E) and annex D of this study, will place this overview in its broader contemporary context in a discussion of relevant issues in contemporaneous congressional consideration of the SALT I Agreements as a whole (with particular focus on the "Jackson Amendment"), will review the history of consideration of the "broad-narrow" issue by subsequent Congresses, and finally, briefly will review the process of subsequent congressional interpretation of the "broad-narrow" issue.

1. An overview of congressional consideration of the "broad-narrow" issue during initial consideration of the ABM Treaty

This section will present an overview summary of Senate (and more broadly congressional) consideration of the "broad-narrow" issue during initial consideration of the ABM Treaty. A more detailed analysis of overall congressional consideration, from which this analysis is drawn, appears as section (III)(E) and annex D of this study.

The ABM Treaty was signed at Moscow on May 26, 1972. On June 10, 1972, Secretary of State Rogers submitted the ABM Treaty (and the Interim Agreement) to the President for transmittal to the Senate. The Secretary's letter of submittal contained a description of the ABM Treaty and was, on June 13, 1972, transmitted by the President to the Senate along with the President's transmittal letter and texts of agreed interpretations and unilateral statements. On June 15, 1972, Dr. Henry Kissinger, the Assistant to the President for National Security Affairs, gave an extensive briefing at the White House for congressional leaders on the ABM Treaty and the Interim Agreement. Subsequently, major hearings were held before the Senate Foreign Relations Committee, the Senate Armed Services Committee, the House Foreign Affairs Committee and the House Armed Services Committee. Following reports from the Senate Foreign Relations Committee and the House Foreign Affairs Committee, the Treaty and Interim Agreement were debated on the Senate floor. The debate on the ABM Treaty began on August 3, 1972, and concluded on the same day when, by a vote of 88-2, the Senate gave its advice and consent to ratification of the Treaty.

It should be noted in putting the congressional consideration of the "broad-narrow" issue in context, that it was not a central issue in either Executive branch presentation or congressional consideration of the ABM Treaty. The ABM Treaty was considered with the Interim Agreement together presenting a host of central strategic issues including overall limits on offensive forces, non-inclusion of MIRVs, the appropriateness of unequal aggregate national limits on offensive forces, the number of ABM sites permitted, the definition of heavy missiles, and verification and compliance issues. The "broad-narrow" issue was not specifically defined or presented to the Congress in either the President's transmission letter, including the Secretary of State's accompanying analysis, or the opening statements of the principal administrative witnesses, including Ambassador Gerard C. Smith as the leader of the United States SALT Delegation, or in Dr. Kissinger's White House briefing for Members of Congress on June 15, 1972. In over four hearings and the brief one-day floor debate the issue seems to have been unambiguously addressed by only two Senators, and one middle level administration witness who had not participated in the negotiation and who had earlier participated in an exchange at least tilting toward the opposite interpretation. The "broad-narrow" issue was not mentioned in either the Senate Foreign Relations Committee or House Foreign Affairs Committee reports nor in the Senate Resolution of Advice and Consent.

a. Executive branch transmittal documents to the Senate

Executive branch transmittal documents, including a thirteen and one-half printed page letter of submittal from Secretary of State Rogers describing the ABM Treaty, and President Nixon's transmittal letter to the Senate, did not identify the "broad-narrow" issue or provide any meaningful guidance on the issue.

b. Congressional Briefing by Dr. Henry A. Kissinger, Assistant to the President for National Security Affairs, at The White House, June 15, 1972

On June 15, 1972, Dr. Henry Kissinger, as Assistant to the President for National Security Affairs, gave a congressional briefing at the White House for leaders of Congress on the ABM Treaty and Interim Agreement as formally submitted to Congress by President Nixon on June 13, 1972. The transcript of the Kissinger opening statement was approximately 16 pages. The transcript of the question and answer discussion ran approximately 27 pages, including questions by nine senators and fifteen congressmen. Not once in this extended discussion, which certainly is a good indication of principal administration and congressional concerns--as well as one source of general information about the Treaty available to congressional leadership, did the issue of ABM "futures" arise in any form.

c. Opening statements and question and answer discussion during Senate committee hearings by principal administration spokesmen on the Treaty

No prepared statement by a principal administration spokesman on the ABM Treaty (Secretary of State Rogers or Ambassador Gerard C. Smith, the head of the SALT Delegation) either specifically raised the "broad-narrow" issue or presented anything but a neutral (that is, neither tilting toward "broad" or "narrow" interpretation) description to the Congress.

During questions and answers in committee hearings, Ambassador Gerard Smith, accompanied by other principal SALT I Delegation members, was given repeated opportunities to clarify the "broad-narrow" issue but did not unambiguously do so. On at least three occasions, however, Ambassador Smith's answers can be fairly characterized as at least "ambiguous leaning to the `broad' interpretation." On no occasion does an Ambassador Smith answer even lean toward the "narrow" interpretation. These occasions of Ambassador Smith responses at least leaning to the "broad" interpretation are:

* the Senator Aiken--Secretary Rogers--Ambassador Smith exchange before the Senate Foreign Relations Committee,
* the Senator Smith--Ambassador Smith exchange before the Senate Armed Services Committee; and
* the Senator Goldwater--Ambassador Smith exchange before the Senate Armed Services Committee.

On no occasion does a White House, National Security Council (NSC), State Department, Arms Control and Disarmament Agency (ACDA), or participating member of the SALT Delegation, personally make a statement or participate in an exchange before the Senate or House in initial consideration of the ABM Treaty that can even be reasonably regarded as leaning toward the "narrow" interpretation. In contrast, the head of the United States SALT I Delegation, Ambassador Gerard C. Smith, with repeated opportunities to clarify the issue and accompanied by other SALT I Delegation principals, on three occasions, once in an exchange before the Senate Foreign Relations Committee and twice in exchanges before the Senate Armed Services Committee, makes remarks that can at least be regarded as "ambiguous but leaning toward the `broad' interpretation."

d. Senate committee hearings in general

Major hearings were held on the ABM Treaty before the Senate Foreign Relations and Senate Armed Services committees. The Foreign Relations Committee had principal jurisdiction over the Treaty.[586] Indeed, Senator John C. Stennis, the Chairman of the Senate Armed Services Committee, repeatedly stressed during the Armed Services Committee hearings that the ABM Treaty was "not before our committee." The substance and military implications of the Treaty, however, were clearly addressed in these hearings. Thus, in opening the Armed Services Committee hearings on June 6, 1972, before the ABM Treaty was formally submitted to the Senate on June 13, 1972, Chairman Stennis said:

> I wrote Chairman Fulbright that we were going to begin hearings today on the budget changes, and afterwards, at some appropriate time after the proposed treaty is submitted, I think that our committee will have hearings on the military application of these proposals. These hearings, as I see them, would be in depth on the military implications, and would be held during or after Chairman Fulbright's committee hearings but would certainly in no way conflict with his. It would be an effort by each committee to get at the matters that pertain to the area or subject matter about which the respective committee is concerned. Hearings on the treaty itself will undoubtedly be held by the Foreign Relations Committee since they have primary jurisdiction.
>
> In other words, there is no jurisdictional question about the treaty.[587]

---

[586]Even Judge Harold H. Greene's recent opinion in the *Rainbow Navigation* case specifically qualified its statement about the obligatory effect of Executive branch representations by adding ". . . to the Senate committee having jurisdiction." See Rainbow Navigation v. Department of Navy, Civil Action No. 88-0992 (Nov. 15, 1988), at 10. The Executive branch statements relied on by Judge Greene in the *Rainbow Navigation* case were made to the Senate Foreign Relations Committee, which has general jurisdiction over consideration of treaties by the Senate.

[587]*Military Implications of the Treaty on the Limitations of Anti-Ballistic Missile Systems and the Interim Agreement on Limitation of Strategic Offensive Arms: Hearing Before the Senate Comm. on Armed Services*, 92d Cong., 2d Sess. 1-2 (June 6, 20, 22, 28; July 18, 19, 21, 24, and 25, 1972) [hereinafter *Military Implications Hearing Before the Senate Armed Services Comm.*].

Similarly Chairman Stennis said in opening the June 20 session:

> The hearings before this committee are, technically, not hearings on the treaty and interim offensive weapons agreement as such. The treaty and agreement have been referred to the Foreign Relations Committee and the committee is holding its hearings in order to make its report to the Senate. The substance of the treaty and agreement, however, is of direct concern to this committee as well because it concerns the national defense and our overall strategic posture. Thus, we will be holding these hearings concerning the military implications of the treaty and the agreement. That is a term that I used in the beginning in reference to the hearings. I recognized the nature of them, the jurisdiction is with foreign relations, but the military implications should be considered by this committee. Of course, I will not attempt to limit the hearings directly to those points, but I believe that is our primary mission in these hearings.[588]

And, in opening the session on July 19th at which General John D. Ryan and General Bruce Palmer, Jr., testified, Chairman Stennis said:

> For the information of the public, this treaty, of course, is not before our committee, nor is the proposed statute before us formally for an official report, but it is before us in substance.
>
> Our committee decided to hold hearings on the military implications of the SALT agreements, and that means just what it says I think we have had splendid hearings. [sic][589]

During these Senate hearings, the following statements either leaned toward one or another interpretation or may be regarded as unambiguous for one or another interpretation. All were in settings in which the issue was incidentally or ambiguously raised during general discussion within the committee hearing.

---

[588]*Id.* at 138.

[589]*Id.* at 423.

Senate Foreign Relations Committee

* Ambassador Smith, the head of the United States SALT I Delegation and accompanied by senior SALT I Delegation members and testifying with the Secretary of State, in the Senator Aiken--Secretary Rogers--Ambassador Smith exchange in the committee hearing at least leans toward the "broad" interpretation and it can be argued that Ambassador Smith's statement on its face should be characterized as unambiguously supporting the "broad" interpretation.

* Statement by Senator Buckley to the Committee is unambiguous in reflecting the "narrow" interpretation while opposing "futures" related treaty constraints in general. Senator Buckley opposes advice and consent to the ABM Treaty.

Senate Armed Services Committee

* Senator Goldwater in posing a question for the record answered from DOD is ambiguous but at least leans to the "broad" interpretation.

* Department of Defense answer to questions for the record by Senator Goldwater during the hearing is ambiguous but leans toward the "narrow" interpretation.

* An answer by Dr. John Foster, Jr., Director of Defense Research and Engineering, during the hearing in exchange between Senator Jackson and Dr. Foster, is ambiguous but can most reasonably be regarded as leaning toward the "narrow" interpretation.

* Additional information interposed for the record during the above Dr. Foster exchange with Senator Jackson is ambiguous but leans toward the "narrow" interpretation.

* Senator Jackson question in the above exchange with Dr. Foster during the hearing might be regarded as unambiguous for the "narrow" interpretation.

* Senator Jackson involvement in an exchange with Ambassador Smith might be regarded as "ambiguous: leans to `broad.'"

* Ambassador Smith statement in an exchange with Senator Smith during the hearing is ambiguous but at least leans toward the "broad" interpretation.

* Ambassador Smith statement in an exchange with Senator Goldwater is ambiguous but leans toward the "broad" interpretation.

* Senator Goldwater--General Palmer, Acting Chief of Staff of the Army--General John Ryan, Air Force Chief of Staff--and Lt. General W. P. Leber, Safeguard Systems Manager--hearing exchange was on all sides at least "ambiguous leaning toward the `broad' interpretation" and could be regarded as unambiguous for the "broad" interpretation. This exchange should be read with General Palmer's subsequent exchange before the Committee supporting the "narrow" interpretation.

* A statement by General Palmer in the hearing exchange between Senators Jackson, Dominick, and Goldwater, and General Leber, General Ryan and General Bruce Palmer, can be regarded as "unambiguous for the `narrow' interpretation" but seems to contradict the contemporary testimony of the Chairman of the Joint Chiefs given before the House Armed Services Committee as to the view of the Chiefs. This exchange should also be read with General Palmer's inconsistent earlier exchange before the

Committee at least tilting toward the "broad" interpretation.[590]

* A statement by General John Ryan, Air Force Chief of Staff, in the above exchange characterized as "narrow" for General Palmer can be characterized as "ambiguous: leans to `narrow.'"

* The involvement of Senator Jackson in the above exchange can be regarded as "unambiguous for `narrow.'"

* The involvement of Senator Dominick in the exchange with Senators Jackson, Dominick and Goldwater, and Generals Leber, Ryan and Palmer, can be characterized as "ambiguous: leans to `broad.'"

* The involvement of Senator Goldwater in the exchange with Senators Jackson, Dominick and Goldwater, and Generals Leber, Ryan and Palmer, can be characterized as "ambiguous: leans to `narrow.'"

Senate Appropriations Committee

* A "minor" hearing on June 13, 1972, before the Senate Appropriations Committee, resulted in no statement that could be meaningfully characterized as supportive of either "broad" or "narrow" interpretation.

e. Report of the Senate Foreign Relations Committee

---

[590]With respect to General Palmer's reference to "[t]he Chiefs" in this testimony, it should also be read with the seemingly contradictory testimony of Admiral Thomas Moorer, the Chairman of the Joint Chiefs, before the House Armed Services Committee discussed *infra*.

The report of the Senate Foreign Relations Committee on July 21, 1972, did not advert to or meaningfully address the "broad-narrow" issue. One significant focus of the report was whether the United States should, as permitted under the ABM Treaty, deploy an ABM defense around the national capital.

f. General "floor" debate

The Senate general "floor" debate, which lasted only one day on the ABM Treaty (in contrast the "floor" debate on the Interim Agreement lasted 16 days), resulted in three statements of significance for the "broad-narrow" debate. As has been discussed, it cannot be known from the official 1972 Senate records of this debate whether the critical portions of each statement were in fact made on the floor during the general debate or whether they were inserted in the record pursuant to the practice of "revising and extending remarks." These three statements are:

* a statement by Senator Buckley opposing the ABM Treaty which is unambiguous in reflecting the "narrow" interpretation;

* a statement by Senator Fong which can reasonably be regarded as "ambiguous but leaning toward the `broad' interpretation"; and

* a statement by Senator Thurmond which can be most reasonably regarded as "ambiguous but leaning toward the `narrow' interpretation."

g. Senate Resolution of Advice and Consent

The Senate Resolution of Advice and Consent on August 3, 1972, adopted by a vote of 88-2, contained no provision adverting to, or of relevance for, the "broad-narrow" issue nor, indeed, any reservation, understanding, or condition of any kind.

h. Significant House action

While the House of Representatives was not involved, as such, in the process of treaty advice and consent on the 1972 ABM Treaty, hearings on the Treaty and the Interim Agreement were held before the House Foreign Affairs and Armed Services committees leading to a joint resolution of general endorsement passed by Congress as a whole. The only meaningful house statements, exchanges or reports that might be reasonably regarded as addressing the issue in more than a neutral fashion involve three incidents. First, an exchange between Admiral Thomas H. Moorer, the Chairman of the Joint Chiefs of Staff, and Congressman Whitehurst during hearings before the House Armed Services Committee. The remark of Admiral Moorer in that exchange probably is most fairly characterized as "ambiguous but leaning toward the `broad' interpretation" but it can reasonably be interpreted as fairly clearly supporting the "broad" interpretation. It should be noted that two members of the United States SALT I Delegation, Ambassador Paul Nitze and Lt. General Royal B. Allison, were both witnesses at this session and apparently neither sought to qualify Admiral Moorer's remark on this issue. Second, Congressman Stratton in a question for Secretary Laird during a hearing before the House Armed Services Committee can be characterized as "ambiguous: leans to `broad.'" And finally, a staff memorandum prepared for the members of the House Armed Services Committee and inserted in the record arguably leans toward the "broad" interpretation in its choice of language to summarize the meaning of Article II of the ABM Treaty. The Report of the House Foreign Affairs Committee on August 10, 1972, (after the August 3 Senate advice and consent vote on the ABM Treaty) did not meaningfully address the "broad-narrow" issue.

i. Overview summary of Senate and House consideration of the "broad-narrow" issue during initial consideration of the ABM Treaty

An overview of Senate and House consideration of the "broad-narrow" issue during initial consideration of the ABM Treaty is as follows:

None of the Executive branch transmittal documents concerning the 1972 ABM Treaty either adverted to or meaningfully addressed the "broad-narrow" issue.[591]

---

[591]The statement in the Senate Foreign Relations Committee report on *The ABM Treaty Interpretation Resolution* that:

> [t]aken together . . . two passages [in the Letter of Submittal] unambiguously present the Treaty as banning the development, testing, and deployment of any mobile or space-based, ABM system, regardless of the technology involved.

The major White House briefing and discussion session with congressional leaders about the ABM Treaty and the Interim Agreement, held on June 15, 1972, by Dr. Henry Kissinger, Assistant to the President for National Security Affairs, neither adverted to nor meaningfully addressed the "broad-narrow" issue.

Neither Secretary of State William P. Rogers nor Ambassador Gerard C. Smith, as the lead Administration witnesses, either adverted to or clearly addressed the "broad-narrow" issue in their prepared written testimony on the Treaty. Ambassador Smith had at least four opportunities during exchanges within committee hearings to clarify the "broad-narrow" issue but did not definitively do so. At least three of these exchanges, however, one before the Senate Foreign Relations Committee and two before the Senate Armed Services Committee, can be fairly characterized at least as "ambiguous but leaning toward the `broad' interpretation." None even lean toward the "narrow" interpretation.

On no occasion in any Senate or House forum during initial consideration of the 1972 ABM Treaty does any White House, NSC, State Department, ACDA, or participating member of the SALT Delegation, either make a statement or participate in an exchange that can be fairly regarded as even leaning toward the "narrow" interpretation.

No administration spokesman participated in any exchange before the Senate committee with principal jurisdiction over the ABM Treaty, the Senate Foreign Relations Committee, that can be fairly regarded as even leaning toward the "narrow" interpretation. The only administration witness before the Senate Foreign Relations Committee that can be reasonably regarded as having addressed the issue, Ambassador Gerard C. Smith, made a statement that can at least be regarded as "ambiguous but leaning toward the `broad' interpretation." Ambassador Smith, the head of the United States SALT I Delegation, was testifying with the Secretary of State and was accompanied by senior members of the United States SALT I Delegation.

Only one administration spokesman, General Bruce Palmer, Acting Chief of Staff of the Army, participated in any Senate or House statement or exchange that can clearly be regarded as unambiguous for the "narrow" interpretation. That exchange before the Senate Armed Services Committee was seemingly at variance with an earlier exchange participated in by General Palmer

---

is a considerable exaggeration. *The ABM Treaty Interpretation Resolution, supra* note 1, at 17. The reader is invited to compare the analysis of the submittal letter in *The ABM Treaty Interpretation Resolution, supra* note 1, at 16-17, with the analysis of that letter in this study.

before the same committee that can most reasonably be regarded as at least "ambiguous but leaning toward the `broad' interpretation." To the extent that General Palmer's testimony referred to a view of "[t]he Chiefs" on the issue, it also should be compared with the seemingly contradictory testimony of Admiral Thomas H. Moorer before the House Armed Services Committee.

No Executive branch or congressional statement before the House even leans to the "narrow" interpretation while at least three incidents, including one at least strongly tilting toward the "broad" interpretation by the Chairman of the Joint Chiefs, all tilt toward the "broad" interpretation.

Neither the Report of the Senate Foreign Relations Committee, nor the Report of the House Foreign Affairs Committee, nor the Senate Resolution of Advice and Consent, adverted to or meaningfully addressed the "broad-narrow" issue.

The total record of hearings before the Senate Foreign Relations Committee, the committee with principal jurisdiction over the Treaty, shows that the issue received only incidental attention before that committee. Of the only two exchanges seeming to at least lean toward one or another interpretation, Senator Buckley, in testimony to the Committee in opposition to the Treaty, seemed to clearly reflect the "narrow" interpretation, and Ambassador Smith, accompanied by other senior SALT I Delegation members and in an exchange in which Secretary of State Rogers was also present, made a remark that can at minimum be regarded as "ambiguous but leaning toward the `broad' interpretation." Thus, the record of hearings before the Senate committee with the principal jurisdiction over the Treaty was sparse on the issue and at least somewhat mixed, certainly so if the testimony of the principal United States negotiator--with the Secretary of State present--is to receive greater weight than that of a Senator in opposition to the Treaty.

The record of hearings before the Senate Armed Services Committee shows approximately eight exchanges involving Executive branch spokesmen that can reasonably be regarded as addressing the "broad-narrow" issue and that at least lean toward one or the other interpretation in the "broad-narrow" debate. Of these, two exchanges involve Ambassador Gerard C. Smith, the head of the United States SALT I Delegation and lead administration witness on the ABM Treaty, and both can most fairly be characterized at least as "ambiguous but leaning toward the `broad' interpretation." Two exchanges (one of which was additional information interposed for the record) involve Dr. John Foster, Jr., Director of Defense Research and Engineering, and both might be regarded as "ambiguous but leans toward the `narrow' interpretation." Two exchanges involve General Bruce Palmer, Acting Chief of Staff of the Army, with the first of these at least "leaning toward the `broad' interpretation" and the second unambiguous for the "narrow" interpretation. One exchange involves General Ryan in the second of these Palmer incidents which can be reasonably characterized as "ambiguous: leans to `narrow.'" And the last is a written response to Senator Goldwater from the Department of Defense that is most reasonably viewed as "ambiguous but leans toward the `narrow' interpretation." These exchanges also demonstrate that Senator Jackson probably believes that the "narrow" interpretation is correct. Indeed, it is possible that his assumption that the "narrow" interpretation is correct may be one factor in the exchanges with Dr. Foster, General Palmer and General Ryan in which they respectively "leaned toward," "unambiguously adopted," and "leaned toward" the "narrow" interpretation. Senator Jackson, after all, was a formidable questioner; and one knowledgeable observer has suggested that he was leading the witnesses. Indeed, it is striking to note that all three administration witnesses at least leaning toward the "narrow" interpretation were participating in an exchange with Senator Jackson. The overall "box score" of administration witnesses or statements on the "broad versus narrow" issue before the Senate Armed Services Committee was three exchanges at least tilting toward the "broad" interpretation, including two of these from the head of the SALT I Delegation, Ambassador Gerard C. Smith, and five exchanges at least tilting toward the "narrow" interpretation, including the one unambiguous statement for the "narrow" interpretation and one written response for the record and an additional information for the record both from DOD leaning toward the "narrow" interpretation.

The record of minor hearings before the Senate Appropriations Committee shows no statements or exchanges even leaning toward one or another interpretation on the "broad-narrow" issue.

The record of the general "floor" debate in the Senate shows that the "broad-narrow" issue was only sparsely addressed, with Senator Buckley, an opponent of the Treaty, reflecting an unambiguous "narrow" interpretation, Senator Fong making a statement that can be reasonably regarded as "ambiguous but leans toward the `broad' interpretation," and Senator Thurmond making a statement that can be reasonably regarded as "ambiguous but leaning to the `narrow' interpretation." It is not known and cannot be known from the record in these cases whether the critical portions of the statements were or were not actually made during "floor" debate or whether they were subsequently inserted in the record as "revised and extended" remarks.

As an indication of the extent to which clear answers were lacking on the "broad-narrow" issue during overall Senate consideration of the ABM Treaty, on at least nineteen occasions that could have clarified the issue during Senate consideration, an exchange, statement or report can most reasonably be characterized only as "ambiguous neutral or does not address" and does not tilt for either "broad" or "narrow" interpretation.

With respect to reasonably clear indications from the overall record of views by members of the consenting Senate as to the "broad-narrow" issue, the record shows that Senator Buckley, an opponent of the treaty, unambiguously articulated the "narrow" interpretation; Senator Jackson, one of the generally most knowledgeable members of the Senate in defense matters, unambiguously articulated the "narrow" interpretation on two occasions (but had one involvement leaning toward the "broad" interpretation); Senator Goldwater was involved in exchanges in which he seemed variously to lean toward both "broad" and "narrow" interpretations (two exchanges leaning toward "broad" and one toward "narrow"); Senator Thurmond (in "floor" debate) seemed to lean toward the "narrow" interpretation and Senators Dominick and Fong (in "floor" debate) seemed to lean toward the "broad" interpretation.

The only unambiguous statements by either senators or Executive branch witnesses for the "narrow" interpretation not occurring in the Senate Armed Services Committee hearing or hearing record were two statements by Senator Buckley, an opponent of the Treaty, in his testimony before the Senate Foreign Relations Committee and in general "floor debate."

With respect to the House of Representatives, initial consideration of the "broad-narrow" issue before the House shows only three statements, exchanges or reports that can reasonably be regarded as tilting toward either "broad" or "narrow" interpretation. That is, first, a remark by Admiral Thomas H. Moorer, the Chairman of the Joint Chiefs of Staff, in an exchange with Congressman Whitehurst during hearings before the House Armed Services Committee. The remark of Admiral Moorer in that exchange probably is most fairly characterized as "ambiguous but leans toward the `broad' interpretation" but it can be reasonably characterized as simply supporting the "broad" interpretation. Second, a question posed by Congressman Stratton for Secretary of Defense Melvin Laird during hearings before the House Armed Services Committee that can be characterized as "ambiguous: leans to `broad.'" And third, a staff memorandum prepared for the members of the House Armed Services Committee and inserted in the record that can be at least arguably characterized as "ambiguous: leans to `broad.'"

With respect to the congressional record as a whole, it can also be reasonably argued that the only clearly unambiguous statements in the record support the "narrow" interpretation. These would be two statements by Senator

Buckley, remarks during questioning of witnesses by Senator Jackson, and remarks in response to Senator Jackson's questioning by General Bruce Palmer, Acting Chief of Staff of the Army.

It should also be noted with respect to the congressional record as a whole that whatever its legal relevance in an overall standard of interpretation, there seems to be no evidence in the record that the Senate *or even any member thereof or Executive branch spokesman* intended that the ABM Treaty should receive Senate advice and consent *conditioned* on adoption of the "narrow" interpretation under national law regardless of the correct international interpretation of the ABM Treaty. Indeed, of the unambiguous statements in the record reflecting the "narrow" interpretation, apparently from only three persons, Senator Buckley opposed the Treaty in significant measure because of what he believed were its restrictions on "futures"; as will be seen in the next section, Senator Jackson was the principal sponsor of a relatively contemporaneous amendment to an authorizing resolution on the SALT I Interim Agreement *which included the language "Congress recognizes the principle of United States-Soviet Union equality reflected in the antiballistic missile treaty"*; and General Palmer neither suggested *conditioning* the treaty on the "narrow" interpretation nor was in a position to significantly reflect a general *Senate* intent to do so. It is at least highly likely that all three persons would have emphatically rejected any suggestion that the "narrow" interpretation should be made binding on the United States as a "domestic condition" of Senate advice and consent regardless of whether it were binding on the Soviet Union.[592]

---

[592]It might be noted with respect to appraisal of the overall record of Senate consideration of the ABM Treaty of relevance to the "broad-narrow" issue, that Judge Abraham D. Sofaer, the Legal Adviser of the Department of State, writes in a forthcoming commentary in the *University of Pennsylvania Law Review* that "the Senate record contains no formal or informal `statement of understanding' that indicates the Senate gave its advice and consent `on the basis of' the `restrictive interpretation' of the ABM Treaty." Sofaer, *supra* note 444, at 1442 (quoted from page proofs subject to final editing). The broader context of Judge Sofaer's conclusion is as follows:

> These were the standards applied in my office's study of the Senate record of advice and consent to the ABM Treaty. We concluded, and it is irrefutable, that the Senate record contains no formal or informal "statement of understanding" that indicates the Senate gave its advice and consent "on the basis of" the "restrictive interpretation" of the ABM Treaty. We did find "indications" in the record -- in Executive testimony and statements of Senators -- that support the restrictive interpretation, along with indications that cast doubt upon that interpretation, or

2. Relevant issues in contemporaneous initial congressional consideration of the SALT I Agreements as a whole

The 1972 ABM Treaty and the SALT I Interim Agreement were transmitted to the Congress as a SALT I package by President Nixon on June 13, 1972. The Senate consented to the ABM Treaty on August 3, 1972, after only one day of general "floor" debate. A principal issue in the debate about the ABM Treaty, at least as reflected in the Senate Foreign Relations Committee hearings and report, was whether the United States should deploy an ABM system around the national capital as permitted by the Treaty.[593] Congress as a

---

> support a broader interpretation. My study concluded that these indications, taken in the context of the record as a whole, were insufficient to establish a duty to respect the restrictive interpretation under domestic law, but were sufficient to require the President to decide, in accordance with the Restatement, whether "they represent a general understanding by the Senate" of the restrictive interpretation. If he found that they did, he "must respect them in good faith." I strongly believe that the Legal Adviser should not preclude the President from exercising the power to decide issues of this sort. In less contentious contexts, I have no doubt that the Senate, and scholars such as Professor Koplow, would readily acquiesce to the view that a Senate record, such as the one developed for the ABM Treaty, is not binding as a matter of law. The issue was briefly addressed by the Senate and was unlikely to have affected the outcome (the vote on advice and consent was 88 to 2).

Id. Similarly, in a conversation of June 14, 1989, with the author of this study, Colonel A. Richard Richstein, who served as ACDA General Counsel from 1981-1983, indicated that he believed the record of initial Senate consideration of the ABM Treaty did not as a whole clearly reflect the "narrow" interpretation, and that at the time several senators had requested, but never received, an article-by-article legal analysis of the Treaty.

[593]It can be argued that this debate reflected a significant failure of United States policy with respect to the ABM Treaty. That is, if the United States was not prepared, politically or otherwise, to deploy around the national capital, should it have negotiated an agreement permitting deployment at two sites? This issue, of course, is complex, involving not only United States interests but also Soviet concerns and differing initial programs for ABM deployment around the national capital for the Soviet Union and around ICBM silo launchers for the United States. Ultimately, however, arms control agreements should be both reciprocal and perceived as reciprocal for maximum long term viability.

whole, by joint resolution of September 30, 1972, authorized the President "to approve on behalf of the United States" the SALT I Interim Agreement with respect to the limitation of strategic offensive arms. The general "floor" debate on the Interim Agreement lasted sixteen days in the Senate.

The joint resolution, approved September 30, 1972,[594] was a product of a revised House Joint Resolution 1227, Senate Joint Resolution 241, and various Senate amendments. The most important of these Senate amendments leading to the joint resolution of September 30, was the so-called "Jackson Amendment." The Jackson Amendment was originally introduced on August 7, 1972, co-sponsored by 24 senators, including Senators Jackson, Buckley, Fong, Thurmond and Hollings.[595] A "revised" Jackson Amendment of September 13, 1972, was co-sponsored by 44 senators, including Senators Jackson, Buckley, Dole, Dominick, Ervin, Fong, Goldwater, Hollings, Magnuson, Stennis, Stevens, Thurmond and Tower.[596] The Jackson Amendment was principally aimed at ensuring United States-Soviet equality in future SALT treaty limits in reaction to the unequal limits within the Interim Agreement and at ensuring a vigorous research and development program for a prudent strategic posture. Both the original and revised Jackson amendments contained the following relevant language:

> Congress recognizes the principle of United States-Soviet Union equality reflected in the antiballistic missile treaty. . . .
>
> Congress considers that the success of these agreements and the attainment of more permanent and comprehensive agreements are dependent upon the maintenance of a vigorous research and development and modernization program leading to a prudent strategic posture.

On August 18, 1972, a House-Senate conference committee withheld authorization of the Administration proposed National Capital ABM site following doubts expressed by a majority of the Senate Foreign Relations Committee in the ABM Committee Report.

[594]Pub. L. No. 92-448, 86 Stat. 746 (Sept. 30, 1972).

[595]S. Amend. 1406 to S.J. Res. 241, 92d Cong., 2d Sess. (Aug. 7, 1972).

[596]S. Amend. 1518 to S.J. Res. 241, 92d Cong., 2d Sess. (Sept. 13, 1972).

With minor amendments to this latter provision proposed by Senators Cranston and Taft and Senators Javits and Mathias and accepted by Senator Jackson, the modified Jackson Amendment was adopted on September 14 by a vote of 56-35 and ultimately became section 3 of the joint resolution of September 30, 1972. Proposals offered by Senator Muskie and Senator Fulbright, that would have softened the Jackson Amendment's principal thrust on equal limits, failed respectively by votes of 35-55 and 38-48. Following adoption of the Jackson Amendment, and several other amendments to S.J. Res. 241, the modified joint resolution was passed by the Senate on September 14, by a vote of 88-2. Following the vote, the Senate moved to insist on its amendment in conference with the House. The House agreed to the Senate amendment on September 25, by a vote of 307-4, and the joint resolution was signed into law on September 30, 1972.

It is clear that the debate surrounding the Jackson Amendment demand for equality and reciprocity in United States-Soviet arms control agreements and maintenance of a vigorous research and development program for a prudent strategic posture was the principal congressional debate in consideration of the overall SALT I ABM Treaty-Interim Agreement package.[597]

It is also clear that that debate was premised on the view that the ABM Treaty itself reflected a principle of equality, equal limits, or parity; that that principle was regarded as important; and that a vigorous program of research and development under the Treaty was also regarded as important. Moreover, much of the relevant debate on the Jackson Amendment occurred prior to the August 3rd Senate vote on advice and consent to the ABM Treaty during simultaneous Senate consideration of the ABM Treaty and the Interim Agreement. Thus, on August 3rd before the Senate vote on the ABM Treaty, Senator Allott, stating his intention to support both the ABM Treaty and the Interim Agreement being considered, also supported the Jackson Amendment, of which he was a cosponsor, saying:

> This language [of the Jackson Amendment] addresses three matters.
>
> First, it endorses the objective of equality in the limits to be negotiated in the second phase of SALT. It urges general

[597]On the legislative history of the "Jackson Amendment," *see generally Legislative History of the Committee on Foreign Relations, 92d* Cong. 29, 30-34 (Comm. Print March 1973); *Strategic Arms Limitation Talks (SALT); Legislative History of the Jackson Amendment, 1972, prepared by the office of Senator Henry M. Jackson* (undated).

> application of *the principle of equality that underlies the ABM Treaty*.
>
> Second, the amendment stipulates that any Soviet action or deployment endangering the strategic deterrent forces of the United States would be contrary to our supreme national interests.
>
> Third, the amendment expresses the view of Congress that pending a more comprehensive and permanent agreement, and in order to facilitate achieving such an agreement, *the United States should maintain a sound national program of research and development and modernization relevant to a prudent strategic posture.* This language is not directed at any specific procurement item.
>
> The language of this amendment constitutes a constructive exercise of congressional responsibility in helping set basic policy for this Nation. This is certainly an appropriate moment for Congress to express itself. [118 *Cong. Rec.* 26,685 (1972) (statement of Sen. Allott) (emphasis added).]

Senator Jackson spoke at length during the August 3rd debate and said in his segment on "The Objective of Equal Limits in SALT II":

> In the treaty covering anti-ballistic-missile defenses *we and the Soviets have clearly established the principle of equal limits on both countries. . . .* Even though our defense requirements differed from those of the Soviets and even though our ABM program had a momentum that the Soviet program lacked, *we and they have undertaken to live by identical limitations. . . .*
>
> It is my view, Mr. President, *that the principle of equality reflected in the ABM treaty* ought properly to be applied to a future treaty on offensive systems as well. I am confident that the Senate of the United States would not wish to see this country undertake, in an international treaty having the force and weight of the Constitution itself, ceilings on U.S. defenses that are greatly inferior to the levels permitted for the Soviet Union. [118 *Cong. Rec.* 26,693 (1972) (statement of Sen. Jackson) (emphasis added).]

And on "Research, Development and Modernization," Senator Jackson said:

> *I know that my colleagues in both parties have supported and will continue to support those essential programs of research and development and force modernization necessary to enable the United States to maintain a prudent strategic posture. Our resolution merely articulates this commitment in the context of the continuing SALT deliberations.* It is not our intention to bind anyone to any particular procurement item in advance. [118 Cong. Rec. 26,694 (1972) (statement of Sen. Jackson) (emphasis added).]

Senator Jackson went on to state in an exchange with Senator Fulbright: "*We agreed on parity on the ABM*" [118 *Cong. Rec.* 26,695 (1972) (emphasis added)]. And Senator Jackson and Senator Pastore exchanged these remarks:

> Mr. JACKSON. I do not have serious doubts [about the interim agreement] and I can support it if we proceed as we go into SALT II on the basis that we are going to ask for parity on strategic arms.
>
> Mr. PASTORE. Would we not be fools if we did not?
>
> Mr. JACKSON. Of course. That is what my amendment says. That is what my proposal involves--parity.
>
> Mr. PASTORE. I do not object to that. It goes without saying we do not have to make an hour's speech to be sure we have to have parity.
>
> Mr. JACKSON. That is what I am arguing about.
>
> Mr. PASTORE. That is what I am arguing about.
>
> Mr. JACKSON. Then, we are in agreement. [118 *Cong. Rec.* 26,696 (1972).]

Also supporting the ABM Treaty and "confident that the United States will be able to maintain a parity with the Soviets," Senator Tower stated during the debate:

> I am fully satisfied that the SALT treaty and agreement should be approved and I lend my support to that end.
>
> In approving the treaty and agreement, however, we must not lose sight of one basic truth. *We have not and must not*

> *accept less than parity with the Soviet Union.* [118 *Cong. Rec.* 26,709 (1972) (statement of Sen. Tower) (emphasis added).]

Senator Allen, one of the two senators who voted against ratification of the ABM Treaty, stated:

> The reasons for my decision are simple and straightforward.
>
> With respect to the treaty, I cannot review the past record of Russia's indifference to treaty obligations with any degree of confidence. . . .
>
> . . . .
>
> . . . There is reason to believe that the United States has the scientific and technological capability of providing adequate defense against nuclear attack, and I consider it immoral and an invitation to nuclear blackmail not to develop defenses against nuclear attack. [118 *Cong. Rec.* 26,765, 26,766 (1972) (statement of Sen. Allen).]

Following Senator Allen's statement, Senator Humphrey, in a speech intended "to challenge the skeptics" of the SALT agreements, emphasized the stabilizing influence of those agreements, stating:

> What is more important is the balance. *What is more important is the degree of equality or parity which you can have so that you can be assured of your own security.* [118 Cong. Rec. 26,767 (1972) (statement of Sen. Humphrey) (emphasis added).]

The final vote on Senate advice and consent to the ratification of the ABM Treaty on August 3, 1972, was 88-2, with Senators Allen and Buckley voting nay [118 *Cong. Rec.* 26,770 (1972)].

Subsequent to the Senate vote on advice and consent to the ABM Treaty, in "Extensions of Remarks" for August 15, 1972, in the House of Representatives, the Honorable Roman C. Pucinski endorsed and placed in the Record speeches made by Senator Jackson on the Jackson Amendment, which include:

> In insisting on equality in any treaty to [e]merge from SALT II, I am certain I am speaking for the good sense of the overwhelming majority of the American people. *We should*

support the principle of equality on which the ABM treaty is based by applying it to offensive systems as well. . . .

. . . .

I am confident that the Senate will give a solid vote of approval to this amendment expressing our determination to secure a stable future strategic relationship with the Soviet Union. [118 *Cong. Rec.* 28,328 (1972) (reprinted "Statement of Senator Henry M. Jackson on Amendment to Senate Joint Resolution 241") (emphasis added).]

And:

Mr. President, my amendment, which is broadly co-sponsored by a bipartisan group of Senators, deals with three issues: (1) the threat to the survivability of the U.S. strategic deterrent under the interim agreement; (2) the need for equality in any follow-up agreement on offensive intercontinental strategic weapons; and (3) the need for research, development and force modernization. These are issues that I have thoroughly discussed with the Administration, with the witnesses before the Armed Services Committee and, in many cases, with my colleagues in the Senate. It is my firm conviction that we ought to state our views with respect to these issues and I believe my amendment is a medium for the expression of views that I am confident are shared by a majority of my colleagues.

. . . .

. . . I believe that we ought to insist *that the principle that was applied in the case of the ABM treaty--the principle of equality* on which the Russians insisted--ought to be applied to a treaty on offensive weapons.

. . . .

Chief of Naval Operations, Admiral Zumwalt, testified:

"It is my view that in SALT II, we must achieve an equality of numbers. Just as the Soviets insisted on symmetry with regard to the ABM treaty, if we are going to go into a permament [sic] treaty on the strategic side, I think we absolutely must insist on symmetry."

> . . . .
>
> My amendment provides the Senate with an opportunity to declare itself in favor of equality in a follow-on agreement and I am certain that in view of the basic good sense of that position and the overwhelming testimony before us we will act to affirm it.
>
> . . . .
>
> *My amendment, in its final sentences, simply points to the need for a vigorous program of research, development and modernization leading to a prudent strategic posture. . . . [I]t is useful for the Senate to go on record to the effect that we must continue our efforts in the research, development and modernization area,* . . . . [118 Cong. Rec. 28,328, 28,330, 28,331, 28,332 (1972) (reprinted "The Senate and the Interim Agreement (Statement of Senator Henry M. Jackson)") (emphasis added).]

In view of this explicit record of concern for *both* equality of obligation *and* maintenance of a vigorous program of research and development, *and* the expressed conviction that the ABM Treaty was based on "the principle of equality," all of which concerns and conviction were expressed *during* the debate on the ABM Treaty, is it reasonable to believe that two-thirds of the members of the Senate--and particularly Senator Jackson--intended to *condition* advice and consent for the ABM Treaty on the "narrow" interpretation, even if that interpretation were not legally binding on the Soviet Union and could thus work an *unequal* restraint on the United States *in development*?

In connection with this debate it should be noted that ultimately the Senate by a vote of 88-2 and the House by a vote of 307-4 adopted language stating:

> Congress recognizes the principle of United States-Soviet Union equality reflected in the antiballistic missile treaty. . . .

And:

> Congress considers that the success of these agreements and the attainment of more permanent and comprehensive agreements are dependent upon the maintenance under present world

> conditions of a vigorous research and development and modernization program as required by a prudent strategic posture.

These votes, coming less than six weeks and eight weeks respectively after Senate consent to the ABM Treaty, and on an issue that began the major SALT I congressional debate the very day of Senate approval of the ABM Treaty, provide substantial evidence that Congress as a whole believed that the ABM Treaty was rooted in equality of obligation and attached importance to that equality, and, moreover, that Congress as a whole attached importance to a vigorous United States program of research, development and modernization. It should also be noted in connection with the Jackson Amendment that all senators involved in an exchange on the "broad-narrow" issue even leaning toward either interpretation, were co-sponsors of the revised amendment, including its judgments about the importance of both equality of obligation and a vigorous program of research, development and modernization. That is, of particular importance, Senators Jackson, Buckley, Goldwater and Thurmond, who may be the only Senators at any time at least leaning toward a "narrow" interpretation in their remarks, were co-sponsors of this resolution. Indeed, of these, Senators Jackson, Buckley, and Thurmond were even co-sponsors of the original Jackson Amendment on August 7, 1972. And, of course, Senator Jackson, who figured so prominently in many of the exchanges on the "broad-narrow" issue within the Senate Armed Services Committee hearings, was the principal initiator and sponsor of the Amendment.

In view of the principal--and double--thrust of the Jackson Amendment, it seems particularly unlikely that the overall intent of the co-sponsors of the Jackson Amendment, and, by virtue of overwhelming congressional passage of the joint resolution embodying the Jackson Amendment, the intent of the Congress as a whole as well as of the Senate individually, could be reasonably said to be to bind the United States to an obligation limiting important future United States strategic development and testing under any circumstances in which the Soviet Union had not accepted the same obligation. Indeed, it is likely that Senator Jackson, who sponsored the Jackson Amendment, and Senator Buckley, who both co-sponsored the Amendment and voted against the ABM Treaty, would have been appalled at an attribution of an intent to them that the United States should be unilaterally bound on such an obligation involving development and testing of strategic systems in a setting where an analysis of the negotiating record were to show that the Soviet Union was not bound.

With respect to the Jackson Amendment as part of an overall related context in which the intention of the Senate or the Congress may be more completely assessed, it should be noted that in his prepared statement during the 1987 joint hearings on *The ABM Treaty and the Constitution*, Senator Hollings, a co-sponsor of the original and revised Jackson Amendment, says of that context:

> I repeat, at the time of the ABM Treaty ratification, no attention was given to a narrow or a broad interpretation. The Treaty was represented as being balanced and verifiable--it sought only to control those things that could be controlled. At the time of the ratification of the Treaty, the discussion and debate for all practical purposes was carried on off the floor and focused almost exclusively on SALT I. We were talking about future technologies and strategies. In connection with SALT I, the Jackson Amendment of August 7, provided:
>
> > ". . . the Congress considers that the success of these agreements and the attainment of more permanent and comprehensive agreements are dependent upon the maintenance of a vigorous research and development and modernization program leading to a prudent strategic posture."
>
> As I saw it, Mr. President, that was the key point to the Jackson amendment.[598]

---

[598]"Prepared Statement of Senator Ernest F. Hollings," *supra* note 212, at 442, 449.

Relevant statements evidencing a consistent Administration stance of supporting a vigorous research and development program may be found in concurrent hearings before varied Senate committees. See "Statement of Adm. Thomas H. Moorer, U.S. Navy, Chairman, Joint Chiefs of Staff; Accompanied by Lt. Gen. Royal S. Allison, U.S. Air Force, Assistant to the Chairman for Strategic Arms Negotiations, and Col. Robert M. Lucy, U.S. Marine Corps, Legal Adviser, Legislative Assistant to the Chairman, JCS" (June 21, 1972), in *Strategic Arms Limitation Agreements: Hearings Before the Senate Comm. on Foreign Relations*, 92d Cong., 2d Sess. 65, 69-70 (1972), where, in the section "Actions Required Now," Admiral Moorer describes important "assurances," which are quoted in part in this section of the study.

See also Fiscal Year 1973 Authorization for Military Procurement, Research and

---

Development, Construction Authorization for the Safeguard ABM and Active Duty and Selected Reserve Strengths: Hearings Before the Senate Comm. on Armed Services, 92d Cong., 2d Sess., on S. 3108, Addendum No. 1, Amended Military Authorization Request Related to Strategic Arms Limitation Agreement (June 6, 22; July 21 and 26, 1972) (U.S. Gov't Printing Office 1972) [hereinafter Senate Armed Services Committee Hearings on *Amended Military Authorization Request Related to Strategic Arms Limitation Agreement*]. See particularly from these hearings pages 4230, 4195, 4245, 4271-72, and 4220-22, excerpts of which will be considered in this section of the study.

It might also be noted that on October 16, 1972, Senator Margaret Chase-Smith inserted in the record a previous statement and an editorial sympathetic to laser defense research. The relevant entry, which does not discuss the ABM Treaty, provides:

> THE IMPORTANCE OF RESEARCH FOR DEFENSE
>
> Mrs. SMITH. Mr. President, on August 6, 1969, when I led the fight in the Senate against the Safeguard ABM system and those of us who opposed it by the record 51 to 50 vote on which we lost, I said, among other things:
>
>> Instead, I have greater confidence and faith in the ability of our scientists to develop a far more effective and far less costly system than the proposed ABM system.
>>
>> I am sure that it is no breach of security when I say that I have great hopes that before too long a sufficiently powerful laser will be developed for the defense not only of our missile sites but as well of our people and our cities.
>
> So it was with great interest that I read the front page editorial of the issue of the Sunday Oklahoman of October 8, 1972, for in reporting that a laser beam shot from the earth had partially melted a rock on the moon, this newspaper rightly stressed the importance of research for defense and the folly and risk of cutting such funds. Finding such support for my prediction of more than 3 years ago and of my warning this year and in past years against cutting research for defense, I ask unanimous consent to have printed in the RECORD pertinent portions of that editorial, and I invite the close and serious attention of everyone to these editorial observations.
>
> There being no objection, the editorial was ordered to be printed in the RECORD, as follows:
>
> [From the Sunday Oklahoman, Oct. 8, 1972]
>
> TO DESTROY MISSILES
>
> On the last trip of our astronauts to the moon, they found on a moon

The Jackson Amendment is certainly subject to a variety of interpretive arguments as it relates to overall Senate intent on the "broad-narrow" matter. It

---

mountain a rock which had been partially melted by a laser beam shot at the speed of light by American scientists 240,000 miles away. The mission of the astronauts was to find this rock and bring it back to our research scientists, which they did.

If a laser beam from the earth can melt a rock on the moon, why can't it destroy missiles in silos or missiles launched through the air? The answer is, it can.

About four years ago observers watched a Russian vehicle in space which overtook another Russian vehicle orbiting around the earth and suddenly, without firing a shot or causing an explosion, the target vehicle disintegrated and portions of it fell in Oklahoma and some in Kansas. These were recovered and sent to White Sands for scientists to examine. Many believe the object was struck down instantaneously by a laser beam.

Laser beams can melt and burn up the hardest steel. They can burn great holes in the thickest and strongest steel vault doors in any bank in America.

The research laboratories of our Department of Defense are known to be working constantly with lasers. Are they up with Russia or two years behind? If Russia can launch satellites or high flying airplanes capable of projecting laser beams, they could destroy missiles in our Minuteman silos or submarines in ports. Laser beans [sic] could destroy and knock down and perhaps explode missiles aimed at Russian targets. This includes Polaris missiles from our submarines. They might be destroyed over the Atlantic or fall in England or West Germany, destroying cities and populations with radiation.

For a good many months Russia has been building a much larger launching structure than used heretofore by the twenty-five megaton missiles. Perhaps the new structures are for powerful laser projectors which could knock down missiles long before they reached the Russian border.

Recently a Russian admiral announced to the world that no ship of any foreign country could now be safe in any ocean anywhere in the world. The question is, did he mean that Russian naval ships are now equipped with powerful laser projectors that could destroy any American naval vessel by a flash of laser power that could explode the ammunition of the ship and blow it to smithereens? Nothing would be left except floating fragments. If the American ship was an aircraft carrier and fifty of its planes were in the air, the laser beams could then slap down some of those planes like so many flies.

Research for Defense is vital for the survival of our country.

118 *Cong. Rec.* 36,632-33 (1972).

is, however, an important part of the immediate context surrounding Senate approval of the SALT I package, including the ABM Treaty, and, as such, must be considered in any complete effort at assessing the Senate or congressional intent on the "broad-narrow" issue.

Consistent with the Jackson Amendment, there is also evidence, reflected in the record of Senate consideration of the ABM Treaty, that the Executive branch presented the ABM Treaty to the Senate in a context supporting a vigorous research and development program under the Treaty. Thus, for example, in the Senate Armed Services Committee hearings on *Amended Military Authorization Request Related to Strategic Arms Limitation Agreement*, during testimony by Secretary of Defense Melvin R. Laird on June 6, 1972, a prepared question from Senator Goldwater was answered by the Department of Defense as follows:

> *Question. Will there be a tendency on the part of Defense or other interests to overinterpret SAL by making cuts in other areas such as the B-1, ULMS, space, R. & D., et cetera. Does the administration agree to pursue vigorous R. & D. in all areas not precluded?*
>
> Answer. While I cannot speak for other interests, we intend to pursue a vigorous program in all areas important to national security, including those areas as appropriate in which R. & D. is not prohibited by the agreements[.]

Note that Senator Goldwater seemed concerned that SALT I not be "overinterpreted" and that R. & D. would be pursued "in all areas not precluded." And, the Department of Defense response talked of "a vigorous program . . . including those areas as appropriate in which R. & D. *is not prohibited by the agreements*" (emphasis added). Secretary of Defense Melvin R. Laird told the Senate Armed Services Committee: Although ABM deployments will be limited to two sites--Grand Forks, N. Dak., and the National Capital area--we can and must continue permitted ABM research, development, test, and evaluation programs in order to preserve future options and to stay abreast of ABM technology.

> We will continue the site defense program, making modifications to accelerate its development and testing. Without further constraints on Soviet offensive programs, which could be achieved in follow-on negotiations but which do not exist now, we

need this hedge for insuring the survivability of our land-based ICBMs.

We will vigorously pursue a comprehensive ABM technology program. This program will provide knowledge of ABM technology potential that will help us understand better Soviet ABM developments, help us insure adequate penetration capability for U.S. offensive missiles, and examine ABM development options that might be exercised if permitted by future agreements, or if otherwise necessary.

Similarly, a prepared question submitted for the record by Senator McIntyre during Secretary Laird's testimony was answered as follows by the Department of Defense:

Question. When Dr. Foster appeared before the committee in support of the fiscal year 1973 request for R & D, he stated that the increase in the fiscal year 1973 request of $1.2 billion over the appropriation for FY '72 was sufficient to eliminate the remaining apparent divergence in the relative technology efforts of the two countries. He concluded that the amount requested would help restore the momentum needed to maintain our security. Isn't it therefore inconsistent to increase R & D funds, particularly when one of the objectives of SAL is to reduce military expenditures?

Answer. There is no inconsistency to an increase in R&D funds, particularly since neither agreement [deleted] places any constraints on modernization of existing stragetic [sic] defensive systems covered by the Interim Agreement. Moreover, the Interim Agreement places no limitations or constraints on certain important strategic offensive systems which are to be the subject of discussion in the follow-on negotiations. Inasmuch as the major objective of SALT is to enhance--and not reduce--the security of the U.S., the need for a vigorous R&D program, as permitted by the two agreements, becomes even more important in view of the numerical imbalance in the quantitative limitations contained in the Interim Agreement.

It is imperative that the level of effort in research and development be sufficient to allow us to maintain technological superiority.

And Admiral Thomas H. Moorer, Chairman of the Joint Chiefs of Staff, accompanied by Lt. General Royal S. Allison and Colonel Robert M. Lucy, told the Senate Foreign Relations Committee during hearings on *Strategic Arms Limitation Agreements* on June 21, 1972, that:

> The Joint Chiefs of Staff, therefore, believe that action to achieve the following assurances must be taken now if the United States is to guard against a degradation of its national security posture:
>
> . . . .
>
> *Assurance II.*--"Aggressive Improvements and Modernization Programs."
>
> Maximize strategic capabilities within the constraints established by the ABM treaty and the interim offensive agreement.
>
> Plan for rapid augmentation of strategic forces beyond the constraints of the treaty and agreement to be made in the event of abrogation, withdrawal, or collapse of negotiations.
>
> *Assurance III.*--"Vigorous Research and Development Programs."
>
> Maintain weapons systems technological superiority.
>
> Continue testing to insure the effectiveness of new and existing nuclear weapons systems.

In a "Summary" to his statement before the Committee on June 22, 1989, Dr. John S. Foster, Jr., Director of Defense Research and Engineering, stated:

> It is essential . . . that support of these agreements be accompanied by approval of the fiscal year 1973 budget request, together with adjustments including the NCA defense and site defense. Other adjustments at this time include programs in the areas of submarine-launched cruise missile development, accelerated bomber rebasing, augmentation of verification capabilities, improved RV's for ICBM's and SLBM's, and advanced technology for command, control, and communications. Such actions are essential to maintain the sufficiency of our forces during the course of the agreements, to maintain the viability of those agreements, and to maintain the position of strength that we must have for the follow-on negotiations to be successful. In particular, I must reemphasize that in my view, the imbalanced

> numerical limitations on offensive missile forces can be accepted only if we maintain our present technological lead. The programs that we have requested, together with a strong technological program in both offensive and defensive systems, are necessary to maintain U.S. security.

It may also be relevant that an exchange between Secretary Laird and Senator Jackson before the Senate Armed Services Committee considering the *Amended Military Authorization Request Related to Strategic Arms Limitation Agreement*, on June 6, 1972, one week prior to formal submission of the ABM Treaty to the Senate, seems to suggest an Administration sensitivity about a charge that a laser contract may have been cancelled as a result of the ABM Treaty. This exchange, presented and discussed in full in section III(E) of this study, and which in its totality seems simply ambiguous on the "broad-narrow" issue, includes the following concerning a charge of cancellation of a laser contract:

> Senator JACKSON. Do I understand that there is no prohibition in any of the understandings--I can't find it in the treaty--on research, tests, and development for the ABM?
>
> Secretary LAIRD. Yes, in the Safeguard and site defense programs, Senator Jackson. I have been concerned about the statements which you made about a laser contract canceled under my direction. I can assure you that there has been no such contract canceled as far as the Army is concerned. When you made the statement I immediately contacted the Army. The Army reports that no laser program has been canceled. The reports about contract cancellation are in error. I had directed the Secretary of the Army to verify this statement with every one of his research agencies coast to coast, east and west, and north and south.
>
> Senator JACKSON. And that includes theoretical research studies?
>
> Secretary LAIRD. There may have been some cancellations on various theoretical research studies unrelated way prior to the SAL agreement. I think you are referring to a program which is known as HIT. That program was changed, and it was that kind of a research contract. But it had nothing to do with a laser contract.
>
> Senator JACKSON. And nothing to do with SALT?

Secretary LAIRD. It had nothing to do with any laser contract cancellation. And I guarantee, when you made the statement, I went out and went through this. And the laser contract cancellation information is in error.

3. Consideration by subsequent Congresses of the "broad-narrow" interpretation issue

As has been seen, while reasons given in support of a particular position would be entitled to weight as they are either persuasive or unpersuasive on the merits of an interpretation dispute, a subsequent Senate or a constituent unit of a subsequent Senate has no constitutional authority to give a legally binding interpretation of a treaty consented to by a prior Senate. Similarly, under normal principles of legislative history as an aid to interpretation the subsequently expressed views of individual members of a Senate or Congress on an interpretation dispute after such a dispute arises are entitled to little, if any, weight on the merits of that dispute as they are simply subsequent views of individual members of the Senate or Congress. They are, of course, largely entitled to be taken into account (or given greater or lesser weight), not as subsequent views of members of the Senate or Congress, but as the reasons given for one or another position are either persuasive or unpersuasive on the merits of an interpretation dispute. Finally, it should be noted that while Congress as a whole has authority to supersede treaty obligations of the United States--as a matter of national law--by passage of subsequent explicitly inconsistent legislation, it is not clear whether such subsequent legislation would be constitutionally effective if, in fact, its purpose is exclusively, or even principally, to interpret a treaty about which an international public law dispute has arisen, the interpretation seeks to establish an international as well as national law standard, and the setting is one in which the Executive has previously given a contrary interpretation.

Whatever the constitutional limits of congressional authority in treaty interpretation, it is clear that absent subsequent legislation compelling a particular interpretation, neither the actions of a subsequent Senate nor House alone, nor of constituent units of the Senate and House alone, nor both alone, that are not embodied in at least facially binding legislation, can have any significant legal effect on the interpretation of a treaty, apart, of course, from whatever persuasive power is present in reasons given for supporting one or another interpretation. Thus, unless enacted into law, the principal subsequent Senate and congressional actions discussed in this section[599] are relevant principally, if not exclusively, for any persuasive power that arguments given for a particular interpretation may have.

As has been seen in an earlier section of this study, the Administration initially announced the "broad" interpretation of the ABM Treaty in a "Meet the Press" interview with Robert McFarlane on NBC Television, October 6, 1985.

The first hearing on the "broad" interpretation was held on October 22, 1985, before the Subcommittee on Arms Control, International Security and Science of the House Committee on Foreign Affairs.[600] Witnesses appearing before the Committee included the Honorable Paul Nitze, Special Advisor to the President and the Secretary of State for Arms Control Matters, the Honorable Abraham D. Sofaer, Legal Adviser to the Department of State, the Honorable Gerard C. Smith, former chief of the United States Delegation to the ABM Treaty negotiations, the Honorable Ralph Earle, former Director of the United States Arms Control and Disarmament Agency, and Mr. John B. Rhinelander, former legal advisor to the ABM Treaty negotiations. Subsequent to his testimony and in response to a question posed during the hearing, the State Department Legal Adviser Abraham D. Sofaer presented to the Committee a memorandum he had prepared for Ambassador Nitze entitled "Analysis of United States and Soviet Postnegotiation Public Statements Interpreting the ABM Treaty's Application to Future Systems."[601]

The "broad-narrow" issue was addressed next in a November 12, 1985, session during general hearings on "Nuclear Strategy, Ballistic Missile Defense, and

---

[599]The full record of subsequent congressional consideration of the "broad-narrow" issue includes statements, letters and other actions not discussed in this section. This section is intended to briefly summarize the principal subsequent congressional actions in relation to the "broad-narrow" issue.

For a history and analysis of the "broad-narrow" dispute from the perspective of Senator Joseph R. Biden, Jr., Chairman of the Senate Judiciary Committee, and John B. Ritch, III, Deputy Director of the Senate Foreign Relations Committee, see their forthcoming commentary in the *University of Pennsylvania Law Review*: Biden & Ritch, supra note 263, at 1529 (reviewed from page proofs subject to final editing).

[600]*See ABM Treaty Interpretation Dispute: Hearing Before the Subcomm. on Arms Control, International Security and Science of the House Comm. on Foreign Affairs*, 99th Cong., 1st Sess., Oct. 22, 1985 (1986).

[601]Sofaer, "Analysis of United States and Soviet Postnegotiation Public Statements Interpreting the ABM Treaty's Application to Future Systems," *reprinted in* 26 *Int'l Legal Mat.* 291 (Jan. 1987).

Arms Control" before the Senate Foreign Relations Committee.[602] During these hearings the Committee heard from Ambassador Gerard C. Smith, Mr. John B. Rhinelander, and the Honorable Richard Perle, then Assistant Secretary of Defense for International Security Policy.

On November 21, 1985, the Subcommittee on Strategic and Theater Nuclear Forces of the Senate Armed Services Committee held a session of a general hearing on the Strategic Defense Initiative that discussed the "broad-narrow" issue. Witnesses included State Department Legal Adviser Abraham D. Sofaer, Ambassador Gerard C. Smith, the former chief of the United States SALT I Delegation, and Mr. John B. Rhinelander, the former legal adviser to the SALT I Delegation.[603]

On January 30, 1986, a Special Panel on Arms Control and Disarmament of the Procurement and Military Nuclear Systems Subcommittee of the House Committee on Armed Services, chaired by Congressman Beverly B. Byron, transmitted its report[604] on *Review of Arms Control and Disarmament Activities 99th Congress, 1st Session* to the Chairman of the Subcommittee, Congressman Samuel S. Stratton, who then transmitted it the same day to the Chairman of the full Committee, Congressman Les Aspin. After a seven printed page discussion of the merits of the "broad-narrow" issue and "how the issue was explained to Congress," the panel summarized its findings as follows:

> OPINIONS OF THE PANEL
>
> Comparing the text of the treaty, the statements made when the treaty was presented to the Congress, the statements

---

[602]*Commitments, Consensus and U.S. Foreign Policy: Hearings Before the Senate Comm. on Foreign Relations*, 99th Cong., 1st Sess. 535-628 (Nov. 12, 1985) (U.S. Gov't Printing Office 1986).

[603]*Strategic Defense Initiative: Hearings Before the Subcomm. on Strategic and Theater Nuclear Forces of the Senate Comm. on Armed Services,* 99th Cong., 1st Sess. 135-270 (Nov. 21, 1985) (U.S. Gov't Printing Office 1986) (hereinafter Strategic Defense Initiative Hearings).

[604]*Review of Arms Control and Disarmament Activities 99th Congress, 1st Session: Report of the Special Panel on Arms Control and Disarmament of the Subcomm. on Procurement and Military Nuclear Systems, House Comm. on Armed Services, Together with Additional Views,* 99th Cong., 1st Sess. (Comm. Print Jan. 1986) [hereinafter *Report of the Special Panel on Arms Control*].

made by those who have researched the negotiating record, and recent statements made by members of the negotiating team, the panel believes that:

(a) The following interpretation is correct:

> The ABM treaty bans the *deployment* of the advanced ABM systems, such as laser and directed energy beams, because Article III, together with "Agreed Interpretation E (sic)', [D], make clear that systems based on "other physical principles" cannot be deployed *without further* discussion, and amendment of the treaty.

(b) There is no basis for Soviet assertions that all SDI research is prohibited by the ABM treaty on the basis that the ultimate results of such research would be prohibited.

(c) The parties did not intend to ban types of ABM research, development, and testing that could not be verified by national technical means.

(d) The Senate gave its advice and consent to ratification of the ABM Treaty based on the representations of members of the Executive Branch, including the U.S. negotiating team. Those representations on the public record should be given more weight than external statements or remembrances made more than a decade after the fact.

(e) Although the weight of the evidence favors a "broad" interpretation that research, development and testing of certain SDI elements is permitted, up to the point of deployment as an ABM system or components of an ABM system, the threshold for such activities will ultimately have to be established *for both parties* either within the SCC, by treaty amendment, or by another agreement.

(f) The U.S. SDI research program as currently constructed, and as controlled by the Congress, does not violate the ABM treaty nor does it approach any reasonable threshold requiring amendment of the treaty. Notwithstanding this, the Reagan Administration has stated that the U.S. program ". . . will continue to be conducted in accordance with a restrictive interpretation of the treaty's obligations." The panel concurs in the

> caveat that followed that statement that there ". . . can be no double standard as to the way we interpret our treaty obligations vis-a-vis the interpretation the Soviets apply to those same treaty obligations. To do otherwise would outline a formula for potential disaster to our national security interests."[605]

The "Additional Comments of Representatives Nicholas Mavroules and John Spratt"[606] to this report did not specifically address the "broad-narrow" issue as such but did conclude that "there is an honest difference of opinion" as to the Panel's conclusion "that `the S.D.I. program' as now structured, will not approach the thresholds of the ABM Treaty until the `early 1990's when flight tests might begin or a decision might be made that a ballistic missile defense is in fact feasible and affordable.'"[607]

On July 25, 1986, Senator Nunn made a lengthy statement on the Senate floor concerning the "broad-narrow" issue and urging Senate access to the negotiating record and related documents.[608]

In August of 1986 the State Department Legal Adviser's Office submitted to the Senate a memorandum analyzing the ABM Treaty negotiating record with respect to the "broad-narrow" dispute, and also transmitted to the Senate excerpts from the negotiating record.

On December 1, 1986, following submission to the Senate of the Sofaer memorandum on the negotiating record of the "broad-narrow" issue and excerpts from the negotiating record, Senator Carl Levin sent a detailed letter to Secretary of State George Shultz disputing the interpretation of Judge Sofaer and urging that the Administration authorize a new and independent review of the ABM Treaty.[609] The letter says in full:

---

[605]*Id.* at 39-40.

[606]*See* "Comments of Representatives Nicholas Mavroules and John Spratt," in *Report of the Special Panel on Arms Control, supra* note 604, at 71-74.

[607]*Id.* at 72.

[608]Nunn, "Access to ABM Treaty Negotiation Record" (July 25, 1986), *reprinted in* 26 *Int'l Legal Mat.* 298-301 (Jan. 1987).

[609]Letter from Senator Carl Levin to Secretary of State George Shultz (Dec. 1, 1986), *reprinted in* 26 *Int'l Legal Mat.* 302-311 (Jan. 1987).

December 1, 1986

Secretary of State George Shultz
Department of State
2201 C. Street, N.W.
Washington, D.C. 20520

Dear Mr. Secretary:

In October of 1985, our government announced that it had arrived at a "new interpretation" of the ABM Treaty which, in essence, would allow for testing and development of space-based "exotic" defensive systems like those envisioned in our Strategic Defense Initiative. This interpretation reversed a view held for 13 years: that the Treaty banned everything other than research on so-called exotic systems which would use future technologies in anything other than a fixed, land-based mode. Since this new interpretation was made public, there has been a good deal of controversy about its legitimacy and its implications for arms control.

Until recently, most discussions of this issue were restricted to idle speculation. Since no one outside the administration had access to the negotiating record on which the new interpretation was based, it was difficult to review the basis for this new view of the Treaty. Similarly, until the meeting in Iceland, questions about the relationship between SDI Testing, the ABM Treaty and future arms control agreements were being asked in more or less of a vacuum.

Now, however, members of the Senate have had an opportunity to review the negotiating record and the United States may have an opportunity to reach an historic arms reduction agreement with the Soviet Union. In this environment, questions about the ABM Treaty and SDI take on a new significance. After all, no matter how one views the value of SDI, it is clear that our claim that we can test and develop such a system (a claim which we can make only by virtue of the new interpretation of the ABM Treaty) has been, and remains, a major obstacle to any meaningful arms control agreement with the Soviets.

Because of the significance of this issue, I have spent a good deal of time studying various questions associated with the new interpretation. When the author of the new interpretation, Judge Abraham Sofaer, the Legal Advisor to the Department of State, testified on this issue before a House Foreign Affairs Subcommittee, I was troubled by a number of statements which I found to be misleading and inaccurate. So when Judge Sofaer testified before the Senate Armed Services Committee in 1985, I asked a number of questions about those statements and other issues associated with his interpretation of the Treaty. I was unsatisfied with his answers. To resolve my concerns, I believed that I had an obligation to carefully review the negotiating record which Judge Sofaer used to justify his interpretation of the Treaty. Accordingly, I joined in the effort to make the negotiating record available to the Senate. Since that battle was won, I have carefully reviewed the negotiating record. In addition, I have had discussions with members of the U.S. negotiating team who developed that record. Specifically, I have met with the following key members of the U.S. delegation: Ambassador Gerard Smith, Raymond Garthoff, Sidney Graybeal, John Rhinelander and General Royal Allison.

Based on my review, I have concluded that Judge Sofaer's interpretation of the Treaty is incorrect, and that the process he used to develop and justify that interpretation was fatally flawed. Specifically, I believe that:

1. Judge Sofaer has provided the Congress with an incomplete and misleading analysis of the record in an effort to justify his interpretation of the ABM Treaty.

2. The process used by Judge Sofaer to review the negotiating record was fatally flawed.

3. Our national interest requires that the administration authorize a new and independent review of the ABM Treaty.

Let me amplify these points.

Judge Sofaer has provided the Congress with an incomplete and misleading analysis of the record in an effort to justify his interpretation of the ABM Treaty.

While ambiguity can be found in the text and context of any Treaty, it is clear to me that Judge Sofaer sought to find areas of uncertainty and to magnify their meaning so that he could then propose a "clarification" which would advance a specific policy interest, to wit, making it possible for us to test and develop SDI. Evidence of Judge Sofaer's selective reading of the record is all too abundant and his intent to minimize or suppress facts which contradict his reading of the Treaty all too apparent. The incomplete and misleading nature of his analysis became clear to me as I carefully examined his testimony and compared it with the available <u>public</u> record. Let me cite just a few examples of this sort of activity.

(a) <u>Past Government Statements</u>

Judge Sofaer repeatedly claims that his interpretation is, in fact, not new at all. He seeks to suggest that those who read the Treaty in a restrictive manner are distorting the historic record.

That is simply not true.

While Judge Sofaer points to some statements which are "consistent" with his view, the bulk of the evidence--evidence which he either ignores or misinterprets--indicates that at the time the Treaty was being negotiated and at the time the Treaty was being debated in the Senate, our government understood it to prohibit the testing or development of space-based exotic systems (systems based on future physical principles). Indeed, the evidence suggests that this had been the case until October, 1985 when then National Security Advisor Robert McFarlane, appearing on a television news show, announced that our reading of the Treaty had changed. (There is, by the way, some anecdotal evidence suggesting that key officials were not even aware that this new view was to be made public at that time.)

In any event, the point is that Judge Sofaer's interpretation did, in fact, contradict previously stated public positions of the United States government. For example, the Arms Control and Disarmament Agency has issued an Arms Control Impact

Statement every year since 1978 in close consultation with the Departments of Defense and State. Each of these statements has included language like the following (quoted from the 1985 report):

> . . . the Treaty allows development and testing of fixed land-based ABM systems and components based on other physical principles. . . The ABM Treaty prohibition on development, testing and deployment of space-based ABM systems, or components for such systems, applies to directed energy technologies (or any other technology) used for this purpose. [emphasis added]

Clearly then, our government has adopted a restrictive view of the Treaty in the past.

(b) Previous Testimony

In a number of cases, while indicating a familiarity with statements which contradict his view, Judge Sofaer at the hearings of the House and Senate displayed a willingness to minimize the damage they do to his position by selectively editing them. These incidents are particularly disturbing because they reflect on his objectivity and cast doubt on his ability to impartially interpret the Treaty. Let me cite three examples.

First, the Department of Defense in a formal answer to a question posed by Senator Goldwater during the 1972 Senate Treaty deliberations indicated that "there are no restrictions on the development of lasers for fixed land-based ABM systems [emphasis added]." DoD's silence on the lack of restrictions on space-based systems is clearly significant; if DoD had been operating under the "new interpretation" in 1972, it would naturally have extended its statement to make the point clear. It did not, and that is significant--and its statement was significantly absent from Judge Sofaer's testimony before Congress.

Second, consider this exchange between Senators Goldwater and Jackson about developing, testing or deploying

ABM systems. Here is the way Judge Sofaer presented it at the Congressional hearings:

> SENATOR JACKSON: The prohibition runs to sea-based, air-based, space-based or mobile-based ABMs.
>
> SENATOR GOLDWATER: Not fixed land?
>
> SENATOR JACKSON: That's right. That is exempt. I am just pointing this out.

Judge Sofaer cited that exchange at the Congressional hearings but left out the balance of Senator Jackson's statement:

> "in those other areas, it is prohibited **and development is also prohibited."**

It is difficult to explain the omission as anything other than willful. Senator Jackson, considered by many to be the most knowledgeable Senator on this issue, was making a statement at odds with the conclusion which Judge Sofaer sought to advance. (Pursuant to my questioning on this issue, Judge Sofaer has corrected this omission in a later classified memorandum. That seems to suggest that, when pressed, he recognized the significance of the statement in question. His failure to either recognize it without prodding or report it to the Senate and the public without urging is bothersome at best.)

A third example: Judge Sofaer's Congressional presentation on this issue contained unjustified editing of the remarks of General Palmer when he was speaking for the Joint Chiefs of Staff. Here is the way Judge Sofaer presented an exchange between General Ryan, General Palmer, and Senator Jackson:

> SENATOR JACKSON: Now what I am saying, General Ryan, is that you are prohibited from developing a system that is sea-based, air-based, space-based, or mobile land-based?

> GENERAL RYAN: That is correct.
>
> SENATOR JACKSON: I just wanted that; so the Chiefs went along with the concept here that involved --
>
> GENERAL PALMER: A concept that does not prohibit the development in the fixed land-based ABM system. We can look at futuristic systems as long as they are fixed and land-based.

Judge Sofaer presents this edited exchange and then seeks to minimize its significance by referring to a previous, less precise statement by General Palmer. That, of course, does not refute the claim made here. But beyond that, Judge Sofaer fails to report on the extremely illuminating exchange which surrounds the portion which he did quote. In context, the testimony went this way:

> SENATOR JACKSON: You are here in a professional capacity and we need your professional judgement.
>
> GENERAL PALMER: On the question of the ABM, the facts are that when the negotiation started the only system actually under development, in any meaningful sense, was a fixed, land-based system. As the negotiations progressed and the position of each side became clear and each understood the other's objectives better, it came down to the point where to have an agreement it appeared that--this is on the anti-ballistic missile side--this had to be confined to the fixed, land-based system. The Chiefs were consulted . . . on the question of qualitative limits on the AB [sic] side and agreed to the limits that you see in this treaty.
>
> SENATOR JACKSON: Even though it can't be monitored?
>
> GENERAL PALMER: Yes.

SENATOR JACKSON: I just wanted that; so the Chiefs went along with the concept here that involved----

GENERAL PALMER: A concept that does not prohibit the development in the fixed land-based ABM system. We can look at futuristic systems as long as they are fixed and land-based.

SENATOR JACKSON: I understand.

GENERAL PALMER: The Chiefs were aware of that and had agreed to do that and that **was a fundamental part of the final agreement** [emphasis added].

The deletion of this critical exchange clearly distorts what is a very clear and very critical addition to the record.

When I discovered these examples of selective editing, I was disturbed by the obvious lack of objectivity displayed by Judge Sofaer.

(c) Statements During the Debate

One of the techniques which Judge Sofaer uses repeatedly is to suggest that many of the statements made during the ratification and negotiating process "are consistent with" his broader, more permissive interpretation. While technically correct, Judge Sofaer's argument is misleading.

Judge Sofaer fails to point out, until pressed, that the statements he identifies as consistent with his interpretation of the Treaty are also consistent with the more restrictive reading. The statements he cites do not focus specifically on the issue of testing and development of exotics in space and are not explicitly inconsistent with the restrictive interpretation. In addition, Judge Sofaer ignores statements in the negotiating record and the legislative history of the Treaty which do specifically set forth a Treaty prohibition of testing and development of space-based exotics.

Indeed, I was so troubled by these representations that I asked him to provide me with any statement in the ratification history which explicitly represents that exotic technologies other than fixed land-based ABM systems or components can be tested or developed. He did not do so; instead he simply referred back to statements which are ambiguous and which do not specifically state that the testing or development of exotic space-based systems or components are authorized by the Treaty. The best he can come up with, then, are statements which are silent on the precise issue--and silence is not enough to overcome the clear expressions of our negotiators and officials who told us, at the time the Treaty was being negotiated and ratified, that it did contain a prohibition on testing and development of exotic space based systems.

(d) Statements by Our Negotiators

Perhaps the most disturbing example of the way in which Judge Sofaer distorts the record is his suggestion that, in general, "the restrictive view became common only after the SDI program was announced." This, he suggests, is evidence of the fact that "opponents of SDI have advanced it [that theory] to prevent the expansion of SDI." Even a casual review of the record (and one would hope for much more than that from Judge Sofaer) reveals that such a claim is simply a fabrication.

The evidence is clear: the traditional, restrictive view of the Treaty was current--and in control of government policy--long before the SDI program was announced.

Judge Sofaer claims that the "American negotiators, particularly 10 years after the event . . . think that they had convinced the Soviets to ban all future systems." He implied thereby that they did not believe they had secured a ban at the time of the negotiations when, in fact, they have clearly stated that they believe they achieved exactly such a ban at that time. In addition to the final memo by Mr. Rhinelander, our Legal Counsel to the negotiations, which was the most extensive contemporaneous summary by the negotiators of their understanding (and which I will discuss in more detail below), Mr. Rhinelander wrote a book published in 1974 (SALT--The Moscow Agreements and Beyond) which states that the treaty bans future ABM systems:

> "The overall effect of the Treaty therefore is to prohibit any deployment of future systems and to limit their development and testing to those in a fixed land-based mode."

As seen above, the ratification debate in the Senate on the ABM Treaty contains a number of statements in support of the restrictive view. In fact, one of the two members voting against the Treaty, former Senator Buckley, did so precisely because he believed it would prohibit "the development and testing of a laser type system based in space. . ."

Interestingly enough, the only example of a "switch" in positions that I can find involves Ambassador Nitze who has recently reversed his support for the restrictive view in favor of the new interpretation. While I shall have more to say about this shift in as [sic] moment, the point here is that there have been no shifts in the views of the other negotiators.

A similar attempt to misrepresent the views of the negotiating team can be found in Judge Sofaer's claim that our team was directed to achieve language which contained a clear prohibition on space-based ABM exotics but they "have not denied that they failed to obtain the clear language that they sought." That is simply not true. In our hearings, Ambassador Smith said very clearly that "the Treaty says, `Thou shall not develop space-based systems' . . . Article V doesn't say `thou shall not, except. . .,' it is a flat categorical ban." And Mr. Rhinelander, the Legal Advisor to our negotiating team, has consistently told us that "the negotiating history, <u>as interpreted in 1972 by the SALT I delegation and the backstopping representatives in Washington</u>, supports the broad ban on space-based `exotic systems' . . ." [emphasis added]. Judge Sofaer's assertion, then, is simply wrong.

In terms of public presentations, then, Judge Sofaer did not fairly report on the issues involved to the Congress or the public. He too often shaded the facts and too frequently distorted the record. While these are perhaps not sufficient grounds to automatically reject his arguments, they are more than adequate to make one extremely skeptical about his conclusions. That skepticism grows to outright disbelief when one examines the kind of analysis Judge Sofaer failed to engage in as he reviewed the negotiating record. And that is the second major point I wish to make:

The process used by Judge Sofaer to review the negotiating record was fatally flawed.

Judge Sofaer suggests that if the language of a treaty is arguably ambiguous, then the circumstances surrounding its drafting become critical in interpreting it. Legal scholars agree and as Ilmar Tammelo of the University of Sydney pointed out in his text, Treaty Interpretation and Practical Reason, "the principal end of interpretation is the establishment of the intention of [the] parties." And as Tsune-Chi Yu points out in his The Interpretation of Treaties:

> ". . . It is the function of the interpreter to ascertain the genuine sense in which the negotiators have employed the words rather than to ascertain the bare meaning of the words themselves."

Treaty interpretation, then, is designed to allow us to discover intent and one of the ways to discover intent is to determine what the negotiators themselves believed they were agreeing to. Indeed, in one celebrated case involving the Jay Treaty between the United States and Great Britain, efforts to resolve an ambiguous point involved taking depositions from John Adams and John Jay, members of the negotiating team. In theory and practice, then, interpreters of treaties are bound to discover the understanding and intent of the parties to an agreement which is arguably ambiguous and, in the process, they may be guided by the understandings and intentions of the negotiators.

Given this established principle of international law, I find it amazing that in developing his interpretation of the ABM Treaty, Judge Sofaer never saw fit to talk to the key negotiators, including the Chairman of the American delegation.

(There was one exception: Judge Sofaer did discuss his work with one member of the delegation, Ambassador Nitze. In that context, it is interesting to note that Mr. Nitze told the House

Armed Services Committee that his concurrence with the new interpretation "differs somewhat from my opinion at one time." I wonder why Judge Sofaer gives greater weight to views Nitze developed 15 years after the event than to views expressed at the time of the event or closer to the event. If, after all, Ambassador Nitze "played a crucial role in [drafting] Statement D," as Judge Sofaer has suggested, then surely the views he held as to its meaning at the time, or closer to the time, he drafted it ought to be given greater weight than views expressed 15 years later. Indeed, as Judge Sofaer has remarked in a different context, "under accepted principles of construction, those statements made nearer the Treaty's drafting should be given more credence, and later statements accorded less weight." Surely Judge Sofaer ought to explain why that principle ought to be rejected or modified in the case of Ambassador Nitze's statements.)

Since Judge Sofaer thought it was important to get Ambassador Nitze's views, I find it incredible that he did not seek the same sort of assistance from other members of the American negotiating team.

*I cannot understand why Judge Sofaer did not speak with Ambassador Gerard Smith. I did speak with Ambassador Smith, and I found his views, based on his experiences as the Chairman of the U.S. negotiating team, to be of enormous help in allowing me to understand just what happened during the ABM negotiations.

*I cannot understand why Judge Sofaer did not speak with the delegation's attorney, John Rhinelander. After I found and read Mr. Rhinelander's detailed summary memo in the negotiating record, I did speak with him. And, again, I found his comments to be extremely helpful and informative.

*I cannot understand why Judge Sofaer did not speak with Ray Garthoff and Sid Graybeal. When I reviewed the negotiating record, I found notes of extraordinary significance describing critical negotiations between these men and their Soviet counterparts on the precise issue of exotics. In my discussions with these men, I got a clear sense and understanding of the intent of the parties negotiating the Treaty.

*I cannot understand why Judge Sofaer did not talk with General Allison, who represented the Joint Chiefs of Staff at the negotiations. I did. And after that conversation, I understood why General Palmer told the Senate in 1972 that the Chiefs believed that a prohibition on exotics was "a fundamental part of the final agreement."

But the problem goes beyond a failure to discuss the issue with the members of our team prior to reaching his conclusion. Even after presenting his analysis, Judge Sofaer has failed to discuss it with members of the negotiating team. He has never pressed them to explain why they believe, as they do, that the US-USSR agreement prohibits the development and testing of space-based "exotic" systems and components. And that failure also raises serious questions about the way he has approached this task.

Beyond his failure to consult with key members of the negotiating team, there is also a failure to report important contemporaneous evidence in that record to the Congress. For example, during the 1972 negotiations, the legal counsel to the negotiating team, Mr. Rhinelander, developed a detailed summary of the agreement which had been reached--a summary whose many drafts were circulated throughout the delegation and was sent to Washington. Mr. Rhinelander has testified that in the final and still classified draft of that summary memo, he specifically stated that an agreement on a broad ban on space-based exotics was reached. That was the most critical contemporaneous conclusion which explicitly addressed the exotics issue. Judge Sofaer's testimony to Congress totally ignored the existence of this document. Indeed, he told the Congress that the "first indication that the Treaty banned the development and testing of future systems came in a book written by John Rhinelander in 1974." That statement, coming from someone who has studied the negotiating record as Judge Sofaer has, simply defies explanation.

Finally, Judge Sofaer sometimes seeks to shift the focus of the intent argument. He states that whatever our intent was, the Soviets did not intend to agree to a ban on development and testing of exotics. He claims that since intent must be mutual, and since the Soviets "can argue" that they are not prohibited from developing and testing exotics in space, then the United States should not feel itself bound either. While the argument is theoretical [sic] interesting, it ignores reality. The public statements of our negotiators, and my own reading of the negotiating record, clearly indicate that both America and the Soviet Union understood the Treaty in the same way. In Congressional testimony, Ambassador Nitze has confirmed his view that there is no evidence that the Soviet Union has violated the restrictive interpretation. Beyond that, the "evidence" Judge Sofaer uses to demonstrate a "non-restrictive" Soviet intent boils down to the fact that no Soviet statement ever made "it clear that they considered themselves bound by the restrictive view." What Judge Sofaer fails to point out is that no Soviet statement even suggests, much less makes it clear, that they viewed the Treaty in the permissive terms that he now urges us to adopt.

Our national interest requires that the administration authorize a new and independent review of the ABM Treaty.

Mr. Secretary, my personal view is that Judge Sofaer's analysis of the ABM Treaty is simply wrong. But you need not share that opinion to initiate a new review of the issue. Whether Judge Sofaer is right or wrong is not the threshold issue; the issue is whether he did an acceptable job of looking at the issue. I believe I have demonstrated that he has not.

In my view, Judge Sofaer had an ax to grind--and after he sharpened it, he buried that ax in the back of the ABM Treaty. The process he used was one of an advocate, not an objective judge. He clearly wanted to stretch the fabric of the Treaty to allow for SDI testing and development. Judge Sofaer's approach, if sanctified by our government, would weaken respect for international law and the regime of treaties as well as threaten the possibility that a reasonable arms control agreement could be reached in the near future.

I simply cannot believe, based on the available evidence, that the government of the United States of America is willing to rest its new interpretation of the ABM Treaty, and all the policy implications which flow from it, on the analysis done by Judge Sofaer.

In fact, Mr. Secretary, this issue has become so contentious and so critical that I believe our national interest requires that an independent panel be appointed and authorized to study the entire complex of issues raised by the new interpretation of the Treaty. Their review should certainly include discussions with all available members of our negotiating team as well as access to the entire negotiating and ratification record.

Appointing such a group would not, of course, bind you to accept their conclusions nor would it bind the President to follow their implications in any ongoing negotiations. But clearly we cannot stand on the analysis done by Judge Sofaer and maintain any degree of international credibility. The stakes are simply too great to allow us to continue to rest American policy on so inadequate a legal analysis.

Some will say that the issue of the new interpretation is "moot." After all, they tell us, the President has agreed (after a storm of protest) to continue to abide by the old interpretation for the time being even though he believes the new interpretation is fully justified.

In reality, however, the new interpretation is a major issue. To begin with, it turns a treaty between two nations into a unilateral position which the President could change any time he decided to implement his new interpretation. We would never -- and should never -- agree that the Soviets could unilaterally make changes in a Treaty because they had changed their mind about what it meant. We should not kid ourselves: the new interpretation dynamites the ABM Treaty; the only question is whether and when the President will decide to push the plunger.

Beyond that, the interpretation issue certainly impacts on the possibility of progress at Geneva. There appears to be clear evidence indicating that the possibility of unilateral American development and testing of SDI is contributing to our lack of progress in various arms control discussions.

Given the significance of the sort of review I am suggesting and given the need for public awareness of the issues involved, I would also ask that you review the currently classified documents surrounding the negotiations with the purpose of making as many of them public as possible. There are some documents, at least, whose release or partial release would serve to

> advance the public debate on this issue without doing any damage to the national interest.
>
> In conclusion, Mr. Secretary, let me simply suggest that the evidence compels a complete and independent review of the issues raised here.
>
> I look forward to hearing from you.
>
> Sincerely,
>
> Carl Levin
>
> cc: Judge Sofaer[610]

On December 1, 1986, the State Department issued a rebuttal to this letter which states in full:

> The Secretary has received Senator Levin's letter concerning the ABM Treaty. Judge Sofaer's evaluation of the ABM Treaty was done at the Secretary's request, and is a thorough, balanced analysis of the issues, more objective and complete than any prior study of the subject. The study was undertaken, not to justify SDI testing and development, but in response to legitimate concerns regarding Soviet activities, differences of views between Administration departments, and the need to develop a coherent view of permitted activities concerning ABM systems and components based on "other physical principles" than those used in the systems and components regulated by the parties in 1972.
>
> Senator Levin's letter was released at a press conference held hours before its delivery to the Secretary or to Judge Sofaer. It is filled with arguments that have been repeatedly raised and answered, and it distorts Judge Sofaer's statements and work in several respects. In particular:
>
> 1. The Administration has made clear that what happened during the Senate <u>ratification process</u> on the ABM Treaty is a different issue from what happened during the

---

[610] *Id.*, the "[emphasis added]" is Senator Levin's.

negotiations themselves. Judge Sofaer was assigned the task of analyzing the negotiating record. In that regard, Senator Levin fails to challenge in a single respect Judge Sofaer's statements about the negotiating record. He asserts that Judge Sofaer is wrong in claiming that the negotiators failed to obtain the language they thought was necessary to establish the so-called narrow interpretation. But the record clearly proves that Judge Sofaer is correct. The negotiators sought to cover "other devices" in the prohibition of Article V, and they failed.

2. Judge Sofaer has written, openly and honestly, that some statements made in the ratification process and later are consistent with the view Senator Levin espouses. Indeed, Senator Levin does not cite a single statement not previously revealed by Judge Sofaer.

3. Any outside study of the ABM Treaty is unnecessary. The full, relevant negotiating record -- in a form that was accepted by the Senate leadership of both parties -- is at the Senate. That is the proper place for any review that is necessary. The Secretary is confident that a more balanced picture will emerge as other Senators familiar with the record state their views of the subject.

4. The interpretation supported by Judge Sofaer, and confirmed by the President as fully justified, has not been implemented.

5. Senator Levin criticizes Judge Sofaer for failing to talk to certain ABM Treaty negotiators. Judge Sofaer was assigned the task of analyzing a written record. He was, moreover, fully familiar with the views of all the persons mentioned by Senator Levin, having read their writings, and having appeared with some of them at congressional hearings and public debates. As Senator Levin notes, Ambassador Paul Nitze, who participated in the ABM

> Treaty negotiations, has studied Judge Sofaer's work and agrees with its conclusions.[611]

On February 5, 1987, Senator Sam Nunn, Chairman of the Senate Committee on Armed Services, sent a letter to the President warning of "a Constitutional confrontation of profound dimensions" absent due consultation with the Senate on adopting the "broad" interpretation. The letter says in full:

> February 6, 1987
>
> Dear Mr. President:
>
> According to press reports, the Administration intends next week to address the question of whether the United States should terminate its policy of observing the traditional, or so-called "restrictive," interpretation of the ABM Treaty limitations pertaining to the development and testing of space-based or otherwise mobile ABM systems and components.
>
> If such a decision is taken, I believe it should be done only after a thorough consultative process, including extensive discussions with the Congress and with our allies. Consultation after the fact would not, in my view, be satisfactory given the central importance of this issue.
>
> Were the Administration now to decide to abandon the traditional ABM Treaty interpretation without having achieved a consensus with NATO and the Congress that such an action was warranted, it would have several extremely adverse consequences. It would clearly cause consternation within the Alliance and create particularly severe problems for our European friends and NATO supporters. It would put immense pressure on SDI funding and in my opinion would cause much deeper SDI cuts than would otherwise occur. Such a decision would also very likely be taken on Capitol Hill as the end of arms control under your administration -- whether accurate or not.
>
> Finally, I am concerned that absent due consultation, a unilateral Executive Branch decision to disregard the interpretation

---

[611]"State Department Rebuttal of Letter, December 1, 1986," 26 *Int'l Legal Mat.* 282, 311-12 (Jan. 1987).

of the Treaty which the Senate believed it had approved when the accord was ratified in 1972 would provoke a Constitutional confrontation of profound dimensions.

Pursuant to the agreement on Congressional access to the ABM record which I helped negotiate last summer, I have been conducting an extensive review of the negotiating record of the ABM Treaty. I intend to complete this review within the next week or two and would hope that there would be an opportunity for a complete exchange of views with the Administration prior to your making any final decisions on this issue.

Sincerely,

Sam Nunn
Chairman

The President
The White House

cc: The Honorable George P. Shultz
The Honorable Frank Carlucci
The Honorable Caspar W. Weinberger[612]

On February 26, 1987, the Subcommittee on Arms Control, International Security and Science of the House Committee on Foreign Affairs held a hearing on *Review of ABM Treaty Interpretation Dispute and SDI.*[613] Witnesses included Representatives Les AuCoin and Norman Dicks, the Honorable Lloyd N. Cutter, Counsel to President Carter during 1979-80, Mr. John B. Rhinelander, former legal adviser to the ABM Treaty negotiations, and William R. Harris, Senior Social Scientist, the Rand Corporation.

On March 11 and 26, and April 29, 1987, a more extensive hearing was held on *The ABM Treaty and the Constitution* jointly by the Senate Committees on

---

[612]Letter from Senator Sam Nunn, Chairman of the Senate Committee on Armed Services, to the President of the United States (Feb. 6, 1987).

[613]*Review of ABM Treaty Interpretation Dispute and SDI Hearing, supra* note 323.

Foreign Relations and the Judiciary.[614] Witnesses included: Lt. General Royal B. Allison (USAF-Ret.), member, U.S. ABM Treaty Negotiating Delegation; the Honorable Raymond L. Garthoff, Executive Secretary and Senior Adviser to the U.S. ABM Treaty Negotiating Delegation; the Honorable J. W. Fulbright, former Chairman of the Senate Committee on Foreign Relations; Senator Pete Wilson; Senator Sam Nunn; Gordon Brewster Baldwin, Professor of Constitutional Law and International Law at the University of Wisconsin; Professor Louis Henkin, University Professor at Columbia University; Professor Laurence H. Tribe; Ralph S. Tyler, Jr., Professor of Constitutional Law at Harvard; Senator Ernest Hollings; the Honorable Richard N. Perle, Assistant Secretary of Defense for International Security Policy; the Honorable Abraham D. Sofaer, Legal Adviser to the Department of State; the Honorable Gerard C. Smith, chief of the 1972 ABM Treaty Negotiating Delegation; the Honorable Abram Chayes, former Legal Adviser to the Department of State and Felix Frankfurter Professor of Law at Harvard Law School; the Honorable Antonia Chayes, former Under Secretary of the Air Force and President of End Dispute, Inc.; Arthur W. Rovine, former Assistant Legal Adviser for Treaty Affairs and currently with Baker & McKenzie; Leonard C. Meeker, former Legal Adviser to the Department of State; William Sims, former Attorney Adviser in the Department of State; and Sydney N. Graybeal, former ABM Treaty Negotiator and current Vice President for the Center for Strategic Policy, Systems Planning Corp. During these hearings Senator Sam Nunn presented a detailed consideration of the "broad-narrow" issue in rebuttal to the interpretation presented by Judge Sofaer.[615] This is by far the most detailed rebuttal to date on this issue by any member of Congress and is probably generally regarded as the most powerful presentation for the "narrow" interpretation.

On April 7 and 8, 1987, Senators Thurmond, Wallop and Cochran made statements on the Senate floor on the "broad-narrow" issue generally supportive of the policy or legal dimensions of the "broad" interpretation or urging avoidance of a "rush to judgment" on the issue.[616]

On May 19, 1987, the Senate Foreign Relations Committee met to mark-up S. Res. 167, concerning constitutional principles relating to the making of treaties and adopting the "narrow" interpretation of the ABM Treaty. The key vote in the

---

[614]*The ABM Treaty and the Constitution, supra* note 1.

[615]*See Nunn, "Interpretation of the ABM Treaty," supra* note 1, at 553-811.

[616]"Senators' Statements on ABM Treaty and the SDI Program," Briefing Memorandum of the United States Arms Control and Disarmament Agency (April 9, 1987).

Committee relating to the Resolution was an amendment offered by Senator Helms, in the nature of a substitute, that was defeated by a vote of 9-10 precisely along political party lines. Subsequently, the Committee voted 11-8 to report S. Res. 167 with a favorable recommendation.[617]

On September 17, 1987, the Senate voted 58-38 for a proposal drafted by Senators Sam Nunn and Carl Levin that the *Washington Post* said "would require congressional approval before the administration could conduct SDI tests based on its reinterpretation of the 1972 Anti-ballistic Missile (ABM) Treaty."[618] According to the Post account the debate and vote were heavily along party lines:

> The Senate, defying veto threats from President Reagan, voted 58 to 38 to approve a Democratic-sponsored move to restrict testing of the administration's space-based Strategic Defense Initiative (SDI).[619]
>
> . . . .
>
> Democrats fell short of the two-thirds vote they would need to override the veto that Reagan has promised if Congress gives final approval to the proposal as part of a defense authorization bill for next fiscal year.[620]
>
> . . . .
>
> . . . Democrats held firm, contending that the White House was treading on the Senate's constitutional turf by attempting to reinterpret the treaty without congressional approval in order to allow tests that would be barred under the traditional reading of the ABM pact that was accepted by the Nixon, Ford and Carter administrations.[621]
>
> . . . .

---

[617]*See The ABM Treaty Interpretation Resolution, supra* note 1, at 37. S. Res. 167 is set out in full in section V(E) of this study.

[618]*Senate Votes to Curb SDI Testing,* Wash. Post, Sept. 18, 1987, at 1, col. 1, A20, col. 2.

[619]*Id.* at 1, col. 1.

[620]*Id.* at 1, col. 2.

[621]*Id.* at A20, col. 2.

> Republicans argued that only the president has the power to interpret treaties and said it would be unprecedented for the Senate to write an interpretation into law.[622]

In the overall vote on this proposal, 50 Democrats voted in favor and only 1 against, and 37 Republicans voted against and only 8 in favor. Three Democrats and one Republican did not vote but according to the Post "had previously signaled support for the proposal."[623]

On September 22, 1987, a report on *The ABM Treaty Interpretation Resolution* was issued by the Senate Committee on Foreign Relations[624] based on three days of testimony on the subject during March and April and also considering S. Res. 167 on the generic issue the "ABM Treaty Interpretation Resolution." The sixty-seven page report of the Committee concluded:

> The Committee can find no evidence to contradict the conclusion that the Reagan Administration's "reinterpretation" of the ABM Treaty constitutes the most flagrant abuse of the Constitution's treaty power in 200 years of American history.
>
> American constitutional principles should apply notwithstanding the ends at issue. The Committee therefore urges that, as Senators weigh the "reinterpretation" question, they isolate the constitutional issue from any position they may hold regarding the deasirability [sic] of ABM systems or the Strategic Defensive Initiative.
>
> The importance of subordinating short-term policy expediency to long-term constitutional principle is perhaps best underscored by way of a hypothetical example that cuts in a different policy direction. Thus, suppose that in the current INF talks the American side secretly agreed to permit the Soviets to convert their SS-20 missiles into intercontinental-range SS-16s. And suppose further that an INF treaty were then ratified with no reference to this secret understanding. Would those who now

[622]*Id.* at A20, col. 4.

[623]*Id.* at A20, col. 3. *The Senate Roll Call vote on SDI Restrictions*, Wash. Post, Sept. 18, 1987, appears at A20, cols. 4-5.

[624]*The ABM Treaty Interpretation Resolution, supra* note 1.

assert the preeminence of the negotiating record seriously contend that ratification of this INF treaty had elevated this secret agreement to the status of a solemn treaty obligation of the United States?

Far less hypothetically, will not the Senate be required to act aggressively to prevent any such occurrence? Indeed, unless the Administration reverses its position, ratification of an INF treaty would require a full exposition of the negotiating record leading up to each and every treaty provision and, in the Senate's resolution of ratification, a formal condition or understanding associated with each provision. Thus, the Administration's theory of treatymaking, having cast a dark shadow over the Senate's consideration of all future treaties, could severely complicate and greatly prolong the Committee's consideration of an INF treaty--and thereby jeopardize early ratification of that treaty.

In the metaphor of the Committee's distinguished former chairman, Senator J.W. Fulbright, those who would dispense with constitutional principles in the interest of furthering an expedient goal are:

> . . . rather like the defenders of a besieged fort firing their artillery through the protecting walls instead of over them: They may blow up some of the attackers on the other side, but in the process they are making a nice opening through which the enemy can pour into the fort in their next attack.

It has been argued that, by threatening to develop ABM technology in violation of the ABM Treaty, the Reagan Administration has strengthened its hand in arms talks with the Soviet Union. In the Committee's view, this is wishful thinking. The Soviet interest in the ABM Treaty is the same as the interest which *both* superpowers reflected when they entered into the Treaty in 1972. Strict limitations on defensive systems are crucial both to limiting the arms race and to negotiated reductions in offensive strategic systems.

The Committee does, however, recognize the possibility that a nation *could* enhance its international leverage by violating

> or threatening to violate international norms. Hitler's success in this regard is well known. And certainly the Iranian regime of Ayatollah Khomeini has succeded [sic] in using illegal acts to gain considerable international bargaining leverage. Indeed, it managed to use such behavior to extract arms transfers from this very Administration.
>
> But such examples hardly vindicate a practice of flouting international obligations. As a nation which subscribes to the rule of law, the United States has purposefully denied itself certain forms of behavior, whether they provided temporary leverage at the bargaining table or not. We have done so because, as a member of the community of nations, we have concluded that ultimately, in a long and halting march toward some form of world order, benefit for all will derive from the elevation of certain standards to a level of general acceptance and practice.
>
> No standard is more fundamental to civilization than the value of honoring a solemn pledge. While the "reinterpretation" debate has raised many complex and technical questions of international and constitutional law, beneath them all is a simple value with which every American is familiar: the value of honesty.
>
> In seeking to distort the ABM Treaty through the sham of a "reinterpretation," the Administration has denigrated this value in the interest of pursuing a Presidential dream--that the United States can find safety in the nuclear age through the erection of an anti-nuclear astrodome. Some in the Senate support this goal; others regard it as naive, futile, and dangerous. But that debate aside, it should be taken as unarguably true that corrupting our own institutions and constitutional processes is not an effective way to defend the United States of America.[625]

A twenty-one page "Additional Views of Senator Helms"[626] rejected the report of the Committee and endorsed the "broad" interpretation as "solidly based in law and the Treaty records."[627] An additional seventeen page "Additional Views of Senators

---

[625] *Id.* at 66-67.

[626] *Id.* at 68-88.

[627] *Id.* at 88.

Helms, Pressler, and Trible"[628] set out a "`Summary of Findings' of a lengthy study developed by the minority staff to the Senate Committee on Foreign Relations"[629] and recommending that, based on the currently known record, the United States should adopt the "broad" interpretation.[630] Apparently the key committee vote on S. Res. 167, on a Helms amendment in the nature of a substitute, was defeated by a vote of 9-10 along purely party lines with all ten Democratic members of the Senate voting in favor of S. Res. 167 and all nine Republican members voting in favor of the Helms amendment. Senator Kassebaum, a Republican from Kansas, did, however, add her vote to the Democratic majority to report S. Res. 167 with a favorable recommendation.[631]

The Defense Authorization Act for fiscal 1988 contains the following provision relating to the "broad-narrow" issue:

> SEC. 225. DEVELOPMENT AND TESTING OF ANTI-BALLISTIC MISSILE SYSTEMS OR COMPONENTS
>
> (a) USE OF FUNDS.--(1) Funds appropriated to the Department of Defense for fiscal year 1988, or otherwise made available to the Department of Defense from any funds appropriated for fiscal year 1988 or for any fiscal year before fiscal year 1988, shall be subject to the limitations prescribed in paragraph (2).
>
> (2) The funds described in paragraph (1) may not be obligated or expended--
>
> (A) for any development or testing of anti-ballistic missile systems or components except for development

---

[628]"Additional Views of Senators Helms, Pressler, and Trible," *supra* note 213, at 89-105.

[629]*Id.* at 90.

[630]*Id.* at 104.

[631]*The ABM Treaty Interpretation Resolution, supra* note 1, at 37.

and testing consistent with the development and testing described in the April 1987 SDIO Report; or

(B) for the acquisition of any material or equipment (including any long lead materials, components, piece parts, test equipment, or any modified space launch vehicle) required or to be used for the development or testing of anti-ballistic missile systems or components, except for material or equipment required for development or testing consistent with the development and testing described in the April 1987 SDIO Report.

(3) The limitation under paragraph (2) shall not apply to funds transferred to or for the use of the Strategic Defense Initiative for fiscal year 1988 if the transfer is made in accordance with section 1201 of this Act and any comparable provision in legislation appropriating funds for military functions of the Department of Defense for fiscal year 1988.

(b) DEFINITION.--As used in this section, the term "April 1987 SDIO Report" means the report entitled "Report to Congress on the Strategic Defense Initiative", dated April 1987, prepared by the Strategic Defense Initiative Organization and submitted to certain committees of the Senate and House of Representatives pursuant to section 1102 of the Department of Defense Authorization Act, 1985 (Public Law 98-525; 10 U.S.C. 2431 note).[632]

The House Conference Report to the fiscal 1988 Defense Authorization Act describes the origins and intent of this provision as follows:

Development and testing of the ABM systems or components (*sec.* 225)

The Senate bill contained a provision (sec. 233) prohibiting the obligation or expenditure of FY 1988-89 funds to develop or test anti-ballistic missile (ABM) systems or components

---

[632]PL 100-180, 101 Stat. 1056 (Dec. 4, 1987). *See U.S. Code Congressional & Administrative News* (No. 11, Jan. 1988), at PL 100-180, 101 Stat. 1056.

which are sea-based, air-based, space-based, or mobile land-based unless the President proposed to conduct such development or testing and the Congress passed a joint resolution under expedited procedures approving the President's proposal.

The House bill contained a provision (sec. 224) prohibiting the obligation or expenditure of any funds to develop, test, or deploy any ABM systems or components which are sea-based, air-based, space-based or mobile land-based unless the President certified to the Congress that extraordinary events related to such ABM systems or components have jeopardized the supreme national interests of the United States, necessitating a repeal of this limitation.

The House recedes with an amendment.

The conferees agreed to a provision requiring that DOD funds for FY 1988 and previous years be spent consistent with the SDI plan presented by the Defense Department to the Congress in the April 1987 SDIO Report. Specifically, the conferees agreed that funds provided to the Defense Department in FY 1988 or prior years for the development or testing of ABM systems or components may not be obligated or expended for any development or testing of ABM systems or components unless such development or testing is consistent with the testing and development described in the April 1987 SDIO report to Congress.

The conferees emphasize that a key declaration in the April 1987 SDIO Report is the statement that: "Since the President has decided as a matter of policy to observe the more restrictive interpretation of the ABM Treaty, all statements in this appendix [Appendix D of the Report] regarding compliance with the treaty provisions should be understood to be based on the more restrictive interpretation." Consistent with this statement, the Report describes no development or testing of space-based or other mobile-based ABM systems or components. The conferees agreed that "consistent with the development or testing described in the April 1987 SDIO Report" means development or testing which does not involve space-based or other mobile-based ABM systems or components. By "development" and "testing", the conferees mean the definition of those terms as used by the United States Government in the ABM Treaty and as applied in Appendix D of the April 1987 SDIO Report.

> The conferees further agreed that funds provided to the Defense Department for FY 1988 or prior years may not be obligated or expended for the acquisition of any material or equipment (including any long-lead materials, components, piece-parts, test equipment, or any modified space launch vehicle) required or to be used for the development or testing of ABM systems or components unless such material or equipment is required for development or testing consistent with the development and testing described in the April 1987 SDIO Report.
>
> In adopting this provision, the conferees agreed that nothing in this limitation is intended or may be construed to preclude SDIO or contractor planning activities (including studies, design activities or computer simulations) related to any development or testing of ABM systems or components, including development and testing not described in the April 1987 SDIO report. In addition, the Defense Department may request, through normal budgeting procedures, authority to acquire material or equipment related to ABM development or testing not described in the April 1987 SDIO Report, but such requests would have to be specifically approved by the Congress. Such approval could take the form either of new legislation or Congressional approval of a transfer of funds. The conferees direct that no such transfer of any amount take place under this provision without prior notification and Congressional approval through the procedures that traditionally have governed transfers.[633]

Apparently also this provision was worked out as a compromise with the President, applying only to the FY 1988 authorization, in order to avoid a presidential veto. Subsequently, however, this provision has been rolled over into the National Defense Authorization Act for FY 1989 in terms nearly identical to those for FY 1988, and is keyed for FY 1989 to the March 1988 SDIO Report.[634]

---

[633] *U.S. Code Congressional & Administrative News* (No. 11A, Jan. 1988), at PL-180, 1706-07.

[634] National Defense Authorization Act, Fiscal Year 1989 (Sept. 29, 1988), Pub. L. No. 100-456, §223, 1988 *U.S. Code Cong. & Admin. News* (102 Stat.) 1918, 1942. Section 223 of this FY 1989 Defense Authorization Act entitled "Development and Testing of Antiballistic Missile Systems or Components" provides in full:

It might also be noted that according to HASC TASKS, a periodic newsletter from the House Armed Services Committee, the House had in approving the Defense Authorization Bill for fiscal year 1988: "[v]oted 262-159 to retain language in the committee bill that would fix in law the narrow or traditional interpretation of the 1972 ABM Treaty, thus limiting SDI testing."[635] This same newsletter reports under "Two views of one defense bill" the following statements by Chairman Les Aspin and ranking Republican Bill Dickinson:

Chairman Les Aspin

> There are some interesting political aspects to the bill.
> On final passage, Democrats voted 227-18. That's 93 percent support for the bill this year and 97 percent support for the

---

(a) USE OF FUNDS.--(1) Funds appropriated to the Department of Defense for fiscal year 1989, or otherwise made available to the Department of Defense from any funds appropriated for fiscal year 1989 or for any fiscal year before 1989, shall be subject to the limitations prescribed in paragraph (2).

(2) The funds described in paragraph (1) may not be obligated or expended--

(A) for any development or testing of antiballistic missile systems or components except for development and testing consistent with the development and testing described in the March 1988 SDIO Report; or

(B) for the acquisition of any material or equipment (including any long lead materials, components, piece parts, test equipment, or any modified space launch vehicle) required or to be used for the development or testing of antiballistic missile systems or components, except for material or equipment required for development or testing consistent with the development and testing described in the March 1988 SDIO Report.

(3) The limitation under paragraph (2) shall not apply to funds transferred to or for the use of the Strategic Defense Initiative for fiscal year 1989 if the transfer is made in accordance with section 1201 of this Act.

(b) DEFINITION.--As used in this section, the term "March 1988 SDIO Report" means the report entitled, "Report to Congress on the Strategic Defense Initiative", dated March 23, 1988, prepared by the Strategic Defense Initiative Organization and submitted to certain committees of the Senate and House of Representatives pursuant to section 1102 of the Department of Defense Authorization Act, 1985 (Public Law 98-525; 10 U.S.C. 2431 note).

Id.

[635]*HASC TASKS* 1 (June 1987).

bill last year. In the previous eight years, only 77 percent of the Democratic Caucus voted for final passage of the defense bill on the average.

The Republicans this year voted 12-160, only the second year in recent history that a majority of the GOP has opposed final passage. In other words, this year, as last year for the first time, we have fashioned a Democratic defense bill. . . .[636]

Ranking Republican Bill Dickinson

The defense authorization bill is a partisan, liberal Democratic exercise in "Reagan bashing" that was achieved at the expense of the national defense of the United States. Chairman Aspin serves as a conduit for the Democratic Caucus and bends to its efforts to impose a variety of liberal "anti-defense" measures onto the bill. More and more, the work of the Armed Services Committee is being polarized and politicized. If Congress produces final legislation that bears any resemblance to the House-passed bill, I would strongly urge the President to veto it.

The objectionable features of the House-passed bill include:

. . .

A series of arms control restrictions that limit the right and ability of the President to conduct U.S. foreign policy while at the same time tying the hands of our negotiators in Geneva. . . .[637]

A continuing dispute, growing out of the "broad-narrow" issue, as to the legal effect of administration witnesses during testimony in Senate consideration of treaties, produced an exchange between Senator Biden and Ambassador Nitze during INF Treaty hearings before the Senate Foreign Relations Committee and an exchange of letters between Senators Byrd and Nunn and Secretary of State George P. Shultz in February of 1988.

On February 1, 1988, the following exchange occurred between Ambassador Nitze and Senator Biden during INF hearings before the Senate Foreign Relations Committee:

---

[636] *Id.*

[637] *Id.*

Senator BIDEN. Well, Mr. Ambassador, in closing I want to ask you a question for reasons that I think you will understand.

Is it fair for the Committee to consider your testimony on the meaning of this treaty as authoritative?

Ambassador NITZE. I believe so. But I would like to go over the transcript and be sure that it is thoroughly corrected and that it is authoritative after it has been reviewed.

Senator BIDEN. Again, I am not in any way questioning your judgment or your knowledge, you understand.

Ambassador NITZE. No, I know what you are talking about. It is a legitimate question.

Senator BIDEN. Well, I would invite you to do that.

Ambassador NITZE. I want to be sure that it is authoritative.

Senator BIDEN. Good, that would be helpful. How should a legal advisor 10, or 15 years from now, who decides that he wants to discount your testimony--

Ambassador NITZE. Want to discount my testimony?

Senator BIDEN. Discount your testimony as to the meaning of the INF agreement and reinterpret it. How should that be viewed?

Ambassador NITZE. I think what he would say is that with respect to domestic law, an authoritative statement by a member of the Executive branch is determinative as to what the meaning of the treaty is from the standpoint of domestic law.

I believe it is also true that from the standpoint of international law, what is determinative is the language of the treaty itself. And the negotiating record with respect to how that language was arrived at, and not the testimony, my testimony before this committee.

Senator BIDEN. Let me make sure that I understand that. You believe your testimony before the Committee would be binding as it relates to domestic law, that is, the Constitution?

Ambassador NITZE. Yes; that is, that I think one should not change that without getting the concurrence of the Congress thereto, as a matter of domestic law. As a matter of international law, I think that is a different matter.[638]

---

[638]This exchange is reprinted from *The INF Treaty Report, supra* note 1, at 449.

On February 5th, Senators Byrd and Nunn wrote Secretary Shultz as follows:

February 5, 1988

The Honorable George P. Shultz
Department of State
Washington, D.C. 20520

Dear Mr. Secretary:

We have received your letter outlining the agreement between the Senate and the Administration on Senate access to the INF negotiating record. We are pleased that we have been able to reach agreement on this matter and look forward to your delivery of the documents identified in the letter. In particular, we welcome your recognition that internal, executive branch deliberative material "cannot be used as a basis for interpretation of obligations" and therefore need not be submitted to the Senate.

This agreement removes one obstacle to prompt consideration by the Senate of the INF Treaty. We deeply regret, however, that your letter is silent with regard to the three key principles we have been discussing over the last two months concerning the relationship between the Senate and the Executive Branch as treaty-making partners. Our agreement on the negotiating record can only be truly effective if it is accompanied by an agreement on these three principles:

(1) The testimony of all Executive Branch witnesses and any submissions for the hearing record by the Executive Branch on a Treaty can be regarded by the Senate as authoritative.

(2) The meaning of the Treaty as presented to the Senate can be regarded by the Senate as authoritative without the necessity of the Senate's incorporating that testimony and material in its Resolution of Ratification through understandings, reservations, amendments, or other conditions.

(3) A meaning for the treaty different from that presented to the Senate by the Reagan Administration cannot be adopted without the approval of the Senate.

As your know, our concerns stem from statements made on this subject by Judge Sofaer, the State Department's Legal Adviser, over the last two years. For example, in response to a question asked by Senator Nunn during a November 21, 1985 Armed Services Committee hearing, Judge Sofaer stated:

> The Senate held extensive hearings to develop a detailed understanding and assessment of the two SALT I agreements. Although this process may have helped to answer questions in particular Senators' minds, it could not result in authoritative clarifications of any ambiguities in the Treaty, because statements made during the hearings were unilateral.

Judge Sofaer has suggested that the testimony of some top Nixon Administration witnesses, including Secretary of Defense Laird and the Director of Defense Research and Engineering, Dr. John Foster, was not authoritative. Moreover, on March 26, 1987, Judge Sofaer told the Senate Foreign Relations and Judiciary Committees:

> When it [the Senate] gives its advice and consent to a treaty, it is to the treaty that was made, irrespective of explanations it is provided.

Under this doctrine, if the Senate is misinformed by Executive Branch officials as to the meaning of a treaty, that is simply too bad. Unless modified, Judge Sofaer's views put the Senate on notice that if it relies upon the testimony of the Administration as to the meaning of the INF Treaty, it will do so at its own risk.

Since you have not assured us that the meaning of the Treaty as presented to the Senate by Administration witnesses is authoritative and that such meaning will be respected in the future even if the Senate has not embodied its understanding of the Treaty in the Resolution of Ratification, we must assume that we will have to review the negotiating record exhaustively, compare it to all Executive Branch testimony, and prepare understandings, reservations or amendments addressing every point of interpretation in the Treaty. At best, such an approach would be unwieldy and time consuming. At worst, it could undermine the treaty ratification process.

Based on our meeting last Monday, we were of the opinion that we were close to reaching a satisfactory resolution through a letter from you addressing the three principles. It is most unfortunate, therefore, that you have apparently changed your mind and do not intend to provide us with such a letter.

The Armed Services Committee had intended to conduct hearings on the Treaty with Administration witnesses over the several weeks and complete its hearings by the end of the month. This plan was based on the expectation that the testimony of Executive Branch witnesses on the Treaty would be in accord with the three principles. However, the Armed Services Committee now has no choice but to clarify the Reagan Administration's position on these questions before hearing from other Administration witnesses. We regret the inevitable delay this will cause.

In an effort to resolve this impasse and avoid undue delay in hearing the Administration's testimony on the Treaty, Senator Nunn hereby requests that you appear before the Armed Services Committee as soon as possible after the February recess.

We hope that we can quickly get these serious questions behind us.

Sincerely,

Robert C. Byrd Sam Nunn[639]

---

[639]Letter from Senators Robert C. Byrd and Sam Nunn to Secretary of State George P. Shultz (Feb. 5, 1988).

And on February 9, 1988, Secretary Shultz responded as follows in identical letters to Senators Byrd and Nunn:

February 9, 1988

[The Honorable Sam Nunn,
United States Senate,
Washington, D.C.]

Dear Senator Nunn:

I am responding to your letter of February 5 concerning the INF Treaty. I am pleased that we have resolved the question of Senate access to the INF negotiating record. I believe that we can also resolve the remaining questions posed by your letter in a manner that accommodates the interests of all concerned and serves the national interest.

Your letter asks for our agreement on three points. Your first point is that the testimony of all Executive Branch witnesses and any submissions for the hearing record by the Executive Branch on the Treaty can be regarded by the Senate as authoritative. We agree. All INF testimony of Executive Branch witnesses, within their authorized scope, is authoritative. We will inform the relevant Committee of any instance in which a witness' testimony is not authoritative in any respect.

Your second point is that the meaning of the Treaty as presented to the Senate can be regarded by the Senate as authoritative without the necessity of the Senate's incorporating that testimony and material in its Resolution of Ratification through understandings, reservations, amendments, or other conditions. Again, we agree. Administration testimony and materials for the record can be regarded as authoritative, as described above, without the need for the Senate to incorporate them in its Resolution of Ratification.

Your third point is that a meaning for the Treaty different from that presented to the Senate by the Reagan Administration cannot be adopted without the approval of the Senate. I can assure you that the Reagan Administration will in no way depart from the INF Treaty as we are presenting it to the Senate.

I hope that this letter will help us resolve these important questions.

Sincerely yours,

George P. Shultz

cc: Senator Robert Dole[640]

A question and answer concerning the effect of this letter on the "broad-narrow" dispute and associated constitutional treaty issues, apparently prepared as talking points in connection with the Shultz letter said:

SEC. SHULTZ LETTERS TO SENATORS BYRD AND NUNN

Q. Do Secretary of State Shultz' February 9, 1988, letters to Senators Byrd and Nunn change the Administration's position that a meaning of the ABM Treaty different from that presented to the Senate by the Nixon Administration can be adopted without the approval of the Senate?

A. As the Secretary of State has said, the testimony during INF ratification of all Executive Branch witnesses within their authorized scope can be regarded to be authoritative by the Senate. In addition, Administration testimony and materials for the record can be regarded as authoritative without the need for the Senate to incorporate them in its Resolution of Ratification. The INF Treaty text is a clear and accurate statement of the obligations of the United States and the Soviet Union. In accordance with international law we should look first to this text to answer any questions about the meaning of these obligations. The Senate in discharging its Constitutional role of considering advice and consent to ratification has access to and may wish to review the INF negotiating record. With regard to

[640]Identical Letters from the Honorable George P. Shultz to Senator Robert C. Byrd and Senator Sam Nunn (Feb. 9, 1988).

> the ABM Treaty, our view remains that the broad interpretation is fully justified.[641]

Finally, as part of the same generic issue of the Senate role in the treaty process, Senate Democratic leaders are said to have reached agreement in late February 1988 to attach a condition to the INF Treaty concerning the Senate's treaty making authority.[642] On March 9, 1988, Senator Richard G. Lugar sent a letter to the Honorable Howard Baker, Chief of Staff to the President of the United States, attaching "the latest version of a draft by Democratic Members of the Foreign Relations Committee" concerning the treaty interpretation condition proposed to be attached to the INF Treaty. Senator Lugar's letter and attachment provided in full:

> March 9, 1988
>
> The Honorable Howard Baker
> Chief of Staff to the
> President of the United States
> The White House
> Washington, DC 20500
>
> Dear Howard:
>
> Attached is the latest version of a draft by Democratic Members of the Foreign Relations Committee seeking to address the "interpretation issue" in the form of an amendment to the INF Treaty. Senators Biden, Cranston and Pell are seeking Republican support for this approach.
>
> Although my own preference for the moment would be for a "clean" INF Treaty, I have indicated that I would not be prepared to discuss the Democratic draft formally until I had received some indication from the White House as to its thinking on the "interpretation" issue as a whole as well as any vehicle that might be employed to express the Senate's interest in the matter.

---

[641] Sec. Shultz Letters to Senators Byrd and Nunn.

[642] H. Dewar, *Byrd, Allies Agree to Smooth Way for INF Pact*, Wash. Post, March 1, 1988, at A15, cols. 1-3.

I would appreciate it if you could share with me the White House's thoughts on this matter as well as any guidance you may wish to offer relative to discussions and negotiations with the Democratic Members of the Committee and the Senate Democratic leadership.

Sincerely,

Richard G. Lugar
United States Senator

RESOLUTION OF RATIFICATION

Resolved, (two-thirds of the Senators present concurring therein), That the Senate advise and consent to ratification of the Treaty between the United States of America and the Union of Soviet Socialist Republics on the Elimination of Their Intermediate-Range and Shorter-Range Missiles and the two Protocols thereto, together referred to as the INF Treaty, all signed at Washington, on December 8, 1987 (Treaty Doc. 100-11), subject to the finding contained in Section 1 and the condition contained in Section 2:

Section 1. Finding Concerning Constitutional Principles.

The following principles derive, as a necessary implication, from the provisions of the Constitution, Article II, section 2, clause 2, for the making of treaties:

(a) the United States shall interpret a treaty in accordance with the understanding of the meaning of the treaty shared by the Executive and the Senate at the time of Senate consent to ratification;

(b) such common understanding is reflected in authoritative representations as to the meaning of the treaty provided by the Executive branch in seeking Senate consent to ratification;

(c) the United States shall not agree to or adopt an interpretation different from that common understanding without the approval of the Senate.

Section 2. Condition of Senate Advice and Consent.

The Senate's advice and consent to ratification of the INF Treaty is subject to the condition that the United States shall interpret the INF Treaty in accordance with the principles cited in Section 1 of this Resolution.

Report Language: "This provision is not designed to resolve the dispute over alleged ambiguities in the genesis, design, and implementation of the ABM Treaty, or to constitute a final disposition of the ABM Treaty `reinterpretation' issue. Rather, the provision is intended to affirm certain constitutional principles which have been brought into question during the `reinterpretation' debate."

On March 17, 1988, Arthur B. Culvahouse, Jr., Counsel to the President, sent the following letter in response to the letter of March 9th from Senator Lugar:

March 17, 1988

[The Honorable Richard D. Lugar
United States Senate
Washington, D.C. 20510]

Dear Senator Lugar:

This letter responds to your letter to Howard Baker of March 9, 1988. The Administration has reviewed the attached March 2 draft of a proposed Senate resolution of advice and consent to the ratification of the INF Treaty.

For reasons discussed below, the Administration believes that sections 1 and 2 of the Resolution (hereinafter these sections are referred to as the "Resolution") are seriously flawed. The Resolution would change the legal rules of treaty interpretation. It would impose an unconstitutional mechanism for the alteration of a treaty interpretation. Moreover, it would greatly increase the risk of inflexible distinctions between the meaning of a treaty for purposes of international law and its meaning for purposes of domestic law -- distinctions that could operate to the disadvantage of the United States.

Therefore, we believe the Resolution is not in the best interests of the United States.

Changing the Rules of Treaty Interpretation

We agree that the Executive is, as a matter of domestic law, required to adhere to the interpretation of a treaty authoritatively shared with, and clearly intended, generally understood and relied upon by, the Senate at the time of its advice and consent to ratification. The Resolution, however, would purport to expand the Executive's obligation beyond this settled principle. Sections 1(b) and 2 of the Resolution apparently would define that shared understanding as encompassing all statements made by officials of the Executive branch during ratification proceedings. These statements presumably include and attribute equal dignity to the Secretary of State's definitive article-by-article analysis and to the extensive testimony of Cabinet Members, treaty negotiators and other Executive branch officials, as well as to the Administration's answers to over 1,000 questions submitted by Members of the Senate, no matter how trivial or how unimportant the issue addressed may be to the Senate's advice and consent deliberations.

This overly broad standard is inconsistent with the principles governing judicial interpretation of treaties as a matter of domestic law. Such a general statement would not in our view provide the guidance required for the President or a court to give meaning to the INF Treaty.

Section 1 of the Resolution focuses solely on the role that Executive representations play in the interpretation of treaties, but fails to acknowledge the most important interpretive tool -- the text of the treaty itself. Ignoring the text of the treaty is inconsistent with bedrock rules of treaty interpretation, which mandate that the text is the best evidence of the parties' intent. Although "authoritative representations" are among the tools for interpreting ambiguous provisions in a treaty under domestic law, the language of the treaty is the primary means by which a treaty is interpreted.

<u>Unconstitutional Mechanism for Altering Treaty Interpretation</u>

Section 1(c) of the Resolution would purport to grant the Senate a role in interpreting treaties not contemplated by the Constitution. Section 1(c) states that the "United States shall not agree to or adopt [a different] interpretation" of a treaty "without the approval of the Senate." This provision of the Resolution and the Section 1(b) incorporation by reference of all Executive statements as critical shared understandings purport to provide the Senate with an ongoing power to accept or reject subsequent Executive interpretations and implementations of the INF Treaty. A "reinterpretation," subject to Senate approval, seemingly would occur each time implementation of the treaty calls into question any Executive statement in the massive ratification record. This section, therefore, interferes with the President's constitutional responsibility to interpret and implement treaties and also constitutes an unprecedented arrogation of treaty power by the Senate.

The Constitution does not provide that treaties may be amended by the Senate and the Executive acting alone after ratification, nor does it permit unicameral "interpretive" legislation. The provisions in Sections 1(c) and 2 that contemplate such a process are not consistent with the Constitution.

<u>Risk of Unilateral Restrictions on the United States</u>

As noted above, when interpreting a treaty, one obviously looks first and foremost to the text of the treaty itself. In instances where the treaty text is not dispositive or is unclear, under <u>international law</u> one looks primarily to the negotiating record and the subsequent practice of the treaty parties. As a matter of <u>domestic law</u>, however, the President is bound by shared interpretations which were both authoritatively communicated to the Senate by the Executive and clearly intended, generally understood and relied upon by the Senate in its advice and consent to ratification. This is true even if the treaty negotiating record and subsequent practice indicate an interpretation contrary to that shared understanding. Exchanges in Senate proceedings in connection with the ratification of a treaty cannot under international law alter the meaning of a treaty where they are not officially communicated to the other treaty party prior to the exchange of instruments of ratification. The result might be two INF treaties, one binding domestically against the President and a second one binding internationally between the United States and the Soviet Union. In our view, the Resolution would substantially increase this risk of a dichotomy between the interpretation of a treaty under international law and the interpretation to which the President constitutionally is bound under domestic law. While we have spared no effort to ensure that Administration statements reflect the correct interpretation of the INF Treaty, the magnitude of the record heightens the risk of divergence between our domestic and international legal obligations. Any such difference will favor the Soviet Union because the Soviet Union is not and cannot be bound by our domestic processes.

The principles of treaty interpretation stated herein in no way contradict the position previously taken by the Administration with respect to the ABM Treaty. The President is obligated to abide by a treaty interpretation clearly intended, generally understood and relied upon by the Senate, based on authoritative Executive Branch representations during its advice and consent to ratification. Our position in the ABM case is not that the President may disregard such clearly intended interpretations, but rather that the ABM Treaty ratification record does not establish as a matter of law that the Senate clearly intended that the restrictive interpretation be followed. Administration witnesses had presented inconsistent and ambiguous views on the reach of these provisions, and the Senate as a whole did not assert a view. The President, therefore, is legally entitled to interpret the ABM Treaty on the basis of materials other than the ratification record, including the negotiating history. As you know, we believe that the negotiating record shows that the Soviet Union did not agree to be bound to the restrictive interpretation.

This letter is presented in a spirit of cooperation and in the hope that the Senate and the Executive can agree that the INF Treaty should receive the advice and consent of the Senate without any conditions. We do not believe that it is necessary or desirable to address broad, free-standing constitutional principles in a resolution of advice and consent. We believe that the proposed Resolution only serves the interests of confusion, ambiguity, confrontation and uncertainty. This Administration, of course, intends to consult closely with the Senate as the INF Treaty, upon ratification, is implemented and interpreted, and we will continue to embark upon such consultation in candor and good faith.

This letter also reflects the views of the legal offices of the Department of State, Department of Defense, the Office of Legal Counsel, Department of Justice, the Arms Control and Disarmament Agency, and National Security Council.

Sincerely,

Arthur B. Culvahouse, Jr.
Counsel to the President

Attachment

And on March 22, 1988, Arthur Culvahouse, Jr., sent the following additional letter:

March 22, 1988

[The Honorable Richard D. Lugar
United States Senate
Washington, D.C. 20510]

Dear Senator Lugar:

Discussions concerning my letter to you of March 17, 1988, have raised a question about the Secretary of State's identical letters of February 9, 1988, to Senators Byrd and Nunn. To clear up any misunderstanding that may exist, I should like to assure you that no inconsistency was intended or in fact exists between my letter and Secretary Shultz' letters. Whereas Secretary Shultz responded to the Senators' request for assurances regarding the "authoritativeness" of Executive branch testimony on the INF Treaty and the Senate's ability to rely on such testimony, my letter addressed a specific draft text setting forth what we believe to be unconstitutional and unworkable rules of treaty interpretation.

As the Secretary of State's February 9 letters pointed out: (1) all INF testimony of Executive branch witnesses, within their authorized scope, is authoritative; (2) Administration testimony and materials for the record can be regarded as authoritative without the need for the Senate to incorporate them in its Resolution of Advice and Consent; and (3) the Reagan Administration will in no way depart from the INF Treaty as we are presenting it to the Senate. Those letters remain an accurate statement of our policy and intention with respect to the INF Treaty.

My March 17 letter is consistent with Secretary Shultz' statement of Administration views.

Sincerely,

Arthur B. Culvahouse, Jr.
Counsel to the President

On March 19, 1988, the *Washington Post* reported that a group of Democratic senators led by Senator Joseph R. Biden, Jr., had agreed to support a condition to the INF Treaty that would "bar the executive branch from telling the Senate one thing and then doing another in treaty implementation, as the Democrats have claimed the administration did in adopting a `broad' or permissive reading of the ABM Treaty in 1985."[643] According to the Post, a four-page critique from White House counsel Arthur B. Culvahouse, Jr., opposed the proposed condition on the grounds that it would force the Executive branch to abide by everything stated by Executive branch officials, no matter how junior the spokesman or unimportant the issue and that it could force the Executive branch to follow an

---

[643] *White House Opposes Condition Democrats Seeking for INF Treaty*, Wash. Post, March 19, 1988, at A11, col. 1.

interpretation under national law diverging from the Nation's international obligations.[644]

On April 14, 1988, the Senate Foreign Relations Committee published its report on *The INF Treaty*.[645] Because of the importance of that report in summarizing committee views on the treaty interpretation issue, the relevant portions of the report are reprinted here in full. Thus, Part IX of the report of the Committee, entitled "Treaty Interpretation," provides as follows:

IX. TREATY INTERPRETATION (CONDITION ADOPTED BY THE COMMITTEE)

> While intent on opposing any unnecessary encumbrance on the resolution of ratification, the Committee felt compelled to address the issue of treaty interpretation. As Senator Cranston put it, the Committee acted on this issue "by necessity, not by choice." The Committee did so by approving a formal Condition which affirms certain constitutional principles relating to the Treaty Power, and requires that these principles govern U.S. interpretation of the INF Treaty.
>
> Some Senators questioned the Committee's need to act on the treaty interpretation issue, particularly in the context of a treaty that will mandate a relatively prompt three-year dismantlement of intermediate-range missiles. Is interpretation of the INF Treaty really an issue? The Committee's answer is affirmative, for three reasons:
>
> > --First, the issue is indeed relevant to the INF Treaty. While involving a three-year missile elimination phase, the INF Treaty is designed to ban a defined class of missiles permanently. Thus, the Treaty's limitations and prohibitions will entail the complexities of interpretation and implementation over a period of unlimited duration.
> >
> > --Second, the issue can hardly be avoided. The Committee could not sidestep the fundamental constitutional question raised by the Administration's recent promulgation of an extraordinary doctrine which

---

[644] *Id.* at A11, cols. 1-2.

[645] *The INF Treaty Report, supra* note 1.

asserts wide presidential latitude for changing the interpretation of a treaty, notwithstanding what the Senate may have been told in consenting to ratification. To ignore this question, while dealing with a major treaty, could imply acquiesence in the doctrine.

--Third, the inclusion of a Condition on treaty interpretation represented the least problematic means of handling a potentially grave problem for the INF Treaty. In the absence of a Condition reaffirming traditional principles of treaty interpretation--under which the Senate can accept Executive explanations as having binding significance--the Senate would face the alternative of considering countless other Conditions designed to formalize the Senate's understanding of various INF Treaty provisions.

A. THE TREATY POWER

The Constitution's Treaty Clause (Article II, section 2, clause 2) states that the President "shall have Power, by and with the Advice and Consent of the Senate, to make treaties, provided two-thirds of the Senators present concur." Because treaties constitute solemn international commitments of the United States, and hold domestic status as "supreme Law of the Land," the Senate's shared role in the Treaty Power is a central constitutional provision. As such, it represents a principal means by which the Senate participates in the shaping of American foreign policy.

In the words of Alexander Hamilton, the Framers of the Constitution considered the division of the Treaty Power between the Executive and the Senate to be "one of the best digested and most unexceptional parts of the plan." It would have been "utterly unsafe and improper," Hamilton wrote, to entrust the power of making treaties in the President alone. Hamilton's most famous dictum applied directly to the Treaty Power:

> The history of human conduct does not warrant that exalted opinion of human virtue which would make it wise in a nation to commit interests of so delicate and momentous a kind as those which

> concern its intercourse with the rest of the world to the sole disposal of a magistrate, created and circumstanced, as would be a president of the United States.

The essence of the Treaty Power is that the President and the Senate are partners in the process by which the United States enters into international obligations. It is fundamental to the logic of the Treaty Clause that it does not envisage that the President may unilaterally re-make a treaty. If he could, the Senate's portion of the shared power inherent in the Treaty Clause would be nullified.

B. ORIGINS OF THE ISSUE

Last year, in seeking to justify the Administration's "broad" interpretation of the 1972 ABM Treaty, the State Department Legal Adviser, Mr. Sofaer, advanced two claims--one factual, the other constitutional:

> (1) The factual claim is that the entire ABM Treaty, in design, genesis, and implementation, was fraught with ambiguity: ambiguity in what the negotiators agreed to, ambiguity in the text they produced, ambiguity in the Executive presentation to the Senate, ambiguity in the Senate's understanding of the Treaty, and ambiguity in the subsequent practice of the parties.
>
> (2) The constitutional claim is that what the Senate is told in the process of consenting to a treaty is not in itself of binding significance in determining the President's obligation in carrying out the treaty.

The constitutional claim was manifest in a number of statements made by Mr. Sofaer, but none more crystallized the issue for Senators than this assertion, made during joint Foreign Relations-Judiciary Committee hearings in early 1987: "When [the Senate] gives its advice and consent to a treaty, it is to the treaty that was made, irrespective of the explanation [the Senate] was provided." Questioning how a treaty could be "made" prior to the Senate's consent, Senators grew increasingly concerned about the Administration's concept of the Treaty Power.

In 1987, the Foreign Relations Committee devoted considerable time and attention to the ABM Treaty dispute in both of these dimensions: factual and constitutional.[13] [[13]For the Foreign Relations Committee's actions and views with regard to the overall ABM Treaty dispute, see the Committee's March-April 1987 joint hearings with the Judiciary Committee, entitled "The ABM Treaty and the Constitution," and the Committee's September 1987 report on S. Res. 167, "The ABM Treaty Interpretation Resolution." The Committee wishes to acknowledge that in the conduct of those hearings, the drafting of that report, and the creation of the Condition herein described, the Committee received extensive and invaluable assistance from its former legal counsel, Professor Michael J. Glennon.] Having done so, the Committee found no reason, while considering the INF Treaty, to debate again the overall validity of the Administration's assertion of a "broad" interpretation of the ABM Treaty as opposed to the traditional "narrow" interpretation. Indeed, in the Committee's view, that issue is being adequately addressed elsewhere:

> --First, as to U.S. defense policy in pursuing the development and testing of ABM systems, that issue is now being addressed through the normal give-and-take of the U.S. *defense budget process*. By means of an amendment to the FY 1988-89 DoD authorization, Congress has employed the power of the purse to assert its view, and similar amendments in the future will succeed or fail on the basis of policy debate.
>
> --Second, and even more to the point, it has become patently clear that what is permitted by the ABM Treaty will ultimately be decided by *superpower negotiation*. Such negotiation is virtually inevitable--and the need for it is now part of the Reagan Administration's own position--because the United States, as a precondition of

agreeing to major reductions in strategic offensive arms, will be required by self interest to achieve its own clear and detailed understanding of which kinds of Soviet ABM systems to anticipate in the future strategic environment. Any Treaty amendment would, of course, be subject to Senate advice and consent.

In sum, the future of U.S. policy with regard to ABM systems, and U.S. participation in the ABM Treaty, will be addressed in the budget process and in negotiations with the Soviet Union. The Committee was unanimous in believing that its action on the INF Treaty required no resolution of the "broad-versus-narrow" ABM Treaty debate.

The one legacy of that debate which the Committee could not overlook, however, was the Administration's *constitutional* assertion of a clearly delineated and unprecedented doctrine under which the President has wide latitude for treaty "reinterpretations," notwithstanding what the Senate may have been told in the course of granting consent to ratification. The Committee was intent upon addressing and refuting this effort at Executive enlargement of its share of the Treaty Power.

As Senator Sarbanes emphasized, "We did not raise this issue to begin with; it was in effect raised to us."

Thus, those who have described the Committee's interest in the treaty interpretation issue as an effort to refight the old ABM battle have missed the point. The Committee is looking forward--to the successful implementation of the INF Treaty and other treaties--and looking backward only to a crucial constitutional provision established 200 years ago, which the Committee feels duty-bound to uphold and affirm.

C. DESCRIPTION OF THE SOFAER DOCTRINE

In defending its new, "broad" interpretation of the ABM Treaty, the Reagan Administration employed a dual-track approach:

(1) In the context of *international* law, it used a new reading of the ABM Treaty text and of internal U.S.

Government memoranda from 1971-72 (the "negotiating record"[14]) [[14]Under international law (and also under domestic law), the primary source of interpretation is the text, which should be interpreted in accordance with the ordinary meaning to be given the treaty's terms in light of their context and in light of the treaty's object and purpose. Another major source of interpretation under international law is practice under the treaty. But the negotiating history--which refers to what happened, as opposed to any particular set of documents--is also recognized as having some interpretive significance insofar as it may reflect what the parties commonly understood about the meaning of the text. For a discussion of the complexities of defining what a "negotiating record" might be, see the Committee's September 1987 report on S. Res. 167, pp. 49-51. See also Restatement of the Law (3d), Foreign Relations Law of the United States, The American Law Institute, 1988; and Reports of the International Law Commission, United Nations, 1966.] as a basis for asserting that the two superpowers had not actually agreed to limit the development of any ABM systems based on new technologies.

(2) In the context of *domestic, constitutional* law, it argued that alleged ambiguities in the Treaty text and in the negotiating history had been reflected in the Executive's presentation to the Senate--and buttressed this claim with a newly-minted doctrine which asserted wide Executive latitude for "reinterpretation" of treaties.

The argument of pervasive ambiguity--in the ABM Treaty's design and its presentation to the Senate--would have been sufficient, in terms of *logic*, to assert Executive latitude for a "broad" interpretation of the Treaty. Such an approach would have emphasized that the ABM Treaty was being interpreted "within the bounds of the ambiguity in the original shared understanding" held by the Executive and the Senate, rather than "reinterpreted."[15] [[15]Because of its interest in avoiding a renewed debate over the "broad-versus-narrow" interpretation of the ABM Treaty, the Committee will not comment here on its evaluation of the persuasiveness of the factual case for the "broad" interpretation; i.e., the assertion that the ABM Treaty--in genesis, design, and presentation to the Senate--was suffused with ambiguity. The Committee notes only that the assertion of such pervasive ambiguity in the original "shared understanding" of the Treaty, held by the Executive and the Senate, is logically sufficient to make the case for a "broad" interpretation without any need for innovative constitutional assertions.]

The additional assertion, however, amounted to a new constitutional doctrine--which the Committee will here call the Sofaer Doctrine--that effectively claims an Executive right of treaty amendment disguised as treaty interpretation.

The essence of the Sofaer Doctrine is the assertion that the Executive is not bound, in implementing a treaty, by what it has told the Senate in seeking consent to ratification. The Executive is only bound, according to the doctrine, by a particular interpretation of a treaty's meaning if that interpretation meets three criteria: the particular interpretation must have been (1) "generally understood" by the Senate, (2) "clearly intended" by the Senate, and (3) "relied upon" by the Senate.

In a letter dated March 17, 1988 (see Appendix), White House Counsel Culvahouse described these criteria as "settled principles." But in fact they have been asserted with no constitutional basis--no reference to the intent of the Framers, to historical precedent, to case law--no reference to any source of constitutional authority. These alleged "principles" have been invented during this Administration, from which they emerged in the course of Mr. Sofaer's various presentations to Congress.[16] [[16]See, for example, Mr. Sofaer's testimony to the Senate Foreign Relations Committee in the previously cited hearing volume entitled "The ABM Treaty and the Constitution."]

Moreover, while such terms as "generally understood," "clearly intended," and "relied upon" may appear straight forward and appealing, in practice such criteria would be so difficult to meet that the Executive would almost never be bound by its own presentation to the Senate:

> --(1) How many Senators must speak on a given interpretation before it can be proven that the Senate "generally understood" that interpretation?

--(2) How, unless the Senate has affirmed a particular interpretation by means of a formal condition, can it ever be demonstrated that the Senate "clearly intended" a particular interpretation?

--(3) And if "relied upon" means (as Administration officials have suggested) that a particular interpretation was crucial to the Senate's action in approving a treaty or refraining from the imposition of a formal condition, how can that negative proposition--"The Senate wouldn't have done x if it weren't for y"--ever be proven?

Yet, under the Sofaer Doctrine, all three of these difficult proofs are required if a particular treaty interpretation is not to be subject to "reinterpretation."

Thus, the Sofaer Doctrine is in effect a claim of wide Executive latitude in treaty interpretation by means of the assertion, in the context of *domestic* law, of unreasonable criteria for what may not be "reinterpreted." If a particular interpretation of a particular provision of a treaty does not meet these criteria, it apparently is subject--according to the Sofaer Doctrine--to any interpretation the President may wish to place upon it.

As subsequent discussion will underscore, the import of this assertion is that the Senate is not a partner in the treaty process, but essentially an adversary--an on-looker of secondary status which, while it may derive some momentary power from its ability to block a treaty or impose formal conditions on its consent, must take extraordinary precautions if what it is told by the Executive about a treaty is to be determinative of the Executive's obligations in interpreting and implementing that treaty.

It bears note that there is no necessary relationship between the Sofaer Doctrine and a treaty's "negotiating record." By way of example, one may imagine circumstances in which the Sofaer Doctrine would be asserted but the "negotiating record" would play no role. Let us say that President Reagan's successor and Secretary Gorbachev wished to "reinterpret" the INF Treaty in a manner inconsistent with what the Senate has been told in consenting to ratification. The Sofaer Doctrine would play the role of helping the Administration loosen its obligations under domestic law, while as between the parties there would be no resistance to the new meaning being put on existing words and thus no need to justify the change by reference to a "record." Indeed, under this scenario the "record" would be assiduously disregarded, because it reflected a meaning contrary to that which the parties wished to adopt.

Against this background one can examine Mr. Sofaer's provocative declaration that "When [the Senate] gives its advice and consent to a treaty, it is to the treaty that was made, irrespective of the explanations [the Senate] was provided."

With the Senate's role denigrated by the Sofaer Doctrine, the essence of a treaty from the U.S. perspective becomes not what the Executive and the Senate jointly understood at the outset but what the Executive at any moment wants to assert was agreed to with the other party. What little constitutional constraint there is on any particular interpretation would require an Executive determination that the Senate has fulfilled the Sofaer Doctrine criteria with regard to that interpretation--criteria the Senate rarely fulfills. Thus, under the Sofaer model, whatever the President can assert within the context of international law acquires a *de facto* supremacy over constitutional law.

There is, of course, a central defect in Mr. Sofaer's supposition that the President unilaterally "makes" treaties which the Senate subsequently is asked to approve. Constitutionally, no treaty is "made" until the Senate has given its consent. This is how a treaty becomes part of "the supreme Law of the Land."

The Legal Adviser's statement implies that the meaning of a U.S.-Soviet treaty is to be gleaned not by examination of what the President and the *Senate* jointly understood, but by examination of what the President and the *Soviets* agreed upon--regardless of what the President may or may not have told the Senate. This is tantamount to saying that a U.S.-Soviet treaty becomes the supreme law of the United States with the advice and consent of the Soviet Union. The Constitution provides otherwise.

D. PROBLEMS WITH THE SOFAER DOCTRINE

The basic problem with the Sofaer Doctrine is that it is founded on the faulty premise that the Senate is not an integral part of establishing the meaning of a treaty under U.S. constitutional law--except insofar as the Senate does so through affirmative steps which impose restrictions on Executive latitude. The doctrine undercuts the basic model of treaty-creation: that the Executive negotiates and signs a treaty,[17] [[17]The signing of a treaty does not bring the treaty into force. Only ratification can do that. Discussion of this and related concepts is contained in the Appendix section entitled "Principles of Treaty-Making and Interpretation."] explains its proposed treaty to a listening Senate, and then on that basis is accorded consent to ratify the treaty that has been explained.

Under the Constitution, the President may only ratify a treaty to which the Senate advised and consented. And it must be taken as axiomatic that the Senate cannot consent to that which it did not understand. Accordingly, the operative principle of treaty-making under the Constitution *must* be that, as co-makers of a treaty for the United States, the Executive and the Senate share a common understanding of a treaty which has binding significance domestically as the treaty, upon ratification, becomes an integral part of United States law.

In the establishment and determination of that common understanding, the concept of legislative intent must be as applicable to treaties as it is to statutory law, in which intent may be explicit or implicit.

Explicit understandings regarding a treaty's meaning are manifest in formal conditions to the Senate's consent. These conditions include amendments to the text of a treaty as well as amendments to the resolution of ratification, such as "reservations," "understandings," and the like.

Implicit understandings represent Senate agreement with and acceptance of the Executive's explanations of the treaty. Whereas explicit understandings may at times entail the Senate's imposition on the Executive of a meaning not originally intended by the Executive, implicit understandings never do; they can only reaffirm the meaning presented by the Executive.

Although not formalized, implicit understandings must necessarily be equal in significance to explicit understandings. To accord them lesser significance would be illogical because implicit understandings commonly occur precisely where there is no disagreement as to meaning and where no issue has arisen. Such understandings are reflected in the various materials traditionally described as legislative history. These sources include hearings and committee reports, as well as debates transcribed into the Congressional Record. Such sources must be regarded as indicia of legislative intent as much for a treaty as for a statute.

What is crucial is that legislative intent, with regard to a treaty as well as a statute, is expressed not only in language drafted by legislators but in unchallenged communications of the Executive. Under longstanding principles of textual construction, Executive communications to the Congress concerning the meaning of a text are evidence of the meaning of that text if Congress (or the Senate) acquiesces in that meaning. In other words, the legislative branch is deemed to be placed on notice by the Executive that certain words will be construed in a certain manner. If Congress wishes a different meaning to obtain, it may act so as to effect that different meaning. If Congress does not act, however, it is properly deemed to have accepted--and to intend--the meaning communicated by the Executive.

In testimony to a joint hearing of the Judiciary and Foreign Relations Committees, Professor Louis Henkin, chief reporter of the new *Restatement of U.S. Foreign Relations Law,*[18] [[18]The full title of this preeminent compendium of U.S. law in the realm of foreign affairs is *Restatement of the Law (3d), Foreign Relations Law of the United States,* 1988.] summarized this concept as follows: "Where several [Executive] statements are made and there is general acceptance of their tenor, that is the Senate understanding. That is true in the case of Senate consent to a treaty, as it would be in the legislative history of a statute."

Clearly, in determining whether the Senate consented to the ratification of a treaty pursuant to an implicit understanding, a rule of reason must apply. Obviously, where the indicia of Senate intent or understanding (including unchallenged Executive communications or explanations) are few or inconsistent, no implicit Senate intent can reasonably be said to exist. On the other hand, where the indicia of intent (again, including unchallenged Executive communications or explanations) are several and largely consistent, an implicit intent can reasonably be concluded to exist. In such circumstances, the President is bound constitutionally to regard that intent as an implicit Senate understanding, and therefore an implicit condition of the Senate's consent. The Chief Executive cannot bring the treaty into force unless it reflects that condition, and subsequent Presidents must interpret the treaty subject to that intent.

The essence of the Sofaer Doctrine is to reject this concept of legislative intent as it has been normally understood, and to replace it with a requirement that the Senate act affirmatively to formally demonstrate what is "generally understood, clearly intended, and relied upon" regarding every provision of a treaty, lest that provision be subject to any interpretation a President may later prefer.

E. IMPLICATIONS OF THE SOFAER DOCTRINE

In very practical terms, the Sofaer Doctrine, if accepted, threatens two far-reaching and dangerous consequences:

> (1) Nullification of the Senate's Treaty Power. A presidential right to adopt a different interpretation of a treaty, irrespective of the understanding on which the Senate based its consent, would tend to nullify the Senate's share of the Treaty Power and thus undermine a basic provision of the Constitution.
>
> (2) Paralysis in Treaty-Making. The Senate's only recourse, to prevent its share of the Treaty Power being nullified, would be to attach elaborate and numerous conditions to treaties in order to have the Senate's understanding become an integral and explicit part of the ratification documents. Such procedure could easily overburden the treaty process to the point of paralysis.

F. THE INF TREATY AND THE SOFAER DOCTRINE

In the context of the Senate's consideration of the INF Treaty, two letters--from Secretary of State Shultz and from White House Counsel Culvahouse (both reprinted in the Appendix)--became the focus of Senate efforts to deal with the Administration's constitutional assertions.

Some originally saw in the Shultz letter (dated February 9, 1988) an indication of Administration willingness to retreat from its assertion of the Sofaer Doctrine, and thus reacted with disappointment when the doctrine was clearly reasserted in the letter (dated March 17, 1988) signed by White House Counsel Culvahouse. Under analysis, however, it becomes clear that the Administration has remained consistent in its adherence to the Sofaer Doctrine.

Accordingly, the Committee agrees with the Culvahouse letter (as he stated in a brief follow-up letter dated March 22, 1988) that the Shultz and Culvahouse letters are consistent on the question of treaty interpretation. The Shultz letter tiptoed around the Sofaer Doctrine; the Culvahouse letter simply stated the Administration's views on the Sofaer Doctrine clearly and boldly.

The key to understanding this consistency is to recognize that the Administration conceded virtually nothing in the Shultz letter, which contained only these three items:

> (1) an assertion that Administration testimony on the INF Treaty is "authoritative" (which appears to mean nothing more than dependably accurate);
>
> (2) a kind of admonition that, because of these dependably accurate statements, the Senate need not incorporate Executive materials and testimony in the resolution of ratification--but no clear statement that this or a future Administration would be bound in any legal sense by such an "authoritative" presentation;
>
> (3) a promise that the Reagan Administration would not depart from the meaning of the INF Treaty as presented to the Senate.

These three elements offer absolutely nothing by way of any agreement on principles as to what would bind the Executive. Thus, while the Culvahouse letter seemed to some to be a step backward, in fact it served only to articulate the premises underlying the vague and essentially noncommittal language in the Shultz letter. The essence of the Culvahouse letter is its clear reiteration of the Sofaer Doctrine, which asserts wide Executive latitude for "reinterpretations" by promulgating unreasonable criteria for what provisions in a treaty may not be "reinterpreted":

> As a matter of domestic law . . . the President is bound by shared interpretations which were both authoritatively communicated to the Senate by the Executive and *clearly intended, generally understood and relied upon* by the Senate in its advice and consent to ratification. [Emphasis added.]

In criticizing the draft Biden Condition under consideration by the Committee, the Culvahouse letter agreed that U.S. treaty interpretation must be based on the "shared understanding" of the Executive and the Senate when a treaty is made. But it rejected any notion that such "shared understandings" of binding significance could be found by examining the record of Executive testimony:

> [The Biden Condition] apparently would define that shared understanding as encompassing all statements made by officials of the Executive branch during ratification proceedings. These statements presumably include and attribute equal dignity to the Secretary of State's definitive article-by-article analysis and to the extensive testimony of Cabinet members, treaty negotiators and other Executive branch officials, as well as to the Administration's answers to over 1,000 questions submitted by Members of the Senate, no matter how trivial or unimportant the issue may be to the Senate's advice and consent deliberation.

In testifying to the Foreign Relations Committee, Senator Nunn saw this sentence as casting doubt on the "authoritativeness" of all Executive branch communications concerning the INF Treaty. But in fact the Culvahouse letter does not deny that all Executive branch communications are "authoritative." Rather, it denies that all "authoritative" communications meet the criteria of the Sofaer Doctrine as to what is binding on the Executive.

This confusion apparently rests on Senator Nunn's eminently reasonable premise that "authoritative" testimony should have binding significance. But this is a premise that the Administration has never formally acknowledged--in the Shultz letter or anywhere else.[19] [[19]One individual exception was Ambassador Nitze, speaking spontaneously. See the final paragraph of this section on "Treaty Interpretation" and also the Appendix of this report.]

G. PURPOSE AND CONTENT OF THE BIDEN CONDITION

The purpose of the condition drafted by Senator Biden--and offered on his behalf by Senator Cranston--is to reaffirm the long-standing practice and long-standing principle that the "shared understanding" of the Executive and the Senate, as reflected in the Executive's formal representations, is indeed fully binding--as opposed to binding only with regard to those provisions and interpretations which the Senate has gone to extraordinary lengths to brand as crucial to its consent, by formal condition or some other means.

Unlike the Sofaer Doctrine, the Biden Condition envisages the Executive and the Senate not as adversaries in the treaty-making process but as partners--co-makers of the treaty on behalf of the United States.

While both the Biden Condition and the Sofaer Doctrine rest upon the premise that a "shared understanding" is required to bind the Executive to a given interpretation of a treaty, the crucial difference is that the Biden Condition envisages that a "shared understanding" will be reflected in all "authoritative" statements by the Executive. Under the Sofaer Doctrine, the Executive is bound only by those "shared understandings" which the Senate has somehow labeled crucial to its consent by fulfilling the criteria of "generally understood, clearly intended, and relied upon."

The Committee's purpose, in adopting the Condition, was to lead the Senate to affirm a set of principles which reflect long-standing constitutional practice. By so doing, the Senate can:

--avoid the need for other conditions pertaining to specific interpretations of the INF Treaty;

--repudiate a pernicious doctrine that was asserted solely for a specific purpose; and

--establish a position with regard to future treaties such that the Senate can avoid repeating the inclusion of a formal condition. The Senate's 1988 action will have been sufficient to reaffirm fundamental constitutional principles of treaty-making.

The Biden Condition was drafted in consultation with Professor Louis Henkin, chief reporter of the *Restatement of U.S. Foreign Relations Law* and the nation's most generally esteemed scholar in this field. The provision was designed to articulate and affirm, as succinctly as possible, these constitutional principles reflected in time-honored practice: to wit, that the original shared understanding of the Executive and the Senate must govern a treaty's subsequent implementation, and that such understanding is reflected in the Executive's presentation to the Senate.

A key consideration in the drafting of the Condition was to strike an appropriate balance between the general and the specific. As stated earlier, the Committee did not wish to see the Senate fight once again a battle over the Administration's "broad" interpretation of the ABM Treaty. The Committee therefore sought to direct this Condition, to the maximum degree possible, to the INF Treaty. At the same time, however, the Committee's purpose, in addressing the treaty interpretation issue, was not to erect *sui generis* barriers against any "reinterpretation" of the INF Treaty, but to affirm principles that *inherently apply* to the INF Treaty.

The Committee notes that, in one respect, its action in including this Condition in the INF Treaty's resolution of ratification was unnecessary insofar as principles which inherently apply to the INF Treaty would apply even in the absence of any Senate action affirming them. Given the circumstances, however, the Committee judged that to fail to affirm such principles could suggest some degree of acquiesence in the Sofaer Doctrine, which the Committee views as an Executive attempt to assert an unconstitutional arrogation of the Treaty Power. In this sense the

Committee views the Biden Condition, paradoxically, as both unnecessary and highly significant.

The Condition, as approved by the Foreign Relations Committee, stipulates as follows:

> That this Treaty shall be subject to the following principles, which derive, as a necessary implication, from the provisions of the Constitution (Article II, section 2, clause 2) for the making of treaties:
>
> (a) the United States shall interpret this Treaty in accordance with the understanding of the Treaty shared by the Executive and the Senate at the time of Senate consent to ratification;
>
> (b) such common understanding is:
>
> (i) based on the text of the Treaty; and
>
> (ii) reflected in the authoritative representations provided by the Executive branch to the Senate and its committees in seeking Senate consent to ratification, insofar as such representations are directed to the meaning and legal effect of the text of the Treaty;
>
> (c) the United States shall not agree to or adopt an interpretation different from that common understanding except pursuant to Senate advice and consent to a subsequent treaty or protocol, or the enactment of a statute.

The Condition also stipulates that "This understanding shall not be incorporated in the instruments of ratification of this Treaty or otherwise officially conveyed to the other contracting Party."

Several concepts in the Condition warrant discussion:

Text of the Treaty: Both domestic and international law give primacy in treaty interpretation to the text of the treaty. International law requires that a treaty be interpreted in accordance with the ordinary meaning to be given the treaty's terms in light of their context and in light of the treaty's object and purpose.

Domestic law does not differ, and is also premised on the assumption that the Executive and the Senate, as co-makers of a treaty for the United States, will share a common understanding of a treaty's text. As a matter of record, that common understanding of the text will be reflected in the Executive's formal presentation of the treaty to the Senate: in formal presentation documents, in prepared testimony, and in verbal and written intercourse regarding the treaty's meaning and effect.

In Professor Henkin's judgment, the phrase "meaning of a treaty" in the original draft Condition included the treaty text. However, in order to underscore that the Biden Condition had not (as alleged in the Culvahouse letter) ignored the primacy of the treaty text as a source of interpretation, the draft Condition was altered at the initiative of Senator Dodd, who worked in consultation with Professor Henkin to refine language that would serve to preempt any further criticism along such lines. Senator Dodd's adjustments in the Condition also served to underscore that the Executive's "authoritative" representations have interpretive significance only insofar as such representations relate to the meaning and legal effect of the treaty text. Thus are excluded the Administration's answers to such questions as "What is the overall effect of the INF Treaty on U.S. security?" and "What will the Administration do to ensure an adequate military balance in Europe?

As Senator Dodd stressed, this wording "binds the Executive only in those parts of its presentation where it analyzes and explains the text itself, such as "This is what these words mean.' and `This is what their effect is under international law'"--in short, where the Executive describes the precise international obligation about to be assumed by the United States.

Authoritative Representations: With regard to what constitutes an "authoritative" representation by the Executive, a rule of reason must apply. Certainly, substantial weight must be accorded the Executive's formal presentation do[c]uments, which include the treaty itself and a detailed explanation of the Executive's understanding of the treaty's terms. Considerable weight must also be accorded the prepared testimony of top Executive officials. Additional information elicited during Executive-Senate interaction regarding the meaning and legal effect of treaty terms will also be important because such discussion and questioning will cover items of particular interest and concern to the Senate, as a co-maker of the treaty for the United States. The overall significance of Executive branch representations makes it incumbent upon the Executive to take great care to avoid or remove any inconsistency in its overall presentation of a treaty. The possibility, however, that the Executive may prove fallible--that an "authoritative" representation could, on rare occasion, be inconsistent with the text of the treaty, or with another "authoritative" representation--is simply an unavoidable fact of life, which does not in any way diminish the crucial role of such representations in providing evidence of the common understanding of the text of a treaty held originally by the Executive and the Senate as co-makers of a treaty.

In this context arises the question of the role of the INF Treaty "negotiating record," access to which was afforded Senators not as a part of the Executive's formal or "authoritative" presentation of the Treaty, but in response to a Senate request. This is discussed in the following section, entitled "The INF Treaty Negotiating Record."

Methods for Establishing New Interpretations: As originally drafted, the Biden Condition stated that the United States would not agree to or adopt a new interpretation of the INF Treaty without the "approval of the Senate." That phrase was intended to encompass three possibilities, each of which would legitimately result in the United States adopting a different interpretation of a treaty:

> (1) an amendment to the treaty, accomplished by protocol or other means and ratified by the Executive with the advice and consent of the Senate;
>
> (2) a change in the treaty's terms of implementation agreed to by the parties under procedures, and within the framework, established by the treaty as originally ratified with the advice and consent of the Senate; and
>
> (3) a subsequent statute.

In response to a concern expressed by Senator Helms that this should be stated more explicitly, Senator Cranston offered new phrasing which substituted the words, "except pursuant to Senate advice and consent to a subsequent treaty or protocol, or the enactment of a statute." Professor Henkin subsequently indicated his judgment that the principle being enunciated had not been altered by the change in language.

With regard to the modality of a statute resulting in a change in U.S. treaty interpretation, the Committee wishes to emphasize that the Condition envisages this possibility not as a matter of advocacy but as a matter of accuracy. In the overwhelming majority of cases, the preferable course for the United States is for the Executive to negotiate an international agreement--a new treaty or a protocol to an existing treaty--which is subsequently ratified with the advice and consent of the Senate. However, as a practical reality, it is a truth of U.S. domestic law that a statute requiring the President to adopt a new interpretation of a treaty is binding on the Executive.[20] [[20]One example, during the Wilson Administration, involved a congressionally-initiated statute requiring a new U.S. policy that contravened existing international arrangements pertaining to the Panama Canal. In successfully persuading Congress to repeal this legislation, President Wilson argued that the United States is simply "too big and powerful and self-respecting" to put a strained interpretation on its promises.]

The Committee notes that paragraph (c) of the Condition is essentially a corollary of the principles in paragraphs (a) and (b). The import of paragraphs (a) and (b) is that the Executive must interpret a treaty in accord with the original Executive-Senate "shared understanding" of the treaty, which is reflected in the Executive's presentation to the Senate, and accordingly that the Executive may not, acting alone, adopt an interpretation outside the bounds of that "shared understanding." Paragraph (c) simply spells out the circumstances under which the Executive would receive a mandate to adopt an interpretation outside such bounds.

Non-Conveyance of Condition to the Other Party: A stipulation that the Condition not be conveyed to the Soviet Union as a part of the instruments of ratification was included in the Condition at the initiative of Senator Helms. The Committee viewed this as a matter of underscoring that the Condition is not directed to U.S. obligations under international law, which provides the context within which the U.S.-Soviet exchange of instruments of ratification will occur. Rather, the Condition is binding under domestic law, and obtains its binding effect because the President, in the absence of the resolution of ratification, lacks authority to participate in the treaty's ratification. He obtains such authority through the resolution of ratification and is governed by any stipulations by which the Senate conditions its consent.

In sum, the President may not act upon the Senate's consent without honoring this Condition. Nothing that he or his Administration does, by statement or action, whether before or after the act of ratification, can alter the binding effect of any condition which the Senate places upon its consent to treaty ratification. If the President brings the INF Treaty into force, the Condition takes effect.

H. THE INF TREATY "NEGOTIATING RECORD"

Because the Sofaer Doctrine and the "negotiating record" were closely tied in the ABM dispute, some Senators demanded the "record" of the INF Treaty by means of underscoring the point that the Administration's assertions about the role of the Senate in treaty-making had destroyed any basis on which the Senate could operate in confidence of Executive good faith. With the INF Treaty "negotiating record" having been provided under these circumstances, both the Administration and the Senate now face the task of ensuring that Senate review of "negotiating records" does not become an institutionalized procedure.

First, a systematic expectation of Senate perusal of every key treaty's "negotiating record" could be expected to inhibit candor during future negotiations and induce posturing on the part of U.S. negotiators and their counterparts during sensitive discussions.

Second, by seeking possession of the myriad internal Executive memoranda comprising the "negotiating record," the Senate would impose upon itself a considerable task with no clear purpose. Because this "record" does not constitute an agreed account of the negotiations, such documents have no formal standing. Accordingly, regularized efforts to reconcile these "snapshots" of the negotiation process with the resulting treaty text as explained by the Executive would serve only to divert the

Senate's attention from the central aim of the ratification process--which is to build, between the Executive and the Senate, a clear "shared understanding" of the treaty text and the obligations which that text entails.

The overall effect--of fully exposed negotiations followed by a far more complicated Senate review--would be to weaken the treaty-making process and thereby to damage American diplomacy.

The traditional approach does not, of course, *preclude* reference to the "record" where such reference can be useful in explaining the effect of treaty provisions which may appear ambiguous or about which questions may arise. The Executive may sometimes wish to initiate such reference to the "record"; on some occasions the Senate may request a detailed account of the interchange which resulted in a particular treaty provision. But this case-by-case approach is far superior to a systematic submission of the "negotiating record," which implies either that treaties tend to be replete with ambiguity or that the Executive cannot be trusted to present an accurate account of the obligations to be assumed by the United States. Neither assumption should be allowed to govern the basic Executive-Senate interaction in the treaty-making process.

Now that the INF Treaty "negotiating record" has been made available to the Senate, the status of these documents requires resolution. In the Committee's view, that resolution would not have been satisfactorily achieved by any stipulation in the resolution of ratification declaring that the Senate had scrutinized the "record" and satisfied itself that the "record" was in harmony with the formal Executive branch presentation of the Treaty. Such an approach could entail three significant problems:

> (a) institutionally, it could imply that such scrutiny is important to the Senate's examination of treaties and thus should be institutionalized;
>
> (b) retroactively, it could imply that such scrutiny should have been exercised in the past; and
>
> (c) specifically, with regard to the INF Treaty, it could leave open the question of what is to be done if, in the future, there is an assertion--for example, by a subsequent Administration--that notwithstanding the

Senate's perception of harmony there was an inconsistency between the "record" and the Executive presentation.

Accordingly, the Committee believes that no formal finding concerning the contents of the INF Treaty "negotiating record" would be wise. In the Committee's judgment, the status of this "record" is established by the basic principles affirmed in the Biden Condition. If U.S. treaty interpretation is to be based upon the shared understanding of the Senate and the Executive at the time of ratification, and if the common understanding is reflected in authoritative Executive branch statements made in seeking Senate consent to ratification, then sources of interpretation which appear at variance must be subordinated to those authoritative statements.

In sum, although internal Executive memoranda and other negotiating materials may have been available to members of the Senate, some of whom have sought to assure themselves that this "record" is consistent with the Administration's formal presentation, the clear corollary of the constitutional principles cited in the Biden Condition is that such documents need not have been examined for consistency and should not be deemed material to U.S. interpretation of the INF Treaty insofar as they are inconsistent with the Executive branch's formal presentation of the INF Treaty.

I. ADMINISTRATION CRITICISMS OF THE BIDEN CONDITION

The Culvahouse letter (previously cited and reprinted in the Appendix) makes three charges against the Condition, which the Committee has considered but to which the Committee can attach little weight:

(1) *"Changing the Rules of Treaty Interpretation"*

Under this heading, the Administration's position makes two false charges and affirms a false principle.

The false charges are that the Condition (a) ignores the text of a treaty as the primary source of meaning[21]; [[21]As discussed earlier, the first draft of the Biden Condition, which is the object of the Culvahouse letter's criticism, used the phrase "meaning of a treaty" on the premise that this phrase is synonymous with "meaning of the text of a treaty." Thus, the concept and central role of the "text" of a treaty were always implicit in the Biden Condition.] and (b) accords "equal dignity" to all sources of interpretation, ranging from the Secretary of State's definitive article-by-article analysis to the written answers to hundreds of Senators' questions.

As to the importance of the text, there is no issue. No one disputes that the text of a treaty constitutes the seminal source of the treaty's meaning. (As described previously, at the initiative of Senator Dodd the original draft text of the Condition was revised before Committee approval to underscore this point.) The Condition simply affirms that the Executive must continue to interpret a treaty in accord with the original understanding of that meaning shared by the Executive and the Senate.

As to the weight to be given to various parts of the Executive presentation, there is also no real issue. The Administration's position itself envisages that "the interpretation of a treaty [will be] authoritatively shared with * * *. the Senate." Obviously a rule of reason must apply. As stated above, the text is the central source of meaning. But that meaning is elaborated upon through various elements of the Executive's presentation. The Condition does not state that the treaty is "defined by" the Executive's presentation. Rather, it affirms that the "common understanding" of the two branches is reflected in--meaning evidenced by--authoritative representations by the Executive.

The Administration, however, does not wish to accept this because it wishes to assert broad latitude for subsequent Executive "reinterpretation." It therefore affirms what, under analysis, proves to be a truly radical constitutional principle: that the Executive must adhere to a given interpretation of a treaty *only if* that interpretation was "clearly intended, generally understood, and relied upon by the Senate."

(2) *"Unconstitutional Mechanism for Altering Treaty Interpretation"*

Under this heading, the Administration alleges that the Condition "interferes with the President's constitutional responsibility to interpret and implement treaties and also constitutes an unprecedented arrogation of treaty power by the Senate." This charge is without foundation.

It is indisputable that the President alone bears the constitutional obligation to interpret and implement treaties, and the principles affirmed by the Condition are perfectly consistent with that. What the President does not have the authority to do is interpret a treaty in a way that constitutes an amendment. His interpretive action must, if he is to behave constitutionally, be in accordance with the original understanding of the treaty. If he wishes to change the meaning of a treaty, he must obtain the agreement of the other party and formalize the change with the established mechanism of Senate advice and consent.

Meanwhile, the President will possess inherent latitude in his capacity as interpreter of every treaty to which the U.S. is a party. In the international context, each such treaty will inevitably provide a measure of flexibility in interpretation and implementation--within the treaty framework. Similarly, in the domestic context, the President will inevitably have latitude for interpretation within the bounds of the "shared understanding" established with the Senate.

(3) *"Risk of Unilateral Restrictions on the United States"*

Under this heading, the White House letter seeks to raise the specter of the United States being bound by constitutional processes to one interpretation of a treaty while the Soviet Union is free to apply a less restrictive interpretation.

This specter--originally raised by Mr. Sofaer while trying to justify the "broad" ABM Treaty interpretation--is highly theoretical. It is a truism that the Executive has different obligations under domestic and international law, and therefore it is possible to hypothesize situations in which those obligations could conflict. However, in practice this has not proven to be a serious problem and there is no basis for the Administration's assertion that the Condition "would substantially increase this risk." The Condition, after all, does no more than state principles which already suffuse the *Restatement of U.S. Foreign Relations Law*.

An apparent premise of the Sofaer Doctrine is that practical difficulties would ensue if the Executive were bound by what it tells the Senate, because it would not be an abnormal circumstance for a difference to exist between what was agreed to with the other party and the explanations provided to the Senate. There should be no such difference. It is the Executive's responsibility to ensure sufficient clarity in a treaty and in its explanations thereof to the Senate so that no conflict exists between the shared understanding of the parties on the one hand and the shared understanding of the Executive and Senate on the other. If, *in extremis*, such conflict should arise and prove not resolvable by discussion or negotiation with the other party, the United States of course has the option of withdrawing from the treaty.

In sum, this largely theoretical problem should be addressed if and when it arises--not by a preemptive alteration of constitutional principles. The Senate should not accept a doctrine that assumes and protects carelessness or deviousness on the part of the Executive.

J. PROPOSED "COMPROMISES" AND OTHER ALTERNATIVES

The Committee takes note of the assertion that the Committee failed to pursue potential "compromises" that might allegedly have resulted in Committee unanimity on the issue of treaty interpretation. The Committee rejects this assertion as unfounded.

The Committee notes first that when Senator Biden initially drafted the Condition he circulated his text to a number of Senators of both parties in hope of engendering bipartisanship on an issue--the Senate's role in the Treaty Power--that should be of concern to all Senators. Moreover, as Senator Cranston stated when offering the proposal, "I have hoped that this simple language . . . could be adopted unanimously, with the support of Senators on both sides of the aisle. I have worked closely over many weeks with a number of Democratic and Republican Senators on and off this Committee . . . in an effort to work out a bipartisan solution."

As to potential "compromises," the Committee takes note of the following text, submitted by supporters of the Administration as a proposed substitute for the Biden Condition:

> (a) that, as a matter of international law, only the mutual obligations assumed by the parties bind the United States;
>
> (b) that the Senate has relied upon the testimony and written submissions, which it regards as authoritative, of witnesses of the Executive Branch concerning the meaning of the Treaty;
>
> (c) that, as a matter of domestic law, the United States is bound by interpretations which the Senate clearly intended and generally understood would bind the United States in giving its advice and consent;
>
> (d) that, the United States being so bound, no interpretation different from that intended and understood by the Senate, as a matter of domestic law, may be agreed to or adopted by the United States without appropriate legislative action.

The Committee points out that, while somewhat masked, the Sofaer Doctrine is clearly present in paragraphs (b) and (c), which have the effect of asserting that the three Sofaer Doctrine criteria--"generally understood, clearly intended, and relied upon"--must somehow be met lest the Executive have a right of "reinterpretation." In the final analysis, the Committee could hardly be expected to affirm the Sofaer Doctrine in a provision the purpose of which was to refute that Doctrine.

To be sure, various members of the Committee and of the Senate leadership displayed a good-faith willingness to discuss possible compromise language. But no compromise was ever reached. Nor was one possible so long as discussions focused on proposals designed to affirm the Sofaer Doctrine and thereby denigrate the Senate's role in exercise of the Treaty Power.

Senator Cranston summarized the situation as follows: "If we settle for a solution that undermines the Senate's role in the treaty process, we who serve together in the Senate now may well be charged with giving away the Senate's treaty powers."

The basic issue remains. On the one hand are those who view the Executive as constrained in treaty interpretation by the original shared understanding of a treaty as reflected in authoritative explanations of the text provided by the Executive in seeking consent to ratification. On the other are those who wish to affirm a radical new doctrine that has the effect of requiring the Senate to meet certain criteria lest the Executive have latitude to "reinterpret" a treaty provision as he may find convenient.

The Committee wishes to emphasize that in asserting the binding significance of the Executive's original representations, it has articulated the principle with great care. Whereas some formulations would have asserted that the Executive is directly and explicitly "bound by" its representations, the Biden Condition makes no such assertion. Rather, beginning with the premise of Executive-Senate partnership in the making of treaties, it asserts only the binding quality of the original "shared understanding" and then asserts a derivative principle: that this "shared understanding" of a treaty's text is "reflected in"--meaning evidenced by--the Executive's authoritative representations "insofar as such representations are directed to the meaning and legal effect of the text" of the treaty.

This construction helps to underscore that a rule of reason must apply in instances where inconsistencies may appear, lest the Executive be "bound by" two inconsistent requirements. Thus, the Biden Condition is precisely and carefully balanced in seeking to articulate the constitutional principles it aims to uphold.

Finally, the Committee notes that any "compromise" of this basic formulation would have the effect of diluting and thereby perverting the provision's basic purpose. The Committee does not wish to be a party to any act of Executive aggrandizement which, however expedient, would have the effect of impairing the treaty-making process or future American diplomacy. Specifically, the Committee wishes to uphold principles and practices of treaty-making under which the Senate is able to accept the Executive's presentation of a treaty in confidence and approve the treaty in good faith solely on the basis of that presentation, without the obligation of creating an elaborate formal record, or imposing formal conditions, to display what it "generally understood, clearly intended and relied upon" as a defense against future Executive "reinterpreters."

The only practical alternative to the Biden Condition is to do precisely that: to lade the INF Treaty and its resolution of ratification with an enormous burden of formal amendments, stipulations, conditions, and the like, which could require months of debate. For example, in response to questions, the Administration provided "authoritative" representations regarding a number of issues of direct concern to the Committee, including:

--the meaning of "weapon-delivery" vehicle in Article II;
--the effect of Article XIV on U.S.-NATO weapons cooperation;
--the effect of Article VII on testing of sea-launched cruise missiles; and
--the effect of Article II on the testing of strategic missiles at INF ranges.

Given the context created by the Sofaer Doctrine, however, the Committee could not--without the countervailing effect of the Biden Condition--have been assured that such Administration representations were determinative of the Executive's obligations in carrying out the Treaty. Accordingly, in the absence of the Biden Condition, some Members would have felt obliged to proposed specific conditions on these and other issues.[22] [[22]By way of a detailed example, the text of the INF Treaty does not clearly state that a "weapon-delivery" vehicle encompasses missiles using future technologies to damage or destroy targets. Nor does the INF Treaty specifically define a "weapon-delivery" vehicle as a missile capable of damaging or destroying a target. The Administration provided the Committee with a specific assurance that the United States defines the term "weapon-delivery" vehicle as a missile capable of destroying or damaging a target and that missiles employing futuristic technologies such as lasers would be covered by the INF Treaty. Since the INF Treaty is a permanent treaty, the question of whether it covers missiles using futuristic technologies is a highly relevant concern. Thus, in the absence of the Biden Condition, the Committee might well have attached a condition to the resolution of ratification on this issue.]

Senator Nunn articulated this in testimony to the Committee when he noted that in the absence of clear confidence that the Senate could regard Executive testimony as having binding significance, "then of course there are a number of us that feel that we would have to come to the floor of the Senate with a number of amendments that would make it clear that the testimony we received on ambiguities was indeed * * * binding on this Administration and future Administrations."

If the Senate is required to consider formal conditions with regard to every such issue, the result would be indefinite delay, a product which might have been contorted beyond any possibility of U.S.-Soviet ratification, and no resolution at all of the current constitutional issue. Against this prospect, it becomes clear that the Biden Condition is a cautious, responsible, and straightforward means of addressing a complex and potentially grave problem.

As Senator Cranston emphasized during the mark-up, "Adoption of this plain and simple language will liberate us from an exhaustive and absurd obligation to speak in the resolution of ratification to our understanding of every word of the Treaty . . . It allows us to rely on the Administration testimony without the cumbersome, time-consuming process of restating it."

In sum, the two categories of alternatives to the Biden Condition are both undesirable. So-called "compromise" language would be perverse to the degree that it embraced the Sofaer Doctrine. And to delete the Biden Condition would be to lay the resolution of ratification open to a plethora of proposed conditions on the specifics of INF Treaty interpretation.

K. RELATIONSHIP TO ABM TREATY DISPUTE

The Committee points out that its interest in avoiding a replay of the ABM Treaty dispute was manifest in its efforts to make this provision as INF Treaty-specific as possible, through the use of the words "this Treaty," although as indicated earlier the Committee recognized that any assertion of principles would have broader meaning.

The Committee therefore reiterates, that, even if passed by the Senate, this Condition would not be dispositive on the issue of ABM Treaty interpretation because the essential argument used to justify the "broad" interpretation is not an assertion of constitutional principle but a factual claim of pervasive ambiguity.

In other words, the Administration's most basic claim is not actually that it is "reinterpreting" that Treaty but that it is interpreting the Treaty within the wide latitude provided by the general ambiguity which, it argues, surrounded the ABM Treaty's meaning at the time of ratification.

Accordingly, as Senator Dodd stressed, "One can vote for [the Biden Condition] and still support the "broad" interpretation of the ABM Treaty because that debate is mostly over facts. You ought to vote against [the Condition] only if you believe that under the Constitution the Executive branch can bring a treaty here, give you an authoritative explanation directed to the meaning of its text, and then after the treaty is ratified return and state that that was not really what the text meant--it meant something else."

In sum, the Biden Condition is not designed to resolve the dispute over alleged ambiguities in the genesis, design, and implementation of the ABM Treaty, or to constitute a final disposition of the issue of Treaty interpretation. Rather, the provision is intended to affirm certain constitutional principles which have been brought into question during the ABM Treaty debate.

At the same time, the Committee wishes to note, on behalf of those who oppose the Administration's "broad" interpretation, that since the issue of Treaty interpretation did not arise during Senate consideration of the ABM Treaty, and was not foreseen at that time, the absence of any action pertaining to interpretation of the ABM Treaty at that time cannot be construed as having any bearing on the interpretation of that Treaty.

L. CONCLUSION: A SUMMARY OF KEY POINTS

In conclusion, the Committee wishes to emphasize what the treaty interpretation issue is and what it is not:

> --The issue addressed by the Biden Condition is not a struggle over who interprets treaties. It is solely and indisputably the President's responsibility to interpret and implement treaties for the United States. At issue is the question of what limits are to govern the President's latitude in exercising that power.

--The issue is *not* whether and what testimony by the Executive is "authoritative." To answer that question is still to be without an answer as to whether "authoritative" representations are in any way binding on the Executive. The issue is whether and how such representations have a binding significance under United States law.

--The issue is *not* whether to have a "clean" resolution of ratification for the INF Treaty. The issue is how, without burdening the resolution with a *plethora* of formal conditions, the Senate can ensure that the current "shared understanding" of the Treaty, as reflected in what the Executive has told the Senate, becomes determinative of the Treaty's future implementation.

--The issue is *not* the "broad-versus-narrow" interpretation of the ABM Treaty. The issue is the Sofaer Doctrine, which asserts unreasonable, highly elastic criteria which must allegedly be met before the Executive may not "reinterpret" a given treaty provision. To reject the Sofaer Doctrine is not to resolve the ABM Treaty dispute, but simply to narrow it to the confines of a debate over facts: that is, to a debate over alleged ambiguities surrounding that particular Treaty.

--The issue is *not* whether the Executive is to be bound by every last utterance of its representatives before Congress, but whether and how the principle of original "shared understanding" is to govern a treaty's implementation. Shall it be axiomatic that such "shared understanding" is reflected in authoritative Executive representations of the treaty's meaning? Or must the Senate deal with the Executive as an adversary, who will not act in good faith and around whom a cage of explicit stipulations must be build?

--The issue is *not* a Senate effort to chart new constitutional ground, but an Executive effort to do so. It is not the Senate but the Executive which seeks to assert constitutional principles in a manner which expresses an aggressively broad claim on power. An adequate response requires no counter-assertion of Senate power but a simple manifestation, as reflected in the Biden Condition, of Senate unwillingness to acquiesce in Administration assertions which, if not refuted, could imply acceptance of a radical aggrandizement of presidential power. As Senator Kerry put it, "if we do *not* say this, we are acquiescing in a new statement of constitutional principles."

The Committee reiterates its intent that the Senate not digress on this question into a replay of the ABM Treaty dispute. That question is not here at issue, and will not be disposed of even by a Senate affirmation of the principles embodied in this Condition. The real issue, simply put, is this: that those who oppose this Condition are, in effect, proposing to concede to the President a power the Constitution does not grant him, and which neither any previous President nor any previous Legal Adviser has ever asserted.

The Foreign Relations Committee seeks not to make the Senate the interpreter of treaties, but to require that the Executive interpret and implement treaties within the boundaries of the Executive's original presentation in obtaining Senate consent to ratification. Senator Sarbanes put the issue clearly: "I dare say that if Members . . . think about it carefully, I do not think anyone would want an Executive to be able to alter the interpretation of a treaty from the representations that were made to the Senate at the time the Executive sought the Senate's approval." Heretofore, this principle has never been placed at issue, and the Committee urges the Senate to uphold the principle against the current ill-considered and unnecessary challenge mounted by Mr. Sofaer.

Finally, the Committee notes the February 1 exchange--at the outset of hearings on the INF Treaty--between Senator Biden and Ambassador Nitze, during which Ambassador Nitze stated that "an authoritative statement by a member of the Executive branch is determinative as to what the meaning of the Treaty is from the standpoint of domestic law."[23] [[23]This exchange is reprinted in full in the Appendix.] Had the Administration subsequently been willing in the Shultz letter, the Culvahouse letter, or any other authoritative representation to affirm this principle--and thereby repudiate the Sofaer Doctrine--the question of treaty interpretation would not now be at issue. The issue of treaty interpretation is the Administration's unwillingness to endorse the principle stated by Ambassador Nitze and affirmed more formally and precisely by the Biden Condition.[646]

The relevant portion of the "Additional Views of Senator Jesse Helms" provides:

B. TREATY INTERPRETATION

The Cranston/Biden condition, before its later modification, was presented on March 29, 1988, in committee markup in the following form:

> That this Treaty shall be subject to the following principles, which derive, as a necessary implication, from the provisions of the Constitution (Article II, section 2, clause 2) for the making of treaties:
>
> (a) the United States shall interpret this Treaty in accordance with the understanding of the Treaty shared by the Executive and the Senate at the time of Senate consent to ratification;
>
> (b) such common understanding is:
>
> (i) based on the text of the Treaty; and
>
> (ii) reflected in the authoritative representations provided by the Executive branch to the Senate and its committees in seeking Senate consent to ratification, insofar as such representations are directed to the meaning and legal effect of the text of the Treaty;
>
> (c) the United States shall not agree to or adopt an interpretation different from the common understanding *without the approval* of the Senate. (Emphasis added.)

[646]"IX. Treaty Interpretation," in *The INF Treaty Report, supra* note 1, at 87-108 (emphasis in original).

During that day, I proposed and the committee accepted two amendments which caused the condition to be modified to read as follows:

> That this Treaty shall be subject to the following principles, which derive, as a necessary implication, from the provisions of the Constitution (article II, section 2, clause 2) for the making of Treaties:
>
> (a) the United States shall interpret this Treaty in accordance with the understanding of the Treaty shared by the Executive and the Senate at the time of Senate consent to ratification;
>
> (b) such common understanding is:
>
> (i) based on the text of the Treaty; and
>
> (ii) reflected in the authori[ta]tive representations provided by the executive branch to the Senate and its committees in seeking Senate consent to ratification, insofar as such representations are directed to the meaning and legal effect of the text of the Treaty;
>
> (c) the United States shall not agree to or adopt [an] interpretation different from that common understanding *except pursuant to Senate advice and consent to a subsequent treaty or protocol, or the enactment of a statute. This understanding shall not be incorporated in the instruments of ratification of this Treaty or otherwise officially conveyed to the other contracting Party*. (Emphasis added.)

The following day on March 30, 1988, the committee adopted the condition in substantially the form previously agreed except that the preamble included a provision that the condition would be "binding upon the Executive." Explaining to the committee immediately prior to the vote that this new clause would indeed bind the President "just like any Senate resolution would bind him," with my support the committee adopted the proposal on a vote of 12 to 6.

I agreed with the modified Cranston/Biden condition because I believed then and I believe now that it is an accurate, albeit somewhat awkward, statement of constitutional law. Furthermore, I agree in a general sense with the majority views regarding the condition, but I regret to say, however, that I find their lengthy exposition on the subject is in some sense somewhat vague and in another claims far too much for the condition than it actually achieves or can achieve.

Throughout the 100th Congress, the Senate has expended enormous time and [e]nergy and written copious volumes on this subject of treaty interpretation. Much of this might better have been left to the high school civics classes where it ought to have been learned.

Nonetheless, the fulminous debate of proper means for construing a treaty has at least helped in the reeducation of us all and brought some clarity to the symmetrical plan that the Framers established for the promulgation of Federal law under the Constitution. For my own use, for example, I asked the lawyers on the committee minority staff to prepare a straightforward statement of the relevant principles unencumbered by any political bias arising from this or that view of the meaning of the ABM Treaty or any other contentious document. They were directed as well, since I have the "misfortune" myself not to be a member of their profession, to "keep it simple" and not to have more information in footnotes than in basic declaratory sentences.

The result was reasonably satisfying, and the memorandum is therefore included at this point as an expression of what appears to be a correct and, for once, clear outline of the relevant considerations surrounding treaty interpretation. It follows:

-- Treaties and Federal statutes are supreme law over State statutes and constitutions. They are *not* supreme law over the U.S. Constitution.

-- Treaties under the American Constitution are therefore both domestic law and international law.

-- The meaning of a treaty at international law is determined primarily from the text of the Treaty itself and, only in the case of ambiguity, from the negotiating record reflecting the intentions of the *contracting* states. Principles of contract interpretation apply when the meaning of a treaty at international law is in question.

-- In terms of domestic law (*called municipal law in international jurisprudence*) in America, the meaning of a treaty is determined primarily by reference to its text and secondarily, in the case of ambiguity only, by reference to its *executive* history both in the Executive Department of Government and in the Senate acting in executive session. Once ratified, the treaty text and its executive history are locked into place much as a statute and its legislative history (including an overridden veto message) are locked into place when the statute becomes law either through the President's signature or passage notwithstanding his objections.

-- In terms of domestic law, once the domestic meaning of a treaty is locked into place upon ratification its meaning cannot thereafter be changed "by reinterpretation." However, each of the three branches of the Federal Government is its own arbiter of what that meaning is to the extent of its own powers under the Constitution.

-- Since the President is charged by the Constitution with seeing that the law--including treaty law--is faithfully executed, he is required as Chief Magistrate under municipal law to execute obligations in a treaty as he determines those obligations to have been at the time of ratification. If another branch of Government disagrees with his determination of those obligations, then it must rely on its own powers to enforce its will. In the case of the Senate, the only principal constitutional method for enforcing its will regarding the meaning of a treaty (when its view as a body is at variance with that of the President) is to act with the House of Representatives to pass a statute (presumably over the President's veto) which requires the President to abide by the meaning asserted by Congress.

-- The Senate could also enforce its will regarding the meaning of an existing treaty by amending the existing treat[y] through amendment of a subsequent proposed treaty with the same foreign sovereign and making its consent to ratification of the latter treaty contingent on the President securing the acceptance by the foreign sovereign of the amendment of the Senate as so propounded. This course of action would obviously require the President's acquiescence in seeking ratification of the latter treaty notwithstanding his objection to the interpretation of the prior treaty made express by the amendment of the Senate.

-- In case of conflict between the meaning of a treaty in domestic law and its meaning in international law, the President is bound by the domestic meaning under municipal law which requires him to execute the treaty faithfully pursuant to its domestic meaning. However, in terms of international relations, he is not limited by a domestic interpretation and has far greater freedom of action because principles of international law (based on contract law) obtain. In American history, this fact has led to numerous illogical situations in which treaties have been "set aside" or "suspended" rather than nullified or voided. In such cases, the purpose has been to maintain the stance that domestic law is neither being ignored or violated.

-- The President's greater freedom of action at international law arises because, in terms of international law, there are a variety of principles related to contract law which operate to change the obligations of the United States as a contracting party even though an affected treaty may be technically valid in all aspects in terms of American domestic law. These principles include changed circumstances (for example, a declaration of war with the other contracting state), impossibility of performance (e.g. the other contracting state ceases to exist, c.f. the Republic of South Vietnam), fraud in the inducement (for example, the provision of false data on which a treaty was presumed to be based), mistake (for example, lack of knowledge of a material fact like *arguendo* the ignorance of a secret treaty between the GDR and the FRG for their reunification), and, of course, material breach (for example, every bilateral treaty ever ratified by the United States and the Union of Soviet Socialist Republics).

-- Also, at international law, change in conduct by one party which is accepted or acquiesced in by the other can vary the obligations of one or both. This last principle is the reason the administration will not confront Russia with her ABM violations in the Standing Consultation Commission since our acknowledgment of the violations without countervailing action would, through acquiescence, confirm the international legitimacy of the Russian actions.

-- In short, it is essential that any attempt by the Senate to enunciate the foregoing principles not be officially transmitted to the Russians because were this to occur principles of international law governing the United States under the Treaty might be deemed to be those of American municipal law and thereby tend to bind the United States to higher standards than those required by international law or observed in practice by other contracting states, particularly the Soviet Union.

-- Moreover, the Senate should avoid any vague provision that a "reinterpretation" must be submitted to the Senate for approval. Unless a "reinterpretation" is in the form of a proposed Treaty amendment between the United States and another contracting sovereign; i.e., in effect a new treaty, this proposal would permit unicameral legislation which is prohibited by the Constitution. Since the Constitution is supreme over treaties (not to mention over precatory material merely incorporated in a resolution of ratification), any condition requiring "reinterpretation" submittal would in any event be a nullity because, in the repeated words of the Supreme Court, "if it is prohibited by the Constitution, then it is void." Such a condition would also contribute to the prevailing and growing lack of understanding in congressional staff of the fundamental principles of lawmaking envisaged by the Constitution.

-- The Framers in Philadelphia in 1787 provided that law at the Federal level (excluding the Constitution itself) could be created by two and only two methods: statute and treaty. At the time of its creation, law (whether treaty or statute) can of course be made self-terminating or self-limiting in the sense that it can be subject to a "sunset" clause or a clause providing that it be deemed void upon the happening of a contingency or effective only upon the happening of a contingency. Nonetheless, it is still positive law until specifically repealed or abrogated.

-- Law, perforce, can be unmade or modified by only two methods: statute and treaty. Since the two forms of law are interchangeable with neither being supreme over the other, it follows that, when latter in time: (1) a statute can modify or void a treaty; (2) a statute can modify or void a statute; (3) a treaty can modify or void a statute; and (4) a treaty can modify or void a treaty. Accordingly, as much as the Senate or some Senators may wish it to be otherwise, without a constitutional amendment, the Senate can neither make nor modify law acting by itself.

-- In summary, so long as nothing on the subject of treaty interpretation is embodied by amendment in the treaty or the instruments of ratification *no law is made* and the President's acceptance of an unincorporated condition as "binding on the Executive" is at best a "gentlemans' agreement" reflecting a present intention to go alone with a view expressed by resolution as the prevailing opinion of the Senate. Even if such a condition were incorrectly deemed to have statutory weight, it would do far less than generally supposed because a statute can neither add to nor subtract from the Constitution.

In view of the principles in the foregoing memorandum, an argument could easily be made that the modified Cranston/Biden condition is mere surplusage and, if so, that it may as well be stricken from the proposed resolution consenting to ratification. I disagree because the condition does serve the purpose of clearing the air in an area of constitutional law which ought never to have been clouded by imprecise declarations of the State Department lawyers. I also give my full support to the condition and urge other Senators to do so as well, because there have already developed numerous controversies regarding the interpretation of the proposed INF Treaty. For example, the Treaty is being interpreted by the Department of State as prohibiting so-called future systems while the Department of Defense appears to assert that it does not and no one, George Shu[l]tz included, has the vaguest notion of what the Russians think of the subject beyond that they will choose at any given point to give the Treaty whatever interpretation best suits their political and military needs.

A final worrisome problem found in the majority view on treaty interpretation is that "authoritative testimony" when clarifying ambi[g]uities, drafting errors, or omissions in the Treaty serves to obviate the need for the Senate to adopt clarifying amendments, reservations, understandings, or declarations. While this may be true insofar as regards those few aspects of the Treaty which have strictly domestic application in the United States, it is decidedly untrue with respect to the meaning of the international obligations undertaken.

Simply because the Executive and the Senate have a "common understanding" of an international obligation does not mean that the other contracting state has the same understanding *nor does it bind it.* The *only* method of ensuring that our internal "common understanding" extends to the other sovereign (unless it is patently clear in the Treaty text or on the face of the negotiating record) is to adopt amendments, reservations, understandings, or declarations (depending on the scope and nature of the problem to be corrected) and to secure the assent (for amendments and some understandings) or the acquiescence (for reservations and declarations) of the other sovereign by incorporation of such provision either in the Treaty text or in the ratification instruments exchanged.

> The Senate should therefore avoid the temptation to forget that not just domestic law but an *international contract* as well is being forged during treatymaking and that "authoritative testimony" while good enough for domestic purposes is generally not sufficient to tie down the behavior of another nation, especially when that nation is the Soviet Union from which at best every sharp practice possible can be expected.
>
> The Senate, therefore, cannot assume, as the majority view implies, that the "authoritative testimony" received by the Senate will serve as any means whatsoever to bind Russia and must take those steps necessary to ensure that there is a meeting of the minds of the *contracting parties* and not just of the minds of the Senate and the President.[647]

The committee report also attached in the "Appendix" a memorandum on "Principles of Treaty-Making and Interpretation."[648] A footnote to the first sentence in the memorandum provides: "The Committee wishes to express particular appreciation to Professors Michael Glennon, Louis Henkin, and Laurence Tribe."[649] This memorandum provides in full:

> Last year, pursuant to hearings involving leading constitutional authorities and with their assistance, the Committee drafted and approved S. Res. 167, which was intended inter alia to identify constitutional principles that govern the Congress, the courts, and the Executive in determining the meaning of a treaty. A discussion of the general principles affirmed in S. Res. 167 (shown below in italics) provides background on treaty-making and treaty interpretation:
>
> (1) *If, following Senate advice and consent, the President proceeds to ratify a treaty, the President may ratify only the treaty to which the Senate advised and consented.* This principle, which

---

[647]"XII. Additional Views of Senator Jesse Helms," in *The INF Treaty Report, supra* note 1, at 179, 246-51 (emphasis in original).

[648]"Principles of Treaty-Making and Interpretation," in "XIV. Appendix," in *The INF Treaty Report, supra* note 1, at 437-41.

[649]*Id.* at 437 n.24.

is fundamental to the meaning and operation of the Treaty Clause, embraces two precepts:

> --First, if the President transmits an international agreement to the Senate for its advice and consent pursuant to the Treaty Clause, the President may not bring that agreement into force without the Senate's advice and consent. Under the United States Constitution, when the President submits the agreement to the Senate, it constitutes an agreement which does not yet have force and effect. It may thereafter become effective as "Law of the Land" for the United States pursuant to the Supremacy Clause of the Constitution (article VI, clause 2); and it may become effective for the United States as an international obligation. But it takes effect in either legal system only if the Senate gives its advice and consent. The President is precluded, constitutionally, from bringing the treaty into force domestically or internationally without the advice and consent of the Senate.
>
> --Second, if, following such transmittal, the Senate accords its advice and consent, the President then has the option of whether to bring the treaty into force: he is not constitutionally bound to do so. Technically, therefore, it is the President, not the Senate, who "ratifies" the treaty, through deposit of an instrument of ratification in accord with procedures specified or envisaged by the treaty. Presidential ratification is carried out pursuant to Senate advice and consent.

(2) *Under the United States Constitution, a treaty is properly interpreted in good faith in accordance with the ordinary meaning to be given its terms in light of their context and in light of the Treaty's object and purpose.* The several terms of art used in this formulation have been developed over the course of many decades by innumerable scholars and tribunals, both international and domestic. It is therefore the central principle of treaty interpretation set forth in the Vienna Convention on the Law of Treaties (Article 31(1)) and is, appropriately, incorporated in the *Restatement of the Law (3d), Foreign Relations Law of the United States* (referred to hereafter as the *Restatement*). This principle

"represents what states generally accept," the *Restatement* comments, "and the United States has also appeared willing to accept it, regardless of differences in nuance."

In effect, this principle serves to describe the scope of the President's authority to interpret a treaty. In the absence of adjudication, the President bears the responsibility to interpret U.S. treaties, and his interpretation of a treaty is entitled to great weight in United States law. But the Constitution permits the President, acting alone, only to interpret existing treaties--not to make new ones. To remain within the scope of his constitutional power, the President must genuinely be engaged in the act of treaty interpretation. He cannot engage--by himself--in the act of treaty creation.

The location of the line between interpretation and creation is the subject of this principle. It provides, in effect, that when the President reasonably construes a treaty in good faith in accordance with the ordinary meaning to be given its terms in light of their context and the treaty's object and purpose, he acts within the scope of his constitutional power. When his construction of a treaty cannot be so described, it represents not construction or interpretation at all, but the making of a new treaty, which he can do only with the advice and consent of the Senate.

(3) *The meaning of a treaty is to be determined in light of what the Senate understands the Treaty to mean when it gives its advice and consent.* This principle follows from the proposition that, if the President elects to ratify a treaty, he cannot ratify a treaty different from the one to which the Senate consented--which means that he cannot ratify a treaty with a meaning different from the meaning to which the Senate consented. If the Senate expressed an understanding as to the treaty's meaning, the President must respect that understanding. He can bring the treaty into force as it reflects the Senate's understanding, but he cannot bring into force a treaty that does not reflect the Senate's understanding. For the United States, the meaning of the treaty that the President ratifies is the meaning on which there existed a meeting of the minds between the President and the Senate at the time of Senate consent.

(4) *The understanding of the Senate is manifested by any formal expression of understanding by the Senate, as well as by*

other evidence of what the Senate understood the treaty to mean, including Senate approval or acceptance of, or Senate acquiescence in, interpretations of the treaty by the Executive branch communicated to the Senate. The essence of this principle is that the Senate's understanding of a treaty's meaning may be explicit or implicit.

Explicit understandings comprise formal conditions to the Senate's consent. These conditions include amendments to the text of a treaty as well as amendments to the resolution of ratification, such as "reservations," "understandings," "declarations," "statements," and the like.

Implicit understandings represent informal--but equally significant--conditions placed on the Senate's consent. They are reflected in the various materials traditionally described as legislative history. These sources include hearings and committee reports, as well as debates transcribed into the Congressional Record. These sources are regarded as indicia of legislative intent concerning the meaning of a legislative instrument, be it a statute or a treaty.

Legislative intent is also expressed in unchallenged communications of the Executive contained in these sources. Under longstanding principles of textual construction, Executive communications to the Congress concerning the meaning of a text are evidence of the meaning of that text if Congress (or the Senate) acquiesces in that meaning. In other words, the legislative branch is deemed to be placed on notice by the Executive that certain words will be construed in a certain manner. If Congress wishes a different meaning to obtain, it may act so as to effect that different meaning. If Congress does not act, however, it is properly deemed to have accepted--and to intend--the meaning communicated by the Executive.

In testimony to a joint hearing of the Judiciary and Foreign Relations Committees, Professor Louis Henkin, chief reporter of the *Restatement*, summarized this concept as follows: "Where several [Executive] statements are made and there is general acceptance of their tenor, that is the Senate understanding. That is true in the case of Senate consent to a treaty, as it would be in the legislative history of a statute."

In determining whether the Senate consented to the ratification of a treaty pursuant to an implicit understanding, a rule of reason must apply. Obviously, where the indicia of intent or understanding (including unchallenged Executive communications or explanations) are few or inconsistent, no implicit intent can reasonably be said to exist. On the other hand, where the indicia of intent (again, including unchallenged Executive communications or explanations) are several and largely consistent, an implicit intent can reasonably be concluded to exist. In such circumstances, the President is bound constitutionally to regard that intent as an implicit understanding, and therefore an implicit condition of the Senate's consent. The Chief Executive cannot bring the treaty into force unless it reflects that condition, and subsequent Presidents must interpret the treaty subject to that intent.

(5) *The Senate's understanding of a treaty cannot be informed by matter of which it is not aware, such as private statements made during the negotiations that were not communicated to the Senate.* While essentially a truism, this proposition is fundamental to the question of treaty interpretation by the United States government. Legislative intent is reflected by legislative history, which is by definition *legislative* history. It does not include history unknown to the legislature, which could not, logically, be part of the "meeting of the minds" between the President and the Senate extant on the date of Senate consent. The events, acts, or interpretations comprising such extraneous activity thus are not properly taken into account in determining what meaning U.S. treaty-makers--the Executive and the Senate--ascribed to the treaty at that time.

This principle does not imply that an untransmitted negotiating record is in all circumstances irrelevant to treaty interpretation. A negotiating record not placed before the Senate at the time of its consent proceedings might conceivably have some bearing on the meaning of a treaty in the event that no meeting of the minds occurred between the President and the Senate with respect to a given issue. In such circumstances, the import of the negotiating record would not displace that of other indicia of the treaty-makers' intent.

In sum, where the Senate had no intent or understanding, a negotiating record could have bearing in resolving a question of treaty interpretation so long as the interpretation derived did not conflict with areas of interpretation where the Senate's understanding was clear. But in areas where the Senate clearly intends or understands--or has been formally apprised by the Executive of a particular meaning--the question of what weight is to be accorded an untransmitted negotiating record can be decisively answered. The answer is, None.

(6) *Any subsequent practice between the parties in the application of the treaty is to be taken into account in interpreting the treaty.* Like principle (2) above, this principle has its origins in the Vienna Convention on the Law of Treaties (Article 31(3)). Also like principle (2), this principle is incorporated into the *Restatement* of U.S. foreign relations law, which repeats this principle and notes that "it represents what states generally accept and the United States has also appeared willing to accept it regardless of differences of nuance and emphasis."

An important aspect of subsequent practice is consistent, subsequent interpretation. Statements made consistently and frequently by a government with respect to the meaning of a treaty provision represent "practice." In the case of the United States Government, this means that statements by Executive branch officials, accepted or acquiesced in by the Congress, constitute subsequent practice to be taken into account in determining the meaning of a treaty.

The period of "practice" to be examined consists of that period beginning on the date of the treaty's entry into force and ending on the date on which a particular question concerning the treaty's meaning is raised. In the case of an international dispute, limiting the relevant period of "practice" in this way is necessary lest a government be permitted to bootstrap its way into the very interpretation in controversy by citing its own disputed claims as authority. Similarly, in a dispute between the Senate and the Executive, the Executive's interpretation constitutes evidence of a treaty's meaning only during that period when the Executive's interpretation is not contested. A challenge to such acts or statements brings about the termination of the period of "practice" properly taken into account in assessing the meaning of a particular treaty provision.

(7) *The President may not amend a treaty without the agreement of the parties and the advice and consent of the Senate.* Both the Vienna Convention on the Law of Treaties and the *Revised Restatement* of U.S. foreign relations law set forth the requirement that agreement between the parties precede any amendment of a treaty. This principle is obviously seminal in international law; treaties are made jointly and can only be modified jointly.

Also fundamental is the requirement of Senate advice and consent. Although not addressed directly by the *Restatement*, support for the proposition is implicit in its declaration that "The power of the President to terminate an international agreement does not imply authority to conclude a new one in its place." Were the President to amend an agreement on his own, he would in effect be terminating an old agreement and entering into a new one.

Constitutionally, the question of treaty amendment is crucial because a unilateral presidential power to amend treaties would vitiate the Senate's power to approve a treaty conditionally. With the agreement of the other party or parties, the President could simply ignore the Senate and remove any Senate-added reservation or any other treaty provision no longer desired. The Constitution does not accord the President such power. Instead, the President possesses a limited power of treaty interpretation, and he acts within the scope of that power when he interprets a treaty in accordance with the principles cited above.

When the President acts beyond the scope of his constitutional authority to interpret a treaty, he is in effect either amending that treaty or making a new one. And he is not entitled to disguise that reality by calling his action an "interpretation" or "reinterpretation" of the existing treaty. He is engaged in the act of treaty amendment or of treaty-making; each such act requires the advice and consent of the Senate.

(8) *All treaties made shall be the supreme law of the land, and the President is required to take care that the laws be faithfully executed.* These constitutional provisions are included for the purpose of recalling the President's solemn obligation to abide by the provisions of treaties. Nothing in the United States Constitution permits the President to flip freely through *Treaties in Force* and, armed with a red pencil and white-out, make such

> additions, deletions, and modifications as he might wish. The President is not empowered to amend U.S. treaty commitments; he is charged to uphold them. Treaties are laws, and the President's duty of faithful execution applies as fully to treaty law as it does to statutory law. The President takes an oath of office in which he swears to "preserve, protect, and defend the Constitution of the United States." When the President violates a treaty provision, he violates his oath of office.[650]

Also of relevance, the committee report attached in the same appendix a "Chronology of Executive/Senate Action on Treaty Interpretation." That chronology provides in full:

> 1. October 1985: The Reagan Administration announces the "broad" interpretation of the ABM Treaty, which would permit extensive testing in space of SDI. The traditional interpretation severely restricts such testing. Subsequently, various Administration rationales are offered.
>
> 2. March 1987: State Department Legal Adviser Sofaer, in testimony before the Foreign Relations Committee, asserts that "When [the Senate] gives its advice and consent to a treaty, it is to the treaty that was made, irrespective of the explanations [the Senate] was provided." This statement is viewed as a threat to the Senate's constitutional role in treaty-making because it implies that treaties are "made" irrespective of the Senate's understanding of a treaty.
>
> 3. May 1987: The Foreign Relations Committee approves the Biden Resolution (S. Res. 167) by a vote of 11-8. The resolution affirms that the President is bound, constitutionally, to an interpretation which the Executive branch presented during ratification proceedings.
>
> 4. May 1987: Mr. Sofaer provides the President with a study on the ratification proceedings of the ABM Treaty. The study asserts that the President is bound to a specific interpretation of a treaty only if that interpretation was "generally understood," "clearly intended," and "relied upon" by Senators during the

---

[650]*Id.* at 437-41 (footnote omitted) (emphasis in original).

ratification proceedings. The assertion of these criteria subsequently comes to be known as the Sofaer Doctrine.

5. September 1987: As part of the FY 1988 Defense Authorization Bill, the House and Senate enact Levin-Nunn legislation prohibiting the President from conducting space-based and other mobile ABM tests which would violate the traditional interpretation on the grounds that such authority was not sought in the submission of the Defense Budget. Authors of the language assert that the vote was not about the validity of the Administration's new interpretation of the ABM Treaty.

6. September 1987: Senator Nunn demands that the Administration provide the Senate with the INF Treaty "negotiating record" as a result of the Sofaer Doctrine.

7. November 1987: Senator Pell, in an effort to finesse the "negotiating record" issue, seeks an authoritative analysis by the Administration of the INF Treaty "negotiating record."

8. January 1988: Negotiations begin between Secretary Shultz and Senators Pell, Byrd, and Nunn. The Senators seek a letter from the Secretary of State asserting that Reagan Administration testimony is authoritative and binding upon the Executive.

9. February 5, 1988: Secretary Shultz sends a letter to Senator Byrd. The letter merely affirms the transfer of the "negotiating record" but does not address the question of whether Executive Branch testimony will be both "authoritative" and "binding."

10. February 5, 1988: Senators Nunn and Byrd respond to the Shultz letter by threatening to hold up the ratification proceedings on the INF Treaty unless the Administration assures the Senate that the testimony of Administration officials is "authoritative" and "binding." Nunn and Byrd say that, without such assurances, the Senate will have to fully examine the "negotiating record" and attach reservations and understandings to the Resolution of Ratification on each provision of the Treaty to ensure that a future President cannot change the meaning of the Treaty as presented by the Executive.

11. February 9, 1988: Secretary Shultz responds to the Byrd/Nunn letter. He asserts the following: (1) all INF testimony is "authoritative," unless the various Committees are told

otherwise; (2) the testimony is "authoritative" without the need for understandings in the Resolution of Ratification; and (3) the Reagan Administration will in no way depart from the meaning of the Treaty presented to the Senate. While the letter states that Administration testimony is "authoritative," it does not state that such "authoritative" testimony is "binding" upon the Executive.

12. February 1988: In testimony before the Foreign Relations Committee, Ambassador Nitze asserts that "with respect to domestic law, an authoritative statement by a member of the Executive Branch is determinative as to what the meaning of the Treaty is from the standpoint of domestic law."

13. March 1988: Secretary Shultz tells the Foreign Relations Committee in a written response that Administration testimony on the INF Treaty "can be regarded as authoritative * * * without the need for the Senate to incorporate them in its resolution of ratification." He adds, however, "Of course, we cannot bind future Administrations." This answer is consistent with the Administration's earlier refusal in the Shultz letter of February 9 to state that all "authoritative" testimony would be "binding."

14. March 17, 1988: White House Counsel Arthur B. Culvahouse, Jr. sends a letter to Senator Lugar commenting on the proposed Biden Condition. The Culvahouse letter asserts that it reflects the views of all the relevant legal counsels in the Administration (State, Defense, ACDA, Justice, and NSC). The Culvahouse letter does not question whether all Administration testimony is "authoritative." Rather, the letter states that all "authoritative" testimony is not "binding" unless the Senate can demonstrate that a given interpretation was "generally understood," "clearly intended," and "relied upon" by the Senate.

15. March 22, 1988: A second letter is sent to Senator Lugar by Culvahouse. The second Culvahouse letter merely states that the first Culvahouse letter is consistent with the February 9 Shultz letter. This assertion of consistency seems correct because the Shultz letter, while stating that all Administration testimony is "authoritative," did not state that all "authoritative" testimony is "binding." Indeed, the key premise of the first Culvahouse letter

is that "authoritative" testimony is not binding unless the Senate has fulfilled the criteria of the Sofaer Doctrine.[651]

Finally, the Resolution of Ratification recommended by the Committee included the following treaty interpretation condition:

XIII. RESOLUTION OF RATIFICATION

Resolved, (two-thirds of the Senators present concurring therein), That the Senate advise and consent to ratification of the Treaty between the United States of America and the Union of Soviet Socialist Republics on the Elimination of Their Intermediate-Range and Shorter-Range Missiles, together with the Memorandum of Understanding and the two Protocols thereto, collectively referred to as the INF Treaty, all signed at Washington on December 8, 1987 (Treaty Doc. 100-11), provided that the Senate's advice and consent to ratification of the INF Treaty is subject to the following condition, which shall be binding on the Executive:

That this Treaty shall be subject to the following principles, which derive, as a necessary implication, from the provisions of the Constitution (Article II, section 2, clause 2) for the making of treaties:

(a) the United States shall interpret this Treaty in accordance with the understanding of the Treaty shared by the Executive and the Senate at the time of Senate consent to ratification;

(b) such common understanding is:

(i) based on the text of the Treaty; and

(ii) reflected in the authoritative representations provided by the Executive branch to the Senate and its Committees in seeking Senate consent to ratification, insofar as such representations are directed to the meaning and legal effect of the text of the Treaty;

---

[651]"Chronology of Executive/Senate Action on Treaty Interpretation," in "XIV. Appendix," in *The INF Treaty Report, supra* note 1, at 447-48.

> (c) the United States shall not agree to or adopt an interpretation different from that common understanding except pursuant to Senate advice and consent to a subsequent treaty or protocol, or the enactment of a statute.
>
> This understanding shall not be incorporated in the instruments of ratification of this Treaty or otherwise officially conveyed to the other contracting Party.[652]

This proposed treaty interpretation condition within the proposed Resolution of Ratification, as with earlier action of the Senate Foreign Relations Committee in support of S. Res. 167, was adopted in a committee vote largely along party lines. Thus, all Democrats on the Committee supported the condition as offered by Senator Cranston on behalf of Senator Biden, and all Republicans on the Committee except Senators Jesse Helms and Frank Murkowski, who voted for the condition, voted against the condition.[653]

In an address to the American Law Institute in Chicago on May 19, 1988, entitled "Treaty Interpretation and the Separation of Powers," Judge Abraham D. Sofaer, the Legal Adviser to the Department of State, said:

> Luncheons are not the time for lengthy lectures. Yet, this body thrives on serious stuff. And I came here, delighted to accept Rod Perkins' invitation, because I knew that you would have some interest in my topic: treaty interpretation and the separation of powers. While this is not generally seen as an exhilarating subject, Perkins has arranged the timing of the INF debate to give the topic special importance.
>
> During October 1985, as you know, President Reagan announced that he had concluded that a broad interpretation of the ABM Treaty was "fully justified." The President also made clear, however, that he would not implement this interpretation until after consulting with Congress and our allies. Intense opposition arose to the interpretation, and while the Administration's position on the ABM Treaty's language and negotiating record became one focus

---

[652]"XIII. Resolution of Ratification," in *The INF Treaty Report, supra* note 1, at 436.

[653]*See The INF Treaty Report, supra* note 1, at 85-86. The final Resolution of Ratification was ordered reported by a vote of 17 to 2 with only Senators Helms and Pressler voting nay. *Id.* at 86.

of attention and debate, even more attention was given in the Senate to whether the President was bound to the restrictive interpretation of the treaty because of certain Executive branch representations made in 1972 during Senate ratification hearings. The particulars of the Senate record need not be examined here. The point presently at issue is whether the condition to the INF Treaty on treaty interpretation, currently proposed by the Senate Foreign Relations Committee, properly states the standards by which the legal effect of such records should be judged.

The rules that have traditionally governed treaty interpretation were recently restated in this Institute's Restatement of the Foreign Relations Law of the United States. A treaty between two or more states is an international agreement, "and is governed by international law." International law establishes rules for the construction of treaties, based on the common understanding that exists or is exhibited between the signatories. Thus, the parties look first to the text, in context, to subsequent conduct, and in appropriate situations to the negotiating history.

The Senate has broad authority to affect the meaning of treaties. It can "exclude, limit, or modify" an obligation of the United States by adopting a "reservation" which, to be effective, must be presented to and accepted by the other party. The Senate may also act by formulating a "statement of understanding" of the treaty's meaning, which it requires the President to present to the other party, but with respect to which it does not require acceptance. "When the Senate gives its advice and consent to a treaty on the basis of a particular understanding of its meaning, the President, if he makes the treaty, must do so on the basis of the Senate's understanding." The President makes a treaty on the basis of a specific understanding by communicating it to the other party prior to ratification. The other party is free to treat the understanding as "a reservation which it is not prepared to accept." Its failure to object is therefore powerful evidence that the understanding is mutual.

The Senate may also adopt particular understandings of a treaty's meaning which it does not require the President to present to the other party prior to ratification. When it does so the "treaty that is ratified or acceded to by the United States . . . becomes effective in <u>domestic law</u> subject to that understanding." The

Restatement makes no claim that "a statement of understanding" not communicated to the other party has any authority under international law on the treaty's meaning. Under domestic law, however, even "if no such statement is made, indication that the President or the Senate ascribed a particular meaning to the treaty is relevant" to its interpretation by a United States court "in much the same way that the legislative history of a statute is relevant to its interpretation." Such statements of understanding might be found, in addition to the Senate's resolution of consent, "in the report of the Senate Foreign Relations Committee and in the Senate debates." The relevant rule, "in that event," according to the Restatement, is that "the President must decide whether they represent a general understanding by the Senate and, if he finds that they do, must respect them in good faith."

The ABM Treaty record of proceedings on advice and consent contains evidence of "particular understandings," which though not adopted as formal "statements of understandings," were generally held by the Senate, and on the basis of which the Senate gave its advice and consent. The Senate adopted no formal or informal "statement of understanding," however, to indicate that it had given its advice and consent to the ABM Treaty "on the basis of" the restrictive interpretation.

"Indications" do exist in the Senate record, however, in Executive testimony and statements of Senators, that support the restrictive interpretation of the ABM Treaty, along with indications that cast doubt upon that interpretation or support a broader interpretation. My report on this subject concluded that these indications were insufficient to establish a duty to respect the restrictive interpretation under domestic law, but were sufficient to require the President to decide, in accordance with the Restatement, whether "they represent a general understanding by the Senate" of the restrictive interpretation, and that if he found they do he "must respect them in good faith."

In this discussion I will review the positions taken by the Administration and its opponents on the two principal issues posed by the proposed condition: first, the effect of informal Senate understandings under international law; and second, the standards by which such understandings are properly treated as binding under domestic law.

I. Effect of Informal Senate Understandings on International Obligations.

The Administration believes that informal Senate understandings based on Executive branch statements have no binding effect on a treaty partner. Senator Sam Nunn disagreed with this view in March 1987, contending that the presence of a Soviet official at Senate ABM hearings put them on notice of what was said; even if the Soviets had not been present, Senator Nunn argued, they "understand how our treaty making process works, monitored the proceedings and reviewed the public records." Their "clear awareness of the interpretation being presented to the Senate," followed by their failure to object prior to ratification, provided the U.S. with "a very strong basis in law for insisting on the original meaning as presented to the Senate. . . ." Senator Nunn concluded, moreover, that "it is contrary to the long-term interests of the United States to assert that statements made to the Senate have no standing with other parties to a treaty." The international community is "on notice that the executive branch explains treaties to the Senate during the ratification proceedings. It is to our national advantage to ensure that such authoritative explanations remain available as powerful evidence of a treaty's meaning in the event of an interpretive dispute among nations."

During March and April 1987, the Senate Foreign Affairs and Judiciary Committees held joint hearings under the chairmanship of Senator Joseph Biden to consider a resolution addressed to the ABM Treaty controversy. During the hearings on this resolution, I testified that, in determining the Soviet Union's international obligations, the President cannot safely rely on the Senate's "understanding" of the treaty, let alone an understanding based on "acquiescence." For the purpose of determining whether a treaty partner is bound, I said, "When [the Senate] gives its advice and consent to a treaty, it is to the treaty that was made, irrespective of the explanation [the Senate] was provided." This single sentence from my testimony, taken out of context, became known as the "Sofaer Doctrine," purporting to state that Presidents may freely disregard prior Executive positions. In actuality, in that testimony, and repeatedly thereafter, I noted with respect to domestic law, that "the President cannot, and should not, disregard views expressed during Senate proceedings. . . ."

During those hearings, the claim that statements made in the Senate can be used to bind another treaty party to the meanings expressed was again advanced. Professor Tribe insisted, for example, that the Soviets could reasonably be expected to know what goes on in the Senate, and must realize that the treaty made is the treaty to which the Senate consents. "It is axiomatic,["] he said, "that the treaty means what the Senate consented to." He rejected what he called "the Legal Adviser's model," which he understood to take the position that "the meaning of the ABM Treaty is to be gleaned not by examination of what the President and the Senate agreed upon, but by examination of what the President and the Soviets agreed upon -- regardless of what the President may or may not have told the Senate about what he had negotiated."

The Joint Committee's report adopted Professor Tribe's view. It approved a resolution that declared that the President must interpret treaties in accordance with the common understanding of the President and Senate, express or implied from acquiescence in Executive representations. While it recognized the possibility of disparate obligations under international and domestic law, the report joined in the claim that the Soviets as well as the President would be bound:

> [I]t is quite reasonable to expect -- indeed, disingenuous to pretend otherwise -- that other nations are sufficiently interested and capable to monitor U.S. ratification proceedings. Can anyone seriously believe that the Soviets have remained studiously oblivious to Senate proceedings with regard to arms control? The Committee is well aware of the contrary; Soviet diplomats are diligent in the extreme in monitoring deliberations of the Senate, most particularly on matters pertaining to U.S. Soviet relations.

The Administration's study on the ABM ratification process was completed during May 1987. It concluded that international practice and governing law in fact lend no support to the notion that statements at proceedings before the Senate are a useful or proper device for binding our treaty partners to specific meanings of a treaty. Our treaty partners are undoubtedly aware of our system of treaty making, but it is hardly disingenuous to question whether they follow with care all Senate proceedings, or derive clear messages from the Senate proceedings as to the meaning of given treaty provisions. Relatively little is clarified about most treaties, due to the lack of time Senators are able to devote to their consideration.

Other nations are in any event unlikely to accept the premise that statements not formally communicated to them have binding effect on them with respect to a treaty's meaning. A particularly cogent illustration of this occurred when U.S. and Soviet negotiators discussed the specific issue of MIRV interceptors in 1981, in a formal bilateral exchange. The U.S. negotiator took the position that anything short of field testing of such interceptors was allowed under the ABM Treaty. The Soviet rejected that view, claiming that the U.S. could not engage in research on such an interceptor, as it could lead to a prohibited system. The U.S. negotiator then reminded the Soviets that Ambassador Smith had testified to the U.S. position at the Senate hearings in 1972, and that the Soviets (who were present for Smith's public testimony) should have objected if they disagreed. The Soviet negotiator responded that the USSR had set forth its view on the meaning of "development" during the ABM Treaty negotiation, and, if it differed from the view advanced in the Senate by Ambassador Smith, that was not the Soviet side's fault; the Smith statement was an internal matter. In 1979, when asked if the Soviets could be held to an agreement "as presented to Congress," Sidney Graybeal (an ABM negotiator) replied: "Presentations to Congress can help explain the language and how it was derived, but they should not change the meaning of the language or the scope of the provisions of the agreement."

The United States has itself rejected suggestions that it is bound internationally by what is said in the Senate. For example, when a German civil court used statements made during U.S.

Senate ratification discussions, to determine the intent of the parties to a treaty, Secretary of State Hughes instructed the U.S. Ambassador in Berlin that "expressions of opinion as to the meaning" of the treaty involved "occurring in general debate, cannot be regarded as affecting the interpretation of that treaty." The U.S. would even more emphatically object to the use by other states of their own internal proceedings as a basis for binding the U.S. to a given meaning. Yet, reciprocity is a guiding principle in international affairs. If the U.S. is going to insist that foreign states follow and object to positions taken by Executive officials or Senators in our internal, advice-and-consent process, we would be obliged to shoulder the same obligations abroad. We could not do so without great additional effort, and in states such as the Soviet Union we could not do so in any meaningful sense. Furthermore, given the frequent ambiguity of such legislative history, this practice would add great uncertainty to the process of treaty formulation and interpretation, and would become a nightmare in connection with multilateral treaties.

The proper and workable rule was stated in a report on treaty procedures, prepared by the professional staff of the Senate Foreign Relations Committee in 1977. The study noted that Senate committee reports, and statements and colloquies by the floor manager, were intended to present the committees' understanding of the meaning of treaty provisions, but that these sources were "purely domestic documents and of no concern to the other party. . . ." This rule is implicit in the accepted Senate practice of formulating statements of understanding in some cases which it does not require the President to communicate to the treaty partner. The recognized legal effect of this practice is to condition the Senate's advice and consent under domestic law without requiring an assurance that the condition also binds the treaty partner.

The Senate did not act upon the ABM Treaty Resolution proposed by the Joint Committee, because Congress incorporated into the Defense Appropriation bill a provision prohibiting spending without specific appropriation on ABM development or testing that is inconsistent with the restrictive interpretation. President Reagan agreed to this provision in advance, thus accepting Congress' role and deferring the underlying controversy.

Submission of the INF Treaty to the Senate led, however, to renewed debate on the treaty-interpretation issue. The Administration received from several leading Senators demands for the treaty's entire negotiating record. These Senators claimed that, in light of the Administration's position in the ABM Treaty debate that the treaty to which the Senate gives its advice and consent is the treaty made by the parties, the Senate would need to check the negotiating record to be confident that the Executive branch had fully and accurately explained the treaty's meaning. Some Senators also threatened to condition their advice and consent with numerous reservations and understandings, because they thought the Administration had claimed it could disregard Executive branch statements.

The Administration responded constructively to both these concerns. First, we agreed that the Senate had a legitimate interest in the negotiating history, and supplied the whole record -- 31 binders of documents. Secretary Shultz also provided a letter to deal with the erroneous assumption that the Executive branch was claiming the freedom to disregard its own presentations. The Committee nonetheless decided to recommend to the Senate as a condition of its advice and consent to the INF Treaty, a declaration of the principles governing treaty interpretation. While acknowledging that the ABM Treaty interpretation dispute should not be revisited unnecessarily, the staff report claims that the committee could not overlook the "constitutional assertion of a clearly delineated and unprecedented doctrine under which the President has wide latitude for treaty `reinterpretations,' notwithstanding what the Senate may have been told in the course of granting consent to ratification." Authority to disregard prior Senate statements would enable the President unilaterally to amend treaties, the report claims, contrary to the Senate's advice-and-consent authority.

In claiming that the "Sofaer Doctrine" entitles the President to disregard Executive representations to the Senate, the INF Treaty Report reiterates the erroneous premise adopted in the earlier Joint Committee Report. In fact, as the record demonstrates, the testimony cited as the Sofaer Doctrine related only to the nation's international obligations, and not to any domestic, constitutional limitation implicit in the advice and consent process. On this point, the INF Treaty report agreed with the Administration by acknowledging that the domestic representations of the Executive branch cannot be relied upon to bind the other party to a treaty under international law. The Committee ordered that its treaty interpretation resolution not be conveyed to the Soviet Union as part of the instruments of ratification, because it "viewed this as a matter of underscoring that the Condition is not directed to U.S. obligations under international law. . . . ."

II. Effect of Informal Senate Understandings under U.S. Law.

The Administration has repeatedly recognized that informal Senate understandings based on Executive representations can result in binding commitments under domestic law. In my testimony before the Joint Committee I said, for example, that "the President cannot, and should not, disregard views expressed during Senate proceedings . . . ." I noted Secretary Shultz's statement that, while what is said during the ratification process in the U.S. is important to the Executive branch, "that has absolutely no standing as far as the Soviets are concerned." I said: "That is the point that we are making here today -- `insofar as the Soviets are concerned.' We do believe that such statements have standing insofar as the Senate is concerned and insofar as our relationship with the Senate is concerned." I noted that my memorandum on the ABM negotiating record "is not addressed to any duties created by the entire ratification process for the President to the U.S. Senate. So, <u>the President cannot and will not and does not disregard those statements</u>." Despite the clarity of these statements, the Administration was accused of having advocated the proposition that the President is free to disregard Executive representations.

After its hearings, the Joint Committee adopted a resolution stating that, under the U.S. Constitution, the President is obliged to interpret all treaties in accordance with the "Senate's understanding." The resolution in effect claims that only one treaty can exist, the one to which the Senate gives its advice and consent. The Administration agrees with this principle; the question is how one goes about determining the meaning of the treaty to which the Senate has given its advice and consent. The Joint Committee's

Report asserts that sources upon which the President must sometimes rely in determining the parties' international obligations, particularly the negotiating history, cannot be relied upon if they have not been given to the Senate. The report rejects the "premise" on which it says the Administration's position is based -- "that a treaty's meaning derives from communications between the parties. This is true," the report states, "under international law. But it is not true under United States law." In the view of the Committee report, the President's broad power of treaty interpretation is limited by the constitutional principle that the President can only interpret treaties as they were understood by the Senate when it voted, and a Senate understanding need not be formally recorded, but may involve mere "acquiescence" in Executive statements or a host of other possibilities under what the report called a "rule of reason."

The INF Treaty report follows in most respects the ABM Joint Committee report in its approach to the domestic law limitations on the President's power to interpret treaties. The proposed condition, as adopted by the Committee, notes that the "principles" it states are necessarily derived from the Constitution, an assertion that could be seen as an attempt to control the outcome of the ABM Treaty debate despite the report's claim to the contrary. The Resolution then goes on to state that "the United States shall interpret this Treaty in accordance with the understanding of the Treaty shared by the Executive and the Senate at the time of Senate consent to ratification." The "common understanding" thus referred to is, in the Resolution, "based on the text of the Treaty," and "reflected in the authoritative representations [concerning meaning or legal effect] provided by the Executive branch to the Senate and its committees" in seeking consent to ratification. The President would be bound to this "common understanding" unless a change was authorized by amendment, in accordance with a procedure authorized by the treaty's terms, or in a subsequent statute. The report continues to rely on the claim that what it calls the Sofaer Doctrine would allow the President to disregard prior Executive statements to the Senate.

Two important questions arise under the proposed condition: what is meant by "common understanding," and when is the evidence concerning a particular meaning sufficient to bind the President. The report explains the condition as intended to give overriding priority in treaty interpretation for domestic purposes to the representations of Executive officials. It states that any negotiating history, and presumably any subsequent practice, that is inconsistent with Executive representations considered binding must be subordinated to the meaning supported by the representations.

In reaching this conclusion, the INF Report had to deal with the fact that the Executive has submitted to the Senate the full INF negotiating record. The Joint Committee Report rejected the relevance to the shared understanding of the Senate and President any negotiating history not submitted to the Senate, in itself a questionable conclusion. But why should the Senate not be assumed to have considered evidence actually received by it, pursuant to its request? The INF Report claims, in effect, with classic circularity, that because it is necessary to make Executive statements binding, any inconsistent materials, although accurate and truly authoritative, must be ignored. Thus, the report states:

> If U.S. treaty interpretation is to be based upon the shared understanding of the Senate and the Executive at the time of ratification, and if the common understanding is reflected in authoritative Executive branch statements made in seeking Senate consent to ratification, then sources of interpretation which appear at variance must be subordinated to those authoritative statements.

The INF report also deals with the standards by which the "common understanding" is to be determined, and at what point the evidence of a particular interpretation is to be deemed binding.

The Administration's position on this question draws once again on the Restatement, concluding that the President would be bound for domestic purposes if the Senate relied on a particular meaning as a basis for granting advice and consent, with the Senate's intent to be ascertained in much the same way courts determine whether Congress intended to bind the Executive in legislation. After examining the standards actually applied by the

Supreme Court in recent cases, combined with the Restatement rules, we concluded that a particular interpretation would bind the President, despite the treaty's actual meaning, when it was "generally held by the Senate, relied upon, and clearly intended." The relevant cases fail to support the notion that acquiescence in Executive statements automatically creates a binding meaning. For legislative history to prevent the President from adopting a construction that is otherwise reasonable, the record as a whole must reflect a positive legislative determination to adopt a different interpretation. In the Japanese Whaling Association case the Court required deference to the Executive's construction of a statute "unless the legislative history of the enactment shows with sufficient clarity that the agency construction is contrary to the will of Congress." Where no such express intent is found, subsequent agency interpretation -- including reinterpretation -- is generally accorded appropriate deference and held to a general standard of reasonableness. And these standards should be applied to treaty interpretation with a special regard for the President's broad authority to interpret treaties and conduct foreign affairs. We did not conclude, however, that the Senate must adopt a formal "statement of understanding" to create a binding obligation. Our study in fact collected several examples from ratification records of cases in which the Senate manifested its intention through reports, in hearings, speeches, and colloquies which thereafter were treated by the Executive as creating binding obligations.

The INF report condemns the criteria relied on by the Administration as having "no constitutional basis - no reference to the intent of the Framers, to historical precedent, to case law - no reference to any source of constitutional authority." Furthermore, the report argues, "while such terms as `generally understood,' `clearly intended,' and `relied upon' may appear straight forward and appealing, in practice such criteria would be so difficult to meet that the Executive would almost never be bound by its own presentation to the Senate. . . ." These "unreasonable criteria," the report claims, would allow the President to "reinterpret" treaties in any way he chose, without constraint, conferring "an effective right of treaty amendment disguised a treaty reinterpretation."

When the report turns, however, to the task of determining the criteria which it would advance to judge whether the President is bound by a particular though informal Senate understanding, the report agrees that the standards should be the same as those used in ascertaining legislative intent. Without citing a single such authority, however,the report asserts that "implicit" intent must be treated as equally significant to explicit intent, stating that "implicit understandings represent Senate agreement with and acceptance of the Executive's explanations of the Treaty. . . , [which] although not formalized . . . must necessarily be equal in significance to explicit understandings. To accord them lesser significance would be illogical because implicit understandings commonly occur precisely where there is no disagreement as to meaning and where no issue has arisen." Congress' failure to act to alter the meaning in "unchallenged communications," expresses "acquiescence" in that meaning, and therefore an intention that it be maintained.

The report is correct in stating that "a rule of reason" -- in which all the relevant circumstances are considered -- should guide the determination of whether an Executive representation is "authoritative." But it is wrong to treat the Senate's "acquiescence" in Executive statements too readily as a basis for implying an intention to bind the President. In the absence of a formal "statement of understanding," the Restatement provides that the President must decide whether a particular understanding was "generally held" by the Senate, and whether the Senate gave its advice and consent "on the basis" of the understanding. This formulation may, in some instances, permit an inference of intent to bind from acquiescence, as where highly authoritative statements are made on an issue of fundamental importance to the treaty. The judicial precedents indicate, however, that binding legislative intent is formed only when Congress "has directly spoken to the precise question at issue." While courts have properly given "great weight" to authoritative statements on issues the record shows to have been a basis for legislative action, no case could be found in which such intent was established merely by Senate acquiescence in Executive testimony. This is hardly surprising, since the silence, for example, of a handful of Senators at a hearing, in the face of testimony of an official, bearing on an issue of less than central importance, is as likely to reflect the absence of any intention as it is an implied decision of the Senate to limit the President for all time.

On this issue, as on the status of informal understandings under international law, the differences between the Administration and Senate advocates of the proposed condition are narrowing. Senator Nunn, for example, recently testified that he agreed completely with the following excerpt from a letter by White House Counsel A.B. Culvahouse, restating the Administration position:

> As a matter of domestic law, however, the President is bound by shared interpretations which were both authoritatively communicated to the Senate by the Executive and clearly intended, generally understood, and relied upon by the Senate in its advice and consent to ratification.

Senator Nunn said: "I don't think we are that far apart on the Constitution itself. I think this letter here comes a long way along that line." (Senator Adams, who supports the proposed condition, agreed with this appraisal.)

The INF report exaggerates the dangers of accepting these standards. The rules to which the Administration agrees it is bound do not allow it to disregard either the Senate's intentions or the treaty's meaning. Where a conflict in fact exists between the treaty as made under international law and understandings generally held and relied on by the Senate in granting advice and consent, the President would be required to abide by his domestic obligation. No constitutional confrontation is created by this rare situation, since U.S. law accords priority to constitutionally based duties. Even where the President is free as a matter of law to construe a treaty in a manner that differs from an Executive representation, he is nonetheless obliged to act within the constraints of international law. He cannot "amend the treaty," but is allowed only to construe it in accordance with the text and negotiating history. Indeed, the freedom he has when these requirements for a binding domestic obligation are not satisfied is to adopt an interpretation that actually reflects the treaty's obligations, rather than being bound by representations that fail accurately to describe those obligations. He is limited here in the same way the Executive is limited in construing a statute; the construction must be reasonable or it can properly be regarded as in excess of his authority. And even though a reasonable basis exists for a particular construction, nothing prevents the treaty partner or Congress from exercising all lawful pressures to prevent its adoption or implementation. An interpretation need not be found unlawful to be deemed unwise.

The actual effects of the condition proposed for the INF treaty would prove detrimental to the nation's interests if adopted. First, the rules proposed would upset established standards of treaty interpretation, based on commonly accepted principles of international law. By insisting on a meaning for treaties derived from unilateral Executive representations the Senate would signal to U.S. treaty partners a broad discretion to invoke domestic law to disregard the treaty actually made. In some instances this may please the treaty partner, which may want to see the U.S. restrained to a particular rule. But as a general matter it will tend to create additional uncertainty in a process that is already complex. We would resist such a claim by any of our treaty partners, to avoid the uncertainties and burdens it would entail. Furthermore, the proposed condition would by definition only have practical effect in situations where the treaty partner is not bound by the same standard to which the condition would bind this nation. This is an undesirable consequence, and it should be restricted to those situations in which the record truly reflects a generally held intention on the Senate's part to rely on the meaning at issue.

It is simply wrong, moreover, to claim that one demeans the Senate's role by saying the Senate gives its advice and consent to the treaty made between the parties. The Senate's constitutional role is to pass on the international agreements that are actually to be made at ratification, not to insist on limiting the U.S. unilaterally on the basis of evidence of a domestic understanding that a Senate majority later deems sufficient to be a binding interpretation. The Senate is entitled to proper respect, and to a full and accurate explanation of treaties. But it is entitled to receive - and obliged to give - far more. It is entitled and obliged to determine the true meaning of treaties, and jointly with the

President to decide whether and in what form they should be ratified. It demeans the Senate's role to suggest that it will rely upon the power to insist that Executive representations be binding irrespective of a treaty's true meaning, rather than participating as a partner in ascertaining the true meaning and shaping it as necessary through proper means.

In fact, the Senate in considering the INF Treaty has acted in accordance with its constitutional responsibilities. On a series of issues concerning which Senators found ambiguity, including the regulation of INF missiles that would be equipped with future forms of weapons, they were unwilling to accept Executive representations, however explicit, authoritative, and often repeated. They wanted to know what the parties to the treaty had actually agreed on each of these issues, and to find that out they examined the relevant negotiating history. When that history failed to satisfy concerned Senators as to the treaty's negotiated meaning, they asked the Executive to go back to the Soviets for clarification. We saw, in short, a demonstration of the Senate playing its intended role by exercising its constitutional authority to assure itself that it understood and found acceptable the treaty to which it was considering giving its advice and consent. The law should not be distorted in order to create a standard for implying binding domestic obligations that is designed to accommodate a record in which the Senate failed to perform this role. If adopted, the Condition could readily be used as a vehicle for binding the President to Senate treaty interpretations based on mere acquiescence in Executive representations, thus impinging upon the President's recognized authority.

III. Conclusion

The treaty interpretation debate continues. This review of the issues shows, however, that the differences have narrowed considerably.

- Both sides in the debate agree that a shared or common understanding in the Senate, if based on Executive representations, cannot be used to bind treaty partners to a meaning other than that established under international law.

- o Both agree that the President cannot disregard Executive statements to the Senate, and may in proper circumstances be bound by such statements under domestic law.

- o Both largely agree on the standards for determining if the President is bound domestically: a rule of reason, reference to cases on legislative intent, and the need to establish a generally held understanding on which the Senate relied.

The remaining differences should be overcome. We intend to keep working so that President Reagan gets to go to Moscow with the INF Treaty ready to ratify, thus concluding a strategic plan that is a bipartisan triumph. We must also succeed, however, in preventing misunderstanding and interbranch rivalry from distorting the law governing treaty interpretation and the advice-and-consent process. I am grateful for this opportunity to address you on this subject.[654]

The INF Treaty interpretation condition precipitated a major debate in the Senate.[655] Reviewing highlights of that debate, on the one hand the Senate majority

---

[654]Address by Abraham D. Sofaer, Legal Adviser to the Department of State, "Treaty Interpretation and the Separation of Powers," given to the American Law Institute in Chicago, Illinois (May 19, 1988) (footnotes omitted).

This address, as well as certain other Executive branch statements, have been included in this section on "consideration by subsequent Congresses of the `broad-narrow' interpretation issue" because of their relevance in an ongoing Senate-Executive interaction on the issues.

[655]For the debate on the INF Treaty on May 26, 1988, most of which concerns the treaty interpretation condition, see 134 *Cong. Rec.* S6725-6809 (daily ed. May 26, 1988).

leader, Senator Byrd, made the following statement in introducing his "Byrd condition" amendment:

> Madam President, the amendment I am offering is intended to clarify and strengthen the Senate's rightful and constitutional role in the approval of treaties. The dispute over the proper interpretation of provisions of the ABM Treaty has thrown a cloud of uncertainty over the definitive meaning of the provisions of a treaty which has been approved by the Senate. This amendment intends to make it crystal clear that common understandings reached by the Senate and the executive branch in the course of the Senate deliberations, and investigations in connection with its advice and consent to the ratification of a treaty, bind any future Presidents. The Senate consents to the ratification of a treaty only on the understanding that the President will interpret a treaty and implement a treaty, in good faith conformity to the meaning arrived at by the Senate, as a result of its deliberations.
>
> Certain administration officials have challenged the role of the Senate in the treaty-making process, and declared that the administration has the right to interpret and implement the provisions of a treaty in a manner inconsistent with that shared by the Senate and the President, through his representatives, when it gave its advice and consent. To accept this proposition would make a mockery of the entire Senate process, and in fact it would reduce the constitutional role of the Senate to a mere nullity. The consent of the Senate would be reduced to a clerical function. This is not what the framers of our Constitution envisioned.
>
> This amendment intends to bind the President, as a condition of Senate approval to his implementing this treaty, to the interpretation understood by this body of the meaning of the provisions of the treaty. If the President does not agree to the common understandings developed in the process of examining the text his negotiators developed, and in the process of the committee's examination of his representatives and their testimony on the treaty, then the President ought not to exchange the instruments of ratification. By his act of exchanging the instruments of ratification, the President is bound by the common understandings developed in the Senate by his representatives. The President and the Senate, through this process entered into a

solemn constitutional contract. This amendment does not break any new legal ground. It does not create any new constitutional roles or duties, nor could it, it merely restates what I believe is the current law and the current responsibilities of the two branches regarding the treaty-making power. It would not have been necessary had not a challenge been mounted to that constitutional arrangement. I regard it as a critically important amendment for this body. I regard this amendment as going to the heart of one of the most important powers that the framers of our Constitution gave to the Senate. A proper resolution of this dispute is of great significance.

The amendment states that the President shall interpret this treaty in accordance with the common understanding, shared by the Senate, that prevails at the time the Senate gave its advice and consent to the ratification. It states further that this common understanding is based on the text of the treaty, any reservations or understandings which the Senate may attach to the resolution of ratification, and on the authoritative testimony of executive branch officials concerning the meaning and legal effect of the treaty. The amendment then states, clearly and explicitly, that no subsequent interpretation of this treaty which is inconsistent with this shared understanding shall be permitted, unless the Senate has participated through the passage of a subsequent treaty or protocol on the enactment of a statute.

Mr. President, the amendment addresses the rules of the game when a common understanding between the two branches has been reached. There can be times when, after the resolution of ratification has been approved, a matter arises about which no interpretation was available and no common understanding was reached. Under those circumstances--and I expect that if both sides do their job well, those will be rare circumstances--then paragraph 4 of my amendment provides that the disputed provision shall be interpreted in accordance with applicable United States law. Those instances then would be outside of the rules pertaining to common understandings which are embodied in clauses 1, 2 and 3 of the amendment. We would not be dealing with a reinterpretation of a common understanding. That is where the problem has heretofore arisen. Instead, we would be dealing with a first interpretation of a case which arose after the consent had been given. The distinguished Senator from Maine, Mr. COHEN, is to be commended for fashioning this provision and I think it fills a necessary GAP in my original formulation in which others participated with me, and I think it is an important contribution to the amendment.

The position which the Senate adopts through the passage of this amendment is based on sound constitutional logic. There is no need to restate that logic as part of the condition, but the Senate is clearly acting in accordance with the treaty clause of the constitution--article II, section 2, clause 2--and in accordance with the powers of the Senate in the making of treaties. The amendment emphasizes this point by reference to the constituting language.

The amendment I offer has the same intent as the amendment proposed by the committee on foreign relations, but I believe that in consideration of the hours that have gone into its formulation and the bipartisan efforts, the time involved and the application of the energies and talents of Senators on both sides of the aisle, it is more focused, specific, and precise. It prevents the President from acting unilaterally in a way inconsistent with the meaning of the treaty as understood by both the Senate and the President. There should be no ambiguity about this.

Why is it important to attach this condition at this time?

Once the Senate has concluded its action on this resolution and has given its advice and consent to ratification, the treaty becomes the law of the land. A treaty becomes law unlike other laws--the House of Representatives does not participate, the President does not have the opportunity to veto, and mistakes are not easily corrected by subsequent legislation. A treaty is thus quite different, in the context of the law of the land, from a bill which becomes a law.

For these reasons, the Senate spends considerable time studying the treaty, holding extensive hearings, examining all issues carefully, and, ultimately, approving the resolution of ratification by a two-thirds vote of those Senators present. Three committees of this Senate, composed of nearly half of the membership of this Senate, conducted what has probably been as exhaustive and responsible a scrutiny as of any treaty that has come before this body in our Nation's history. I believe this process has produced a better treaty, and the committees are to be commended

> for their diligence. In this process. We examine the test [sic] of the treaty very carefully. We rely upon executive branch officials to testify as to the meaning of the treaty.
>
> The testimony of these officials as to the meaning of the treaty is authoritative, and any inconsistencies or problems should be detected by the committees or the executive branch and clarified prior to final action by the Senate.
>
> As we all know, several problems were discovered in the course of examination of this treaty, and they did require the negotiation of diplomatic notes and agreements to clear them up.
>
> All of this contributes to what the Senate and the administration understand to be the legal meaning and effect of the treaty.
>
> After all of this, if any administration comes along later and attempts to change the interpretation of the treaty, then that future administration is determining for itself what should be the law of the land.
>
> The Senate's approval of the treaty is based on the proposition that the President will act in good faith to implement the treaty in accord with the common understandings of its terms when that approval was given. If the administration decides later, after the instruments have been exchanged, that it does not like those understandings and decides to interpret the treaty differently, then it breaks the constitutional contract. The Senate, in reaching its decision, based that decision on the testimony and on the record that was made before it in duly constituted hearings, has no opportunity at that time to give its advice and consent to the reinterpretation of that treaty.
>
> That is why it is necessary at this time to state clearly and irrevocably that the Senate insists on its rights and its duty under the Constitution to bind the President to the interpretation of the treaty which the Senate accepted at the time it gave its advice and consent to ratification.[656]

And Senator Nunn said:

---

[656] 134 *Cong. Rec.* S6725-26 (daily ed. May 26, 1988) (statement of Sen. Byrd).

The necessity for this provision stems from the effort by the State Department's legal advisor, Judge Abraham Sofaer, to radically alter the relationship between the Senate and the President in the treatymaking process.

Under the Constitution, the President makes treaties "by and with the advice and consent of the Senate, provided two-thirds of the Senators present concur." Hamilton, in the Federalist (No. 75) clearly illustrated the intent of the framers that treatymaking be a shared power between the Senate and the President, based on mutual trust:

> The power, in question seems . . . to form a distinct department, and to belong, properly, neither to the legislative nor the executive. The qualities elsewhere detailed as indispensible in the management of foreign negotiations, point out the Executive as the most fit agent in those transactions; while the vast importance of the trust, and the operation of treaties as laws, plead strongly for the participation of the whole or a portion of the legislative body in the office of making them.

Because the Senate is an equal partner with the President in the treaty-making process, we have a direct, constitutional interest in ensuring that treaties are accurately presented and faithfully upheld. The executive branch, however, has challenged the Senate's role by inventing a novel theory--that the President has the power to reinterpret treaties and change obligations that were clearly understood and accepted by the Senate at the time of ratification.

We first encountered this doctrine in 1985 during hearings before the Senate Armed Services Committee. Judge Sofaer was asked if he agreed "that the purpose of the Senate's extensive ratification hearings on the ABM Treaty was to clarify ambiguities of interpretation." In his response, he argued that: "Although this process may have helped answer questions in particular Senators' minds, it could not result in authoritative clarifications of any ambiguities in the treaty, because statements made during the hearings were unilateral." In other words, because the testimony on the treaty was not offered in a joint United States-Soviet forum, Judge Sofaer viewed it as nothing more than interesting information which could be freely disregarded by the exectuive [sic] branch in the future.

Judge Sofaer expanded his assault on the role of the Senate in March 1987 when he told the Foreign Relations Committee:

> When [the Senate] gives its advice and consent to a treaty, it is to the treaty that was made, irrespective of the explanations it is provided.

Under this version of the Sofaer doctrine, the executive branch could treat prior testimony to the Senate as irrelevant. Indeed, under Judge Sofaer's approach, the executive branch is free to mislead the Senate as to the meaning of a treaty simply because the statments [sic] in ratification hearings are "unilateral."

PROBLEMS POSED BY THE SOFAER DOCTRINE FOR THE SENATE'S CONSIDERATION OF THE INF TREATY

In a letter to the President last September, I noted the grave implications of the Sofaer doctrine for the Senate's consideration of the INF Treaty:

> In effect, the Sofaer doctrine holds that if the Senate is misinformed by Executive Branch officials as to the meaning of a proposed treaty, that is simply too bad. Judge Sofaer has put the Senate on notice that if Congress relies upon the testimony of your Administration as to the meaning of an INF treaty, it will be at its own risk * * *.

The effect of the Sofaer doctrine for the INF Treaty in particular and the treaty making process in general would have been disastrous. Because treaties are the supreme law of the land, the Sofaer doctrine--if not repudiated--would compel the Senate to incorporate into its resolution of ratification on every treaty and amendment for every explanation given by an executive branch official lest it be disavowed as "unilateral" after ratification. Treaties so laden would sink of their own weight. This would be very damaging, not only to the Senate but also, more important, in the long run, to the Presidency itself, in the conduct of foreign policy. You cannot conduct foreign policy through treaties if these are the rules of the game.

THE AGREEMENT WITH SECRETARY SHULTZ

In an effort to expedite consideration of the INF Treaty, Senators BYRD, PELL, BOREN, and I worked with Secretary Shultz to address the Treaty interpretation issue. The Secretary, in a letter dated February 9, 1988, assured us that--

> All INF testimony of executive branch witnesses, within their authorized scope, is authoritative. We will inform the relevant committee of any instance in which a witness' testimony is not authoritative in any respect.
>
> Administration testimony and materials for the record can be regarded as authoritative, as described above, without the need for the Senate to incorporate them in its resolution of ratification.
>
> The Reagan administration will in no way depart from the INF Treaty as we are presenting it to the Senate.

THE ADMINISTRATION CASTS DOUBT UPON THE SHULTZ AGREEMENT

We began our hearings on the assumption that the administration was prepared to agree that the executive branch would be bound by the authoritative testimony of its witnesses. As our hearings drew to a close, however, the administration undermined our confidence in that assumption, in a letter from the counsel to the President, Arthur B. Culvahouse, Jr. The letter suggested that it would be wrong to treat testimony as authoritative if it is received from officials below the level of Secretary of State or if it is addressed to trivial or unimportant issues. The Culvahouse letter would have had the effect of leaving the executive in the future with the freedom to reinterpret the INF Treaty by claiming that the administration's testimony only addressed a trivial or unimportant issue.

The Colvahouse [sic] letter also suggested that the administration testimony would not be binding unless "the Senate as a whole" asserted a view on the subject of the testimony. This completely undermined the assurance from Secretary Shultz that the Senate need not incorporate administration testimony in its resolution of ratification, because the only way that "the Senate as a whole" can assert a view is to attach a condition on the resolution of ratification.

In addition, the Culvahouse letter implied that the Shultz letter was intended merely to serve as an expedient means of dealing with the INF Treaty and that the commitments by Secretary Shultz would apply only to the Reagan administr[a]tion. By denying that the Shultz letter had any constitutional foundation, the Culvahouse letter would have served as a invitation for a future administration to disavow the Shultz assurances at the earliest opportunity.

Finally, Mr. Culvahouse stated that the President could only be bound by testimony that was "generally understood, clearly intended and relied upon by the Senate." As the New York Times noted in an editorial: "Since it is hard to know what this mumbo-jumbo means, Presidents would be free to do with treaties as they wish." (May 5, 1988).

Mr. Culvahouse issued a subsequent letter which asserted that there were no conflicts between his letter and the assurances we received from Secretary Shultz. This simply underscored our concern that the commitment from Secretary Shultz would expire next January, leaving future administrations free to reinterpret the INF Treaty and give it a meaning contrary to the interpretations presented to the Senate by the Reagan administration.

In the report of the Armed Services Committee on the INF Treaty, we noted the problems presented by the Culvahouse letter and said: "If the matter is not satisfactorily resolved, Members of the Committee may find it necessary to offer appropriate measures during consideration of the Treaty by the Senate, including understandings or amendments to the Treaty."

THE ADOPTION OF THE BIDEN CONDITION AND ITS BENEFICIAL EFFECT IN EXPEDITING SENATE CONSIDERATION OF THE TREATY

Recognizing the serious difficulties that the Sofaer doctrine would present for the ratification process, the Foreign Relations Committee--under the guidance of Senator PELL, with the leadership of Senator BIDEN, Senator SARBANES, and others--wisely added a treaty interpretation condition to its resolution of ratification.

As we noted in the report of the Armed Services Committee on the treaty: "All Administration testimony and material submitted for the record have been regarded by the Committee as significant, and will form an essential element of the body of evidence before the Senate as it determines whether to give its consent to the INF treaty." Because the Foreign Relations Committee included a treaty interpretation condition on its resolution of ratification, there has been no need to clutter the resolution with issues satisfactorily addressed by the administration in its testimony before the Senate.

My approach to the ratification debate would have been much different had the Foreign Relations Committee not included the treaty interpretation condition in its resolution of ratification. Rather than signing a cloture petition, I would have vigorously opposed cloture until every aspect of the administration's testimony had been incorporated in the resolution. This would have required extensive floor debates on both the form and content of amendments governing--

the effect of article XIV on assistance to our allies;

the impact of the double negative in article VI on interchangeable stages;

the definition of range of new type of INF missiles;

the GLCM range definition;

the relationship between the treaty and Pershing 1A missiles;

the ability of the parties to make technical changes to the protocols without using the treaty's formal amendment procedures;

the definition of "force majeure" for purposes of canceling an inspection;

the inspection of SS-20 cannisters [sic] prior to elimination;

and literally hundreds of other issues raised by the members during our hearings.

If the Foreign Relations Committee had not recommended a treaty interpretation condition, there would have been hundreds of issues we would have had to incorporate on the floor of the Senate, indeed, rather than attempting to complete the INF Treaty debate this week, we would be planning for an exhaustive debate throughout the summer.

THE BYRD AMENDMENT

The Byrd amendment is consistent with the condition recommended by the Foreign Relations Committee. The committee, in its report, went to great lengths to state that the condition was not intended "to be dispositive on the issue of ABM Treaty interpretation." While the Byrd amendment does not resolve the ABM Treaty issue, it affirms enduring constitutional principles which apply to the interpretation of all treaties, including the ABM Treaty. I understand that differences may persist as to factual issue of ambiguity as to the text, ratification debate, and negotiating history of the ABM Treaty. But this amendment repudiates the Sofaer [sic] it clear that the executive branch is bound by authoritative representations as to the meaning of a treaty, and that such meaning cannot be changed by resort to the negotiating record or otherwise without the approval of the Congress through a subsequent statute or treaty.

The Byrd amendment must be understood in the following context:

All executive branch testimony is regarded by the Senate as important to its consent.

The negotiating documents provided to the Senate have not been presented in such a way that they constitute representations by the executive branch as to the meaning of the treaty.

> The Senate has relied on executive branch representations in the hearings on the treaty, and has therefore deemed it unnecessary to make a detailed review of the negotiating documents or to attach to the resolution of ratification understandings, amendments, or reservations embodying all such testimony.
>
> The Senate reserves the right to obtain any element of the negotiating history necessary to meet the consitutional [sic] obligations of the Senate should an issue arise as to treaty interpretation involving the President's reliance on the negotiating history.
>
> Nothing in the treaty interpretation condition shall be construed to imply, with respect to any prior or subsequent treaty, that the President can interpret such treaty in a manner contrary to or inconsistent with the meaning of the treaty presented to the Senate, regardless of whether such a condition was placed in the resolution of ratification.
>
> The treaty interpretation condition provides a sensible approach to a critical problem. Newsday, in an editorial on May 23, observed that this issue is "central to our constitutional system * * *. The Constitution says treaty making is a shared responsibility. The * * * condition simply says that the executive branch cannot decide by itself to reinterpret the INF Treaty." According to the Association of the Bar of the City of New York, the principles set forth in the treaty interpretation condition "are fundamental to our constitutional scheme and cannot reasonably be questioned." By including the treaty interpretation condition on the resolution of ratification, we will confirm the constitutional significance of the Senate's proceedings in the ratification process, thereby ensuring that this treaty will be respected by the executive branch in the future.[657]

Senator Specter, in opposition to the condition, said:

> Mr. President, the Byrd condition, like the Biden condition, stands the international law of treaty interpretation on its head, because international law in treaty interpretation has, as a

[657] 134 *Cong. Rec.* S6773-75 (daily ed. May 26, 1988) (statement of Sen. Nunn).

fundamental requirement, mutuality. The United States cannot be bound, realistically, if the Soviet Union is not bound. But the Biden condition and the Byrd condition impose upon the United States a greater obligation by holding the United States to what some may say is the Senate's understanding. There is no question that the Soviet Union is not bound by the Senate's understanding.

Some references have been made to that by the distinguished Senator from Georgia, and perhaps in this debate we will have an opportunity to see if he really contends that the Soviet Union is bound by what goes on in Senate ratification proceedings; but the clear law is that the Soviet Union is not so bound.

What is endeavored here today is to make the United States bound on tighter restrictions than those which apply to the Soviet Union.

Mr. President, the thrust of the Biden condition and the Byrd condition has the same fatal flaw, but the thrust of the Biden condition is to render irrelevant the negotiating record, which is a cardinal principle of international law treaty interpretation.

The distinguished Senator from Georgia [Mr. NUNN] was on the floor a few moments ago--and I have sent notice through staff that I would be referring to this--saying that the negotiating record is important. Certainly it is under all standards of international law. But what does the Biden condition and what does the Byrd condition do with the negotiating record?

According to the Foreign Relations Committee report, it makes it immaterial. At page 101 of that report:

"Such documents"--referring to the negotiating record--"need not have been examined for consistency and should not be deemed material to U.S. interpretation of the INF Treaty insofar as they are inconsistent with the executive branch formal presentation of the INF Treaty."

Can you imagine that under a condition adopted by this body today the negotiating record is immaterial?

I have already introduced into the RECORD voluminous authorities from the Supreme Court of the United States, the prestatement [sic] of foreign relations law, consented to by most Members of this body, that state that the negotiating record is an indispensable tool on treaty interpretation. But under the Biden condition and the Byrd condition the negotiating record is deemed irrelevant and that is an underlying fallacy of this condition.

The Biden condition and the Byrd condition as well turn upside down U.S. constitutional law interpretation because they develop a new theory, a new approach on what they call implicit understandings. I have sought to find any authority for the so-called implicit understandings. We know of reservations. We know of expressed understandings. We know of a managers report. We know of dialog [sic] on the floor where a question is asked of the managers of a bill.

But this condition brings forward a new concept which is revolutionary and extremely destructive because it is up to anyone's guess as to what will happen with respect to such implicit understandings.[658]

He then introduced into the record the following "statement of law on the implications of the Biden condition which will be equally applicable to the Byrd condition":[659]

IMPLICATIONS OF THE BIDEN CONDITION

Mr. President, I am opposed to the so-called Biden condition, which I more appropriately refer to as the ABM reinterpretation condition, because it revises international law on treaty interpretation, confuses U.S. constitutional law on treaty ratification, and interjects in the deliberations on the INF Treaty an attempt to resolve the continuing dispute over the ABM Treaty.

As I stated on this floor on May 18, inclusion of the ABM reinterpretation condition in the resolution of ratification by the Senate Foreign Relations Committee has proven to be a detrimental factor in debate on the INF Treaty which continues to threaten the treaty's ratification.

The ABM reinterpretation condition poses three serious implications for treaty interpretation. The condition would: First,

---

[658]134 *Cong. Rec.* S6745-46 (daily ed. May 26, 1988) (statement of Sen. Specter).

[659]*Id.* at S6746 (statement of Sen. Specter).

fundamentally change international law on treaty interpretation; second, change and confuse U.S. constitutional law regarding the Senate's role in the treaty ratification process; and third, necessarily implicate the complex facts of the ABM Treaty and its interpretation.

I. INTERNATIONAL LAW ON TREATY INTERPRETATION

Mr. President, the ABM reinterpretation condition fundamentally changes international treaty interpretation.

The ABM reinterpretation condition establishes, in effect, a two-treaty doctrine, where there is a treaty between the executive branch and the Soviet Union and simultaneously a second treaty between the executive branch and the U.S. Senate. This concept is discussed at length in chapter IX of the Senate Foreign Relations Committee report on the INF Treaty entitled "Treaty Interpretation, condition adopted by the committee," which, in effect, gives primacy to the agreements reached between the executive branch and the Senate. The committee report's analysis of the ABM reinterpretation condition creates confusion and contradiction in the treaty ratification process, and represents a turf battle between the two branches.

Although it includes reference to the "common understanding" between the executive branch and the Senate "based on the text of the treaty" and "authoritative representations," the ABM reinterpretation condition elevates the provisions of the understanding reached between the executive branch and the Senate, making them paramount to the understanding between the executive branch and the foreign nation. Subsection (a) of the condition reads:

The United States shall interpret this treaty in accordance with the understanding of the treaty shared by the executive and the Senate at the time of Senate consent to ratification.

Chapter IX of the Senate Foreign Relations Committee report includes a number of references establishing the committee's priorities in the treaty ratification process. For example, the committee report states:

The Legal Adviser's statement implies that the meaning of a U.S.-Soviet treaty is to be gleaned not by examination of what the President and the Senate jointly understood, but by examination of what the President and the Soviets agreed upon--regardless of what the President may or may not have told the Senate. Report at 92.

This statement and other similar statements throughout chapter IX of the committee report establish the committee's view and the underlying doctrine of the ABM reinterpretation condition that the paramount consideration in treaty interpretation is what was agreed upon between the President and the U.S. Senate.

Mr. President, a treaty is valid and binding only if it establishes mutual obligations between the two contracting parties--in the case of the INF Treaty, the United States and the Soviet Union. Although the Senate's understanding plays a critical role in what the United States agrees to in the treaty process, it certainly is not the dominant factor to be considered in interpreting a treaty.

In this regard, the ABM reinterpretation condition turns the international law of treaty interpretation on its head, because the dominant consideration in interpreting an international treaty is what was agreed upon between the two nations--the intent of the parties. The committee report, however, reads:

In sum, although internal Executive memoranda and other negotiating materials may have been available to Members of the Senate, some of whom have sought to assure themselves that this "record" is consistent with the Administration's formal presentation, the clear corollary of the constitutional principles cited in the Biden Condition is that *such documents need not have been examined* for consistency and *should not be deemed material to U.S. interpretation* of the INF Treaty insofar as they are inconsistent with the Executive Branch's formal presentation of the INF Treaty. Report at 101 (emphasis added).

The committee's conclusion that such documents are not material flatly contradicts firmly established principles of treaty interpretation. The committee report notes that only the Senate's understanding matters, and does not mention the subsequent practices of the parties--thereby inferentially deeming them irrelevant as well.

The committee's attempt to exclude the negotiating record and the subsequent practices of the parties by placing sole reliance on what the committee defines as the Senate's understanding clearly revises treaty interpretation under international law, which recognizes that a treaty reflects the intent of the parties. The parties to the INF Treaty are the United States and the Soviet Union; the Senate is not, nor should be considered, an independent party. The committee report, however, requires a treaty to be in accordance with what the committee determines the Senate's understanding to be regarding that treaty.

By elevating the Senate's understanding of the agreements between the executive branch and the Senate, the ABM reinterpretation condition subordinates the agreements reached between the President and the other contracting country--the Soviets in the case of the INF Treaty--to the indicia of the Senate's intention.

The condition's effect of elevating the Senate's understanding of agreements reached between the President and the Senate may instill reluctance in other nations to negotiate treaties with the United States. Nations like the Soviet Union may be far less willing to enter into treaties with the United States if we claim that such treaties will be interpreted in light of the intentions of the U.S. Senate. The United States certainly would object--vociferously--if another country asserted a similar condition.

The ABM reinterpretation condition also has the effect of proposing a dramatic and one-sided change in the interpretation of international law, by urging that international agreements should be interpreted without regard to the intent of the parties, whenever that intent conflicts with the intent of the U.S. Senate.

Mr. President, to the contrary, the Supreme Court of the United States and established constitutional doctrine clearly recognize the following vital factors in treaty interpretation: the negotiations, the terms of the treaty, the negotiating record, and the practical construction adopted by the parties, also referred to as the "subsequent practice" of the parties.

The U.S. Supreme Court recently restated this fundamental tenet of treaty interpretation. In *Societe Nationale Industrielle Aerospatiale v. U.S. District Court for the Southern District of Iowa*, slip op. 85-1695 (1987), the Supreme Court stated:

In interpreting an international treaty, we are mindful that it is "in the nature of a contract between nations" . . . [and] The treaty's history, "the negotiations, and the practical construction adopted by the parties" may also be relevant. Id at 10.

The Senate Foreign Relations Committee report on the INF Treaty is inconsistent with this firmly established principle. It is possible that the understanding between the Senate and the President may be at variance with what the United States agreed to with the other contracting country. In such cases, the Senate's understanding is an important, but not the determinative factor--or even the factor to be considered first.

In cases of ambiguity regarding interpretation of a treaty, the law is clear that the negotiating record and the subsequent practices of the parties are the critical factors in resolving the ambiguity. The Senate should reject contrary statements included in the committee report.

II. U.S. CONSTITUTIONAL LAW

The ABM reinterpretation condition changes and confuses U.S. constitutional law regarding the Senate's role in the treaty ratification process.

Mr. President, the law is well established that the executive interprets the meaning of a treaty. The "Restatement of the Foreign Relations Law of the United States," section 326, sets forth U.S. law on the authority to interpret international agreements:

(1) The President has authority to determine the interpretation of an international agreement to be asserted by the United States in its relations with other states.

(2) Courts in the United States have final authority to interpret an international agreement for purposes of applying it as law in the United States, but will give great weight to an interpretation made by the executive branch. "Restatement of the Law Third," American Institute (1987) at 202.

The "Restatement's" Comment elaborates on Presidential authority to interpret treaties:

The President has authority to interpret international agreements for the purpose of United States foreign relations since he is the country's "sole organ" in its international relations and is responsible for carrying out agreements with other nations. . . . The Senate, whose consent is necessary for the United States to conclude a treaty, has no special role in the implementation of the treaty after it is made, though, of course, it participates equally with the House of Representatives in enacting implementing legislation or appropriating funds. Interpretation by the Senate of a treaty after it has been concluded may have no special authority, but understandings expressed by the Senate in giving its advice and consent must be respected. *Id.*, comment a.

Professor Henkin, who is extensively relied upon by the Foreign Relations Committee, has posited a similar doctrine:

The obligation and authority to implement or enforce a treaty involve also the obligation and authority to interpret what the treaty requires. For international purposes, no doubt, the President determines the United States position as to the meaning of a treaty. Domestically, too, since the President has usually the principal, often the sole, responsibility to execute a treaty, the treaty means what he says it means. Henkin, "Foreign Affairs and the Constitution" 167 (1972).

The Supreme Court also addressed subsequent Senate interpretation of a treaty in *Fourteen Diamond Rings v. United States*, 183 U.S. 176 (1901). The Court considered the Senate's adoption of a resolution, subsequent to ratification of a peace treaty between the United States and Spain, which attempted to clarify the application of customs duties to the Philippines, and determined "that it is absolutely without legal significance on the treaty interpretation question before the us." Id. at 180. The Supreme Court held:

The meaning of the treaty cannot be controlled by subsequent explanations of some of those who may have voted to ratify it. Id.

In a concurring opinion, Justice Brown stated that the Senate resolution "cannot be regarded as part of the treaty, since it received neither the approval of the President not the consent of the other contracting power." Id. at 182. Justice Brown also discussed at length the treaty ratification process and the authority to interpret treaties:

A treaty . . . [i]n its essence is a contract. It differs from an ordinary contract only in being an agreement between independent states instead of private parties. . . . Obviously, the treaty must contain the whole contract between the parties, and the power of the Senate is limited to a ratification of such terms as have already been agreed upon between the President, acting for the United States, and the commissioners of the other contracting power. The Senate has no right to ratify the treaty and introduce new terms into it, which shall be obligatory upon the other power, although it may refuse its ratification, or make such ratification conditional upon the adoption of amendments to the treaty. Id. at 182-83.

Justice Brown concluded that the resolution at issue "can be considered only as expressing the individual views of the Senators voting upon it." Id at 184.

Mr. President, the principles of treaty interpretation which apply in cases of ambiguity are similar to those used in determining the legislative intent of a statute. This standard was outlined by the Supreme Court in *Japan Whaling Association v. American Cetacean Society*, slip op. No. 85-954 (1986):

If a statute is silent or ambiguous with respect to the question at issue, our long-standing practice is to defer to the "executive department's construction of a statutory scheme it is entrusted to administer" [quoting *Chevron U.S.A. Inc. v. Natural Resources Defense Council, Inc.*, 467 U.S. at 843] unless the legislative history of the enactment shows with sufficient clarity that the agency construction is contrary to the will of Congress. Id. at 11.

The Court continued:

It may be that the legislative history of these amendments [at issue] there are scattered statements hinting at the per se rules advocated by respondents, but read as a whole, we are quite unconvinced that this history clearly indicates, contrary to what we and the Secretary have concluded is a permissible reading of the statute. . . . Id. at 18.

In this case, the Supreme Court clearly indicated that it is the executive branch which interprets the statute, just as it is the executive branch which interprets a treaty.

The U.S. Supreme Court articulated the same doctrine in *Chevron U.S.A. Inc. v. Natural Resources Defense Council, Inc.*, 467 U.S. 837 (1984). The Court stated:

When a court reviews an agency's construction of the statute which it administers, it is confronted with two questions. First, always, is the question whether Congress had directly spoken to the precise question at issue. If the intent of Congress is clear, that is the end of the matter; for the court, as well as the agency, must give effect to the unambiguously expressed intent of Congress. If, however, the court determines Congress has not directly addressed the precise question at issue, the court does not simply impose its own construction on the statute, as would be necessary in the absence of an administrative interpretation. Rather, *if the statute is silent or ambiguous with respect to the specific issue, the question for the court is whether the agency's answer is based on a permissible construction of the statute.* Id. at 842-43 (emphasis added).

Mr. President, the committee report is inconsistent with U.S. constitutional law on the Senate's role in the treaty ratification process.

A. THE SOFAER DOCTRINE

The Committee report rejects the so-called Sofaer doctrine which articulates three criteria which must be met for the executive to be bound by the Senate's understanding of a treaty:

The particular interpretation must have been: first, "generally understood" by the Senate; second, "clearly intended" by the Senate; and third, "relied upon" by the Senate. Committee report at 90.

These criteria, however, are based on principles set forth in section 314 of the "Restatement of the Foreign Relations Law of the United States["] and on well-established constitutional doctrine.

During the March 22, 1988, hearing on the INF Treaty before the Senate Foreign Relations Committee, Senator NUNN himself agreed with those three criteria when he quoted with approval the following sentence from a March 17 letter from the President's Counsel, Mr. Culvahouse, to Senator LUGAR:

"As a matter of domestic law, however, the President is bound by shared interpretations which were both authoritatively communicated to the Senate by the Executive and clearly intended, generally understood, and relied upon by the Senate in its advice and consent to ratification."

Senator NUNN stated: "That sentence there I agree with completely." Hearings at 144. Senator NUNN again quoted this sentence and the following sentence from the Culvahouse letter, id. at 153, and stated: "Now, I think those two sentences are something we can build on here." Id. at 154.

B. EXPLICIT/IMPLICIT CONDITIONS

Mr. President, the Senate traditionally performs its constitutional function by expressing any particular views of a treaty in the form of explicit conditions.

The committee report discusses at length how the Senate reaches its understanding, both explicit and implicit, of a treaty's meaning. The report noted that explicit understandings "are manifest in formal conditions to the Senate's consent. These conditions include amendments to the text of a treat [sic] as well as amendments to the resolution of ratification, such as `reservations,' `understandings,' and the like." Report at 93.

"Implicit understandings" are much more complicated. The committee report noted that "implicit understandings represent Senate agreement with and acceptance of the executive's explanations of the treaty." Id. at 93. The committee report refers to testimony by Professor Henkin to help define this concept: "Where several executive statements are made and there is general acceptance of their tenor, that is the Senate understanding." Id. at 93. The report continued:

Clearly, in determining whether the Senate consented to the ratification of a treaty pursuant to an implicit understanding, a rule of reason must apply. Obviously, where the indicia of Senate intent or understanding (including unchallenged executive communications or explanations) are few or inconsistent, no implicit Senate intent can reasonably be said to exist. On the other hand, where the indicia of intent (again, including unchallenged executive communications or explanations) are several and largely consistent, an implicit intent can reasonably be concluded to exist. Id. at 93-94.

These statements are illustrative of repetitious ambiguity in the committee report; they also reflect that implicit understandings realistically have no meaning where there is "a factual claim of pervasive ambiguity"--see id. at 106.

Mr. President, the committee report seeks to elevate implicit understandings * * * to be equal in significance to explicit understandings. Id. Such a doctrine of implicit understandings is obviously tailored to buttress the narrow interpretation of the ABM Treaty. It acknowledges that there is no implicit understanding where the executive communications are few or inconsistent, id. at 94, and then refers to the ABM controversy as a factual claim of pervasive ambiguity. Id. at 106. As to the ABM Treaty, and treaty interpretation generally, such a doctrine of implicit understandings inevitably will raise complex--and probably insolvable--arguments about what is sufficient to imply an understanding. It is precisely for that reason that explicit understandings are formulated to remove such ambiguities and disagreements.

Had there been an explicit understanding of the scope of the ABM Treaty's application--narrow or broad--this issue would not now be before us. This Senator and many others have illustrated the lack of an explicit understanding in the ABM Treaty record--the text of the treaty, committee proceedings and floor debate. The ABM Treaty debate would not be a part of the INF Treaty debate today had there been an explicit understanding on narrow versus broad application of the ABM Treaty.

III. THE ABM TREATY

Mr. President, debate on the ABM reinterpretation condition necessarily will implicate the complex facts of the ABM Treaty and its interpretation.

While its proponents maintain otherwise, the condition necessarily rekindles--and, realistically viewed, seeks to resolve--the substance of the ABM Treaty reinterpretation debate. This is so because the Constitution obviously binds the President with respect to interpretation of all treaties and the condition purports to state principles of constitutional law. Its intent, quite clearly, is to bind the President generally, including his interpretation of the ABM Treaty. This is obvious from reading chapter IX on the condition, which refers repeatedly to the ABM controversy.

Mr. President, Chapter IX of the Senate Foreign Relations Committee report on the INF Treaty clearly is an attempt to discredit the so-called Sofaer doctrine and influence the argument on the narrow versus broad interpretation of the ABM Treaty. Apart from these two purposes, the committee acknowledges that this condition is unnecessary. The report reads:

The committee notes that, in one respect, its action in including this condition in the INF Treaty's resolution of ratification was *unnecessary* insofar as principles which inherently apply to the INF Treaty would apply even in the absence of any Senate action affirming them. Given the circumstances, however, the committee judged that to fail to affirm such principles could suggest some degree of acquiescence in the Sofaer doctrine, which the committee views as an executive attempt to assert an unconstitutional arrogation of the treaty power. In this sense the committee views the Biden Condition, paradoxically, as both *unnecessary* and highly significant. Report at 97, emphasis added.

The committee report repeatedly raises the interpretation issue, only to discuss at length what the interpretation is not. The extended discussion in chapter IX of the so-called Sofaer doctrine clearly reflects the committee's attempt to interject the ABM Treaty debate into the INF Treaty ratification debate.

The ABM reinterpretation condition clearly implicates the ABM controversy when the ultimate question was asked of Senator CRANSTON on May 18:

Mr. SPECTER. When the distinguished Senator from California says that there is no objection to the current interpretation of the INF Treaty, only as to issues of reinterpretation, the sole issue in the Senate today is the interpretation of the INF Treaty, why bring up the question of reinterpretation of treaties? CONGRESSIONAL RECORD, May 18, 1988, at S6064.

Had Senator CRANSTON replied that there is no reason to bring up the question of reinterpretation of treaties, the debate on this condition would be over. However, Senator CRANSTON's answer brought up ABM and the Sofaer doctrine and that is where the extensive debate necessarily leads if the condition is pursued.

Mr. President, the debate over interpretation of the ABM Treaty highlights the importance of treaty interpretation principles. The ratification record of the ABM Treaty contains only a few statements on the issue of narrow versus broad, and these statements are themselves inconsistent. This Senator suggests that if a full debate of the ABM Treaty is pursued in the context of the INF Treaty ratification process, the record will reveal the degree of ambiguity on the narrow versus broad issue, which thus requires deference to the executive branch's interpretation given established principles of international law and U.S. constitutional law.

The only issue before the Senate today, however, is the interpretation of the INF Treaty, as to which there is no real dispute.

IV. CONCLUSION

Mr. President, inclusion of the ABM reinterpretation condition in the INF Treaty's resolution of ratification threatens to embroil the Senate in a protracted debate over the constitutional treaty power and continues to threaten ultimate ratification of this historic agreement. The concern I expressed on this floor on May 18--that the condition would be a detrimental factor in the ratification of the INF Treaty--unfortunately and regrettably still may prove accurate.

Ratification of the INF Treaty prior to the President's departure for the Moscow summit is too important to the Nation to be ensnared in a turf battle between a few individuals in the Senate and a few in the executive branch. The Senate should reject the ABM reinterpretation condition in the INF Treaty's resolution of ratification, and should continue to follow established principles of international law and U.S. constitutional law regarding treaty interpretation.[660]

In introducing this statement of law, Senator Specter said:

---

[660]*Id.* at S6746-49 (statement of Sen. Specter, "Implications of the Biden Condition").

> So, it may be that in terms of what we are doing here today, those of us who are advancing legal arguments and resisting the changes in international law and changes in U.S. constitutional law, may be putting into the CONGRESSIONAL RECORD the statements which will be picked up another day, very much as Plessy versus Ferguson may be picked up.[661]

The record of this debate repeatedly indicates that the INF Treaty interpretation condition leaves the "broad-narrow" issue unresolved. Thus, in an exchange between Senators Wilson and Byrd it was said:

> [Mr. WILSON.] I commend Senator COHEN and the majority leader for the effort to deal with that problem because it is a real problem. In my judgment, it does not go far enough for the reason that it fails to deal with the situation in which we discover that there is an inconsistency between a so-called authoritative representation, and not other conflicting testimony by another administration witness but rather the negotiating record, the very situation which, indeed, we dealt with last year at great length in terms of the debate as to whether the broad or narrow was the correct legal interpretation of the ABM Treaty.
>
> Having prefaced my question with that, and I thank the majority leader for his graciousness and patience, my question is this: During the negotiations to which the majority leader referred in his remarks, which occurred last night, there were repeated efforts by the majority leader, by Senator NUNN, by Senator WARNER, by Senator COHEN to make a point which was that the Byrd amendment does not seek to dispose of the debate on the broad and narrow interpretation of the ABM Treaty. Rather, I gather that it is the opinion of the sponsor that the Byrd amendment leaves that particular question unresolved. It does not seek to settle the question.
>
> Mr. BYRD. The Senator is preeminently correct.
>
> Mr. WILSON. I thank the majority leader.
>
> I think that is correct--that it does not. I point out that the language that has been chosen in the Byrd amendment speaks to the INF Treaty. It states that the Senate's advice and consent to

---

[661]*Id.* at S6746.

ratification of the INF Treaty is subject to the condition and does not purport to speak to any other treaty--not the ABM Treaty, not a future treaty, but simply to the INF Treaty.

Is that a correct interpretation?

Mr. BYRD. Mr. President, I am not interested in fighting or refighting the battle concerning the ABM Treaty; but I am interested in establishing clearly the standard by which we all ought to be guided in connection with the making and the interpretation of treaties.

The Senate has a clearcut, vital role in the making of treaties, by virtue of the "advice and consent" which it gives. I believe that the language that has been carefully crafted here establishes that standard, and it in no way, in my judgment, is intended to deal with the ABM Treaty dispute.[662]

Senator Cranston said:

> Mr. President, I want to begin by making clear that the issue before us is one which we must confront by necessity, not by choice.
>
> It is an institutional issue, which goes to the heart of the meaning of the long treaty ratification exercise in which we, as Members of the U.S. Senate, are engaged.
>
> It is not--or at least it need not and should not be--a partisan issue.
>
> The question simply put, is:
>
> > How can we ensure that the Senate and the President share a common understanding of our obligations under the INF Treaty?
>
> It is not an academic question. And it is not one devised as a means of introducing an element of complexity into our INF deliberations. Rather, it is a question thrust upon all Senators by the awkward efforts certain State Department lawyers have made to reinterpret U.S. obligations under a previous nuclear arms agreement, the 1972 ABM Treaty.

---

[662] 134 *Cong. Rec.* S6726-27 (daily ed. May 26, 1988) (statements of Sen. Wilson and Sen. Byrd).

> We are not trying to resolve that ABM dispute today. Indeed, as we in the Senate Foreign Relations Committee made crystal clear, the language on interpretation of the INF Treaty which was adopted by the committee is not dispositive of the "ABM reinterpretation issue"--nor, I should note, should the failure of Senators to address treaty interpretation principles during the 1972 ratification be deemed to prejudice subsequent debate and decisionmaking.
>
> The ABM/SDI traditional interpretation versus broad interpretation debate has become charged with emotion--despite the fact that the funding issue has been, for all intents and purposes, resolved on Department of Defense authorization measures. We must set the ABM issue aside if we are to resolve the task before us--which is to vote on consenting to ratify the INF Treaty.
>
> Having said what our amendment to the resolution of ratification does not do, let me briefly clarify what it does seek to accomplish.
>
> Our amendment is an understanding which governs Senate consent to ratification. It is a "category one condition" which the President is obliged to accept as governing on his authority to exchange INF instruments of ratification with the Soviets.
>
> It is treaty-specific. It applies only to this INF debate.
>
> . . . .
>
> I had honestly hoped that this simple language--which does not dispose of the past ABM dispute--could be adopted with the strong bipartisan support of Senators on both sides of the aisle.[663]

And, as we have seen, Senator Nunn said:

> THE BYRD AMENDMENT
>
> The Byrd amendment is consistent with the condition recommended by the Foreign Relations Committee. The committee, in its report, went to great lengths to state that the condition was not intended "to be dispositive on the issue of ABM Treaty interpretation." While the Byrd amendment does not resolve the ABM Treaty issue, it affirms enduring constitutional

---

[663] 134 *Cong. Rec.* S6749 (daily ed. May 26, 1988) (statement of Sen. Cranston).

> principles which apply to the interpretation of all treaties, including the ABM Treaty. I understand that differences may persist as to factual issue of ambiguity as to the text, ratification debate, and negotiating history of the ABM Treaty. But this amendment repudiates the Sofaer [sic] it clear that the executive branch is bound by authoritative representations as to the meaning of a treaty, and that such meaning cannot be changed by resort to the negotiating record or otherwise without the approval of the Congress through a subsequent statute or treaty.[664]

During the debate, Senators Specter and Hollings each introduced the following letter from Professor Louis Henkin, whose work provides the principal intellectual underpinning of the "dual" approach:

> MAY 24, 1988.
>
> MR. JOHN B. RITCH III,
> *Deputy Staff Director, Senate Foreign Relations Committee, Washington, DC.*
>
> DEAR MR. RITCH: It has come to may [sic] attention that I have been quoted as saying that the Senate Foreign Relations Committee Report on the INF Treaty misrepresented my views. I have made no such statement and that is not my view. I did express some concern that, in view of the way my name was used in the Report, a reading--surely a quick reading--of the Report might lead the reader to believe that I was behind the Report's statement of, and attack on, the so-called Sofaer Doctrine and that I favored the addition of the Condition on interpretation.
>
> Let me make my position clear. I discussed the substance of the statement of Constitutional principle with you and others; I agree that what has emerged in that respect is substantively sound.

---

[664]134 *Cong. Rec.* S6775 (daily ed. May 26, 1988) (statement of Sen. Nunn). While the debate on the INF Treaty interpretation condition contains repeated statements that the condition is not intended to resolve the ABM Treaty interpretation issue, the language in the condition that "the condition, based on the Treaty Clauses of the Constitution," seems to be intended to produce an effect going beyond principles of interpretation solely for the INF Treaty. *See*, for example, the statements by Senators Nunn, Levin and McClure set out in text at *infra* note 751.

> As I said from the beginning, however, I am not in favor of making a statement of Constitutional principle a condition of Senate consent. If the Senate thinks it is necessary or desirable to declare its views of Constitutional principle--which in the present instance I agree are sound--it should put them into a separate Resolution.
>
> The Committee draft in effect combines two resolutions: it combines an understanding, stated as a condition, on the interpretation of the particular INF Treaty (which condition is binding on the President, and on future Presidents) with a statement of general Constitutional principle (which is not binding on anyone). If there is insistence that the reference to Constitutional principle should be included, the text as it appears in the Committee Report is not unsound. The condition is applicable to the interpretation of this Treaty and as such is binding on this and any later President; the statement of Constitutional principle is included only parenthetically in a kind of editorial reference in passing. Perhaps it would be better to make the parenthetical character of the reference to the Constitutional principle even clearer by adding a few words, so that the introductory phrase would read:
>
> That the Treaty shall be subject to the following principles, which, in the judgment of the Senate, derive, as a necessary implication, etc.
>
> All good wishes.
>
> Sincerely,
> LOUIS HENKIN.[665]

Note that in this letter Professor Henkin takes the position that:

> The Committee draft in effect combines two resolutions: it combines an understanding, stated as a condition, on the interpretation of the particular INF Treaty (which condition is binding on the President, and on future Presidents) with a

[665]134 *Cong. Rec.* S6763 (daily ed. May 26, 1988) (letter from Louis Henkin to John B. Ritch, III (May 24, 1988), introduced by Sen. Hollings) (also in *id.* at S6746, introduced by Sen. Specter).

statement of general Constitutional principle (which is not binding on anyone).[666]

Of particular interest, during the debate Senators Wilson, Nickles, Quayle, Dole, Lugar, Warner and McCain introduced the following amendment:

> The PRESIDING OFFICER. Under the previous order the Senator from California is recognized for the purpose of making an amendment.
>
> AMENDMENT NO. 2325
>
> (Purpose: To provide that the only interpretations of the Treaty which bind the United States are those which are equally binding on the Soviet Union under applicable international law)
>
> Mr. WILSON. Mr. President, there is an amendment at the desk which [I] offer on behalf of myself, Senators NICKLES, QUAYLE, DOLE, LUGAR, WARNER, and MCCAIN.
>
> The PRESIDING OFFICER. The clerk will report.
>
> The legislative clerk read as follows:
>
> > The Senator from California (Mr. WILSON), for himself, Mr. NICKLES, Mr. QUAYLE, Mr. DOLE, Mr. LUGAR, Mr. WARNER, and Mr. MCCAIN, proposes an amendment numbered 2325
> >
> > At the end of the resolution of ratification, add the following:
> >
> > The Senate's advice and consent to ratification of the Treaty is further subject to the following:
> >
> > ( ) CONDITION.--The United States shall not be bound to any interpretation of this Treaty that is not equally binding on the Soviet Union under applicable international law.

---

[666] *Id.*

> Mr. WILSON. Mr. President, I did not ask for a suspension of the reading. It took him a very brief time to read the entire amendment. It is a single sentence. It states:
>
>> The United States shall not be bound to or constrained by any interpretation of this treaty that is not equally binding or constraining upon the Soviet Union.
>
> Mr. President, a great Senator, a great Democrat, "Scoop" Jackson, at the time of the SALT I agreement, offered an amendment that said essentially the same thing. His concern at that point had to do with mutuality of obligation in terms of quantity, in terms of the number of units that we were concerned with, but the principle was the same.
>
> Mr. President, I can think of no reason, frankly, why this amendment is not acceptable, and would be happy to have it accepted. It simply says that the United States and the Soviet Union shall operate under mutuality of obligation with respect to an interpretation of this treaty.[667]

In support of this amendment Senator Nickles said:

> Mr. NICKLES. Mr. President, I rise in support of this amendment and as a cosponsor of it. I appreciate and compliment my good friend and colleague, Senator WILSON from California.
>
> This amendment is simple, but probably as important as any amendment which we have discussed over the last couple of weeks. It says and states very frankly and very briefly that the United States should not be constrained by any interpretations of the treaty that are not equally binding upon the Soviet Union.
>
> We should not be more binding on the United States than we are on the Soviet Union. Very often, despite the fact that the United States adheres to treaties very strictly and closely, the Soviet Union has taken advantage of us and "driven a truck" through a very broad or gray area of various treaties.

---

[667] 134 *Cong. Rec.* S6804-05 (daily ed. May 26, 1988).

> This amendment says we will not be held bound by any interpretation in any way that the Soviet Union is not also equally bound. It is a very common sense amendment, a very important amendment, one that I would hope would be passed by an overwhelming majority of the Senate tonight.[668]

In opposition to this amendment Senator Nunn said:

> Mr. NUNN. I thank the Senator.
>
> Mr. President, this looks like an amendment that everyone should immediately go down and say, "I am in favor of this." But I think it is important for the Senate to understand what it does. This basically sets up international law, applicable international law, and says by implication that international law will override domestic law. That has the effect of severely undermining, if not completely diluting the Byrd amendment, which was passed by 72 votes a few minutes ago, maybe a few hours ago.
>
> It also is contrary to the Culvahouse letter that was sent to Senator LUGAR. The Culvahouse letter states clearly, and I quote from that letter:
>
>> The President is bound by authoritative interpretations * * * and relied upon by the Senate.
>
> Quoting from the letter:
>
>> * * * even if the treaty negotiating record and subsequent practice indicate an interpretation to the contrary.
>
> This is also contrary to the Cooper memo which was a Justice Department memo which came out about a year ago which states, and I quote from that Cooper memo:
>
>> Obviously a President could not negotiate a treaty with other nations on the basis of one

[668]*Id.* at S6805 (statement of Sen. Nickles).

> understanding of its import, submit the treaty to the Senate on the basis of a wholly different understanding, and then in implementing the treaty rely solely on the understanding he had reached with other parties.
>
> Such results would essentially eviscerate the Senator's constitutional advice and consent role, because it would deprive the Senate of a fair opportunity to determine whether or on what conditions the treaty should become the supreme law of the land.

So I say about the Wilson amendment, for those who voted for the Byrd amendment, I urge them to vote against this amendment.

We do not believe that the Senate of the United States and the authoritative representations given to the Senate of the United States should be rolled back by international law. What this basically says is that if you have a negotiating history or a negotiating record that is contradicted by the administration's own authoritative testimony, the international law principle would set up a negotiating history. That may not be what the author means, but that is the clear import of this amendment.

It basically would mean that the ratification process we go through in the Senate, no matter what we are told, is forbidden by international law or could be interpreted that way, and we could go back to the negotiating history.

So an administration could come up here and say: "We have agreed to treaty A. We want you to give consent to ratification of treaty A." We could give consent to ratification of treaty A. They could sign that--let us say the INF Treaty. They could sign the INF Treaty and then testify before the Senate what it meant. Then they could go to Moscow, with the Senate's consent, and could exchange the articles of ratification, and we could have a treaty. They could come up a year later and say: "Wait a minute, fellows. Locked in the State Department's safe, we forgot to give you part of the negotiating history. Under the rules of international law, we now have a treaty we explained to you as treaty A, but it is really treaty B, because we didn't give you

> that, or at least you didn't catch it. So what we have here is that the Soviet Union is not bound, because of negotiating history, by treaty A, and they are bound by treaty B. We are sorry, and we are now bound by treaty B. We will help you next time, Senate, but right now we're going to go with another treaty, even though we testified that this was the treaty we agreed to."
>
> So anyone who believes that the Senate of the United States has a role in this matter should vote against this amendment.[669]

Following debate, this amendment to the treaty interpretation condition to require mutuality of obligation was defeated in a close, largely party line, vote of 53-45 to table the amendment.[670] The largely party line nature of the vote and the tough stance taken by the Senate majority leader in linking approval of the INF Treaty to passage of the INF Treaty interpretation condition is suggested in the following statement by Senator Byrd, the Senate majority leader, immediately after the vote to table this amendment:

> Mr. BYRD. Mr. President, I thank all Senators for their patience and attention.
>
> This is a very beautifully worded amendment on its face. It almost had me voting for it. But this amendment will not uphold the role of this Senate under the Constitution and the making of treaties.
>
> Mr. President, I warned Senators before this vote that if this amendment were not tabled, the President would not have the treaty before he leaves the summit. That is no empty threat. But Senators did not listen. I think we had three votes from the other side, three or four. The rest voted a party line vote, against their own President's having that treaty approved before he leaves the summit.
>
> I have had a good bit to do with helping to save this treaty and helping the President to have it approved. I resisted the pressure to bring up this treaty until the faults could be corrected. The administration's negotiators went back to Geneva and

---

[669]*Id.* at S6805 (statement of Sen. Nunn).

[670]*Id.* at S6809.

> corrected those faults. It is now a better treaty than it ever was before. If this is the kind of cooperation we are going to get, if we are going to continue to have to deal with Mickey Mouse amendments like this one that was tabled, the President is not going to have his treaty before he leaves the summit. And that is no empty threat.[671]

The Democratic leadership proposal, which became known in its final version as the "Byrd amendment on treaty interpretation," or the "Byrd-Biden" amendment, was adopted as a condition to Senate advice and consent to the INF Treaty. As adopted on Thursday, May 26, 1988, by a vote of 72-27 it provided in relevant part:

> that the Senate's advice and consent to ratification of the INF Treaty is subject to the condition, based on the Treaty Clauses of the Constitution, that --
>
> (1) the United States shall interpret the Treaty in accordance with the common understanding of the Treaty shared by the President and the Senate at the time the Senate gave its advice and consent to ratification;
>
> (2) such common understanding is based on:
>
> (A) First, the text of the Treaty and the provisions of this resolution of ratification; and
>
> (B) Second, the authoritative representations which were provided by the President and his representatives to the Senate and its Committees, in seeking Senate consent to ratification, insofar as such representations were directed to the meaning and legal effect of the text of the Treaty; and
>
> (3) the United States shall not agree to or adopt an interpretation different from that common understanding except

[671]*Id.* at S6809 (statement of Sen. Byrd).

pursuant to Senate advice and consent to a subsequent treaty or protocol, or the enactment of a statute; and

(4) if, subsequent to ratification of the Treaty, a question arises as to the interpretation of a provision of the Treaty on which no common understanding was reached in accordance with paragraph (2), that provision shall be interpreted in accordance with applicable United States law.[672]

---

[672]*See* "ACDA Briefing Memorandum, Final Senate Action on the INF Treaty" (May 31, 1988); *also* 134 *Cong. Rec.* S6724 (daily ed. May 26, 1988) (Amendment No. 2305), 134 Cong. Rec. S6937 (daily ed. May 27, 1988) (Resolution of Ratification of the INF Treaty) (Treaty Doc. No. 100-11); *Senate Approves Historic INF Treaty on 93-to-5 Vote*, Wash. Post, May 28, 1988, at 1, col. 5.

A forthcoming commentary by Senator Sam Nunn in the *University of Pennsylvania Law Review* discusses the background of the INF Treaty condition, "the Byrd-Biden Amendment." It also discusses the Culvahouse letter and Senate action rejecting an amendment offered by Senator Specter to qualify "the Byrd-Biden Amendment." Nunn, *supra* note 281, at 1523 (reviewed from page proofs subject to final editing).

Some of the legislative history of Senate Resolution 167 and the "Biden resolution" is discussed in a forthcoming commentary by Professor Phillip R. Trimble in the *University of Pennsylvania Law Review. See* Trimble, *supra* note 158, at 1461 (reviewed from page proofs subject to final editing). In this discussion, Professor Trimble notes that:

> Senator Specter offered an amendment to the effect that neither the Biden Condition, as amended, nor the Foreign Relations Committee Report on the INF Treaty would change existing constitutional law. That amendment was rejected, by a vote of 64-33, arguably creating a negative implication that the Senate did seek to change constitutional law.

Id. at 1472 n.39 (quoted from page proofs subject to final editing). Professor Trimble also writes that:

> [b]y declining to act on the Foreign Relations Committee recommendation, the Senate laid the foundation for a negative implication; it did not wish to endorse the constitutional law principles embodied in S. Res. 167, as amended.

The lead *Washington Post* article on Senate approval of the INF Treaty gave the following description of passage of this condition:

> The only major condition attached to the treaty was a Democratic proposal, stemming from a fight with Reagan over whether Strategic Defense Initiative (SDI) testing is permitted under the 1972 Antiballistic Missile (ABM) Treaty, to ban future administrations from reinterpreting the INF pact without Senate approval. Slightly modified to win Republican support, it was attached to the treaty Thursday by a vote of 72 to 27.[673]

The *Washington Post* article also pointed out that the Senate:

> [r]ejected, 64 to 33 and 67 to 30, two proposals from Sen. Arlen Specter (R-Pa.) to dilute the impact of the previously approved treaty interpretation proviso.[674]

On May 26, 1988, the "Byrd-Biden" condition to the INF Treaty was adopted by a vote of 72-27. On May 27, 1988, an amendment offered by Senator Specter that

---

Id. at 1468. And to the same effect he writes:

> [T]he congressional proponents of formal entrenchment and curtailment of executive power lost the battle over constitutional principle. The Biden resolution was first amended and then abandoned. The Senate did not approve S. Res. 167, S. Res. 167 as amended, or the Biden Condition as initially proposed. Therefore, the resulting constitutional common law of treaty interpretation was to reject the general statements of constitutional law embodied in the Biden Resolution and Condition with their formal entrenchment assumptions.

Id. at 1475.

[673]*Senate Approves Historic INF Treaty on 93-to-5 Vote, supra* note 672, at 1, col. 5.

[674]*Id.* at A23, col. 3. Note that if subject to the presentment clause as legislation, at least one of these proposals by Senator Specter obtained sufficient votes to sustain a presidential veto.

seemed generally intended to modify the "Byrd-Biden" condition by the *Restatement (Third)* approach was defeated 67-30. (Both votes include an at least two-thirds Senate majority). The Specter amendment would have provided:

> Such common understanding means a shared interpretation which is both authoritatively communicated to the Senate by the Executive and clearly intended, generally understood and relied upon by the State [sic "Senate" ?] in its advice and consent to ratification.[675]

Following Senate ratification of the INF Treaty with the attached condition on treaty interpretation, President Reagan released a statement on May 27, 1988, saying:

> STATEMENT BY THE PRESIDENT
>
> I am very pleased with the action of the United States Senate in consenting to ratification of the INF Treaty.
>
> In two days, I will arrive in the Soviet Union to meet with General Secretary Gorbachev to discuss our four-part agenda. Today's action by the Senate clearly shows support for our arms reduction objectives.
>
> I want to express my appreciation for the leadership demonstrated by Majority Leader Bob Byrd and Republican Leader Bob Dole in securing the timely approval of this treaty. I have invited them to join me for the exchange of ratification documents in Moscow.
>
> I continue to have concerns about the constitutionality of some provisions of the Resolution of Ratification, particularly those dealing with interpretation, and I will communicate with the Senate on these matters in due course.[676]

---

[675]134 *Cong. Rec.* S6884 (daily ed. May 27, 1988) (Amendment No. 2328).

[676]"Statement by the President" (The White House, Office of the Press Secretary (Helsinki, Finland), May 27, 1988).

Subsequently, on June 10, 1988, the President released a more detailed statement concerning the Senate condition on treaty interpretation. The statement "To the Senate of the United States" provided in full:

> I was gratified the United States Senate gave its advice and consent to the ratification of the Treaty Between the United States of America and the Union of Soviet Socialist Republics on the Elimination of Their Intermediate- and Shorter-Range Missiles (INF Treaty). It was my honor to exchange instruments of ratification on June 1 in Moscow, and the Treaty has now entered into force.
>
> During the past 4 months, the Senate has performed its constitutional duties with respect to the advice and consent to this Treaty in an exceptionally serious and diligent manner. On the Administration's part, we spared no effort to respond to the Senate's needs, and to do our best to ensure that the Senate had all the information it needed to carry out its constitutional responsibilities. Administration witnesses appeared in more than 70 formal hearings and many more informal briefings; we provided detailed written answers to over 1,300 questions for the record from the Committees and individual Senators; and we provided access to the negotiating record of the Treaty, comprising 31 bound volumes.
>
> In short, I believe the Executive branch and the Senate took their responsibilities very seriously and made every effort to work together to fulfill them in the common interest of advancing the national security of the United States and our Allies and friends. The Treaty will bear witness to the sincerity and diligence of those in the Executive branch and the Senate who have taken part in this effort.
>
> As noted in my statement issued on May 27, the date of final Senate action, one provision of the Resolution to [sic] Ratification adopted by the Senate causes me serious concern.
>
> The Senate condition relating to the Treaty Clauses of the Constitution apparently seeks to alter the law of treaty interpretation. The accompanying report of the Committee on Foreign Relations accords primacy, second only to the Treaty text, to all Executive branch statements to the Senate above all other

sources which international forums or even U.S. courts would consider in interpreting treaties. It subordinates fundamental and essential treaty interpretative sources such as the treaty parties' intent, the treaty negotiating record and the parties' subsequent practices.

Treaties are agreements between sovereign states and must be interpreted in accordance with accepted principles of international law and United States Supreme Court jurisprudence. As a practical matter, the Senate condition only can work against the interests of the United States by creating situations in which a treaty has one meaning under international law and another under domestic law. Unilateral restrictions on the United States should be avoided, especially in a treaty affecting vital national security interests. With respect to U.S. law, the President must respect the mutual understandings reached with the Senate during the advice and consent process. But Executive statements should be given binding weight only when they were authoritatively communicated to the Senate by the Executive and were part of the basis on which the Senate granted its advice and consent to ratification. This is in accordance with the legal standards applied by our courts in determining legislative intent. I commend the thoughtful statements made during the Senate debate by Senators Specter, Roth, Wilson, and others which amplify these concerns.

This Administration does not take the position that the Executive branch can disregard authoritative Executive statements to the Senate, and we have no intention of changing the interpretation of the INF Treaty which was presented to the Senate. On the contrary, this Administration has made it clear that it will consider all such authoritative statements as having been made in good faith. Nonetheless the principles of treaty interpretation recognized and repeatedly invoked by the courts may not be limited or changed by the Senate alone, and those principles will govern any future disputes over interpretation of this Treaty. As Senator Lugar pointed out during the debate, the Supreme Court may well have the final judgment, which would be binding on the President and Senate alike. Accordingly, I am compelled to state that I cannot accept the proposition that a condition in a resolution to ratification can alter the allocation of rights and duties under the Constitution; nor could I, consistent with my oath of office, accept

> any diminution claimed to be effected by such a condition in the constitutional powers and responsibilities of the Presidency.
>
> I do not believe that any difference of views about the Senate condition will have any practical effect on the implementation of the Treaty. I believe the Executive branch and the Senate have a very good common understanding of the terms of the Treaty, and I believe that we will handle any question of interpretation that may arise in a spirit of mutual accommodation and respect. In this spirit I welcome the entry into force of the Treaty and express my hope that it will lead to even more important advances in arms reduction and the preservation of world peace and security.
>
> RONALD REAGAN
>
> THE WHITE HOUSE,
> June 10, 1988.[677]

On June 16, 1988, Senator Pell responded to the President's statement to the Senate as follows:

> [O]n Friday, June 10, President Reagan conveyed a formal message to the Senate concerning the Senate's action in approving

---

[677]Statement by President Ronald Reagan to the Senate of the United States (The White House, Office of the Press Secretary, June 10, 1988).

For a relevant recent article by a key supporter of the "narrow" interpretation and the INF condition, see J. Biden, Jr., & J. Ritch, III, "The End of the Sofaer Doctrine: A Victory for Arms Control and the Constitution," 18 *Arms Control Today* 3 (Sept. 1988).

This article, while written by a strong participant in the debate, provides useful information on the background of the INF condition and the Reagan Letter. It also adds the following to the previous harsh criticism of the "reinterpretation":

> . . . There is indeed little left of the ABM Treaty "reinterpretation," other than the memory of a failed and disgraced effort to distort the Constitution and a solemn treaty obligation of the United States. . . .

Id. at 8.

the INF Treaty. Much of that statement was devoted to commentary on the so-called Biden condition, which the Foreign Relations Committee attached to the INF Treaty resolution of ratification and which the Senate upheld by a vote of 72 to 27 after minor modification. Because the President's formal statement criticizes the Biden condition--and in ways which I judge to be inaccurate--I believe it important to clarify where matters now stand.

Let me comment first on the status of the President's postratification message. What weight or significance does it have? Can the President's statement alter the effect of the Biden condition? I quote from the relevant section of the Foreign Relations Committee report on the INF Treaty:

> * * * the [Biden] condition is binding under domestic law, and obtains its binding effect because the President, in the absence of the resolution of ratification, lacks authority to participate in the Treaty's ratification. He obtains such authority through the resolution of ratification and is governed by any stipulations by which the Senate conditions its consent.
>
> In sum, the President may not act upon the Senate's consent without honoring this condition. Nothing that he or his Administration does, by statement or action, whether before or after the act of ratification, can alter the binding effect of any condition which the Senate places upon its consent to treaty ratification. If the President brings the INF Treaty into force, the [Biden] Condition takes effect.

Mr. President, I think this portion of the committee report demonstrates quite clearly that the Biden condition is binding on the administration, notwithstanding anything in the President's statement. Nonetheless, the President's message to the Senate warrants comment, because it demonstrates a continuing unwillingness of [sic "on"?] the part of this administration to recognize or acknowledge what was truly at issue.

What was at issue, Mr. President, was the Sofaer Doctrine, a constitutional assertion promulgated by this administration in the course of its efforts to fabricate a rationale for the so-called reinterpretation of the ABM Treaty of 1972. According to the Sofaer Doctrine, executive branch representations to the Senate concerning the meaning of a treaty have binding weight only if such statements meet three criteria: they must, in the judment [sic] of the Executive, have been "generally understood, clearly intended, and relied upon" by the Senate.

These criteria may sound innocent enough, and indeed no one would disagree that if the criteria are met the Executive is bound. But the Sofaer Doctrine asserts much more: that the Executive is bound only if the criteria are met. The implication of this doctrine is profound. For if accepted, it would place upon the Senate a burden of proof to demonstrate its fulfillment of these critieria [sic]--a burden that, in practical terms, could only be carried by formal and elaborate Senate conditions on each and every treaty's resolution of ratification.

Clearly, such a practice, if regularized, would have devastating consequences for the treaty process. Yet, in the absence of such explicit assertions of Senate purpose, the Executive could in most cases argue that the Senate had not fulfilled all three of the criteria concerning a particular treaty provision. This would mean that the practical effect of the Sofaer Doctrine, if accepted explicitly or by Senate acquiescence, would be to accord the Executive virtually free reign, in interpreting a treaty, to ignore its own representations to the Senate.

According to the President's June 10 statement, the Biden condition "seeks to alter the law of treaty interpretation." But in fact nothing could be further from the truth. The Biden condition represents a Senate effort to uphold the law, by affirming the clear constitutional principle that a treaty must be interpreted and implemented by the Executive in accord with the original understanding of the treaty shared by the Executive and the Senate when the Senate gives its consent to ratification.

In addition, and very importantly, the condition denotes where evidence of that shared understanding is to be found. According to the Biden condition:

> Such common understanding is based on:
>
> First, the text of the treaty and the provisions of this resolution of ratification; and
>
> Second, the authoritative representations which were provided by the President and his representatives to the Senate and its committees, in seeking Senate consent to ratification, insofar as such representations were directed to the meaning and legal effect of the text of the treaty.

The President's statement strongly implies that this formulation would drastically alter the traditional approach to treaty interpretation because it "subordinates fundamental and essential treaty interpretative sources such as the treaty parties' intent, the treaty negotiating record and the parties' subsequent practices." But let us examine each of these three elements against the accusation that they have been unduly subordinated by the Biden condition.

First, "the treaty parties' intent." Is the administration suggesting that it is constitutionally acceptable for the Executive to enter into a treaty in which the intent of the treaty or a provision thereof may be absent from the text of the treaty or the Executive explanation of the treaty, and then later to assert that this theretofore hidden intent may suddenly supersede the text and the Executive's original explanation to the Senate thereof? If that is the administration's implied assertion, then it is not the Biden condition which subordinates the treaty parties' intent; it is the Constitution.

Next, the treaty negotiating record, which is a precise-sounding phrase for what in reality is no more than the aggregate of any and all internal U.S. Government memoranda which may pertain to the positions adopted by the United States during a negotiation and the events which occur in the negotiation--all as recorded by various U.S. negotiators. Is the administration suggesting that it is constitutionally acceptable for the Executive to enter into a treaty and then to assert at some subsequent point that some paragraph from one of these internal U.S. Government memoranda must take precedence over the text of the treaty and the Executive's explanation to the Senate thereof? If that is the administration's implied assertion, then it is not the Biden condition which subordinates the treaty negotiating record; again, it is the Constitution.

Finally, the parties' subsequent practices. Of course, under international law subsequent practice is a well recognized, albeit secondary, criterion of treaty interpretation. But is the administration suggesting that it is constitutionality [sic] acceptable for the Executive to engage in subsequent practice which is at odds with the text of the treaty or with the explanation of that text as presented to the Senate? If that is the administration's implied assertion, then it is not the Biden condition which subordinates the parties' subsequent practices; once again, it is the Constitution.

Mr. President, no one disputes that all three of these elements--intent of the parties, negotiating history, and subsequent practice--may have interpretive significance in the implementation of a treaty. When a question arises which cannot be answered by reference to the treaty text or to the Executive's original description and analysis of the treaty as presented to the Senate, such criteria may be useful in clarifying a fine point of treaty interpretation. But under the Constitution those elements cannot be used to subordinate the text, or the original shared understanding of the text held by the Executive and the Senate when a treaty is ratified. To accept that would be to overturn the essential logic of treatymaking, and to negate the Senate's constitutional role under the Treaty Clause.

This brings us, Mr. President, to the administration's principal claim against the Biden condition, a charge encapsulated in the following sentence in the President's letter:

> As a practical matter, the Senate condition only can work against the interests of the United States by creating situations in which a treaty has one meaning under international law and another under domestic law.

This specter, Mr. President, of "two treaties"--one highly restrictive on the United States and the other less restrictive on the other party--is essentially a false alarm raised by the administration on the basis of argumentation that is neither consistent nor persuasive.

As to consistency, the President's letter itself states that "the administration does not take the position that the executive branch can disregard authoritative Executive statements to the Senate." Indeed, the letter appears to acknowledge that binding weight must be accorded to Executive statements if such statements were "authoritatively communicated to the Senate by the Executive" and if such statements "were part of the basis on which the Senate granted its advice and consent to ratification." Thus, by its own acknowledgment, the administration accepts the principle that some statements by the Executive have binding significance. Accordingly, the administration cannot logically contend that it is the Biden condition which creates the possibility that U.S. obligations under domestic and international law could, under extraordinary circumstances, conflict. Rather, it is the Constitution. The possibility of a conflict between domestic and international obligations inheres even in the administration's model.

What is at issue--and what is solely at issue--is precisely which statements by an administration shall be accorded binding weight. By its assertion of the so-called Sofaer Doctrine, the Reagan administration endeavored to establish criteria which are so difficult to meet that the Executive would, in practice, be bound by few if any of its statements. The Biden condition in contrast affirms in effect that all of the Executive's authoritative explanations are relevant to the Executive's obligations in interpreting and implementing a treaty. Each such authoritative executive branch statement may not in and of itself be binding. But taken collectively, an administration's representations constitute a substantial body of evidence as to what the Executive and the Senate jointly understood a treaty to mean at the time of ratification. And that shared understanding cannot be ignored; it is binding in setting the limits of a President's latitude in treaty interpretation.

I would stress that any potential doubt about the Senate's view on this question was eliminated during consideration of the Biden condition, when administration supporters offered amendments explicitly intended to incorporate into the Biden condition the very elements of the Sofaer Doctrine which the Biden condition was designed to repudiate. I am pleased to note that these amendments were defeated by virtually the same overwhelming Senate majority which upheld the Biden condition.

As to the "two treaties" specter raised by the President's letter, I think it appropriate to quote once again from the Foreign Relations Committee report on the INF Treaty:

> * * * the White House * * * seeks to raise the specter of the United States being bound by constitutional processes to one interpretation of a treaty while the Soviet Union is free to apply a less restrictive interpretation.
>
> This specter--originally raised by Mr. Sofaer while trying to justify the broad ABM Treaty interpretation--is highly theoretical. It is a truism that the Executive has different obligations under domestic and international law, and therefore it is possible to hypothesize situations in which those obligations could conflict. However, in practice this has not proven to be a serious problem and there is no basis for the administration's assertion that the condition "would substantially increase this risk" * * *.
>
> An apparent premise of the Sofaer Doctrine is that practical difficulties would ensue if the Executive were bound by what it tells the Senate, because it would not be an abnormal circumstance for a difference to exist between what was agreed to with the other party and the explanations provided to the Senate. There should be no such difference. It is the Executive's responsibility to ensure sufficient clarity in a treaty and in its explanations thereof to the Senate so that no conflict exists between the shared understanding of the parties on the one hand and the shared understanding of the Executive and the Senate on the other. If, in extremis, such conflict should arise and prove not resolvable by

> discussion or negotiation with the other party, the United States of course has the option of withdrawing from the treaty.
>
> In sum, this largely theoretical problem should be addressed if and when it arises--not be a preemptive alteration of constitutional principles. The Senate should not accept a doctrine that assumes and protects carelessness or deviousness on the part of the Executive.

In closing, Mr. President, let me say that I agree with certain of the conclusions in President Reagan's message to the Senate. The President states as follows:

> I cannot accept the proposition that a condition in a resolution to ratification can alter the allocation of rights and duties under the Constitution; nor could I, consistent with my oath of office, accept any diminution claimed to be effected by such a condition in the constitutional powers and responsibilities of the Presidency.

Unfortunately, while this particular statement by the President is unarguably true, it contains a false implication: that the Biden condition was aimed at altering the Constitution. In fact, quite the opposite is the case. The sole and fundamental purpose of the Biden condition was to uphold the Constitution by repudiating assertions made by this administration that would, if accepted explicitly or by acquiescence, have undercut the Constitution's allocation of a joint Executive-Senate role in the exercise of the Treaty Power.

Let me then reiterate: The aim of the Biden condition was not to alter constitutional principles or create them, but to defend and reaffirm principles inherent in the Constitution but threatened by the Executive aggrandizement implicit in this administration's promulgation of the Sofaer Doctrine. Fortunately, by means of the Biden condition, that defense and reaffirmation have now been accomplished. The Sofaer Doctrine has been formally and overwhelmingly rejected. And nothing in the President's postratification letter has changed or could change that fact.

Mr. President, I ask that there appear in the RECORD at this point the text of the President's June 10 letter. I also call attention to the relevant section of the Foreign Relations Committee report which warrants special attention as a definitive refutation of the points made in the President's letter.[678]

A forthcoming commentary in the *University of Pennsylvania Law Review* to be published during 1989 describes the position of Judge Abraham D. Sofaer, the Legal Adviser of the Department of State, in the following terms:

> The Administration has also recognized, however, from the outset of this debate, that the Senate may adopt particular understandings of a treaty that are not formally communicated to the treaty partner. When the Senate acts in this manner, while it cannot change the meaning of the treaty under international law, its understandings may be effective in binding the President under domestic law.
>
> . . . .
>
> The Reagan Administration's position on this issue, as on the others in the ABM Treaty debate, was based upon the principles expressed in the Restatement (Third) of Foreign Relations Law. The Restatement recognizes the possibility that the Senate might reach an understanding of a treaty, even though that understanding has not been communicated to the treaty partner. In that event, while the understanding cannot be relied upon to alter the treaty's meaning among or between the countries involved, the Restatement concludes that the "treaty that is ratified or acceded to by the United States with a statement of understanding becomes effective in domestic law . . . subject to that understanding." If a formal statement of the Senate's understanding is made, then the Senate's position is clearly on record. Where no such statement is made, however, the technique to be applied in ascertaining the

---

[678] 134 *Cong. Rec.* S8034-36 (daily ed. June 16, 1988) (statement of Sen. Pell). For a discussion of the response of Senator Pell to the letter from President Reagan on "the Biden condition," see Biden & Ritch, *supra* note 263, at 1552 (reviewed from page proofs subject to final editing).

> President's or the Senate's understanding is to look at all the indications of such an understanding "in much the same way that the legislative history of a statute is relevant to its interpretation." The Restatement notes, moreover, some of the possible sources of such "indications" of an informal understanding, including the Senate's resolution of consent, "the report of the Senate Foreign Relations Committee," and "the Senate debates."[13] [[13] RESTATEMENT, *supra* note 5, § 314 comment d (emphasis added, citation omitted).]
>
> The Restatement also offers a specific legal standard to govern situations in which an informal understanding should be given binding weight. The Restatement provides that "*the President* must decide whether they [indications of an informal understanding in the Senate record] represent *a general understanding by the Senate*, and, if he finds that they do, he must respect them in good faith."[14] [[14] *Id.* (emphasis added).] Finally, it is essential to remember that the understanding involved not only must be generally held by the Senate, but must be an understanding "on the basis" of which the Senate gave its advice and consent.[15] [[15] RESTATEMENT, *supra* note 5, § 314(2).] The Restatement does not require the President to defer to understandings on which the Senate could not be said to have conditioned its approval of the treaty. This is entirely consistent with the notion that a treaty's history should be analyzed in much the same way legislative history is analyzed.[679]

It should be noted that this comment stresses that for a Senate understanding to create a binding obligation under national law: "the understanding involved not only must be generally held by the Senate, but must be an understanding `on the basis' of which the Senate gave its advice and consent."[680] This is an important and easily overlooked issue in considering the position of the *Restatement (Third)* and Judge Sofaer. While Judge Sofaer's comment does not develop this issue in detail, possibly, under the *Restatement (Third)* position, the authority of the Senate to create an obligation binding under national law is rooted in any authority of the

---

[679]Sofaer, *supra* note 444, at 1440, 1441-42 (quoted from page proofs subject to final editing).

[680]*Id.* at 1441-42.

Senate to condition its advice and consent. That, in turn, may suggest that to become legally binding under national law, even under the *Restatement (Third)* view, an informal understanding must not only be "generally held by the Senate," but must also be generally held by the Senate as a condition or "`on the basis'" of which the Senate gave its advice and consent. *Both* requirements would be ascertained "`in much the same way that the legislative history of a statute is relevant to its interpretation.'"[681]

---

[681]*Id.* at 1441 (quoting the *Restatement (Third)*, § 314, comment *d*).

Section 314 of the new *Restatement (Third)* and its accompanying comment *d* provide in full:

§ 314. Reservations and Understandings: Law of the United States

(1) When the Senate of the United States gives its advice and consent to a treaty on condition that the United States enter a reservation, the President, if he makes the treaty, must include the reservation in the instrument of ratification or accession, or otherwise manifest that the adherence of the United States is subject to the reservation.

(2) When the Senate gives its advice and consent to a treaty on the basis of a particular understanding of its meaning, the President, if he makes the treaty, must do so on the basis of the Senate's understanding.

. . . .

d. *Understandings.* A treaty that is ratified or acceded to by the United States with a statement of understanding becomes effective in domestic law (§ 111) subject to that understanding. If no such statement is made, indication that the President or the Senate ascribed a particular meaning to the treaty is relevant to the interpretation of the treaty by a United States court in much the same way that the legislative history of a statute is relevant to its interpretation. See § 325, Reporters' Note 5; § 326, Reporters' Note 2.

Although the Senate's resolution of consent may contain no statement of understanding, there may be such statements in the report of the Senate Foreign Relations Committee or in the Senate debates. In that event, the President must decide whether they represent a general understanding by the Senate and, if he finds that they do, must respect them in good faith.

And in a forthcoming commentary in the *University of Pennsylvania Law Review*, Senator Joseph R. Biden, Jr., Chairman of the Senate Judiciary Committee, and John B. Ritch, III, Deputy Director of the Senate Foreign Relations Committee, cite the following excerpt from the *INF Treaty Report* as emphasizing where the "common understanding is to be found" which is binding domestically:

> In the establishment and determination of that common understanding, the concept of legislative intent must be as applicable to treaties as it is to statutory law, in which intent may be explicit or implicit . . . .
>
> What is crucial is that legislative intent, with regard to a treaty as well as a statute, is expressed not only in language drafted by legislators but in unchallenged communications of the Executive. Under longstanding principles of textual construction, Executive communications to the Congress concerning the meaning of a text are evidence of the meaning of that text if Congress (or the Senate) acquiesces in that meaning. In other words, the legislative branch is deemed to be placed on notice by the Executive that certain words will be construed in a certain manner. If Congress wishes a different meaning to obtain, it may act so as to effect that different meaning. If Congress does not act, however, it is properly deemed to have accepted -- and to intend -- the meaning communicated by the Executive.
>
> . . . Professor Louis Henkin, chief reporter of the new *Restatement of U.S. Foreign Relations Law*, summarized this concept as follows: "Where several [Executive] statements are made and there is general acceptance of their tenor, that is the Senate understanding. That is true in the case of Senate consent to a treaty, as it would be in the legislative history of a statute."
>
> Clearly, in determining whether the Senate consented to the ratification of a treaty pursuant to an implicit understanding, a rule of reason must apply. Obviously, where the indicia of Senate intent or understanding (including unchallenged Executive communications or explanations) are few or inconsistent, no implicit Senate intent can reasonably be said to exist. On the other hand, where the indicia of intent (again, including unchallenged Executive communications or explanations) are several and largely

---

Restatement (Third), supra note 235, § 314 and comment *d*, at 186, 188.

consistent, an implicit intent can reasonably be concluded to exist. In such circumstances, the President is bound constitutionally to regard that intent as an implicit Senate understanding, and therefore an implicit condition of the Senate's consent. The Chief Executive cannot bring the treaty into force unless it reflects that condition, and subsequent Presidents must interpret the treaty subject to that intent.

The essence of the Sofaer Doctrine is to reject this concept of legislative intent as it has been normally understood . . . .[682]

4. A brief review of the process of subsequent congressional interpretation on the "broad-narrow" issue

It is, of course, fundamental that a process of interpretation of a major treaty ratified by the United States should be conducted thoroughly and with great care and should not be a political exercise. As such, it is relevant to briefly review strengths and any weaknesses of the process by which Congress has sought to interpret the 1972 ABM Treaty on the "broad-narrow" issue. Such a review may also be useful in appraising the functional suitability under the Constitution of the Senate or Congress engaging in an exercise of complex legal interpretation. Finally, such a review would not seem unfair in light of the extraordinary criticism of the role of the State Department Legal Adviser contained in the report of the majority of the Senate Foreign Relations Committee on The ABM Treaty Interpretation Resolution reflecting certainly that the majority would accept the need for standards of great care and rejection of political determination in interpretation on an important treaty dispute.[683]

---

[682]Biden & Ritch, *supra* note 263, at 1539-41 (quoting *The INF Treaty: Report of the Senate Comm. on Foreign Relations, S. Exec. Rep. No.* 15, 100 Cong., 2d Sess. 93-94 (1988)).

[683]*See The ABM Treaty Interpretation Resolution, supra* note 1, at 62-67. It is, of course, appropriate for Congress to uphold high standards of legal interpretation and the rule of law. If, however, criticism moves from the merits of process to allegations of improper motive, particularly in a complex and emotional issue requiring substantial courage to review *de novo*, there is a serious risk that such criticism could itself inhibit the process of future legal analysis and thus impair the rule of law.

On the strength side, as has been seen, both the Senate and House have held hearings on the issue in which proponents of both "broad" and "narrow" views have testified. In that process several senators, particularly Senator Sam Nunn for the "narrow" interpretation and Senator Fritz Hollings for the "broad" interpretation, have invested substantial time and energy in reviewing the issues and testifying. Several senators, including Senator Levin, have discussed the issues with former members of the United States SALT I Delegation. And Senator Specter, among others, devoted substantial time to assessment of constitutional issues surrounding the resulting dispute concerning the national law of treaty implementation. Moreover, the report of the Senate Committee on Foreign Relations on *The ABM Treaty Interpretation Resolution*, supporting the "narrow" interpretation, was a detailed document of some 67 pages and it was accompanied by two additional substantial reports for, respectively, Senator Helms and Senators Helms, Pressler and Trible, making the case for the "broad" interpretation.

Despite these significant strengths, however, there are several weaknesses that call into question the congressional process as a serious decision mode in objective legal decision--as required by the rule of law--about a complex treaty interpretation matter.

First, there is a significant issue as to how many members of Congress have carefully reviewed--or even reviewed at all--the treaty text, negotiating record, congressional consideration and subsequent practice relevant to the interpretation issue, even apart from the relevant international legal and constitutional law applicable to interpretation of the "broad-narrow" issue. According to Ambassador Raymond L. Garthoff in his monograph on the "broad-narrow" issue:

> Even in the Senate, by the time of new hearings in March 1987--seven months after the administration very reluctantly provided a segment of the classified negotiating history--only five of the one hundred senators had personally consulted the documents.[684]

---

[684]*R. Garthoff, Policy Versus the Law: The Reinterpretation of the ABM Treaty* 99 n.4 (1987).

In contrast, Senator Nunn notes in his study on "Interpretation of the ABM Treaty" that all Senators had access to the negotiation record as transmitted to the Senate. Thus, he writes: "Under an arrangement negotiated with Secretary Shultz, all Senators and six cleared staff members have had access to the negotiating record in Room S-407 of the Capitol, a secure facility under the direct control of the majority and minority leaders." S. Nunn, "Interpretation of the ABM Treaty," supra

In contrast, whatever the process criticism of the studies by the State Department Office of the Legal Adviser, the Legal Adviser personally spent a substantial amount of time reviewing the negotiating record. It should also be noted that a key combined Senate Judiciary and Foreign Relations Committees hearing was held prior to completion by the State Department Office of the Legal Adviser of the portion of the overall treaty review process relating to "subsequent practice." Indeed, according to the Foreign Relations Committee report, the Legal Adviser was forced to testify over his objection that the "subsequent practice" study was not yet completed.[685] Moreover, the centrally important testimony of Senator Sam Nunn in these hearings apparently took place prior to completion and availability of the portion of his study relating to review of the negotiating record.[686]

---

note 1, at 567 (page 8 of Senator Nunn's numbering).

Similarly, in a forthcoming commentary in the *University of Pennsylvania Law Review*, Senator Joseph R. Biden, Jr., Chairman of the Senate Judiciary Committee, and John B. Ritch, III, Deputy Director of the Senate Foreign Relations Committee, write the following concerning the state of Senate information about the "negotiating record" in the "broad-narrow" debate:

> After its receipt by the Senate, the voluminous "record" was stored in a special room in the Capitol, where interested Senators could view this collection of documents. Only an astute and dedicated reader, however, could master such an amorphous body of information -- a fact from which one reasonably may infer that, in the Senate as in the Executive Branch, opinions about the content of the "negotiating record" were more numerous than informed opinions.

Biden & Ritch, *supra* note 263, at 1537 n.18 (quoted from page proofs subject to final editing).

[685]*See The ABM Treaty Interpretation Resolution, supra* note 1, at 63. To the extent that it is a fair criticism that the Legal Adviser's views on the interpretation issue may have been formed prior to a full study of "subsequent practice," the Senate Judiciary and Foreign Relations Committees would seem subject to the same criticism in not waiting for the full review by the Office of the Legal Adviser to be completed.

[686]The author of this study requested ACDA to obtain this paper at the time of the hearings and it was not available.

Second, there is a high "coincidence" in congressional consideration of the "broad-narrow" issue of decision along political party lines. Thus, as we have seen, the key vote in the Senate Foreign Relations Committee on S. Res. 167 which adopted the "narrow" interpretation divided the Committee precisely along party lines with all Democrats voting for the majority report and all Republicans voting for an amendment in the nature of a substitute. The final vote to report S. Res. 167 with a favorable recommendation was 11-8 with only Senator Nancy L. Kassebaum breaking party ranks to vote for the majority report.[687] Similarly, as we have seen, the votes in both House and Senate most closely related to the issue divided in substantial measure along party lines. The vote in the Senate was characterized by the *Washington Post* as "a Democratic-sponsored move,"[688] and 50 Democrats voted in favor while only one, Senator Hollings, voted against, and on the Republican side 37 senators voted against while only 8 voted in favor.[689] And on the House side, in approving the Defense Authorization Bill for fiscal year 1988, a bill containing language that would fix in law the "narrow" interpretation of the 1972 ABM Treaty for fiscal year 1988, 227 Democrats voted in favor while only 18 voted against, and 160 Republicans voted against while only 12 voted in favor. The House Armed Services Committee Chairman Les Aspin noted of this bill that "this year, as last year for the first time, <u>we have fashioned a Democratic defense bill</u>"; and Ranking Republican Bill Dickinson stated: "The defense authorization bill is a partisan, liberal Democratic exercise in `Reagan bashing'. . . . More and more, the work of the Armed Services Committee is being polarized and politicized."[690]

---

[687]*The ABM Treaty Interpretation Resolution, supra* note 1, at 37.

Although related only to a treaty interpretation issue arising from the "broad-narrow" dispute, the 12-7 vote within the Senate Foreign Relations Committee on the INF Treaty condition was also largely along party lines. All Democrats on the Committee voted for the condition as offered by Senator Cranston on behalf of Senator Biden; and all Republicans on the Committee except Senators Helms and Murkowski, who voted for the condition, voted against the condition. *See The INF Treaty Report, supra* note 1, at 85-86.

[688]*Senate Votes to Curb SDI Testing, supra* note 436, at 1, col. 1.

[689]*Senate Roll Call Vote on SDI Restrictions, supra* note 441, at A20, cols. 4-5.

[690]*HASC TASKS* 1 (June 1987).

See also the largely party line vote *defeating* an amendment to the INF Treaty interpretation condition that would have added mutuality of obligation with the

Finally, of the major process weaknesses, while the report of the Senate Foreign Relations Committee did append two reports as to additional views disagreeing with the report's support for the "narrow" interpretation and other positions particularly as to treaty interpretation questions in general, the report did not develop arguments supporting the "broad" interpretation and its presentation and tone is adversarial.[691] To give but one example, it summarizes the Senate advice

---

Soviet Union as an essential element of the condition, discussed in text at notes 667-71 *supra* and note 742 *infra*.

[691]*See The ABM Treaty Interpretation Resolution, supra* note 1.
It can also be argued that the raised level of rhetoric concerning congressional consideration of the issue did not contribute to objective appraisal. Examples of this rhetoric include:

> The Committee can find no evidence to contradict the conclusion that the Reagan Administration's "reinterpretation" of the ABM Treaty constitutes the most flagrant abuse of the Constitution's treaty power in 200 years of American history.

Id. at 66.

> The Committee does, however, recognize the possibility that a nation *could* enhance its international leverage by violating or threatening to violate international norms. Hitler's success in this regard is well known.

Id. at 67.

> Constitutionally, the Reagan Administration's challenge to this Treaty--the effort to alter the Treaty fundamentally without the consent either of the other party or of the Senate--represents not merely an attack on one treaty but a cavalier disregard for the rule of law itself, domestic and international.

Id. at 47.

> We cannot change the rules in the middle of the game simply by ordering lawyers of the State Department to find some loophole, as if they were high-paid counsel to some tycoon who wants to welsh on a bad deal. . . .

and consent record by saying: "[I]t is possible to conclude without qualification that nothing in the Senate ratification proceedings offers a scintilla of evidence in support of the `reinterpretation.'"[692]

Statement by Senate Judiciary Committee Chairman Biden on March 11, 1987, in the hearings on *The ABM Treaty and the Constitution, supra* note 1, at 3.

> . . . action to implement the "reinterpretation" without formal acceptance by the Senate would provoke a constitutional crisis. . . .

"Prepared Statement of Senator Joseph R. Biden, Jr.," *supra* note 207, at 152, 162.

This raised level of rhetoric has continued in the debate on the INF Treaty condition. Thus, on May 26, 1988, during that debate Senator Bumpers said:

> I want to say that it is an absolute mystery to me why we are here. We are here for a simple reason. That is Judge Sofaer was told to find a loophole of some kind that will allow us to test in violation of what we believe in the preceeding [sic] 15 years was the ABM Treaty and to give the President on the Sofaer doctrine the right to literally lie to the U.S. Senate and say, "Just because I said it does not make it so" is offensive to me.
>
> How can you expect nations like the Soviet Union to negotiate with us? No self-respecting nation is going to negotiate with you seriously when you have a negotiating record, when you have a clear understanding of the clear intent of a treaty and you can come back 15 years later for whatever reason because you want to test SDI or some other reason in the future and literally unilaterally abrogate a solemn compact.
>
> It is offensive to me as a Senator.

134 *Cong. Rec.* S6775 (daily ed. May 26, 1988) (statement of Sen. Bumpers).

[692] *The ABM Treaty Interpretation Resolution, supra* note 1, at 19.

It might also be noted of this committee report that in reprinting part of the report, the *American Journal of International Law* included the following Editor's Note at the end:

> *Editor's Note*: The Journal has found it necessary to correct the large number of typographical errors in this document.

It should be kept in mind that the point of this review as to strengths and weaknesses of the congressional process of consideration of the "broad-narrow" issue is to provide information that may be relevant in appraising congressional conclusions and the suitability of a congressional role in interpreting treaties. It is emphatically not a criticism of the sincerity of distinguished Americans on all sides of the most complex treaty interpretation issue--and perhaps even foreign policy law issue--of our time. Indeed, it is the author's conclusion, after more than several thousand hours reviewing this issue, that the many distinguished Americans within both Congress and the Executive branch with differing conclusions on the issue are all sincere and motivated by high principle and a dedication to the rule of law. Moreover, given the extraordinary complexity of the issue, the time required to do a full appraisal, and the reality that legal conclusion on this issue has long been felt by many to be of immediate significance for policy, holding proponents on any side of the issue to standards of perfection in review may be to set a standard that none could pass.[693]

D. Application to the "Broad-Narrow" Debate

This section will develop the principal arguments applying the legal issues under national law to the "broad-narrow" dispute. Arguments will first be developed for the "narrow" interpretation and then for the "broad" interpretation. Finally, arguments for both "narrow" and "broad," rooted in national law, will be appraised. Because of the complexity of the legal and policy issues engaged in this national law component of the "broad-narrow" debate, the more detailed discussion appears in the above discussion for both "broad" and "narrow" positions and the reader interested in other than summary discussion is urged to review this material in detail.

1. Arguments that the President is bound to the "narrow" interpretation under national law

---

"The ABM Treaty Interpretation Resolution," 82 *Am. J. Int'l L.* 151, 165 (Jan. 1988).

[693]It should also be recalled that there may well be a legal obligation to inform Congress of any mistake in interpretation of an arms control agreement and that this obligation may require sharing of tentative conclusions with Congress, with suspension of action on a new interpretation pending completion of a full legal review.

Arguments that the President is bound to the "narrow" interpretation under national law (ignoring for the moment yearly subsequent congressional constraints enacted initially in the Defense Authorization Act for FY 1988) are summarized effectively in the careful appraisal by Senator Sam Nunn, "Interpretation of the ABM Treaty,"[694] and in the report of the Senate Committee on Foreign Relations *The ABM Treaty Interpretation Resolution*.[695] The reader is urged to review the arguments presented in these two sources.

With the inevitable oversimplification in presenting complex views, the principal arguments that the President is bound in the "broad-narrow" dispute to the "narrow" interpretation are rooted in a double conclusion/premise: first that the Senate understood the "narrow" interpretation in giving advice and consent to the 1972 ABM Treaty as a result, at least in part, of representations of Executive branch officials; and second, that this informal Senate understanding, even if not embodied in the instrument of ratification, is binding on the Executive branch as a matter of national law regardless of the appropriate international interpretation of the treaty.[696] A variant of this second element would argue that Executive branch representations to the Senate supporting the "narrow" interpretation should be regarded as authoritative and thus binding on the Executive branch or that there should be an "estoppel" against the Executive branch from any such statements.[697]

---

[694]Senator Sam Nunn, "Interpretation of the ABM Treaty," *supra* note 1, at 553-811.

[695]*The ABM Treaty Interpretation Resolution, supra* note 1, at 16-19, 33-34, 46-62, 66-67.

[696]Supporters of this approach in the "broad-narrow" debate have, of course, also taken the position that the "narrow" approach is the correct international interpretation but, if this national law argument is to have any separate legal effect, it must assert the primacy of an informal Senate understanding or Executive Branch representation to the Senate under national law regardless of the appropriate international legal interpretation.

This discussion, for the moment, is ignoring the action of the Congress on this matter in the Defense Authorization Act for fiscal 1988 and--as rolled over--fiscal 1989 (and any successor legislation) which, of course, is of great importance on the issue at the present time.

[697]In a meeting with the author of this study on July 7, 1989, Mr. Robert G. Bell, Professional Staff Member for the Arms Control Observer Group of the Senate

---

Committee on Armed Services, stressed the importance of the Senate ratification record in the "broad-narrow" debate. He suggested that perhaps the most important questions are: "Was the Senate Presented with the Narrow Interpretation?" and "Does It Matter Which Version Was Presented to the Senate?" In response to these questions which he posed, he reviewed for the author a brief summary memorandum supporting his conclusions that the Senate was presented with the "narrow" interpretation and that that presentation was binding under national law. This summary memorandum, as given to the author, provides:

II. Was the Senate Presented with the Narrow Interpretation?

1. Exchange between Senator Kerry and Judge Sofaer at a April 29, 1987 joint hearing of the Senate Foreign Relations and Judiciary Committees:

Senator Kerry:

> Do you have one statement, Judge, that you could put in front of us of a Senator or a member of the executive who were defining it that specifically says they were permitted? Do you have one? . . . That development and testing of mobile, or space-based exotics is permitted?

Judge Sofaer:

Affirmatively, in those words; no.

2. Statement by Richard Perle at same hearing:

> I think that Senator Jackson had to go on what was said to him by various officials of the executive branch and the view they presented was the narrow interpretation.

3. May 1987 report by Judge Sofaer on the Senate ABM ratification proceedings:

> The [ratification] record contains Executive Branch representations to the Senate which support the restrictive interpretation, which were apparently cleared by NSC [National Security Council] staff, and upon which Senators could justifiably have relied in granting advice and

---

consent.

4. October 1987 testimony before House Armed Services Committee by Lt. Gen. Brent Scowcroft:

> [The Treaty] was presented to the Congress in the narrow interpretation, [and] we have behaved for most of its existence on the narrow interpretation."

5. Statement by President Nixon following April 1988 speech:

> As far as what was presented to the Senate was concerned, it was what we call the narrow interpretation; there is no question about that. And so Senator Nunn is absolutely correct on that point.

III. Does It Matter Which Version Was Presented to the Senate?

1. November 1985 Armed Services Committee hearing:

> Senator Nunn:
>
> Would you agree that the purpose of the Senate's extensive ratification hearings on the ABM Treaty was to clarify ambiguities of interpretation?
>
> Judge Sofaer:
>
> Although this process may have helped answer questions in particular Senators' minds, it could not result in authoritative clarifications of any ambiguities in the treaty, because statements made during the hearings were unilateral.

2. March 1987 joint hearing of the Senate Foreign Relations and Judiciary Committees:

Judge Sofaer: "When it [the Senate] gives its advice and consent to a treaty, it is to the treaty that was made [i.e., negotiated], irrespective of the explanations it is provided."

---

3. April 9, 1987 Justice Department opinion written by Assistant Attorney General Charles Cooper:

> If . . . the ratification record unequivocally shows that the President presented the treaty to the Senate based on specific, official representations regarding the meaning of an ambiguous provision, that the Senate regarded that understanding as important to its consent, and that the Senate relied on the representations made by the executive branch in approving the treaty (and thus in refraining from attaching a formal reservation setting forth the understanding), we believe that the President would, in effect, be estopped from taking a contrary position in his subsequent interpretation of the treaty, just as he would be bound by a formal reservation or understanding passed by the Senate to the same effect.

4. March 17, 1988 letter to Senator Lugar from White House Counsel Arthur B. Culvahouse, Jr.:

> As a matter of domestic law, however, the President is bound by shared interpretations which were both authoritatively communicated to the Senate by the Executive and clearly intended, generally understood and relied upon by the Senate in its advice and consent to ratification. **This is true even if the treaty negotiating record and subsequent practice indicate an interpretation contrary to that shared understanding**. [emphasis added]

5. Byrd-Biden "Treaty Interpretation" Amendment to INF Treaty, Approved 72-27:

> The United States shall interpret the Treaty in accordance with the common understanding of the treaty shared by the President and the Senate at the time the Senate gave its advice and consent to ratification;
>
> Such common understanding is based on:
>
> (A) First, the text of the Treaty and the provisions of this resolution of ratification; and

Factually, the premise that the Senate understood the "narrow" interpretation and that this interpretation was presented by the Executive branch is

---

> (B) Second, the authoritative representations which were provided by the President and his representatives to the Senate and its Committees in seeking Senate consent to ratification, insofar as such representations were directed to the meaning and legal effect of the text of the Treaty.

6. Specter Amendment to INF Treaty, May 27, 1988, defeated 67-30:

> "Common understanding" means a shared interpretation which is both authoritatively communicated to the Senate by the Executive and clearly intended, generally understood, and relied upon by the Senate in its advice and consent to ratification.

7. June 10, 1988 Message to the Senate from President Reagan (10 days after entering into force on INF Treaty):

> . . . one provision of the Resolution to Ratification adopted by the Senate causes me serious concern. The Senate condition relating to the Treaty Clauses of the Constitution apparently seeks to alter the law of treaty interpretation. . . . Executive statements should be given binding weight only when they were authoritatively communicated to the Senate by the Executive and were part of the basis on which the Senate granted its advice and consent to ratification.

8. Justice Department Docketing Statement in appeal of Rainbow Navigation case, March 6, 1989:

> Statement of Issues to be Raised on Appeal:
>
> What degree of weight **(if any)** in the context of treaty interpretation must be accorded statements by representatives of the Executive Branch during the treaty ratification process before the United States Senate. [emphasis added]

Summary memorandum given to the author of this study by Mr. Robert G. Bell during an interview on July 7, 1989.

supported by a statement of General Bruce Palmer, Acting Chief of Staff of the Army, unambiguously for the "narrow" interpretation, in an exchange with Senators Jackson, Dominick, and Goldwater, unambiguous statements for the "narrow" interpretation by Senator Buckley and Senator Jackson, two exchanges leaning toward the "narrow" interpretation by Senators Goldwater and Thurmond, and a Department of Defense written response to questions from Senator Goldwater, an answer by General John Ryan, Air Force Chief of Staff, in the above exchange involving General Palmer, and an answer by Dr. Foster, Jr., Director of Defense Research and Engineering, in an exchange with Senator Jackson (and additional information interposed for the record) all leaning toward the "narrow" interpretation. It can also be reasonably argued that there were no unambiguous statements in the Senate hearing record supporting the "broad" interpretation. It should be noted that Senator Sam Nunn has concluded in connection with Senator Buckley's testimony before the Senate Foreign Relations Committee, in which Senator Buckley unambiguously adopted the "narrow" interpretation, that Senators Fulbright, Sparkman and Cooper, three senior members of the Committee, "well-understood the basis for Senator Buckley's opposition." Finally, it should be noted that because Senator Jackson had a reputation as a particularly knowledgeable observer as to arms control matters, the view apparently held by Jackson that the "narrow" interpretation was correct should be given particular weight. It might also be noted that the published record of the session on July 19, 1972, before the Senate Armed Services Committee in which General Bruce Palmer, Jr., makes a statement unambiguously supporting the "narrow" interpretation, does suggest in Senator Stennis's reference to: "[f]or the information of the public,"[698] that this session may have been public, and it lists the following senators and staff as present: "Senators Stennis (presiding), Jackson, Ervin, Byrd, Jr., of Virginia, Bentsen, Smith, Tower, Dominick, and Goldwater"; and staff members "T. Edward Braswell, Jr., chief counsel and staff director; John T. Ticer, chief clerk; Edward B. Kenney,

---

[698]*Military Implications Hearing Before the Senate Armed Services Comm., supra* note 587, at 423.

In this connection it seems the case from the published record of the Armed Services Committee hearing that some closed sessions were held in the overall committee hearing. Similarly, Senator Nunn's analysis of the Senate ratification proceedings says: "The published records of all of these proceedings, as well as the classified transcripts of the Senate Armed Services Committee and the Foreign Relations Committee hearings, have been examined as part of this study." Senator Sam Nunn, "Interpretation of the ABM Treaty," *supra* note 1, at 584.

professional staff member; and Nancy Bearg, research assistant, and Richard Perle, special assistant to Senator Jackson."[699]

In support of the conclusion that the Senate understood the "narrow" interpretation when it gave advice and consent to the ABM Treaty, Senator Sam Nunn has written:

> I have concluded that the Nixon Administration presented the Senate with the Traditional Interpretation of the Treaty's limits on mobile/space-based exotics and the Senate clearly understood this to be the case at the time it gave its advice and consent to the ratification of the Treaty. In my judgment, this conclusion is compelling beyond a reasonable doubt.[700]

---

[699]*Military Implications Hearing Before the Senate Armed Services Comm., supra* note 587, at 423. This of course, cannot confirm that these senators and staff were present for the relevant exchanges during question and answer in this session.

[700]Senator Sam Nunn, "Interpretation of the ABM Treaty," *supra* note 1, at 614 (page 55 of Senator Nunn's numbering).

In his 1987 exchange with Judge Sofaer on the "broad-narrow" issue in the *Washington Quarterly*, Senator Sam Nunn summarizes the Senate ratification record as follows:

> The Senate plays a full and critical role in the treaty-making of the United States, and consonant with these responsibilities, it carefully considered the ABM Treaty in 1972. It was the subject of nine days of hearings held by the Senate Armed Services Committee, six days of hearings by the Senate Foreign Relations Committee, and a thorough floor debate.
>
> Nowhere in this record is there a single statement in which any senator or executive branch official explicitly states that the development or testing of mobile/space-based exotics is permitted under the treaty--a point Sofaer conceded at the March 26, 1987 joint Foreign Relations/Judiciary hearing. In contrast, the record does contain a series of authoritative statements and insertions for the record explicitly supporting the traditional view that the treaty prohibits testing and development of mobile/space-based exotics--a point which, as previously noted, Sofaer also concedes.
>
> Futhermore, Senator Henry M. Jackson went to considerable lengths to address the question of exotics during the ratification debate. Senator

---

Jackson elicited a written clarification of the meaning of the treaty on the subject of exotics from Dr. John Foster, director of defense research and engineering, a clarification that directly contradicts the reinterpretation of the treaty. Senator Jackson also elicited the testimony of the Joint Chiefs of Staff that "we can look at futuristic systems as long as they are fixed and land based." General Bruce Palmer, Jr., acting army chief of staff, declared that "The Chiefs were aware of that and had agreed to that and that was a fundamental part of the final agreement."

The record also contains various general statements about the development, testing, or deployment of exotics, without reference to their basing mode. But because these statements do not distinguish between fixed, land-based systems and mobile/space-based systems, they carry little probative value either way with respect to the correct interpretation.

> In brief, the record clearly demonstrates that the key figures in the Senate debate--Senators Henry Jackson, James Buckley, Barry Goldwater, Strom Thurmond, John Sherman Cooper, and John Sparkman--understood that the development, testing, or deployment of space-based exotics was not permitted under the treaty. Moreover, there was clearly a perception within the Senate that the ratification hearings had served a crucial function in clarifying the treaty's terms. Senator Jackson, for example, observed in his final speech on the treaty just prior to the vote that "some of these provisions had been interpreted in several different ways depending on the witness commenting upon them. I believe the hearings were helpful both in clarifying the obligations we have undertaken and in understanding the implications for our future security."

The record of these proceedings makes a compelling case for the conclusion that the Nixon administration presented the Senate with the traditional interpretation of the treaty's limits on mobile/space-based exotics and that the Senate clearly understood this to be the case at the time it gave its advice and consent to the ratification of the treaty. In my judgment, this conclusion is compelling beyond a reasonable doubt.

S. Nunn, "The ABM Reinterpretation Issue," 10 *Wash. Q.* 45, 47-48 (Autumn 1987) (footnotes omitted).

Similarly, on November 21, 1985, Elliot L. Richardson, together with Erwin N. Griswold, Shirley M. Hufstedler and Cyrus R. Vance sent a statement for inclusion

Also former President Richard Nixon recently stated: "As far as what was presented to the Senate was concerned it was, what we call, the narrow interpretation. There is no question about that, and so Senator Nune [sic] is absolutely correct on that point."

Legally, the premise that if the Senate informally understood the "narrow" interpretation the United States is bound under national law to that informal understanding regardless of whether that understanding is or is not the appropriate international legal understanding is supported by a constitutional argument that the President can only make a treaty as it has received the advice and consent of the

---

in the record of hearings on the Strategic Defense Initiative to the Senate Armed Services Subcommittee on Strategic and Theater Nuclear Forces. The statement contains the following characterization of the Senate advice and consent record on the "broad-narrow" issue:

> The ABM Treaty, like all treaties, is legally recognized as the supreme law of the land. When the Senate approved ratification of the Treaty without qualification by a vote of 88-2, it acted on the clear understanding presented by the President, the Secretary of State, the Secretary of Defense, and the Chief Negotiator that the Treaty banned the development and testing of all space-based ABM systems and components, including "exotic systems" based on new physical principles. This view of the Treaty was understood by all, including critics like Sen. Jackson, who voted for the Treaty, and Sen. Buckley, who voted against it.

E. Griswold, S. Hufstedler, E. Richardson & C. Vance, "Statement on the Reinterpretation of the ABM Treaty by Four Lawyers and Former Government Officials Submitted to the Senate Armed Services Subcommittee on Strategic and Theater Nuclear Forces" (Nov. 21, 1985), *reprinted in Strategic Defense Initiative Hearings, supra* note 603, at 196, 196. (It is recommended that this characterization of the record, including the statements that the Senate "acted on the clear understanding presented by the President, the Secretary of State, the Secretary of Defense, and the Chief Negotiator" and that this view "was understood by all," be compared with the record as discussed in greater detail in this study.)

The hearing record of this 1985 hearing on the *Strategic Defense Initiative* contains questions and answers for the record submitted by Senators Nunn and Levin for Judge Sofaer which touch upon characterization of the Senate advice and consent record. *Strategic Defense Initiative Hearings, supra* note 603, at 267-70.

Senate, by statements of several constitutional scholars at least strongly suggestive of this conclusion, by provisions of the revised *Restatement of the Foreign Relations Law of the United States* suggestive of this conclusion, and by a number of policy arguments. It is also at least analogously supported by a recent opinion of Judge Harold H. Greene in the *Rainbow Navigation*--now on appeal--case and the final sentence of footnote 7 in the recent Supreme Court decision in *United States v. Stuart.*

Under Article II, section 2 of the Constitution the President is empowered "to make Treaties" but this power is to be exercised "by and with the Advice and Consent of the Senate." Thus, if the President decides to ratify a treaty he can only ratify the treaty to which the Senate has consented. Professor Louis Henkin of Columbia Law School, one of the Nation's preeminent experts on constitutional aspects of foreign policy, has testified that: "[i]n my view, if the Senate's understanding is clear, the President can make the treaty only in accordance with that understanding, whether or not that understanding is expressed as a condition of consent." That is, Professor Henkin supports the position that for purposes of national law a clear informal Senate understanding is just as binding as a formally adopted Senate condition. Similarly, the *Restatement (Third) of the Foreign Relations Law of the United States*, of which Professor Henkin is Chief Reporter, adopts the position in section 314(2):

> **When the Senate gives its advice and consent to a treaty on the basis of a particular understanding of its meaning, the President, if he makes the treaty, must do so on the basis of the Senate's understanding.**

Comment *d* to this section more specifically takes the position that in the event of informal indications of Senate intent with respect to a treaty "the President must decide whether they represent a general understanding by the Senate and, if he finds that they do, must respect them in good faith."

It can also be argued that the recent District Court decision of Judge Harold H. Greene in the *Rainbow Navigation* case and the final sentence of footnote 7 of Mr. Justice Brennan's opinion for the Supreme Court in the recent case of *United States v. Stuart* support the position that informal Senate understandings or Executive branch statements to the Senate during Senate consideration of a treaty are binding. In the *Rainbow Navigation* case Judge Greene cited section 314 of the *Restatement* as well as the report of the Senate Foreign Relations Committee on *The ABM Treaty Interpretation Resolution* and said: "This Court has no doubt about the obligation of the Executive branch to stand behind the representations made by its officials to the Senate committee having jurisdiction, and to comply with the conditions attached, formally or informally, by the Senate as part of its ratification." And the final sentence of footnote 7 in the *Stuart* case said: "A treaty's negotiating history, which JUSTICE SCALIA suggests would be a better interpretive guide than preratification Senate materials . . . would in fact be a worse indicator of a treaty's meaning, for that history is rarely a matter of public record available to the Senate when it decides to grant or withhold its consent."

There are also a number of policy arguments supporting this position. These include that such a position arguably would most effectively protect the meaningfulness of the Senate role in the treaty process and prevent abuse by the Executive branch in representations to the Senate and that the Senate would be more relaxed about not seeking formal reservations or understandings or having access to an entire negotiating record.

It can also be urged that quite apart from the general principle of the legal effect under national law of informal Senate understandings, the Executive branch should be held to an interpretation presented to the Senate by an Executive branch official whether because such statements should be regarded as "authoritative" or because there should be an "estoppel" of the Presidency in such settings. Senator Sam Nunn has emphasized this point in its "authoritative" mode both in his testimony on "Interpretation of the ABM Treaty" and in his recent efforts concerning the status of testimony by Executive branch officials on the INF Treaty. Thus, in his important testimony he says:

> By asserting that the Executive Branch may now disregard the views of those who spoke for the Administration and those who debated the issue in the Senate, the State Department is arguing, in effect, that Administration witnesses need not accurately reflect the executive's understanding of a treaty; instead, they are free to keep that understanding a secret and may mislead the Senate into consenting to a treaty which has a secret interpretation different from the meaning presented to the Senate. This line of argument has profound implications for the legislative process in general and the constitutional role of the Senate in particular. . . .[701]

Arguments for the "narrow" interpretation would further point out that regardless of whether the President was initially bound to follow the "narrow" interpretation, he is bound once Congress as a whole requires action consistent with

---

[701]Senator Sam Nunn, "Interpretation of the ABM Treaty," *supra* note 1, 618-19.

this interpretation, as seems to be the case under the 1988 Defense Authorization Act for fiscal year 1988 and--as rolled over--fiscal year 1989, or if extended by Congress as a ban into fiscal year 1990 or beyond. Under this view, it would be assumed that the enumerated and reasonably implied powers of Congress, coupled at least with the appropriations power, would provide a constitutional basis for congressional regulation of activities inconsistent with the "narrow" interpretation.

2. Arguments that the President may elect to act on the "broad" interpretation under national law

Principal arguments that the President may elect to act on the "broad" interpretation under national law are as follows (ignoring for the moment the effect of subsequent congressional constraints):

At the outset, it should be noted that in order for the proponents of the "narrow" interpretation to succeed in the argument that even without subsequent congressional action the President is bound to the "narrow" interpretation under national law they must prevail at minimum on each of three important issues: to establish that the "narrow" interpretation represented a general understanding of at least two-thirds of the advising Senate under recognized rules of legislative and "treaty" history as an extrinsic aid to interpretation; to establish in the full context of Senate consideration of the ABM Treaty that that two-thirds majority would have supported the "narrow" interpretation restriction on development and testing even in a setting where the United States were unilaterally bound to it and the U.S.S.R. was not; and to establish that under the Constitution the "dual" theory, postulating in settings of informal Senate understanding that such understandings would serve as the standard for treaty interpretation under national law rather than the appropriate international standard for interpretation, is correct. Rather than prevailing on all three of these necessary points in their argument, however, the argument fails on each ground and thus fails independently on three grounds, each of which is a sufficient condition to negate the argument. In the alternative, proponents of these national law arguments for the "narrow" interpretation must establish some *ipso facto* binding Executive branch statement. Again, any such arguments fail both factually and legally in relation to the record of initial Senate consideration of the ABM Treaty.

First, the record of ratification proceedings of the 1972 ABM Treaty does not establish, using normal rules of legislative and treaty history as extrinsic aids to interpretation, that a two-third's majority of the consenting Senate gave consent on the informal understanding that the "narrow" interpretation was correct.[702]

The record as a whole shows that none of the Executive branch transmittal documents either adverted to or meaningfully addressed the "broad-narrow" issue. The major White House briefing and discussion session with congressional leaders about the Treaty neither adverted to nor meaningfully addressed the issue. Neither Secretary of State William P. Rogers nor Ambassador Gerard C. Smith, as the lead administration witnesses, either adverted to or clearly addressed the "broad-narrow" issue in their prepared written testimony. Ambassador Smith had at least four opportunities during exchanges within committee hearings to clarify the "broad-narrow" issue but did not definitively do so. Moreover, at least three of these exchanges, one before the Senate Foreign Relations Committee and two before the Senate Armed Services Committee, can be fairly characterized at least as "ambiguous but leaning toward the `broad' interpretation." None even lean toward the "narrow" interpretation. On no occasion in any Senate or House forum during initial consideration of the Treaty does any White House, NSC, State Department, ACDA, or participating member of the SALT Delegation, either make a statement or participate in an exchange that can be fairly regarded as even leaning toward the "narrow" interpretation. No administration spokesman participated in any exchange before the Senate committee with principal jurisdiction over the ABM Treaty, the Senate Foreign Relations Committee, that can be fairly regarded as even leaning toward the "narrow" interpretation. The only administration witness before the Senate Foreign Relations Committee that can be reasonably regarded as having addressed the issue, Ambassador Gerard C. Smith, the head of the United States SALT I Delegation during testimony with the Secretary of State and accompanied by senior members of the SALT I Delegation, made a statement that can at least be regarded as "ambiguous but leaning toward the `broad' interpretation." Only one administration spokesman, General Bruce Palmer, the Acting Chief of Staff of the Army, participated in any Senate or House statement or exchange that can clearly be regarded as unambiguous for the "narrow" interpretation. That exchange before the Senate Armed Services Committee was seemingly at variance with an earlier exchange participated in by General Palmer before the same committee that can most reasonably be regarded as at least "ambiguous but leaning toward the `broad'

---

[702]It should be noted that during the recent debate on the INF Treaty interpretation condition, Senator Hollings, a member of the original Senate which consented to the ABM Treaty, presented an analysis of the Senate advice and consent record in support of the "broad" interpretation. *See* 134 *Cong. Rec.* S6758-60 (daily ed. May 26, 1988) (statement of Sen. Hollings).

interpretation." It was also inconsistent with contemporary testimony before the House Armed Services Committee by the Chairman of the Joint Chiefs as to the view of the Chiefs. Neither the report of the Senate Foreign Relations Committee, nor the report of the House Foreign Affairs Committee, nor the Senate resolution of advice and consent, adverted to or meaningfully addressed the issue. The total record of hearings before the Senate Foreign Relations Committee, the committee with principal jurisdiction over the Treaty, shows that the issue received only incidental attention. Of the only two exchanges seeming to at least lean toward one or another interpretation, Senator Buckley, in testimony to the committee in opposition to the Treaty, seemed to clearly reflect the "narrow" interpretation, and Ambassador Smith, in an exchange in which Secretary of State Rogers was also present, made a remark that can at minimum be regarded as "ambiguous but leaning toward the `broad' interpretation." Thus, the record of hearings before the Senate committee with principal jurisdiction over the Treaty was sparse on the issue and at least somewhat mixed, certainly so if the testimony of the principal United States negotiator--with the Secretary of State present--is to receive greater weight than that of a senator in opposition to the Treaty. The record of hearings before the Senate Armed Services Committee, not the lead committee on the ABM Treaty, shows approximately eight exchanges involving administration spokesmen that can reasonably be regarded as addressing the issue and that at least lean toward one or the other interpretation. Of these, two exchanges involve Ambassador Smith, the head of the SALT Delegation and lead administration witness on the ABM Treaty, and both can most fairly be characterized at least as "ambiguous but leaning toward the `broad' interpretation." Two exchanges (one of these involving additional information interposed for the record) involve Dr. John Foster, Jr., Director of Defense Research and Engineering, during questioning by Senator Jackson and can be regarded as "ambiguous but leaning toward the `narrow' interpretation." Two exchanges involve General Bruce Palmer, Acting Chief of Staff of the Army and not a member of the SALT Delegation, with the first of these exchanges most reasonably characterized as "ambiguous but leaning toward the `broad' interpretation" or even arguably "clear for the `broad' interpretation" and the second, involving questioning by Senator Jackson, "clear for the `narrow' interpretation." One exchange involving General John Ryan during questioning by Senator Jackson can be regarded as "ambiguous but leans toward the `narrow' interpretation." And the last is a written response to Senator Goldwater from the Department of Defense that is most reasonably viewed as "ambiguous but leans toward the `narrow' interpretation." These exchanges before the Armed Services Committee also demonstrated that Senator Jackson probably believed that the "narrow" interpretation was correct. Indeed, it is possible, if not probable, that his assumption that the "narrow" interpretation is correct may be a factor--if not the principal cause--in the exchanges with Dr. Foster, General Ryan and General Palmer in which they respectively "leaned toward," "leaned toward," and "unambiguously adopted" the "narrow" interpretation. Senator Jackson, after all, was a formidable questioner; and one knowledgeable observer, Mr. John B. Rhinelander, has noted even that Senator Jackson seemed to be leading the witnesses during at least some of the overall hearing. In this connection, it is striking that the only three administration witnesses appearing in person and even leaning toward the "narrow" interpretation all did so under questioning by Senator Jackson. The overall "box score" of the administration witnesses or statements on the "broad-narrow" issue before the Senate Armed Services Committee was three exchanges at least tilting toward the "broad" interpretation, including two of these from the head of the SALT Delegation, Ambassador Gerard C. Smith, and five exchanges at least tilting toward the "narrow" interpretation, including one clear statement for the "narrow" interpretation and one written response and an interposition for the record from DOD at least leaning toward the "narrow" interpretation. The record of minor hearings before the Senate Appropriations Committee shows no statements or exchanges even leaning toward one or another interpretation. The record of the general "floor" debate in the Senate, lasting only one day, shows that the "broad-narrow" issue was only sparsely addressed with Senator Buckley, an opponent of the Treaty, unambiguously reflecting the "narrow" interpretation, Senator Fong making a statement that can be reasonably regarded as "ambiguous but leans toward the `broad' interpretation," and Senator Thurmond making a statement that can be reasonably regarded as "ambiguous but leans toward the `narrow' interpretation." It is not known, and cannot be known from the record, whether the critical portions of these statements were or were not actually made during "floor" debate or whether they were subsequently inserted in the record. As an indication of the extent to which clear answers were lacking on the "broad-narrow" issue during overall Senate consideration of the ABM Treaty, on at least nineteen occasions that could have clarified the issue during Senate consideration, an exchange or statement can most reasonably be characterized only as "ambiguous neutral or does not address." Finally, with respect to reasonably clear indications from the overall record of views by members of the consenting Senate as to the "broad-narrow" issue, the record shows that Senator Buckley, an opponent of the treaty, unambiguously articulated the "narrow" interpretation, Senator Jackson, one of the generally most knowledgeable members of the Senate in defense matters but also the leader of the Jackson Amendment in the overall SALT context, unambiguously articulated the "narrow" interpretation (but on one occasion can be characterized as "ambiguous: leans to the `broad' interpretation"), Senator Goldwater was involved in exchanges in which he seemed variously to lean toward both "broad" and "narrow" interpretations (two for "broad" and one for "narrow"), Senator Thurmond seemed to lean toward the "narrow" interpretation and Senators Dominick and Fong (in "floor" debate) seemed to lean toward the "broad" interpretation. That is three senators either clearly believed that the "narrow" interpretation was correct or leaned toward it, and three senators seemed to lean toward the "broad" interpretation. Of these, two senators seemed variously at different times to lean both ways. The only unambiguous statements by either senators or Executive branch witnesses reflecting the "narrow" interpretation not occurring in the Senate Armed Services Committee hearing or hearing record were two statements by Senator Buckley, an opponent of the Treaty, in his testimony before the Senate Foreign Relations Committee and in general "floor" debate.

One potentially significant point in appraisal of the hearing record in Senate consideration of the "broad-narrow" issue has not been generally noted in the debate. That is, *some* of the relevant hearings before the Senate Armed Services Committee may have been held in closed session. As has been seen, however, the only Executive branch statements to the Senate characterized in this study as even "ambiguous: leans to the `narrow' interpretation" occurred in this hearing before the Armed Services Committee. If any of these statements occurred in a closed session it could as a practical matter further affect the extent to which they would have been known to the Senate as a whole. At minimum, closed hearings would likely reduce the dissemination of information within the Senate by reducing staff attendance. Yet another question is whether the sanitized hearing record would be available, or available with adequate lead-time, to be taken into account in overall Senate deliberations on advice and consent during the floor debate and resulting Senate resolution of advice and consent on August 3rd. In this respect, it should be recalled that no report on the ABM Treaty was available from the Senate Armed Services Committee. It should also be noted that the final session in the overall hearings before the Senate Armed Services Committee did not occur until July 25, 1972, only nine days before the Senate vote on the ABM Treaty, August 3. And it should be noted that the important session in which the published record shows that General Bruce Palmer, Jr., testified unambiguously for the "narrow" interpretation occurred on July 19, only fifteen days before the Senate vote on the ABM Treaty.

In appraising the overall record of Senate consideration of the "broad-narrow" issue, it also should be understood that the Foreign Relations Committee, and not the Armed Services Committee, was the lead committee in Senate consideration of advice and consent to the ABM Treaty. Hearings before the Armed Services Committee were jurisdictionally rooted in considering the military implications of the Treaty. As Senator John Stennis, Chairman of the Armed Services Committee, stated during the Armed Services Committee hearings:

> The hearings before this committee are, technically, not hearings on the treaty and interim offensive weapons agreement as such. The treaty and agreement have been referred to the Foreign Relations Committee and the committee is holding its hearings in order to make its report to the Senate. The substance of the treaty and agreement, however, is of direct concern to this committee as well because it concerns the national defense and our overall strategic posture. Thus, we will be holding these hearings concerning the military implications of the treaty and the agreement. That is a term that I used in the beginning in reference to the hearings. I recognized the nature of them, the jurisdiction is with foreign relations, but the military implications should be considered by this committee. Of course, I will not attempt to limit the hearings directly to those points, but I believe that is our primary mission in these hearings.[703]

And:

> For the information of the public, this treaty, of course, is not before our committee, nor is the proposed statute before us formally for an official report, but it is before us in substance.
>
> Our committee decided to hold hearings on the military implications of the SALT agreements, and that means just what it says I think we have had splendid hearings. [sic][704]

Pursuant to this committee jurisdictional distinction, the Foreign Relations Committee, and not the Armed Services Committee, issued a report on advice and consent to the ABM Treaty.

While former President Richard Nixon did respond to a question asked at his appearance on April 15, 1988, before the ASNE Convention by saying that "[t]here is no question" but that "the narrow interpretation" "was presented to the

---

[703]*Military Implications Hearing Before the Senate Armed Services Comm., supra* note 587, at 138.

[704]*Id.* at 423. *See also supra* note 587 and accompanying text.

Senate," this response was made almost seventeen years after the ABM Treaty was presented to the Senate and well after a substantial public debate addressing the issue. As with subsequent statements by former legislators arising after an interpretation issue is presented, this response is of only limited interpretive significance apart from specifics, which were notably absent from Nixon's response, as to how the "narrow" interpretation was presented to the Senate. Moreover, President Nixon's response did not say that the "narrow" interpretation was the *internationally* correct interpretation of the ABM Treaty and pointedly focused on, without conclusion, the constitutional issue raised in what this study refers to as the "dual" versus "unitary" theories of treaty interpretation.

Summarizing this factual record, and applying to it the generally recognized law of legislative and treaty history as extrinsic aides in interpretation, it is evident that the record does not support the conclusion that a two-thirds majority of the Senate consented to the ABM Treaty on the informal understanding that the "narrow" interpretation was correct. That is, the record does not support a conclusion of general intent on the part of at least two-thirds of the Senate on this point. In application of the law of legislative and treaty history to this record it should initially be noted that none of the principal indicators of legislative or treaty history in this record are supportive of the "narrow" interpretation. That is, there is no support for that interpretation in Executive branch transmittal documents, statements of the lead administration witnesses, committee reports, textual changes during enactment, or the Senate resolution of consent to the Treaty. Indeed, the failure of all of these principal sources to clearly address the issue is itself a substantial argument that a two-thirds majority of the Senate was highly unlikely to have formed an opinion for or against the "narrow" interpretation. That is, these sources that have not clearly addressed the issue are the very sources entitled to greatest weight in interpreting legislative and treaty history and that are most likely to have been known to a two-thirds majority in the Senate. With respect to Executive branch statements to the Senate, of particular concern in treaty history, only one statement by a subsidiary Executive branch witness--and one not a member of the SALT Delegation--during the Armed Services Committee hearing can be said to be clearly adopting the "narrow" interpretation and that occurred in a setting where the same witness previously testified before the same committee in a way at least leaning toward the "broad" interpretation and that some might even interpret as clear for the "broad" interpretation, in which the witness was pressed by Senator Jackson who seemed to believe the "narrow" interpretation was correct, and where the witness was contradicted by contemporary testimony from the Chairman of the Joint Chiefs of Staff before a House committee. And on the other side of this equation, on at least three occasions the lead administration witness and head SALT negotiator made statements at least leaning toward the "broad" interpretation. No committee hearing in which relevant exchanges occurred was free from ambiguity in the record on the point and, in any event, the record of general committee consideration is only a weak indicator of general intent. This should be particularly true of the Armed Services Committee where most relevant exchanges occurred since it was not the lead committee on the ABM Treaty and did not issue a committee report on it. Similarly, the "floor" debate was not free from ambiguity on this point and it is not known whether any of the relevant "floor" statements were in fact made on the floor. In any event the floor debate, except for statements by principal sponsors, also is recognized to be only a weak indicator of overall general intent. Moreover, of the two senators making statements anywhere in the record clearly supportive of the "narrow" interpretation, Senators Buckley and Jackson, Senator Buckley was a treaty opponent and, as such, his interpretive statements are entitled to particularly little weight, and arguably Senator Jackson may be at least analogous to a treaty opponent on the development and testing issues as the principal sponsor of the Jackson Amendment embodying a strong interest in supporting strategic research and development in general. The argument that the record supports the conclusion that an at least two-thirds majority of the Senate adverted to and had adopted the "narrow" interpretation as correct is an argument that, despite the failure of the transmittal documents, the lead administration witness on the treaty, and the committee reports or the Senate resolution of consent to address the issue, despite statements in the record suggesting that three senators made ambiguous statements leaning toward the "broad" interpretation, and despite a tilt on at least three occasions toward the "broad" interpretation by the lead administration witness Ambassador Smith, if it is fair to ascribe any position to him, an at least two-thirds majority of senators was aware of and supported the "narrow" interpretation based on a series of mostly ambiguous exchanges occurring in the non-lead committee hearings before the Armed Services Committee and statements by a strong opponent of the Treaty, Senator Buckley, one in committee hearings and one that may or may not have actually been made on the Senate floor. The burden of such an argument seems, in common experience, rather great.

Second, the record as a whole lends no support to the proposition that an at least two-thirds majority of the Senate intended in consenting to the 1972 ABM Treaty to bind the United States to the "narrow" interpretation even if the Soviets were not bound. Indeed, a virtually contemporaneous legislative action in pari materia, the Jackson Amendment, passed on September 30, 1972, less than eight weeks after Senate consent to the ABM Treaty, said quite specifically that "Congress recognizes the principle of United States-Soviet Union equality reflected in the antiballistic missile treaty." Moreover, principal motivations for the Jackson

Amendment were to ensure at least equality in general strategic arms limits between United States and Soviet forces and to promote "a vigorous research and development" program, both at least suggestive that the approving Congress would not have been sympathetic to an interpretation in an important strategic area relating to testing and development unilaterally binding only on the United States. That is, the Jackson Amendment is certainly strongly suggestive of a congressional concern, and particularly a Senate concern, that important arms control agreements be reciprocally limiting and that a vigorous research and development program proceed up to treaty limits binding on all parties. With respect to Senate intent, the key votes to modify the Jackson Amendment failed by margins of 35-55 and 38-48 and the modified joint resolution embodying the Jackson Amendment was passed by the Senate on September 14, less than six weeks after approval of the ABM Treaty, by a vote of 88-2. It should also be noted in connection with the Jackson Amendment and the "broad-narrow" interpretation that all senators involved in a relevant exchange on the "broad-narrow" issue whose remarks seemed to even lean toward either interpretation were co-sponsors of the Jackson Amendment. That is, of particular importance, Senators Jackson, Buckley, Goldwater and Thurmond, who seemed to be the only senators at any time at least leaning toward a "narrow" interpretation in their remarks, were co-sponsors of this resolution. Indeed, of these, Senators Jackson, Buckley, and Thurmond were even co-sponsors of the original Jackson Amendment on August 7, 1972, four days after Senate consent to the ABM Treaty. And, of course, Senator Jackson, who figures so prominently in the series of exchanges on the "broad-narrow" issue before the Armed Services Committee, was the principal initiator and sponsor of the Amendment. In the face of this record of contemporary legislation in pari materia, it would even seem grotesque to ascribe an intention to Senators Jackson, Buckley, Thurmond or a two-thirds majority of the ABM Treaty consenting Senate that the United States should be bound by a "narrow" interpretation even if the Soviets were not bound. That is, the Jackson Amendment and its legislative history demonstrated that the Senate that consented to the 1972 ABM Treaty was particularly concerned about issues of equality in United States-Soviet arms control agreements and specifically believed that the ABM Treaty was premised on equality of obligation. As such, even if the record showed a general intent of a two-thirds Senate majority that the "narrow" interpretation were correct--which it does not, the overall Senate intent was certainly not to unilaterally bind the United States to that interpretation if it turned out that the international legal interpretation were otherwise. And if this issue were conceptualized as one of mistake it would seem reasonably clear that the consenting Senate, which also supported the Jackson Amendment as its principal SALT I message, would not have wanted to be unilaterally bound by a mistake in interpretation into a posture of non-reciprocity of legal obligation with the Soviet Union in an important area of strategic development.

Third, whatever the interpretation of a general Senate intent with respect to any informal understanding, as opposed to a formal Senate condition on consent, the appropriate constitutional standard for treaty interpretation is, in fact, the meaning of the treaty under recognized interpretive principles of international law. Arguments supporting this approach and rejecting a "dual" approach to treaty interpretation (or a rule that Executive branch statements to the Senate *ipso facto* create legally binding national law) include arguments rooted in constitutional theory, case law, scholarly opinion and policy.

As a matter of constitutional theory the treaty power is a power to make international agreements. It is probably not a general legislative power to make laws, apart from the international agreement, that would be binding under domestic law. When the framers bestowed the general legislative power it was bestowed on the Congress as a whole and the President was given a qualified veto. Certainly the framers did not intend that a record of informal "legislative" history of the Senate alone, as embodied in the "dual" approach, could create binding rights, privileges, powers and immunities under United States domestic law apart from the underlying international agreement. Moreover, when in fact the result of the "dual" approach would be to hold the United States to an obligation not shared by the other party (or conversely to be in violation of its international obligations) would such a result protect the integrity of the Senate which by definition would in such a case have believed the United States and the other treaty parties mutually bound?

As a matter of constitutional theory the treaty power is a power to make international agreements. It is probably not a general legislative power to make laws, apart from the international agreement, that would be binding under domestic law. When the framers bestowed the general legislative power it was bestowed on the Congress as a whole and the President was given a qualified veto. Certainly the framers did not intend that a record of informal "legislative" history of the Senate alone, as embodied in the "dual" approach, could create binding rights, privileges, powers and immunities under United States domestic law apart from the underlying international agreement. Moreover, when in fact the result of the "dual" approach would be to hold the United States to an obligation not shared by the other party (or conversely to be in violation of its international obligations) would such a result protect the integrity of the Senate which by definition would in such a case have believed the United States and the other treaty parties mutually bound?

With respect to case law as primary authority, while, with one possible exception, there are no cases squarely addressing the "unitary vs. dual" issue, there are a number of cases strongly supporting the principal theoretical underpinnings of the "unitary" approach and seemingly none[705] squarely--at least in holding rather than dictum--supporting the "dual" approach. The one case which can fairly be read to have rejected the "dual" approach, at least as a blanket theoretical requirement, is the 1898 decision of the Supreme Court in *New York Indians v. United States*.[706] That case held that a Senate proviso, even formally adopted as a condition of Senate consent to a treaty but not published with the treaty nor apparently conveyed to the other party, was not binding and could not "be considered as a legislative act, since the power to legislate is vested in the President, Senate and House of Representatives."[707] Similarly, there is a considerable line of Supreme Court decisions referring to a treaty as a compact or contract between nations, a substantial line of Supreme Court decisions refers to international law or mutuality of obligations between the parties as the appropriate standard for interpretation of a treaty, and another substantial line of such cases roots the scope of the treaty power in matters of negotiation among nations. And, Mr. Justice Brown, concurring in the important *Fourteen Diamond Rings* case in 1901 said of the Senate role in "consent" to treaties:

> [T]he power of the Senate is limited to a ratification of such terms as have already been agreed upon between the President, acting for the United States, and the commissioners of the other contracting power. The Senate has no right to ratify the treaty and introduce new terms into it, which shall be obligatory upon the other power, although it may refuse its ratification, or make such ratification conditional upon the adoption of amendments to the treaty.[708]

---

[705]Proving a negative in legal research for case authority is, of course, a proposition on which caution is in order. To date, however, neither this researcher nor, to my knowledge, any proponent of the "dual" approach has found case holding squarely supportive of that approach (although the recent opinion of Judge Harold H. Greene in the *Rainbow Navigation* case has been argued as such).

[706]170 U.S. 1 (1898).

[707]170 U.S. 1, at 23.

[708]183 U.S. 176, 183 (1901).

Similarly, the opinion of the United States Court of Appeals for the District of Columbia Circuit in the famous 1957 *Niagara Reservation* case,[709] while ultimately vacated as moot by the Supreme Court, upheld a treaty with Canada about the waters of the Niagara River while setting aside a clear Senate *formal* reservation to the treaty on the grounds that "[i]t was merely an expression of domestic policy which the Senate attached to its consent" and, as such, was beyond the power of the Senate.[710] And the 1984 decision of the United States Claims Court in *Coplin v. United States*,[711] while reversed on other grounds mooting a direct dual v. unitary clash, seemed clearly to reject a "dual" approach and to take the position that informal expressions of Senate intent not included in the instrument of ratification and communicated to the other treaty party could have no legal effect. It should also be noted in the *Coplin* case that the court, including the Court of Appeals, examined a negotiating record in detail including materials not presented to the Senate in seeking to ascertain "the intention of the two governments"[712] as the appropriate standard for treaty interpretation. And the Claims Court rejected any informal Senate understanding as a legal basis even in a setting where there was testimony by the State Department Legal Adviser during treaty consent proceedings that a concern expressed by a senator on the issue would be dealt with and where an Executive branch analysis of the treaty on the issue was embodied in the Senate Foreign Relations Committee report. The recent District Court decision by Judge Harold H. Greene in the *Rainbow Navigation* case--now on appeal, while containing sweeping language about informal Senate conditions and Executive branch statements to the Senate, is principally a case concerning the legal effect of "domestic conditions" rather than the international meaning of a treaty. And on that point it is in conflict with the higher Court of Appeals decision in the *Niagara Reservation* case (as well as the theory of the Supreme Court in the *New York Indians* case). And footnote 7 of the opinion of Mr. Justice Brennan for the Supreme Court in the recent *Stuart* case addresses the issue of the permissibility of

---

[709]Power Authority of the State of New York v. Federal Power Commission, 247 F.2d 530 (D.C. Cir. 1957); *vacated as moot sub. nom.* in American Pub. Power Assn. v. Power Authority of the State of New York, 355 U.S. 64 (1957).

[710]247 F.2d 538, 541 (D.C. Cir. 1957).

[711]Coplin v. United States, 6 Cl. Ct. 115 (1984), *rev'd on other grounds,* 761 F.2d 688 (Fed. Cir. 1985).

[712]6 Cl. Ct. 115, at 126.

using Senate preratification materials in a search for the intent of the treaty parties and does not decide whether informal Senate understandings or conditions or Executive branch statements to the Senate are "binding." Indeed, it should be pointed out that the thrust of this decision, reflected in at least three separate places in the text of the Court's opinion, is that the intent of the parties to the treaty is the basic standard for treaty interpretation.

With respect to scholarly authorities, a detailed ninety-six page opinion prepared by the distinguished international lawyers, Professors Philip C. Jessup and Oliver J. Lissitzyn of the Columbia Law faculty, in the *Niagara Reservation* case, did set out at length a theoretical discussion supportive of the proposition that the treaty power is rooted in international agreement rather than legislative act. Paradoxically, Professor Philip C. Jessup, who became a judge of the International Court of Justice and was one of the United States' most distinguished international lawyers, was then holding a chair at Columbia subsequently held by Professor Louis Henkin (Hamilton Fish Professor of International Law and Diplomacy) whose testimony on the "ABM Treaty Interpretation Resolution" was interpreted by the majority of the Senate Foreign Relations Committee in favor of the "dual" approach. With respect to the revised *Restatement* position relied on by the supporters of the "dual" approach, it cites no case authority for its position and it departs from the predecessor *Restatement* which clearly reflected the position that informal indications from the record of Senate intent, as opposed to formal statements of understanding either attached at signature or included in the instrument of ratification, would not ipso facto become "effective as domestic law" but rather would only be "taken into account." It should also be noted in this connection that the Chief Reporter of the *Revised Restatement* is Professor Henkin, whose views on an analogous issue in the *Niagara Reservation* case were rejected in 1957 by Judge Bazelon writing for the Court of Appeals for the District of Columbia Circuit and were contradicted by his then senior colleagues at Columbia, Professors Jessup and Lissitzyn.

Finally, with respect to policy arguments supporting the view that the appropriate constitutional standard for treaty interpretation should be the international legal obligation, under this approach informal Senate ratification history will not serve to create discrepancies between the Nation's international and domestic legal obligations. While the record of Senate ratification consideration will be taken into account and accorded weight pursuant to the international standard for treaty interpretation, the interpretation then reached will be identical under both international and national law. In contrast, the "dual" approach will always require that the United States adopt an interpretation under national law either in violation of its international legal obligations or an additional unilateral obligation not assumed by the other treaty party. In addition, the core circumstance in which the "dual" versus "unitary" issue is likely to arise is one in which an issue was only peripherally considered during the ratification process and/or one on which there is a mistake of fact or law. To adopt an approach in such a setting that would require the United States under national law either to void a treaty (and thus in most settings be in violation of our international legal obligations) or to adopt an interpretation either in violation of the treaty or unilaterally imposing a non-reciprocal legal obligation on the United States, rather than serving to protect the Senate intent, could, and perhaps even in most cases would, grotesquely subvert the intent of the original ratifying Senate. Moreover, it is unclear as a matter of constitutional law why a "dual" approach would not simply void United States adherence to a treaty as a whole, as opposed to holding the United States to an obligation not understood in its international dimensions by the consenting Senate. And the "dual" approach, to the extent that it permits creation of binding domestic legal obligations inconsistent with or not embedded in the Nation's treaty obligations solely by informal Senate action, would, at least in some settings, seem inconsistent with the constitutional notion of shared powers clearly reflected in the treaty power. It can also be argued that the most effective way to strengthen the Senate role in the process of treaty advice and consent is precisely the rule that will require the Senate to act only through formal conditions, which in turn maximizes the opportunity for addressing the issue within the international agreement process. The "dual" approach could also substantially complicate United States participation in international adjudication. Finally, the "unitary" approach is supported by a substantial policy underpinning of the constitutional framers as they addressed the new Nation's treaty commitments. That is, one of their motivations was to create a mechanism that would reduce the internal difficulties experienced under the Articles of Confederation in ensuring adherence to the Nation's treaty obligations. They believed that it was important for the Nation to take its treaty obligations seriously and to seek to structure internal processes to enhance observance of those obligations. This, of course, reflects both pragmatic underpinnings that to be taken seriously a nation must respect its international obligations, and elements of fairness and honor that the Nation should deal fairly and honorably in its relations with other nations. Both of these objectives are supported by the "unitary" approach and are harmed by the "dual" approach. Under the "unitary" approach there is a single standard for treaty interpretation and that standard coincides with the Nation's international obligations. In contrast, under the "dual" approach the Nation would be establishing a process with the potential for not complying with treaty obligations through proceedings not communicated to the other party. Certainly we would not regard that process by others as honorable or conducive to the rule of law among nations.

With respect to any argument that the views of Executive branch witnesses expressed during Senate consent proceedings should be regarded as "authoritative" and binding or that such views might work an "estoppel" against the Presidency, given the ratification record such arguments are not applicable in the "broad-narrow" dispute even if in some settings they would arguably be applicable. Moreover, the argument, focusing on settings of abuse in which an Executive branch official might deliberately seek to "mislead the Senate into consenting to a treaty which has a secret interpretation different from the meaning presented to the Senate" obscures the more likely setting of simple mistake as to a provision initially given only peripheral attention by both the Executive branch and the Senate and it also obscures the cost for the Senate and the Nation of using this tool as an instrument to police the Executive branch in any setting. There has been no charge, and there is no evidence, that the Nixon Administration sought to mislead the Senate as to the meaning of the ABM Treaty and thus invoking this "horrible" in the ABM context seems overkill. Perhaps most importantly, this general line of argument obscures again the underlying constitutional issue as to whether the test for treaty interpretation is the international meaning.

The actual setting of the Senate record in the "broad-narrow" debate simply does not present a credible occasion for asserting that the Administration presented an "authoritative" position to the Senate or that it should be "estopped" by Executive branch communications to the Senate. That record suggests that only one statement by an Executive branch official to the Senate can be clearly categorized as "unambiguous for the `narrow' interpretation." That was a statement during question and answer by General Bruce Palmer, Acting Chief of Staff of the Army, in a hearing exchange in the Senate Armed Services Committee (not the lead committee within the Senate on the ABM Treaty) between Senators Jackson, Dominick, and Goldwater and General Leber, General Ryan and General Palmer. The overall setting, however, was one in which General Palmer was previously involved in a hearing exchange before the same committee that at least "leans toward the `broad' interpretation" and could be regarded as "clearly adopting the `broad' interpretation." That is, on different occasions General Palmer seemed to convey opposite messages on the issue to the same committee. And to the extent that his testimony referred to a view of "[t]he Chiefs" on the issue, it should be compared with the seemingly contradictory testimony of Admiral Thomas Moorer, the Chairman of the Joint Chiefs, before the House Armed Services Committee. General Palmer was not a lead witness for the Administration on the ABM Treaty or a member of the SALT Delegation that negotiated the treaty, did not make any written representation on the "narrow" interpretation, was testifying before a committee that was not the lead Senate committee on the ABM Treaty, and was pushed in the exchange by Senator Jackson who seemed to believe that the "narrow" interpretation was correct. Most importantly, neither the Administration transmitted documents on the ABM Treaty nor any lead administration witness made any statement clearly supporting the "narrow" interpretation and, in contrast the lead administration witness, Ambassador Gerard C. Smith, participated in three question and answer exchanges that could at least be regarded as "leaning to the `broad' interpretation." Moreover, Ambassador Smith recollects that he was accompanied by the key delegation members during his testimony. Arguably, these three at least "ambiguous leaning to the `broad' interpretation" exchanges by the administration lead witness in testimony before both Foreign Relations and Armed Services committees, apparently accompanied by other key delegation members, should count for more than arguably contradictory statements from a DOD non-lead representative together with four other "ambiguous but leaning toward the `narrow' interpretation" indications from other DOD non-lead representatives or statements.

In connection with any "estoppel" or "authoritative testimony" argument, it should also be noted that Secretary of State Rogers fully informed the Senate considering the ABM Treaty that:

> [i]f questions of interpretation arise in the future, we certainly will go back and look at the memoranda because there wasn't a complete transcript kept of the plenary sessions. . . .[713]

In any event, arguments about Executive branch statements necessarily being "authoritative" or giving rise to an "estoppel" prove too much. Of course any administration has an obligation to carefully and candidly present treaties to the Senate for its consideration. It can be expected that the Senate will rightly be troubled by subsequently discovered discrepancies between any international obligations and communications about the treaty by Executive branch witnesses. But what should happen in the setting where the few cases to arise here will likely be concentrated? That is, a setting precisely such as the "broad-narrow" issue where both Executive branch and Senate only peripherally addressed an issue, or a setting where at least some Executive branch official in good faith makes a mistake about a complex interpretation matter. Does it protect the role of the Senate in such cases to bind the United States when the other party is not so bound? Is it an appropriate cost paid by the Nation as a whole in resolving the issue? It seems more likely that

---

[713]*See* Sofaer memorandum of April 10 at page 16.

the Senate, and the Nation as a whole, would be better served in such cases by encouraging a subsequent administration to come forward when mistaken interpretations are discovered and to adopt the position that the United States is bound only to the extent the other treaty partner is bound. Indeed, arguably at least in the arms control area, there is a legal obligation on the Administration to promptly come forward with issues it discovers to have been mistakenly interpreted, and that it would be a violation of law to limit the Nation's arms by obligation except pursuant to a treaty approved by the Senate and reciprocally binding on the other treaty party or authorized by affirmative legislation of the Congress. It should be recalled that section 33 of the Arms Control and Disarmament Act of 1961 provides in part:

> [N]o action shall be taken under this or any other law that will obligate the United States to disarm or to reduce or to limit the Armed Forces or armaments of the United States, except pursuant to the treaty making power of the President under the Constitution or unless authorized by further affirmative legislation by the Congress of the United States.[714]

In this connection it should be noted that the Administration promptly came forward with the "broad" interpretation when, after more careful internal review of the issue than any previous administration, it determined that the "narrow" interpretation was not the most appropriate interpretation. To speak of an "estoppel" against a subsequent administration which discovers a mistake, or even an outright fraud, of an earlier administration, is to lose a potentially powerful tool in uncovering mistake and fraud and is a meaning of "estoppel" not normally associated with the term. And arguably such an estoppel would violate the spirit of section 33 of the Arms Control Act as well. It should also be noted that it is by no means clear whether there is any "estoppel" argument operating between the branches on major issues of separation of powers. Indeed, as previously discussed, even the existence, or at least the parameters, of any doctrine of "estoppel against government" are at present unclear.

---

[714]Arms Control and Disarmament Act of 1961, Pub. L. No. 87-297, § 33, 75 Stat. 631 (1961), 22 U.S.C. § 2573. This Act, it might be noted, refers to "the treaty making power of the President under the Constitution," which certainly is a power rooted only in agreement with another actor in international relations, not a general legislative power.

It should also be noted that it is clear that the President has authority to interpret treaties, at least in the absence of congressional action. It is also clear from the decision of the Supreme Court in the Fourteen Diamond Rings case[715] that a subsequent Senate, Senate committee, or member of the Senate, acting alone, has no authority to interpret a treaty consented to by a prior Senate. And it is clear that a treaty interpretation by the Executive branch is entitled to at least "great weight" before both the courts and the Congress. Given these absolutely clear legal principles, it would seem more political hyperbole than legal analysis to assert that "action to implement the 'reinterpretation' without formal acceptance by the Senate would provoke a constitutional crisis"[716] when a subsequent administration comes forward with what it believes to be, after more careful analysis of the issue than any previous administration, a legally permissible interpretation of a treaty, even if that interpretation sets aside an earlier interpretation as mistaken. Indeed, it can be said with considerably greater legal justification, that any action by the Senate to insist on formal Senate approval of a treaty interpretation in a specific dispute about international interpretation, with that interpretation intended to be binding on the President both nationally and internationally, and inconsistent with a prior executive interpretation, could "provoke a constitutional crisis."

Finally, it should, of course, be noted that Congress seems to have acted in the Defense Authorization Act of 1988 to limit Administration actions to those consistent with the "narrow" interpretation, at least for fiscal year 1988 and as rolled over into future fiscal years, as it has been in the National Defense Act for FY 1989. This action was apparently initially agreed by the Administration as a compromise to avoid a veto of the entire Defense Authorization Act without compromising the legal position of the Administration on the issue. It will, of course, expire absent an affirmative joint congressional-presidential understanding to extend it or a law passed over the President's veto. While apparently a short legal limit was at least minimally acceptable to the Administration, as has been seen, there is an issue as to whether this congressional action is constitutional. If the purpose of this provision is in fact solely to interpret a treaty in a specific interpretation dispute in opposition to a prior determination by the President, there is a significant constitutional issue as to whether Congress can do so. Under Article II, section 3, the President is directed to "take Care that the Laws be faithfully executed" and it can be questioned whether an action by Congress solely to interpret a treaty in

---

[715]Fourteen Diamond Rings v. United States, 183 U.S. 176 (1901).

[716]"Prepared Statement of Senator Joseph R. Biden, Jr.," *supra* note 207, at 152, 162.

opposition to a prior Executive branch decision would be an infringement on this executive power. It should also be recalled in this connection that executing the law, including its initial interpretation, is a core component of the executive function, and that Alexander Hamilton wrote in his first "Pacificus" letter of June 29, 1793, that "[t]he legislative department . . . is charged neither with making nor interpreting treaties." Indeed, Hamilton stated emphatically in this letter that as to non-litigated cases involving "external political relations of Treaties between Government and Government" the interpretation of treaties was not even shared by the judicial branch and that this authority was executive in nature. Jefferson told M. Genet in a conversation of July 10, 1793, that "the Constitution had made the President the last appeal" in seeing that treaties are observed. It also should be recalled that even Madison's "Helvidius" letter adopted the view that the President's power "[t]o see the laws faithfully executed constitutes the essence of the executive authority." Finally, it can be urged that if it is important to avoid politicization of treaty interpretation issues it would be preferable, on balance, that issues purely of interpretation should be viewed as exclusively executive.[717]

---

[717]One other argument of lesser weight might be made for the "broad" interpretation concerning congressional action in writing the "narrow" interpretation into law through the Defense Authorization Acts. While only a peripheral and arguable issue, action as presently being taken under the Defense Authorization Acts to limit the Executive branch to the "narrow" interpretation could, if that interpretation is not legally binding under the ABM Treaty, also present an issue of inconsistency with the letter or underlying policy of section 33 of the 1961 Arms Control and Disarmament Act. It should be recalled that section 33 contains an important proviso:

> [t]hat no action shall be taken under this or any other law that will obligate the United States to disarm or to reduce or to limit the Armed Forces or armaments of the United States, except pursuant to the treaty making power of the President under the Constitution or unless authorized by further affirmative legislation by the Congress of the United States.

The issue presented, of course, is whether action under the Defense Authorization Acts to write into national law the "narrow" interpretation, and without specifically adverting in the law to this as a purpose, is not simply a regular exercise of the appropriations power to withhold funding from a non-favored weapons system, but does instead as an authorizing law "obligate the United States . . . to limit the . . . armaments of the United States" based on a belief that the "narrow" interpretation

3. Appraisal

Issues concerning the treaty power within the "broad-narrow" debate occur within a broader context of separation of powers in foreign policy that has spawned debate across a broad range of issues throughout American history. It is clear, however, that the President has broad authority with respect to treaties, including the authority to interpret treaties and to suspend treaties in whole or in part in response to prior material breach of agreement,[718] in the absence of inconsistent congressional action. It is also clear that a subsequent Senate or Senate committee or other sub-unit, including individual senators, has no constitutional authority, acting alone, to authoritatively interpret a treaty previously consented to. It is also clear that both Congress and the judiciary should give "great weight" to treaty interpretations by the Executive branch, although at least in the private law area the courts have not necessarily viewed such interpretations as conclusive. It is unclear whether a subsequent Congress, as opposed to a subsequent Senate acting alone, can act solely for the purpose of interpreting a treaty provision contrary to a prior Executive branch interpretation in a specific interpretation dispute. This issue, involving the scope of the President's power to "take Care that the Laws be faithfully executed" is likely to remain uncertain and vigorously debatable. This issue is also complicated by the factual difficulty of determining whether a particular congressional action is solely for the purpose of treaty interpretation as

---

is correct but without either an underlying treaty obligation or "affirmative legislation" which would ensure a full congressional debate--with its enhanced congressional visibility--in both houses on the limitation and a realistic opportunity for presidential participation under the presentment clause. Substantial potential problems with this argument, at least as creating a legal obligation, apart from the underlying debate on the correct interpretation of the ABM Treaty, include whether the action taken under the Defense Authorization Acts would not constitute "affirmative legislation" within the meaning of the Arms Control and Disarmament Act, whether the action could be interpreted as "obligating" the United States within the meaning of the Act, and whether, in any event, a later congressional action would not take precedence over the earlier in time Arms Control and Disarmament Act.

[718]With respect to suspension of treaties in whole or in part in response to prior material breach of agreement there has, however, been some individual opinion to the contrary as discussed earlier in this part.

opposed to other congressional motivations. In the real world it is probably advisable to seek to comply with full congressional actions affecting treaty interpretation matters and to deal with such proposals through either acquiescence or veto while recognizing that congressional claims to interpret a treaty provision, solely for the purpose of interpreting a provision contrary to a previous Executive branch determination in a specific interpretation dispute may well be on shaky constitutional ground. Finally, the "broad-narrow" issue has focused a constitutional issue as to whether the appropriate focus of treaty interpretation is the meaning of the agreement under international law (the "unitary" approach) or whether if it can be shown that an at least two-thirds majority of the Senate informally adverted to and understood a different interpretation, even if such interpretation were not made a part of a Senate resolution of consent and communicated to the other party, then the informal Senate understanding would prevail as a matter of national law (the "dual" approach). The majority report of the Senate Foreign Relations Committee in *The ABM Treaty Interpretation Resolution*[719] seems to support the "dual" approach and this conclusion also seems to be supported by at least one knowledgeable constitutional scholar, Professor Louis Henkin of Columbia, and by the revised *Restatement of the Foreign Relations Law of the United States*, for which Professor Henkin served as Chief Reporter. The weight of authority, however, including at least one generally analogous decision in the *New York Indians* case, as well as the weight of policy argument and constitutional theory, would seem to support the "unitary" approach; and it is at least more likely than not that any direct test of this issue by the Supreme Court would hold for the "unitary" approach, contrary to the arguments in the report of the Senate Foreign Relations Committee.[720] Neither the recent opinion of Judge Harold H. Greene of the District Court for the District of Columbia in the *Rainbow Navigation* case--now on appeal--nor footnote 7 in Mr. Justice Brennan's opinion for the Court in the recent *Stuart* case, which at least arguably lend analogous support to the "dual" approach, addresses a setting of an interpretation dispute with a different meaning under the normal international law standard for treaty interpretation on the one hand and an informal Senate understanding or Executive branch statement to the Senate on the other. In both cases the evidence of treaty intent from all sources seemed congruent. Moreover, *Rainbow Navigation* is not only on appeal but seems principally a case concerning the legal effect of "domestic

---

[719]*The ABM Treaty Interpretation Resolution, supra* note 1.

[720]In light of the importance of these issues the Executive branch might want to consider a strategy for submitting them to the Supreme Court.

conditions" or Executive branch statements concerning such "domestic conditions" and on that issue is a single District Court decision seemingly at odds with a higher Court of Appeals ruling in the *Niagara Reservation* case (and the theory of the Supreme Court in the *New York Indians* case). And footnote 7 in the Stuart case deals principally with the proposition that Senate preratification materials may be considered in seeking to ascertain the intention of the treaty parties. Indeed, to the extent that it is a decision directly on point it suggests merely that at least one Justice of the Supreme Court would reject the "dual" approach since Justice Scalia's rejection of even the use of Senate preratification history would necessarily preclude such materials being given controlling weight.

What may be the principal policy argument for the "dual" approach, the argument that any other approach would require the Senate to concern itself in detail with the treaty negotiating record and endless understandings, may prove too much. For even if the "dual" approach were adopted, it would seem that a Senate should be concerned as to whether it is simply unilaterally obligating the United States or whether its interpretations are understood by and binding upon the other treaty parties and to achieve this latter objective it must also be concerned with the international negotiating record (or a detailed article-by-article treaty legal analysis) and materials clearly communicated to the other parties incident to United States ratification of the treaty. Moreover, the policy arguments for the unitary approach seem, on balance, quite strong, including the point that by definition whenever the issue arises the "dual" approach would always either mean that the United States would be in breach of its treaty obligations or bound more strictly by a treaty than its treaty partners. Since many, if not most, such issues will arise, as seemingly in the "broad-narrow" dispute, in a context in which both an Executive branch and a Senate have given an issue only peripheral attention, it seems preferable to follow the international meaning of the treaty as a means of curing oversight or mistake. Indeed, it can be asked with some force for the health of our foreign relations and arms control process, whether we should not encourage administrations to come forward with subsequently discovered mistakes in treaty interpretation where there is reason to believe another party never accepted a treaty obligation being followed as binding by the United States. That is, is there any more compelling reason to bury our mistakes in the treaty process than anywhere else? Particularly in the arms control area, do we wish as a nation to adopt a rule that a mistake or oversight in initial Senate consideration could mean that the United States will assume unilateral arms control restraints not binding on another party? It should be noted here that under the "dual" approach a purely Senate mistake or oversight would inflict the same cost on the Nation in this respect as an Executive branch oversight or mistake. And it should be noted that the "dual" approach could potentially seriously complicate United States participation in international adjudication. Whatever the appropriate legal rule, "dual" or "unitary," it is clear that any administration must proceed candidly and fully to inform a Senate of the meaning of a treaty.

While the weight of authority, policy, and constitutional theory would seem to lend greater support to the "unitary" than to the "dual" approach to treaty interpretation under the Constitution, there is a possible but seemingly still less desirable "intermediate" approach that seems not to have been adverted to in the debate and that may also present a reasonable resolution of this difficult issue. That is, an approach requiring that any treaty obligation binding on the United States under national law be *both* an internationally agreed obligation (usually binding on each side to the treaty but in some settings reflecting reciprocal *quid pro quos* and asymmetrically binding) *and* understood as such by a consenting Senate (interpreted as understood from a Senate vote for advice and consent unless formal Senate action, or the record of informal "treaty history" in the Senate as interpreted by normal rules for ascertaining the concurrence of a two-thirds majority of the Senate, indicate otherwise). Under such an "intermediate" approach the United States would, *for purposes of national law*, never be bound to a treaty obligation which formal Senate action (never a problem under any theory, of course), or the normally interpreted record of informal "treaty history" in the Senate, shows was specifically not believed by the Senate to be an obligation binding on the United States. That is, a demonstration, whether through formal or informal action (in the case of informal action as demonstrated pursuant to the normal rules for ascertaining "legislative" or "treaty" history within the Senate), that a Senate believed the United States was not obligated by a treaty to a particular action or inaction would suffice to render such obligation not binding under national law but, of course, the Nation would still be bound under international law unless either formal Senate action had been communicated to the other treaty party or the informal action were of a kind and circumstance that falls under the recognized "manifest" violation of "a rule of its internal law of fundamental importance" principle of international law. Conversely, a Senate informal expectation of obligation would not be binding nationally or internationally absent an objectively based assessment that the treaty did in fact create an underlying obligation (usually binding on both sides of the treaty but in some settings intentionally asymmetrical). That is, to be binding under national law there must be *both* an international treaty obligation and an absence of a specific contrary indication of Senate intent. This would, of course, have the virtue of eliminating that class of settings under the "dual" approach which would bind the United States to a treaty obligation that is not binding on the other side of the treaty. Such an "intermediate" approach deals with the two logically possible categories of divergence between national and international law under the "dual" approach by treating as binding under national law that class where informal Senate action (as normally demonstrated by examination of "legislative" or "treaty" history) results in the United States violating an international treaty obligation but would not bind the United States in that other class of cases where the underlying treaty itself creates no obligation binding on the United States. In support of such an "intermediate" approach, it would ensure that no treaty obligation would become nationally binding on the United States (as, of course, opposed to internationally binding) in settings where a two-thirds majority of a consenting Senate specifically believed there was no such obligation (whatever the underlying international reality), and it would ensure that, whatever a consenting Senate believed, the United States would not be obligated under national law by the treaty approval process where it was not obligated under the underlying treaty. This "intermediate" approach might be supported by a theoretical constitutional argument that action to be binding under the treaty clause requires two independent and necessary conditions. First, that the obligation in question is an obligation created by the treaty in fact, and second, that the record of Senate advice and consent not demonstrate that the Senate had a different understanding.

In opposition to this "intermediate" approach, it might be argued from the perspective of the "unitary" approach that such an approach still sets up a constitutional process in the United States which, whenever it were to create a gap between national and international law in a setting of international obligation, would compel the Nation to violate its solemn treaty commitments by virtue of a process not conveyed to the other treaty party. This would not be consistent with the United States setting a high standard in support of the rule of law among nations and fairness in international dealings. Moreover, it can be argued that the Senate should be encouraged to act through formal means such as reservations or understandings conveyed to the other treaty party on issues of importance which will enhance these goals while fully protecting Senate action. And in this connection it can also be noted that encouraging formal Senate action reduces the risk of uncertainty as, for example, has plagued the "broad-narrow" issue. From the perspective of the "dual" approach it might be argued that this approach would unfairly disregard an understanding of a Senate that a treaty created a particular obligation binding on the United States (even if the underlying treaty reality was that it did not, and thus the United States, if bound under national law by the informally expressed Senate understanding, would be bound to an obligation not binding on the other treaty party).

The author of this study regards the "unitary" rule as the approach reflecting the stronger constitutional bases and supporting policy reasons, and particularly would stress the importance of a constitutional process concerning treaty approval which would uphold the rule of law in the international obligations of the United States. Nevertheless, the "intermediate" approach offers an alternative meeting several of the strongest policy concerns underlying both "unitary" and "dual" approaches. It can also be argued that its theoretical constitutional underpinning requiring *both* that an obligation be created by the underlying treaty *and* that it not be inconsistent with a Senate understanding to the contrary best effectuates the bifurcated nature of the treaty adoption and approval process in the Constitution and respects both the presidential role in negotiating treaties and the Senate role in approving treaties. As such, this "intermediate" approach may be a reasonable alternative for resolution of a difficult issue. In this connection, it should be noted that even if the "intermediate" approach were adopted over the "unitary" approach, the "broad-narrow" setting is one in which the issue is whether the treaty itself created a binding obligation. Thus, for this setting both "unitary" and "intermediate" approaches would reach the same result. That is, a treaty obligation could be binding on the United States only in settings where the treaty itself contains such an obligation.

With respect to the specifics of the "broad-narrow" debate, on balance the arguments that the President may elect to act on the "broad" interpretation under national law seem stronger than those that he may not, leaving aside for a moment the recent congressional action associated at least initially with the 1988 Defense Authorization Act and in place for fiscal year 1988 and--as rolled over--fiscal year 1989[721] or later years. To prevail, an argument that the President may not elect to

---

[721]Or, of course, future fiscal years if this restriction is further rolled over into future Defense Authorization Acts. See Halverson, "House Passes Defense Budget Bill, Endorsing Traditional Interpretation," 18 *Arms Control Today* 16 (1988). This news note reports:

> As in 1987, the House restricted SDI to activities which would not violate the "narrow" or traditional interpretation of the ABM (Antiballistic Missile) Treaty. Last year, the Congress and the President compromised on language limiting SDI to tests outlined in its 1987 Annual Report to Congress, which asserted that all planned tests complied with the narrow interpretation, rather than referring directly to the treaty. This year, the House voted to hold the SDI Organization to similar commitments made by DOD Undersecretary of Defense for Acquisition Robert B. Costello in congressional testimony.

Id. See also House Votes to Restrict Missile Defense Program, Wash. Post, Apr. 28, 1988, at A3, cols. 1-6. According to this report of the House action:

act on the "broad" interpretation as a matter purely of national law must show both that as a matter of constitutional law the "dual" approach is correct and that under recognized principles of "legislative" or "treaty history" as an extrinsic aid to interpretation an at least two-thirds majority of the 1972 consenting Senate adverted to and adopted the "narrow" interpretation, or for some other reason the Executive branch is bound to the "narrow" interpretation by statements made to the 1972 consenting Senate. But, as we have seen, on balance the "unitary" and not the "dual" approach is probably constitutional law. And, on balance as well, the available record is not most reasonably read as demonstrating that an at least two-thirds majority of the Senate both adverted to and adopted the "narrow" interpretation as binding on the United States regardless of Soviet intentions to be bound. Finally, the law and the factual record of Senate consideration does not, on balance, support an argument that a subsequent administration is bound to the "narrow" interpretation by statements made to the 1972 consenting Senate by the Nixon Administration.

One element largely lacking to date in assessment of the record of Senate consideration of the "broad-narrow" issue is careful appraisal of the overall record under recognized principles for assessing "legislative or treaty history." The most

---

> As with last year's compromise, the amendment makes no specific mention of the treaty itself or how it ought to be interpreted, but bars spending on any antimissile defense program that "is inconsistent" with stated Pentagon SDI plans for next year. Pentagon officials testified before Congress this year that they do not plan any testing that would violate the traditional interpretation of the treaty, but the administration has taken no position on the amendment adopted by the House yesterday.

Id. at cols. 1-2. This report also suggests that the action on the "broad-narrow" issue significantly reflected party lines. Thus, the report says: "Democratic leaders of the House are pressing arms control restrictions because of continuing disagreements with the White House"; and "Republican lawmakers argued unsuccessfully yesterday that the Democratic restrictions represent an outmoded partisan reflex"; but "Aspin [House Armed Services Committee Chairman Les Aspin] also defended the ABM Treaty amendment as a continuation of last year's rapprochement with the administration. `All of us know we are kicking the can down the road' until the next administration takes office, said Aspin." *Id.* at cols. 4, 6.

For a discussion of action on the 1989 fiscal year provision, see *supra* text at note 634. *See also* the final FY 1989 restriction set out in full, *supra* note 634.

important indicators of "treaty history" intent during Senate consideration are Executive branch transmittal documents, statements of knowledgeable lead administration witnesses--particularly their prepared statements, committee reports, and the Senate resolution of consent. None of these principal indicators of "treaty history" intent unambiguously support either "broad" or "narrow" interpretations. Their failure to do so strongly suggests that it was highly unlikely that an at least two-thirds majority of the 1972 consenting Senate both adverted to and understood the "narrow" interpretation as correct. To the extent that there are indicators in this category they are the three exchanges by Ambassador Gerard C. Smith, the head of the SALT I Delegation, during committee hearings at least tilting toward the "broad" interpretation while probably most fairly regarded as ambiguous. With respect to hearings before the lead committee, the Senate Foreign Relations Committee, Senator Buckley gave testimony unambiguously embracing the "narrow" interpretation, and one of the exchanges involving Ambassador Smith and at least tilting toward the "broad" interpretation, with senior SALT I Delegation members accompanying Ambassador Smith and with the Secretary of State present, occurred in this hearing. Given the probable principle of "treaty history" that a statement of the lead United States negotiator is almost certainly entitled to considerably greater weight than that of a Senator in opposition to the treaty, it would seem that this hearing should be regarded as at least mixed. And the hearing before the Senate Armed Services Committee, not the lead committee on the treaty, shows approximately eight exchanges that can reasonably be regarded as addressing the issue and that at least lean toward one or the other interpretation. Of these, two exchanges involve Ambassador Smith, the lead and most knowledgeable administration witness on the ABM Treaty, and both can most fairly be characterized at least as "ambiguous but leaning toward the `broad' interpretation." Two exchanges (including as one of these additional information interposed in the record) involve Dr. John Foster, Jr., Director of Defense Research and Engineering, and might be regarded as "ambiguous but lean toward the `narrow' interpretation." Two exchanges involve General Bruce Palmer, Acting Chief of Staff of the Army and not a member of the SALT Delegation, with the first of these exchanges most reasonably characterized as "leaning toward the `broad' interpretation" and even arguably characterizable as "clear for the `broad' interpretation" and the second "clear for the `narrow' interpretation." One exchange involves General John Ryan, Air Force Chief of Staff, in a setting involving questioning by Senator Jackson, that can be most fairly characterized as "ambiguous but leaning toward the `narrow' interpretation." And the last is a written response to Senator Goldwater from the Department of Defense that is most reasonably viewed as "ambiguous but leans toward the `narrow' interpretation." These exchanges before the Armed Services

Committee also demonstrate that Senator Jackson probably believed that the "narrow" interpretation was correct. This record suggests that there was also less than great clarity on the issue before this non-lead Armed Services committee, with only Senator Jackson and General Palmer, who was not a member of the SALT I Delegation, making unambiguous statements supporting the "narrow" interpretation and Ambassador Smith, the lead administration witness tilting toward the "broad" interpretation twice. Even apart from any ambiguity, with respect to the hearing records before both committees, it is reasonably clear that committee hearings are entitled to less weight than other principal indicators, in part because it is a considerable leap from views of individual witnesses and committee members to a view shared by an at least two-thirds majority of the Senate. And with respect to the "floor debate" on the ABM Treaty, the record of the debate, lasting only one day, suggests that the "broad-narrow" issue was only peripherally addressed, with Senator Buckley, an opponent of the Treaty making an unambiguous statement reflecting the "narrow" view, Senator Thurmond making a statement most reasonably characterized as "ambiguous but leaning to the `narrow' interpretation," and Senator Fong making a statement that can be reasonably regarded as "ambiguous but leans toward the `broad' interpretation." Statements in floor debate, even if it can be demonstrated that they were actually made on the floor, are generally not entitled to great weight as an indicator of overall legislative intent, and this would be particularly so if made by an opponent of a measure. Thus, an overview of the Senate record shows that the indicators that are entitled to principal weight on an interpretation issue did not support either "broad" or "narrow" interpretation and that only committee hearings and floor statements yielded any unambiguous statements for the "narrow" interpretation. Two of these were by an opponent, Senator Buckley, and, as such, are under recognized legislative history principles entitled to reduced weight; those by Senator Jackson occurred only in hearings before the Armed Services Committee and, in any event, Senator Jackson did not represent the Executive branch on treaty interpretation, and only a question and answer exchange with a non-lead administration witness in a non-lead committee hearing, where the witness had earlier participated in an exchange at least leaning toward the "broad" interpretation represented an "unambiguous" Executive branch exchange for the "narrow" view. On balance, this is not an overall "treaty history" record that can be fairly characterized as demonstrating that an at least two-thirds majority of the 1972 consenting Senate adverted to and understood the "narrow" interpretation as correct.

Even if the record could be read as demonstrating that an at least two-thirds majority of the Senate adverted to and understood the "narrow" interpretation, the overall context of the SALT "treaty history" record shows an unmistakable contemporary intention (because embodied in the Jackson Amendment adopted by both houses of Congress) that "Congress recognizes the principle of United States-Soviet Union equality reflected in the antiballistic missile treaty," and that Congress sought, at least in general terms, such equality in arms control agreements, and supported in particular "a vigorous research and development" program to follow United States acceptance of the SALT I agreements. Thus, it would almost certainly do violence to the intent of the 1972 consenting Senate, and particularly Senator Jackson as the principal sponsor of the Jackson Amendment and Senator Buckley as a supporter of the Jackson Amendment, to interpret the Senate as intending that the United States unilaterally adhere to the "narrow" interpretation even if, in fact, the Soviets had not accepted this interpretation. Given the legislative history of the Jackson Amendment as the principal legislative issue addressed by the Senate with respect to the SALT I agreements as a whole, it would seem important in any meaningful search for Senate intent on the "broad-narrow" issue to root that search in the overall context of Senate concerns and actions.

With respect to any argument that the views of the Executive branch witnesses expressed during Senate consent proceedings should be regarded as "authoritative" and binding or that such views might work an "estoppel" against the Presidency, neither legal authority nor factual application in the "broad-narrow" dispute lends significant weight to this view and, on balance, it should be rejected. Factually, the record of Senate consideration of the "broad-narrow" issue suggests that only one statement by an Executive branch official to the Senate can be clearly characterized as "unambiguous for the `narrow' interpretation." That was a statement during question and answer by General Bruce Palmer, Acting Chief of Staff of the Army, in a hearing exchange in the Senate Armed Services Committee between Senators Jackson, Dominick and Goldwater and General Leber, General Ryan and General Palmer. The overall setting, however, was one in which General Palmer was previously involved in a hearing exchange before the same committee that at least "leans toward the `broad' interpretation" and that could be regarded as "clearly adopting the `broad' interpretation." That is, on different occasions General Palmer seemed to convey opposite messages on the issue to the same committee: one way when questioned by Senator Goldwater who seemed to lean toward the "broad" interpretation, and another way when questioned by Senator Jackson who seemed to believe that the "narrow" interpretation was correct. General Palmer was not a lead witness for the Administration on the ABM Treaty, or a member of the SALT I Delegation that negotiated the treaty, did not make any written representations on the "narrow" interpretation, was testifying before a non-lead Senate committee, and was contradicted in testimony before the House by the Chairman of the Joint Chiefs. Indeed, the reader interested in reviewing the full context of General Palmer's testimony might at this point wish to refer to the considerably more detailed discussion of that testimony both set out and referenced in section III(E). Most importantly, neither the administration transmitted documents on the ABM Treaty nor any lead administration witness made any statement clearly supporting the "narrow" interpretation and, in contrast, the lead administration witness, Ambassador Gerard C. Smith, participated in three question and answer exchanges that could at least be regarded as "leaning to the `broad' interpretation." This is not a factual setting, even if there is any doctrine of "authoritative" administration witnesses or "estoppel" of the Presidency, that seems to reasonably present any such issue. But there is also at least great doubt as to whether there is any such doctrine in American constitutional law that would prevent a subsequent administration from raising a mistake or oversight--or indeed even the intentional fraud--of a prior administration occurring during presentation of a treaty to the Senate. Such a doctrine would require disregarding the international agreement as the root of the treaty obligation under the supremacy clause (an issue raised also in connection with the "broad-narrow" dispute) and would require a policy trade off either binding the United States to an obligation not accepted by the other treaty party or disregarding national treaty obligations for protecting original Senate intent in a setting where the Senate in any event could not know the cost to be imposed by the tradeoff. Every administration should take with great seriousness its obligation to fully and accurately inform the Senate in submission of treaties to the Senate. Arguments made in the "broad-narrow" dispute about "authoritative" statements of administration witnesses or "estoppel" of the Presidency by such statements seem, on balance, however, not to reflect sound law or sound policy.

Finally, it should be understood that the 1988 Defense Authorization Act seems to have adopted a formula widely regarded as writing the "narrow" interpretation into law at least for FY 1988, 1989, and as it may be extended by Congress into future years. As we have seen, while the authority of Congress is not clear when it acts solely to reverse a prior treaty interpretation by the President in a specific interpretation dispute, there is a significant constitutional argument to be made both for and against such authority, and together with inevitable uncertain associated factual issues as to the reason for the congressional action, prudence would suggest a policy of following such laws, even while the Executive branch is amply constitutionally justified in presenting its arguments that such congressional action may unconstitutionally interfere with the President's authority to "take Care that the Laws be faithfully executed" and, at least, fails to give the "great weight" due Executive branch treaty interpretations.[722] The President, of course, may veto the extension of any such laws to future fiscal years.

E. A Postscript on Constitutional and Other Issues Posed by S. Res. 167, the INF Treaty Interpretation Condition, and Related Proposals

The "broad-narrow" dispute has given rise to continuing demands by some members of Congress and supporters of the "narrow" interpretation that the Senate or Congress write the "narrow" interpretation into law.[723] There has, however, also been a demand by some members of Congress to codify what they view as principles concerning the relationship between Congress and the Executive branch with regard to treaties growing out of the "broad-narrow" dispute. This latter demand has stemmed from a central concern on the part of those favoring codifying certain treaty law principles that a treaty should be interpreted "as understood by the Senate." Both of these objectives were evident in S. Res. 167, the "ABM Treaty Interpretation Resolution." In introducing this resolution on March 11, 1987, Senator Joseph R. Biden, Jr. said:

> Mr. President, I am today introducing a Resolution entitled the "ABM Treaty Interpretation Resolution," designed to provide the vehicle for the Senate to make a formal and forceful statement concerning the treaty power in general and the ABM Treaty in particular. Since October 1985, the Administration has, through its pronouncements concerning a new and so-called "broad" interpretation of the Treaty, moved slowly but inexorably toward a constitutional confrontation with the Senate. The time is nearing for the Senate to be heard.
>
> Introduction of this resolution is timed to coincide with joint hearings conducted by the Judiciary and Foreign Relations Committees on its subject matter. These hearings have been

---

[722]Indeed, there may well be a better than even chance that an Executive view of the constitutional issues here would be upheld by the Supreme Court were it ever to be squarely addressed by the Court.

[723]As has been seen this has been done, at least in part, by a restriction contained in the FY 1988 Defense Authorization Act and operative during FY 1988 and--as rolled over--FY 1989 and in any future years when rolled over into successive fiscal year authorization acts.

designed to treat thoroughly the issues involved, and to establish a basis for action on the Resolution. The hearings will elicit testimony concerning the interpretation of the ABM Treaty as it was presented by the Executive branch in 1972, the interpretation as then understood by the Senate, and the constitutional imperatives which flow from the Senate having approved the Treaty on the basis of that interpretation. . . .

One considerable obstacle, however, blocks the way of this unilateral Executive action [adoption of the "broad" interpretation]: it is called the United States Constitution. Interpretation of the ABM Treaty, or any other, is not, constitutionally, subject to whim. In 1972, the ABM Treaty was formulated through the negotiation of a text of considerable clarity of meaning and purpose. Subsequently, representatives of the Executive branch presented the Treaty to the Senate with equal clarity, whereupon the Senate deliberated at length, reflecting through its questioning and debate an understanding of the Treaty consistent with the Executive presentation. And it was on that basis that the Senate, in the performance of its constitutional role, approved the Treaty's ratification -- enabling the Chief Executive to "make" the Treaty to which the Senate had consented.

During the 15 years since the ABM Treaty's entry into force, the United States and the Soviet Union have, in practice and with limited exceptions, abided by its terms as explained by the Executive and understood by the Senate in 1972. This "subsequent practice" has given the Treaty's original and long-standing interpretation additional weight under international law. Accordingly, the situation today may be plainly stated. Unilateral Executive action to implement a new interpretation of the ABM Treaty would represent not only a cavalier arrogance toward international law but a direct challenge to the Constitution's delineation of the treaty power. . . .

-- <u>Constitutional Confrontation.</u> Finally, action to implement the "reinterpretation" without formal acceptance by the Senate would provoke a constitutional crisis. The clarity of the ABM Treaty text, as explained by the Executive branch in 1972 and as understood by the Senate in consenting to ratification, leaves the Executive no latitude for the adoption of a changed interpretation, particularly one so drastic as has been promulgated. For the Executive branch to act on its "reinterpretation" would represent a severe challenge to the Constitution's delineation of the treaty power.

The Imperative of a Strong Senate Response

In the event of such a challenge, the Senate would face the question of recourse. One technique -- that of legislating compliance with the Treaty's correct interpretation -- could be effective on a policy level but would fail to meet the constitutional issue head-on. On the other hand, to bring the issue to resolution in the courts -- to render the question "justiciable" -- could be complex and time-consuming. It is therefore important, both to avoid court action if possible and to provide a basis for such action if necessary, that the Senate speak clearly and forcefully at an early point. Passage of the "ABM Treaty Interpretation Resolution" would provide that statement.

While the text of the Resolution is self-explanatory, one aspect within it warrants emphasis. In recent weeks public attention has been focused on the significance of the negotiating record -- inevitably, since the Administration cited that record in justifying the "reinterpretation" and then proceeded to deny Senate requests for access to the record. The general impression thereby created was that the negotiating record held a decisive significance as to the proper interpretation of this Treaty.

To accept that proposition, however, was to take a bite of the Administration's apple. For as eminent constitutional scholars have affirmed and as the Resolution expressly states, "during the period in which a treaty is in force, the meaning of that treaty is what the Senate understands the treaty to mean when it gives its advice and consent, a meaning which is informed by reference to expressions of intent by the Senate as well as Senate acquiescence in any interpretation communicated to the Senate." And, to the extent such meaning is clear, "anything not transmitted to the Senate, including the negotiating record, is not relevant to the meaning of the treaty."

In the case of the ABM Treaty, there can be little doubt that the harmony of the Treaty text, the presentation of the Executive branch in 1972, and the clearly evident interpretation of the Senate as a whole leaves no latitude at all for the kind of "reinterpretation" the Administration, with its lawyers, has conceived. The negotiating record -- while conceivably a relevant reference on minor, technical issues -- cannot in any way be determinative of proper interpretation of the ABM Treaty on the major questions the Administration's actions have brought to issue. In the absence of a formal Treaty amendment, which would require the formal consent of the Senate, those questions have been decided unalterably.

Conclusion: A Profound Strategic and Constitutional Issue

Mr. President, what is at issue here is decidedly not a lawyer's quarrel. We are witnessing a major assault on the premises and structure of a national nuclear strategy which a decade ago was supported overwhelmingly by the Senate, which on Monday of this week was reaffirmed by six former Secretaries of Defense, but which has been brought to issue by this Administration. We are also witnessing a subtle but equally significant assault on the Constitution's allocation of the treaty power. . . .[724]

---

[724]Excerpts from "Prepared Statement of Senator Joseph R. Biden, Jr.," supra note 207, at 252, 254, 262-63.

A statement of William R. Harris before the Committee on Foreign Relations develops the following arguments, among others, against proposals such as that contained in S. Res. 167:

> It is important that the Senate seek to interpret treaty rights and duties that apply equally to both parties. The record of the Senate can be designed to do so, or it can be designed to interpret only U.S. rights and place restrictions upon them. But this is, over the long run, self-defeating.
>
> A treaty is fundamentally a contract between sovereign nations. As John Jay put it in *The Federalist* No. 64, "a treaty is only another name for a bargain".
>
> Under international law, the Soviet Union may consult the negotiating records of a treaty to ascertain rights and duties that are not dispositively treated by the treaty instruments. Secretary of State Rogers indicated during this Committee's hearings on SALT I, "if questions of interpretation arise in the future, we certainly will go back and look at the memoranda because there wasn't a complete transcript kept of the plenary sessions...."
>
> Proposals to prohibit an equal right for the U.S. to consult the negotiating record

of a treaty (e.g. S. Res. 167) or to bind the United States but not the Soviet Union to an interpretation that may give greater rights to the Soviet side are contrary to the foreign policy and national security interests of the United States. Moreover, Senators who seek to facilitate treaty verification should bear in mind that interpretations that can bind only the United States will not be dispositive in verifying Soviet treaty compliance.

For nearly two centuries the Senate has assured that there are mutual obligations and rights under a treaty, and that the ratification process not leave the United States with fewer treaty rights and more onerous treaty duties than other treaty parties. The Senate is free to later restrict U.S. rights by inconsistent legislation, but the Senate has heretofore sought to assure mutuality of rights and obligations in the treaty ratification process.

The Continental Congress made sure that the ratification process was not an impediment to an effective foreign policy by delegating negotiating powers to three negotiators, including Benjamin Franklin, "promising in good faith to ratify whatsoever our said commissioners should transact in the premises..."

Under the U.S. Constitution, the President and the Senate initially avoided greater restrictions than provided by a treaty through a process of prior consultation. In the period 1790 to 1795 the Senate consulted with the President and gave its advice and consent before a treaty was signed. Thereafter, with rare exceptions, the President signed a treaty and then submitted it for Senate advice and consent before presidential ratification. But the Senate was careful to place any qualifications in the resolution of advice and consent to ratification. This assured that restrictions that might affect the United States would also affect other treaty parties if the qualification were included in the exchange of protocols of ratification.

In the 1806 revision of the Senate rules, the predecessor of Rule XXX - then Rule XXXVII -- provided that the Senate as a whole would, if at all, modify the whole or any part of a treaty. Combining this rule with Rule XXXVI, requiring secrecy for the treaty and its proceedings, the Senate had in place procedural safeguards to assure that an interpretation of a treaty in committee would not result in fewer rights and greater duties for the United States than for other treaty parties. From 1806 to 1929 these two rules -- XXXVI and XXXVII -- assured mutuality of obligations and avoided conflicts between interpretation of Senators in committee and qualification of a treaty by the Senate as a whole.

It was a prior disarmament treaty -- the Kellogg-Briand Peace Pact aimed at the outlawry of war among nations -- that raised the problem later confronted in interpretation of the ABM treaty: should the Senate impose a set of treaty restrictions and interpretations by giving peremptory status to statements before or findings of a Senate Committee. In other words, should the Senate modify its rules and customary practices of two centuries so as to bind the United States alone, or should the Senate assure equal rights and duties among all treaty parties?

The demand for public testimony and a public report on the "multilateral peace pact" of 1928 led to a revision of the Rules affecting the Committee on Foreign Relations, S. Res. 11 of January 1929. Nearly sixty years ago, for the first time, the Senate Foreign Relations Committee decided to write a public report interpreting a treaty and submit that report to the Senate prior to consideration of the resolution of ratification. The distinguished Chairman of the Committee on Foreign Relations, Senator William E. Borah of Idaho, indicated that "the treaty as signed is that which is to guide." Senator Barkley explained, "...this treaty cannot mean one thing for one nation and another thing for another nation..."

Senator Borah made sure that the report filed with the Senate not create inconsistent restrictions under domestic law than those established by the treaty under international law. The report read:

> "This report is made solely for the purpose of putting upon record what your committee understands to be the true interpretation of the treaty, and not in any sense for the purpose or with the design of modifying or changing the treaty in any way or effectuating a reservation to the same."

Senator William H. King of Utah considered the Report an explanation of the views of the committee members of what the treaty meant. His remarks have a pertinence today as some would propose to leave the United States with fewer treaty rights than its treaty partners by arbitrarily binding the United States to a set of limits that may not bind other parties:

> "...Mr. President, I have respect for the members of that [Foreign Relations] committee, but their interpretation of the treaty, I submit, should not be controlling upon Senators. If the treaty is ambiguous and uncertain then it should perhaps be amended, or at any rate, ambiguities should be removed by explanatory reservations. Where an instrument is clear and unambiguous, then interpretations are not needed. The duty rests upon Senators to determine as best they can the meaning of measures presented for their consideration. The responsibility rests upon them for their action... whatever information that bears on the treaty they are entitled to possess. Indeed, it is their duty to secure all available information, and having secured it and acquainted themselves with the treaty, the responsibility rests upon them when they vote upon the question of its ratification."

If the Senate has a set of concerns about the INF treaty or another treaty, and reduces these to an interpretative reservation that other treaty parties would find reasonable, then two advantages accrue to the United States: first, the United States acquires equal rights and duties relative to the interpreted provisions; and second, the interpretations will assist in verification of the other parties' compliance with their treaty duties.

In the alternative, U.S. unilateral statements -- as we have found with seven of them under SALT I -- have been recurringly disregarded by the Soviet Union without breaching a treaty duty.

A rule of peremptory limitation of U.S. treaty rights could occur if the Senate insists that statements made before it or interpretations by its Committees displace the contract terms between the treaty signatories. A peremptory limitation of U.S. treaty rights by a revised Senate rule -- a seeming shortcut on the path towards interpretative reservations that does not risk Soviet refusal to ratify -- has a variety of long term disadvantages.

The first is that diverging limits under domestic law will at best give the U.S. equal rights under a treaty, and may often gives [sic] the United States lesser rights.

Under the INF Treaty, for example, one may be concerned that Article II(3) and II(4) do not prohibit retention of multi-part launching systems for either ballistic or cruise missiles. Would it be illegal to convert SS-20 transporter-erector-launchers into ICBM transporters and to associate them with other equipment capable of erecting and launching ICBMs? If an official witness states that this type of conversion is illegal, then by providing peremptory status to these statements, the United States will be restricted from this type of conversion. But if the treaty does not unequivocally bar the Soviets from a similar conversion, only an interpretative reservation that is included in the instruments of ratification can assuredly bind both parties.

. . . .

An example of an executive agreement that could have fared far worse for the United States in treaty form, under S.Res. 167, involves the agreement on occupation zones for Germany, negotiated in the European Advisory Commission in 1944-45. The written records set forth with clarity the zones of occupation and the air corridors to Berlin. But the commitment to assure access over land was based on commitments by the Soviet Ambassador Gusev. Since the documentary records that would have been submitted to the Senate might have been "clear," i.e. access was provided by air, a "restrictive interpretation" of U.S. occupation rights in Germany might have led to the conclusion that access along the autobahn was not provided. If the memorandum quoting Ambassador Gusev were not considered during ratification, some would bar a later claim that the United States was entitled to access along the autobahn. The Berlin blockade of 1948-49 placed this right in temporary jeopardy. Recourse to the negotiating record and the success of the Berlin airlift combined to aid in the ultimate reaffirmation of this important right. Rules to limit U.S. rights through treaty interpretation will limit U.S. incentives to enter into treaties.

If there are ambiguities that are important and that may be resolved by reasonable interpretation, then if such interpretation should be acceptable to both treaty parties, the prudent course is to qualify the resolution of ratification with an interpretative reservation. Another prudent alternative is to set forth the findings of what the Committee understands the object and purpose and treaty clauses to mean, but to allow the executive department the latitude it has had for two centuries to reinterpret, subject to a duty of good faith, treaty obligations and rights in the light of changing circumstances. Given that a treaty is a contract, and that not all contingencies are foreseeable, this is a course the Senate might wish to consider.

Far less sensible, in my judgment, is the concept of proffering advice and consent to ratification upon the condition that the Senate be required to approve any change in an interpretation of treaty rights and duties by a sitting or subsequent President. In the field of trusts and estates, it is common for a person contemplating a will to attempt to impose his personal inclinations upon future generations, even under unforeseeable circumstances. The "rule against perpetuities" bars perpetual restraints upon the use of property as contrary to sound public policy. Do we need a similar rule to protect the treaty process from an unsustainable impairment?

One of the adverse consequences of conditioning advice and consent upon a Senate right of Senate veto over later reinterpretation is that this procedure would tend to encourage postponement of clarification of treaty rights and duties before the treaty is ratified. But this was one of the functions that the Founders considered a valuable aspect of the shared treaty making powers. If the Senate does not clarify the meaning of a treaty before it advises on its ratification, then the Senate has not met its constitutional responsibilities. Senator King's remarks of January 1929, quoted earlier, indicate a sound view: every Senator must seek to understand a treaty, help to make changes or interpretative reservations if necessary, and render a constitutionally based judgment on whether the treaty should be ratified.

Further, it is worth remembering that a treaty is not just a contract between or among nations but also an instrument of diplomacy. Hence, an effort of one Senate to condition and limit a later President's right to interpret the treaty in the light of diplomatic developments is to seek to impose a degree of inflexibility that is simply incompatible with the rapidly changing world in which we live.

There are powerful instrumentalities by which the Congress can affect public policy after a treaty has been ratified. First, the Congress can enact an inconsistent law that supersedes a treaty (without expunging its obligations). Second, the Congress can refuse to provide appropriations, or can provide appropriations with restrictions upon their application. These mechanisms have the advantage of complying with the procedures of the Constitution, including the presentment of legislation for approval or veto by the President.

Harris, *supra* note 348, at 9-12, 14-15 (footnotes omitted).

S. Res. 167 as reported by the majority of the Senate Foreign Relations Committee provided:

RESOLUTION CONCERNING CONSTITUTIONAL PRINCIPLES PERTINENT TO THE MAKING OF TREATIES, AND FURTHER CONCERNING THE INTERPRETATION OF THE TREATY BETWEEN THE UNITED STATES OF AMERICA AND THE UNION OF SOVIET SOCIALIST REPUBLICS ON THE LIMITATION OF ANTI-BALLISTIC MISSILE SYSTEMS

Resolved, That this Resolution may be referred to as the "ABM Treaty Interpretation Resolution."

THE TREATY POWER

SEC. 2. The Senate finds as follows:

(1)(A) Article II, section 2, clause 2 of the United States Constitution provides that the President "shall have power, by and with the advice and consent of the Senate, to make treaties, provided two-thirds of the Senator [sic] present concur".

(B) If, following Senate advice and consent, the President proceeds to ratify a treaty, the President may ratify only the treaty to which the Senate advised and consented.

(2) Under the United States Constitution--

(A) a treaty is properly interpreted in good faith in accordance with the ordinary meaning to be given its terms in light of their context and in light of its object and purpose;

(B) the meaning is to be determined in light of what the Senate understands the treaty to mean when it gives its advice and consent;

(C) the understanding of the Senate is manifested by any formal expression of understanding by the Senate, as well as by other evidence of what the Senate understood the treaty to mean, including Senate approval or acceptance of, or Senate acquiescence in, interpretations of the treaty by the Executive branch communicated to the Senate;

(D) the Senate's understanding of a treaty cannot be informed by matter of which it is not aware, such as private statements made during the negotiations that were not communicated to the Senate; and

(E) any subsequent practice between the parties in the application of the treaty is to be taken into account in interpreting the treaty.

(3) The President may not amend a treaty without the agreement of the parties and the advice and consent of the Senate.

(4)(A) Article VI of the Constitution provides that "All Treaties made . . . shall be the supreme Law of the Land".

(B) Under Article II, section 3, clause 4 of the Constitution, the President is required to "take Care that the Laws be faithfully executed".

SENATE CONSIDERATION OF THE ABM TREATY

SEC. 3. The Senate further finds as follows:

(1) On May 26, 1972, the Treaty between the United States of America and the Union of Soviet Socialist Republics on the Limitation of Anti-Ballistic Missile Systems (hereafter in this Resolution referred to as the "Treaty") was signed by the two parties.

(2) On June 13, 1972, the President of the United States transmitted the Treaty to the Senate and requested that the Senate advise and consent to its ratification.

(3) On August 3, 1972, the Senate, by a vote of 88-2, gave its advice and consent to ratification of the Treaty.

(4) Between June 6, 1972, and August 3, 1972, representatives of the President communicated to the Senate the interpretation of the President concerning various provisions of the Treaty.

TEXT OF THE ABM TREATY

SEC. 4. The Senate further finds as follows:

(1) Article I of the Treaty provides that "Each party understakes [sic] not to deploy ABM systems for a defense of the territory of its country and not to provide a base for such a defense," except for certain limited deployments of fixed, land-based systems as stipulated in Article III.

(2) Article II of the Treaty provides that an "ABM system is a system to counter strategic ballistic missiles or their elements in flight trajectory" and notes that such systems "currently" consist of ABM interceptor missiles, ABM launchers, and ABM radars.

(3) Article V of the Treaty provides that "Each party undertakes not to develop, test, or deploy ABM systems or components which are sea-based, air-based, space-based, or mobile land-based."

(4) Article XIV of the Treaty provides that "Each party may propose amendments to this Treaty."

(5) Article XV of the Treaty provides that "This Treaty shall be of unlimited duration."

(6) Article XV of the Treaty provides further that "Each party shall, in exercising its national sovereignty, have the right to withdraw from this Treaty if it decides that extraordinary events related to the subject matter of this Treaty have jeopardized its supreme interests."

(7) Agreed Statement D, which was transmitted to the Senate as part of the Treaty, is intended "to insure the fulfillment of the obligation not to deploy ABM systems and their components except as provided in Article III of the Treaty," by providing that, if fixed land-based "ABM systems based upon other physical principles and including components capable of substituting for ABM interceptor missiles, ABM launchers, or ABM radars are created in the future," their deployment would be subject to amendment by the parties in accordance with Article XIV.

INTERPRETIVE COMMUNICATIONS OF THE EXECUTIVE DURING SENATE CONSIDERATION OF THE TREATY

SEC. 5. The Senate further finds that during Senate consideration of the Treaty, representatives of the President communicated to the Senate--

(1)(A) with respect to Article II thereof, that the term "ABM systems and components" should be construed functionally, meaning that the term was not limited to currently existing technology or any specific technology, but applied to any ABM systems and components functionally able to counter strategic ballistic missiles or their elements in flight trajectory;

(B) that among such representations affirming that Article II should be construed functionally was the Secretary of State's formal Letter of Submittal, dated June 10, 1972, which stated (in a section entitled "Future ABM Systems") that "Article II(1) defines an ABM system in terms of its function as a `system to encounter strategic ballistic missiles or their elements in flight trajectory,' noting that such system `currently' consist of ABM interceptor missiles, ABM launchers, and ABM radars"; and

(2) consequently, with respect to Article V thereof, that the undertaking not to develop, test, or deploy any sea-based, air-based, space-based, or mobile land-based ABM systems or components should be construed as applicable to any ABM system functionally able to counter strategic ballistic missiles or their elements in flight trajectory.

INTERPRETIVE COMMUNICATIONS OF THE EXECUTIVE FOLLOWING RATIFICATION OF THE ABM TREATY

SEC. 6. The Senate further finds as follows:

(1) After ratification of the Treaty, representatives of the President formally and consistently reaffirmed that the prohibition in Article V of the Treaty applies to the development, testing, and deployment of any sea-based, air-based, space-based, or mobile land-based ABM systems and components designed to counter strategic ballistic missiles or their elements in flight trajectory.

(2) Beginning in 1978 (the first year an annual Arms Control Impact Statement was required to be submitted to Congress), the Arms Control and Disarmament Agency, on behalf of the President, consistently reaffirmed that the Treaty prohibits the development, testing, and deployment of all types of sea-based, air-based, space-based, or mobile land-based ABM systems and components, including ABM systems and components involving technologies not in existence when the Treaty was ratified.

(3) Among such statements was the 1985 Arms Control Impact Statement, which stated that "The ABM Treaty prohibition on development, testing, and deployment of space-based ABM systems, or components for such systems, applies to directed energy technologies (or any other technology) used for this purpose."

OBJECT AND PURPOSE OF THE ABM TREATY

SEC. 7. The Senate further finds as follows:

(1) The object and purpose of the ABM Treaty is set out in Article I of the Treaty, in which each party undertakes "not to deploy ABM systems for a defense of the territory of its country and not to provide a base for such a defense."

(2) Inasmuch as Article XV stipulated a Treaty of unlimited duration, the functional interpretation of Article II is central to such object and

purpose of the Treaty because technological advancement would render significant prohibitions in the Treaty inoperative if Article II were construed to apply only to ABM systems and components existing on the date of ratification.

(3) Also central to such object and purpose is the prohibition against the development, testing, or deployment of any sea-based, air-based, space-based, or mobile land-based ABM systems or components for the purpose of countering strategic ballistic missiles or thir [sic] elements in flight trajectory, including ABM systems or components involving exotic technologies.

(4) This prohibition was communicated to the Senate during its consideration of the Treaty.

(5) This prohibition is supported by interpretive communications of the Executive while the Treaty was under consideration, by expressions of Senate intent during such period, and by subsequent, consistent practice and interpretation by both parties to the Treaty.

DECLARATION OF POLICY

SEC. 8. The Senate therefore declares that--

(1) under the United States Constitution, the meaning of the ABM Treaty is properly determined in accordance with the principles set forth in paragraph (2) of section 2 of this Resolution.

(2) the development, testing, or deployment of any sea-based, air-based, space-based, or mobile land-based ABM systems or components for the purpose of countering strategic ballistic missiles or their elements in flight trajectory, including ABM systems or components involving technologies not in existence when the ABM Treaty was ratified, would be inconsistent with the provisions of the Treaty and would require an amendment to the Treaty; and

(3) no amendment to the ABM Treaty may occur without the agreement of the parties and the advice and consent of the Senate.[725]

---

[725]"Text of S. Res. 167 (as reported)," in *The ABM Treaty Interpretation Resolution, supra* note 1, at Appendix B, 117-20.

In a forthcoming commentary in the *University of Pennsylvania Law Review*, Professor Phillip R. Trimble rejects what he refers to as "the entrenchment principle" he sees embodied in Senate Resolution 167. Thus, he writes:

The major premises underlying S. Res. 167 seem to be that the "narrow" interpretation of the ABM Treaty is not a legally permissible interpretation--indeed it is not an interpretation at all but rather an act of treaty creation or amendment,[726] that a two-thirds majority of the 1972 consenting Senate clearly adverted to and understood the "narrow" interpretation, and that the standard for treaty interpretation is "what the Senate understands the treaty to mean when it gives its advice and consent." While arguments can be made for each of these premises, such arguments are not helped by attacks on the State Department Legal Adviser,[727] by righteous invocation of the rule of law,[728] by charges of "constitutional confrontation,"[729] or

---

> Despite persistent efforts by Senator Biden and his allies to secure Senate endorsement of some form of the entrenchment principle, the Senate declined to do so -- for perfectly good reasons. The notion that a legal rule -- whether it is a constitutional provision, a contract term, or a treaty interpretation -- can be fixed or "entrenched," subject to change only by formal process, is clearly unsound. The idea of entrenchment, based on the shared understanding of the Executive branch and the Senate, is closely related to the nostalgic appeal to "original intent" as a way of ascertaining the meaning of the Constitution, and is subject to the same criticism.

Trimble, *supra* note 158, at 1465 (quoted from page proofs subject to final editing).

[726]*See also The ABM Treaty Interpretation Resolution, supra* note 1, at 39.

[727]*Id.* at 62-67.

[728]*See, e.g., id.* at 65.

[729]*See, e.g.,* the introductory statement of Senator Biden in introducing S. Res. 167 as set out above (*supra* note 724).

Professor Henkin, whose work provides the principal intellectual underpinning of the "dual" approach to treaty interpretation, writes in a recent article:

> In two hundred years of history under the Treaty Power there have been few issues of constitutional dimension. The ABM and INF controversies of 1987-88 masqueraded as issues of constitutional construction but were essentially, I think, reflections of political differences between independent constitutional bodies in the exercise of a shared role, which neither is happy to share.

Henkin, "Treaties in a Constitutional Democracy," *supra* note 402, at 426.

In a forthcoming commentary in the *University of Pennsylvania Law Review*, Professor Eugene V. Rostow, the former Dean of the Yale Law School, characterizes "[t]he real constitutional crisis of our times" in the following terms:

even by efforts to analogize the Administration position in the debate to the Iran-Contra affair.[730] More importantly, as this study concludes, on balance, the facts and law suggest that all three premises are incorrect, at least as restated to more accurately present the real issues. That is, that there is a significant interpretation issue concerning the "broad-narrow" debate (it is, after all, what the debate is about); that, on balance, the record of Senate consideration of the ABM Treaty under the facts and legal rules of "treaty history" interpretation does not support the conclusion that an at least two-thirds majority of the 1972 consenting Senate adverted to and understood the "narrow" interpretation, much less that in considering the full context of Senate action on the SALT I agreements a two-thirds majority of the Senate believed that the United States did or should adopt the "narrow" interpretation and restrict United States development even if the Soviets were not bound by this provision; and that, on balance, there is greater constitutional and policy support for the proposition that the appropriate standard for treaty interpretation is the single or "unitary" standard as to the meaning of the

---

> The real constitutional crisis of our times is not the tempest in a teapot which exercises Senator Nunn and Professor Koplow. More ominous even than the Court Packing Plan of 1937, it has been gaining in momentum for some forty or fifty years. Madison analyzed the crisis in several of his Federalist Papers, particularly Numbers 47 and 48. The greatest danger to the constitutional order and to the liberty of the citizen, Madison warned, was not the risk of a Presidential tyrant, which he regarded as slight, but the possibility that Congress would take over the powers of the other two branches of government. "The accumulation of all powers, legislative, executive, and judiciary, in the same hands," Madison wrote, "may justly be pronounced the very definition of tyranny." Power, in Madison's view, "is of an encroaching nature" and ought to be "effectually restrained from passing the limit assigned to it." The risk of encroachment by Congress is great, far greater than the risk from the President or the Courts. Congress "alone" has access to the pockets of the people. Its supposed influence over the people is an inducement to act, and it can expand its powers in many ways, "mask[ing], under complicated and indirect measures, the encroachments which it makes on the coordinate departments." Madison states that "it is against the enterprising ambition of this department that the people ought to indulge all their jealousy and exhaust all their precautions," and concludes by noting that "[t]he legislative department is everywhere extending the sphere of its activity, and drawing all power into its imperious vortex."

E. Rostow, *supra* note 351, at 1457-48 (footnotes omitted) (quoted from page proofs subject to final editing).

[730]*R. Garthoff, supra* note 684, at 1-2, 100-105.

treaty under recognized principles of international law, taking account of informal Senate understandings as they are incorporated under these rules. To the extent that S. Res. 167 also reflects the view that materials not before the Senate in its advice and consent deliberations may not be considered in treaty interpretation it is also, on balance, legally wrong.[731]

While the principal shortcomings of S. Res. 167 stem from its erroneous assumptions, a number of other more minor points may be usefully noted. "The treaty power" section states in section 2(B):

> If, following Senate advice and consent, the President proceeds to ratify a treaty, the President may ratify only the treaty to which the Senate advised and consented.

While this statement rolls off the tongue nicely and seems to be self-evident, in reality it is a verbal formulae concealing the serious legal and policy issues concerning the legal effect of informal Senate understandings, the legal effect of oversight or mistake in consideration--on the part of the Senate, a presenting administration, or both, and the constitutional and policy issues underlying the "unitary" and "dual" approaches. Just to ask one equally illusory seemingly self-evident question in response: If the President can not do so but does so anyway why is not the treaty void as a matter of national law rather than in force pursuant to the erroneous Senate understanding? Similarly, "the treaty power" section contains a classic example of what legal realists call legal rules travelling in pairs of complementary opposites in its sections 2(2)(A) and (B) that provide:

> (2) Under the United States Constitution--
>
> (A) a treaty is properly interpreted in good faith in accordance with the ordinary meaning to be given its terms in light of their context and in light of its object and purpose;
>
> (B) the meaning is to be determined in light of what the Senate understands the treaty to mean when it gives its advice and consent . . . .

While one can imagine interpretations squaring these provisions, it is certainly not

---

[731]This issue has been discussed earlier in this part, but to cite one recent case where materials not before the Senate have been considered in treaty interpretation at both original and appellate levels, *see Coplin v. United States*, 6 Cl. Ct. 115 (1984); and Coplin v. United States, 761 F.2d 688 (1985) (reversing the Claims Court decision).

evident on their face and this underlying complementarity may suggest that the draftsmen were aware of the risks in unambiguously embracing the "dual" approach looking solely to Senate intent for interpretation of treaties under national law while the international standard of interpretation would apply in the Nation's international obligations. Also, with respect to "the treaty powers" section, if the understanding of the Senate must be ascertained from information communicated to the Senate, as is suggested by section 2(2)(D), and "the meaning is to be determined in light of what the Senate understands the treaty to mean when it gives its advice and consent," as provided by section 2(2)(B), then how, and on what constitutional theory, is "subsequent practice," which is self-evidently not before the consenting Senate, "to be taken into account in interpreting the treaty" as provided by section 2(2)(E)? One is tempted to believe, perhaps unfairly, either that the draftsmen had not fully thought through their constitutional theory of treaty interpretation or, that as argued by many supporting the "narrow" interpretation, they believe that subsequent practice supports their position and, as such, it must be included prominently in the resolution, or both. Finally, with respect to "the treaty power" section, section 2(3) does not seem to appropriately take into account, as at least one complexity, that treaties may expressly or, in some settings where evident from context, implicitly permit amendment by act of Congress or the Executive branch through congressional-executive agreements or executive agreements pursuant to treaty.[732] Indeed, discussions of the Soviet Union and the United States within the Standing Consultative Commission (SCC) about the ABM Treaty may, in theory at least, provide such opportunities. It also does not specify that Senate "advice and consent" requires an at least two-thirds concurrence, although this may be implicit from section 2(1)(A) which does.

The section on the "Text of the ABM Treaty" rather blatantly restates the text using the device of commentary interspersed with quotes to support the "narrow" interpretation desired by the committee majority. Thus, the critical ambiguity in Article II reflected in the comma after "trajectory" with the language then appearing "currently consisting of:" is rewritten for the "narrow" interpretation by adding the language "and notes that such systems" in place of the comma without more between "trajectory" and "currently consisting of:" in the original text. And Agreed Statement D is rewritten to state that it was:

> intended "to insure the fulfillment of the obligation not to deploy ABM systems and their components except as provided in Article III of the

---

[732]*See, e.g.*, Moore, "Executive Agreements and Congressional Executive Relations," *supra* note 60, at 414-25.

> Treaty," by providing that, if fixed land-based "ABM systems based upon other physical principles and including components capable of substituting for ABM interceptor missiles, ABM launchers, or ABM radars are created in the future," their deployment would be subject to amendment by the parties in accordance with Article XIV.

The real text of Agreed Statement D, it should be recalled, provides:

> In order to insure fulfillment of the obligation not to deploy ABM systems and their components except as provided in Article III of the Treaty, the Parties agree that in the event ABM systems based on other physical principles and including components capable of substituting for ABM interceptor missiles, ABM launchers, or ABM radars are created in the future, specific limitations on such systems and their components would be subject to discussion in accordance with Article XIII and agreement in accordance with Article XIV of the Treaty.[733]

Thus, S. Res. 167 adds the critical language "fixed land-based" to modify ABM systems and components and substitutes for the ambiguous scope language of Agreed Statement D that "their deployment would be subject to amendment by the parties in accordance with Article XIV."[734] Surely, for a section beginning with the heading "Text of the ABM Treaty" this is rather disingenuous.

Section 5 on communications of the Executive branch to the Senate, section 6 on subsequent practice of the United States, and section 7 on object and purpose of the treaty all present the available argumentation on the "broad-narrow" issue incompletely and in an adversarial fashion for the "narrow" interpretation. The reader is invited to compare these statements with the discussion of arguments on both sides of the issue for each of these areas as previously discussed in this study.

The degree of liberty taken with the text of the ABM Treaty by S. Res. 167, coupled with the adversarial presentation of summary arguments for the "narrow" interpretation as presented in sections 5, 6, and 7 of that resolution hardly seem

---

[733]"Agreed Statement D" of the Treaty between the United States of America and the Union of Soviet Socialist Republics on the Limitation of Anti-Ballistic Missile Systems, May 26, 1972, 23 U.S.T. 3435, T.I.A.S. No. 7503 [the ABM Treaty].

[734]Even the provisions within quotes are wrongly quoted in several minor respects. The reader is invited to compare the description of Agreed Statement D in S. Res. 167 with the actual Agreed Statement D.

consistent with the high standards of scholarly integrity recommended in the majority report in its criticism of the study by the State Department Legal Adviser.

Senate Resolution 167 has not been enacted into law and at least this reviewer believes that it will be unlikely ever to be so enacted. While significant constitutional arguments can and have been made in its support,[735] on balance it would seem an unconstitutional effort to enact what this study has described as a "dual" approach, or some part of such an approach, into the constitutional law of treaty interpretation. Moreover, its provisions specifically interpreting the provisions of the ABM Treaty in the "broad-narrow" debate would at least present a constitutional issue as discussed previously concerning whether Congress may specifically take action overturning an Executive branch interpretation of a treaty in a specific interpretation dispute that would be consistent, among other issues in separation of powers, with the President's power and duty to "take Care that the Laws be faithfully executed."[736]

While S. Res. 167 has not been enacted into law, a second, informal effort to obtain Executive branch agreement to some of the tenets of the "dual" approach has taken the form of a request from Senators Robert C. Byrd and Sam Nunn to agree to three principles. As set out in their letter of February 5, 1988, to Secretary of

---

[735]The "Preface" to the hearing record on *The ABM Treaty and the Constitution* expresses appreciation to the following "for their assistance in the preparation of these hearings and for their consultation in the drafting of Senate Resolution 167. . . ." Professors Abram Chayes, Michael Glennon, Louis Henkin, Laurence Tribe and Seth Tillman and Mr. James Rubin, research director for the Arms Control Association. The *ABM Treaty and the Constitution, supra* note 1, at iii.

[736]In a November 1987 panel discussion on "The Treaty Power," Judge Abraham D. Sofaer, the State Department Legal Adviser, takes the view that section 8 of this resolution embodies an unconstitutional attempt at declaring "how the ABM Treaty should be interpreted." He says with respect to section 8:

> The committee asserts that "this section does not constitute a Senate interpretation of the ABM Treaty. The interpretation of treaties is the President's prerogative, so long as he interprets a treaty within constitutional parameters." Notwithstanding the committee's assertion, section 8 is a declaration as to how the ABM Treaty should be interpreted. As such, it is an unprecedented interference with the President's power to interpret treaties, and is inconsistent with treaty practice and Supreme Court precedent.

"Abraham D. Sofaer" in Koh, Nowak, Rees, Sofaer, "The Treaty Power," 43 *U. Miami L. Rev.* 101, 105-6 (Sept. 1988) (footnote omitted).

State George P. Shultz these three principles are:

> (1) The testimony of all Executive Branch witnesses and any submissions for the hearing record by the Executive branch on a Treaty can be regarded by the Senate as authoritative.
>
> (2) The meaning of the Treaty as presented to the Senate can be regarded by the Senate as authoritative without the necessity of the Senate's incorporating that testimony and material in its resolution of Ratification through understandings, reservations, amendments, or other conditions.
>
> (3) A meaning for the treaty different from that presented to the Senate by the Reagan Administration cannot be adopted without the approval of the Senate.[737]

Presumably, proposed principles 1 and 2 incorporate at least some of the tenets of the "dual" approach, although principle 1 focuses on an emphasis of Senator Nunn that the testimony of all Executive branch witnesses should be regarded as "authoritative." While the legal effect of "authoritative" is not defined, one possible meaning is that such Executive branch testimony would bind the delivering and all future administrations to the interpretation as presented. If that is intended by Senator Nunn to be the meaning, as seems to be suggested by his March 1988 testimony before the Senate Foreign Relations Committee on the INF Treaty, then it may well be a request to agree to an unconstitutional condition. First, as we have seen, such a requirement at least partially embodies the "dual" approach to treaty interpretation that, while debatable, on balance does not seem as strong as a matter of constitutional law and policy as the opposing "unitary" approach. Second, to ascertain the meaning of a treaty by any material presented to a Senate by the Executive branch, however informed or uninformed, informal or incidental, whether or not contradicted elsewhere in the overall record, and whether or not that material gives rise to a shared understanding by an at least two-thirds majority of the Senate, would not seem consistent with the constitutional requirement that a two-thirds majority of the Senate must consent and could easily do violence to the overall intent of the Senate. This is at least as clear a constitutional process defect as the one-house veto struck down in the *Immigration and Naturalization Service v.*

---

[737] Letter from Senators Robert C. Byrd and Sam Nunn to Secretary of State George P. Shultz (Feb. 5, 1988).

Chadha case. Note that such a rule could potentially create an obligation binding under national law by the action of a single Executive branch official--no matter how junior or uninformed. In contrast, however, our constitutional processes clearly do not permit a committee of Congress, or even a single house of Congress, acting alone, to create binding national law. Similarly, section 33 of the Arms Control and Disarmament Act of 1961 embodies a congressionally established policy that even the entire Executive branch acting on clear presidential instructions cannot obligate the United States to limit its armaments "except pursuant to the treaty making power of the President under the Constitution or unless authorized by further affirmative legislation by the Congress of the United States." And by the Constitution the treaty power is given to *the President* by and *with the Advice and Consent of the Senate*. It is not given to a single Executive branch official absent a showing that a President has "made" such a treaty obligation and that an at least two-thirds majority of a Senate understood and consented to such an obligation. Indeed, would such a rule permitting a binding national obligation by the action of a single Executive branch official, whether or not authorized by the President, two-thirds of the Senate, or the normal legislative process, be at all consistent with the concepts of separation of powers and checks and balances which serve as cornerstones of the American constitutional system? And third, to seek to "bind" a future administration to an oversight, mistake, or even deliberate fraud of an earlier administration as to a legal meaning of a treaty may well be inconsistent with the power and duty of the President to "take Care that the Laws be faithfully executed." As discussed earlier, apart from these considerable constitutional issues, there is a substantial policy issue as to why a Senate should prefer that an Executive branch mistake or oversight as to the precise meaning of a treaty should be dealt with by a solution either requiring the United States to violate its treaty obligations or unilaterally adhere to an obligation not binding on the other treaty party, an outcome as alien and unknown to the consenting Senate as the fact that the information presented to it was erroneous. While not a constitutional concern, the Byrd-Nunn first condition would also seem inconsistent with recognized legal principles of "legislative history" as an extrinsic aid to interpretation. Such history differentiates contextually as to the setting of any such statement within an overall record and all statements are not treated alike as they are under the Byrd-Nunn condition. Indeed, this very contextuality denied by the Byrd-Nunn condition is a critical element in modern theories of "interpretation."

One other paradox of the proposed Byrd-Nunn principle is would the Senators propose, as this principle would seem to, that a subsequent treaty interpreter should give greater weight--because presumably it is binding--to any statement in the record, no matter how minor, from an Executive branch official, than to a clear and important statement from the Senate embodied, for example, in the principal committee report? If so, why should the Senate support a doctrine that would so alter normal rules of construing legislative history as to denigrate the authority of statements and actions of the Senate during consideration of treaties? If, to the contrary, Senators Byrd and Nunn do not intend that "authoritative" means "binding," what is the intent of the proposal and what standard differing from normal "treaty history" rules are they proposing?

The Byrd-Nunn second condition is largely the functional equivalent of the first because the issue does not arise in any setting where a Senate understanding is formally adopted as a condition to Senate consent and is then communicated to and accepted by the other treaty partners. As such, the constitutional and policy concerns previously explored in this part would also apply here. It should be noted that this second condition mirrors in conception the position in the revised *Restatement of the Foreign Relations Law of the United States*, adopted without citation of authority, of the "dual" approach concerning the effect of informal Senate understandings under national law. Yet it changes that focus to "[t]he meaning of the Treaty as presented to the Senate" rather than the revised *Restatement's* standard of a "statement of [Senate] understanding." Moreover, it even leaves out the important *caveat* in the revised *Restatement* that "the President must decide whether they [the indicators of an informal Senate understanding] represent a general understanding by the Senate and if he finds that they do, must respect them in good faith."[738] Thus, this second condition would also seem to present formidable issues of constitutional law and policy as well as of important general legal principles of "interpretation." Indeed, it should be emphasized that other than sweeping language in a recent District Court opinion by Judge Harold H. Greene in the *Rainbow Navigation* case in a setting concerning "domestic conditions" and not involving any discrepancy between an Executive branch statement and the international meaning of a treaty--and now on appeal, there seems no significant authority, even by analogy, for the proposition that such Executive branch statements are *ipso facto* "binding" regardless of Senate understanding or intent of the treaty parties.

The Byrd-Nunn third condition mirrors the assumptions underlying the first two but adds a new element. That is, if a future change in the meaning of a treaty different from that presented to the Senate by a presenting administration is to be made, it can only be made with "the approval of the Senate." As we have seen, however, it is clear constitutional law that a subsequent Senate, as such, has no constitutional authority to give an interpretation of a treaty consented to by a prior Senate. Thus this condition would seem to embody an additional reason for

[738] *1985 Revised Restatement, supra* note 187, § 314, comment d, at 82 (314-3).

regarding it as at least constitutionally suspect. Moreover, this third condition simply requires "approval of the Senate," as opposed to the constitutional standard for "advice and consent" of an at least two-thirds majority. It is unknown by what theory of law Senators Byrd and Nunn propose to give a simple majority of the Senate, acting alone, a law or treaty making role.[739]

---

[739]Would it be any more unfair than the continuing invocation of a "Sofaer doctrine" based largely on two sentences in testimony by Judge Sofaer and ignoring substantial subsequent clarifications of his position, to regard this remarkable assertion in point three of the Byrd-Nunn three principles as the "Byrd-Nunn doctrine"? The author of this study suggests instead setting aside labels in favor of careful on-the-merits review of the complex underlying legal issues in this dispute.

The "Sofaer doctrine" label seems to largely stem from two specific statements by Judge Sofaer. The first such statement was in response to a written question from Senator Nunn during a November 1985 Senate Armed Services Committee hearing. The relevant exchange provided:

> Senator NUNN. Would you agree that the purpose of the Senate's extensive ratification hearings on the ABM Treaty was to clarify ambiguities of interpretation?
>
> Judge SOFAER. The Senate held extensive hearings to develop a detailed understanding and assessment of the SALT I agreements. Although this process may have helped to answer questions in particular Senators' minds, it could not result in authoritative clarifications of any ambiguities in the Treaty, because statements made during the hearings were unilateral.

"Questions [for the record] Submitted by Senator Sam Nunn" (Nov. 21, 1985), in *Strategic Defense Initiative Hearings, supra* note 603, at 267. The second was a statement made by Judge Sofaer during the 1987 joint hearings of the Senate Foreign Relations and Judiciary Committees on *The ABM Treaty and the Constitution*:

> When it [the Senate] gives its advice and consent to a treaty, it is to the treaty that was made, irrespective of the explanations it is provided.

"Statement of Hon. Abraham D. Sofaer, Legal Adviser, Department of State," in *The ABM Treaty and the Constitution, supra* note 1, at 122, 130.

Judge Sofaer rejects the "alleged `Sofaer doctrine'" as "a polemical device . . . [without] any basis in fact." In a commentary entitled "Treaty Interpretation: A Comment" scheduled for publication in the *University of Pennsylvania Law Review*, Judge Sofaer writes:

> The alleged "Sofaer doctrine" is no more than a polemical device, utilized in a

One point of comparison for the Byrd-Nunn "three principles" proposal to make all administration communications to the Senate during consideration of a treaty "authoritative" no matter how minor the matter or the spokesman or whether or not the issue had been vetted by the Administration and regardless of the overall "treaty history" record, is that despite their importance for the Presidency (or State Governors), even formal and carefully considered opinions of the Attorney General are generally not "binding." That is, an Attorney General or a subsequent Attorney General is free to adopt a different legal opinion if it is felt that the first opinion was mistaken or overlooked an element of the problem. Yet *all* matters of treaty interpretation involve an element of legal judgment and under the Byrd-Nunn "three principles" the legal judgment of even non-lawyers who are addressing an issue possibly for the first time even during a brief Question and Answer would become legally binding and assume greater significance and legal weight than a careful opinion of the Attorney General. Moreover, it is useful to apply this doctrine to the factual setting of the "broad-narrow" dispute. As we have seen, no written administration documents or testimony for the Senate unambiguously addressed the issue. The most knowledgeable and lead administration witness, Ambassador Gerard C. Smith, had at least four opportunities to clarify the issue and did not do so. Yet in that setting somehow we should make "authoritative" the answer of a non-lawyer Department of Defense witness addressing the issue briefly and under pressure during question and answer when earlier in question and answer the same witness at least tilted toward the opposite answer?

The "Byrd-Nunn proposal" could also have a chilling effect on administration spokesmen fully discussing the issues. This is a potential cost of the proposal that would, if anything, lessen information available to the Senate. Although speculative, it might also lead to enhanced interagency disputes as each agency sought in its own testimony to put a different "authoritative" spin on a treaty.

The "Byrd-Nunn proposal," and other proposals concerning principles of treaty interpretation growing out of the "broad-narrow" dispute, coalesced into what

---

> political controversy, and has never had any basis in fact. I realize that disputes between the political branches will not always be fought by Roberts' Rules. I take responsibility, in fact, for any misunderstandings that might have existed on the part of certain Senators. But I cannot accept Professor Koplow's reliance on the "Sofaer Doctrine," as he purports to present a scholar's account. He should have limited his criticisms to those areas in which we truly hold different positions, rather than exploiting a politically generated mischaracterization of my position.

Sofaer, *supra* note 444, at 1437 (quoted from page proofs subject to final editing).

became known as the "Biden condition" or the "Byrd amendment on treaty interpretation" or the "Byrd-Biden condition" adopted on May 26, 1988, as a condition of Senate advice and consent to the INF Treaty. That condition provides in relevant part:

> that the Senate's advice and consent to ratification of the INF Treaty is subject to the condition, based on the Treaty Clauses of the Constitution, that --
>
> (1) the United States shall interpret the Treaty in accordance with the common understanding of the Treaty shared by the President and the Senate at the time the Senate gave its advice and consent to ratification;
>
> (2) such common understanding is based on:
>
> (A) First, the text of the Treaty and the provisions of this resolution of ratification; and
>
> (B) Second, the authoritative representations which were provided by the President and his representatives to the Senate and its Committees, in seeking Senate consent to ratification, insofar as such representations were directed to the meaning and legal effect of the text of the Treaty; and
>
> (3) the United States shall not agree to or adopt an interpretation different from that common understanding except pursuant to Senate advice and consent to a subsequent treaty or protocol, or the enactment of a statute; and
>
> (4) if, subsequent to ratification of the Treaty, a question arises as to the interpretation of a provision of the Treaty on which no common understanding was reached in accordance with paragraph (2), that provision shall be interpreted in accordance with applicable United States law.[740]

---

[740]*See* "ACDA Briefing Memorandum, Final Senate Action on the INF Treaty" (May 31, 1988); *Senate Approves Historic INF Treaty on 93-to-5 Vote,* Wash. Post, May 28, 1988, at 1, col. 5.

According to the *Washington Post* account of the legislative struggle within the Senate engendered by the move to attach this treaty interpretation proviso as a condition to the INF Treaty, the issue was significantly polarized along party lines. Thus, an account on March 29, 1988, reported that "Democrats are pushing to add a proviso to the INF Treaty to block any post-ratification reinterpretation of its provisions without congressional consent." *INF Treaty Called Unclear on Futuristic Weapons*, Wash. Post, Mar. 29, 1988, at A8, col. 2, 5. And an account on May 9, 1988, reports:

> In the case of the treaty-interpretation issue, which will be considered when the Intermediate-Range Nuclear Forces (INF) pact comes to the Senate floor this week or soon thereafter, most Republicans are expected to oppose a Democratic proviso to require a president to get congressional approval for any future reinterpretation of the pact.

GOP Senators Side with President in Power Struggle, Wash. Post, May 9, 1988, at A13, col. 3.

It should be noted that by its terms the INF Treaty interpretation condition would seem to apply solely to the "core" issue of treaty interpretation addressed by this study rather than to the legal effect of "domestic conditions" in treaty implementation.

This INF Treaty condition, as reported in the report of the Senate Committee on Foreign Relations on April 14, 1988, provided:

> XIII. RESOLUTION OF RATIFICATION
>
> *Resolved, (two-thirds of the Senators present concurring therein)*, That the Senate advise and consent to ratification of the Treaty between the United States of America and the Union of Soviet Socialist Republics on the Elimination of Their Intermediate-Range and Shorter-Range Missiles, together with the Memorandum of Understanding and the two Protocols thereto, collectively referred to as the INF Treaty, all signed at Washington on December 8, 1987 (Treaty Doc. 100-11), provided that the Senate's advice and consent to ratification of the INF Treaty is subject to the following condition, which shall be binding on the Executive:
>
> That this Treaty shall be subject to the following principles, which derive, as a necessary implication, from the provisions of the Constitution (Article II, section 2, clause 2) for the making of treaties:
>
> (a) the United States shall interpret this Treaty in accordance with the understanding of the Treaty shared by the Executive and the Senate at the time of Senate consent to ratification;
>
> (b) such common understanding is:
>
> (i) based on the text of the Treaty; and
>
> (ii) reflected in the authoritative representations provided by the Executive branch to the Senate and its Committees in seeking Senate

This condition, formally adopted by the Senate as a condition to its advice and consent to the INF Treaty, like S. Res. 167 and the "Byrd-Nunn proposal" with which it seems to share certain premises, raises serious constitutional and policy issues.[741]

---

consent to ratification, insofar as such representations are directed to the meaning and legal effect of the text of the Treaty;

(c) the United States shall not agree to or adopt an interpretation different from that common understanding except pursuant to Senate advice and consent to a subsequent treaty or protocol, or the enactment of a statute.

This understanding shall not be incorporated in the instruments of ratification of this Treaty or otherwise officially conveyed to the other contracting Party.

"XIII. Resolution of Ratification," in *The INF Treaty Report, supra* note 1, at 436.

[741]A recent *Occasional Paper* from the American Enterprise Institute for Public Policy Research (AEI) on the INF Treaty takes the position that "[t]he Biden Condition" on treaty interpretation linked with the INF Treaty is not consistent with the Constitution. The discussion of this condition says:

> The Biden Condition would fundamentally alter . . . settled principles of treaty interpretation and implementation, and it would arrogate to the Congress a cumbersome, intrusive role in the President's prerogatives not contemplated by the United States Constitution.

The AEI Working Group on the INF Treaty, "A Further Review of the INF Treaty: Seven Critical Issues," *AEI Occasional Papers* 54-68, 68 (May 18, 1988).

An opinion editorial in the *Christian Science Monitor* on April 6, 1988, by two former Defense Department officials opposes the approach reflected in the treaty interpretation condition to the INF Treaty in the following terms:

> As the Senate moves into the decisive phase of its consideration of the Intermediate-Range Nuclear Forces Treaty, one controversy threatens to dominate the debate: the issue of retrospective interpretation of ambiguous or unclear treaty commitments. Several senior Democratic senators have successfully insisted that the Reagan administration accept certain principles as the price for streamlined action on the INF Treaty. It appears that that price is about to increase sharply.
>
> Citing the conflict between themselves and the administration over how to interpret the 1972 Antiballistic Missile Treaty, Sens. Robert Byrd, Claiborne Pell, and Sam Nunn extracted written promises from the secretary of state by threatening

a long and comprehensive ratification process. Chief among these promises was a declaration that the testimony of administration officials will define "authoritatively" the terms and obligations of the treaty.

At the same time, however, the senators (and here they are in step with the administration) oppose the Senate's adding any reservations or clarifications that would oblige the Soviet Union to reveal whether it *agrees* with the administration's self-certified "authoritative" reading of unclear provisions.

The senators' approach implies that they regard the INF Treaty as an agreement not between the United States and the USSR but between a president and the Senate. The senators evince little concern as to whether the USSR accepts obligations that administration officials tell the Senate arise from the treaty. The senators seem to want perfect assurance only that such obligations will constrain US programs. Indeed, it now appears that the assurances provided by Secretary of State George Shultz are considered inadequate; an amendment has been attached by the Foreign Relations Committee to the resolution of ratification that would make the current administration's unilateral interpretation of these obligations part of permanent US law.

Ironically, this approach turns on its head the true lesson of the ABM Treaty controversy. If the Senate in 1972 had plumbed the murky points of the ABM Treaty and demanded express US-Soviet agreement on clarifications, we all could have been spared the current constitutional clash over that treaty.

Gaffney and Feith, *INF: Does Anyone Care What the Soviets Think?*, Christian Sci. Monitor, Apr. 6, 1988, at 13, col. 1.

A statement by Senator Pete Wilson published in the *Washington Post* on the INF treaty interpretation condition calls attention, in the context of presenting policy arguments against the condition, to the way uncertainties concerning future technologies were actually handled by the Senate in consideration of the INF Treaty. Thus, Senator Wilson writes:

I couldn't help noticing the self-contradictory positions you took in an editorial titled "A New INF Treaty Flap" [April 24].

The logic you employ to analyze the current problem of "futuristic" technologies and the INF Treaty runs directly counter to your position on the "interpretation issue"--namely, that the Senate may rely only upon authoritative administration testimony to establish the meaning of a treaty --the view incorporated in the Biden-Pell-Nunn condition to the INF Treaty.

You properly point out that the INF Treaty text is ambiguous on the meaning of "weapons delivery" as it applies to futuristic technologies. Quite naturally, you refer to the negotiating record as the next best source of evidence--or in this case a lack of evidence--that the two parties reached agreement on futuristics.

If the Biden-Pell-Nunn condition were in effect, however, the negotiating record-

-which you refer to to help clarify the futures problem--would neither be an admissible source of information nor could it offer any useful evidence on the issue.

To unravel the futures issue, the sources you cite include "the INF text, international law and the negotiating record." But, ironically, you exclude the *only* source of evidence the Biden-Pell-Nunn condition would allow--the authoritative testimony of administration witnesses!

The reason, of course, is that the authoritative testimony provided to the Senate is all over the map; sometimes an assistant secretary of defense testified "yes," the chief negotiator "no" and the vice chairman of the Joint Chiefs of Staff "maybe."

This is the ultimate flaw in the Biden-Pell-Nunn solution to the interpretation flap. If *all* administration testimony is authoritative and exclusive in determining the meaning of a treaty, then all 3,000 pages of administration testimony is binding domestic law regardless of contradictions, misstatements and wishful thinking. And the futuristics problem is a perfect example.

Sen. Sam Nunn *has* authoritative testimony from administration witnesses regarding future technologies. But Biden-Pell-Nunn notwithstanding, that was not enough for Nunn.

He checked the negotiating record himself, and then he wanted it in writing from the Soviets. He is right to have done so because the negotiating record shows that the Soviets never explicitly agreed to chief U.S. negotiator Ambassador Maynard Glitman's definition of a "weapon."

If Biden-Pell-Nunn were law, however, it wouldn't matter. What the ambassador said goes. And the Senate could either take or leave the whole treaty. Period. There would be no need and no ability to look elsewhere for agreement or meaning, and no means to register any "understandings" or conclusions once the Senate decided the issues.

Clearly such a position would be absurd, and that's why the Biden-Pell-Nunn condition to the INF Treaty is so dangerous.

The Senate needs to rely upon all manner of evidence in establishing the meaning of a treaty. And it needs the flexibility to attach understandings to the resolution of ratification so it can express itself on the meaning of unclear provisions just like the futures issue of INF. Both of these options would be undercut by your solution to the interpretation issue.

Finally, the futures flap raises another interesting point. Suppose Ambassador Glitman had, in fact, tried to protect future technologies in the INF Treaty. Suppose the president had directed him to "keep future technology options open."

Clearly, the way to accomplish this task would have been to insert the phrase "currently consisting of nuclear, conventional and chemical warheads" in the definitions section of Article II, and then add a new article to the effect that "if new weapons technologies, based on other physical principles, are developed, then deployment of these new technologies would be the subject of discussions at the

First, paragraph 1 of this condition seems to direct that any interpretation of the INF Treaty in essence follow the "dual" interpretation approach under which "the common understanding of the Treaty shared by the President and the Senate at the time the Senate gave its advice and consent to ratification" would be determinative as the standard for treaty interpretation, as opposed to the meaning of the treaty between the parties as interpreted by the normal principles of international law. For the reasons discussed in full earlier in this section this is more likely than not an unconstitutional condition. In this connection, one of the most extraordinary events in the INF Treaty interpretation debate was the rejection (by a relatively close and largely party line vote on a motion to table) of the amendment offered to the condition that would have added:

> The United States shall not be bound to any interpretation of this Treaty that is not equally binding on the Soviet Union under applicable international law.[742]

There seemed no real understanding in the debate on this amendment that *neither* the "dual" nor "unitary" approaches can restore the full original understanding of a Senate in any setting in which the approach chosen would make a legal difference. For by definition in such settings there is a difference between an informal understanding of the Senate and the correct international meaning of a treaty. And since it was by definition a *treaty* the Senate was considering, the Senate certainly had a *dual* expectation in its original understanding: that *a particular meaning was correct* and that *it was the correct binding interpretation between the parties*. To reject this amendment, then, could no more police the integrity of the advice and

---

Special Verification Commission."

Interestingly, this is precisely the formulation included in the ABM Treaty.

The futures debate dramatically illustrates the need to carefully examine a treaty and seek clarification of ambiguous terms and meanings before final ratification. Importantly, it also shows the bankruptcy of the Biden-Pell-Nunn approach to the Senate's role in establishing the meaning of a treaty and the necessarily correct position taken by the administration in support of the broad interpretation of the ABM Treaty.

Wilson, *INF Treaty Flap: The Testimony That Counts*, Wash. Post, May 7, 1988, at A21, cols. 2-4.

[742] 134 Cong. Rec. S6805 (daily ed. May 26, 1988).

consent process and the original Senate understanding than to accept it. But to reject this amendment does elevate the understanding as to a particular meaning above the understanding that it was reciprocally binding as part of a treaty with another nation. *That* is a judgment which would seem highly questionable in accurately reflecting the thoughts of either the senators voting for advice and consent to the ABM Treaty or in most settings where the "dual" versus "unitary" issue would arise. Is it a reasonable inference about overall Senate intent in considering treaties that more often that not an at least two-thirds majority of a Senate voting for a treaty would prefer to adhere to an informal understanding as to meaning even if that means they could not adhere to their understanding that the meaning was mutually binding as reflecting Senate advice and consent to a *treaty*? Significantly, in this connection, the 45 votes for this "mutuality of obligation" amendment provide a clear record that even as adopted in connection with the INF Treaty there was not a two-thirds majority of the Senate as necessary for treaty approval which shared this set of priorities about the most important elements of a prior Senate understanding to protect if a choice must be made between the elements as to meaning or reciprocity.

Second, to the considerable constitutional issue presented by the "dual" interpretation approach, paragraph 2(B) seems to incorporate the core of the "Byrd-Nunn proposal" on "authoritative" representations with its major associated problems already discussed. It should be particularly noted that since paragraph (2), which seems to be the sole standard for determining what a shared "common understanding is based on," does not incorporate a standard (as even the Henkin revised *Restatement (Third)* seems to) that a representation to be binding must have produced a setting in which the interpretive record as a whole reasonably suggests that the Senate generally (at least two-thirds of the members) understood the issue as described by the Administration representation, it is constitutionally suspect for yet a second major reason.[743] The Constitution contemplates Senate advice and

---

[743]At a recent conference on "Treaty Implementation and Interpretation Under the Constitution," *supra* note 1, Robert E. Dalton, the Counselor on International Law with the Office of the Legal Adviser in the Department of State, pointed out that the Senate even specifically rejected an amendment to the INF Treaty interpretation condition that would have generally incorporated even this *Restatement* rule. Subsequently, pursuant to a request from the author of this study, Mr. Dalton wrote to the author:

> In accordance with our discussion, I have reviewed the record of the debate in the Senate on advice and consent to the INF Treaty. Senator Specter introduced two amendments dealing with interpretation that were rejected.
>
> Amendment Number 2328 was designed to clarify the meaning of "common

consent to the treaty as an international agreement by an at least two-thirds majority of the Senate and not by isolated understandings or representations by administration spokesmen. There is simply no mechanism in the American constitutional system for treaty advice and consent by Executive branch spokesmen or individual members of the Senate in place of a two-thirds majority of the Senate (as reasonably supported by the interpretive record as a whole). Why the Senate would agree to work such a transfer or whether it was even fully aware that the INF treaty interpretation condition would apparently do so is unclear. Again, this would seem at least as clear a constitutional process defect as the one-house veto struck

---

understanding" as used in the Byrd amendment. This would have been done by inserting the following language at the appropriate place in the resolution of advice and consent: "Such common understanding means a shared interpretation which is both authoritatively communicated to the Senate by the Executive and clearly intended, generally understood and relied upon by the Senate in its advice and consent to ratification." In the debate on his amendment Specter explained that it was based on the Culvahouse letter. On May 27 the Senate adopted a motion to table Specter's amendment by a vote of 67 yeas to 30 nays (*Congressional Record* S6890, May 27, 1988).

Senator Specter introduced a second, more categorical amendment, numbered 2329. He later modified the amendment in the course of debate. The modified text appears on the enclosed copy of page S6890 of the *Congressional Record* of May 27, 1988. The Senate tabled Specter's second amendment by a vote of 64 yeas to 33 nays.

Letter from Robert E. Dalton to John Norton Moore (Mar. 14, 1989) (regarding Senate debate on advice and consent to the INF Treaty).

The *Congressional Record* material supplied by Mr. Dalton with this letter provides:

The Senator from Pennsylvania (Mr. SPECTER) proposes an amendment numbered 2329.

At the appropriate place insert the following:

"Notwithstanding any provision in the Resolution of Ratification, or the Biden Condition as amended by the Byrd Condition, or any statement in the Senate Foreign Relations Committee Report on the INF Treaty, there is no intent by the Senate to change the heretofore accepted constitutional law of the United States on treaty ratification as interpreted by the Supreme Court of the United States or the heretofore accepted international law on treaties as interpreted by the Supreme Court of the United States."

134 *Cong. Rec.* S6890 (daily ed. May 27, 1988) (as read by the assistant legislative clerk).

down by the Supreme Court in the *Immigration and Naturalization Service v. Chadha* case.

Third, to the extent that sections 3 and/or 4 may interfere with the President's authority to interpret treaties, absent specific congressional action in a particular case, they too may be constitutionally suspect.

Fourth, unlike S. Res. 167 and the "Byrd-Nunn proposal" which did not seek their legal effect as a condition to a treaty, this "Biden condition" or "Byrd amendment" does and, as such, squarely presents the issue of the *Niagara Reservation* case. That is, the condition has effect, if at all, under national law and, as such, is arguably or even probably a "legislative act" rather than advice and consent to a treaty. Indeed, this conclusion seems supported by the language of the April 14, 1988, report of the Senate Foreign Relations Committee incorporating a proposed INF Resolution of Ratification with a similar treaty interpretation condition which concluded: "This understanding shall not be incorporated in the instruments of ratification of this Treaty or otherwise officially conveyed to the other contracting Party."[744] As a "legislative act," however, such a condition would be unconstitutional since not approved by the House and Senate and presented to the President subject to the bicameralism and presentment clauses of the Constitution. That is, this condition would affect national law (and probably national law alone) solely by an action of the Senate, without the major checks on legislative action built into our constitutional system of concurrence by both the Senate and House of Representatives and presentment to the President with the opportunity to veto and requirement of subsequent two-thirds roll call vote in both houses to override any such veto. It may be useful to remind ourselves that Article I, section 1 of the Constitution provides:

> All legislative Powers herein granted shall be vested in a Congress of the United States, which shall consist of a Senate and House of Representatives.

And Article I, section 7, clause 3 provides:

> Every Order, Resolution, or Vote to which the Concurrence of the Senate and House of Representatives may be necessary (except on a question of Adjournment) shall be presented to the President of the United States; and before the Same shall take Effect, shall be approved by him, or being disapproved by him, shall be repassed by two thirds of

---

[744]"XIII. Resolution of Ratification," in *The INF Treaty Report, supra* note 1, at 436.

> the Senate and House of Representatives, according to the Rules and Limitations prescribed in the Case of a Bill.

Moreover, the "Biden condition" or "Byrd amendment" is not simply a garden variety effort at pinning down a national law issue that might be associated with a treaty, but rather is using the vehicle of treaty advice and consent to compel the Presidency to accept its view of the precise parameters of the treaty power under the Constitution. It is, in major respects, as though the Senate sought to bring the War Powers Resolution (with all of its associated constitutional issues) into effect as domestic law without either concurrence of the House of Representatives or presentment to the President. It should be recalled that even the 1985 draft of the *Revised Restatement* suggests in comment d to section 303 that the Senate "ought not to impose a condition that has no relation to the treaty before it, for example a requirement that the President accept the Senate's view on some constitutional principle.[745] For yet another major reason, then, this amendment is constitutionally suspect.[746]

In this connection, it might be noted that in a letter of May 24, 1988, to Mr. John B. Ritch, III, Deputy Staff Director of the Senate Foreign Relations Committee, even Professor Henkin said: "I am not in favor of making a statement of Constitutional principle a condition of Senate consent."[747] Professor Henkin's letter also said that the "statement of general Constitutional principle [in this

---

[745] *1985 Revised Restatement, supra* note 187, § 303, comment d, at 30-31 (303-3 to 303-4). *The Restatement (Third) of Foreign Relations Law of the United States*, under Professor Louis Henkin as Chief Reporter, as finally adopted seems to have dropped without explanation this key phrase about imposing "the Senate's view on some constitutional principle." *See Restatement (Third), supra* note 235, § 303, comment *d,* at 160.

[746] Even if some or all "domestic conditions" attached to Senate advice and consent, that is those which would achieve effect if at all under national law, are not legally binding, this would not mean, for example, that as a political or policy matter an Executive should not normally honor conditions freely accepted by the Executive branch at the time of Senate advice and consent and which do not infringe on the constitutional structure of separation of powers or otherwise seek to override the law. This would likely frequently be the case with "domestic conditions" associated with treaty implementation.

[747] 134 *Cong. Rec.* S6746 (daily ed. May 26, 1988) ("Text of Letter Mailed on May 24, 1988" from Louis Henkin to John B. Ritch, III).

condition] . . . is not binding on anyone."[748]

> Let me make my position clear. . . .
>
> The Committee draft in effect combines two resolutions: it combines an understanding, stated as a condition, on the interpretation of the particular INF Treaty (which condition is binding on the President, and on future Presidents) with a statement of general Constitutional principle (which is not binding on anyone).[749]

It should also be noted that in a recent essay Professor Louis Henkin, whose work provides the principal intellectual underpinning of the "dual" approach, seems to suggest that the INF Treaty condition is not a legally binding "condition of consent but only an expression of the Senate's view of the Constitution." Thus, he writes:

> In my view the constitutional principle declared by the Senate [attached to the INF Treaty] is sound and its implications for treaty interpretation unexceptionable. But its title as a condition is dubious. The President, eager to make the treaty, accepted the Senate's consent subject to the Senate's "condition," but issued a statement declaring the condition to be "improper." Proper or not, such conditions are not very significant except as a salvo in President-Senate warfare in the conduct of their shared treaty power. Attaching a constitutional principle as a "condition" of consent to a treaty does not bind future Presidents to that principle. A future President might not agree that there is such a constitutional principle. The principle may not bind even the President who ratified that particular treaty. The principle is not really a condition of consent but only an expression of the Senate's view of the Constitution. The Senate's view may be disputed by the President and must stand or fall on its merits.
>
> Non-amending conditions sometimes reflect distrust between the United States and the other party to the treaty, or Senate mistrust of the Executive (or of later Executives). Sometimes such conditions are blows in larger battles with the President. They reflect and inevitably aggravate friction in the treaty process and beyond, another consequence of our

---

[748] *Id.*

[749] *Id.*

bifurcated treaty procedure.[750]

It should also be noted with respect to the INF treaty interpretation condition that a recent article by a strong supporter and principal initiator of the condition, Senator Joseph R. Biden, Jr., seems to take the position that the condition--sometimes called the Biden condition--was intended to apply to interpretation of all treaties, past, present (the INF Treaty), and future, including those advised and consented to prior to passage of the condition which, of course, would include the ABM Treaty. Thus, Senator Biden writes:

> As its supporters repeatedly emphasized, the Biden Condition was not designed to resolve the question of alleged ambiguities in the genesis, design, and implementation of the ABM Treaty. Accordingly, it could not constitute a final disposition of the issue of ABM Treaty interpretation. Rather, the provision was intended to repudiate the Sofaer Doctrine by affirming certain constitutional principles that were brought into question during the ABM Treaty debate.
>
> The implications for the ABM Treaty, however, are clear and profound. As the floor debate drew to a close, senators on both sides of the "reinterpretation" issue recognized this significance:
>
> Senator Nunn: "[The Condition] affirms enduring constitutional principles which apply to the interpretation of all treaties, *including the ABM Treaty.*"
>
> Senator Levin: "[T]he principles set forth in this amendment apply to all treaties. That is why we fought so hard to keep the words in this amendment `the Treaty Clauses of the Constitution.'"
>
> Senator McClure (a Condition opponent): "This is not some one-time deal. . . . This amendment would affect all treaties, not just the treaty at hand."[751]

And Senator Biden concludes: "In my judgment, the facts of the case are such that the Senate, by enacting the Biden Condition, has effectively declared the

---

[750]Henkin, "Treaties in a Constitutional Democracy," *supra* note 402, at 417.

[751]Biden & Ritch, "The End of the Sofaer Doctrine: A Victory for Arms Control and the Constitution," 18 *Arms Control Today* 3, 8 (Sept. 1988).

`reinterpretation' of the ABM Treaty to be invalid and unconstitutional."[752]

This makes clear that at least one key supporter--as well perhaps as at least those cited in the above quotations by Senator Biden--interpret the INF Treaty interpretation condition as applying also to treaties other than the INF Treaty. In turn, this would seem to clarify the intended "legislative" effect of the condition and that it is not simply a provision relating to the INF Treaty. Moreover, if intended to apply to treaties given Senate advice and consent prior to passage of the condition, it would present even heightened constitutional difficulty in attempted binding application to actions of prior Senates not aware of the condition. Finally, it might be noted in view of Senator Biden's article, that at least one strong supporter of the condition would seem to adopt the view that at least future interpretations, including interpretations of the ABM Treaty relating to the "broad-narrow" issue, could only proceed under the framework of the INF condition.

And, as a policy matter, without repeating the previous discussion with respect to S. Res. 167, the "Byrd-Nunn proposal," and the extensive policy problems associated with a "dual" approach inherent in these proposals, it should be noted that the condition has very serious policy questions associated with it. To summarize several of these: First, why would the Senate wish to create a setting in which, if the condition means anything, it will require the United States either to violate its legal obligations under the INF Treaty or adopt an obligation under the Treaty not binding on the Soviets? Second, why would such a setting protect the integrity of the process of Senate advice and consent when, if the condition means anything different than the international obligation, it means that application would run counter to a critically important Senate understanding that the interpretation meant the same thing internationally for both parties under the treaty? Third, is it honorable for the United States in its treaty relations with other nations to adopt an internal rule that an interpretation known to the Senate, but by the condition not necessarily communicated to the other treaty party, will become binding on the United States in its national law? Fourth, is it consistent with the Nation's interest in strengthening the rule of law in international relations to adopt a rule that could further complicate the use of binding third party dispute settlement? Fifth, why should the Senate create a rule quite counter to normal principles of legislative and treaty history that could weight a single incidental Executive branch representation more than substantial evidence of the views of a two-thirds majority of the Senate? Does a rule possibly weighting the views of a minor Executive branch witness appearing before a non-lead committee more than a clear statement in the report of the Senate Foreign Relations Committee on the Treaty serve to protect the integrity

[752] *Id.* at 8.

of the advice and consent process? Particularly in a setting as vital to the Nation as arms control, why would the Nation be served by a rule that a binding legal obligation restricting national options could be adopted by a single "authoritative representation" of an Executive branch official, no matter how junior or uninformed the spokesman, presented to a committee of the Senate "at the time the Senate gives its advice and consent to ratification," apart from any showing that the issue was reflected in an understanding of a two-thirds majority of the Senate or even reflected a unified Executive branch position? Should such a rule be followed creating an obligation binding on the Nation even in a setting where it were shown that the other party or parties to an arms control agreement were not so bound? It might be recalled that section 33 of the Arms Control and Disarmament Act of 1961 embodies the congressionally expressed policy that not even a clearly unified Executive branch acting under specific instructions from the President can "obligate the United States to disarm or . . . limit the . . . armaments of the United States, except pursuant to the treaty making power of the President under the Constitution or unless authorized by further affirmative legislation by the Congress of the United States." Should the House of Representatives, or the Nation as a whole, welcome a rule that the views of a single Executive branch official, no matter how minor and even if not reflecting a unified Executive branch position, could obligate the United States to limit its armaments apart from any underlying treaty obligation, showing of an understanding shared by an at least two-thirds majority of the Senate considering a treaty, or action pursuant to the normal legislative process of action by both houses of Congress and presentment to the President?[753]

Senate Resolution 167, the "Byrd-Nunn proposal," and the INF Treaty interpretation condition also all present policy issues associated with a generic class of congressional actions designed to legislatively define the congressional role under the Constitution in particular areas, whether the war powers, information flow, treaty interpretation, treaty termination, or some other. This approach, which elsewhere the author has defined as a "legislative/definitional" approach to separation of powers in foreign policy, has a number of disadvantages over possible alternative approaches for strengthening cooperation between Congress and the President in the conduct of foreign policy. During 1979 hearings before the Senate Foreign Relations Committee on "Treaty Termination" in a separation of powers context, the author of this study described this broader policy concern in developing more effective approaches for strengthening executive-congressional cooperation

[753]It might also be asked exactly how subsequent practice, such as United States-U.S.S.R. efforts at resolving interpretation differences within treaty consultation mechanisms, will be handled under the condition.

in foreign policy in the following terms:

> Despite the attention in the last decade, and particularly since the Indo-China War, focused on defining the Congressional and Executive roles for a broad range of foreign policy issues, I doubt that we have materially strengthened needed cooperation between the two branches.
>
> The Executive, with some exceptions, such as revision of "Circular 175 procedures" and offers to more broadly consult with the Congress on the forms of international agreements, has not suggested meaningful new measures or procedures to allay Congressional concerns heightened (perhaps even too much so) by the Indo-China experience. And Congress has focused on line drawing by statute (as evidenced in the national commitments, war power, executive privilege, and treaty power debates among others) without in turn suggesting a broader approach. This present "legislative/definitional" approach seems to have at least the following disadvantages as an exclusive option for strengthening needed cooperation:
>
> --acts of Congress (or declarations of the Executive) cannot alter the constitutional balance so there is room to question what authority they add and whether in some instances they would not even introduce an additional source of uncertainty and argument;
>
> --efforts at capsuling the authority of Congress and the President in statute form may encourage both branches to state and adhere to their most extreme position of constitutional authority;
>
> --a legislative/definitional approach passed over the veto of the President forces him in time of national crisis either to consent to an assertion of congressional authority he may believe to be unconstitutional or to challenge the act at a time when the Nation can least afford confusion as to the legal authority of the President;
>
> --a legislative/definitional approach can be overly rigid for situations required by changed circumstances or not anticipated;

--a legislative/definitional approach may lack realism to the extent not based on a full negotiation with the Executive;

--legislative/definitional approaches to date have focused on defining precise parameters of authority rather than encouraging procedures to strengthen consensus on foreign policy issues at the earliest point in the foreign policy process. For example, a purely definitional approach to treaty negotiation would declare that such negotiation is the exclusive province of the President. Yet the reality seems to be that we need procedures to encourage more meaningful congressional participation in assessing the acceptability of negotiating positions at an early stage in the process. Similarly, we are in perennial need of meaningful procedures for an Executive who does seek to consult "Congress." Who is to be consulted and how and with what guidelines and understandings?

There is, I believe, an alternative to this purely "legislative/ definitional" approach that does not share these shortcomings. That is to encourage the President and Congress to agree before specific crises on a broad range of non-binding flexible guidelines and procedures for the conduct of foreign policy. Although building on the constitutional structure these guidelines and procedures would be aimed not at precise definition of constitutional parameters but rather at strengthening the Nation's ability to function effectively in foreign policy. They would, of course, also not rule out certain new legislative measures where most useful for that objective.

As possible procedures for instituting such an alternative approach the following are illustrative of initiatives the Congress might take:

--establish by act of Congress negotiated with the Executive a joint Executive-Congressional Task Force charged with preparing and recommending a set of flexible guidelines and procedures for strengthening Executive-Congressional cooperation in foreign policy. Such an act could provide for half of the Task Force members to be appointed by Congress and half by the Executive. As Counselor on

International Law, I drafted a bill to establish such a Task Force generally along these lines and urged sponsorship by the Executive Branch. I continue to favor such an approach;

--encourage a cooperative project between the Senate and House Foreign Relations Committees and the Office of the Legal Adviser in the Department of State (perhaps also the Justice and Defense Departments, the National Security Council, and other concerned Congressional Committees such as the Judiciary and Armed Services Committees) aimed at preparation of draft guidelines and procedures for consideration by both branches across the range of foreign policy participation issues (i.e., national commitments, the war powers, executive privilege, information flow, secrecy and accountability, conclusion of agreements, reporting of agreements, termination of agreements, negotiation of agreements, crisis consultation, etc.); or

--request preparation by the Executive Branch of such a broad range of draft procedures and guidelines for consideration by the Congress.

There is nothing magical in these procedures and many others might be suggested that could also do the job. The important point is that to really effectively strengthen cooperation between the Executive and Congress in foreign policy will take more than exercises in constitutional line drawing. It is time we got on with the broader task.[754]

Issues concerning the proper interpretation of the 1972 ABM Treaty, and, even more importantly, the appropriate operation of the treaty power under the

---

[754]"Statement of John Norton Moore for Treaty Termination Hearings," *supra* note 60, at 410-13. To this 1979 list of disadvantages with the generic "legislative/definitional" approach to separation of powers in foreign policy, the author would now add that such measures may also serve the Nation poorly by shifting congressional and Executive branch attention from the merits of policy to compliance with internal procedural requirements. If anything, the experience with the War Powers Resolution has demonstrated the cogency of these policy disadvantages of the generic "legislative/definitional" approach to strengthening inter-branch cooperation in foreign policy.

Constitution, are correctly understood as of great complexity and significance. It is particularly important in such a setting that we lower the rhetoric on all sides and realize that these issues lead honorable observers, indeed some of the Nation's intellectual leaders on the issues, to different conclusions. Future consideration of these issues should encourage focus on the merits, tolerance and receptivity toward serious arguments advanced on the merits by all,[755] and an appropriate humility in seeking to maintain the constitutional balance as bequeathed to us by the wisdom of the constitutional framers.

---

[755]It should also be noted that the Byrd-Nunn letter invoked a specific linkage with Senate consideration of the INF Treaty in its effort to obtain Administration agreement to its "three principles." *See also* the tough linkage statement by Senator Byrd, the Senate majority leader, during Senate debate on the INF Treaty interpretation condition, following the largely party line vote defeating an amendment to the condition that would have added mutuality of obligation with the Soviet Union as an essential element, quoted in text at *supra* note 671.

Annex
The National Law of Treaty Implementation

Annex

Summary Chart of Congressional Consideration of the "Broad-Narrow" Issue in Initial Consideration of the ABM Treaty[1]

Document, Meeting, Statement or Exchange	Unambiguous for "Narrow"	Ambiguous: Leans to "Narrow"	Ambiguous Neutral or Does Not Address	Ambiguous: Leans to "Broad"	Unambiguous for "Broad"
		I. Statements by Executive Branch Officials or Other Executive Branch Actions			
			(A) Congressional Briefing and Transmittal of the ABM Treaty To the Senate		
1. White House SALT briefing by Dr. Henry A.Kissinger, Asst.to the President for National Security Affairs for Congressional leaders, June 15, 1972.			**X**		
2. Secretary of State Rogers' "Letter of Submittal", June 20, 1972[2]			**X**[2]		
3. President Nixon's transmittal letter of June 13, 1972			**X**		

---

1 This chart is based on the analysis contained in section III (E) of the original study prepared for ACDA. While the author has sought to be as careful as possible in characterization, the reader is cautioned that such characterization is not an exact science and that individual characterizations may reasonably differ.

2 Paradoxically, arguments can be made both that this letter is "ambiguous: leans to 'narrow" and that it is "ambiguous: leans to 'broad'".

Document, Meeting, Statement or Exchange	Unambiguous for "Narrow"	Ambiguous: Leans to "Narrow"	Ambiguous Neutral or Does Not Address	Ambiguous: Leans to "Broad"	Unambiguous for "Broad"
			(B) Committee Hearings: Statements And Responses by Members of the Executive Branch		
				(1) Hearings before the Senate Foreign Relations Committee (the lead committee in consideration of the ABM Treaty)	
4. Secretary of State Rogers' opening Statement			**X**		
5. Secretary Rogers in the Sen. Aiken–Secretary Rogers–Amb. Smith exchange[3]			**X**[3]		
6. Amb. Smith in the Senator Aiken – Amb. Smith Exchange[4]				**X**[4]	
				(2) Hearings before the Senate Armed Service Committee	

[3] It can be argued that Secretary Rogers's failure to discuss a "mobiles-futures" development and testing ban suggests that this statement should be characterized as "ambiguous: leans to 'broad'".

[4] It can be argued that Ambassador Smith's statement on its face should be characterized as "unambiguous for 'broad'".

Document, Meeting, Statement or Exchange	Unambiguous for "Narrow"	Ambiguous: Leans to "Narrow"	Ambiguous Neutral or Does Not Address	Ambiguous: Leans to "Broad"	Unambiguous for "Broad"
7. Dept. of Defense answer to questions for the record by Senator Goldwater[5]		**X**[5]			
8. Dr. John Foster, Jr., Dir. of Defense Research & Engineering, in an exchange with Sen. Smith (publically avail. transcript)[6]			**X**[6]		
9. Dr. John Foster, Jr., in an exchange with Senator Jackson		**X**			
10. Dr. John Foster, Jr. in an exchange with Sen. Jackson (additional information interposed for the record)[7]		**X**[7]			

---

[5] It can be argued that this answer for the record should be regarded as "unambiguous for 'narrow'".

[6] It can be argued that this answer should be regarded as "ambiguous: leans to 'broad'" interpretation.

[7] It can be argued that this additional information interposed for the record–if taken as a statement applying to laser technology–should be characterized as "unambiguous for 'narrow'".

Document, Meeting, Statement or Exchange	Unambiguous for "Narrow"	Ambiguous: Leans to "Narrow"	Ambiguous Neutral or Does Not Address	Ambiguous: Leans to "Broad"	Unambiguous for "Broad"
11. Amb. Smith prepared statement before the Senate Armed Service Committee			**X**		
12. Amb. Smith in an exchange with Sen. Smith[8]				**X**[8]	
13. Amb. Smith in exchange with Sen. Goldwater				**X**	
14. Amb. Smith in an exchange with Sen. Jackson			**X**		
15. Gen. Bruce Palmer, Acting Chief of Staff of the Army, Gen. John Ryan, Air Force Chief of Staff, and Lt. Gen. W.P. Leber, Safeguard System Manager, in an exchange with Sen. Goldwater[9]				**X**[9]	

---

[8] It can be argued that, since Ambassador Smith's answer is unqualified by reference to fixed land-based systems, on its face it should be characterized as "unambiguous for 'broad'".

[9] It can reasonably be argued that the statements of all three Generals in this exchange with Senator Goldwater, by not specifically being qualified by a "fixed land-based" referent, should be regarded as "Unambiguous for 'broad'".

Document, Meeting, Statement or Exchange	Unambiguous for "Narrow"	Ambiguous: Leans to "Narrow"	Ambiguous Neutral or Does Not Address	Ambiguous: Leans to "Broad"	Unambiguous for "Broad"
16. Gen. Bruce Palmer in an exchange involving Senators Jackson, Dominick, and Goldwater and Generals Leber, Ryan, and Palmer[10 & 11]	**X** [10 & 11]				
17. Gen. Ryan in the above exchange involving Senators Jackson, Dominick, and Goldwater and Generals Leber, Ryan, and Palmer [11 &12]		**X** [11&12]			

---

[10] This statement should be read with General Palmer's earlier ambiguous statement on the issue characterized as at least "ambiguous: leans to the 'broad' interpretation and that can be reasonably argued to be "unambiguous for 'broad'". In placing it in its fullest context it should also be read with several factors not known to Congress at the time, including a report by Mr. James L. Malone of ACDA reporting "some confusion" by General Palmer during his testimony and Admiral Thomas H. Moorer's interview with the author in which he said that General Palmer's testimony was simply wrong in so far as it invoked the Chiefs. For the full context of issues surrounding General Palmer's testimony see sections III (E) (1) (e), III (E) (1) (h) (2), III (F) (2) (h) and III (G) (2) (c) (1) of this study.

[11] It might be more appropriate to regard the Generals Palmer, Ryan, & Leber participation in this exchange as a single exchange, and it is sometimes treated so in discussion in this study.

[12] Paradoxically, arguments can be made both that the answers of General Ryan in this exchange should be characterized as "unambiguous for 'narrow" and "ambiguous: leans to

Document, Meeting, Statement or Exchange	Unambiguous for "Narrow"	Ambiguous: Leans to "Narrow"	Ambiguous Neutral or Does Not Address	Ambiguous: Leans to "Broad"	Unambiguous for "Broad"
18. Gen. Leber in the above exchange involving Senators Jackson, Dominick, and Goldwater and Generals Leber, Ryan, and Palmer [11]			**X** [11]		
				(3) Hearings before the House Foreign Affairs Committee	
19. Prepared Statement of Secretary of State Rogers			**X**		
				(4) Hearings before the House Armed Services Committee	
20. Secretary of Defense Melvin Laird in exchange with Congressman Stratton			**X**		

'broad'". It should also be noted that the Malone internal ACDA memo reporting on this testimony speaks of "some confusion" with respect to General Ryan's testimony, as well as that of General Palmer above. And, of course, this subsequent testimony of General Ryan should be read in conjunction with the earlier exchange in which General Ryan's answers were characterized as "ambiguous: leans to 'broad'" and in which arguments can be made that his answers should be characterized as "unambiguous for 'broad'".

Document, Meeting, Statement or Exchange	Unambiguous for "Narrow"	Ambiguous: Leans to "Narrow"	Ambiguous Neutral or Does Not Address	Ambiguous: Leans to "Broad"	Unambiguous for "Broad"
(5) Full Committee hearings on the military implications of the Strategic Arms Limitation Talks Agreements before the House Armed Services Committee					
21. Testimony of Amb. Smith			X		
22. Adm. Thomas Moorer, Chairman of the Joint Chiefs of Staff, in an exchange with Congressman Whitehurst[13]				X [13]	
(6) Hearings before the Senate Appropriations Subcommittee on the Dept. of Defense Appropriations					

---

[13] A strong argument can be made that this series of answers by Admiral Moorer should be characterized as "unabiguous for 'broad'". Indeed, it is quite possible, if not probable, that this would be a fairer characterization of Admiral Moorer's answers. An ACDA memorandum reporting on Admiral Moorer's testimony and not then available to Congress reinforces such a characterization. It should also be noted in connection with this exchange that witnesses appearing with Admiral Moorer were Mr. Paul H. Nitze, Member, SALT Delegation and Lt. General Royal B. Allison, Member, SALT Delegation. There is no evidence that either witness sought to qualify Admiral Moorer's remarks. Admiral Moorer has indicated in an interview with the author of this study that he believes his testimony includes the "broad" interpretation and that he recalls no subsequent intervention by either Paul Nitze or General Allison suggesting that his testimony was incorrect in this respect.

Document, Meeting, Statement or Exchange	Unambiguous for "Narrow"	Ambiguous: Leans to "Narrow"	Ambiguous Neutral or Does Not Address	Ambiguous: Leans to "Broad"	Unambiguous for "Broad"
23. Sec. Laird and Adm. Moorer in an exchange with Sen. Young June 13, 1972			**X**		

II.
Statements by Members of Congress

(A) Committee Hearings: Statements or Other Actions of the Congressional Branch

(1) Hearings before the Senate Foreign Relations Committee (the lead committee in consideration of the ABM Treaty)

Document, Meeting, Statement or Exchange	Unambiguous for "Narrow"	Ambiguous: Leans to "Narrow"	Ambiguous Neutral or Does Not Address	Ambiguous: Leans to "Broad"	Unambiguous for "Broad"
1. Sen. Aiken in an exchange with Sec. Rogers and Amb. Smith			**X**		
2. Statement by Sen. Buckley[14]	**X**[14]				

(2) Hearings before the Senate Armed Services Committee

[14] It should be noted that Senator Buckley was an opponent of the ABM Treaty in part because of his opposition to "precluding the possibility of developing at some future date new approaches to antiballistic missile defenses which could offer protection to substantial numbers of our people."

It should also be noted in connection with Senator Buckley's testimony that Senator Sam Nunn has concluded: "[t]he record of the [Buckley] hearing indicates that these three senior members of the committee of principal jurisdiction over the Treaty [Senators Fulbright, Senator Sparkman and Senator Cooper] well-understood the basis for Senator Buckley's opposition."

Document, Meeting, Statement or Exchange	Unambiguous for "Narrow"	Ambiguous: Leans to "Narrow"	Ambiguous Neutral or Does Not Address	Ambiguous: Leans to "Broad"	Unambiguous for "Broad"
3. Sen. Goldwater in posing a question for the record answered from DOD[15]				**X**[15]	
4. Sen. Smith in an exchange with Dr. John Foster, Jr.			**X**		
5. Sen. Jackson in an exchange withDr. John Foster, Jr.[16]	**X**[16]				
6. Sen. Smith in an exchange with Amb. Smith			**X**		
7. Sen. Goldwater in an exchange with Amb. Smith[17]			**X**[17]		

[15] It should be noted that this question from Senator Goldwater was posed in the form of a question asking: "Am I correct?" Otherwise it might most appropriately be characterized as "unambiguous for 'broad'".

[16] It can be reasonably argued, if not even most reasonably, that in view of Senator Jackson's raising this issue for clarification with a witness his statements in this exchange should be regarded as "ambiguous: leans to 'narrow'" rather than "unambiguous for 'narrow'".

[17] It can be reasonably argued, if not even most reasonably, that the most appropriate characterization of Senator Goldwater's understanding in this exchange is that he moved from an understanding of narrower than "narrow" (that is laser development was precluded for all ABM systems, eve including fixed land-based systems) to one possibly consistent with the "broad" interpretation of no restrictions on laser development. Senator

Document, Meeting, Statement or Exchange	Unambiguous for "Narrow"	Ambiguous: Leans to "Narrow"	Ambiguous Neutral or Does Not Address	Ambiguous: Leans to "Broad"	Unambiguous for "Broad"
8. Sen. Jackson in an exchange with Amb.Smith				**X**	
9. Sen. Goldwater in an exchange with Generals Palmer, Ryan, & Leber[18]				**X**[18]	
10. Sen. Jackson in an exchange with Senators Jackson, Dominick, & Goldwater and Generals Leber, Ryan and Palmer[19]	**X**[19]				
11. Sen. Dominick in the exchange with Senators Jackson, Dominick and Goldwater and Generals Leber, Ryan and Palmer[20]				**X**[20]	

Goldwater's subsequent statement in the exchange with Generals Palmer, Ryan, and Leber supports this interpretation.

[18] This series of statements by Senator Goldwater might be reasonably characterized as he believed, following his earlier exchange with Ambassador Smith, that research and development was permitted for ABM laser systems without qualification, and he learned during this exchange (and disapproved) that deployment of such systems was prohibited.

[19] It can be reasonably argued, if not even most reasonably, in view of Senator Jackson's request to "Tell me what it means," that his statements in the exchange should be regarded as "ambiguous: leans to 'narrow'" rather than "unambiguous for 'narrow'".

[20] Since Senator Dominick's statement is technically inaccurate under both "broad" and "narrow" interpretations it can be reasonably argued that it should be characterized as "ambiguous neutral or does not address". Conversely, if he was addressing only laser technology, it would be consistent only with the "broad"interpretation.

Document, Meeting, Statement or Exchange	Unambiguous for "Narrow"	Ambiguous: Leans to "Narrow"	Ambiguous Neutral or Does Not Address	Ambiguous: Leans to "Broad"	Unambiguous for "Broad"
12. Sen. Goldwater in the exchange with Senators Jackson, Dominick & Goldwater and Generals Leber, Ryan and Palmer[21]		**X**[21]			
				(3) Hearings before the House Foreign Affairs Committee	
		[No Relevant Congressional Indications]			
				(4) Hearings before the House Armed Services Committee	
13. Congressman Stratton in a question for Sec. Laird[22]				**X**[22]	

---

[21] It can be reasonably argued that this exchange clarifies for Senator Goldwater that development of lasers would be permitted for fixed land-based systems, but does not squarely address the prohibition, if any, on development and testing of exotic "mobiles" and thus should be characterized as "ambiguous neutral or does not address". In this connection, it should also be noted that Senator Goldwater's conclusion from the exchange that "[w]e could then replace the Sentry with the laser if it became effective" is inconsistent with both "broad" and "narrow" interpretations since it involves deployment and not solely development and testing. Paradoxically, it can be reasonably argued that this exchange should be characterized as "unambiguous for 'narrow'" since Senator Goldwater seems to focus on a distinction between "mobiles" and fixed land-based systems within the context of laser development and Article V of the ABM Treaty.

[22] It can be reasonably argued that since this intervention by Congressman Stratton was asked in the form of a question and, moreover, that it is technically incorrect under both "broad' and "narrow" interpretations, that it should be characterized as "ambiguous neutral or does not address".

Document, Meeting, Statement or Exchange	Unambiguous for "Narrow"	Ambiguous: Leans to "Narrow"	Ambiguous Neutral or Does Not Address	Ambiguous: Leans to "Broad"	Unambiguous for "Broad"
				(5) Supplementary hearings on defense procurement authorization relating to the SALT Agreement before the House Armed Services Committee	
14. Staff memorandum prepared for the members of the House Armed Services Committee & inserted in the record[23]				**X**[23]	
				(6) Full Committee hearings on the military implications of the SALT Agreements before the House Armed Services Committee	
15. Congressman Whitehurst in an exchange with Adm. Moorer			X		

[23] This staff prepared memorandum does not specifically address the "broad-narrow" issue and can reasonably be argued to be simply "ambiguous neutral or does not address".

Document, Meeting, Statement or Exchange	Unambiguous for "Narrow"	Ambiguous: Leans to "Narrow"	Ambiguous Neutral or Does Not Address	Ambiguous: Leans to "Broad"	Unambiguous for "Broad"
				(7) Hearings before the Senate Appropriations Subcommittee on defense appropriations	
16. Sen. Young in an exchange with Sec. of Defense Laird & Adm. Moorer			**X**		
			<u>(B) Committee Reports</u>		
				<u>(1) Report of the Senate Foreign Relations Committee (The lead committee in consideration of the ABM Treaty)</u>	
17. Report			**X**		
				<u>(2) Report of the House Foreign Affairs Committee</u>	
18. Report			**X**		
			<u>(C) Congressional Debates</u>		
				<u>(1) Senate consideration of the ABM Treaty</u>	
				<u>(a) statements by proponents of the Treaty</u>	

Document, Meeting, Statement or Exchange	Unambiguous for "Narrow"	Ambiguous: Leans to "Narrow"	Ambiguous Neutral or Does Not Address	Ambiguous: Leans to "Broad"	Unambiguous for "Broad"
19. Sen. Fulbright			X		
20. Sen. Thurmond[24]		X[24]			
21. Sen. Fong[25]				X[25]	
22. Sen. Kennedy			X		
(b) statements by opponents of the Treaty					
23. Senator Buckley	X				
(2) House consideration					
24. Congressman Morgan summary of August 18			X		

(D) Senate Resolution of Advice and Consent

---

[24] Since this statement says flatly that the ABM Treaty "also prevents us from developing new kinds of systems to protect our population" arguably it can be regarded as "unambiguous for 'narrow'". Paradoxically, however, since this statement is inaccurate under both "broad" and "narrow" interpretations (that is, even under the "narrow" interpretation such systems can be developed if fixed land-based) arguably it can also be regarded as simply "ambiguous neutral or does not address".

[25] Since this statement on research and development contains no qualifying language limiting it to "fixed land-based" system and components it can reasonably be argued to be "unambiguous for 'broad'". Moreover, arguably its inclusion of a deployment ban on "exotic" or "future" systems in the same sentence would support such a characterization. Paradoxically, since this statement contains no specific "mobiles-futures" link on development and testing and since it is technically inaccurate under both "broad" and "narrow" interpretations it can also reasonably be argued to be "ambiguous neutral or does not address".

Document, Meeting, Statement or Exchange	Unambiguous for "Narrow"	Ambiguous: Leans to "Narrow"	Ambiguous Neutral or Does Not Address	Ambiguous: Leans to "Broad"	Unambiguous for "Broad"
25. Senate resolution of advice and consent			**X**		

Annex

Overall Characterizations by Category

I

Statements by Executive Branch officials or Other Executive Branch Actions

Unambiguous for "narrow"	1*
Ambiguous: leans to "narrow"	4
Ambiguous: neutral or does not address	13
Ambiguous: leans to "broad"	5**
Unambiguous for "broad"	0

---

*This statement is by General Bruce Palmer who earlier gave testimony characterized here as "ambiguous: leans to 'broad'".

**Three of these statements are by Ambassador Gerard C. Smith, the head of the United States SALT I Delegation. Ambassador Smith has indicated to the author of this study that he believes he was accompanied by other senior SALT I Delegation members during his testimony. One of these statements is by Admiral Thomas H. Moorer, the Chairman of the Joint Chiefs of Staff, before the House Armed Services Committee. Witnesses appearing with Admiral Moorer were Mr. Paul H. Nitze and Lt. General Royal B. Allison, both members of the SALT I Delegation. And one of these statements is by General Bruce Palmer who later gave testimony characterized here as "unambiguous for 'narrow'".

If the statements of Generals Palmer, Ryan and Leber in an exchange with Senator Goldwater during a hearing before the Senate Armed Services Committee were treated as three rather than one incident in this study then two additional instances would be added to the "ambiguous: leans to 'broad'" category.

II

Statements by Members of Congress or Other Congressional Actions

Unambiguous for "narrow"	4*
Ambiguous: leans to "narrow"	2
Ambiguous: neutral or does not address	12
Ambiguous: leans to "broad"	7**
Ambiguous for "broad"	0

---

*Two of these statements are by Senator Jackson during hearings before the Senate Armed Services Committee and two are by Senator Buckley, an opponent of the ABM Treaty, first in testimony before the Senate Foreign Relations Committee and then during Senate consideration of the ABM Treaty. Senator Jackson, who is widely regarded as a defense expert, also participated in an exchange with Ambassador Smith in which Jackson's position is here characterized as "ambiguous: leans to 'broad'".

It should be noted in connection with Senator Buckley's testimony before the Senate Foreign Relations Committee, that Senator Sam Nunn has concluded: "[t]he record of the [Buckley] hearing indicates that these three senior members of the committee of principal jurisdiction over the treaty [Senators Fulbright, Senator Sparkman and Senator Cooper] well-understood the basis for Senator Buckley's opposition." The totals given here do not include Senators Fulbright, Sparkman and Cooper, as is suggested by Senator Nunn's analysis.

**Two of these are statements by Senator Goldwater who also participated in an exchange before the Senate Armed Services Committee in which his position is characterized here as "ambiguous: leans to 'narrow'". One is a statement by Senator Jackson who also participated in two exchanges in which his position is characterized here as "unambiguous for 'narrow'". One is by Senator Dominick in hearings before the Senate Armed Services Committee. One is by Senator Fong during the Senate debate on the ABM Treaty. One is a staff memorandum prepared for the members of the House Armed Services Committee and inserted in the record. And one is by Congressman Stratton in posing a question for Secretary of Defense Melvin Laird.

III

Combined Totals of Executive Branch and Congressional Indications Concerning the "Broad-Narrow" Issue in Congressional Consideration of the ABM Treaty

Unambiguous for "narrow"	5
Ambiguous: leans to "narrow"	6
Ambiguous: neutral or does not address	25
Ambiguous: leans to "broad"	12
Unambiguous for "broad"	0

It might be noted, as is discussed in sections V (B (3) (b) & (d) and V(B) (7) of this study, that simply adding together these indications without reference to where in the treaty advice and consent process they occurred, and particularly whether made by Executive branch or Congressional sources, is not an appropriate mechanism, taken alone, for seeking the intent of an at least two-thirds majority of the Senate on a matter of treaty interpretation. The reader should also review footnotes * and ** under both parts I and II of this overall characterization.

It might also be noted that the combined totals of all categories at least tilting toward either "broad" or "narrow" interpretations is, at 23, less than the 25 instances characterized as "ambiguous neutral or does not address", and that if all characterizations at least tilting toward the "broad" interpretation and the "narrow" interpretation were combined for each position the figures would be 11 for the "narrow" interpretation and 12 for the "broad" interpretation. In connection with this latter comparison, however, at least this study has characterized a5 of these instances as unambiguous for the "narrow" interpretation and none as unambiguous for the "broad" interpretation.

IV

Combined Totals of Executive Branch and Congressional Indications Concerning the "Broad-Narrow" Issue in Congressional Consideration of the ABM Treaty Modified by Adding Arguable Characterizations

The combined totals in this annex do not capture the uncertainty in characterization of many of the just discussed categories I - III of the instances characterized. As one very rough additional indicator of this uncertainty, it may be useful to provide a combined total adding in other arguable interpretations. This would provide a rough indication of total arguably possible interpretations in each category. Doing so roughly adds the following additional instances in each category (not removing characterizations already made in this study) based on footnotes discussed in this annex:

Unambiguous for "narrow"	5
Ambiguous: leans to "narrow"	3
Ambiguous: neutral or does not address	6
Ambiguous: leans to "broad"	5
Unambiguous for "broad"	8

Combining these additional instances with the total of interpretations as previously characterized in this study produces the following rough grouping of arguable interpretations as a very rough measure of some of the inherent ambiguity in characterization of these incidents:

Unambiguous for "narrow"	10
Ambiguous: leans to "narrow"	9
Ambiguous: neutral or does not address	31
Ambiguous: leans to "broad"	17[***]
Unambiguous for "broad"	8

[***]If the statements of Generals Palmer, Ryan and Leber in an exchange with Senator Goldwater during a hearing before the Senate Armed Services Committee were treated in initial characterization in this study as three rather than one incident (as they are in the above additions) then two additional instances would be added to the category of "ambiguous: leans to 'broad'": bringing the total to 19 in this category.

It should be noted that this combined total of arguably possible interpretations by category does not reflect the conclusions of this study as to the most reasonable characterization of instances. Totals based on the characterizations in this study are provided in I, II and III above in the final "Overall Characterizations by Category" section of this annex D.

V

Summary Analysis of Overall Positions of Principal Participants
[see main Annex D footnotes for greater nuance in position]

Principal Participant	Unambiguous for "Narrow"	Ambiguous: Leans to "Narrow"	Ambiguous Neutral or Does Not Address	Ambiguous: Leans to "Broad"	Unambiguous for "Broad"
Principal Executive Branch Participants					
1. President Nixon			1		
2. Dr. Henry A. Kissinger, Ass't to the President for National Security Affairs			1		
3. Sec. Rogers			4		
4. Amb. Smith*			3	3*	
5. Sec. of Defense Melvin Laird			2		

*Ambassador Smith's testimony should be particularly weighted in view of the fact that he was the head of the United States SALT I Delegation and his statement to the author that he believes he was accompanied by the principal members of the SALT I Delegation during his testimony. It should also be noted that at least two of Ambassador Smith's statements can arguably be regarded as "unambiguous for 'broad'".

Principal Participant	Unambiguous for "Narrow"	Ambiguous: Leans to "Narrow"	Ambiguous Neutral or Does Not Address	Ambiguous: Leans to "Broad"	Unambiguous for "Broad"
6. Adm. Thomas Moorer**				1**	
7. Dr. John Foster, Jr.		2	1		
8. Gen.Bruce Palmer***	1			1***	
9. Gen. Ryan****		1			****
10. Gen. Leber****			1		
11. Dept. of Defense written answer for the record		1			

**A strong argument can be made that Admiral Moorer's participation should be characterized as "unambiguous for 'broad'".

***It can reasonably be argued that this exchange by General Palmer should be regarded as "unambiguous for 'broad'".

****It can be reasonably argued that Generals Ryan and Leber should also be scored as participating in an exchange that was "unambiguous for 'broad'".

Principal Participant	Unambiguous for "Narrow"	Ambiguous: Leans to "Narrow"	Ambiguous Neutral or Does Not Address	Ambiguous: Leans to "Broad"	Unambiguous for "Broad"
Principal Congressional Participants*****					
1. Sen. Aiken			1		
2. Sen. Buckley	2				
3. Sen. Dominick				1	
4. Sen. Fong *****				1 *****	
5. Sen. Fulbright			1		
6. Sen. Goldwater *****		1	1	2 *****	
7. Sen. Jackson *****	2 *****				
8. Sen. Kennedy			1		
9. Cong. Morgan			1		
10. Sen. Smith			2		
11. Cong. Stratton				1	

*****See footnotes in the main annex D for greater nuance in positions of principal Congressional participants and the staff memorandum. For example, it can be argued that individual statements or exchanges by Senators Fong and Goldwater should be characterized as "unambiguous for 'broad':.

It should be noted in connection with Senator Buckley's testimony before the Senate Foreign Relations Committee, that Senator Sam Nunn has concluded: "]t]he record of the [Buckley] hearing indicates that these three senior members of the committee of principal jurisdiction over the Treaty [Senators Fulbright, Senator Sparkman and Senator Cooper] well-understood the basis for Senator Buckley's opposition." This chart does not include Senators Fulbright, Sparkman and Cooper for the "narrow" interpretation, as is suggested by Senator Nunn's analysis.

Principal Participant	Unambiguous for "Narrow"	Ambiguous: Leans to "Narrow"	Ambiguous Neutral or Does Not Address	Ambiguous: Leans to "Broad"	Unambiguous for "Broad"
12. Sen. Thurmond		1			
13. Cong. Whitehurst			1		
14. Sen. Young			1		

Annex

Report	Unambiguous for "Narrow"	Ambiguous: Leans to "Narrow"	Ambiguous Neutral or Does Not Address	Ambiguous: Leans to "Broad"	Unambiguous for "Broad"
Principal Congressional Reports and Other Actions[*****]					
1. Senate Resolution of Advice and Consent			1		
2. Report of the Senate Foreign Relations Committee			1		
3. Report of the House Foreign Affairs Committee				1	
4. Staff memorandum prepared for the members of the House Armed Services Committee & inserted in the Record[*****]				1[*****]	

[*****]See footnotes in the main annex D for greater nuance in positions of principal Congressional participants and the staff memorandum. For example, it can be argued that individual statements or exchanges by Senators Fong and Goldwater should be characterized as "unambiguous for 'broad':.

It should be noted in connection with Senator Buckley's testimony before the Senate Foreign Relations Committee, that Senator Sam Nunn has concluded: "]t]he record of the [Buckley] hearing indicates that these three senior members of the committee of principal jurisdiction over the Treaty [Senators Fulbright, Senator Sparkman and Senator Cooper] well-understood the basis for Senator Buckley's opposition." This chart does not include Senators Fulbright, Sparkman and Cooper for the "narrow" interpretation, as is suggested by Senator Nunn's analysis.

NOTE

Two early exchanges on June 6, 1972, prior to formal transmittal of the ABM Treaty to the Senate, involving Secretary of Defense Melvin R. Laird before the Senate Armed Services Committee, and added to section III (E) after completion of this chart, are not included in it or in the numerical totals incorporated from the chart throughout this study. Both exchanges are characterized in section III (E) of this study as "ambiguous neutral or does not address". Paradoxically, Secretary Laird's participation in the first exchange, however, could arguably be characterized as either: "ambiguous: leans to 'narrow'" or "ambiguous: leans to 'broad'". Moreover, Senator Jackson's early questioning in this exchange might arguably be characterized as: "ambiguous: leans to 'broad'".

About the Author

John Norton Moore is the Walter L. Brown Professor of Law at the University of Virginia School of Law. He also directs the University's Center for National Security Law and the Center for Oceans Law & Policy and was the Director of the Graduate Law Program at Virginia for more than twenty years. Viewed by many as the founder of the field of national security law, Professor Moore chaired the prestigious American Bar Association's Standing Committee on Law and National Security for four terms. He is the author or editor of 20 books and over 140 scholarly articles and served for two decades on the editorial board of the *American Journal of International Law*. He is a member of the Council on Foreign Relations, the American Law Institute, the American Society of International Law, the Order of the Coif, Phi Beta Kappa, and numerous other professional and honorary organizations.

In addition to his scholarly career, Professor Moore has a distinguished record of public service. Among seven Presidential appointments, he has served two terms as the Senate-confirmed Chairman of the Board of Directors of the United States Institute of Peace and, as the first Chairman, set up this new agency. He also served as the Counselor on International Law to the Department of State, and as Ambassador and Deputy Special Representative of the President to the Law of the Sea Conference, Chairman of the National Security Council Interagency Task Force on the Law of the Sea, and as a member of the United States' legal team before the International Court of Justice in the *Gulf of Maine* and *Nicaragua* cases (a Deputy Agent for the United States in the *Nicaragua* case). Professor Moore currently serves as a Member of the Director of Central Intelligence's Historical Review Board.

In the recent past, he has served as a Consultant to both the President's Intelligence Oversight Board and the Arms Control and Disarmament Agency. He has also been a member of the National Advisory Committee on Oceans and Atmosphere, the United States Delegation to the Conference on Security and Cooperation in Europe, and the Presidential Delegation of the United States to observe the elections in El Salvador. In 1990, he served, with the Deputy Attorney-General of the United States, as the Co-Chairman of the United States-USSR talks on the Rule of Law. He also served as the legal advisor to the Kuwait Representative to the United Nations Iraq-Kuwait Boundary Demarcation Commission.

Professor Moore's wife, Barbara, is the Director of the National Undersea Research Program in the National Oceanic and Atmospheric Administration (NOAA), and is a former NOAA aquanaut. Professor and Mrs. Moore are the proud parents of two daughters, Victoria and Elizabeth.

Rule of Law

The love of order and obedience to the laws, which so remarkably characterize the citizens of the United States, are sure pledges of internal tranquility....

Thomas Jefferson
Letter to Benjamin Waring, Esq., and Others (March 23, 1801) in 10 *The Writings of Thomas Jefferson* 235 (Mem. ed. 1903)

[W]hile the laws shall be obeyed all will be safe.

Thomas Jefferson
Original draft of first Inaugural Address, March 4 1801 in 8 *The Writings of Thomas Jefferson* 1 (P. Ford ed. 1897)

It is of high importance to the peace of America, that she observe the laws of nations ....

John Jay
The Federalist No. 3 at 14 (J. Cooke ed. 1961)

I think with others, that nations are to be governed with regard to their own interests, but I am convinced that it is in their interest, in the long run, to be...faithful to their engagements, even in the worst of circumstances, and honorable and generous always.

Thomas Jefferson
Letter to the Marquis De Lafayette (April 2, 1790), in 8 *The Writings of Thomas* Jefferson 12 (Mem. Ed. 1903).